Contents

Preface

This book is aimed primarily at law students in their second or third year of study at university. Although it is not intended to be merely an introductory book, I take the view that it is not necessary to take 800 pages to cover the law of equity and trusts at university or equivalent level, and that the traditional textbook can be made far shorter. In particular, many go into far greater detail over the facts of cases, which are often of only marginal relevance, than is really necessary.

The aim has been to state the law as shortly and clearly as possible, without (I hope) sacrificing clarity of exposition in the more complex areas. I have attempted to concentrate on principle rather than detail, because it is easy to allow obsession with detail to obscure the main principles. I have also confined detailed coverage to those areas which are commonly covered in trusts courses at university level, rather than attempting to encompass, for example, everything that can possibly be said on the entire subject of equity and trusts. Lengthy, comprehensive (and expensive) reference books on all aspects of equity exist, and it is not my intention here to compete with them.

I have also tried to take account of the fact that some aspects of equity are usually covered on other courses (e.g., land law, contract and the English legal system), and therefore require less extensive coverage here. Equitable remedies, for example (except proprietary remedies), are extensively and excellently covered in *The English Legal Process*, 6th edn (1996), by Terence Ingman, and since most readers of this book will already be familiar with the English legal system, I have decided to cover them in outline only here (see 19.1). Proprietary remedies, however, which will probably not have been covered on any other course, are dealt with in greater depth (see 19.2). I have also expanded coverage of *Mareva* injunctions, and in particular the worldwide-*Mareva* injunction, partly because of its increasing importance in combating international fraud, and partly because of the emphasis on equitable remedies in the new Law Society requirements.

Assuming that the subject matter has been concisely defined, and material of peripheral relevance omitted, it is surprising how much detail it is possible to encompass within 390 pages or so.

There is, of course, another (obvious) advantage of a short book. All other things being equal, long books cost more than short books, and my experience of teaching law for 20 years suggests that many students like to have some of their grant left after buying books, in order to enjoy the other attractions offered by university life.

Occasionally I write articles in academic journals, and I have to remind myself that the function of an article differs from that of a chapter of a textbook, in that description and explanation are not enough. There needs also to be a thesis or argument, and of course, the material is arranged so as best to advance the argument. By the same token, however, a chapter of a textbook, such as this one, differs from an academic article in that description and explanation are paramount and it is not the function of a book such as this to advance far-reaching academic arguments. To describe and explain what the law is is by no means a trivial task, incidentally, although often much-underrated, since the law can rarely be stated with certainty, particularly on areas on which academic courses tend to concentrate.

In this book, therefore, I have, on occasions, deliberately sacrificed conceptual neatness for ease of explanation. For example, although for the most part the organisation of this book is conventional, there is no separate chapter on either resulting or constructive trusts. Of course, resulting and constructive trusts are covered in detail in the book, but in the disparate areas where they naturally arise. For example, constructive trusts are referred to in chapters 8 (beneficial interests in shared homes), 9 (secret and half-secret trusts), 10 (equitable fraud doctrine), 14 (breach of fiduciary duty) and 19 (knowing receipt). Even if common principles apply to all of these areas (which is by no means certain), each area is self-contained in the sense that, for example, you do not find in cases on *Lloyds Bank plc* v *Rosset* [1991] 1 AC 107 (in chapter 8) references to the development of secret trusts or knowing receipt (in chapter 19), and the same is generally true of each of the other discrete areas. A separate chapter on constructive trusts would therefore contain much disparate material, and would require extensive cross-referencing, by no means a useful aid to understanding by students.

The same arguments apply to resulting trusts, which are described in 2.4, but detailed applications of which are described in chapters 5 (unincorporated associations) and 8 (*Lloyds Bank plc* v *Rosset* again). Again, these areas are largely self-referential, and you do not find in cases on *Lloyds Bank plc* v *Rosset* references to unincorporated associations, or *vice versa*. Nor is there even a conceptual argument for treating them together, because what were commonly, before the House of Lords decisions in *Westdeutsche Landesbank Girozentrale* v *Islington London Borough Council* [1996] 2 All ER 961, described as automatic resulting trusts (2.4 and chapter 5) are quite different, even conceptually, from presumed resulting trusts (chapter 8). There is some cross-fertilisation between 2.4 and chapter 5, but I shall argue quite strongly that this is misconceived, because the judges have failed fully to understand (in chapter 5) the implications of Cross J's judgment in *Neville Estates Ltd* v *Madden* [1962] Ch 832, which ought to rule out a resulting trust analysis in most cases involving unincorporated associations (see 5.3).

Also for ease of explanation, where areas which are conceptually disparate are developed through the same cases, I have again sacrificed conceptual neatness and dealt with them together. For the first time in this edition, therefore, I have given the topic of beneficial interests in shared homes a chapter to itself (chapter 8). This also accounts for the inclusion of knowing receipt and knowing assistance in the remedies chapter (chapter 19). Although conceptually they are unrelated to tracing, many of the recent authorities on tracing also develop the law of knowing receipt and knowing assistance, and *vice versa*. An excellent (but by no means the only) example is *Agip (Africa) Ltd* v *Jackson* [1991] Ch 547, which is an important authority on common law and equitable tracing, and knowing receipt and knowing assistance. To deal with knowing receipt and knowing assistance separately would not be good for clarity, and it might also be borne in mind that where the same fact situations in reality raise a number of different issues, the same is likely to be true of fact situations in examination problem questions.

It is taken as axiomatic among publishers (or at any rate by the staff at Blackstone Press) that books tend to expand (and hence increase in price) with each successive edition, so in order to keep this edition affordable I have been quite ruthless with areas that are peripheral to the law of trusts. Duress and undue influence came out in 1993. In this edition I have also cut out the details (but not the principles) of part performance. While the principles are still of considerable importance, especially in relation to chapter 10 (equitable fraud doctrine), the details, which in any case have been curtailed, if not abolished, in contracts for the sale of land, by the Law of Property (Miscellaneous Provisions) Act 1989, are more at home in a land law textbook. The separate treatment of trusts for sale has also come out of this edition, again because of the overlap with land law, although discussion is retained, for particular purposes, in chapters 2 and 8. In 1991 I dropped the separate chapter on trusts and taxation, which students seemed to find of little use, preferring instead to explain the taxation consequences of a transaction, where relevant, in the appropriate part of the book.

On the other hand, since the main aim of this book is to be of use to law students, I have tried to cover all the areas that are covered in traditional trusts courses, including arguably arcane areas, such as secret trusts, mutual wills, *donatio mortis causa* (DMC) and perpetuities. Modularisation may eventually affect the traditional coverage, but writing in May 1996 it is difficult to predict how, as I suspect that there will be little consistency among law schools. There have in any case been new cases on DMC and mutual wills (so perhaps they are not after all so arcane); secret trusts are a good example of the application of the equitable fraud doctrine, and trusts still have to satisfy perpetuity requirements, however much some feel them to be out of date. Some knowledge of perpetuities is in any case required to appreciate the problems of applying a trust analysis to non-charitable unincorporated associations, where the members of the association can fluctuate (see, e.g., 5.3.4).

The apparently large number of people who think that the law of trusts does not change very quickly will be surprised at how much re-writing I have done for this edition. Chapter 8 has been entirely re-written, since there have been important Court of Appeal decisions, such as *Huntingford* v *Hobbs, Savill* v *Goodall, McHardy* v *Warren, Drake* v *Whipp, Lloyds Bank plc* v *Carrick*, and the case which may (but I suspect will not) become a landmark decision, *Midland Bank plc* v *Cooke*.

I have also entirely re-written sections 19.2 and 19.3, on tracing, knowing receipt and knowing assistance. These areas have seen a great deal of recent development, and although some of the most important cases, such as *Agip (Africa)* v *Jackson* and *Polly Peck International* v *Nadir (No. 2)*, were in time for the previous edition, the *Bank Tejarat* case, *Goldcorp Exchange* and the three *El Ajou* cases were not. The law may also be in the embryonic stage of developing around coherent restitutionary principles, itself justifying a total re-write.

Apart from those areas, important new cases which are covered in this edition are *Tinsley* v *Milligan*, *Tribe* v *Tribe*, *Hunter* v *Moss*, *Attorney-General for Hong Kong* v *Reid*, *Target Holdings* v *Redfern*, and *Halifax Building Society* v *Clark*. There has also been new charities legislation (in particular, the Charities Act 1993).

A common difficulty with the law of trusts is that it seems to (some!) students to be further removed from the everyday world than other subjects, a major (but by no means the only) role of the trust being a device to enable the wealthy to hang on to their wealth. Sometimes in particular, students are confused by the terminology, especially in the cases; sometimes they cannot see the point of certain types of transaction. I have tried to explain these. Some of the legal concepts are also fairly abstract, and I have tried to explain such concepts as fully as possible.

Finally, a great many trustees and beneficiaries today are women. This was not the case until a hundred years or so ago, but is especially so now that many matrimonial homes, and homes of unmarried co-habitees, are in joint names, or where at least wives and female co-habitees contribute to the purchase money of their home. The use of 'he or she' can lead to clumsy sentences, however, quite apart from greatly lengthening the book. So I have used 'he' pretty well throughout as shorthand, and not because of any assumption that those about whom I am talking are, or should be, male.

The best law students are not necessarily those who do the most work, but those who think hardest about the subject. They have inquiring minds, and immerse themselves in law in the sense that questions continue to bother them when they are shopping, walking to work, or drinking in the pub. Among some students there is a tradition of discussion of the substantive law, which feeds these ideas and questions, but unfortunately this does not seem to be universal. I encourage my own students to e-mail me, and each other, since it is quite a good way of discussing things. It also gives me an idea of what people find difficult, and sometimes gives me ideas which otherwise I would probably not have had, so it probably improves my teaching (and writing). I reply fairly quickly to e-mail (although I suppose that would change if I were inundated). Below are my Internet and CompuServe addresses (Internet is faster, because I do not use my CompuServe account very often). Also below is the URL of my World Wide Web page, which I am planning to use for interactive teaching of trusts, and the other subjects I teach. At the time of writing, there is not much on this page, but by the time the book is published, I am reasonably confident that there will be, and there are also links there to other useful sites on the World Wide Web.

The law is stated as at 31 May 1996. However, I was able to make alterations at proof stage to take account of the important new cases of *Westdeutsche*

Landesbank Girozentrale v *Islington London Borough Council* [1996] 2 All ER 961 and *Trustee of the Property of F. C. Jones and Sons (a Firm)* v *Jones*, (1996) *The Times*, 13 May 1996.

Paul Todd

slapnt@cf.ac.uk
CompuServe: 100433,2016
http://ourworld.compuserve.com/homepages/pntodd/

Table of Cases

Table of Statutes

ONE

History and Outline of Equitable Jurisdiction

1.1 DIVISION OF OWNERSHIP INTO LEGAL AND EQUITABLE ELEMENTS

A surprising feature of English law, and one that is peculiar to it, is that it has two completely different concepts of ownership of property. Even more surprising is that both types of ownership can arise simultaneously. In other words, a single item can be owned, and frequently is, at the same time, by more than one person in more than one way.

Most personal property (i.e., goods) is owned by one person absolutely, and in that case the ownership of the item is not split up. It will be, however, where a person (or persons) holds property on trust for another (or others). In the simplest variety of trust, there will be two people simultaneously owning the property, though the relationship of each to it will be quite different. There is a legal owner, who is called a trustee. He has essentially a management role, and is subject to quite stringent duties. There is also an equitable owner, who is called a cestui que trust, or beneficiary. It is the beneficiary who is entitled to enjoy the property, and whose position is therefore closest to being what a layman might consider to be an owner. It is to the beneficiary that the trustee's duties are owned, and he can enforce them against the trustee.

Figure 1.1 is a diagrammatic representation of this division of ownership.

Figure 1.1

	Creation of trust	
	Before	After
Legal title — burdensome (managerial in nature)	Settlor	Trustee
Equitable title (beneficial: provides enjoyment)	None	Beneficiary or cestui que trust Note: either trustee or beneficiary may also be settlor

Everything that is capable of being owned is capable of being held in trust. This includes not only goods, and freehold and leasehold estates in land, but also lesser interests. For example, it is possible to own a right of way over the land of another (this is an example of an easement), and rights of way can be held in trust. It is even possible for the beneficiary's equitable ownership itself to be held in trust, in which case a sub-trust is created.

1.1.1   Terminological difficulties over land

In previous editions of this book, the diagram indicated that the settlor also had equitable title prior to the creation of the trust, and this analysis can still be found in many textbooks, but in *Westdeutsche Landesbank Girozentrale* v *Islington London Borough Council* [1996] 2 All ER 961, Lord Browne-Wilkinson said, probably as part of the *ratio* of the case:

> A person solely entitled to the full beneficial ownership of money or property, both at law and in equity, does not enjoy an equitable interest in that property. The legal title carries with it all rights. Unless and until there is a separation of the legal and equitable estates, there is no separate equitable title.

Since one cannot argue with House of Lords *rationes*, the analysis in the previous editions has had to be changed.

The purpose of this paragraph is simply to clarify terms which are used later on. All the above applies to land, as well as goods, money, shares, etc. However, for technical reasons, which for the most part do not affect the law of trusts (insofar as they do they are summarised in 1.2.7), it is not possible to own land. This may also come as a surprise to students who are unfamiliar with land law. The technical position is that one can have title to an estate in land. The term 'title', for the purposes of this book, can be taken to mean the same as ownership — the differences between title and ownership are irrelevant to the law of trusts. The title is not to the land itself, however, but to an estate in land. Title to an estate can be divided, by means of a trust, into separate legal and equitable elements.

An estate in land can be regarded as a right to possess land for a period of time. Leasehold estates, for example, are often for a fixed number of weeks, months or years. The period of time can be infinite, as with the usual freehold estate, which is called the fee simple absolute in possession — this is the estate most people buy when purchasing freehold property. But there are also lesser freehold estates. For example, a settlement of land, intended to keep the land in the family, may be in the form of a life estate to the surviving widow, followed by a fee simple in favour of the eldest son. Both the widow and eldest son have estates immediately, even though the son has no right to possess the land yet. All settlements must inevitably contain an estate which does not give an immediate right to possession. It is also possible to have entailed estates, which pass automatically on death, usually to a male heir, and which cannot therefore be left by will.

Subject to the provisions of the 1925 property legislation, which is discussed at the end of this chapter (1.6), it is possible for estates in land to be held in trust, thereby splitting legal and equitable title. The real point of this section, however, is to explain the terms that will be used when talking about trusts involving land, and why I shall not refer to ownership of land, except on occasions as a convenient shorthand.

1.2 EARLY HISTORY OF EQUITY

The English legal system divides into common law and equity: two different systems and until recently two separate jurisdictions. Equity and trusts are found exclusively in England and in other non-Roman legal systems, and neither has any place, for example, on the Continent. That a legal system should develop two separate concepts of ownership, both of which can apply simultaneously to the same property, and effectively two separate legal systems, is by no means self-evident. The reason lies in historical differences between England and Continental countries, dating from the feudal era, and in particular the Norman Conquest.

1.2.1 Feudalism and the Norman Conquest
Though equity is English in origin, and though it developed as an incidental result of feudalism, feudalism was by no means an exclusively English phenomenon. Indeed, although feudalism existed even before 1066 in England, it was probably more developed on the Continent at this time, and it was a modified form of European feudalism that was imposed on England by the Norman Conquest.

Furthermore, true feudalism in England did not last very long after 1066; in its original form it was inefficient, and so had pretty well died out by around 1150, long before the conception of equity. It is none the less important in the development of equity, because of its indirect consequences, especially regarding methods of holding land. These resulted, for example, in transfers of land at common law becoming very difficult, and hence to the impetus for the growth of a new and separate system, of equity, the principles of which remain today. Other indirect consequences, such as the development of the doctrine of estates, and leasehold title, are mainly of interest to land lawyers.

In pre-feudal times land was owned absolutely. The essence of the feudal system was that, in relatively lawless times, landowners collectively and for their mutual protection, bound themselves to an overlord, who was often a military expert, offering service (often of a military nature) to the overlord or produce in exchange for protection. Eventually the land became held on condition that services or produce was provided, and tenure of land became the exclusive bond between overlord and tenant. The system probably developed faster in Europe than in England because of a greater degree of anarchy overseas at that time.

Feudal structures were initially developed well before 1066, possibly by the smallholders themselves, rather than externally imposed upon them. Though feudalism became universal, it was not centralised; each great estate or manor had its own overlord and its own law and customs. It is true that the Crown in Europe granted some of its own land to lords in exchange for money or military services, so the Crown became supreme lord of some, but not all, of the land. But the system was essentially *ad hoc*, and indeed came into being *because* of the lawlessness resulting from the lack of a strong central government.

The peculiarity of English feudalism after 1066 came about because the chief landowners forcibly resisted the attempt of William I to assert supremacy over them. William therefore confiscated all land following his successful conquest, and subsequently allowed it to be held (or often redeemed) only from the Crown (directly by overlords), in exchange for money or services. So *all* land came to be held from the Crown, in exchange for money or services. It is still technically so held, though the services have usually not been collected for so long that they are barred by limitation (i.e., time-barred). Thus in England alone feudal land tenure became centralised, and was imposed from above with the Crown as supreme landlord.

The large landowners or overlords, holding directly (or immediately) from the Crown, allowed others to hold from them, also as tenants in exchange for personal services. These tenants thus held *immediately* from their lords, and *mediately* from the Crown. They allowed yet others to hold some of their land from them on similar bases, and so on, so large tenurial chains developed. Figure 1.2 is a simplified diagrammatic representation.

As can be seen from the figure 1.2, those who held from other lords, and were not themselves in occupation, were called 'mesne lords'. It is likely that many of those at the bottom of these chains ('tenants in demesne') had been holding the same land, from the same immediate lords, before the Conquest; though some evidence of dispossessions has recently come to light, a large-scale movement of people would surely have achieved little. So for many the effect of the Conquest was merely to add the Crown to the top of the chain.

1.2.2 *Quia Emptores* 1290

The creation of subtenancies in this way was called subinfeudation, whereas an out and out transfer of a tenancy (which was not originally allowed) was called substitution. Eventually the system became so complex that it created problems for the overlords in collecting their feudal dues, and subinfeudation was therefore abolished (except for the Crown) by the statute *Quia Emptores* 1290. This statute is still in force, having survived an attempt to repeal it in 1967, and is often regarded as being a pillar of the law of real property. After 1290, therefore, no new freehold subtenancies could be created; those existing remained (a few still remain in rural areas where manorial lords remained active), but as the feudal dues became less valuable many of the intermediate lords did not bother to collect them, and eventually were time-barred. The result is that today nearly all land is held directly from the Crown.

1.2.3 Demise of feudalism

The original services were personal in nature; tenure was therefore for life only, and was inalienable. It soon became clear, however, that it was more

Figure 1.2

Feudal tenures

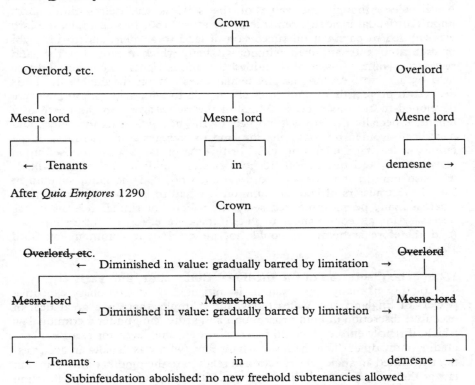

Before *Quia Emptores* 1290

```
                              Crown
        ┌───────────────────────────────────────────────┐
  Overlord, etc.                                      Overlord
    ┌──────────────────────┬─────────────────┐          │
  Mesne lord            Mesne lord        Mesne lord
    │                       │                 │
  ┌──────┐              ┌──────┐          ┌──────┐
  ← Tenants                in              demesne  →
```

After *Quia Emptores* 1290

```
                              Crown
        ┌───────────────────────────────────────────────┐
  ~~Overlord, etc.~~                                  ~~Overlord~~
        ← Diminished in value: gradually barred by limitation →
    ┌──────────────────────┬─────────────────┐          │
  ~~Mesne lord~~        ~~Mesne lord~~     ~~Mesne lord~~
        ← Diminished in value: gradually barred by limitation →
    │                       │                 │
  ┌──────┐              ┌──────┐          ┌──────┐
  ← Tenants                in              demesne  →
```

Subinfeudation abolished: no new freehold subtenancies allowed

efficient to allow families to remain in possession of land over successive generations if they so wished, or if they did not, to allow them to alienate (e.g., sell) the land, and to convert the services into money payments, with which equivalent services could be hired in the general market. Certainly this was a better way, for example, of raising armies, because it mattered that the best soldiers were recruited, and they were not necessarily, after the first generation, holding land on military tenures. Unfortunately (for the lords at any rate), as soon as services became converted into money payments, they quickly lost their value through inflation; it is for this reason that most feudal dues had lost their economic value by about 1150, and were not collected for a sufficiently long period to be time-barred. Many remaining dues were eventually abolished by the Tenures Abolition Act 1660, after the Civil War. The Crown was the main beneficiary by then, as supreme landlord, of the remaining feudal incidents; they were abolished because they effectively constituted extra-Parliamentary revenue for the Crown, and military tenures promoted the creation of private armies.

1.2.4 The remaining feudal dues

Nevertheless, though the value of the services themselves diminished, important feudal incidents remained long after 1150. For example, the lord was entitled to payment on succession of land to an heir, and to the right of escheat if a tenant died without an heir, which meant that the land reverted to him. He was also entitled to various rights when the land was held by a minor. As long as any feudal dues remained valuable the lords desired to protect them, and rules about title to land at common law were developed to aid this process. Many of the rights arose on the death of a tenant, especially if there was no heir or the heir was a minor, and could have been avoided by conveying the land to younger adult members of the family, or leaving the land by will. For this reason taxes were imposed upon conveyances, and until 1540 freehold estates could not be left by will. It was also important to be able to ascertain who held the land, so until at least 1535 transfers of land at common law had to be open and notorious, whereas many people preferred secret transfers. For similar reasons it was necessary for all conveyances to take immediate effect, so future interests (and therefore settlements) could not be created at common law until 1540.

1.2.5 The discretion of the medieval Chancellor, and early equity

The rigidity of many legal systems is mitigated by discretionary executive power. In England and Wales today, for example, there is a great deal of executive discretion in both prosecution and sentencing under a criminal law which, if rigidly enforced, could be very burdensome, even for relatively law-abiding individuals. The medieval Chancellor (who was usually an ecclesiastic) performed an analogous function in relation to the rigidity of the common law at the time; he had the power to issue the royal writs, and this function came to be exercised in a discretionary manner, based on notions of conscience and justice. He also had powers to act against individuals, and to enforce his orders against them by imprisonment. This discretionary use of power was the foundation of equity. Eventually, probably during the 15th century, the Chancellor's office took on many of the features of a court, and the Court of Chancery was born.

Equity originally developed to avoid the restrictions placed on transfers by the common law, and to avoid feudal dues. Its character in this regard has not altered significantly to this day; equitable doctrines still develop where common law doctrines are regarded as inflexible, although as we shall see equity no longer retains the full extent of its original flexibility. For example, the recent development of the promissory estoppel doctrine has mitigated against the supposed rigidity of common law consideration in contract. There are also current developments in land law, whose eventual outcome is still uncertain, in an attempt to avoid the rigours of common law privity of contract: the estoppel licence and possibly a new variety of the constructive trust. It should also not be forgotten that the trust has always been, and is, capable of being used as a tax avoidance device, just as early equitable intervention was used as a device to avoid feudal dues.

The Chancellor's power could theoretically be exercised without altering the substance of the common law, though in practice his jurisdiction significantly affected the exercise of common law rights. For example, he might refuse to issue a writ to a claimant at common law, or compel a common law owner to convey his property to someone else. One might have thought that conflict between the two systems was therefore inevitable, but it should be remembered that in these early days the common law was not itself a very well defined system, and it was not thought odd that the King, through the Chancellor, should exercise a residual discretion. Conflicts between common law and equity did eventually arise, but not until some centuries later.

1.2.6 Uses

One of the most important early developments was the use, which was the predecessor of the modern trust. In fact, even before the Conquest, land was sometimes held by one person on behalf of another for a particular purpose or use. General uses originated probably around or before 1230: land was conveyed to X to the use of Y, where, for example, Y was a community of Franciscan friars which at that time was not allowed to hold property. Later uses became more common generally as conveyancing devices, often specifically to avoid the common law restrictions. The difficulty was that X had legal title; the common law did not recognise the use. Clearly, however, Y was intended to enjoy the property. From about 1400 the Chancellor ensured, by acting on the conscience of X, that X held the land for the benefit of Y. X, who became known as the 'feoffee to uses', therefore retained legal title, and indeed the common law was theoretically unaffected, but Y, the 'cestui que use', came to be regarded as equitable owner. Hence the division of ownership (or title), and hence the development of two separate legal systems.

The device was used to avoid the feudal dues described above; the legal estate could be vested in a number of feoffees to uses as joint tenants. Jointly held estates pass automatically to the survivors on the death of a joint tenant, so it was possible to avoid the dues on death and ensure that a minor never had title at common law, while allowing equitable title to pass from, say, father to son on the father's death. Legal estates also needed rarely to be transferred, because the joint tenants at law held the land merely in a nominal or managerial role, the right to enjoy the property taking effect behind the use. It was also possible to devise the equitable estate, and to create settlements by means of future interests.

Figure 1.3 is a diagrammatic representation of legal and equitable titles during a possible transfer over four generations. Ideally, it should not have been necessary to transfer legal title at all.

Figure 1.3

Legal title
(managerial in nature — rarely changes)

Feoffees to uses as joint tenants

Grandfather ———▶ Father ———▶ Son ———▶ Grandson ———▶ Etc.

Equitable title
(beneficial in nature — often changes)

1.2.7   Equity follows the law

One of the consequences of the early feudal tenurial system was that no one
could be said to own land. The lord was not in possession, and owed
obligations to the tenant. Tenure, on the other hand, was subject to obligations to the lord. An appropriate analogy today might be the tenure of a High
Court judge in office — however secure the post may be, it cannot sensibly
be said that anyone owns it, either judge or Crown, and this would continue
to be so even in the unlikely event that such posts became inheritable. So far
as early landholding was concerned the very concept of ownership was
meaningless, and certainly no such concept was protected by the common
law. Some of the consequences of this, which still remain, are of greater
interest to students of land law than trusts, for example, that title to land is
to this day a relative concept. But the impossibility of owning land also
influenced the development of uses, and later trusts. In particular, as land
became marketable, and some concept similar to ownership was therefore
required, the doctrine of estates developed. An estate is the right to hold
tenure for a period of time, and many estates can exist in the same land
simultaneously. The concept, which for these historical reasons is peculiar to
common law, as opposed to Roman law systems, is very useful in its own
right.

When the Chancellor created the use it was necessary to decide which
equitable estates would be protected. One meaning of the maxim 'equity
follows the law' (on equitable maxims, see 1.4.1) is that equity recognises all
the estates (and other interests in land) recognised by the common law. In
fact, for a greater part of equity's history, and today, equity has also
recognised estates and interests which are not recognised at common law;
today, however, this is mainly because limits have been placed on the number
of possible legal estates in land by the 1925 property legislation (see 1.6.1).

1.3   STATUTE OF USES 1535

It is clear from the above that one of the functions of the use was to enable
feudal dues to be avoided, and soon a great proportion of land was held to
uses. Obviously this affected the Crown most adversely, as supreme landlord.
Henry VIII therefore decided to counter the device, and the effect of the
Statute of Uses 1535 was to 'execute' many uses, that is to say to convey the

legal estate to the cestui que use. Henry was unable to get his way entirely, and the Act was a compromise. It was not of universal application, as it did not apply to leaseholds or to situations where the feoffees to uses had active duties to perform. Where it applied, however, the advantages of the device were negated, because the feoffees to uses disappeared. Figure 1.4 illustrates this, and it can also be seen that the number of transfers of the legal estate is necessarily increased to achieve the same result.

The eventual solution, which seems to have been reached by around 1700, was to employ a second use, called a 'trust'. An example might be a conveyance 'to X unto the use of Y and his heirs in trust for Z and his heirs'. Though the first use was executed the second (trust) was not. Hence Y held the legal estate in trust for Z, who became equitable owner. In later conveyances X would have been omitted completely. The effect of this statute in this regard, therefore, was to do little more than change the name of the use to trust and to add a few words to conveyances. The terminology has also changed. The legal owner has become the trustee: the equitable owner the cestui que trust, or beneficiary.

The legal history of, and even the legal basis for the subversion of an Act of Parliament by the Court of Chancery is obscure. Certainly by 1700 the political situation had completely changed, with the abolition of many feudal dues in 1660 and a more satisfactory Parliamentary basis for royal finances.

Figure 1.4

Before 1535

ABC as joint tenants	Legal title
D→E→F→G→	Equitable title

After 1535

D→E→F→G→	Legal title
	Equitable title

The statute had incidental effects, which made it necessary eventually for the common law to develop a rule against perpetuities. These incidental effects, and the rule itself, are considered in chapter 7.

1.4 AN OUTLINE OF MODERN EQUITABLE PRINCIPLES

In its early days equitable jurisdiction was exercised on an *ad hoc* basis, and its transformation into a modern system did not come about until after around 1700, by which time Chancellors tended to be lawyers rather than ecclesiasts and a system of precedent was beginning to develop. Yet many features of the early use remain in the modern trust. Indeed it was necessary for equity to retain many of its early features to avoid conflict with the common law (a major problem in the 17th century). It should be noted, however, that today's trust applies to goods, as well as land.

It may be that the development of principles some 200 years ago, followed by increased rigidity in the law more recently, has had undesirable consequences. The 18th century was, after all, before modern banking practices and limited liability companies (as presently constituted) existed. Most trusts tended to be of the family settlement variety. Yet the principles that were well-suited to such settlements also apply in essence today. We shall see in chapter 4 how assumptions based on family-type trusts impeded until very recently the development of the law relating to certainties, and it may also be that trustees' duties are too onerous for similar reasons. The nub of the problem is that family trusts are not in their nature intended as risky ventures, and a significant difficulty is in guarding against fraud of the trustees. To apply similar principles to professional trustees, who may well be expected to take business risks, is arguably inappropriate.

1.4.1 The equitable maxims

As equity shook off its *ad hoc* origins, certain principles developed which became embodied in the form of equitable maxims. These are not rules to be construed like statutes, but rather a general basis around which much of the law of equity has formed. They frequently appear as part of the reasoning in judgments. All have relevance to the law of trusts — the first was a rationalisation of the basis of the jurisdiction exercised originally by the medieval Chancellor, and the second we have already come across. Many of the rest will appear in later sections and chapters, so for convenience all of the 12 usually quoted are listed below, though their full explanations will be at the appropriate part of the book.

1. Equity will not suffer a wrong without a remedy.
2. Equity follows the law.
3. Where there is equal equity, the law shall prevail.
4. Where the equities are equal, the first in time shall prevail.
5. He who seeks equity must do equity.
6. He who comes to equity must come with clean hands.
7. Delay defeats equities.
8. Equality is equity.
9. Equity looks to the intent rather than the form.
10. Equity looks on that as done which ought to be done.
11. Equity imputes an intention to fulfil an obligation.
12. Equity acts *in personam*.

Though only the above 12 are usually regarded as the definitive equitable maxims, equity has developed additional principles which may be treated to all intents and purposes as if they were among the maxims. The following may not be an exhaustive list, but all these principles will appear again in the book.

13. Equity will not assist a volunteer (see chapter 3).
14. Equity will not perfect an imperfect gift (see chapter 3).
15. Equity will not construe a valid power out of an invalid trust (see 2.5 and 4.4).
16. Equity will not permit the provisions of a statute intended to prevent fraud to be used as an instrument for fraud (see chapter 8, and 6.5 and 9.8).
17. Equity will not permit a trust to fail for want of a trustee.

The exact language of these maxims and principles appears to vary slightly between different authorities.

1.4.2 Equity acts *in personam*

One feature of equitable jurisdiction has always been that it is exercised against specific persons — equity acts *in personam*. This is also an important maxim of equity. In the case of the use the remedy was personal against the feoffee to uses, who held the legal estate in the land. Also in a modern trust the action is against the owner of the legal estate in land, or the legal owner of money or goods. Consequently it does not matter, for example, if the land, money or goods are themselves situated abroad, so long as the legal owner or trustee can be found.

Nevertheless, as equity developed it acted not only against the original legal owner of the property, but also against subsequent owners in certain circumstances. The exact nature of this development is considered in 1.4.6. As a result of this it is reasonable to describe certain equitable rights as property rights, and to talk about equitable title to land, and equitable ownership of goods. It is also the case that various statutory provisions, and in particular the 1925 property legislation (see 1.6) and some taxation legislation (see, e.g., 6.4.4) treat equitable interests as property interests. So although it is still accurate to say that equity acts *in personam*, some equitable rights also have the characteristics of rights *in rem*. As will appear from the following sections, however, there are significant differences between legal and equitable title or ownership.

1.4.3 Nature of legal and equitable ownership

To return again to the use, it is clear that it was the equitable ownership which was enjoyed; the feoffee to uses merely managed the property on behalf of the cestui que use. The same position obtains with the modern trust. Legal ownership, or trusteeship, is a management function. So far from being desirable, a trustee undertakes onerous duties (on which, see chapters 14 to 17), and is often paid for undertaking trusteeship (e.g., banks, solicitors — for conditions attaching to payment, see 14.3.2). The equitable owner, or beneficiary, on the other hand, is entitled to enjoy the property. Of course, where no trust is imposed, the same person will be both legal and equitable owner, as is the case with the majority of ordinary possessions owned absolutely by one person (see figure 1.1). In this event legal ownership is by no means a burden, because there is nobody to whom any duties are owed, and most owners of goods would be surprised if it were otherwise. Here also, though, the correct analysis is probably that it is the equitable title, which is also enjoyed by the absolute owner, which gives rise to the enjoyment right.

1.4.4   Other equitable interests

The equitable principles discussed in this section do not apply only to full equitable ownership of chattels or estates in land arising out of the types of transactions already considered. Equity also recognises other interests in property which are less than full ownership, and some of the following cases and examples are about equitable interests, rather than full equitable ownership.

For example, suppose A has freehold legal title to land, and contracts to lease the land to B for seven years. Under the contract B is entitled to possession and enjoyment of the land for that period. The contract is enforceable at common law, just like any other contract, and if a lease is not executed, or B is denied possession or enjoyment of the land, he can claim damages. The common law does not recognise B as actually being lessee, however, until the lease is executed in the prescribed formal manner. But unlike many contracts, this arrangement is also enforceable in equity, allowing B to claim the equitable remedies of specific performance, which forces A to execute the lease, and injunction, which stops A acting in a manner inconsistent with the grant of the lease. Furthermore, 'equity looks on that as done which ought to be done' (see the equitable maxims in 1.4.1), and B is treated as if he were *already* a lessee in equity, even if no formal lease has yet been executed (*Walsh* v *Lonsdale* (1882) 20 ChD 9). So a contract for a lease can create an immediate equitable interest in land, called an estate contract (a lease being an estate in land), to which the equitable principles discussed below apply.

The same applies to contracts for lesser legal rights in land. A contract to create a legal easement (e.g., a right of way — a right much less extensive than legal ownership) can give rise to an equitable easement, which is another equitable interest less than full ownership. Additionally, there are some interests in land which exist only in equity, for example, restrictive covenants, which are a narrowly defined specialist type of contract between landowners. The principles discussed in this section apply to these interests also.

Terminologically, so far as land is concerned, an *estate*, whether legal or equitable, connotes an interest akin to ownership; an *interest in land* can include an estate, but also includes rights that are much less extensive than ownership.

1.4.5   Equitable remedies

Some specific applications of equitable remedies are discussed in chapter 19, but it is necessary even at this stage to introduce the equitable remedies, and consider the general principles applicable to them.

Originally equity developed its own remedies, which were not available to the common law. Nor did equity administer common law remedies. This position was to some extent altered by the Common Law Procedure Act 1854, which gave the common law courts some jurisdiction to give equitable remedies, and the Chancery Amendment Act 1858, which allowed the Court of Chancery to award the common law derived remedy of damages, but only in addition to, or in substitution for an equitable remedy. See further 1.5.

In 1873–5 the courts were fused (see 1.5), but the principles governing the grant of equitable remedies were not changed by that legislation, and are still applicable to actions to protect equitable interests or estates, and other rights having an equitable origin. Thus, it is still necessary to consider the equitable remedies separately from the common law remedies.

The main equitable remedies are the injunction and specific performance. For breach of fiduciary duty (see chapter 14) there is also the remedy of account, and sometimes equity imposes a constructive trust (see chapters 10 and 19). Damages could not originally be awarded, and can be now only on the basis of the 1858 Act. In any event the quantum of equitable damages may differ from that appropriate in a common law action.

Equitable remedies are available for breaches of equitable obligations, such as those considered in chapters 10 and 14, but in addition injunctions can be used to prevent the commissions of torts. For some torts, such as negligence claims arising out of road accident cases, the remedy is obviously inappropriate, but it can be useful for continuing torts, such as trespass or nuisance. As will be seen in chapter 14, it can be used to prevent abuses of confidential information.

1.4.5.1 Equitable remedies discretionary A major difference between the two systems is that whereas common law remedies are available as of right, equitable remedies retain the discretionary nature of early equitable jurisdiction. Although for the creation of wholly new equitable rights and principles, the onset over the last two centuries or so of defined systems of precedent and law reporting has curtailed the early discretion somewhat, the remedies are nevertheless still discretionary, even though that discretion is now exercised in accord with fairly clear and even rigid principles. The discretionary nature of the remedies can lead to dire consequences. If an equitable estate or interest depends on the award of an equitable remedy, the refusal to grant the remedy destroys the interest.

1.4.5.2 Exercise of the discretion A common ground for refusal of a remedy is the behaviour of the party claiming the equitable remedy: 'he who comes into equity must come with clean hands' — see 1.4.1. For example, in *Coatsworth* v *Johnson* (1886) 54 LT 520, CA the plaintiff was in possession of land under a contract for a lease, where no lease that would be recognised at common law had been executed. The landlord in fact turned the plaintiff out, and the plaintiff sued for trespass. He would have won the action had he been regarded as a lessee, either at common law or in equity. As we saw above, equity in principle enforces contracts for leases, and would normally regard the plaintiff as being an equitable lessee. In the particular case he was in breach of various covenants under the agreement, however. In these circumstances, the Court of Appeal held, the equitable remedy would have been refused, and the plaintiff *therefore lost his interest*. Thus he was thrown back on his common law rights, and of course he had no lease at common law. So he lost. Not only is this case a good example of the discretionary nature of equitable remedies, but also emphasises the need to treat common law and equitable rights and remedies separately. Also, the entire interest was lost because the remedy was refused.

The behaviour of the party claiming the remedy is not the only factor. Innocent plaintiffs can also lose their remedies. For example, a remedy might also be refused if to grant it would put the other party in breach of a contract with a third party (*Warmington* v *Miller* [1973] QB 877). Other grounds for refusing the remedy are that severe hardship might be caused to the defendant, or in a contract action where the contract has been forced upon the defendant through unfair pressure (even in the absence of undue influence or duress).

The existence of a discretion does not, however, imply that it is unlimited. In *Mountford* v *Scott* [1975] Ch 258, an argument was advanced that equity ought not to enforce an option, granted for £1, to purchase a house for £10,000. The argument was based on the undoubted rule that equity will not specifically enforce a promise at the instance of a volunteer, although the promise, if under seal, may found an action for damages at common law (see further chapter 3). It was argued by the defendants that this rule should be extended to this situation, where the consideration for the grant of the option was a token payment, and that the plaintiffs should therefore have been left to their remedy in damages. Brightman J summed up the issue thus:

As the plaintiffs had made no more than a token payment for the defendant's promise, are the plaintiffs, so far as the equitable remedy of specific performance is concerned, in the position of volunteers who ought to be left to their remedy in damages?

The argument was rejected by Brightman J, whose decision was upheld in the Court of Appeal.

1.4.6 Equitable rights and third parties
So far we have considered only remedies against the trustee or, where the interest arises out of a contract, as in 1.4.4, the other contracting party. For equitable rights to be regarded in any sense as property rights, however, it is necessary also to consider the extent to which they can bind third parties.

1.4.6.1 Equitable notice doctrine in land transactions
Common law title is in principle enforceable against anyone. Suppose, however, that property is conveyed to X on trust for Y, as in figure 1.5, and that X disposes of the legal estate in the property to Z. If equitable rights are proprietary, then Z (and not just X) should normally be bound by Y's interest.

Figure 1.5

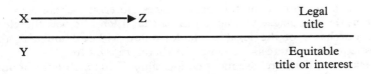

It might be objected that there is no need for Z to be bound, since X has clearly acted in breach of trust, and Y will have a perfectly good action against X. Or suppose, for example, that Y had an estate contract enforceable against X. Obviously X has broken the contract and can be sued by Y for damages. This is of little use, however, if X has gone bankrupt, or disappeared, or spent the purchase money. In any event Y does not want the common law damages; he wants the land at the agreed price.

As far as the common law is concerned, the only title it recognises is that of Z, and because of the privity of contract doctrine (see 2.3.2.4) Y cannot sue Z on the contract at common law. However, equity imposes obligations on Z as well as on X, and it is in this sense that equitable rights can be regarded as proprietary.

However, whereas legal title and legal interests in land are enforceable against anyone, Z can, in some circumstances, take free of Y's equitable interest. The basis of the action against Z is the same as that of the action against X — equity imposes on the conscience of the third party. But this depends on Z's conscience being affected, and it is not when Z is a bona fide purchaser of the legal estate for value, without notice of Y's title or interest (in which case Z is also described as 'equity's darling'). Here Z is as much an 'innocent' victim of X's breach of trust as is Y. The equities between them are equal, and the law, or Z's legal title, prevails over Y's title, which is merely equitable: 'where there is equal equity, the law shall prevail' (see 1.4.1). This is the basis of the equitable notice doctrine.

In *Cave* v *Cave* (1880) 15 ChD 639, Charles Cave, as sole trustee and family solicitor, stole trust money and purchased a house with it. As a result of this transaction, the moneys in the trust fund were converted into land, so that the beneficiaries of the fund became beneficiaries of the land (upon principles which are similar to those applied in *Re Hallett's Estate* (1880) 13 ChD 696, on which see further 19.2). The fraudulent trustee/solicitor then raised money by way of legal mortgage. This transaction took place before the enactment of the 1925 property legislation, at a time when a legal mortgage took effect by way of a conveyance of the entire freehold estate to the mortgagee, with a covenant to re-convey the property to the mortgagor if the money loaned, plus interest and administration charges, was repaid to the mortgagee on a fixed date. Equity enforced this covenant and also allowed the mortgagor to demand a later re-conveyance, subject to repayment of the capital loaned, plus interest and administration charges. (Had the transaction taken place today, since the 1925 property legislation, the only difference would have been that the mortgagee would have obtained a legal lease on the property, rather than the freehold estate.) Hence, the mortgagee obtained legal title. He also provided value, in the form of the money advanced. Fry J held that he had no notice of the beneficiaries' interest. There was no suggestion that the mortgagee was acting in bad faith, and he was therefore a bona fide purchaser of the legal estate for value without notice of the beneficiaries' equitable interests, of which he therefore took free.

For Z to take free, the purchase must be for value. Value includes not only consideration recognised at common law, but also equitable consideration. Thus, for example, as well as value in terms of money or money's worth (which are recognised as consideration by both systems), equity also recognises a future marriage as consideration, and so it constitutes value for the purposes of the bona fide purchaser rule. On the other hand, the common law allows contracts under seal to be enforced even in the absence of consideration; equity does not take the same view, and such contracts do not provide value for the purposes of this rule (nor incidentally can such contracts be enforced using equitable remedies). Where the value is money, the purchaser must pay all the money before receiving notice of the equitable interest.

Notice itself includes not only actual, but also constructive notice. For dealings in land this means that the purchaser must inquire about equitable interests with no less diligence than he would inquire of legal interests, and these standards are determined by ordinary conveyancing practice. Thus a careless purchaser is not protected, neither is one who could have discovered the existence of an interest by inspecting the land. Additionally, knowledge of an agent (e.g., solicitor) is imputed, so that the purchaser is treated as having any knowledge that his agent acquires. In *Cave* v *Cave*, however, Charles Cave acted as solicitor for both the mortgagor and the mortgagee, and obviously he knew the truth, but Fry J held that his notice would not be imputed to the mortgagee since he was party to a fraud. Fry J said (at p. 644):

> . . . the act done by the agent [Charles Cave] is such as cannot be said to be done by him in his character of agent, but is done by him in the character of a party to an independent fraud on his principal [mortgagee], and that is not to be imputed to the principal as an act done by his agent.

The details of precisely what constitutes notice is covered in land law textbooks and is beyond the scope of this book, but it is worth observing that the notice doctrine developed from land transactions, which are characterised by their thoroughness and lack of haste. For this reason, the notice doctrine works strictly against purchasers. The courts have shown a marked reluctance to apply quite so rigorous a doctrine in ordinary commercial transactions, which are characterised by their informality and speed: see further 19.3.

The notice doctrine applies not only to full equitable ownership or title, but also to any lesser form of equitable interest in property. One consequence of this is that trusts, which can therefore affect third parties, can be used as a device to avoid the privity of contract doctrine; see further 2.3.2.4. However, it does not follow that whenever Y has an equitable remedy against

X, and assuming that Z is not 'equity's darling', Z will always take subject to X's rights. In *National Provincial Bank Ltd* v *Ainsworth* [1965] AC 1175, the House of Lords held that some equitable rights were personal, or 'mere equities', which did not create proprietary interests capable of binding third parties. *Ainsworth* concerned the right of a spouse to occupy the matrimonial home, which (prior to the Matrimonial Homes Act 1967) was a personal right, enforceable only against her husband. It is now clear that contractual licences to occupy land fall into this category — see *Ashburn Anstalt* v *Arnold* [1989] 1 Ch 1, considered in detail in chapter 10. They are correctly described as equities, since they are enforceable using equitable remedies, and the principles discussed in 1.4.5 apply to them, but they are not equitable interests, since contractual licences are purely personal rights.

1.4.6.2 Priorities between successive equitable interests The equitable maxim 'Where there is equal equity, the law shall prevail', applies only where Z purchases a legal estate or title. A purchaser of an *equitable* estate or interest will not generally, therefore, take priority over a prior equitable interest. Another maxim applies: 'Where the equities are equal, the first in time shall prevail.' In other words, priorities of equitable interests generally rank according to the order of time in which they have been created (there is a limited number of exceptions concerning mortgages, which are outside the scope of this book).

The general position is illustrated by figure 1.6.

Figure 1.6

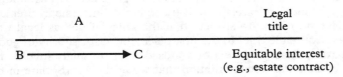

It is assumed in the diagram that B and C have both entered estate contracts with A to purchase his legal estate in land. As we have seen, estate contracts are equitable interests in land. Clearly A cannot sell the same land to both B and C, so B's estate contract will prevail in equity. C can still sue A for damages for breach of contract at common law, of course.

In *Cave* v *Cave*, the value of the property was greater than the amount raised on the first mortgage, so Charles Cave raised further money on a second mortgage. The second mortgagee, like the first, had no notice of the beneficiaries' interests. However, he could not obtain a legal estate, since that had already been conveyed to the first mortgagee (the usual position prior to the 1925 legislation). His mortgage took effect as a mortgage in equity only. Even though he had acted bona fide, therefore, had given value and had no notice of the prior equitable interests of the beneficiaries, he was not a bona fide purchaser of the *legal* estate for value without notice. He therefore took subject to the plaintiffs' prior equitable interest, Fry J observing (at p. 648):

As between persons having only equitable interests, if their equities are in all other respects equal, priority of time gives the better equity, or, '*Qui prior est tempore potior est jure*'.

It can be seen that this is merely a restatement, in slightly different language, of equitable maxim 4 (see 1.4.1).

1.4.6.3 Application to property apart from land The notice doctrine originally developed from land transactions, but has been extended to all other forms of property. Indeed, today it is far more important in relation to other forms of property than it is to land, since the importance of the doctrine in relation to land has been much reduced by the 1925 property legislation (see 1.6.2).

The same fundamental distinction between legal and equitable ownership applies also in the case of goods and other property. In the case of goods, common law ownership can be enforced against anyone at all (subject, in the case of sale of goods, to the exceptions contained in the Factors Act 1889, ss. 2, 8 and 9, and the Sale of Goods Act 1979, ss. 21–26, which are discussed in detail in textbooks on sale of goods). Equitable ownership, by contrast, can be lost to a bona fide purchaser for value who does not know of the equitable ownership. Note that I have deliberately not adopted the same wording as for the notice doctrine, since it seems that many of the detailed workings of the notice doctrine (e.g., constructive and imputed notice — see 1.4.6.2) may well apply only to land. The position with personal property is similar, but probably not identical.

Yet although the doctrine theoretically applies to goods as well as land, in practice, buyers of goods are rarely bound by equitable interests in them, as they generally have no reason to suspect that the seller, if he has legal title, does not also have equitable title. In the first place, the vast majority of goods are not held in trust. Also, transfers of goods do not normally involve the degree of investigation and documentation that would be appropriate in the case of land, so an assumption of absolute ownership is normally reasonable.

If the seller does not have legal title, such title can nevertheless pass to the buyer in certain circumstances (under the Factors Act and Sale of Goods Act sections mentioned above), but these circumstances are so drawn up that it is almost inconceivable that a buyer who acquires title in this way would be acting in bad faith, or have any notice of an equitable interest. On the other hand, if the seller has no title, and the buyer also acquires no title, because the Factors Act, etc. provisions do not apply in his favour, he will necessarily be bound by any prior equitable interests. This will be so whether or not he acts in good faith, and whether or not he has notice, because he does not acquire any legal title.

It is possible to conclude in the case of goods, that in practice the determining factor will be whether the buyer acquires legal title to the goods, rather than the presence or absence of good faith or notice.

The position is quite different where money is concerned, at least where it is being used as currency, however, and there has been quite a spate of recent litigation (see further 19.2.1.2). Where money is stolen, or a cheque forged by altering the name of the payee, the thief can pass legal title in the money, even though he has no title to it himself, because of an exception to the common law principle that a man cannot pass a title that he does not have (*nemo dat quod non habet*). Money stolen in this way may be (for example) laundered through bank accounts, given to friends, spent at gambling clubs or used to purchase tangible property. The legal title will be passed on by the thief, and in general, the thief will disappear or not be worth suing. The victim of the theft may in certain circumstances be able to assert equitable title in the money against the recipients, however, and the precise circumstances where this can be done are considered in 19.2.2, where again the distinction between legal and equitable ownership is of fundamental importance. One of the main issues there considered is the state of knowledge required to bind the recipient, which probably differs in some respects from the notice doctrine as it applies to land (on which see 1.4.6.2).

1.4.6.4   Equitable rights as right *in rem*   To conclude this discussion, equity began by acting *in personam*, without affecting common law title or ownership. This is similar to the situation today, where let us say the owner of a ship charters it for a period to a time charterer. The charterer can assert contractual rights against the owner, but these are simply personal rights against the owner, and although the charterer is entitled to use the vessel, the ownership of the vessel remains entirely unaffected by the charterparty. Furthermore, the charterer cannot enforce his charterparty against a purchaser of the vessel, at any rate directly (see further 2.3.2.4).

It may well be that equitable rights began like present-day contractual rights, enforceable only against the original feoffee to uses. Equity developed, however, as contract has not, to allow wide-ranging enforcement against subsequent legal owners. It is therefore not a full description of equitable rights to say that they are merely rights *in personam*. Some (classified as mere equities) undoubtedly are merely rights *in personam*, but others have many of the properties of rights *in rem*, and it is not unreasonable to describe these as giving additionally rights of ownership.

So it is reasonable to describe certain equitable rights as property rights, and to talk about equitable title to land, and equitable ownership of goods. It is also the case that various statutory provisions, and, in particular, the 1925 property legislation and some taxation legislation, treat equitable interests as property interests. Thus, s. 53(1)(c) of the Law of Property Act 1925 (on which see 6.2) provides:

[A] disposition of an equitable interest or trust subsisting at the time of the disposition must be in writing signed by the person disposing of the same, or by his agent thereunto lawfully authorised by writing or by will.

This clearly suggests the existence of equitable interests, which are presumably property interests, and which therefore have the characteristics of rights *in rem*.

The courts have also accepted that at any rate some equitable rights can have the characteristics of rights *in rem*. In *Baker* v *Archer-Shee* [1927] AC 844, a beneficiary was considered to be the owner of dividends for tax purposes. In *National Provincial Bank Ltd* v *Ainsworth* [1965] AC 1175, the House of Lords distinguished between equitable interests in land, which were full property rights capable of binding third parties as overriding interests under s. 70(1)(g) of the Land Registration Act 1925, and 'mere equities', which were not capable of binding third parties at all. (See 1.4.6.5).

In *Tinsley* v *Milligan* [1994] 1 AC 340, Stella Tinsley and Kathleen Milligan jointly purchased a home which was registered in Tinsley's name alone. On the principles set out at 8.1.4.1, the beneficial interest would have been shared between Tinsley and Milligan in equal shares; but to both Tinsley's and Milligan's knowledge, the home was registered in Tinsley's name alone to enable Milligan to make false claims to the Department of Social Security for benefits. After a quarrel Tinsley moved out, and claimed possession from Milligan. Milligan counterclaimed, seeking a declaration that the house was held by Tinsley on trust for both of them in equal shares. Tinsley argued that Milligan's claim was barred by the common law doctrine *ex turpi causa non oritur actio* and by the principle that 'he who comes to equity must come with clean hands'.

The House of Lords held (Lord Keith and Lord Goff dissenting) that because the presumption of resulting trust applied (see 8.4.1), Milligan could establish her equitable interest without relying on the illegal transaction, and was therefore entitled to succeed. The case supports the argument, it is suggested, that Milligan's resulting trust interest was a property interest in its own right, which had an existence that was independent of the precise arrangement between the couple. Had it been no more than merely a collection of personal rights against Tinsley, Milligan would surely have failed, since she would have been unable to assert those rights without disclosing the fraud. Lord Browne-Wilkinson went so far as to say:

> More than 100 years have elapsed since the fusion of the administration of law and equity. The reality of the matter is that, in 1993, English law has one single law of property made up of legal and equitable interests. Although for historical reasons legal estates and equitable estates have differing incidents, the person owning either type of estate has a right of property, a right *in rem* not merely a right *in personam*. If the law is that a party is entitled to enforce a property right acquired under an illegal transaction, in my judgment the same rule ought to apply to any property right so acquired, whether such right is legal or equitable.

Even if (as this author would suggest) this statement goes too far, it is clear at the very least that some equitable rights also have the characteristics of rights *in rem*.

Similar principles were applied by the Court of Appeal in *Rowan* v *Dann* (1992) P & CR 202. Rowan was a farmer in financial difficulties, who entered into sham leases of his land with somebody with whom he intended to go into a joint business venture (cattle-embryo transplanting). His sole intention in granting the leases was to keep the land out of hands of creditors, and no rent was ever paid, but no creditors were in the event actually defrauded. When the joint venture failed to get off the ground, the farmer successfully claimed his land back on a resulting trust. The resulting trust arose in Rowan's favour by reason of the failure of the joint venture project, on principles similar to those in 2.4, and, as in *Tinsley* v *Milligan*, it was unnecessary for Rowan to rely on the illegal purpose.

Like *Tinsley* v *Milligan*, *Rowan* v *Dann* supports the view that Rowan's interest was not merely a personal right against Dann, but an independent property interest. Legal title will not be lost merely because it has been obtained as part of a fraudulent transaction, and these cases suggest that the same is true for equitable titles.

1.4.6.5 Equitable rights as rights *in personam*

It is also still true to say, however, that equitable rights have some of the characteristics of rights *in personam*. Indeed, some equitable rights, such as the 'mere equities' considered by the House of Lords in *National Provincial Bank Ltd* v *Ainsworth* (above), do not have the characteristics of rights *in rem* at all.

In *Richard West and Partners (Inverness) Ltd* v *Dick* [1969] 2 Ch 424, the Court of Appeal held that the English courts had jurisdiction to grant a decree of specific performance of a contract for the sale of land abroad (in Scotland). The defendant was within the jurisdiction, and Harman LJ observed:

> . . . that the Court of Chancery, acting as it does *in personam*, is well able to grant specific performance of a contract to buy or sell foreign land, provided the defendant is domiciled within its jurisdiction.

The ability of equity to act *in personam* can be useful in any case where the property is situated abroad. The worldwide *Mareva* injunction (see 19.1.2.4) depends on equity acting *in personam*, as does equity's ability to trace property through civil law jurisdictions (see 19.2.2.1). In these cases, however, the personal rights are presumably additional to any real rights created. If the land or other property were in England, beneficial interests in it would surely not be defeated merely because the trustee was abroad.

However, there may be situations where the beneficiary's rights are limited by the personal nature of the action. It is also often the trustee, not the beneficiary, who takes action against a third party in respect of the trust property. For example, where property is leased it is the trustee who sues for rent: *Shalit* v *Joseph Nadler Ltd* [1933] 2 KB 79. Of course, the trustee is accountable to the beneficiary, and can be required by the beneficiary to sue, but the beneficiary cannot sue the third party directly. This really is a case where the trustee's rights are rights *in rem*, whereas those of the beneficiary are limited to a personal action against the trustee.

Generally speaking, only the owner of property at the time that it is damaged can sue in negligence. It is probable that an equitable owner does not count for these purposes, and that only the legal owner can sue. Again, of course, the equitable owner can require the legal owner to sue. In *Leigh & Sillivan Ltd* v *Aliakmon Shipping Co. Ltd, The Aliakmon* [1986] AC 785, buyers of a quantity of steel coils failed in a negligence action against the shipowners who had badly stowed the cargo aboard *The Aliakmon*, as a result of which it suffered damage, because property in the cargo had not passed to them by the time the damage occurred. The buyers alternatively claimed that they were equitable owners of the cargo (on the grounds that equity treats as done that which ought to be done, and that property ought to pass to them). However, Lord Brandon thought that even if they were equitable owners, that would not give them the right to sue in negligence:

> My Lords, under this head Mr Clarke [for the buyers] put forward two propositions of law. The first proposition was that a person who has the equitable ownership of goods is entitled to sue in tort for negligence anyone who by want of care causes them to be lost or damaged without joining the legal owner as a party to the action. . . .
>
> In my view, the first proposition cannot be supported. . . . If . . . the person is the equitable owner of the goods and no more, then he must join the legal owner as a party to the action, either as co-plaintiff if he is willing or as co-defendant if he is not. This had always been the law in the field of equitable ownership of land and I see no reason why it should not also be so in the field of equitable ownership of goods.

He also held that the buyers in fact had no equitable ownership, so that these remarks are techically *obiter dicta*, but it is suggested that there is no reason to doubt their correctness.

This author would suggest, therefore, that although for many purposes equitable rights have the charactersitics of rights *in rem*, vestiges of their personal origins still remain.

1.5   JUDICATURE ACTS 1873–5

One of the main defects of the English system of justice up until the mid-19th century was that common law and equity were administered in separate courts. The Court of Chancery had no power to grant common law remedies, nor did the common law courts have power to grant equitable remedies. This meant that litigants might have to commence two separate actions in order to obtain justice.

Some slight improvement was introduced by the Common Law Procedure Act 1854, which gave the common law courts the power to award certain equitable remedies. The most useful of these was an order for specific delivery. Up to 1854, a common law court had no power to order a defendant to hand over property which did not belong to him. The court could only compel the defendant to pay a sum of money as damages for wrongful detention of the property. The 1854 Act allowed the court to compel the defendant to hand over the property itself.

On the Chancery side, the major defect was the inability of the Court of Chancery to award a sum of money as damages in lieu of granting an equitable remedy. The Chancery Amendment Act 1858 (Lord Cairns' Act) gave the Court of Chancery a discretion to award 'equitable' damages where no other remedy was appropriate.

The effect of these two Acts was to make it easier for a plaintiff to bring his action to a satisfactory conclusion in a single court.

However, this did nothing to improve a second major defect. The main complaint about the courts was that they were agonisingly inefficient. The Court of Chancery in particular had a terrible reputation for delay and needless technicality (see, e.g., Charles Dickens, *Bleak House*).

In spite of the 1854 and 1858 enactments, until 1873 common law and equity continued to be administered in different courts, equity being administered only in the Court of Chancery. The legislation of 1873–5 provided that subsequently the High Court, though divided for convenience into divisions, would administer both systems. Section 25 of the 1873 Act, now replaced by the Supreme Court Act 1981, s. 49, provided that in a case of conflict the rules of equity were to prevail: this was effectively the position also before 1873.

The 1873–5 Acts were almost certainly intended to be procedural only, and that was probably their only effect — the generally held view is that they did not alter the substantive law.

There are those who argue, however, that as a result of the procedural fusion of the two systems equity's freedom to develop has been fettered, by virtue of its closer association with the common law. It is probably true that its original flexibility and rapid development have been largely curtailed, and that it is now almost as rigid and rule-bound as the common law. Of course it still continues to develop: see, for example, chapter 8 for developments in the application of resulting and constructive trusts to new situations. The doctrine of promissory estoppel has already been mentioned. The pace of equitable development today, however, is little (if any) faster than that of the common law.

At least three observations can be made about this argument. First, it is probable that legislation, whose role and extent have increased greatly since 1875, today takes on many of the functions once taken on by equity; where the law appears rigid and unjust, legislation is now a possible and realistic answer. It may well be better suited to modern democratic conditions than the exercise of discretionary power by a court. Megaw LJ, for example, expressed this view in *Western Fish Products Ltd* v *Penwith District Council* [1981] 2 All ER 204, 218. Additionally, the nature of case law makes it inevitably uncertain as a method of law reform.

The second observation is that the curtailment of equitable discretion is explicable as a simple consequence of the development of effective law reporting inevitably leading to precedents coming to be regarded as binding. Probably it has little to do with the 1873–5 legislation.

The third observation is that unfettered judicial discretion may nowadays be a bad thing; it is arguably better to promote certainty, in a society in which expectations are relied upon, than discretion. Not only is the latter quality inherently unpredictable, but if administered by a court is also retroactive. Its exercise can therefore cause considerable injustices, especially where commercial and property transactions are concerned.

It has been suggested by Lord Diplock in *United Scientific Holdings Ltd* v *Burnley Borough Council* [1978] AC 904, that since 1875 law and equity should themselves be considered as being fused, and that it is no longer meaningful to speak as though rules of equity still retain a separate identity. Whether or not this is correct (and it is difficult to see it as being more than a semantic argument), there are practical reasons for continuing to treat the two systems separately. Rights which owe their derivation to equitable principles differ, as we saw in 1.4, from those which derive from the common law. Both types of right can exist simultaneously in a given situation, and it is without doubt more convenient to continue to subject them to a separate analysis.

In *Walsh* v *Lonsdale* (1882) 20 ChD 9, for example (see 1.4.4), the tenant had a periodic tenancy at common law, and a 17-year equitable lease. If the landlord had sold the land to a third party, the common law tenancy, as a right *in rem,* would certainly have bound the purchaser, whereas the equitable lease would only have done so on the basis of the notice doctrine discussed in 1.4.6. The conclusion that I would draw is that it is still sensible to consider common law and equity separately, even after both doctrines have been administered in the same court for 120 years.

1.6 THE 1925 PROPERTY LEGISLATION

The 1925 property legislation comprised the Law of Property Act, Settled Land Act, Land Charges Act and Land Registration Act. The Land Charges Act was amended and re-enacted in 1972. They are mainly of interest to land law students, but their effect on trusts and equitable doctrines was also quite considerable.

Perhaps the main purpose of the 1925 property legislation was to make it easier for people to sell or otherwise alienate land. The ability to alienate land easily had become increasingly necessary following the social upheavals brought about by the First World War, and much of the legislation was directed towards improving the conveyancing process.

The effect on equity and trusts of this legislation was threefold. In the first place, many estates in land can now exist only in equity. Secondly, the notice doctrine (see 1.4.6) was severely curtailed. Thirdly, the trust for sale, which was used as a conveyancing device before 1925, was substantially enhanced in importance.

1.6.1 Reduction in number of legal estates

Many estates in land can now exist only in equity (i.e., as beneficial interests under a trust), because of the reduction in 1925 (in order to aid conveyancing) in the number of possible legal estates. We have seen that though before 1535 the number of legal estates that could exist in land was very limited, and no future interests could be created at common law, this changed with the Statute of Uses, because on the execution of uses the common law came to recognise most of the wider range of equitable estates. This in turn led to difficulties for purchasers, who might have a great number of legal titles to investigate, in addition to equitable estates and interests. For example, if land was settled in order to keep it in a family, the present tenant's life estate and the future tenant's entailed estate could both be legal estates.

Even greater complexity could arise where there were concurrent interests in the same land (i.e., where land was shared, but not divided, as for example, where a matrimonial home was held jointly by husband and wife). In this situation each party to the arrangement often had a separate legal estate. Furthermore, each of these estates could be further split, and frequently would be where land was held by large partnerships, or settled equally among sons and grandsons over several generations. Thus, a prospective purchaser would have to investigate, and buy, large numbers of legal estates, before investigation of equitable title had even begun. Effectively, this could render shared land unsaleable.

The Law of Property Act 1925, s. 1, reduced the number of possible legal estates in land to two, those that are now commonly known as freehold (fee simple absolute in possession), which must take immediate effect, and leasehold (term of years absolute). Future freehold interests and life interests, as are commonly found in settlements, can exist only in equity, and concurrent interests in land take effect only behind a trust for sale (i.e., in equity: see further 1.6.3 and 2.8). In this respect, therefore, the 1925 legislation increased the contribution of equity to the law of real property.

1.6.2 Notice doctrine

So far as the equitable estates and interests themselves were concerned, the notice doctrine (described in 1.4.6) was not altogether satisfactory. Innocent owners of equitable interests could lose them to a bona fide purchaser for value without notice through no fault of their own; there was no way of being sure that they would be brought to his notice, and if they were not he would take free (i.e., without being bound by those interests). Purchasers, on the other hand, were put to great expense to discover the existence of all possible equitable interests, in case they should find themselves bound. The system was lucrative for lawyers, but not conducive to safe and rapid alienation of land.

Broadly speaking, the 1925 legislation distinguishes between equitable estates in land (i.e., those akin to full ownership), and interests less than ownership. For most equitable interests, but not estates, the 1925 legislation replaced the notice doctrine with registration provisions; such interests today generally can be and have to be registered for protection against purchasers. The idea is that if the interest is registered the purchaser has notice; if it is not registered, the purchaser is not bound whether or not he has notice in fact.

The details of the registration systems, provided for by the Land Charges and Land Registration Acts, are dealt with in land law textbooks, and are beyond the scope of this book. Trusts lawyers need to be aware of them in as much as they reduce the importance of the notice doctrine.

The long-term aim was for all titles and interests to be registered under the provisions of the Land Registration Act 1925. As far as interests are concerned, some are made overriding interests under s. 70, in which case they bind purchasers irrespective of registration. Some are overreachable (see 1.6.3), but all others are registrable as minor interests. If they are not so registered, then by virtue of s. 20(1), they will not bind a transferee for valuable consideration. Since there are no other types of interest, there is no room under these provisions for the application of the notice doctrine, there being no requirement under s. 20(1) for either good faith or lack of notice.

It was not possible to register all titles immediately, however, and a transitional system was set up, the provisions of which are now to be found in the Land Charges Act 1972, which still applies to unregistered titles. Under these provisions, land charges on a list (in s. 2 of the Act) have to be registered for protection, registration constituting actual notice (under the Law of Property Act 1925, s. 198) and the effect of non-registration depending on the class of charge concerned: Land Charges Act 1972, s. 4. Estate contracts, for example (Class C(iv)), are void if not registered against any purchaser, for money or money's worth, whether or not he has notice or even acts in good faith. In *Midland Bank Trust Co. Ltd* v *Green* [1981] AC 513, a sham sale between husband and wife, intended specifically to defeat their son's valuable option to purchase a farm, succeeded in its purpose, solely because the option had not been properly registered as an estate contract under the Act. The purchaser had actual notice, and was acting in bad faith. In *Lloyds Bank plc* v *Carrick*, CA, 28 February 1996, an unregistered estate contract (between a widow and her brother-in-law) was held void against a mortgagee, which would certainly have had notice on an application of the pre-1925 notice doctrine.

The notice doctrine has not in fact been completely abolished for dealings involving land. It still exists at the margins. Indeed, the courts have been unhappy with the logic of *Midland Bank Trust Co. Ltd* v *Green* and have been at some pains to bring back good faith requirements where they can. For example, for land still covered by the regime of the Land Charges Act, not all equitable interests are expressly covered by the statute. For those that are omitted the old rules apply, and the courts have been unenthusiastic about extending the legislation to cover them by implication (see, e.g., *E.R. Ives Investments Ltd* v *High* [1967] 2 QB 379; *Shiloh Spinners Ltd* v *Harding* [1973] AC 691). Equity has also developed new interests since 1925, such as that in *Binions* v *Evans* [1972] Ch 359 (see 10.4), which are obviously not covered by the legislation.

Another situation where the notice doctrine continues to apply, at any rate unless and until the law is changed by the Trustees of Land and Appointment of Trustees Act 1996, is where there is a statutory trust for sale (see 1.6.3) but a receipt is not obtained from two trustees, and hence the equitable interests are not overreached: see, e.g., *Caunce* v *Caunce* [1969] 1 WLR 286 and *Kingsnorth Trust Co. Ltd* v *Tizard* [1986] 1 WLR 783. Bare trusts of land are neither overreachable nor registrable under the Land Charges Act scheme, so the notice doctrine applies to them too (bare trusts of land are rare, but see *Hodgson* v *Marks* [1971] 1 Ch 892, considered at 8.2). In *Lloyds Bank plc* v *Carrick*, the widow, Mrs Carrick, unsuccessfully argued a claim based on the first category in *Lloyds Bank plc* v *Rosset* (see 8.5); but had she succeeded, her brother-in-law would have held the property on bare trust for her, and her interest would not have been one of the registrable interests under the Land Charges Act.

Under the Land Registration Act, all interests that are not overriding or overreachable are registrable, so there is no similar scope for the application of the notice doctrine (*Hodgson* v *Marks* was actually a Land Registration Act case, the purchaser being bound by Mrs Hodgson's overriding interest.) However, it might be argued that the overriding interests, which bind irrespective of registration, have been defined in such a way as to create a doctrine similar to notice. For example, s. 70(1)(g) protects as an overriding interest:

> The rights of every person in actual occupation of the land or in receipt of the rents and profits thereof, save where inquiry is made of such person and the rights are not disclosed; . . .

This is certainly similar to the notice doctrine as developed in *Hunt* v *Luck* [1991] 1 Ch 45, as was observed by the House of Lords in *Williams & Glyn's Bank Ltd* v *Boland* [1981] AC 487 (although the Court of Appeal in *Hodgson* v *Marks* had suggested that it might operate less favourably for the purchaser than the notice doctrine). However, the decision in *Boland* was the same as in the later case of *Kingsnorth Trust Co. Ltd* v *Tizard*, above, which was decided on the basis of the equitable notice doctrine. It was accepted in the Court of Appeal in *Lloyds Bank plc* v *Carrick*, above, that had the land been registered the mortgagee would have been bound, Mrs Carrick having not only paid the entire purchase price but also gone into possession of the property.

Section 70(1)(g) protects only those who are in occupation, however, but there are authorities importing a good faith requirement into the statute (a purchaser being defined in s. 3(xxi) as 'a purchaser in good faith ...'), and a purchaser, at any rate with express notice, may be regarded as not being in good faith (see, e.g., *Peffer* v *Rigg* [1977] 1 WLR 285; *Lyus* v *Prowsa* [1982] 1 WLR 1044). In the former case, after citing s. 3(xxi), Graham J said that a purchaser who was not in good faith would not therefore take free of unregistered interests, and observed that 'He cannot in my judgment be in good faith if he has in fact notice of something which affects his title as in the present case'. To a limited extent, therefore, a doctrine similar to the notice doctrine survives even the Land Registration Act 1925.

1.6.3 Trusts for sale; overreaching

Full equitable estates in land are treated differently by the 1925 legislation. In the case of land held concurrently (i.e., shared), the Law of Property Act

1925 requires that it be held on a statutory trust for sale, and the interests of the co-owners thus become beneficial interests under a trust for sale. Trusts for sale are described in detail in 2.8 and 8.9, but it should be noted that their purpose in this context is simply as a conveyancing device; in other words, the theoretical intention to sell is for all practical purposes merely a legal fiction.

The main effect is that on sale the interests of those with concurrent interests cease to be interests in land, and become interests in the purchase money only. Indeed, because of the equitable doctrine of conversion, on which see further 2.8 and 8.9, for some purposes their interests become interests in the money only even before the sale takes place. A purchaser is thus enabled to 'overreach' them. This means that he is relieved from having to inquire about them so long as he pays the purchase money to at least two trustees (and obtains a receipt from them) because they take effect as interests in the purchase money only rather than in the land itself. Thus the beneficiaries are protected by being able to take a share of the purchase money, and the purchaser is not concerned with their interests. A large proportion of matrimonial and cohabited property is now held in this manner, and the notice doctrine is no longer relevant to this situation.

1.6.4 Settled land
The Settled Land Act 1925 was also directed towards easier alienability of land, but a more specific aspect of the problem. It dealt with the difficulties encountered when (as commonly used to be the case) land was settled for generations in families, and continued the policy of the earlier Settled Land Acts 1882 to 1890.

Settled land is considered in more detail at 8.8. For present purposes we need only note that it is another area where the notice doctrine no longer has any application.

When the Trusts of Land and Appointment of Trustees Act 1996 comes into force, then the regime for concurrent interests in land, and for settled land, will be considerably changed, but the notice doctrine will continue to be inapplicable to them.

TWO

Nature and Classification of Trusts

2.1 REASONS FOR CREATING TRUSTS

Trusts arise in many everyday situations, which cover widely differing social circumstances. It is perhaps unfortunate, therefore, that similar (but, as we shall see, not identical) principles are applicable to each variety of trust.

2.1.1 Family settlements

The purpose of many express trusts (i.e., those which are deliberately created by a settlor) is the retention of wealth by the wealthy. Probably the majority of trusts we shall meet in this book have this purpose as their main aim. They are often family settlements, which tie up wealth within the family, and are also drafted to minimise liability to taxation. Sometimes they are made by will, but it can be advantageous from a taxation viewpoint for them to be constituted during the life of the settlor (i.e., *inter vivos*). Although they were more important historically than they are today, family settlements are still common, and frequently give rise to litigation. It is not, of course, the function of this book to comment on the desirability or otherwise of these schemes. This is a political question, upon which views may validly differ. Only the legal consequences are appropriate for discussion in this book.

The trustees may be members of the family, and in the early days of such settlements often were. They may be solicitors who are familiar with the family business. Neither of these appointments is considered by the courts to be very desirable, however, because of the likelihood of conflicts of interest where the trustee is too closely connected to, or involved with the beneficiaries. There is even a possibility of fraud, especially where family members are constituted trustees. So in the rare cases where the court has to appoint trustees (say, where the existing trustees fail to carry out their duties — see further chapters 4 and 15), such people are unlikely candidates. Further, it was probably because the modern law of trusts largely developed at a time when this sort of trust was exceedingly common, and when the trustees were normally family members, that the nature of trustees' duties (on which, see chapters 14 to 17) is so stringent.

Family trusts may also be administered by the trustee and executor departments of banks. Proper professional administration can be of the greatest importance if tax benefits are to be maximised. Banks charge quite heavily for taking on these duties, by way of a charging clause that they insist on putting into the trust instrument. The charges are therefore usually fixed at the outset, and do not depend on how the trust is administered. This, as we shall see, is very important when we come to consider conflicts of interest in 14.3.

The terminology relating to settlements will arise again throughout the book. All settlements involve the creation of successions of interests, and the simplest form would be where A leaves property to B for life and thereafter for C. B is the *life tenant,* and is usually entitled to the immediate income from the property. He is sometimes referred to as an income beneficiary. C is entitled in remainder. He is the *remainderman,* sometimes referred to as a capital beneficiary.

In this case the extent of C's interest is known at the outset, and so it is a *vested* interest. Suppose on the other hand the gift is to B for life and then to the first of C, D and E to marry. It is unknown yet which will marry first, and the interests of C, D and E are said to be contingent. More is made of this distinction in chapter 7.

In citations of cases 'ST' indicates a settlement trust and 'WT' a will trust.

2.1.2   Shares

Shares are often owned out and out by the shareholder, but they may be held by nominees, this practice being more common in holdings of shares in public, rather than private companies. The nominee is often a bank. In this case the legal estate is held by the nominee in trust for the shareholder. One reason for this might be if it is intended that the trustee should manage the portfolio, as would be the case, for example, with a unit trust. Pension funds may only be held by trust corporations.

2.1.3   Charities, trade unions and unincorporated associations

Trusts can also be used to enable property to be held for the benefit of people who for some reason cannot hold it themselves. Interestingly, some of the earliest uses for Franciscan friars had this as their main purpose. Incorporated bodies, such as companies, which are incorporated under the Companies Acts, and universities, which are incorporated by charter, have legal personality, and can therefore hold property themselves. So there is no need, for example, for treasurers or directors to hold the property on their behalf as trustees, and normally they do not do so. As we shall see in 14.3, however, they may owe fiduciary duties, which are akin to those of trustees.

Charities (on which, see chapters 11 and 12) can also be incorporated, in which case they too may hold property in their own right. If they do so, the courts are undecided whether they hold absolutely, subject to the articles of association under the Companies Acts, or whether they are held on trust for charitable purposes. We will come upon purpose trusts again in chapter 4, and we shall see that they are rather unusual in that there are no true beneficiaries.

Not all charities are incorporated, however. Unincorporated bodies have no legal personality, and cannot hold property themselves. In the case of unincorporated charities, the property is held by trustees, who are often individuals, for the purposes of the charity. Donations to charity therefore commonly give rise to trusts.

A trust can also be, in theory, a method of enabling property to be held by members' clubs, which are also unincorporated. Nominated trustees (who would usually be officers of the club) could hold the property on trust for the members. This gives rise to no difficulties so long as the membership is fixed, or the club is of short duration (e.g., a club which is geared to a specific, one-off event). Most clubs have a fluctuating membership, however, and in this case, as we shall see, the trust solution can give rise to perpetuity problems, because the interests of future members may not vest until outside the perpetuity period (on which, see further chapter 7). This is not a problem that arises in the case of charities, because they are exempt from the perpetuity rules.

The usual analysis for members' clubs is not based on the trust, therefore. The usual analysis is that the present members hold the club property absolutely, subject to their *contractual* rights and duties arising from membership. These may, for example, prevent them taking their share of the club property for themselves on resignation, or at any other time. They may allow the officers to decide how the property is to be used. If property is held by officers, they will hold it as agents of the members, not as trustees.

Trade unions are in a peculiar (and unique) position, being regarded as unincorporated for most purposes, though sharing some of the features of corporate bodies. Section 2 of the Trade Union and Labour Relations Act 1974 (re-enacting earlier legislation) prevents them from being corporate entities, but also provides that the trustees of a union hold on trust *for the union itself*, not for the members. So a union, unlike other unincorporated bodies, can be an equitable owner, though not a legal owner of property. Another feature of unions is that the trustees are nominal owners of the property only, and have no significant discretion, because rule books nearly always provide that they act under the directions of the executive.

2.1.4 Trusts arising from marriage or cohabitation
Unlike express trusts, resulting and constructive trusts, as we shall see, can arise in quite different circumstances from those described above. Resulting trusts (see 2.4) often arise from informal family arrangements. A common variety is where a wife or female cohabitee (X) provides money towards the purchase of a home, which though intended to be jointly occupied, is conveyed into the name of the man alone (Y). Y holds X's interest in the home on resulting trust, so that both parties share equitable title. Furthermore, as we saw in chapter 1, a statutory trust for sale arises in this situation under the provisions of the Law of Property Act 1925. A statutory trust for sale also arises where the home is originally conveyed to X and Y jointly, and we may suppose that these are among the commonest trusts in existence today. See further chapter 10.

2.1.5   Reason for distinguishing similar concepts

Trusts, then, are used in widely differing social situations, of which the above examples are by no means exhaustive. Sometimes, however, wholly different concepts are applicable instead, in similar situations. We have already seen, for example, that members' clubs are normally based on contract not trust, whereas the property of charities which are unincorporated is held by trustees. Banks may be trustees if they are specifically constituted as such, but ordinary accounts create only a debtor-creditor relationship. Company directors are not usually trustees, but share many of the trustees' duties.

It is necessary, then, not only to describe the nature of the trust, but also to distinguish it from other concepts that can arise in similar situations.

2.2   NATURE OF A TRUST

As we saw in chapter 1, a trust involves a division of the ownership of property. An example of a typical express trust is as follows. The settlor is the original owner of property, and creates a trust by conveying it to one or more trustees, and manifesting an intention that it is to be held on trust for one or more beneficiaries. The trustees become owners at common law, and are given control of the property. No trust is created, whatever intention the settlor has manifested, unless legal title is vested in (i.e., given to) the trustee (see further on this, chapter 3). This is called 'constituting' the trust. The trustees come under an equitable obligation enforceable by the beneficiaries.

Though this example describes the essence of a trust, there are several possible variations and qualifications.

First, it is not necessary for settlors, trustees and beneficiaries to be different people. A settlor can validly constitute a trust by declaring *himself* trustee of his own property, on behalf of one or more beneficiaries. This is discussed in detail in chapter 3.

The settlor may be a beneficiary, and will always be in the case of a resulting trust (see 2.4). A trustee may be the beneficiary, or one of a number of beneficiaries. Settlors can even be trustees *and* beneficiaries, and this is normal in the case of statutory trusts for sale (see 2.7).

A second qualification is that the property settled can include an equitable interest. In other words a beneficiary under a trust may constitute a further trust of his equitable interest, thereby creating a subtrust. Subtrusts are common in tax avoiding settlements. The beneficiary under the subtrust can himself repeat the process, creating a further subtrust, and there is no limit to the number of times this process may be repeated.

Thirdly, the example at the beginning of the section is of a private (i.e., non-charitable) trust. If the trust is charitable (see chapters 11 to 13), there may be no true beneficiaries at all. Yet charitable trusts are perfectly valid, enforcement being by the Attorney-General.

Fourthly, the example above also assumes that the beneficiary has a full equitable interest in the property, and that there is no restriction, for example, on the purposes to which he can put it. As we will see in chapter 5, however, it may be possible to have private purpose trusts, benefiting a defined group of people. Arguably, these people are not true beneficiaries, because they are constrained to use the property for a particular purpose. An example might be a conveyance of land to A and B, in trust to be used as a football pitch for the employees of X Ltd. The employees are arguably not true beneficiaries, because they cannot use the land in any way they wish. Nevertheless, the trust is probably valid, because in spite of this, they have sufficient interest in the property to be able to enforce the equitable obligations owed by the trustees.

Fifthly, there may also be an anomalous category of unenforceable trusts, which, however, share the other characteristics of ordinary trusts. These seem to be limited to trusts for the benefit of animals and the maintenance of tombs, and should be regarded as exceptional. They are considered in Chapter 5.

2.3 TRUSTS DISTINGUISHED FROM SIMILAR COMMON LAW CONCEPTS

The division of ownership, and the nature of the enforcement, serve to distinguish the trust from other concepts, with which trusts share common factors.

2.3.1 Trust and bailment
For example, possession of personal property is often separated from ownership of the property, as in common law bailment, for example, hiring or hire-purchase, but both legal and equitable ownership remain in the bailor or hirer; so the relationship of the bailee to the property is quite different from that of a trustee, who is the legal owner.

To some extent this is manifested in differences in the duties of bailees and trustees — those of bailees are beyond the scope of this book, while those of trustees are considered in chapters 14 to 17. Additionally, the position of third parties is different. If a bailee sells the goods, where this is unauthorised by the terms of the bailment, then unless the buyer can benefit from the provisions of the Factors Act 1889, ss. 2, 8 and 9, or the Sale of Goods Act 1979, ss. 21 to 26, he gets no title, even if he acts in good faith, and has no notice of the existence of the bailment. This is because a bailee has no title, legal or equitable, to sell, so a purchaser from him gets neither legal nor equitable title. The statutory provisions, incidentally, allow transfer of title by non-owners (as here) in limited circumstances, and are dealt with in detail in sale of goods textbooks.

If, on the other hand, a trustee sells goods in breach of trust, the buyer obtains legal title from the trustee, and is bound by any equitable title and interests only if he is unable to show that he is a bona fide purchaser for value without the knowledge requirement in 1.4.6.4. If he is a bona fide purchaser etc., he obtains legal title unencumbered by equitable interests.

Another difference between trust and bailment is that trusts can apply to land and goods, whereas bailment can only apply to goods.

A diagrammatic representation can be found in figure 2.1.

Figure 2.1

Comparison between trust and bailment

	Bailment	Trust
Legal title	Remains in bailor. If bailee tries to sell, purchaser obtains no title unless Factors Act, etc., operate.	Trustee obtains legal title
Equitable title		If trustee disposes of legal title, equitable title defeated by bona fide purchaser (of legal title) for value without the knowledge requirement in 1.4.6.4

2.3.2 Trust and contract

A private trust, then, is created either by a declaration of trust by the settlor, in which case he becomes trustee himself, or by his arranging for someone else to act as trustee. The beneficiary (or if a purpose trust, the person who can enforce it) need not be a party to the arrangement at all. Yet it is he, and not the settlor, who can enforce the trust, because the settlor retains no interest in the property (*qua* settlor — he can, of course, be beneficiary). This is so whether or not the beneficiary has given any consideration, because he is in effect the recipient of a gift. So it is only the third party to the arrangement who can enforce it.

While a third party (X) can benefit from a contract, on the other hand, he generally cannot enforce it himself by legal action, by virtue of the privity of contract doctrine. However, the creation of a trust in favour of X is similar to making him a gift: X need do nothing in return, the gift gives him enforceable rights, and a gift once made cannot be revoked.

As a general conclusion, then, whereas contracts cannot be enforced by third parties, trusts are enforceable by beneficiaries who need not be parties to the arrangement. Furthermore, trusts are unenforceable by anyone else, even the settlor, who is always party to the arrangement.

Of course, if the trustee is acting by virtue of a contract with the settlor, for example, if he is acting as his solicitor or banker, then the settlor can enforce this contract. It may also be that a settlement of property by A on B, subject to a condition that B holds it for the benefit of X, always leads to the implication of a contract between A and B. A's remedies are in contract, however, and these are quite different from those available to a beneficiary for breach of trust.

2.3.2.1 A contract example Suppose, for example, A contracts with B that, in consideration of a payment by A to B of a sum of money, B pays X an annuity for his (X's) life. No trust is constituted, however. Assume also that X does not provide consideration for this benefit, and is not party to the arrangement. X is therefore unable to enforce the contract in his own right. This is shown diagrammatically in figure 2.2.

Figure 2.2

Trust and contract

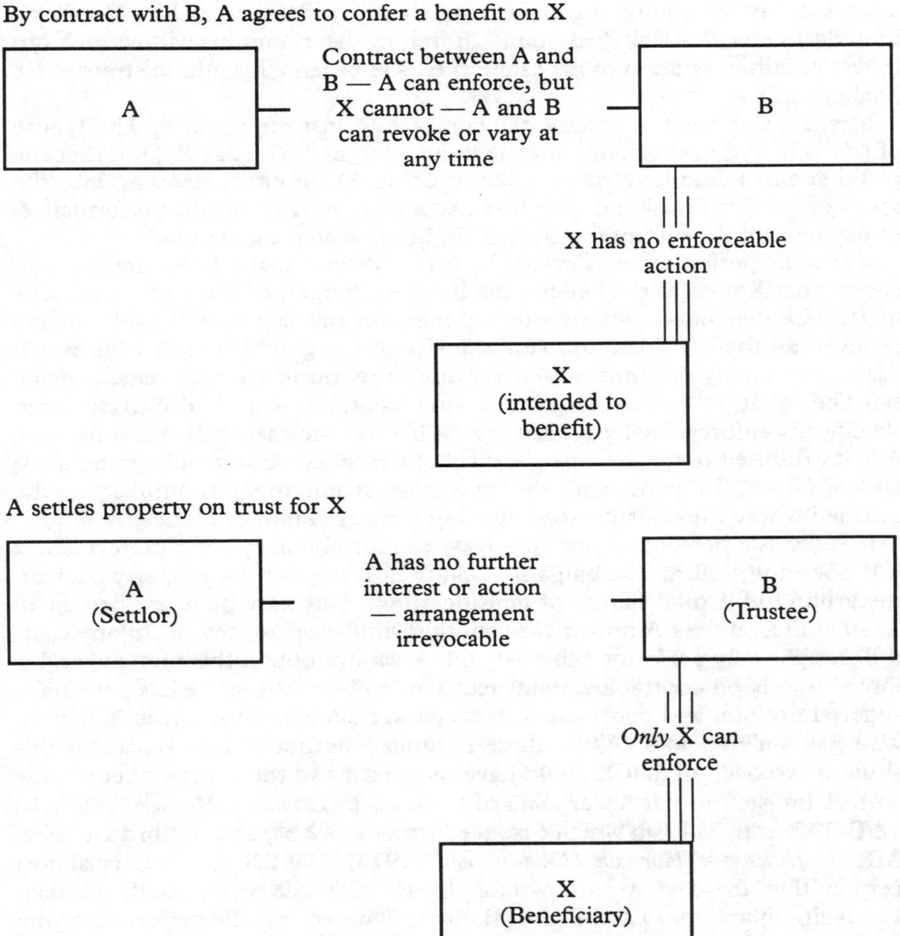

By contract with B, A agrees to confer a benefit on X

```
┌──────────────┐   Contract between A and   ┌──────────────┐
│              │   B — A can enforce, but   │              │
│      A       │─  X cannot — A and B      ─│      B       │
│              │   can revoke or vary at    │              │
└──────────────┘         any time           └──────────────┘
                                                    │││
                                            X has no enforceable
                                                  action
                                            ┌──────────────┐
                                            │      X       │
                                            │ (intended to │
                                            │   benefit)   │
                                            └──────────────┘
```

A settles property on trust for X

```
┌──────────────┐   A has no further         ┌──────────────┐
│      A       │   interest or action       │      B       │
│  (Settlor)   │─  — arrangement           ─│  (Trustee)   │
│              │   irrevocable              │              │
└──────────────┘                            └──────────────┘
                                                    │││
                                            *Only* X can
                                               enforce
                                            ┌──────────────┐
                                            │      X       │
                                            │ (Beneficiary)│
                                            └──────────────┘
```

A can enforce the contract, but often such arrangements are made in favour of wives, sons or daughters, in which case A may well predecease them. In that event, after A's death A's personal representatives will be able to enforce the contract on A's behalf. As a third party, X cannot force them to do so, however, or sue B directly. Of course, if X is A's personal representative, X can sue in that capacity, but not as a third party.

The leading authority is the House of Lords decision in *Beswick v Beswick* [1968] AC 58. A coal merchant (Peter Beswick), who was over 70 years old, transferred his business to his nephew, who in return agreed, among other things, that he would, after Peter Beswick's death, pay £5 a week to his widow. (This may not sound like a great deal of money, but the agreement was made almost 30 years ago. It would be the equivalent of some £50–£60 a week today, or enough to make a substantial difference to Mrs Beswick's lifestyle.) Peter Beswick died about 18 months later, and his widow took out letters of administration to his estate (i.e., she became his administratrix: see further, 2.7).

Mrs Beswick sued to enforce the contract against the nephew. The House of Lords held that she could not sue in her own right (i.e., as X), but that she could sue as administratrix of estate (i.e., as A), in effect stepping into the shoes of her dead husband. She was also able to obtain specific performance, of payment of the annuity to herself (in her personal capacity).

If specific performance is available, A (or A's personal representatives) can ensure that X obtains the benefit that has been bargained for. But the remedy in *Beswick* depended, among other things, on the fact that B had actually received all the consideration (the transfer of the goodwill in A's business). Also, the remedy depends in general upon the mutuality requirement being satisfied, that is to say that the same contract would also have been specifically enforceable by B against A. This was the case in *Beswick*, because A had promised to transfer the goodwill of a business, but it will by no means always be so. In particular, the mutuality requirement is unlikely to be satisfied where the consideration moving from A is money alone.

If A (or A's personal representatives) cannot obtain specific performance, if B does not perform the bargain at all, then A can get the property back on the ground of a total failure of consideration. This may be of no benefit to X, of course, unless A now makes another similar arrangement. In any case, if B has partially performed the bargain, A cannot obtain this remedy, and is forced to rely on contractual damages. The problem is that he has personally suffered no loss, and contractual damages are compensatory. It is X, not A, who has suffered loss. While there is limited authority that A can in this situation recover all that X could have recovered had the contract been made with X himself, in particular *dicta* of Lush LJ in *Lloyd's v Harper* (1880) 16 ChD 290, at p. 321 (on which case see further 2.3.2.3), and of Lord Denning MR in *Jackson v Horizon Holidays Ltd* [1975] 1 WLR 1468, it is almost certain that these views are wrong. In *Beswick v Beswick* itself, all their Lordships apart from Lord Pearce thought that had specific performance not been available, the administratrix would have been entitled to nominal damages only, as Mr Beswick's estate had suffered no loss. A similar view was taken by all members of the House of Lords in *Woodar Investment Developments Ltd v Wimpey Construction (UK) Ltd* [1980] 1 WLR 277, where the *dicta* referred to above in *Lloyd's v Harper* and *Jackson v Horizon Holidays Ltd* were disapproved. A's damages will therefore be nominal, and unless specific performance is available his action will generally be of limited value. The view was also expressed in *Woodar Investment Developments Ltd* v *Wimpey Construction (UK) Ltd* (in particular by Lords Salmon, Keith and Scarman) that the law was very unsatisfactory, but could be altered only by statute.

There are a limited number of exceptions to the *Woodar* principle, as in (for example) *Darlington Borough Council* v *Wiltshier Northern Ltd* [1995] 1 WLR 68, but they are not relevant to the present discussion.

Because X has no enforceable rights, A and B may subsequently agree to vary the agreement to X's detriment. Indeed, the most plausible reason for not setting up a trust in the first place would be that A and B wish to retain such flexibility.

2.3.2.2 A trust example

If B is constituted trustee for X, however, the position is quite different. Not only can X sue B in his own right, but A and B can no longer vary the arrangement to X's detriment: to do so would be akin to making X a gift, and taking it back again. In effect, the creation of a trust avoids the privity of contract rules. There is no objection to this, of course, so long as A and B clearly intend this to happen.

2.3.2.3 Trusts of promises

It is even possible to create trusts of promises. In other words, a cause of action in contract can itself be held in trust for a third party, at least if the contract involves payment of money or transfer of property. Again, this device avoids the privity doctrine. This is frequently done with the benefits of life insurance policies.

In *Beswick* v *Beswick* [1968] AC 58, Lord Reid compared the case before him with the position had A declared himself trustee of the promise for X (at pp. 71–2):

> For clarity I think it best to begin by considering a simple case where, in consideration of a sale by A to B, B agrees to pay the price of £1,000 to a third party . . .
>   . . . I assume that A has not made himself a trustee [of the promise] for X . . . So, if X has no right, A can at any time grant a discharge to B or make some new contract with B. If there were a trust the position would be different. X would have an equitable right and A would be entitled and, indeed, bound to recover the money and account for it to X. And A would have no right to grant a discharge to B.

From this passage it is clear that in the absence of a trust, X has no enforceable rights at all, and that A and B can vary the contract as they please. If, however, A constitutes himself trustee of the promise, X has an enforceable right (against A), and A no longer has any right to enter into an agreement with B, to vary the contract or discharge B.

This device would obviously not help if A's remedy in contract was itself useless, and the position in 2.3.2.1 was that if A were confined to a damages claim, his damages would be nominal only. There is authority, however, that if A contracts as trustee the position is different, and he can claim substantial damages to hold on trust for X. In *Lloyd's v Harper* (1880) 16 ChD 290, a father agreed with Lloyd's (prior to their incorporation) to act as guarantor for his son, who was an underwriting member of Lloyd's (underwriting marine insurance policies). A guarantee was required before the son could be accepted as an underwriter, in accordance with Lloyd's practice. The Court of Appeal took the view that the father's guarantee contract with Lloyd's was made by Lloyd's acting as trustees of the benefit of the guarantee for the property-owners. On the son's later bankruptcy, the father's estate was liable on the guarantee, which was enforced by Lloyd's on behalf of those who were insured under the marine insurance policies. Note that the insured were not party to the guarantee contract. Hence they were in the position of X above. Lloyd's were in the position of A and the father was in the position of B.

The point of interest for present purposes is that Lloyd's as contracting parties were able to obtain substantial damages, but this depended on them having contracted as trustees. Note that although the views of Lush LJ in this case have been disapproved (see 2.3.2.1), the case has been accepted as authority where A contracts as trustee. Note also that the trust is of the contract not the property itself. The arrangement was not that Lloyd's would become trustees of any tangible property, and it was never envisaged that any property should be transferred to Lloyd's for them to hold on trust for others.

In *Lloyd's v Harper*, Lloyd's contracted as trustees from the start, and all parties were at all times aware of the nature of the arrangement. It must be assumed (although it has never been clearly held) that the authority is limited to this situation. Otherwise A, who had originally contracted otherwise than as trustee, could by the later unilateral act of declaring himself trustee of the promise affect B's damages liability. As long as A was not trustee of the promise B's liability would be limited to nominal damages, whereas once A had declared himself trustee of the promise B would become liable to substantial damages. This cannot possibly be correct.

A will not lightly be regarded as trustee of the promise, however. The evidential requirement is high, and it seems that a clear intention to create an irrevocable trust benefiting the third party must be shown: it was not, for example, in *Re Schebsman* [1944] Ch 83 (which was approved in *Beswick v Beswick*). Schebsman had entered into an agreement with his ex-employers whereby they agreed (by way of compensation for Schebsman's loss of employment) to pay money to Schebsman's wife and daughter. Schebsman was adjudicated bankrupt just under two years later, and died soon after. The trustee in bankruptcy claim all the sums which remained payable to Schebsman's wife and daughter as part of Schebsman's estate. Schebsman's wife and daughter argued that they were beneficiaries under a trust (of Schebsman's chose in action). The Court of Appeal held that Schebsman had not contracted as trustee, Lord Greene MR observing (at p. 89):

> It is not legitimate to import into the contract the idea of a trust when the parties have given no indication that such was their intention. To interpret this contract as creating a trust would, in my judgment, be to disregard the dividing line between the case of a trust and the simple case of a contract

made between two persons for the benefit of a third. That dividing line exists, although it may not always be easy to determine where it is to be drawn. In the present case I find no difficulty.

Du Parcq LJ (at p. 104) thought the crucial consideration to be that no *irrevocable* arrangement had been agreed:

> . . . [U]nless an intention to create a trust is clearly to be collected from the circumstances of the case, I think that the court ought not to be astute to discover indications of such an intention. I have little doubt that in the present case both parties (and certainly the debtor) intended to keep alive their common law right to vary consensually the terms of the obligation undertaken by the company, and if circumstances had changed in the debtor's lifetime injustice might have been done by holding that a trust had been created and that those terms were accordingly unalterable.

In spite of there being no trust in their favour, however, the wife and daughter still prevailed over the trustee in bankruptcy. The rights of the trustee in bankruptcy were no greater than those of Schebsman himself (had he still been alive). Although Schebsman could no doubt by fresh agreement with his ex-employer deprive his wife and daughter of their benefits under the arrangement, he could not do so unilaterally without being in breach of contract. The same restriction applied also to the trustee in bankruptcy.

2.3.2.4   Privity — burdening third parties
Since trusts bind not only the original trustee, but also anyone else who comes into control of the property, subject to the notice doctrine rule discussed in 1.4.6, they can also be used to bind third parties to contracts, avoiding the privity rules.

For example, suppose X owns an aircraft, and agrees to charter it to Y for two years, Y paying a single lump sum in advance. If X now sells the aircraft to Z, Y can sue X in contract, but cannot sue Z. If, on the other hand, X has declared himself a trustee of the aircraft in Y's favour, Z may find himself bound by the agreement. This may not be unjust in cases where a trust has been clearly created, but equally obviously, if the courts were over-zealous to infer trusts, it would become more difficult to sell aircraft, or other property.

2.3.3   Trusts and loans
When you lend money to a friend or business partner, or deposit money in a bank account, your friend, business partner or bank becomes a debtor, not a trustee, and you become a creditor, not a beneficiary. It should be clear from the above that a debtor will be in a very different position from a trustee. A debtor's liability to repay a loan is contractual, and therefore strict, subject to the terms of the loan. In other words, it does not require proof of negligence or bad faith. It is not avoided, for example, by the theft by a third person either of the money loaned, or of any property purchased with the money, however innocent the debtor may be. On the other hand the property the creditor has loaned passes to the debtor, so if the debtor goes bankrupt, the

creditor takes his place as one among many unsecured creditors, and is unlikely to see the return of any or all his money.

A trustee's duties are less strict (see chapters 14 to 17), but in the event of a trustee's bankruptcy, a beneficiary is in the position of a secured creditor, because he has retained equitable property, which will be protected from the claims of the general creditors. In effect, the property never becomes part of the debtor's estate.

Both legal and equitable obligations can coexist, however, so that a loan can also constitute a trust. Thus, a creditor can also be a beneficiary, and this protects him in the event of the debtor's bankruptcy.

2.3.3.1 Express declaration of trusteeship by debtor The most certain method of doing this is to require the debtor to declare himself trustee on behalf of the creditor. A common commercial transaction where this is routinely done is the bankers' documentary credit, where the bank, on releasing to its customer the shipping documents, which are its security, to enable the customer to re-sell the goods (and hence obtain the money to repay the bank), protects itself against the bankruptcy of its customer by taking a trust receipt, under which the customer (typically) declares himself trustee for the bank of the goods until they are sold, and of the proceeds of sale once the goods are sold. Thus the bank becomes both creditor and beneficiary under the trust, and hence retains equitable title in the goods and (if sold) the proceeds of sale. Since the customer obtains the goods only as trustee, if he goes bankrupt, whether before or after the goods are sold, the bank will be able to claim the goods or the proceeds of sale (so long as they are traceable under the equitable rules described in 19.2) in preference to the general creditors.

Other examples of the use of trusts to protect against bankruptcy are considered at the end of 3.1.4.

2.3.3.2 No express declaration of trusteeship by debtor Even where words of trust are not expressly used, the courts have held, in a line of authorities going back at least 150 years, that where A advances to B an identifiable sum of money for a particular purpose, the obligations of trusteeship are imposed upon B.

The leading authority is the House of Lords decision in *Barclays Bank Ltd* v *Quistclose Investments Ltd* [1970] AC 567. The case revolved around Rolls Razor Ltd, who were in serious financial difficulties, and had an overdraft with Barclays Bank of some £484,000, against a permitted limit of £250,000. If Rolls Razor were to stay in business, it was essential for them to obtain a loan of around £210,000 in order to pay dividends which they had declared on their ordinary shares, and which in the absence of such a loan they were unable to pay. They succeeded in obtaining the loan from Quistclose Investments Ltd, who agreed to make the loan on the condition 'that it is used to pay the forthcoming dividend due on July 24, next'. The sum was paid into a special account with Barclays Bank, on the condition (agreed with the bank) that the account would 'only be used to meet the dividend due on July 24, 1964'.

Rolls Razor went into voluntary liquidation on 27 August, without having paid the dividend. Barclays wanted to count the money in the special account against Rolls Razor's overdraft, but the House of Lords held that Barclays held the money on trust for Quistclose, so that Quistclose was able to claim back the entire sum. Lord Wilberforce stated (at p. 580):

> The mutual intention of the respondents [Quistclose] and of Rolls Razor Ltd, and the essence of the bargain, was that the sum advanced should not become part of the assets of Rolls Razor Ltd, but should be used exclusively for payment of a particular class of creditors, namely, those entitled to the dividend. A necessary consequence from this, by process simply of interpretation, must be that if, for any reason, the dividend could not be paid, the money was to be returned to the respondents: the word 'only' or 'exclusively' can have no other meaning or effect.
>
> That arrangements of this character for the payment of a person's creditors by a third person, give rise to a relationship of a fiduciary character or trust, in favour, as a primary trust, of the creditors, and secondarily, if the primary trust fails, of the third person, has been recognised in a series of cases over some 150 years.

The effect of the decision, of course, was that the money loaned by Quistclose was secured from the consequences of Rolls Razor's bankruptcy, since it never became part of Rolls Razor's general assets.

Note that it was Barclays, who as bankers had legal title to the money, who were held to be trustees. This raised the issue of the bank's notice of the trust since, on the principles in 1.6.4, they would have taken free of Quistclose's interest in the absence of notice. Lord Wilberforce commented (at p. 582):

> It is common ground, and I think right, that a mere request to put the money into a separate account is not sufficient to constitute notice. But [in this case] . . . there is no doubt that the bank was told that the money had been provided on loan by a third person and was to be used only for the purpose of paying the dividend. This was sufficient to give them notice that it was trust money and not assets of Rolls Razor Ltd: the fact, if it be so, that they were unaware of the lender's identity (though the respondent's name as drawer was on the cheque) is of no significance.

He went on to say that the bank were also aware that Rolls Razor could not themselves, without a loan from an outside source, provide the money to pay the dividend, and that the bank never contemplated that the money so provided could be used to reduce the existing overdraft.

2.3.3.3 Money must be for a specific purpose

The decision in *Quistclose* seems to depend on the fact that the money was to be used for a specific purpose, that that purpose was known to the recipient, and that the money was paid into a special account, which could be used for no other purpose. The last requirement, for a special account, may not be absolutely rigid, but at the very least the money must be earmarked for the particular purpose *and no other*, in order to negative the inference that the payments are to be included in the general assets of the company. In the absence of such a requirement, a prospective purchaser through a car import company, for example, who pays a deposit of £1,000 for the purpose of importing a car, would be able to reclaim that £1,000 in the event of the car import company going into liquidation before the car is obtained. The payment, after all, is made for a particular purpose, which is known to the recipient (the company), but except in the unlikely event that the company can use that money for *no purpose other* than obtaining the car, the prospective purchaser is not protected on *Quistclose* principles. The position is somewhat similar to cases where money has been paid to a company for the purpose of obtaining an allotment of shares, but no trust has been held to have been created. Commenting on those cases, Lord Wilberforce said (at p. 581):

> I do not think it necessary to examine these cases in detail, nor to comment on them, for I am satisfied that they do not affect the principle on which this appeal should be decided. They are merely examples which show that, in the absence of some special arrangement creating a trust . . . , payments of this kind are made upon the basis that they are to be included in the company's assets. They do not negative the proposition that a trust may exist where the mutual intention is that they should not.

The setting up of a special fund negates the inference that the payments are to be included in the company's assets, but so long as that inference is negated, it may be that a special fund is not absolutely necessary. In *Re EVTR* [1987] BCLC 646, for example, the appellant, Barber, who had just won £240,000 on premium bonds, agreed to assist a company for whom he had worked in purchasing new equipment. He accordingly deposited £60,000 with the solicitors to the company, and authorised them to release it 'for the sole purpose of buying new equipment'. The money was not paid into a special fund, but was paid out by the company in pursuit of the purpose. Before the new equipment was delivered EVTR went into receivership. The Court of Appeal held that Barber was entitled to recover his money (or at any rate, the balance of £48,536, after agreed deductions) on *Quistclose* principles. Dillon LJ also thought (at p. 649):

> in the light of *Quistclose*, that if the company had gone into liquidation, or the receivers had been appointed, and the scheme had become abortive before the £60,000 had been disbursed by the company, the appellant would have been entitled to recover his full £60,000, as between himself and the company, on the footing that it was impliedly held by the company on a resulting trust for him as the particular purpose of the loan had failed.

At this stage, however, the money would not have been held in a special account, but the inference that it was intended to be included as part of the general assets would have been negated by other factors. The existence of a special account does not appear, then, to be absolutely essential, so long as the inference that the payments are to be included in the company's assets is negated.

The reality is, however, that *Quistclose* trusts are used when the trustee is in liquidation. Merely to have a personal action against the trustee is therefore useless; it is essential for the lender to be able to point to a fund of money held by the trustee and say 'that money is my property'. To be able to do this it is necessary to be able to identify the money, and this is clearly easiest where the money has been paid into a special account. It is not essential, however, so long as the money can be traced on the principles discussed in 19.2. In *Re Kayford Ltd* [1975] 1 WLR 279 (see 3.1.4), where it was held that a trust fund had been set up for customers of an insolvent company, Megarry J did not think it fatal that the money had been mixed with small amounts of other money. The case was not decided on *Quistclose* principles, but it was essential to be able to establish that the money belonged in equity to the customers; a personal action against the company would have availed them nothing. The money in *Kayford* was clearly traceable, however, so there was no problem even though there were other small sums in the account.

2.3.3.4 Position where money already owed to trustee For the purposes of *Quistclose* type trusts, it does not seem to matter where the money comes from. In *Quistclose* itself it was a loan made voluntarily by a third party. *EVTR* also involved a voluntary disposition. In *Carreras Rothmans Ltd* v *Freeman Mathews Treasure Ltd* [1985] Ch 207, on the other hand, the money paid into the special account was money that Carreras Rothmans (CR) were contractually obliged to pay to Freeman Mathews Treasure (FMT) in any event. Applying *Quistclose*, however, Peter Gibson J held that the money in the special account was held on trust.

The plaintiff (cigarette manufacturers) engaged the defendant advertising agency. The defendant contracted as principal with production agencies and advertising media. The arrangement was that CR paid a monthly fee to FMT, which was used:

(a)   as payment in arrears for FMT's services, and
(b)   to enable FMT to pay debts incurred to agency and media creditors.

The defendant (FMT) got into financial difficulties, but needed funds to pay its production agencies and advertising media, if it was to carry on acting for the plaintiff.

Carreras Rothmans also knew that if FMT went into liquidation still owing money to media creditors, the media creditors would have sufficient commercial power to compel CR to pay, and therefore (although they were not legally obliged to do so) they would in practice have to pay twice over. An agreement was therefore made between CR and FMT whereby the plaintiffs would pay a monthly sum into a special account at the defendant's bank, the money to be used:

only for the purposes of meeting the accounts of the media and production fees of third parties directly attributable to CR's involvement with the agency.

The first payment (of just under £600,000) was made at the end of July, covering debts incurred in June. Unlike the position in the cases discussed above, however, this was money which CR owed to FMT in any event.

The defendant went into liquidation before the debts were cleared. CR immediately found another advertising agency, and so that its advertising campaign would not be jeopardised, paid the debts of the media creditors, taking assignments of those debts. Of the money in the special account, Peter Gibson J held that it was held by FMT (and hence by the liquidator) on trust, since it had been paid for a specific purpose, and he made an order requiring the liquidator to carry out that purpose (i.e., payment to the third parties). He did not think it relevant (at pp. 221–2) that CR was under a contractual obligation to pay the money to FMT in any event, noting (at p. 222C–E) that:

> if the common intention is that property is transferred for a specific purpose and not so as to become the property of the transferee, the transferee cannot keep the property if for any reason that purpose cannot be fulfilled. I am left in no doubt that the provider of the moneys in the present case was the plaintiff. True it is that its own witnesses said that if the defendant had not agreed to the terms of the contract letter, the plaintiff would not have broken its contract but would have paid its debt to the defendant, but the fact remains that the plaintiff made its payment on the terms of that letter and the defendant received the moneys only for the stipulated purpose. That purpose was expressed to relate only to the moneys in the account. In my judgment therefore the plaintiff can be equated with the lender in *Quistclose* as having an enforceable right to compel the carrying out of the primary trust.

2.3.3.5 Enforcement of *Quistclose* trusts In both *Quistclose* and *EVTR*, the provider of the money was able to claim it back, the primary purpose of the trust having failed. In *Carreras Rothmans* the primary trust could still be carried out, and the order made was to that effect (presumably the court would have been reluctant in any event to order repayment to Carreras Rothmans themselves, given that this was money owed by CR under contract). Peter Gibson J even thought (at p. 223) that the third party creditors might themselves have had enforceable rights, but at the end of the day it was CR, as provider of the money, who was able to apply for the order. It is also clear from *Quistclose* itself (at p. 581) that it is the provider of the money who can enforce the trust, that:

> the lender acquires an equitable right to see that [the money advanced] is applied for the primary designated purpose . . . if the primary purpose cannot be carried out, the question arises if a secondary purpose (i.e.,

repayment to the lender) has been agreed, expressly or by implication: if it has, the remedies of equity may be invoked to give effect to it . . .

It is also the view of P J Millett QC (as he then was), counsel for CR, that the provider of the moneys, and only he, can usually enforce a *Quistclose* trust: (1985) 101 LQR 269, at pp. 290–91.

Nonetheless, other views are possible. As has been observed, Peter Gibson J thought that the third party creditors could enforce the primary trust. It is necessary then to explain why CR, rather than the third party creditors, were able to obtain the order. They had taken assignments of the third party creditors' debts, and one might argue that they were suing as assignees. The problem with this view is that debt actions against a company which is in liquidation are valueless, and (at least as far as it is possible to tell from the report) CR had not taken assignments of any other rights the third party creditors might have. I do not think it is possible to escape the conclusion that if the third party creditors were the beneficiaries under, and hence able to enforce, the primary trust, the actual decision in *Carreras Rothmans* is wrong. That is also a tenable view; after all, it is a first instance decision which has not been followed, where the decision appears inconsistent with the reasoning in the judgment.

Another possible view is that the primary trust in *Quistclose* cases is a pure purpose without true beneficiaries at all. This view was taken by Megarry J in *Re Northern Developments (Holdings) Ltd*, unreported, 6 October, 1978, but considered in *Carreras Rothmans* and discussed by P J Millett QC in the article referred to above. It is subject to the criticisms advanced in chapter 5.

2.3.3.6 Loans for purchase and improvement of dwelling-houses So far as dwelling-houses are concerned, contributions to the purchase or improvement of such houses have been held to give rise to resulting or constructive trusts, where the purpose of the contribution has been to enable the creditor to live in the house. It seems that if there is no intention that the money be repaid, the trust will attach to the house itself, whereas if the money is advanced as a loan (as in *Hussey* v *Palmer* [1972] 1 WLR 1286 and *Re Sharpe* [1980] 1 WLR 219), the trust attaches to the money. In either case the creditor becomes secured against the bankruptcy of the debtor. *Re Sharpe*, in particular, has been heavily criticised, however, and indeed the general creditors could justifiably have felt hard done by. The case, which may well be wrong, is discussed further in 10.6.

2.4 EXPRESS, IMPLIED, RESULTING AND CONSTRUCTIVE TRUSTS

So far we have considered only express trusts, where the settlor has expressed an intention to set up a trust. They are not the only variety, however, and the distinctions are important because implied, resulting and constructive trusts are not subject to the same formality requirements as express trusts (see chapter 6).

An implied trust arises where the settlor's intention is inferred from his words or conduct, rather than being expressed. A constructive trust is imposed by the courts irrespective of the owner's intention. A particular variety of these will be considered in detail in chapter 8.

Resulting trusts require more detailed consideration. The factual situations in which they can occur are very diverse, but the common factor is this. Although legal title is vested in a trustee, either the equitable title never leaves the settlor (for example, because the settlor never properly disposes of his equitable title), or if it is properly divested, because of some later occurrence, it returns to the settlor. In the latter situation the contingency will have been unforeseen by the settlor and hence (or perhaps because of bad drafting) not provided for. Because there is therefore nowhere else for the equitable interest to go, it goes back to the settlor under a resulting trust.

In *Re Vandervell's Trusts (No. 2)* [1974] Ch 269 (see 2.4.1.2), Megarry J distinguished between presumed and automatic resulting trusts, as follows:

(a)   The first class of case is where the transfer to B is not made on any trust . . . there is a rebuttable presumption that B holds on resulting trust for A. The question is not one of the automatic consequences of a dispositive failure by A, but one of presumption: the property has been carried to B, and from the absence of consideration and any presumption of advancement B is presumed not only to hold the entire interest on trust, but also to hold the beneficial interest for A absolutely. The presumption thus establishes both that B is to take on trust and also what that trust is. Such resulting trusts may be called 'presumed resulting trusts'.

(b)   The second class of case is where the transfer to B is made on trusts which leave some or all of the beneficial interest undisposed of. Here B automatically holds on resulting trust for A to the extent that the beneficial interest has not been carried to him or others. The resulting trust here does not depend on any intentions or presumptions, but is the automatic consequence of A's failure to dispose of what is vested in him. Since *ex hypothesi* the transfer is on trust, the resulting trust does not establish the trust but merely carries back to A the beneficial interest that has not been disposed of. Such resulting trusts may be called 'automatic resulting trusts'.

In this chapter we are concerned only with the second type, that is to say automatic resulting trusts. Presumed resulting trusts are considered in detail at 8.2–8.4.

In *Westdeutsche Landesbank Girozentrale* v *Islington London Borough Council* [1966] 2 All ER 961, Lord Browne-Wilkinson doubted whether the second class of case operated automatically, but thought that it too depended on intention. He did not doubt the validity of the distinction between the two types, however.

2.4.1 Incomplete disposal of the equitable interest
The settlor may have made it clear that property is intended to be held on trust and may even have transferred the legal title to the trustee. There may

be some reason, however, why the equitable interest is not properly disposed of. Obviously the trustee cannot keep the trust property for himself and so he holds it on resulting trust for the settlor. There is nowhere else for the equitable interest to go.

2.4.1.1 Formalities and certainty Sometimes this can arise for technical reasons. For example, we shall see in chapter 6 that formalities may be required for the disposal of an equitable interest. If these formalities are not complied with, there will be no effective disposal. In that case the equitable interest never leaves the settlor and there is a resulting trust. A similar result obtains if the certainty of objects requirement (see chapter 4) is not complied with.

2.4.1.2 Equitable interest undefined Another possibility is where property is settled on trust but details of the trust are left unclear (i.e., the terms of the trust fail to provide for the totality of the beneficial interest). In *Vandervell* v *IRC* [1967] 2 AC 291, a case considered in greater detail in chapter 6, Mr Vandervell made arrangements to endow a chair of pharmacology by transferring shares to the Royal College of Surgeons, to enable it to take the dividends declared on those shares. He did not wish to make an out-and-out transfer, however, and so gave an option to purchase (at a nominal cost) to a trustee company which was under his control. He left no clear instructions with the trustee company as to the terms on which the option was to be held by them.

As will be explained in chapter 6, Vandervell's liability to surtax on the dividends depended on whether he had divested himself of his entire interest in both the shares and the option. The Revenue failed to show that he had not divested himself on the entire interest in the shares. The point that arises in the present context, however, is that they succeeded in showing that he had not divested himself of his equitable interest in the option, the legal title to which was now in the trustee company. The option was therefore held on resulting trust for him along with liability to pay surtax on the dividends.

Lord Wilberforce said that the trusts upon which the option was supposed to be held were undefined and in the air, possibly to be defined later. The trustee company itself was clearly not a beneficiary. An equitable interest cannot remain in the air and so the only possibility was a resulting trust in favour of the settlor. This is an example, then, of the trust being insufficiently defined.

To counter the Revenue's claims to surtax on the dividends declared on the shares, Mr Vandervell in 1961 instructed the trustee company to exercise the option, and repurchase the shares. The shares were then placed by the trustee company on the trusts of the children's settlements. The Court of Appeal held in *Re Vandervell's Trusts (No. 2)* [1974] Ch 269, that Vandervell had now succeeded in divesting himself of the entire interest in these shares, there being no longer a resulting trust in his favour. The later trusts were precisely defined, in favour of the children's settlements, so that it was no longer necessary for this reason for the equitable interest to remain in the settlor.

2.4.1.3 Necessary pre-condition absent There can be other reasons, apart from a defective trust instrument, for a failure to dispose of an equitable interest. One possibility is that the body upon which money or property is settled has never existed or has ceased to exist. If a general or paramount charitable intention is shown on the part of the donor, a cy près scheme may be applied (see chapter 13). Otherwise the property will be held on resulting trust for the settlor.

Another situation is where money or property is given for a purpose, and the circumstances necessary to achieve the purpose fail to materialise. For example, in *Essery* v *Coulard* (1884) 26 ChD 191, a trust for the parties to an intended marriage, and the issue of the marriage, could not take effect when the parties decided to live together without marrying, so Pearson J held that the property was to be held on resulting trust for the settlor. The intention of the settlor (the intended wife) had been to provide for all the issue of the relationship, and this was inevitably defeated by failure to marry, even if a marriage were later to take place: children had already been born, and at that time illegitimate children could not take. Since a subsequent marriage would not legitimate the children who had already been born, the settlor's intention to provide for all the children had been irrevocably defeated by the failure of the parties to marry.

A similar result was reached in *Re Ames' Settlement* [1946] Ch 217, where although Mr Ames and Miss Hamilton went through a ceremony of marriage, the Supreme Court of Kenya later declared the marriage void *ab initio*, a decree of nullity having at that time retrospective effect. In other words, there had never been a valid marriage. There were no issue, and those who were entitled under the trust in default of issue claimed the trust property. Vaisey J held that the parties never having been validly married, the fund should be held on resulting trust for the settlor (or rather, his representatives).

The same result would not obtain on the same facts today: since 31 July 1971, a decree of nullity in respect of a voidable marriage has not had retrospective effect, so the marriage would not be regarded as void *ab initio*.

2.4.1.4 Partial disposal of equitable interest Sometimes the settlor disposes of some, but not all, of the equitable interest. Usually this occurs because some contingency is unprovided for, perhaps because it is unforseen, or perhaps because of sloppy drafting. In this case also, the undisposed of residue 'results' to the settlor.

A good example is *Re Cochrane* [1955] Ch 309, which concerned a marriage settlement of funds for the wife:

> during her life so long as she shall continue to reside with the said W.J.B. Cochrane . . . and after [her] decease or the prior determination of the trust in her favour . . . upon trust to pay the said income to the said W.J.B. Cochrane (if then living) during his life and after the decease of the survivor of them . . . in trust for

such of their issue as they should jointly or as the survivor of them should appoint, and in default of appointment equally at the age of 21, or in the case of daughters, earlier marriage.

The draftsman appears to have assumed that even if Mrs Cochrane ceased to reside with Mr Cochrane, Mr Cochrane would live long enough either for an appointment to be made, or for his children to take in default of appointment. In the event, however, this did not happen, the timing of events being as follows. First, Mrs Cochrane stopped living with Mr Cochrane. Her interest accordingly terminated. Then Mr Cochrane died, before either any appointment in favour of the children had been made, or the default conditions had occurred. The issue before the court was what should happen to the income from the fund between Cochrane's death and the children reaching 21 or, in the case of daughters, their marriage if earlier.

It can be seen that the contingency that occurred had simply not been provided for, so that for a time there was no clear disposition of the equitable interest. Not only had it not been provided for, but the deed gave no guidance to the court as to what could have been intended. Harman J held that for the period unprovided for there was a resulting trust of the income to the settlor.

2.4.2   Necessary condition ends

2.4.2.1   The general position
It may be that the trust pre-supposes the existence of a condition which comes to an end. In that case, again there will be a resulting trust of any surplus. For example, in *Hussey* v *Palmer* [1972] 1 WLR 1286 a payment of £607, for improvements to property to enable a widow to live with her daughter and son-in-law, was held on resulting trust for her when differences arose and she had to leave the house.

In this situation, however, there will be a resulting trust only if the surplus is undisposed of at the end of the precondition. Another possibility is that the donor made an unconditional gift, and did not intend to retain any interest in the surplus should the necessary conditions for the gift cease.

In *Re the Trusts of the Abbott Fund* [1900] 2 Ch 326, a fund was collected for the relief of two deaf and dumb ladies (who had been defrauded out of their rights under an earlier settlement). No provision was made for disposal of the fund on the death of the survivor. A surplus of some £367 remained when they died, and Stirling J held that this should be held on resulting trust for the subscribers. It can be seen that the case is not unlike *Re Cochrane* [1955] Ch 309 (see 2.4.1.4), in that the contingency of the death of the ladies had not been provided for.

In reaching his decision in *Re the Trusts of the Abbott Fund*, Stirling J held that the ladies themselves never became absolute owners of the fund. Nor did the trustees once the purposes were accomplished. No resulting trust occurs if either beneficiary or trustee is intended to take absolutely, however.

The fund in *Abbott* was subscribed to by various friends of the Abbotts. On the other hand, where the whole of a specific fund is left by a single individual for the maintenance of given individuals, the courts are more likely to construe the transaction as an absolute gift to those individuals, even where the fund is expressed to be left for a particular purpose (although it depends, of course, on the intention of the donor, which is ultimately a question of fact). An example is the Court of Appeal decision in *Re Osoba* [1979] 1 WLR 247, where a testator left the whole of a fund on trust for the education of his daughter up to university level. On completion of the daughter's university education she was held entitled to the surplus beneficially, the educational purpose being regarded merely as a statement of the testator's motive — in other words, there was no resulting trust in favour of the testator's estate.

The other possibility is a gift to the trustee. *Re the Trusts of the Abbott Fund* applies only where the property was intended to be held on trust, and so does not apply where the intention is to make an out-and-out gift subject to trusts (as opposed to a gift 'on trust', which is subject to the *Abbott* principle). In such cases the trustee is clearly intended to keep the surplus. An example is *Re Foord* [1922] 2 Ch 519, where the testator left in his will: 'all my effects including rubber and other shares I leave absolutely to my sister on trust to pay my wife £300 p.a., etc.'.

2.4.2.2 Anonymous subscriptions to funds Where money has been given to a fund, say a disaster appeal fund, one might infer the donor's intention from, among other considerations, whether the donation was anonymous (e.g., small change in a street collecting box). If so, and no means of tracing the donor exists, then the contribution might be construed as an out-and-out gift. Clearly the donor cannot have intended that any surplus left over be held on resulting trust for him, when he has left the organisers no means of finding him in the event of there being a surplus. If there is a surplus left over after the fund has fulfilled his purposes, therefore, and the fund is not charitable, that part of the surplus attributable to his donation will have no owner. It therefore goes to the Crown as *bona vacantia*.

Note that the position is different where the purpose of the fund is charitable. In that event the Charities Act 1960, s. 14 applies (see 13.5), and a cy près scheme could be invoked. For present purposes, however, we are assuming that the purpose of the fund is not charitable.

In spite of the general principle suggested above, *Re the Trusts of the Abbott Fund* [1900] 2 Ch 326 was followed in *Re Gillingham Bus Disaster Fund* [1958] Ch 300 (upheld on a different issue [1958] 2 All ER 749), and such donations were directed to be held on resulting trust. The case concerned a fund collected to defray funeral and other expenses incurred as a result of a disaster involving the deaths of 24 Royal Marine cadets in Gillingham. The town clerk of Gillingham wrote a letter to *The Daily Telegraph* in the following terms:

> Cadets' memorial. To the editor of '*The Daily Telegraph*'. Sir, The mayors of Gillingham, Rochester, and Chatham have decided to promote a Royal Marine Cadet Corps Memorial Fund to be devoted, among other things, to defraying the funeral expenses, caring for the boys who may be disabled, and then to such worthy cause or causes in memory of the boys who lost their lives, as the mayors may determine.

Harman J held that this was not a charitable purpose, and that the last purpose, 'to such worthy cause or causes in memory of the boys who lost their lives, as the mayors may determine', was void for uncertainty (see further chapter 5). The purposes were therefore taken to be defraying the funeral expenses of the boys who lost their lives, and caring for the boys who were disabled.

Far more money (about £9,000) was collected than was necessary for these purposes, especially as there were common law actions available against the bus company. The question therefore was who owned the surplus: was it the donors, represented by the Official Solicitor, or the Crown (represented by the Treasury Solicitor), as *bona vacantia*? Harman J, following *Re the Trusts of the Abbott Fund*, held that the surplus should be held on resulting trust for the donors.

The difficulty was that although some of the money had been provided by identifiable people, most had been obtained from street collections. So many of the donors were anonymous and the trustees were therefore required to hold the fund on resulting trust for unknown people. Obviously this is most inconvenient administratively. As we will see in chapter 13, had the gifts been charitable, the cy près doctrine could have provided a way of avoiding this difficulty but the gifts in *Gillingham* were not charitable. As explained above, if people give money in an anonymous collection, surely it can be assumed that they do not intend to see it back again. In other words, an out-and-out gift seems a more sensible inference than a gift on trust. Had that inference been drawn by Harman J, the surplus would of course have gone to the Crown as *bona vacantia*.

This result (i.e., the out-and-out gift construction) was indeed reached by Goff J in *Re West Sussex Constabulary's Widows, Children & Benevolent (1930) Fund Trusts* [1971] Ch 1. The case concerned a fund for widows and dependants, to which the members contributed, but there were also outside contributions. In this section we are concerned only with the outside contributions. The division of the surplus among the members themselves is considered in chapter 5.

The purpose of the fund was to provide allowances for the widows and dependants of deceased members. Some of its revenue was derived from contributions from its own members. Some was also raised from outside sources, by:

(a)   entertainments, raffles and sweepstakes;
(b)   collecting boxes;
(c)   donations, including legacies.

The fund was wound up at the end of 1967, upon the amalgamation of the constabulary with other police forces, and the question arose as to how to divide it up.

Goff J held that the outside contributions raised from category (c) were held on resulting trust for the contributors. Those raised by categories (a) and (b) were clearly intended to take effect as out-and-out gifts to the fund, and therefore the resulting trust doctrine did not apply to them.

So far as identifiable donations and legacies were concerned (category (c)), Goff J thought these indistinguishable from *Re the Trusts of the Abbott Fund* (but see further 5.3), so the proportion of the surplus attributable to that source was held on resulting trust. But there were also identifiable collections from raffles and sweepstakes (category (a)), which Goff J thought were out-and-out payments subject only to a (contractual) hope of receiving a prize. Thirdly, however, there were the proceeds of street collecting boxes (category (b)), and here Goff J declined to follow Harman J's earlier judgment, again on the grounds that the intention to be inferred was also that of an out-and-out gift. Thus, nobody could lay claim to the proportion of the surplus attributable to the last two categories, so it went to the Crown as *bona vacantia*.

Clearly the *West Sussex* case is easier to justify in conceptual terms than the earlier case, and of the two *West Sussex* is, I suggest, more likely to be followed in the future. Understandably, however, Harman J was concerned in the earlier case to ensure that the Crown was not the main beneficiary of a fund collected in highly publicised and tragic circumstances.

Another aspect of the *West Sussex* case is discussed in chapter 5. Further discussion of resulting trusts (in a different context) can be found at the beginning of chapter 8.

2.5 TRUSTS AND POWERS

2.5.1 Fixed and discretionary trusts

So far the assumption has been made that the extent of the beneficial interests under a trust has been known at the outset, and indeed many trusts are of this nature. An example might be property divided equally among the sons of the settlor. Each son has an interest which is fixed and ascertainable from the outset. Statutory trusts for sale, arising from undivided shares in land, are normally fixed trusts, because each co-owner will have a defined share from the start. On statutory trusts for sale, see further chapter 10.

This situation is by no means universal, however. With many trusts, the trustees are given a discretion as to how the property is to be distributed, usually within a defined class of possible beneficiary. This type of trust is usually termed a discretionary trust, although the term 'trust power' is also sometimes used. Obviously, nobody within the class of possible beneficiaries (such people are referred to as 'objects', as we shall see in 4.4), can claim a defined interest, or indeed any interest at all, unless and until the trustees' discretion is exercised in his favour. Yet though the trustees have a discretion as to how the property is distributed, that discretion does not extend to a refusal to distribute it at all. The trustees *must* administer the trust. They *must* appoint (i.e., decide who from within the class will benefit, and also the size of each beneficial interest). Who they appoint, and in what proportions, is up to them.

Family trusts used often to be of this nature for tax reasons. There were a number of advantages in giving discretion to the trustees. One was to enable them to alter the beneficial interests to take advantage of changing tax circumstances. Another was that tax liability attached in some circumstances only where rights were created, and none of the beneficiaries has any right to the property at all unless and until the discretion is exercised in his favour. Discretionary trusts have been hard hit by recent tax legislation, however, and are probably less common today.

As we shall see in chapter 4, the distinction between fixed and discretionary trusts is important, as the orthodox view is that different requirements of certainty of object apply.

2.5.2 Nature of powers

A power (sometimes called a mere power) differs from a discretionary trust in the following respects. First, the legal title is given, not to trustees, but to donees of the power. They have a discretion not only as to *how* to distribute the property, but also as to *whether* to distribute it. They are under no obligation to appoint at all. In other words, whereas a trust is imperative, because the trustees have to appoint, a power is discretionary, because the donees of a power need not appoint at all — the choice is theirs.

There may be limited exceptions to this position. In *Klug* v *Klug* [1918] 2 Ch 67, a mother who disapproved of her daughter's marriage without her consent capriciously refused to exercise a power in her favour. On application by the public trustee, the court ordered that the power should be exercised. This case was relied on in *Mettoy Pension Trustees* v *Evans* [1991] 2 All ER 513. noted [1991] Conv 364, where Warner J held that the court could enforce a fiduciary power in the same manner as a discretionary trust. The case is unusual, however, in that there was nobody else who was capable of exercising the power. Assuming that these cases are correct, they create limited exceptions where non-exercise of a power is capricious, and where there is nobody available to exercise a power. The cases do not affect the general principle that where donees of a power make a bona fide decision not to exercise it, the courts will not compel them to do so.

If the donees of a power do not appoint, a gift or trust over may have been provided for in default of appointment. A gift or trust over is a gift or trust which takes effect where the property has not otherwise been fully disposed of. It must be provided for in the original trust instrument, and if it has, it will take effect. If not, the property goes on resulting trust to the settlor.

A power to distribute property to a limited class of persons (called the objects of the power) is called a 'special power of appointment'. If there is no limit on who the objects may be, it is called a 'general power of appointment'. There is also a category of intermediate, or hybrid powers, where a donee is given power to appoint to anyone except those within a particular class. In each case a donee may also be an object of the power. Obviously, a donee under a general power of appointment is in a position akin to that of an absolute owner. The distinction between general and special powers of appointment is of importance when considering perpetuities (chapter 7).

The purpose of mere powers is not immediately apparent. Probably they are a hangover from days when testators did not trust wives and eldest sons to administer family property in the manner that they regarded as sensible. So, although the settlor in general terms wished to benefit his wife or eldest son, he did not wish to give them enforceable rights. Therefore the property was settled on somebody else, who had the power to appoint to the wife or eldest son, but need not do so if such appointment appeared unwise.

In recent years the practice has arisen of creating powers with discretionary trusts over, in default of appointment, where the donees under the power are the same people as the trustees under the discretionary trust. In most respects this has an identical effect to a discretionary trust. For example, if A is given power to appoint to B, C or D, with a trust over in default, in favour of E and F, A cannot avoid appointing altogether, and this is no different from a discretionary trust in favour of B, C, D, E and F. The only exception might be where A refuses to carry out his duties at all, and the court is required ultimately to distribute the property. In the case of a power with trust over, B, C and D would have no claim. If the instrument was in the form of a single trust, they would. But it is unlikely that settlors have frequent regard to this extreme and pathological situation.

So why use a power and trust over in default? As we shall see in chapter 4, between 1955 and 1971 the certainty of object test for powers was thought to be less stringent than that for discretionary trusts. In other words, an instrument which was valid as a power might be invalid as a discretionary trust, if there was a wide range of objects. It therefore became common practice to draft powers with a wide range of objects, which were valid, while confining the trust over to a narrow range of objects. Such an instrument could be valid, whereas if drafted as a trust alone it would fall foul of the certainty of object requirements. If this is indeed the explanation for such instruments, one might expect that they will become less common now that, since 1971 the certainty tests for trusts and powers have been regarded as being practically the same.

As with discretionary trusts, the objects of the power have no definable interest in the property unless that power is exercised in their favour. The objects can come to court to enforce the power, however, to the very limited extent that the court will restrain disposal of the property otherwise than in accordance with the terms of the power.

2.5.3 The extent of the discretion and the nature of enforcement

For mere powers, the donee's discretion seems to be unfettered except to the extent that he must not dispose of the property otherwise than in accordance with the terms of the power.

So far as discretionary trusts are concerned, though members of the class of possible beneficiaries have no defined interest in the property unless and until the trustees' discretion is exercised in their favour, nevertheless, they have sufficient *locus standi* to come to court to enforce the trust. Clearly the degree to which enforcement is possible is limited by the discretionary nature of the arrangement, but the courts will restrain the trustees from acting contrary to the terms of the trust instrument. And if they refuse to distribute at all, a court can remove them and appoint new trustees, or in the final analysis distribute the property itself. Furthermore, unlike donees of mere powers, the trustees' discretion is not absolute. In considering its exercise, they must make a survey of the entire field of objects, and consider each individual case responsibly, on its merits: per Lord Wilberforce in *Re Baden's Deed Trusts, McPhail v Doulton* [1971] AC 424. The requirement that discretion must be properly exercised is not merely academic. In *Turner v Turner* [1984] Ch 100, the trustees (who were relatives of the settlor, without any previous experience or understanding of trusts) simply acted on the instructions of the settlor (i.e., did not exercise their own discretion at all, but effectively delegated it to him). Mervyn Davies J held that the appointments they made were invalid.

Where a power with discretionary trust over is created, where the donees of the power and the trustees are the same people, we saw above that this is very like a discretionary trust. On principle, therefore, the exercise of the power should be controlled in the same way as that of a discretionary trust, rather than a mere power. Sir Robert Megarry V-C provides some support for this view in *Re Hay's ST* [1982] 1 WLR 1202, holding that the extent of the duty to consider both whether or not a power should be exercised, and how it should be exercised, is stronger when the power is given to someone who is also a trustee, than when a mere power is exercised. For example, it is not sufficient simply to appoint to the objects who happen to be at hand, whereas the donee of a mere power can do this. It seems that it is necessary periodically to consider whether or not to exercise the power, and at least to appreciate the width of the field of objects, even if it is not possible to compile a list of all the objects or ascertain accurately their number. Also, individual appointments need to be considered on their merits. It is not clear whether Sir Robert Megarry V-C regarded this duty as the same as in the case of discretionary trusts, or a lesser duty, though still more stringent than in the case of a mere power.

The extent of the duty is important, at least on the orthodox view, when considering certainty of objects, and we shall return to it in chapter 4.

2.5.4 Distinguishing between trusts and powers

The distinction between discretionary trusts and powers is often extremely fine. It is a matter of construing the settlor's intention, and therefore no precise criteria can be laid down. The courts have no particular presumption one way or the other, and in the days when certainty requirements used to be much stricter for discretionary trusts than powers, the courts refused to spell valid powers out of invalid trusts (see the equitable maxims referred to in 1.4.1).

If the settlor provides for a gift over or trust over in default of appointment, or has otherwise provided for this contingency, a power must be intended. This is because a trustee *must* appoint. The converse statement does not follow, however, and the courts will by no means presume a trust because there is no gift over in default. If in this case a power is construed, a failure to appoint leads to a resulting trust in favour of the settlor.

There are a number of reasons why it is necessary to distinguish between trusts and powers:

(a) The duties of donees and trustees and method of enforcement are different (see above).

(b)   The certainty of object rules used to be different, and may still be in detailed respects (see chapter 4).

(c)   Suppose an appointment has become impossible, perhaps because the donee or trustee has died. In default of appointment under a power, either the instrument will provide for a gift over, or there will be a resulting trust back to the settlor. The objects have no claim. In the case of a discretionary trust, however, the property will ultimately be distributed among the objects. If the discretion is given to one person in particular, say a particular member of a family, and he dies without exercising that discretion, the court itself must do so, and in *Burrough* v *Philcox* (1840) 5 My & Cr 72, Lord Cottenham held that the property should be divided equally among the objects. This solution will not always be sensible except in family-type trusts, however, and where it is not the courts will not adopt it (*Re Baden's Deed Trusts, McPhail* v *Doulton* [1971] AC 424, see chapter 4).

2.6   PROTECTIVE TRUSTS

This special type of trust was developed as a method of protecting family property against the consequences of the family falling into debt. Generally speaking, any property owned by a debtor can be taken to satisfy his creditors, and in the extreme event of bankruptcy, all of the debtor's property becomes vested in his trustee in bankruptcy, including of course any interest under a family settlement.

In the 19th century, when family settlements were commoner than today, such an interest would usually be a life interest, and where improvidence was feared, this interest might be made determinable upon the bankruptcy or attempted alienation of the interest on the part of its owner. At first, the practice was to provide for a gift over to some other member of the family if the life interest was thus brought to an end, but by the latter part of the 19th century a more satisfactory solution was discovered, and today a protective trust consists of a determinable life interest, the determination of which brings into play a discretionary trust in favour of the former life tenant, his spouse and children (if any), and ultimately his next of kin who would inherit in the event of his death.

The obvious advantages are that upon the bankruptcy or alienation of the interest, that interest simply ceases to exist, and cannot be claimed by creditors or the trustees in bankruptcy. The property itself remains in the hands of the trustees who can distribute the income as they see fit in the circumstances. If the reason for the determination is the actual indebtedness of the former life tenant, it would clearly be pointless to make payments to him, as the creditors could then seize the money, but the lifestyle of the family can be maintained by paying the income instead to the wife, or directly to those who supply his needs, since they can apply it for the 'use and benefit' of the former life tenant without placing money directly into his hands. It is not even necessary to set out in express terms the nature of the trusts, since s. 33 of the Trustee Act 1925 provides a model form which can be invoked simply by directing that the property shall be held on 'protective trusts' for the benefit of the person who is to be the life tenant (called 'the principal beneficiary' in the section).

There are two main limitations. First, it is not possible to settle property upon oneself upon such trusts, and protective trusts would usually be created by the parent of the principal beneficiary on his behalf. Secondly, the life interest must be made *determinable* upon the relevant event — that is, so defined that it ends naturally upon the happening of the event. If on the other hand it is made subject to a *condition subsequent,* that condition may be void as a device to defeat one's creditors. The difference is purely one of language, and is devoid of moral principle.

2.7 SUCCESSION

Trusts have a limited role to play in succession, but the main function of this section is to explain terms which will be used later in various parts of the book.

When a person dies, the legal and beneficial entitlement to all his property passes to his 'personal representatives'. If he made a will in which he appointed specific persons to be his personal representatives, they are known as his 'executors', and their first task is to obtain probate of the will (i.e., have the will registered by the registrar). Thereafter, their duty is to meet the debts and funeral expenses of the deceased out of his property, and then to distribute the rest in accordance with the instructions given in the will.

When a person dies intestate (i.e., without making a will), a statutory scheme provided by the Administration of Estates Act 1925 comes into play. This attempts to give effect to what most people are assumed to intend to happen to their property after their deaths, by providing first for any widow or widower, then for children and so on, so that the closest relations obtain the benefits which the deceased would probably have wished for them. The scheme extends outwards, so that if the deceased has no close relatives, his more distant relations will benefit. If he has no relations at all, the property passes to the Crown.

Since there is no will, his personal representatives will not be executors, but 'administrators', i.e., the persons who have obtained a grant entitling them to administer the estate. These will usually be the persons who are entitled to the property. If the deceased left a widow, she is entitled to a grant of administration, permitting her to distribute the property; if there is no widow, the right passes to the children, and so on.

The distinction between executors and administrators was material to the discussion in *Re Gonin* [1979] Ch 16 (see chapter 3).

Whether the personal representatives are executors of a will or administrators upon an intestacy, their duties are the same, and many of the rules which apply to trustees (see chapters 14 to 16) apply also to them. They hold their office for life, but the active duties are usually completed within one or two years. They must collect in all the deceased's assets, pay all debts and expenses, and then distribute the property either in accordance with the terms of the will or the statutory scheme, as the case may be.

Wills commonly provide for specific gifts to relatives or friends. A gift of land is called a 'devise', and its recipient a 'devisee'; a gift of personal property, including money, is a 'legacy', and its recipient a 'legatee'. Property which is not specifically disposed of by will is called 'the residue', and the person(s) entitled the 'residuary legatee(s)'. If a specific gift fails for any reason (possible reasons appear in chapter 4), it is added to the residue. In practice, this often comprises the bulk of the property, as it is usual to provide small specific gifts to selected friends and relatives, and simply leave the rest to the person whom one most desires to benefit.

Trusts may arise on a death, either because the will specifies that some property is to be held on trust, or because the intended recipient is under 18, so that the legal title must be held for him until he reaches that age. Where trusts are deliberately created, it is usual to name the persons who are to act as trustees, and when the executors have completed their administration, they must transfer that property to the trustees. Often, the same persons will be named as both executors and trustees, and will continue to hold the legal title in their new capacity.

It is important to appreciate that the legatees, devisees and beneficiaries under any trust created by the will have no beneficial interest in that property until such time as the executors appropriate (i.e., earmark) property to meet the gifts or trusts created by the will. What they have is merely a right to demand the proper administration of the estate by the executors. Similarly, persons entitled upon an intestacy have no beneficial interest in the property until the administrators have paid off all the liabilities affecting the deceased's property and prepared their accounts, showing what is available for those persons. For the sake of convenience, the persons entitled under an intestacy are referred to as the 'next of kin' rather than legatees, etc.

It is possible for a partial intestacy to occur, e.g., where the deceased failed to specify in his will who the residuary legatee is to be, or where the residuary gift fails. In such a case, the property will pass to the next of kin, as provided by the statutory scheme.

2.8   TRUSTS FOR SALE

In a trust for sale, the trustees are directed to sell the trust property and to hold the purchase money on trust as directed.

The original purpose of the trust for sale, dating from around the beginning of the last century, was in settling commercial land. Unlike rural aristocratic estates, commercial land was not normally settled entirely on the eldest son and thereafter down the male line, but the intention rather was to share the wealth among all the sons equally. The best way to achieve this was to direct that the business be sold, each son to take a share of the proceeds.

Settlements nowadays are rare, however, and by far the most important function of the trust for sale today is where land is shared. Matrimonial homes are frequently jointly held by husband and wife, so this may well be one of the commonest forms of trust. The term 'shared land' is used in this context as shorthand to denote that there are concurrent interests in property, in undivided shares.

The Law of Property Act 1925, ss. 34–36 provide that all shared estates in land be held on trust for sale, with powers to postpone sale. The people with concurrent interests in the land will usually be both trustees and beneficiaries (except that the legislation allows a maximum of only four trustees). As long as the purchaser pays the purchase money to at least two trustees he overreaches the beneficial interests in the property. The reason for this device being adopted by the legislature in 1925 was to simplify conveyancing, a policy generally apparent throughout the 1925 legislation. The conveyancing difficulties to which concurrent interests could give rise have already been explained (see 1.6.1).

It is not intended in this section to examine the differences between joint tenancies and tenancies-in-common. That is the preserve of land lawyers, and is dealt with in textbooks on land law.

2.8.1 Overreaching and conversion

We have already come across the concept of overreaching in chapter 1 (see 1.6.3). The effect of overreaching is that on sale of the shared land (or any other land subject to a trust for sale) the interests of the co-owners cease to be interests in land and become interests in the purchase money only. It is this feature that provides a purchaser of such land with protection, as long as he obtains receipts for the proceeds from at least two trustees. The equitable doctrine of conversion goes further, however, in that for some purposes the interests of the co-owners become interests in the money only even before the sale takes place.

This is based on the maxim 'Equity looks on that as done which ought to be done' (see 1.4.1). Most contracts for the sale of legal estates in land are specifically enforceable, and therefore from the moment the contract is made, equity treats as done that which ought to be done and regards the property as if it were already sold. (See 1.4.4).

Applying the doctrine to trusts for sale, consider an old-fashioned settlement of commercial property, where a trust for sale was expressly imposed by the settlor with the intention that the property be sold and the proceeds divided equally among his sons. Equity regarded the interests of the sons as having been converted into personalty (i.e., money, not land) from the time of the creation of the trust, even before the land was actually sold. This could have consequences, for example, for taxation purposes, or if 'all my personalty' is left in a will. In *Re Kempthorne* [1930] 1 Ch 268, a phrase in a will 'all my personal estate and effects' was held by the Court of Appeal to include shared land held under a statutory trust for sale.

The consequences would be startling, however, if interests in shared land were regarded as interests in money even before the land was sold. It seems that the conversion doctrine is not taken to its logical conclusion in this case, however (see further 8.9).

When the Trusts of Land and Appointment of Trustees Act 1996 comes into force, then the regime for concurrent interests in land will be considerably changed, and the conversion doctrine will cease to apply to them.

THREE

Constitution of Trusts and Covenants to Settle

One of the major themes of the law of trusts (which has already been touched on in chapter 2) lies in a comparison between contracts and trusts. A beneficiary under a fully constituted trust (let us call him A) is in a very different position from someone (B) who is entitled to benefit as a party to a contract, but who is not a beneficiary under a trust. Somebody (C) who merely expects to receive a benefit as a third party to a contract between two other people is in a different position again. This chapter is essentially concerned with an analysis of those differences.

3.1 details the requirements necessary for someone (let us call him X) to be in the position of A. If these requirements are not met, in other words if there is not a fully constituted trust, X may still be in the position of B or C. A likely possibility is that there is a contract to create a trust in X's favour, and if so X's rights and remedies (if any) are covered in 3.2. X may have either legal or equitable rights and remedies, or both, and they will differ. Both therefore have to be distinguished and considered.

Yet another possibility is that there is a fully constituted trust, not of tangible property, but of contractual rights themselves. This possibility is considered, along with its implications, in 3.3.

3.1 CONSTITUTION OF TRUSTS

In general, the legal title to trust property must be transferred to trustees for a valid trust to be constituted. The trustees must have control of the property. If formalities are required for this transfer, for example, in the case of land or shares, then they must be complied with. In the case of land in an area of compulsory registration of title, the relevant registration of title must be carried out.

3.1.1 Effect of constitution of trust
The effect of constituting a trust is:

(a)   Irreversible by the settlor; a gift once given cannot be revoked (unless the settlor has, by the terms of the trust, specifically granted himself or someone else a power to revoke the settlement).

(b)   To give beneficiaries enforceable rights in relation to the property (assuming a private non-purpose trust), whether or not they have provided any consideration: *Paul* v *Paul* (1882) 20 ChD 742. Indeed, it is only the beneficiaries, and not the settlor, who can enforce the trust, because the settlor retains no interest in the property (assuming he is not also a trustee or beneficiary).

(c)   To give beneficiaries an equitable interest in the property which forms the subject matter of the trust.

3.1.2   Vesting of property in trustees

In order for a valid private trust to come into existence, these two elements are both necessary and sufficient:

(a)   There must be a manifest intention on the part of the settlor to create a trust (and not to effect some other kind of transaction, such as making an outright gift or loan). The intention must be expressed in a way which complies with the certainty requirements (see chapter 4).

(b)   The trust property must be properly vested in trustees who hold it in that capacity on behalf of the beneficiaries. A trust involves a division of the ownership of property. The trustees become owners at common law, and are given control of the property. The beneficiaries become owners in equity, and in effect it is they who may enjoy the property.

It is not necessary that the property be transferred in the manner that the settlor intended. If it is conveyed to trustees in any manner, even accidentally, this is sufficient to constitute the trust: *Re Ralli's WT* [1964] Ch 288 (see 3.4) and see also *Strong* v *Bird* (1874) LR 18 Eq 315 (see 3.5.2).

Usually, the property will be transferred to third parties as trustees, although the settlor may alternatively constitute himself trustee (see 3.1.4).

3.1.3   Equity will not perfect an imperfect gift

Conversely, if the trust property is not properly vested in trustees, then there is no trust: equity will not pefect an imperfect gift. *Milroy* v *Lord* (1862) 4 De GF & J 264 is the leading authority.

The settlor had executed a voluntary deed, purporting to transfer shares to a trustee on trust for the plaintiffs. The voluntary deed was incapable of transferring legal title, however, since that could only be achieved by registering the name of the transferee in the books of the bank.

The Court of Appeal in Chancery held that no trust had been constituted, Turner LJ stating that there is no equity to perfect an imperfect gift:

in order to render a voluntary settlement valid and effectual, the settlor must have done everything which, according to the nature of the property comprised in the settlement, was necessary to be done in order to transfer the property and render the settlement binding upon him. He may of course do this by actually transferring the property to the persons for whom he intends to provide, and the provision will then be effectual, and it will be equally effectual if he transfers the property to a trustee for the purposes of the settlement, or declares that he himself holds it on trust for those purposes; . . . but, in order to render the settlement binding, one or other of these modes must . . . be resorted to, for there is no equity in this Court to perfect an imperfect gift. The cases I think go further to this extent, that if the settlement is intended to be effectuated by one of the modes to which I have referred, the Court will not give effect to it by applying another of those modes. If it is intended to take effect by transfer, the Court will not hold the intended transfer to operate as a declaration of trust, for then every imperfect instrument would be made effectual by being converted into a perfect trust.

Where the settlor does not constitute himself trustee (on which, see 3.1.4), generally speaking, the legal title has actually to be transferred to the trustees, but Turner LJ requires only that the settlor must have done everything which was necessary to be done in order to transfer the property. It is possible, therefore, for a trust to be constituted where the settlor has done all that is within his power to constitute the trust by transferring the property to a trustee, but has been thwarted by formalities which are outside his control. Equity regards the trust as constituted by the last act of the settlor.

This principle was applied in *Re Rose* [1952] Ch 499, CA, where the settlor intended to transfer shares, but where the directors of the company had an effective veto over any transfer. Rose executed transfers in shares in the required form in March 1943, but they could not take effect (at any rate at common law) until the directors of the company had registered them. They did this in June 1943. Rose died more than five years after executing the transfers, but less than five years after they were registered. If the effective date of the transfer was June 1943 then estate duty was payable, whereas if the transfer took effect in March it was not.

The Court of Appeal held that the date of constitution of the trust was when the settlor had done all he could, rather than when the directors consented to, and registered the transfer. Equity regarded the property as transferred by Rose's last act. Evershed MR said (at pp. 511–12) that he adopted in full the words of Jenkins J in *Re Rose* [1949] 1 Ch 78:

I was referred on that to the well known case of *Milroy* v *Lord*, and also to the recent case of *In re Fry* [see below]. Those cases, as I understand them, turn on the fact that the deceased donor had not done all in his power, according to the nature of the property given, to vest the legal interest in the property in the donee. In such circumstances it is, of course, well settled that there is no equity to complete the imperfect gift. . . . In *Milroy* v *Lord* the . . . document was not the appropriate document to pass any interest in the property at all. In this case, as I understand it, the testator had done everything in his power to divest himself of the shares in question . . .

In *Re Fry* [1946] 1 Ch 312, by contrast, more may have been required from the testator effectively to transfer legal title to the shares. The reason in this case that the shares could not be registered was because Treasury consent had not been obtained, as required by the Defence (Finance) Regulations 1939, under which shares could not be registered until Treasury consent was obtained. Although all the requisite forms had been filled in by the donor, the required Treasury consent had not been obtained before he died.

This may appear, at first sight, to be similar to *Rose*, but as Romer J explained (at pp. 317–18):

> Now I should have thought it was difficult to say that the testator had done everything that was required to be done by him at the time of his death, for it was necessary for him to obtain permission from the Treasury for the assignment and he had not obtained it. Moreover, the Treasury might in any case have required further information of the kind referred to in the questionnaire submitted to him, or answers supplemental to those which he had given in reply to it; and, if so approached, he might have refused to concern himself with the matter further, in which case I do not know how anyone else could have compelled him to do so.

In this case, therefore, the testator may not have done all that was required, so the principles later elaborated in *Re Rose* could not apply.

It is not entirely clear what mechanism is operating in *Re Rose*. One possibility is that once the settlor has done all that he needs to do to constitute a trust (or effect an out-and-out transfer), he is treated as if he has declared himself trustee of the property until legal title is actually transferred to the trustees (or transferee). Another is that equity imposes a constructive trust over the intervening period. It will not normally matter which of these approaches is correct, but arguably declarations of trust of land must be in writing unless they can be categorised as implied, resulting or constructive trusts (see 6.2 and 8.5.2). In *Mascall v Mascall* (1984) 50 P & CR 119, the Court of Appeal applied *Re Rose* to registered land, but since the requisite writing was present the categorisation argument was not further advanced. The transferor had executed a transfer and sent it to the Inland Revenue, and also handed to the transferee the land certificate. At this stage, before the transfer and land certificate had been sent to the Land Registry for registration of the transferee as proprietor, the transferor changed his mind, after a quarrel with the transferee. The Court of Appeal held the transfer effective, since it was for the transferee to apply to the Land Registry for registration as proprietor, and the transferor had done everything he had to do to complete the transfer.

Mascall v Mascall suggests that the trust in *Re Rose* is constructive, then, but it is difficult to see on what principle equity imposes on the conscience of the donor, especially in the light of Lord Browne-Wilkinson's insistence in *Westdeutsche Landesbank Girozentrale* v *Islington London Borough Council* [1966] 2 All ER 961 that it is a fundamental principle of the law of trusts that equity only operates on the conscience of the owner of the legal interest.

This is hardly a case like those considered in chapter 10, or at 8.5.2 or 19.3. The alternative solution, that the donor is taken to have declared himself trustee for the intervening period, also looks wrong in principle, given that he had intended a gift, and equity will not normally infer a declaration of trusteeship from an incomplete gift (see next section). Furthermore, on closer examination, *Re Rose* is not that easy to distinguish from *Re Fry* since the directors were under no obligation to register the shares (although they may well have done so routinely in practice), and so could presumably, had they so wished, have refused to do so or required further particulars from the donor.

However much *Re Rose* appears wrong in principle, however, it must be regarded as good authority, not only because it was applied in *Mascall* v *Mascall*, but also because it was approved by the House of Lords in *Vandervell* v *IRC* [1967] 2 AC 691 (see 6.4.4.1).

3.1.4 Declaration of self as trustee

In *Milroy* v *Lord*, Turner LJ also allows for the settlor to declare himself trustee, in which case no transfer of the legal title is necessary. The courts are not keen, however, except in the clearest cases, to infer on the part of a settlor an intention to declare himself trustee, because of the onerous nature of trusteeship. An intention must be shown to create a trust, rather than to effect some other transaction (e.g., an outright gift). By contrast, an intention to make an outright gift will more easily be inferred.

Thus, in *Jones* v *Lock* (1865) LR 1 Ch App 25, the father of a baby boy handed a cheque to his nine-month old son, uttering words which made it clear that he meant the child to have the sum represented by the cheque, although he immediately removed the cheque from the baby for safe-keeping. He died some days later, without having endorsed the cheque, which would have been necessary to pass title in it to the child. The court refused to construe his actions as amounting to a declaration of trust, with himself as trustee, in favour of the child.

Lord Cranworth LC did not think that an irrevocable intention to part with the property had been manifested. There was an intention to make an outright gift, but no gift had actually been made. It was not, therefore, a declaration of trust.

A similar result obtained in *Richards* v *Delbridge* (1874) LR Eq 11. Delbridge wished to give his infant grandson, Richards, the lease he had on his place of business as a bone manure merchant. He indorsed on the lease: 'This deed and all thereto belonging I give to Edward Benetto Richards from this time forth, with all the stock-in-trade'. He gave the lease to Richards' mother to hold for Richards, but died before the lease was actually delivered to Richards himself. It was held that there had been no transfer of the lease to Richards, nor a declaration of trust in his favour. Sir George Jessel MR refused to infer a declaration of trust from the failed gift:

The principle is a very simple one. A man may transfer his property . . . in one of two ways: he may do such acts as amount in law to a conveyance or assignment of the property, and thus completely divest himself of the legal ownership, in which case the person who by those acts acquires the property takes it beneficially, or on trust, as the case may be; or the legal owner of the property may, by one or other of the modes recognised as amounting to a valid declaration of trust, constitute himself a trustee, and, without an actual transfer of the legal title, may so deal with the property as to deprive himself of its beneficial ownership, and declare that he will hold it from that time forward on trust for the other person. It is true that he need not use the words, 'I declare myself a trustee,' but he must do something which is equivalent to it, and use expressions which have that meaning . . . for a man to make himself trustee there must be an expression of intention to become a trustee, whereas words of present gift shew an intention to give over property to another, and not to retain it in the donor's own hands for any purpose, fiduciary or otherwise.

This passage emphasises the difference between gift and trust, that the donor retains no interest after the property has been transferred, whereas a trustee's fiduciary obligations continue. It is no surprise, therefore, that the courts will not infer a declaration of trusteeship from a failed gift.

In the above passage, however, Jessel MR observed that the settlor need not use the words, 'I declare myself a trustee', but he must do something which is equivalent to it. It is possible to infer declaration of trusteeship from conduct, or from words which can be construed as equivalent to a declaration of trusteeship, or from a mixture of the two. In *Paul v Constance* [1977] 1 WLR 527, Constance was injured at work, and obtained £950 in damages, which he put into a bank account in his name alone. The evidence suggested, however, that the money was intended for himself and Mrs Paul, with whom he was living, but he was not married to Mrs Paul, and the reason for not opening a joint account was to save her embarrassment (this was apparently on the instigation of the bank manager).

Subsequent additions were made to the account, in particular from bingo winnings which Constance and Paul played as a joint venture. One withdrawal of £150 was also made, which was divided equally between them.

Constance died, and the question at issue was whether Mrs Paul could claim any share of the fund. If the money in the account had belonged solely to Constance, then his wife, Mrs Constance, from whom he had parted, would be entitled to it on his death.

The Court of Appeal held that Constance held the money on trust for Mrs Paul. No words of trust were used, but regard was had to the unsophisticated character of Constance, and the nature of his relationship with Mrs Paul. Scarman LJ said:

. . . there must be clear evidence from what is said or done of an intention to create a trust . . . 'an intention to dispose of property or a fund so that somebody else to the exclusion of the disponent acquires a beneficial interest in it.' . . .

When one looks at the detailed evidence to see whether it goes as far as that — and I think that the evidence does go as far as that — one finds that from the time that the deceased received his damages right up to his death he was saying, on occasions, that the money was as much the plaintiff's as his. When they discussed the damages, how to invest them or what to do with them and when they discussed the bank account, he would say to her: 'The money is as much yours as mine'. . ..

It might, however, be thought that this was a borderline case, since it is not easy to pinpoint a specific moment of declaration, . . .

There are two further points to make regarding *Paul v Constance*. First, in addition to Constance's conduct, there are his words: 'The money is as much yours as mine'. These may not obviously seem equivalent to a declaration of trusteeship, but surely what he is really saying is that although (because the bank manager advised it) legal title to the money would be vested in Constance, the money in fact belonged to both of them. Since Constance had legal title, it could only be the equitable title that was shared, so, in fact, these words are exactly appropriate for a declaration of trusteeship. We discuss similar informal words of declaration at 8.5.2.

The second point is that Scarman LJ thought it difficult to pinpoint a specific moment of declaration. If it had been impossible to do so, I would suggest that there ought to have been no trust. Trusts are, in principle, irrevocable, and there must be a moment at which the irrevocable commitment is made. Before that moment, Constance could have changed his mind. Afterwards, he could not. That is essential to the nature of a trust, although in the case itself it was difficult to pinpoint exactly which moment this was.

There are also a number of cases where companies in financial trouble have been held to have declared themselves trustee of various moneys for their customers, or others with whom they deal. The result has been that the beneficiaries have taken in preference to the general creditors. In *Re Kayford* [1975] 1 WLR 279, a mail order company was in financial difficulties. In order to protect customers in the event of insolvency, the company considered setting up a separate bank account, called the 'Customers' Trust Deposit Account' to hold the customers' deposits and payments until their goods were delivered, the intention of the company being that this money should be kept separate from the company's general funds. But the company took the advice of the bank, and instead of opening a new account, used a dormant account (with a small credit balance) in the company's name. On the winding-up of the company Megarry J held that the money in the account (apart from a small credit balance) was held on trust for the customers. Hence, the customers were not mere creditors of the company but beneficial owners of the moneys which they had paid until such time as their goods were delivered. Megarry J observed that:

it is well settled that a trust can be created without using the words 'trust' or 'confidence' or the like: the question is whether a sufficient intention to create a trust has been manifested.

Nor did he consider it fatal that the money had not been put into a separate account, but mixed with other moneys:

In *Re Nanwa Gold Mines Ltd* [1955] 1 WLR 1080 the money was sent on the faith of a promise to keep it in a separate account, but there is nothing in that case or in any other authority that I know of to suggest that this is essential. I feel no doubt that here a trust was created. From the outset the advice (which was accepted) was to establish a trust account at the bank. The whole purpose of what was done was to ensure that the moneys remained in the beneficial ownership of those who sent them, and a trust is the obvious means of achieving this. No doubt the general rule is that if you send money to a company for goods which are not yet delivered, you are merely a creditor of the company unless a trust is created. The sender may create a trust by using appropriate words when he sends the money (though I wonder how many do this, even if they are equity lawyers), or the company may do it by taking suitable steps on or before receiving the money. If either is done, the obligations in respect of the money are transformed from contract to property, from debt to trust. Payment into a separate bank account is a useful (though by no means conclusive) indication of an intention to create a trust, but of course there is nothing to prevent the company from binding itself by a trust even if there are no effective banking arrangements . . . I should, however, add one thing. Different considerations may perhaps arise in relation to trade creditors; but here I am concerned only with members of the public, some of whom can ill afford to exchange their money for a claim to a dividend in the liquidation, and all of whom are likely to be anxious to avoid this.

Re Nanwa Gold Mines Ltd was an early *Quistclose*-type trust, the requirements of which doctrine are considered at 2.3.3.3. As in the *Quistclose* situation, however, it is essential to be able to establish that the money belongs in equity to the customers; a personal action by them against the company after it had been wound up would clearly have availed them nothing. Therefore the money must be traceable on the principles in 19.2. It was in *Kayford*, since the amount in the account never dropped below the amount of the small initial deposit, so that the excess could be clearly identified as trust property. Obviously, where the money is kept entirely separate, in a separate account, no difficulties of identification arise.

Re Kayford was applied by the Court of Appeal in *Re Chelsea Cloisters Ltd* (1980) 41 P & CR 98, where a 'tenants' deposit account' was set up to hold deposits against damage and breakages. Even in the absence of words of trust, however, there has to be evidence of an intention to create a trust, which is an irrevocable step, depriving the company of all beneficial interest in the money. It is not enough merely to put the money into a separate account. The requisite intention was not present in *Re Multi Guarantee Co. Ltd* [1987] BCLC 257, where the Court of Appeal distinguished the two previous cases. It had not been finally decided what to do with the money in the account, so an irrevocable intention was not established.

These cases have been criticised by Professor Michael Bridge (1992) 12 OJLS 333, at pp. 355–7.

3.1.5 Sub-trusts

A further point to note is that the property settled can include an equitable interest. In other words, a beneficiary under a trust may constitute a further trust of his equitable interest, thereby creating a sub-trust. Sub-trusts are common in tax avoiding settlements. The beneficiary under the sub-trust can himself repeat the process, creating a further sub-trust, and there is no limit to the number of times this process may be repeated.

3.2 CONTRACTS TO SETTLE

3.2.1 Common law and equitable remedies

Even if there is not a fully constituted trust, that may not be the end of the matter. Sometimes would-be settlors make contracts, either with would-be trustees or would-be beneficiaries or both, to settle property. Assume for the moment that the contract has not yet been carried out. Though some of the books, and indeed the cases themselves, refer to settlors, trustees and beneficiaries in this context, this is confusing where no trust is yet in existence. If the parties had actually become trustees and beneficiaries the position would be fundamentally different. I will therefore, for clarity, preface the terms with 'would-be' to indicate that no trust has yet been constituted. Clumsy English seems a reasonable price to pay for clarity of analysis, especially in an area where lack of clarity causes most of the difficulties.

Contracts to settle are especially common if the property has yet to be acquired by the would-be settlor, for example an expected inheritance yet to be received, or expected royalties on a book, because to make a contract is the best that the would-be settlor can do. He has no existing property with which he can constitute the trust, and the courts have held, e.g., in *Re Ellenborough* [1903] 1 Ch 697, that future property, or expectancies, cannot form the subject matter of a trust (see also *Re Brooks* [1939] Ch 933, considered in 3.4). Additionally, however, such contracts are sometimes made to settle existing property, which is already owned by the settlor, especially where the deal is that it will be settled by will, on the death of the would-be settlor.

In principle, such contracts to settle ought to be enforceable by whoever is party to them. It may be that would-be trustees cannot enforce them, however, and even if they can, they may not always have a worthwhile remedy.

As any student of the law of contract knows, a contract is enforceable if it is made by deed, and also if it is supported by consideration, but a gratuitous promise (not made by deed or under seal) cannot be enforced. Most contracts (or covenants) to settle property are made either by deed or where the parties are within the marriage consideration (on which, see below). There is no reason why they should not be made for conventional (i.e., common law) consideration in money or money's worth, but in practice this is uncommon. This is important in relation to the availability of remedies.

It should be noted that whereas contracts under seal (or covenants by deed) are recognised as valid by the common law, even where no consideration moves from the promisee, they are not recognised as valid in equity. The result is that whereas the common law remedy of damages can be obtained for breach of such covenants by the would-be settlor, the equitable remedy of specific performance, which would require him actually to constitute the trust, is not. Further, as we shall see, a damages remedy is not always useful, especially at the suit of the would-be trustee.

Equity, on the other hand, recognises marriage consideration as valid, whereas the common law does not. Thus, even if they do not provide consideration in the conventional common law sense (e.g., money or money's worth), the husband, wife or issue of a marriage can sue in equity on a contract agreed to be made before, and in consideration of, the marriage. In such cases specific performance can be obtained to force the would-be settlor to constitute the trust, or damages in lieu thereof under the Chancery Amendment Act 1858 (see 1.4.5). Marriage consideration is considered in greater detail in the next section.

Of course, if the contract is for ordinary common law consideration, (i.e., money or money's worth) conventional contractual principles apply, except for a possible exception in the case of would-be trustees. In this area, contracts for conventional common law consideration are uncommon, but an example of such a contract is *Re Cook's ST* [1965] Ch 902 (see 3.2.4).

3.2.2 Factual situations in which the cases arise

Nearly all the cases are of essentially the same type, and it is worth briefly examining the factual nature of the situation in order to explain the issues which have arisen.

The cases have typically involved marriage settlements, and the agreements to settle are usually therefore made in consideration of marriage. The parties may also enter into a deed of covenant, to which trustees, or intended trustees, may also be party. A typical arrangement might be where the husband-to-be agrees to settle not only the property he owns now, but also *property yet to be acquired* (for example, an expected inheritance yet to be received), on the terms of the settlement. Under the terms of the settlement, the beneficiaries will usually include the issue of the marriage, and in default of such issue, the next of kin of the wife.

The first point to note is that the settlement usually covers not only existing, but also after-acquired property. As observed in the previous section, future property, or expectancies, cannot form the subject matter of a trust, because there is insufficient certainty of subject matter. There is not usually, therefore, a failure by the settlor properly to constitute the trust: the trust *cannot* be properly constituted, since the trust property does not yet exist.

The second point to note is that the agreement is made, not in consideration of money or money's worth, as with most contracts, but in consideration of marriage. The relevance of marriage consideration is that not only the parties to the contract, but also any issue *of that marriage* (who are said to be within the marriage consideration) can sue on the contract. This is, in effect, an exception to the privity of contract doctrine (on which, see 2.3.2), and is usually regarded today as a narrow and anomalous exception to the rule that equity will not assist a volunteer. Historically, it appears to have been a device to impose upon the conscience of the husband (forcing him to settle the property he had agreed to settle) at a time (before the Married Women's Property Act 1882) when the wife herself had no economic independence (and could not sue in her own right). For example, Lee argues that ((1969) 85 LQR p. 227):

> [the] doctrine of marriage consideration survives as a fossil of the long era of the wife's economic subjugation to her husband. The Married Women's Property Act and the Inheritance (Family Provision) Act sounded the death knell of that era; and so the reasons of public policy which accounted for the courts' ambivalent attitude to the covenant to settle after-acquired property belong to a closed chapter of legal history.

Nevertheless, the doctrine still survives, although it is unlikely, I would suggest, that the courts are ever likely to extend it beyond its present narrow boundaries.

For example, the marriage must actually constitute the consideration for the contract, and must therefore be a future marriage. It also seems probably that only the issue of the marriage can sue, although there are (rather inconclusive) authorities to the contrary, suggesting, for example, that step-children are within the marriage consideration. Certainly however, the next-of-kin of the wife, who will typically be the intended beneficiaries in the event of failure of issue, are not within the marriage consideration (see *Re Plumptre's Marriage Settlement* [1910] 1 Ch 609, below). The clearest recent statement of the law can be found in Buckley J's judgment in *Re Cook's ST* [1965] 1 Ch 902:

> It is an elementary general rule of law that a contract affects only the parties to it and their successors in title and that no one but a party or the successor in title to a party can sue or be sued upon it. There are, however, exceptions to this rule, some legal, some equitable and some statutory. . . .
>
> It has long since been recognised that if marriage articles or a marriage settlement contain an executory agreement to settle property, equity will assist an intended beneficiary who is issue of the marriage to enforce the agreement. Such a beneficiary is described as being within the marriage consideration. . . . On the other hand, an intended beneficiary who is not issue of the marriage is not within the marriage consideration, is not treated as though any consideration moved from him, and will not be assisted to enforce a contract to make a settlement. Thus the next-of-kin of the covenantor who are intended to take the property which is to be brought into settlement in the event of a failure of issue cannot enforce a covenant to settle . . . , nor can the children by a previous marriage of one of the parties . . . , nor can the children of the marriage, if the settlement is a post-nuptial one, for in such a case, though there may be consideration as between the husband and the wife, that consideration would not be their marriage but consideration of some other kind to which their children would be strangers . . . .

Furthermore, the policy behind marriage consideration would probably not go beyond providing an action against the husband, and indeed there is no authority on whether the issue of the marriage, who though parties to the marriage consideration are otherwise volunteers, can sue anyone *apart* from the husband.

The third point to note is that the parties may also have entered into a deed of covenant, to which indeed, the intended trustees may also be party. At common law, parties to a deed can sue on it even in the absence of consideration, but they are limited to common law remedies (i.e., damages), and cannot obtain specific performance of the covenant. It is in any case very unlikely that the intended *beneficiaries* will be party to the covenant, at any rate if they are the issue of the marriage, since at the time of the covenant they wll not have been born. For an unusual example, where a beneficiary *was* party, see *Cannon* v *Hartley* [1949] Ch 213 (3.2.3, below).

The final point to note is that although the cases usually arise because a trust has not been constituted, the intended trustees under the settlement are often actually trustees of other family property. Another possibility is that trusts of the settlement *have* been constituted, but not of the particular property in dispute. It is likely that although no trusts had been constituted of the property in dispute, the decisions in *Kay* and *Pryce* (3.2.4, below) may well have been influenced by the fact that the intended trustees of the settlement were actually trustees of other property.

3.2.3 Would-be beneficiary party to the contract

If the would-be beneficiary is himself party to a covenant to settle, no problems arise, and he can enforce the contract, in the same way as he could enforce any other contract. If he is party to a covenant by deed, he can obtain substantial damages at law if the would-be settlor fails fully to constitute the trust.

As has already been explained, it would be unusual under the conventional form of marriage settlement for the intended beneficiaries to be party to the deed, but an unusual case, where an intended beneficiary was a party, was *Cannon* v *Hartley* [1949] Ch 213, where on the breakdown of a marriage, a father (would-be settlor) covenanted to make provision for a daughter (would-be beneficiary) by settling on her property expected later to be acquired under the will of his parents. When he received the property he refused to settle it on the agreed terms. The daughter was not of course within the marriage consideration, as the covenant itself was not made prior to or in consideration of marriage. But as a party to the deed, she could enforce the contract at common law, and obtain substantial damages. Romer J observed (at p. 223):

> In the present case the plaintiff, although a volunteer, is not only a party to the deed of separation but is also a direct covenantee under the very covenant upon which she is suing. She does not require the assistance of the court to enforce the covenant for she has a legal right herself to enforce it. She is not asking for equitable relief but for damages at common law for breach of covenant.

The second complication is that marriage consideration is recognised only by equity, and where the beneficiary relies on this form of consideration, he must seek an equitable remedy: specific performance or damages in lieu. As stated in chapter 1, these remedies are discretionary, although this causes no difficulty in a straightforward case.

Thus in *Pullan* v *Koe* [1913] 1 Ch 9 the children of the would-be settlor, being within the marriage consideration, could obtain specific performance of a covenant in consideration of marriage that the husband and wife would settle the wife's after-acquired property of the value of £100 or upwards. More remote kin, however, not being within the consideration, would be volunteers in the eyes of equity unless they had provided other consideration of value.

If, on the other hand, the would-be beneficiary is neither party to a deed nor within the marriage consideration, and has not provided any other consideration, he will be without remedy: 'equity will not assist a volunteer' (see the equitable maxims in 1.4.1). Authority for this proposition can be found in *Re Plumptre's Marriage Settlement* [1910] 1 Ch 609, the facts of which were similar to those in *Pullan* v *Koe*, except that the would-be beneficiaries were the next of kin of the wife, and hence not within the marriage consideration.

The case concerned a marriage settlement made in 1878, covering presently owned and after-acquired property. The settlement was of the conventional type, so that, there having been a failure of issue, the intended beneficiaries were the next of kin of the wife. In 1884, the husband made a gift of stock to his wife. On the death of the wife, intestate, in 1909, the intended beneficiaries attempted to enforce the covenant. Eve J held that the gift of stock should have been settled on the terms of the settlement, so that the husband was in breach of covenant by making an outright gift in favour of his wife. He also held, however, that the next of kin could not enforce the covenant in equity because they were volunteers.

It was also noted, in passing, that the would-be trustees, who were party to the deed of covenant, would be unable to sue at common law, because they were time-barred. The breach had occurred in 1884, when the husband had used money which should have been caught by the settlement, to make an outright gift to his wife. The case was not brought until after the wife's death in 1909. It is obvious that in cases of this type, there is often a long delay between the breach and the case being brought, and that limitation is therefore often a problem in this type of case (the intended trustees' action would also have been time-barred in *Pullan* v *Koe*).

The result was that the stock represented by the original gift (the original stock having been sold and the money reinvested) went to the husband on the intestacy of his wife, and the next of kin could not enforce the covenant.

The only way in which would-be beneficiaries in a *Plumptre* situation could benefit from the covenant would be if there were other beneficiaries who were not volunteers (as in *Pullan* v *Koe*), such as the children of the marriage, who could enforce the covenant on behalf of the would-be beneficiaries as well as on their own behalf, or the would-be beneficiaries were themselves parties to the covenant.

These cases appear in diagrammatic form in figure 3.1 below.

Figure 3.1

A is the would-be settlor
B is the would-be trustee
C is the would-be beneficiary

Cannon v *Hartley: Pullan* v *Koe*

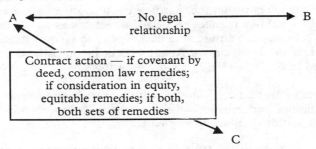

Re Plumptre's Marriage Settlement

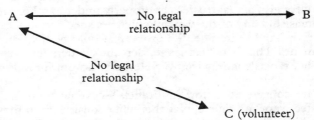

3.2.4 Would-be trustee party to the contract

The problem discussed in this section appears in diagrammatic form in figure 3.2.

Figure 3.2

Re Pryce; Re Kay

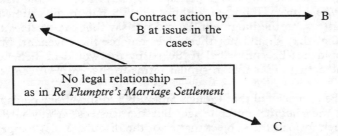

It might be thought that the same position should apply and that the would-be trustee should be able to sue. Of course, the initiative would lie with him; the would-be beneficiary could not force him to sue (assuming he has no action in his own right, on the principles outlined above). There are *dicta*, however, that he will not be allowed to bring the action. In *Re Kay's Settlement* [1939] Ch 329, the would-be trustees (though they were actually trustees of other property) were party to a covenant under seal with the would-be settlor to settle after-acquired property. No consideration moved from them, however. The would-be beneficiaries were not party to the covenant, nor were they within the marriage consideration, so were therefore volunteers. The would-be trustees requested directions as to whether or not they ought to take steps to enforce the covenant or to recover damages. The court directed them not to do so. At the end of his judgment, Simonds J, following Eve J in *Re Pryce* [1917] 1 Ch 234, said:

> . . . it appears to me that . . . I must direct the trustees not to take any steps either to compel performance of the covenant or to recover damages through [the settlor's] failure to implement it.

This *dictum* was followed by Buckley J in *Re Cook's ST* [1965] Ch 902, an unusual case in which, as part of a resettlement of family capital, Sir Francis Cook covenanted with his father, Sir Herbert Cook, and with would-be trustees (who were also actual trustees of property under another settlement), that if Sir Francis sold any of the valuable pictures specified in a schedule to the agreement, during his lifetime, the proceeds would be held on the terms of the settlement. The beneficiaries under the settlement were various members of Sir Francis's family (but Sir Herbert was not himself one of the beneficiaries).

There was no consideration for Sir Francis's covenant moving from the would-be trustees; nor, of course, was there any consideration moving from Sir Francis's children (who were beneficiaries). Buckley J found that there *was* consideration moving from Sir Herbert.

Sir Francis married several times, and gave (or purported to give) one of the pictures to one of his subsequent wives. The subsequent wife, after her divorce from him, wanted to sell it, and the trustees of the settlement sought directions from the court. The issue was whether the would-be trustees were obliged to take steps to enforce the covenant against Sir Francis. Buckley J thought not, which on the facts is perhaps not surprising, on the basis that the *Re Pryce/Re Kay's ST* line of authority was a bar to an action by the would-be trustees. In the judgment, he did not say that the trustees had no remedy, or that they should not themselves enforce the covenant, but only that they could not be compelled to do so by the would-be beneficiaries. However, the actual order was in similar terms to that in *Re Pryce/Re Kay's ST.*

It should be appreciated that though Simonds J in the above passage talks of 'trustees', the plaintiffs never in fact became trustees, at any rate of the property which formed the subject matter of the dispute. What happened in

Pryce, *Kay* and *Cook* was that a would-be settlor refused to add, to an already constituted trust, further property which was yet to be acquired. The *would-be* trustees of this new property were therefore *already* trustees of a perfect trust (of other property), and the question seems to have been treated as one in which they were contemplating taking steps (as is of course perfectly proper) to get in property which is owed to a trust. The court appeared to regard them as acting on behalf of the trust (which however was of *other property*), thereby obscuring the fact that as parties to the covenant they were acting in a purely personal capacity.

The apparent effect of *Pryce*, *Kay* and *Cook* is to deprive a plaintiff of an otherwise perfectly valid common law contract action. It is one thing for equity to refuse to assist a volunteer, but surely quite another for it to deprive others (not the volunteers) of actions which they would otherwise have. I would suggest that we need first to consider whether the cases really do have this effect. If they do, it is necessary further to consider whether this can possibly be justified. If it cannot, then it seems perfectly plausible to argue that what is after all first instance *dicta* is wrong. Let us consider first whether the cases really do have the effect described here.

It is important to note that in none of the cases did the courts decide what the outcome would have been if the trustees had actually sued. The trustees did not do so, but merely requested directions. Obviously, the court would not direct them to sue, and force upon them the onerous burdens of trusteeship, in favour of volunteers. A further point to bear in mind is that had the would-be trustees been directed to sue, the cost of the suit would presumably have fallen on the trust fund (this is one reason why trustees seek directions before suing in the first place: if they obey the court, they are not personally liable for costs in an action which goes against the trust). With the outcome presumably uncertain, it would have been arguably inapposite for a court to direct trustees to engage in speculative litigation.

Perhaps, then, the position is not that would-be trustees are prohibited from bringing an action, but only that the court would not direct them to sue, and force upon them the onerous burdens of trusteeship, in favour of volunteers. Professor Elliott has argued that the would-be trustees should have been directed that they need not sue, not that they ought not to sue: (1960) 76 LQR 100. It would indeed be perfectly proper for the court to leave the decision as to whether to exercise one's rights to the private individual, just as in any other case where a person has a right of action. On the other hand, they had requested directions, and arguably these ought to be mandatory in form.

Let us now suppose that this is wrong, and that would-be trustees would be prevented from bringing their common law action. Can this be justified? It can be argued that to allow them to sue gives them a discretion as to whether or not to enforce the trust, and that this is inconsistent with the very nature of a trust. Since the court will not force the trustees to act in favour of a volunteer, the only possibility is to deprive them of action. The problem with this view is that they are *not yet* trustees, at any rate of the disputed property, so objections based on giving trustees discretion cannot apply. The choice given to a *would-be* trustee is not whether to carry out his/her duties under a trust — there is no trust yet — but whether or not to become a trustee at all. This is a perfectly proper choice which anyone faced with a request to become a trustee is entitled to make.

If the would-be trustees choose to sue, and obtain specific performance (not a remedy available in any of the cases, since in none had the would-be trustees provided consideration), then they become trustees. But at that point they no longer have a discretion; once they have taken this step, they have to carry out the trust. In other words, to allow them to sue does not give trustees a discretion as to whether or not they enforce the trust. The choice is given to people who are not trustees, as to whether or not they undertake the onerous duties of trusteeship. That choice is always given to would-be trustees, and is perfectly proper.

Another argument is that, at any rate where the covenant is voluntary, it is for the settlor voluntarily to constitute the trust. There may be good policy reasons for taking this approach, especially when it is remembered that the covenants are usually entered into when the would-be settlor is young and the property covered often includes much of what he or she will acquire over an entire lifetime. Where the contract is for consideration, then arguably different considerations apply.

One problem with this view is that there is little if any authority for the proposition that it is for the settlor voluntarily to constitute the trust. There is, however, contrary authority in *Re Ralli's WT* [1964] Ch 288 (see 3.4). Another problem is that a different position ought to obtain where the contract is for consideration, but the cases do not seem to distinguish. Certainly, *Re Kay* concerns what appears to be a genuine voluntary settlement by a spinster, who only married much later. There was no marriage consideration, and hence the children of the marriage were volunteer beneficiaries. The covenant in *Re Pryce* also appears at first sight to have been voluntary, but closer examination shows that it actually formed part of a marriage settlement, with consideration moving from both husband and wife (but admittedly none from the trustees). There was no issue and the beneficiaries in default of issue were volunteers. There was consideration in *Re Cook*, but again none moving from the trustees. It does not seem that the cases distinguish between voluntary covenants and covenants for consideration, although whether consideration moving from the trustees themselves would make any difference has not been tested.

It is also pertinent to point out that equity does not generally interfere with common law contract actions, even when they are only covenants by deed, and regardless of the age of the covenantor. If it interferes here, special considerations would have to apply.

Let us now suppose, for the sake of argument, that the cases do not have the effect of preventing the would-be trustees from suing. Suppose also that they do sue. What remedy do they get? Let us first suppose that specific performance is, in principle, available. The action for specific performance would have the effect of constituting the trust. Arguably, the equitable remedy would be being used to assist the volunteers, and that could be an argument for equity refusing to grant the remedy. It would not be an argument for interfering with the common law remedy for damages.

Where the covenant is voluntary, damages are in this case the only available remedy. Damages compensate for loss suffered (see 2.3.2.1), and since it is the would-be beneficiary who is intended to receive the benefit, arguably the would-be trustee personally suffers no loss, if the trust is not constituted. Indeed, if the duties under the putative trust are of an onerous nature, as they will often be, the would-be trustee may actually be seen as gaining from the settlor's breach (by virtue of being relieved of an onerous obligation). On this argument the damages will be nominal.

However, Goddard argues ([1988] Conv 19) that this situation is not comparable with *Beswick* v *Beswick* [1968] AC 58 or *Woodar Investment Developments Ltd* v *Wimpey Construction (UK) Ltd* [1980] 1 WLR 277 (see 2.3.2.1), since here the would-be settlor has covenanted to transfer property to the would-be trustee, whereas in *Beswick* v *Beswick* the contract was to transfer money directly to the third party, without any intermediate transmission to the other contracting party. Arguably, therefore, the breach has deprived the would-be trustee of property to which he or she is entitled, and damages should compensate for that. No doubt, the would-be trustee is not intended to obtain the benefit of that property, but rather to hold it on trust, rendering the would-be trustee's loss nugatory, but this is irrelevant as far as the common law is concerned. Goddard notes that there are pre-Judicature Act authorities that the common law would grant substantial damages, and ignore equitable obligations.

If this analysis is correct, the next question is whether the would-be trustee holds the damages as trustee. If equity requires him or her to hold them on the trusts of the covenant equity will be assisting a volunteer, so this seems an unlikely solution. But the would-be trustee was never intended to keep the damages beneficially. The only possible solution would be to require him or her to hold them on resulting trust for the settlor.

The conclusion that I would draw is that whatever *Pryce, Kay* and *Cook* decide, it is unlikely that a would-be trustee would have a useful remedy even were he or she allowed to sue.

3.3   TRUSTS OF PROMISES

There is no reason in principle why a covenant made to would-be trustees to settle property should not of itself form the subject matter of a trust. The benefit of such a covenant, i.e., the right of the other party to sue on it, is itself a form of property: a chose in action. If a settlor so wishes, he can settle (i.e., create a fully constituted trust) of that chose in action in just the same way as he could settle any other property. All he has to do is to transfer that property — the benefit of the covenant — to the intended trustees. This will perfect the trust, and the beneficiaries can now enforce that trust just as if the subject matter were land or cash, even if they are not party to the covenant.

We know that in *Re Kay's Settlement*, for example, no trust of the after-acquired *property* was constituted. But had it been decided that a valid trust had been constituted of the *covenant* (or promise), the result would have been very different: the beneficiaries, though volunteers, would have enforceable rights against the trustees of the covenant. Far from the trustees being directed not to sue on it, the beneficiaries could have required them to do so. A diagrammatic representation of this situation appears in figure 3.3.

We have to consider, then, on what basis will the courts construe a trust of a promise, and whether there are any limits on the doctrine.

Figure 3.3

Substantive property as in Figure 4.2
B's action in contract against A

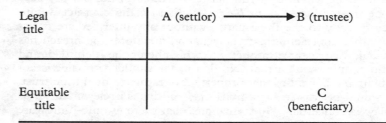

B holds the benefit of the contract on constituted trust for C, who can therefore force B to enforce it

3.3.1 When do trusts of promises arise?

The leading case, where a trust of a promise arose, was *Fletcher* v *Fletcher* (1844) 4 Hare 67. Ellis Fletcher covenanted with trustees by deed to pay £60,000 to his trustees, on trust for his illegitimate sons, who were outside the marriage consideration, and were thus volunteers. The surviving son, Jacob, was able to compel the trustees (note that the term is here correctly used) to enforce the covenant on his behalf. Though the *money* was never settled, Wigram V-C held that the *covenant* was held on a fully constituted trust for Jacob. Thus Jacob could enforce it in his own right, despite being a volunteer. Substantial damages were recoverable, amounting to the promised £60,000.

It seems from this case that the beneficiary can force the trustee to sue on the covenant, and that substantial damages can be recovered (at any rate where the covenant concerns the settlement of money), which will be held in trust for the beneficiary.

Although the principle of *Fletcher* v *Fletcher* is no doubt sound, there are difficulties in construing a trust of the promise on the facts. A point often made is that the trustees knew nothing of the covenant until the death of the settlor, Ellis Fletcher, and then were unwilling to enforce it. Even so, Jacob could compel the trustees to sue. However, it could be argued that the ignorance of the trustees, or their unwillingness to accept the trust, should not be a bar to a finding that Fletcher has meant to give his trustees a chose in action rather than the money itself, so creating a valid trust. The relevant intention is surely that of the settlor, not of the trustees. If a trustee is unwilling to act, 'Equity will not allow a trust to fail for want of a trustee' (maxims, at 1.4.1), and the courts will appoint another trustee.

Accepting that the relevant intention is that of the settlor, however, we still have to ask who this is. After all, this is a trust of the promise, not of the property to be settled. It is arguably the would-be *trustee* of the property who owns the contractual cause of action, since he can enforce it, so surely he rather than the settlor of the property is settlor of the contract. Indeed, on this view the would-be trustee of the property is both settlor and trustee of the promise, declaring himself trustee of it.

Now there is no doubt that the would-be trustee of the property is the *legal* owner of the contract, but who owns it in equity? Clearly not the would-be trustee, since he is not intended to take the benefit beneficially. Surely the position is that if the settlor of the property contracts with the would-be trustee as trustee of the promise, then the would-be beneficiaries of the property under the settlement are *true* beneficiaries of the promise. There is a fully constituted trust of the promise. But if the settlor of the property contracts with the would-be trustee *otherwise* than as trustee of the promise, the position is exactly as in *Pryce, Kay* and *Cook*. The would-be beneficiaries under the settlement are clearly not in that case beneficiaries of the promise, nor is the would-be trustee. The only possible beneficial owner of the promise is the settlor himself. In other words, in the absence of a declaration of a trust of the promise in favour of the volunteer beneficiaries, *the trustees hold the chose in action on resulting trust for the settlor.*

It would seem to follow, therefore, that although the would-be trustee is legal owner of the promise, the settlor is beneficial owner unless it (the promise) is settled in trust. It is therefore for the settlor to create the trust of the promise, and his intention is the relevant intention. Were it otherwise the would-be trustees in *Pryce, Kay* and *Cook* could at any time declare themselves trustees of their promise, thereby significantly improving the position of the volunteers.

Nevertheless, in cases since *Fletcher* v *Fletcher* the courts have demanded much more conclusive evidence that the settlor really did intend to settle the benefit of the covenant, before construing trusts of promises: e.g., *Re Schebsman* [1944] Ch 83, see 2.3.2.3, and see Smith [1982] Conv 352. It is probable that were the same facts to arise today, no trust would be construed, and *Fletcher* v *Fletcher* would be considered wrongly decided in this regard.

3.3.2 Limits to *Fletcher* v *Fletcher*
Fletcher v *Fletcher* involved a covenant to settle money. No doubt covenants to settle other property can also form the subject matter of a trust, but there is some doubt as to whether a covenant to settle after-acquired property (i.e., mere expectations of the settlor) can be. Buckley J thought that it could not, in *Re Cook's ST* [1965] Ch 902:

Counsel for the second and third defendants have contended that on the true view of the facts there was an immediate settlement of the obligation created by the covenant, and not merely a covenant to settle something in the future . . . He relied on *Fletcher* v *Fletcher* (1844) 4 Hare 67 . . . I am not able to accept this argument. The covenant with which I am concerned did not, in my opinion, create a debt enforceable at law, that is to say, a property right, which, although to bear fruit only in the future and upon contingency, was capable of being made the subject of an immediate trust, as was held to be the case in *Fletcher* v *Fletcher*. Nor is this covenant associated with property which was the subject of an immediate trust . . . Nor did the covenant relate to property which then belonged to the covenantor . . . In contrast to all these cases, this covenant upon its true construction is, in my opinion, an executory contract to settle a particular fund or particular funds of money which at the date of the covenant did not exist and which might never come into existence. It is analogous to a covenant to settle an expectation or to settle after-acquired property. The case, in my judgment, involves the law of contract, not the law of trusts.

The view that a covenant to settle after-acquired property cannot form the subject matter of a trust has also been taken by Lee (1969) 85 LQR 213, and Barton (1975) 91 LQR 236, but this reasoning has been criticised: e.g., Meagher and Lehane (1976) 92 LQR 427. Perhaps this is the explanation for no trust of a promise being constituted in *Re Kay*, which concerned after-acquired property.

Nevertheless, it by no means obvious why a *contract* to settle after-acquired property cannot form the subject matter of a trust, even though it is impossible to create an immediate trust of after-acquired property (see 3.2.1). The contract after all is existing not future property. The reasoning in *Re Ellenborough* [1903] 1 Ch 697 does not apply to it. There may be a remedies problem, however. We saw in 2.3.2.3 that a party who contracts as trustee for another can claim substantial damages to hold on trust for that other, and where the contract is to settle existing property (or an existing sum of money as in *Fletcher* itself), there is no difficulty in calculating those damages. In *Re Cavendish Browne's ST* [1916] WN 341, Catherine Cavendish Browne made a voluntary settlement containing a covenant to 'convey and transfer to the trustees all the property, both real and personal, to which she was absolutely entitled by virtue of the joint operation of the wills of' two named persons. She died without having settled property to which she was so entitled in trust. Younger J, 'without delivering a final judgment, held . . . that the trustees were entitled to recover [from Catherine's administrators] substantial damages for breach of the covenant . . ., and that the measure of damages was the value of the property which would have come into the hands of the trustees if the covenant had been duly performed'. Although it is not entirely clear, it appears that Catherine was *already* entitled to the property at the time that the contract was made.

In the above passage from *Cook*, Buckley J talks of the covenant in *Fletcher* creating a debt enforceable at law, and the same is presumably true in *Re*

Cavendish Browne's ST: see also Friend [1982] Conv 280. The trust of the promise constituted the settlor as debtor of the trustees. This reasoning may not be possible where the covenant is to settle after-acquired property, however, since it will be difficult or impossible to assess damages based on the value of property which has not yet been acquired, may never be acquired, and indeed need not even yet exist. Perhaps this is the real reason for limiting the principle in *Fletcher* v *Fletcher* to covenants for existing property (but see the contrary argument by Meagher and Lehane (1976) 92 LQR 427).

3.4 PROPERTY ACTUALLY TRANSFERRED

Whether or not the contract to settle property is enforceable, and whether or not the trustees will be allowed to enforce it, if the settlor actually transfers the property as promised, he cannot later reclaim it, because the act of transfer will have created a perfect trust of the money. In *Re Ellenborough* [1903] 1 Ch 697 (see 3.2.1), the court would not compel Miss Emily Towry Law to pay over the legacy when it arrived, but there was no argument in favour of allowing her to reclaim earlier payments which she had made in fulfilment of the same covenant which she now declined to perform.

Nor, if *Re Ralli's WT* [1964] Ch 288 is correct, would it prevent the trust from becoming fully constituted if the property came into the trustee's hands in some other capacity than that of trustee. In *Ralli's WT* the trust was constituted by the accident that the would-be trustee was also trustee under an earlier will, and so obtained legal title by those means.

Helen's father left his residue on trust for his wife for her life, thence to his two daughters, Helen and Irene. Helen, by her marriage settlement, covenanted with trustees, of whom the plaintiff (Irene's husband) was one, to settle all her existing and after-acquired property on Irene's children.

On Helen's death, in 1956, the plaintiff, who was the sole surviving trustee under the marriage settlement, was also appointed a trustee under Helen's father's will, and hence obtained title to Helen's residuary estate under her father's will, on the death of Helen's mother (in 1961). He brought an action to determine whether he held the property on the terms of Helen's will, or on the trusts of Helen's marriage settlement.

Buckley J held that the trust of the after-acquired property in the marriage settlement was completely constituted, since the plaintiff held the property under Helen's father's will. It was irrelevant that the plaintiff came by the property under Helen's father's will, rather than under Helen's marriage settlement itself:

> In my judgment the circumstances that the plaintiff holds the fund because he was appointed a trustee of the will is irrelevant. He is at law the owner of the fund, and the means by which he became so have no effect upon the quality of his legal ownership. . . . It is also true that, if it were necessary to enforce performance of the covenant, equity would not assist the beneficiaries under the settlement, because they were mere volunteers; and

that for the same reason the plaintiff, as trustee of the settlement, would
not be bound to enforce the covenant and would not be constrained by the
court to do so, and indeed, it seems, might be constrained by the court not
to do so. As matters stand, however, there is no occasion to invoke the
assistance of equity to enforce performance of the covenant.

The logic of *Re Ralli's WT* extends to all cases where the trustee acquires legal
title, and so long as he does so the method of acquisition is irrelevant. Thus,
the principle ought still to apply if, for example, he comes by his legal title
not as his executor, but as the settlor's trustee in bankruptcy, or even as a
judgment creditor, or where the settlor has mortgaged his property to the
would-be trustee, and the would-be trustee forecloses. However, it seems that
transfer of legal title is required, and not merely physical possession.

One of the arguments considered in 3.2.4 was that it is for the settlor under
a voluntary settlement voluntarily to settle the property. Yet clearly in *Re
Ralli's WT* Helen took no steps at all to settle the property, yet a fully
constituted trust was held to have been created. If *Re Ralli's WT* is correct,
and this is the true explanation of it, a trust can be constituted without any
action at all by the settlor.

So is *Re Ralli's WT* correct, and is this is the true explanation of the case?
Rather surprisingly, *Re Brooks* [1939] Ch 993 was not cited, Buckley J reasoning
instead from *Re James* [1935] Ch 449, a *Strong* v *Bird* authority (see 3.5.2) which
is not on all fours since that doctrine requires an intention, continuing until
death, to transfer on the part of the transferor. By contrast, *Re Ralli's WT*
required no intention of any kind on Helen's part. It is, however, very difficult to
reconcile *Re Ralli's WT* with *Re Brooks*, which is pretty well on all fours with *Re
Ralli's WT*. *Re Brooks* concerned the property of a mother and her son, and in
particular a voluntary settlement of after-acquired property by the son. Lloyds
Bank were the trustees under this voluntary settlement. Later, because of the
exercise by his mother of a power of appointment in his favour, the son acquired
property which should have been caught by the voluntary settlement. The power
of appointment had been granted to his mother under her marriage settlement.
But Lloyds Bank were also trustees under the marriage settlement, and hence
already had legal title to this property. The issue was whether Lloyds Bank held
the property for the son, or on the trusts in the son's voluntary settlement. It was
held that they held the property for the son. The main issue was whether this
property was existing or after-acquired property at the time the son's voluntary
settlement was made. It was held that it was after-acquired property until the
appointment was actually made in his favour. It could therefore not form the
subject matter of a trust. *Re Ellenborough* (see 3.2.1) was followed.

The problem is that Lloyds Bank's position was exactly analogous with that
of the plaintiff in *Re Ralli's WT*; they had acquired the property which was
subject to the son's voluntary settlement otherwise than in their capacity as
trustees under that settlement. Yet the opposite decision was reached to that
in *Re Ralli's WT*. Both sets of reasoning cannot be correct.

There is only one way of reconciling the cases. In *Re Ralli's WT* Helen
settled a reversionary interest, which counts as existing property, even though

enjoyment of it was postponed until after her mother's death. Existing property is not subject to *Re Ellenborough*, and the alternative view adopted by Buckley J was that Helen had declared herself trustee of it from the moment of her marriage settlement. If this is right there is no need to treat *Re Ralli's WT* as an authority on covenants to settle at all. It was simply an immediate declaration of trust of existing property. Trusts do have to be constituted by some act of the settlor. Of course, one would have to regard the covenants reasoning in *Re Ralli's WT* as wrong.

The only other possibility is that *Re Brooks* is wrong. With two conflicting first instance authorities, and no other clearly relevant authorities, it is impossible to reach a clear conclusion.

3.5 'EXCEPTIONS' TO THE PRINCIPLE THAT EQUITY WILL NOT ASSIST A VOLUNTEER

In this section two apparent exceptions are considered to the principle that equity will not assist a volunteer. It can be argued that they are not genuine exceptions, but merely additional methods by which a trust can be fully constituted, but whether or not this is the case, they operate as if they were exceptions to the general rule.

It should also perhaps be mentioned that it would be very rare for either of the exceptions considered below to occur. No settlor would deliberately invoke them. Problems in this area, in so far as they occur at all in practice, arise *ex post facto* because of competing claims to a deceased person's property.

3.5.1 *Donatio mortis causa*

A *donatio mortis causa* (which, translated from Latin, broadly means 'gift by reason of death') is a gift made in contemplation of, and conditional upon, the death of the donor. It is different from an ordinary, immediate gift, for the donee's title does not come into existence until the death occurs: until such time, the donor may revoke. Nor is it a testamentary gift taking effect under the terms of a properly attested will. Suppose, for example, that A is terminally ill, or about to engage in a dangerous activity and, realising that death is a possibility, entrusts some of his property to B, telling him that if A should die, B may keep the property as his own. Although B has custody of the property he will not own it unless and until A dies.

If that happens, equity regards B's title as perfected, and he may claim the property in preference to anyone to whom A may have chosen to bequeath it in his will. So if A has already made a will in which all his personal property, which would otherwise include the property entrusted to B, is left to X, B has a better claim by virtue of the conditional gift.

The situations in which *donationes mortis causa* (note Latin plural) are most likely to occur are variations on something like this: A is a man and B is his mistress. A wishes to benefit B on his death, but does not wish to leave property in his will because he does not wish to disclose her existence to his 'legitimate' family. Nor, possibly for the same reason, does he wish to make an *inter vivos* transfer in her favour. The *donatio mortis causa* is the obvious device for him to use.

To permit the making of a disposition which is neither an immediate perfect gift nor a formal testamentary disposition is to invite fraudulent claims intended to defeat the expectations of legatees, and it is therefore not surprising that equity hedges a *donatio mortis causa* with stringent conditions.

The necessary conditions for a *donatio mortis causa* were set out by Farwell J in *Re Craven's Estate* [1937] Ch 423:

(a)   The transfer must be with the intention of giving, and not simply of securing, the goods. There is no *donatio mortis causa* if A simply wants B to look after his property.

(b)   It must be clear that the property was handed over in contemplation of a real possibility of death, and some specific focus upon the possibility of death must be shown. The donor must anticipate some hazard to life. This is usually a serious illness, but extreme hazard (such as motor racing) is also probably covered, but not normal, everyday risks, e.g., air travel.

The gift must be conditional upon death occurring, and otherwise revocable, i.e., A must intend to keep the property himself if he survives. This requirement is superfluous where the property is a chattel which could be transferred by simple delivery, since A could obviously have made a valid immediate gift if he chose, but it is relevant where some further formal step is required to perfect the title, as for example, in the case of land (see 3.5.1.1 below).

(c)   The donor must have effectively parted with dominion over the subject matter of the gift. In other words, the property must have been handed over, or the means of access to it transferred, for example, by giving B the key to the bank deposit box where the property is lodged. The test is whether the donor has put it out of his power between the dates of gift and death to alter the subject matter of gift and substitute other property for it: see also *Re Lillingston* [1952] 2 All ER 184, at p. 191. In *Woodard* v *Woodard* [1995] 3 All ER 980, the Court of Appeal inferred a *donatio mortis causa* of a car from the handing over of its keys, where the donor had also said: 'You can keep the keys, I won't be driving it any more.' It was immaterial that the car was already in the donee's possession as bailee, or that another set of keys (which the donor was in any case in no position to use) might have existed.

It is also possible to transfer property which is not capable of physical delivery, e.g., by handing over *indicia* of title, such as a savings bank book, or (presumably) a bill of lading covering a consignment of cargo aboard a ship. The test is whether handing over the document 'amounted to a transfer', in which case possession or production of the document would entitle the possessor to the money in the account.

3.5.1.1 *Donatio mortis causa* and land

Long after most students of the law of trusts must have thought that *donatio mortis causa* cases were ancient history, a *donatio mortis causa* was successfully argued before the Court of Appeal in *Sen* v *Headley* [1991] Ch 425. It had long been thought that it was impossible to have a *donatio mortis causa* of land, because the third of Farwell J's conditions cannot be satisfied, even by delivery of the title deeds; but on the assumption that *Sen* v *Headley* is correct, this view must now be regarded as wrong.

Mr Hewett, who was, at the age of 86, on his death-bed, gave the plaintiff, Mrs Sen, the keys to a steel box with the title deeds to his house inside, saying to her:

> The house is yours, Margaret. You have the keys. They are in your bag. The deeds are in the steel box.

It appeared that Mr Hewett and Mrs Sen had, for some 30 years, lived together as if married. Title to the house was unregistered.

After Hewett's death, the gift was challenged by his next of kin. There were no difficulties over Farwell J's first two criteria set out above, but at first instance ([1990] Ch 728), Mummery J thought that the third was not satisfied: Hewett had not parted with dominion over the house. He concluded, in effect, that land cannot form the subject matter of a *donatio mortis causa*.

Clearly, the transfer of title deeds could not amount to a transfer of the land itself during Hewett's lifetime, since no deed was executed, and a declaration of trust would require writing. This is because it would have to be a declaration of trust of land (see chapter 6). Here there was no documentation at all, and Margaret could at most acquire a 'mere *spes*' (hope or expectation) of obtaining the property. Mummery J's view was that the entire doctrine was anomalous, and that judicial caution should be exercised before extending it, that the policy of the law required formality for dispositions of land and interests in land, and that, accordingly, the *donatio mortis causa* doctrine would not be extended so as to allow an attempt at disposition on death which avoided the Wills Act formalities (on which, see chapter 9), or the perfection of an imperfect *inter vivos* gift.

The clear inference from Mummery J's judgment was that *donatio mortis causa* could *never* apply to land. This view, at any rate, was in line with the orthodox views that had been long held.

Mummery J was reversed in the Court of Appeal, however, on analogy with extensions of the doctrine in previous cases. In *Snellgrove* v *Bailey* (1744) 3 Atk 213, the doctrine had been applied to a gift of money secured by a bond, by delivery of the bond; in *Duffield* v *Elwes* (1827) 1 Bli (NS) 497, the House of Lords had applied the doctrine to a gift of money secured by a mortgage of land, by delivery of the mortgage deed. In each case, transfer of *indicia* of title was all that was required. (However, one problem is that, in *Duffield* v *Elwes*, Lord Eldon thought the doctrine would not apply to a gift of land by delivery of the title deeds.)

No doubt the doctrine was anomalous, but in the view of Nourse LJ, that did not justify creating anomalous exceptions to the admittedly anomalous doctrine. The only reason why, with unregistered land, transfer of the title deeds did not transfer title to the property was because of a formality statute.

All *donationes mortis causa* avoid formality provisions, usually the Wills Act (on which, see further, chapter 9). There was no reason why the formality provisions relating to land should be regarded as presenting any greater obstacle than any other formality provisions, and no reason why this case should be treated differently from the cases alluded to in the previous paragraph.

It does not necessarily follow that shares in private companies, which cannot be physically transferred, can also be the subject of a *donatio mortis causa*, since registration of a new owner may be refused. They are therefore not directly analogous to land.

3.5.1.2 Death sooner than expected   It seems on the basis of *Wilkes* v *Allington* [1931] 2 Ch 104 that the gift is valid even if A dies sooner than expected, and even if from a different cause. The donor was suffering from an incurable disease, and made the gift knowing that he had not long to live. In fact he died even earlier than expected of pneumonia, but the gift was held to be valid. Whether the same principle would apply even if the death were completely different from A's expectation is less clear (e.g., he dies of food poisoning).

3.5.2   The rule in *Strong* v *Bird*
The other exception to the principle that equity will not assist a volunteer (and an example of the presumption that equitable title follows legal — see further 8.4.2) is the rule in *Strong* v *Bird* (1874) LR 18 Eq 315, and it could arise in some such fashion as this. A hands B his share certificates but fails to procure the transfer and registration of B as owner. He then dies, leaving a will which appoints B as his executor but makes X the legatee of all his personal property. Again, equity treats the gift as perfected, this time by the vesting of A's property in B in his capacity as executor, and the claims of the beneficiaries under the will (in this case X) are overridden.

The same principle operates if B owes A money, but A makes no effort to collect his debt and appoints B his executor: these were the facts of *Strong* v *Bird* itself. The appointment is, as it were, a conclusive release of the debt. But it must be clear that there was an intention to make the gift or release the debt, and that this intention continued until death.

In *Strong* v *Bird*, the defendant borrowed £1,100 from his step-mother. His step-mother lived in his house and paid rent at £212 quarterly. The money borrowed by the defendant was to be repaid by 11 deductions of £100 from quarterly rent. The step-mother made two deductions, but after that made no more, and continued to pay full £212 until her death. Orally, she forgave the defendant the remainder of debt (but this was ineffective as a release at law). The defendant was appointed executor under her will. The residuary legatees claimed the remainder of the debt, but Jessel MR held the defendant not liable. His appointment as an executor extinguished the debt at common law since it is impossible for an executor to sue himself. It seems that equity acquiesces with the common law position, subject to the other requirements of doctrine.

In *Re Stewart* [1908] 2 Ch 251, Neville J applied the same principle to perfect imperfect *inter vivos* gift of bonds by appointment of the intended donee as executor. Equity would not interfere with the common law transfer of title. The doctrine depends on an attempt to make an immediate *inter vivos* gift of specific property, a continuing intent to make the gift until death, and the vesting of legal title in the donee.

One might argue that the logic of the rule in *Strong* v *Bird* requires that B be *voluntarily* appointed executor by A, but there is some authority that the rule operates if B becomes A's administrator, instead of his executor. This was the view of Farwell J in *Re James* [1935] Ch 449, where a housekeeper had herself appointed one of two administratrices of the testator's estate.

In *Re Gonin* [1979] Ch 16, Walton J cast doubt on *Re James*. In *Re Gonin*, the plaintiff alleged that, in return for her returning home after being called away during the Second World War, and going to live with and look after her parents, her parents had orally agreed that the parental home and its contents should become hers on their deaths. The plaintiff's father died in 1957, leaving no estate. After the death of the plaintiff's mother in 1968, the plaintiff took out letters of administration to her estate, and began an action to determine whether she was entitled, as administratrix, to vest the freehold in the property in herself.

She claimed both land and contents (furniture) under the rule in *Strong* v *Bird*, on the basis that the plaintiff's mother intended to give the plaintiff the house on her death, and by the plaintiff taking out letters of administration, the gift was perfected.

Walton J took the view that the appointment of an administrator was quite different to the appointment of an executor, since it is not a voluntary act of the deceased, but of the law. It was also often a matter of pure chance which of many persons entitled to a grant of letters of administration actually took them out:

> Why, then, should any special tenderness be shown to a person so selected by law and not the will of the testator, and often indifferently selected among many with an equal claim? It would seem an astonishing doctrine of equity that if the person who wishes to take the benefit of the rule in *Strong* v *Bird* manages to be the person to obtain a grant then he will be able to do so, but if a person equally entitled manages to obtain a prior grant, then he will not be able to do so.

Walton J did not need actually to decide whether the earlier authority was correct, however, since he also held that even if the rule in *Strong* v *Bird* applied to administrators, the evidence did not point to a continuing intention on the part of the plaintiff's mother to give the house to the plaintiff.

It is nevertheless possible to defend *Re James*. Kodilinye argues [1982] Conv 14, at p. 17) that the criticisms of *Re James* by Walton J cannot stand, for a number of reasons. He argues that the crux of Jessel MR's principle is that the gift (or release in *Strong* v *Bird* itself) is perfected by the vesting of the legal title in the donee, and it is immaterial whether that vesting is brought about by the act of the donor or by the operation of law. He also points out that the need to give effect to the will of the testator is already satisfied by the requirement that the donor must have shown an intention to give *inter vivos* until his death. Therefore, there is no need for any *additional* voluntary act by the testator, such as appointing the donee executor. It must be admitted that there is some force in these arguments.

Re James was applied in *Re Ralli's WT* (see 3.4), but the situation there was different because no intention at all was needed on the part of the transferor. It is easier to support Farwell J's views in *Re James* than those of Buckley J in *Re Ralli's WT*.

FOUR

The Three Certainties

Chapter 3 was about the vesting of property in trustees, a prerequisite to the existence of any trust. Chapters 4 to 7 are about further requirements for validity, assuming the property is so vested. This chapter deals with the requirement for certainty.

The requirements considered in this chapter apply not only to trusts which are expressly created, but also to resulting and constructive trusts. Charitable trusts are exempt from certainty of object requirements, and they are also incidentally largely exempt from the perpetuity rules (see chapter 7). For convenience, certainty of objects requirements for powers also are included in this chapter, by way of comparison with those for discretionary trusts.

4.1 CERTAINTY

4.1.1 Reasons for certainty requirements
There are two main reasons for certainty requirements. The first and obvious reason is to ensure that the property is correctly identified and is dealt with in accordance with the wishes of the settlor. Thus, a doubt as to those wishes leads the courts to play safe rather than risk an unauthorised disposition of a person's property. Additionally, it must be clear to the trustees themselves exactly what their duties are. The difficulty is most acute in the case of testamentary trusts, where those who have the duty of administering the estate have to rely for guidance upon whatever terms the testator may have chosen to express his desires, since obviously it is not possible to ask him.

The second reason is less obvious. Whereas today trustees usually act in a professional capacity, the typical trust of 200 years ago was very different in nature, and the rules originally developed around the older type of trust. These were often family arrangements, and one of the main concerns of the courts was that the trustees might be fraudulent and keep the trust property themselves. Equity has been criticised for making essentially the same assumptions about, e.g., banks and company directors today; the problem stems from adapting to a modern situation a set of principles which were originally developed for quite a different purpose. Certainly a limited degree

of successful adaptation has occurred, but the same basic assumption remains, namely that trustees are likely to be fraudulent.

At least until very recently, the courts have tended to over-emphasise the
pathological situation, in which the trustees refuse to carry out the trust. The
courts have insisted that there must exist someone with sufficient interest in
the trust property to be able to come to court to compel the trustees to carry
out the trust and in the final analysis the courts must be able to administer
the trust themselves. This emphasis has led (at least until recently) to much
more rigid certainty requirements than might otherwise have been the case.

4.1.2 The three certainties

The classification for certainty usually cited is that of Lord Langdale in *Knight*
v *Knight* (1840) 3 Beav 148, 173: while the classification has been criticised,
there is no doubt that it is the one adopted by the courts. The essential
prerequisites of a valid private express trust are certainty as to the intention
of the settlor to create a trust of property (sometimes misleadingly termed
certainty of words), certainty as to the property to which the trust is to attach
(also referred to as certainty of subject matter), and certainty as to the persons
or 'objects' who are to benefit (certainty of object).

4.1.3 Effect of absence of certainty

If any of the certainties is absent then no valid express trust will be created,
but the precise consequences will depend upon the circumstances. If the
settlor attempts to declare himself trustee, the declaration will be invalid
whichever certainty is not satisfied. If legal title has been transferred but there
is uncertainty as to the intention to create a trust (i.e., to separate the legal
and equitable titles) then the transferee will hold it free of any trust. If either
of the other certainties is absent, there will be a resulting trust to the settlor
(or residuary legatees, in the case of an attempt to establish a trust by will),
subject to one exception: *Hancock* v *Wilson* [1902] AC 14 establishes that
where there is an absolute gift of property in the first instance and trusts are
subsequently imposed on that property, then if the trusts fail for any reason
the property is not held on a resulting trust for the settlor or his estate but
will vest absolutely in the person to whom the property was given. We can see
this in, e.g., *Palmer* v *Simmonds* (1854) 2 Drew 221 (see 4.3).

4.2 CERTAINTY OF INTENTION

4.2.1 Words or intention?

Although Lord Langdale spoke of certainty in relation to the words alleged
to establish the settlor's intention, this is misleading in two respects. First, it
is possible to establish a trust without any writing whatever, except where the
statutory formality requirements obtain (see chapter 6). A trust need not even
be orally declared, as it is possible to establish an intention of a settlor to
create a trust (i.e., to separate legal and equitable titles) from words or
conduct; this may be inferred from the nature of the gift as a whole. No doubt
in fact most express trusts are created by means of written documents, since

they arise either by will or in a formal settlement, carefully documented to meet the settlor's tax planning needs. A modern trust precedent will be highly intricate and will attempt to provide for almost all conceivable contingencies. But in principle technical words are not necessary, since equity looks to the intention rather than the form of the transaction. It is not even necessary that the word 'trust' should have been employed, if the intention to create a trust is clear.

The second reason why Lord Langdale's statement is misleading is that even where words are present, the courts do not have regard to them alone, though they are important in construing the intention of the would-be settlor. Indeed, to rely on words alone as binding precedent would be dangerous, as the attitude of the courts has changed considerably over the last 150 years or so, especially regarding precatory words (i.e., words expressing a wish, hope or request, rather than being imperative).

4.2.2 History of precatory words

So far as testamentary gifts are concerned, up to about the middle of the 19th century the courts were disposed to find that almost any expression of desire by a testator that his property should be used in a given manner was intended to create a binding trust of that property in the hands of an executor or legatee. The reasons historically can be traced to the fact that the administration of estates lay formerly with the ecclesiastical courts, which permitted the executor to keep for himself any undisposed-of residue of property left after the specific bequests had been satisfied. When this jurisdiction was taken over by the Court of Chancery, it preferred to treat the executor as trustee of such residue for the testator's family. Almost any expression of desire or hope would be seized upon to effect this policy. Even this solution was not entirely satisfactory. Widows and eldest sons of gentry were often provided for in any event by a marriage settlement, or entail of the estate, and the courts were suspicious of their ability to manage the family property in prudent fashion (that is to say, keeping it in the family). Therefore a similar principle was applied to legatees as had formerly been applied to executors. The outcome was that precatory words like 'wish', 'hope' or even 'in confidence' that the legatee would use the gift to benefit others, were taken to create binding trusts.

The rationale for the lenient view taken of precatory words largely disappeared with the Executors Act of 1830, which specifically required executors to hold property in an appropriate manner. Since 1830, therefore, the courts have felt able to tighten up their attitude, the modern view being derived from the judgment of Cotton LJ in *Re Adams and the Kensington Vestry* (1884) 27 ChD 394, 410, where it was established that beneficiaries were no longer to be made trustees unless this was the testator's clear intention, and a gift to the widow 'in full confidence that she would do what was right as to the disposal thereof between my children, either in her lifetime or by will after her decease' was treated as giving the widow an absolute interest unfettered by any trust in favour of the children. Cotton LJ thought that many of the older authorities had gone too far; he also thought that one should consider the total effect of the instrument (not only the particular words) to ascertain the testator's intention. Other cases around the same time made it clear that the attitude of the courts towards precatory words had changed.

4.2.3 Law relating to precatory words

Since intention is all important, however, a trust may still be created by precatory words, if such intention appears from the document (or settlor's conduct) as a whole. See, for example, the cases considered at the end of 3.1.4.

Because the whole document or transaction is to be considered, it does not follow that the same precatory words will always have the same effect. Thus in *Re Hamilton* [1895] 2 Ch 370, 373, Lindley LJ said (of a testamentary gift):

> You must take the will which you have to construe and see what it means, and if you come to the conclusion that no trust was intended, you say so, although previous judges have said the contrary on some wills more or less similar to the one you have to construe.

In *Cominsky* v *Bowring-Hanbury* [1905] AC 84, the House of Lords found a trust on the basis of words very similar to those employed in *Re Adams and the Kensington Vestry:* 'absolutely in full confidence that she [the widow] will make such use of [the property] as I would have made myself and that at her death she will devise it to such one or more of my nieces as she may think fit'.

If on the other hand, a testator reproduces the exact language of an earlier will which has previously been held to create a trust, it may be possible to infer that he intended to use the earlier will as a precedent. If so, there is authority that the court in construing the later will should follow the earlier decision, at least unless that decision was clearly wrong (*Re Steele's WT* [1948] Ch 603). Though this case attaches great significance to the actual precatory words used, it is not really an exception to the flexible approach described above, because all the circumstances do indeed point to an intention to create a trust. It follows that draftsmen should make clear beyond doubt that precatory words are intended to indicate desire alone, unless of course a trust is indeed intended.

A further, somewhat technical, consideration is that the creation of a gift in a will, followed by the inclusion of a precatory expression in a codicil, raises a stronger inference of intention to create a trust than would be the case were both gift and precatory words to appear in the same instrument (*Re Burley* [1910] 1 Ch 215). Lastly, it should not be forgotten that the testator, while not intending to create a trust, may have subjected the property to a power of appointment (on which, see chapter 2) instead of making an outright gift to the legatee. In any case, the decision as to the testator's intention is a matter of construction of the document, and no hard and fast rule can be laid down for determining when this intention is present.

4.3 CERTAINTY OF SUBJECT MATTER

To satisfy the test it appears to be necessary that the trust property be defined in objective rather than subjective terms, or, in other words, so as not to be a matter on which opinions may reasonably differ. In *Palmer* v *Simmonds* (1854) 2 Drew 221, a testatrix left on trust 'the bulk' of her residuary estate, and Kindersley V-C, after consulting a dictionary, concluded that the word 'bulk' was inadequate to specify any portion of the property as trust property:

> What is the meaning then of bulk? The appropriate meaning, according to its derivation, is something which bulges out . . . Its popular meaning we all know. When a person is said to have given the bulk of his property, what is meant is not the whole but the greater part, and that is in fact consistent with its classical meaning. When, therefore, the testatrix uses that term, can I say that she has used a term expressing a definite, clear, certain part of her estate, or the whole of her estate? I am bound to say that she has not designated the subject as to which she expresses her confidence; and I am therefore of opinion that there is no trust created; that [the residuary legatee] took absolutely, and those claiming under him now take.

Since it was not possible to carve out from the residue that portion which was to be held on trust, the trust failed and the residuary legatee took the whole absolutely. This is an application of what later became the rule in *Hancock* v *Wilson* [1902] AC 14 (see 4.1.3).

The same result was reached in *Curtis* v *Rippon* (1820) 5 Madd 434, where not only was there uncertainty as to the property to be subject to the trust, but also as to the identity of the beneficiaries themselves. The widow received all her husband's property under his will, subject to an exhortation (using precatory words that were valid at the time) that she should use the property for the spiritual and temporal good of herself and the children, 'remembering always, according to circumstances, the Church of God and the poor.' The clause rendered uncertain even who was to benefit.

An approach similar to that in *Palmer* v *Simmonds* was taken in *Re Kolb's WT* [1962] Ch 531, where the testator referred, in an investment clause in his will, to 'blue-chip' securities, a term generally used to designate shares in large public companies which are considered an entirely safe investment. The term has no technical or objective meaning, however, and Cross J held that its meaning in the context must depend on the standard applied by the testator, which could not be determined with sufficient certainty to enable the clause to be upheld. The case was considered in a different context in *Trustees of the British Museum* v *Attorney-General* [1984] 1 WLR 418, which is discussed in chapter 18.

In *Re Golay's WT* [1965] 1 WLR 969, the testator had directed his trustees to allow 'Totty' to 'enjoy one of my flats during her lifetime and to receive a reasonable income from my other properties'. Ungoed-Thomas J felt able to uphold the gift, as the trustees could select a flat, and the income to be received by Totty could be quantified objectively by the court. If, on the other hand, Totty had been entitled to receive what the testator or a specified person considered to be reasonable, then the trust would fail, since the test would be subjective.

The judgment in *Re Golay's WT* is very short, and the case appears to be out of line with the others considered. The test cannot simply be whether the income could be objectively quantified by the court, since a court could equally well quantify 'the bulk' or 'blue-chip securities'. Can it really be supposed that a court, faced with a statutory provision which applied to 'blue-chip securities' would be unable to apply the provision? The courts can define the reasonable man. Surely they would not be defeated by 'blue-chip securities'.

I would suggest that in *Re Golay's WT,* Ungoed-Thomas J misunderstood the function of a certainty test. It is not, I would suggest, to make life easier for courts, but to ensure that the trustees can administer the trust. That is why precise objective definitions are required, so that the trustees know exactly which property is subject to the trust, and which property is not. A 'reasonable income' would not seem sufficiently certain to satisfy that criterion, unless the view were taken that the trustees should forever be coming to court to obtain directions.

In *Hunter* v *Moss* [1994] 1 WLR 452 (followed in *Re Lewis's of Leicester Ltd* [1995] 1 BCLC 428), an oral declaration of trusteeship of 50 shares of a company's issued share capital of 1,000 shares succeeded, even though the particular shares were not ascertained or identified. However, the company was precisely identified, all the shares in that company were identical, and the quantification (50 shares) was obviously precise. Moreover, as long as the trustee retained all 1,000 shares there would be no point in identifying which 50 shares were subject to the trust.

Difficulties in a case like *Hunter* v *Moss* could arise if the trustee later split up the fund, sold the shares and invested some of the proceeds in fund A and some in fund B, one of which funds would then have performed better than the other. I would suggest that this problem would not arise if the settlement had been of 5 per cent of the issued share capital, since then it would be clear that the trust owned 5 per cent of fund A and 5 per cent of fund B.

On the assumption that the case is correct, then the applicable principles ought to be those in 19.2. The trustee is mixing trust funds with his own, and the decision in *Re Hallett's Estate* (1880) 13 Ch D 696 suggests that the beneficiaries could choose which fund held their share of the proceeds. If, however, the trustee had declared other trusts of the remaining shares, the contest would be between competing beneficiaries, and there would be no reason to apply *Hallett's Estate*. *Re Diplock* [1948] Ch 465 suggests that in such circumstances, a *pari passu* distribution would be appropriate.

4.4   CERTAINTY OF OBJECTS

Certainty of objects rules serve two main functions. First, if a trustee, or donee of a power fails to carry out his duties, or exercises his discretion in an improper manner, it is important to be able to ascertain who has *locus standi* to come to court to remedy the situation. Secondly, a trustee, or donee of a power, has to be able to ascertain who are the objects in order to able to exercise his discretion in a proper manner.

4.4.1   Rationale of the rules: enforcement
Once a settlement has been made, whether it creates a trust or a power, the settlor ceases to have any interest in the property. Indeed, in the common

case of a settlement by will he will naturally be unable to have any further personal say. The question then arises as to what happens if the trustee, or the donee of the power, does not carry out the trust or power. Sometimes a trustee will have agreed to act for consideration (e.g., a bank acting under a remuneration clause). In that case the settlor, or his personal representatives can sue at common law in contract. It is not an altogether satisfactory action, however, as we saw in chapter 3: unless he can obtain specific performance, he will be limited to claiming damages for his own loss, which will probably be nominal only. Therefore the courts have always been very concerned that someone who benefits in equity is able to enforce the trust.

The certainty requirements to achieve this end depend on the nature of enforcement by the courts. They have taken a more realistic and less rigid view in recent years of the manner in which trusts are to be ultimately enforced. This has led to a relaxation of certainty rules, which in most respects is to be welcomed.

Generally speaking, all that is now required for this purpose is for it to be possible to tell, with certainty, whether any individual coming to court to enforce a trust or power has sufficient interest to do so: in other words whether or not he is within the class of objects. This test is called the 'individual ascertainability test'. It is not necessary to be able to draw up a list of all the objects, a much more stringent requirement called the 'class ascertainability test'. Further, in applying the individual ascertainability test, it is necessary only that definitions in the settlement be conceptually certain. The court itself can deal with evidential difficulties when an application for enforcement arises. See further 4.4.5.2–4.4.5.4.

4.4.2   Rationale of the rules: administering the trust
Some writers argue (e.g., Matthews [1984] Conv 22) that this is not a proper function of certainty of objects rules at all, but the orthodox view is otherwise (see, e.g., Jill Martin in her reply in [1984] Conv 304). The certainty test required to enable trustees or donees of powers to discover all that is necessary for them to be able to carry out the trust depends on the nature of their discretion. Generally speaking, however, if a trustee or donee has to get any impression of the size or composition of the entire class in order to carry out his duties, a more stringent test is required than individual ascertainability.

4.4.3   Operation of the rules
The manner in which a settlement is ultimately enforced, and the nature of the discretion given to trustees or donees of powers, depend on whether a fixed trust, discretionary trust or power has been created (see 2.5 for the distinctions). The certainty of objects requirements vary accordingly, so it is necessary to consider separately the certainty requirements for each of these categories.

4.4.4   Powers
The nature of mere powers has been considered in 2.5.2. Donees of a power (unlike discretionary trustees — see 4.4.5) have a discretion not only as to

how to distribute the property, but also as to *whether* to distribute it. They are under no obligation to appoint at all, subject to the limited exceptions at the beginning of 2.5.2. In other words, whereas a trust is imperative, because the trustees have to appoint, a power is discretionary, because the donees of a power need not appoint at all — the choice is theirs.

If there is a gift over in default of appointment, the disposition must take effect as a power, not a trust, since the existence of the gift over is obviously inconsistent with an imperative duty to appoint. The absence of a gift over in default is not necessarily indicative of a trust, however, since the alternative construction, of a power with a resulting trust in favour of the settlor in the absence of appointment, is also possible. It will all depend on the words used in the instrument.

In the case of mere powers (i.e., a power not given to a fiduciary), the donee's discretion seems to be unfettered except insofar that he must not dispose of the property otherwise than in accordance with the terms of the power. The objects can come to court to enforce the power, therefore, only to the limited extent that the court will restrain disposal of the property otherwise than in accordance with the terms of the power.

This limited negative duty can be carried out and enforced so long as 'it can be said with certainty that any given individual is or is not a member of the class'. No more stringent test of certainty than the individual ascertainability test is required.

It is probably more common for powers of appointment to be given to trustees, in which case the donees of the power will not enjoy an unfettered discretion. Sir Robert Megarry V-C took the view in *Re Hay's ST* [1982] 1 WLR 1202, that the extent of the duty to consider both whether or not a power should be exercised, and how it should be exercised, is stronger when the power is given to someone who is also a trustee, than when a mere power is exercised. For example, it is not sufficient simply to appoint to the objects who happen to be at hand, whereas the donee of a mere power can do this. It seems that it is necessary periodically to consider whether or not to exercise the power, and at least to appreciate the width of the field of objects, even if it is not possible to compile a list of all the objects, or ascertain accurately their number. Also, individual appointments need to be considered on their merits:

> The trustee must not simply proceed to exercise the power in favour of such of the objects as happen to be at hand or claim his attention. He must first consider what persons or classes of persons are objects of the power within the definition in the settlement or will. In doing this, there is no need to compile a complete list of the objects, or even to make an accurate assessment of the number of them: what is needed is an appreciation of the width of the field, and thus whether a selection is to be made merely from a dozen, or, instead, from thousands or millions . . .

Nevertheless, if at the end of the day the donees of the power refuse to exercise it, that is a choice that they are entitled to make, and there is no reason why the courts should be required to distribute on their behalf. It is still necessary to be able to ascertain of any given individual whether or not he or she is an object of the power, since only objects of the power will have *locus standi* to enforce it, even to the limited extent of preventing the donees acting otherwise than in accordance with its terms. It is also necessary for the objects to be defined so that the donees can, as required by Sir Robert Megarry V-C above, get a feel for the width of the class.

Despite this, the duty to consider is not so stringent as to require the donees, in order to carry it out, to draw up a list of the entire class of potential beneficiaries, and there is therefore no reason in principle to apply the class ascertainability test to powers.

In *Re Gestetner's Settlement* [1953] 1 Ch 672, Harman J had to consider the validity of a power given to trustees to distribute among a very wide class, including directors and employees or former employees of a large number of companies, with a gift over in default. Since membership of the class constantly fluctuated, it was impossible to draw up a list of the entire class at any one time. He held that it was not necessary to know all the objects in order to appoint, and that it was not fatal that the entire class could not be ascertained.

In *Re Gulbenkian's Settlements* [1970] AC 508, trustees were given a power to apply income from the trust fund to maintain, among others, any person in whose house or in whose company or in whose care Gulbenkian may from time to time be residing, and there was a gift over in default of appointment. In upholding the power, the House of Lords held that the individual ascertainability test was the applicable test for powers: a power would be valid if it could be said with certainty whether any given individual was *or was not* a member of the class, and would not fail simply because it was impossible to ascertain every member of the class.

There are two points specifically to note about the *Gulbenkian* test. First, the italicised words, *or was not*, are important. Secondly, the House of Lords expressly rejected Lord Denning MR's test in the Court of Appeal in *Gulbenkian* [1968] Ch 126, at pp. 132–4. On the basis that a power would only be held void for uncertainty if it was impossible to carry it out, he had taken the view that it should be necessary only to be able to identify one single beneficiary as being clearly within the class. The House of Lords disagreed, primarily because this test took no account of the trustees' duty to carry out the power in a fiduciary manner. The Denning test would only really be appropriate were the trustees at liberty to distribute to the first person who came to hand, and as we have seen that is not the case.

The importance of these two points will become apparent later in the chapter.

4.4.5 Discretionary trusts

The nature of discretionary trusts (sometimes called 'trust powers'), and the reasons for using them, were considered in 2.5.1. As with mere powers, nobody who is an object can claim a defined interest, or indeed any interest at all, unless and until the trustees' discretion is exercised in his favour. But they differ from mere powers and fixed trusts in that the trustees are under an obligation to distribute the property.

Clearly the extent to which a discretionary trust can be enforced is limited by its discretionary nature. The courts will, however, restrain the trustees from acting contrary to the terms of the trust instrument. And if they refuse to distribute at all, a court can remove them and appoint new trustees, or in the final analysis distribute the property itself.

Since 1971 the test for discretionary trusts has been assimilated to that for powers (i.e., individual ascertainability). However, the test is still slightly more stringent than that for powers because the trustees must distribute, and in order to exercise their discretion must have at least some idea of the range of objects. Also, at the end of the day, if they refuse to distribute, the court must be able to distribute in their place.

4.4.5.1 The pre-1971 approach   Before 1971 the approach of the courts was dictated by their view of ultimate enforcement. They took the view that if the trustees refused to distribute, the court could not itself exercise any discretion on their behalf (see, e.g., the view of Jenkins LJ in *IRC* v *Broadway Cottages Trust* [1955] Ch 20). The court could remove the trustees and appoint others in their place, but in theory it could be impossible to find any other trustees prepared to execute the trust. It followed that, however unlikely this eventuality might be, at the end of the day a court had be prepared to carry out the trust itself. Since it refused to exercise any discretion it could only divide the property equally among all the objects.

Although there is a logic to this conclusion, given the premises, equality of distribution will often not implement the intentions of the settlor, and indeed is quite likely to frustrate them. It seems that the equality principle originated in 19th-century family settlements (e.g., *Burrough* v *Philcox* (1840) 5 My & Cr 72), where it may have been the most reliable method of carrying out the settlor's intention. It is much less likely to be appropriate, however, in modern settlements, for example, dividing proceeds among employees of a company.

Nevertheless, equality of distribution was the rule, and of course it could only be done if it was possible to draw up a list of all the objects. For this reason, *Broadway* applied the class ascertainability test to discretionary trusts.

The class in *Broadway* was undoubtedly extremely wide, consisting mostly of remote issue, as well as a number of charities. Two charities (Broadway Cottages Trust and Sunnylands Trust) had received income under the settlement, and claimed an income tax exemption on it, but in order to do so they had to show that the settlement was valid. The class was never held to be unascertainable, since the charities conceded the point (perhaps unwisely, since it was conceptually certain, and only evidential difficulties prevented drawing up an entire list of objects: see further, the discussion on fixed trusts, below). The Crown for its part conceded that the individual ascertainability test was satisfied. On the basis of these concessions, the Court of Appeal held that the trust failed: *Gestetner* did not apply, since here there was no gift over, there was an obligation to distribute, and the whole range of objects had to be ascertainable.

Jenkins LJ took the view that if the court was called upon to enforce the trust 'it could not mend the invalidity of the trust by imposing an arbitrary distribution amongs some only of the whole unascertainable class.' The court could only effect a distribution to all the objects equally. The irony of this is that, given that some of the objects were charities and others people, equality of distribution was probably the last thing the settlor would have wanted.

One result of this case was that the test for certainty was much more stringent for discretionary trusts than for powers (on which, see above). This had two main consequences: first, many perfectly reasonable trusts failed; secondly, the courts were at pains to construe doubtful dispositions as powers, rather than discretionary trusts.

4.4.5.2 *Re Baden's Deed Trusts (No. 1), McPhail v Doulton*

In *Re Baden's Deed Trusts (No. 1), McPhail v Doulton* [1971] AC 424, however, the House of Lords decisively rejected the principle of equality of distribution in a case where equal distribution would have made a nonsense of the settlor's intention. The House accepted that even in the final analysis (in other words even assuming that no trustee can be found who is prepared to execute the trust), the court could exercise the necessary discretion itself. Therefore, the reasoning in the *IRC v Broadway Cottages Trust* [1955] Ch 20 was inapplicable (and indeed, *Broadway Cottages* was overruled). All that is required is for it to be possible to tell, with certainty, whether any individual coming to court to enforce a trust or power has sufficient interest to do so: in other words whether or not he is within the class of objects. This requirement is of course satisfied by the individual ascertainability test.

The *ratio* of *Re Baden's Deed Trusts (No. 1)* is that the test for certainty for discretionary trusts is essentially the same as that for powers, the individual ascertainability test, not the class ascertainability test.

Lord Wilberforce also made the point that in applying the test the courts are concerned only with conceptual uncertainty. A trust will not fail merely because there are evidential difficulties in ascertaining whether or not someone is within the class, as the court is never defeated by evidential uncertainty, and can deal with problems of proof when an application for enforcement arises:

> I desire to emphasise the distinction clearly made . . . between linguistic or semantic uncertainty which, if unresolved by the court, renders the gift void, and the difficulty of ascertaining the existence or whereabouts of members of the class, a matter with which the court can appropriately deal on an application for directions.

Thus, a trust in favour of the first 20 people who crossed Clifton suspension bridge in 1996 should be enforceable: the class is conceptually certain even though proof may be difficult. A trust in favour of 'all my friends' is different, however. It is conceptually uncertain, because 'all my friends' is not a phrase capable of precise definition. Such a trust ought therefore to fail even on the *McPhail v Doulton* test.

4.4.5.3 Problems of applying the individual ascertainability test The outcome in *Re Baden's Deed Trusts (No. 1)* was largely consequential on the court changing its views about the ultimate enforcement of a discretionary trust. Unfortunately, the relaxation may lead to difficulties over administration. Unlike donees of mere powers, the trustees' discretion is not absolute. In considering its exercise, they must, according to Lord Wilberforce in *McPhail* v *Doulton* itself, make a survey of the entire field of objects, and consider each individual case responsibly, on its merits. This ought to require a more rigourous certainty test than individual ascertainability. For example, the Clifton suspension bridge example should fail (assuming no central record is kept of people walking over Clifton bridge), because the trustees could not possibly survey the entire field.

Since under the new test trustees may be unable to discover the identities of all the possible beneficiaries, they will sometimes be unable to carry out their duties. Some discretionary trusts could be very difficult to administer were the trustees unable to survey the entire field of possible beneficiaries. An example might be a discretionary trust to distribute property 'according to the age and ability of the potential beneficiaries'.

Lord Wilberforce himself suggested a way out of the difficulty. He thought that even if a disposition satisfied the individual ascertainability test, it might fail if the class is so widely drawn as to be administratively unworkable. An example he gave was a gift to 'all the residents of Greater London', but the acceptable width of the class presumably depends on the exact nature of the trustees' duties, and whether they must actually survey the entire field. See further, 4.4.5.5.

Another possible solution is that if the terms of a trust negative any sensible intention on the part of the settlor, it may fail on the grounds of capriciousness. This was suggested *obiter* by Templeman J in *Re Manisty's Settlement* [1974] Ch 17. The same applies, incidentally, to powers, and indeed *Manisty* actually concerned a valid power (see further below, 4.4.5.5).

I would suggest that the real problem is the distinction, drawn by Lord Wilberforce, between on the one hand, linguistic or semantic uncertainty which, if unresolved by the court, renders the gift void, and on the other hand, evidential difficulties of ascertaining the existence or whereabouts of members of the class (see 4.4.5.2). I would suggest that this distinction is irrational, and loses sight of the purposes of certainty tests. As we saw in 4.3, the court (which is happy to apply the reasonable man test when required to do so) is no more defeated by linguistic or semantic uncertainty than it is by evidential difficulties. Trustees administering the trust, on the other hand, will be equally defeated by both types of uncertainty. Unfortunately, there are traces of the distinction in *Gulbenkian*, and it has been adopted by at least one of the judges in *Re Baden's Trusts (No. 2)* [1973] Ch 9 (see 4.4.5.4), so it may well become entrenched in the law.

Another problem with the new certainty test is how, if at all, the doctrine in *Saunders* v *Vautier* (1841) 10 LJ Ch 354 applies. Under this doctrine (on which, see further chapter 18), all the beneficiaries, collectively entitled, can (so long as they are adult and *sui juris*) terminate the trust and distribute or resettle the trust property. It is difficult to see how this doctrine can operate if the entire class of beneficiaries cannot be ascertained.

One possible answer is that *Saunders* v *Vautier* applies only to fixed trusts, on the grounds that the objects of a discretionary trust do not have full beneficial interests unless and until the trustees' discretion is exercised in their favour, but Lord Upjohn in *Gulbenkian* suggests otherwise. The other possible answer is that the courts would use a device similar to the *Benjamin* order discussed below (in 4.4.6, on fixed trusts).

4.4.5.4 *Re Baden's Deed Trusts (No. 2)*

The disposition in *Re Baden's Deed Trusts* was remitted to the Chancery Division so that the House of Lords test could be applied. Eventually it came again to the Court of Appeal, where differing opinions were given: *Re Baden's Deed Trusts (No. 2)* [1973] Ch 9. By this time some 12 years had passed since Mr Baden's death, the fund was still sterilised by litigation, and a considerable proportion had been dissipated in legal costs. Sachs LJ observed that the situation 'lacks attraction'.

The disposition was 'to or for the benefit of any of the officers and employees or ex-officers or ex-employees of the company or to any relatives or dependants of any such persons'. It was argued by John Vinelott QC, who was challenging the disposition on behalf of the executors, that it could not be shown that any person definitely is or *is not* within the class (as required by the *Gulbenkian* test). Had this ingenious argument been accepted it would have meant virtually returning to the rejected class-ascertainability test, as Megaw LJ observed. The Court of Appeal rejected the argument, but not on identical grounds.

Sachs LJ avoided the difficulty by emphasising that the court was concerned only with conceptual certainty, so that it should not be fatal that there might be *evidential* difficulties in drawing up John Vinelott QC's list. This effectively destroys the Vinelott argument, which was addressed primarily towards *evidential* difficulties in drawing up the class. Sachs LJ also took the view that the courts would place the burden of proof, in effect, on someone claiming to be within the class. This seems acceptable if ultimate enforcement is the issue, and the test is of the *locus standi* of the claimant, but it does not help the administration of the trust.

Megaw LJ adopted a different solution requiring that as regards a substantial number of objects, it can be shown with certainty that they fall within the class. This is rather a vague test — clearly it is not enough to be able to show that *one* person is certainly within the class, as this test was rejected in *Gulbenkian* (see the discussion of powers, above). Presumably, the test requires evidential, as well as conceptual certainty. Maybe Megaw LJ adopted it simply because he could find no other way of rejecting Mr Vinelott's argument without returning either to the rejected *Broadway* test, or to the Denning test which had been rejected in *Gulbenkian*. Indeed, none of the judges in the Court of Appeal was able to find a satisfactory solution to this difficulty. The test may have the merit, however, of ensuring that the trustees will be able to get a feel for the width of the class, which they need properly to be able to exercise their discretion.

Stamp LJ's test is probably the strictest of the three, and he seemed to be quite impressed by the Vinelott argument. He emphasised that it must be possible for the trustees to make a comprehensive survey of the range of objects, but he did not think it would be fatal if at the end of the survey it was impossible to draw up a list of every single beneficiary. He would have taken the view that the trust failed, had he not felt compelled to follow an early House of Lords authority, which had held that a discretionary trust for 'relations' was valid, 'relations' being defined narrowly as 'next of kin'.

Of the three tests, that of Sachs LJ will usually be the easiest to satisfy, but it relies heavily on an additional administrative unworkability test, the extent and application of which, as we will see in the next section, are quite unclear. I would also suggest that:

(a)   The distinction drawn by Sachs LJ between conceptual and evidential uncertainty has its origin in Lord Wilberforce's speech in *McPhail* v *Doulton*, and indeed, there are traces of a similar distinction in *Gulbenkian*. The justification is that evidential distinctions can always be resolved by the courts, but, as we saw in 4.3, the courts can also resolve conceptual uncertainties. But surely, once the *Broadway* equality of distribution principle has been abandoned, the justification for certainty rules is not to assist the courts but rather the trustees in administering the trust. And trustees will be defeated just as easily by evidential as they will by conceptual difficulties.

(b)   If a class is conceptually certain, then the only reason why a list of the entire class cannot be drawn up is evidential. The class ascertainability test, if it was ever meaningful at all, must have been an evidential test; if the test were simply conceptual, then there would be no difference between the individual and class ascertainability tests.

(c)   I would suggest, therefore, that no good basis can be found for the conceptual/evidential distinction. Proponents of Sachs LJ's view would respond that the test of administrative workability is sufficient to ensure that the trust is workable, but in that case it is reasonable to ask why any test is needed at all apart from administrative workability. In any case, evidential issues would now need to be dealt with by the administrative workability test, and it is not obvious that that is an improvement over dealing with them as part of the individual ascertainability test itself.

(d)   Megaw LJ's test is evidential and addresses the problem of making the trust workable for trustees. It is therefore (I would suggest) preferable to Sachs LJ's test.

(e)   Stamp LJ's test is also evidential (indeed, entirely so, since 'next-of-kin' is not itself conceptually certain), but once the *Broadway* equality of distribution principle has been rejected, it is difficult to justify a test as strict as Stamp LJ's, since his test amounts virtually to a return to the class ascertainability test.

This, then, is an argument for preferring Megaw LJ's test, or at any rate a test similar to it.

4.4.5.5 Administrative unworkability The question of administrative unworkability was considered in *Re Manisty's Settlement* [1974] Ch 17, where a power given to trustees was upheld where they were able to appoint anyone in the world apart from a small excepted class (a power where the objects are defined only by reference to an *excepted* class is called an intermediate or hybrid power). A similar decision was reached in *Re Hay's ST* [1982] 1 WLR 1202. These decisions suggest that very rarely will a power fail on grounds of administrative unworkability, simply because of the width of the class.

The courts are not concerned with questions of ultimate enforcement with a power, however, and it is arguable that the decisions in *Kay* and *Manisty* ought not to apply directly where, as here, the instrument is drafted as a trust. Indeed, in *Re Hay's ST* [1982] 1 WLR 1202 itself, Sir Robert Megarry V-C noted that: 'The words of Lord Wilberforce [about administrative unworkability] . . . are directed towards trusts, not powers'.

The problem arose directly in the Divisional Court in *R* v *District Auditor, ex parte West Yorkshire Metropolitan County Council* [1986] RVR 24. Prior to the abolition of the Metropolitan County Councils, they were prohibited from incurring expenditure under the Local Government Act 1972, s. 137(1):

> which in their opinion is in the interests of their area or any part of it or some or all of its inhabitants

after 1 April 1985.

When West Yorkshire Metropolitan County Council realised that they were going to have a large surplus on 1 April 1985, they sought to find ways of ensuring that this money could still be spent after the 1 April deadline. In their attempt to achieve this aim, they purported to set up a discretionary trust of £400,000, having a duration of 11 months, 'for the benefit of any or all or some of the inhabitants of the County of West Yorkshire'. The trust also directed the trustees to use the fund specifically:

(a)   To assist economic development in the county in order to relieve unemployment and poverty.
(b)   To assist bodies concerned with youth and community problems.
(c)   To assist and encourage ethnic and other minority groups.
(d)   To inform all interested persons of the consequences of the proposed abolition of the Council (and the other Metropolitan County Councils) and of other programs affecting local government in the county.

This was held to be administratively unworkable. The inhabitants of the County of West Yorkshire numbered about two and a half million. The range of objects was held to be so hopelessly wide as to be incapable of forming anything like a class.

There are clear statements in the case that trusts may be treated differently from powers in this regard, since a court may be called upon ultimately to execute a trust, whereas it will not, of course, be required to execute a power.

The second possibility is that the terms of the trust negative any sensible intention on the part of the settlor. Indeed, in *Manisty*, Templeman J thought this was the real problem over 'residents of Greater London':

The settlor neither gives the trustees an unlimited power which they can exercise sensibly, nor a power limited to what may be described as a 'sensible' class, but a power limited to a class, membership of which is accidental and irrelevant to any settled purpose or to any method of limiting or selecting beneficiaries.

In addressing these issues the width of the class is not the only factor, since other factors may make clear what the intention of the settlor was. For example, in *Re Hay's ST* [1982] 1 WLR 1202, Sir Robert Megarry V-C said of this passage:

In *Re Manisty's Settlement* [1974] Ch 17 at 27 Templeman J appears to be suggesting that a power to benefit 'residents in Greater London' is void as being capricious 'because the terms of the power negative any sensible intention on the part of the settlor'. In saying that, I do not think that the judge had in mind a case in which the settlor was, for instance, a former chairman of the Greater London Council, as subsequent words of his on that page indicate.

Alternatively, suppose that trustees were directed to use the fund, in their discretion, to provide library facilities for the residents of Greater London. It might also be perfectly possible to infer a sensible intention on the part of the settlor. On the other hand, fairly precise guidelines were laid down in *R v District Auditor, ex parte West Yorkshire Metropolitan County Council*, but this was still insufficient to save the trust.

Suppose that even the class ascertainability test is satisfied. Then it could not be said that the disposition was administratively unworkable, because clearly the trustees could survey the entire class. Presumably the disposition could still fail, however, if the terms were such as to negative any sensible intention on the part of the settlor.

4.4.6   Fixed trusts
It is usualy argued that, since it is of the essence of a fixed trust that the property is to be divided among all the beneficiaries in fixed proportions (e.g., in equal shares), it can only be workable if the entire class of beneficiaries is known; the conventional view, therefore, is that the test of certainty is the class ascertainability test.

This was certainly the view of Jenkins LJ in *IRC v Broadway Cottages Trust* [1955] Ch 20, at p. 29:

There can be no division in equal shares amongst a class of persons unless all the members of the class are known.

In other words, a complete list of objects must be able to be drawn up. From the fact that in *McPhail v Doulton* [1971] AC 424, the House of Lords was concerned only to assimilate discretionary trusts and powers, the implication usually drawn is that the reasoning was not intended also to apply to fixed trusts.

However, there are fairly convincing contrary arguments (see, e.g., 1 thews [1984] Conv 22). The orthodox view presupposes that *Broadway* still stands insofar that later cases have not directly detracted from it, but it is arguable that even when it was decided, *Broadway* was wholly out of line with other authorities, in which case there is no reason for it still to be regarded as authority for anything at all.

The central issue, I would suggest, is the basis upon which the trust property is distributed by the trustees, or if the issue becomes one of ultimate enforcement, by the courts. It is often assumed that distribution is impossible unless the entire class can be ascertained, but this need not be the case, and even if it is, application of the class ascertainability test may not necessarily resolve the difficulty.

Suppose, for example, that in 1986 Michael settled property upon trustees with directions that in 1991 the property was to be sold, and that the proceeds of sale were to be distributed equally, in favour of those of his three sons, Paul, Quentin and Richard, who are still then living. Assuming that in 1986 all three of the settlor's sons were known to be alive, it is obvious that this is a fixed trust, and that it satisfies the class ascertainability test.

Suppose now that at some time after 1986 Richard went on an Antarctic expedition, from which by 1991 he has not returned. He is thought (but not known definitely) to have perished on the expedition. The trustees sell the property, and wish to distribute it in accordance with their directions. Despite the fact that the class ascertainability test was clearly satisfied, and that the trust did not fail for want of certainty, they clearly have a problem.

If at this point the trustees asked for directions, it is likely that the court would resolve the difficulty by making a *Benjamin* order (based on *Re Benjamin* [1902] 1 Ch 723). The trustees would be directed to distribute on the basis that Richard was dead. If Richard later turned up alive, he would still have an interest in the proceeds of sale, which he would be able to claim from Paul and Quentin if it were still traceable, and assuming that his claim was not barred by limitation. The trustees personally would be protected from any action, however.

It is clear, then, that evidential difficulties, even in the distribution of fixed trusts, can be resolved by the courts. Is there any reason of logic or principle why the position should be any different if by the time of the settlement in 1986, Richard had already embarked upon the expedition, and it was not known even then whether he was alive or dead? In those circumstances it would not after all, be possible at the date of the settlement, to draw up a list of all the objects, since it would not be possible to say with certainty whether Richard should be included or not. A strong argument can therefore be made that there is no need to apply the class ascertainability test, even to fixed trusts.

As was explained in 4.4.5.2, in applying the individual ascertainability test, Lord Wilberforce distinguished between evidential and conceptual uncertainty, on the ground that the courts are never defeated by evidential uncertainty. Does it follow that, if the class ascertainability test does still apply to fixed trusts, the same distinction also applies? If so, it leads to some interesting consequences.

In *Broadway* (see 4.4.5.1), although the class was very large, it was not conceptually uncertain. There was no problem over defining the class conceptually, and *it was conceded* in *Broadway*, rather than concluded from rational argument, that the class could not be ascertained. Perhaps the concession was wrongly made, and that in reality, even in *Broadway* itself, the class ascertainability test was satisfied. *Broadway* was indeed criticised in *Re Gulbenkian's Settlements* [1970] AC 508 (in particular, by Lords Reid and Upjohn), and by Lord Wilberforce in *McPhail v Doulton* (above), on the grounds that the Court of Appeal had confused conceptual and evidential uncertainty.

If, however, the distinction between conceptual and evidential uncertainty applies equally to the class as to the individual ascertainability test, it is difficult to see any difference between the two tests. If it can be said of any individual that he or she falls outside the class, then there can be no conceptual difficulty in defining the class as a whole. Indeed, there is no *conceptual* difficulty in defining the class in the above example, merely an evidential difficulty in ascertaining whether Richard is a member. In principle, however, evidential difficulties, as in *Broadway* and the example, are capable of resolution by the courts.

I would suggest, however, that the class ascertainability test has always been an evidential test, and that the distinction between conceptual and evidential uncertainty has only ever been applied to the individual ascertainability test. Even there, I have already argued that it is inappropriate. Further, if it is accepted that a function of the certainty of object test is to ensure that the trust is administratively workable, then even if one accepts that there is no need to apply the class ascertainability test to fixed trusts, one can argue for a more rigorous test than for discretionary trusts. One way of achieving this is to apply different tests of administrative workability, since it does not follow that merely because a discretionary trust is administratively workable with a given class of objects, a trust with the same class of objects will necessarily be so if the trustees' discretion is removed. It is probably more satisfactory, however, to have a stricter certainty test for fixed trusts, albeit perhaps a test not as strict as the class ascertainability test.

Figure 4.1

Fixed trusts, discretionary trusts and mere powers

Duties of trustees	Arguments for class ascertainability	Arguments for individual ascertainability
	Fixed trusts	
Must distribute according to instrument.	Necessary to enable trustees to distribute.	Distribution on basis of *Benjamin* order.
	Discretionary trusts	
Must distribute — discretion as to how.	Ultimate enforcement. Trustees need to ascertain entire class in order to decide how to exercise their discretion.	*Locus standi.* Class ascertability test leads to unjust results. Administrative unworkability/ capriciousness safeguards sufficient.
	Powers	
Need not distribute, but must consider whether to do so and if so how.	As above, except that ultimate enforcement no longer an issue.	As above, except that *locus standi* only to prevent distribution inconsistent with power.

FIVE

Private Purpose Trusts and Unincorporated Associations

The principles relating to private (i.e., non-charitable) purpose trusts and unincorporated associations follow on naturally from the discussion on certainty of objects in the chapter.

5.1 PRIVATE PURPOSE TRUSTS

Purpose trusts may either be for a pure purpose (for example, a trust to advance a cause), where no individual directly benefits, or for the benefit of an ascertainable group of people (for example, a trust to build a school swimming-pool). A private (non-charitable) purpose trust of the first type is usually struck down, because it is not enforceable by anyone. Charitable trusts (which are dealt with in chapters 11 to 13) are always purpose trusts, and are valid, but problems of enforcement do not arise as the Attorney-General has *locus standi* to sue.

Where an ascertainable group of people is intended to benefit, it appears that the trust is valid.

5.1.1 No identifiable object
Where the purpose is not intended directly to benefit any identifiable human being, nobody can enforce the trust. Dispositions of this nature are therefore generally void.

A classic example is *Re Astor's ST* [1952] Ch 534, where trustees were instructed to hold a fund upon various trusts including 'the maintenance of good relations between nations [and] . . . the preservation of the independence of newspapers'. The purposes were not charitable, but the settlement was drafted expressly (by limiting its duration) so as to be valid under the perpetuity rules (see chapter 7). The trust was held by Roxburgh J to be void because there were no human beneficiaries capable of enforcing it.

A similar case to *Astor*, where there were no clearly identifiable human beneficiaries, was *Re Shaw* [1957] 1 WLR 729, where Harman J held void on the same principle a trust to research into the development of a 40-letter alphabet. The case concerned the will of George Bernard Shaw, and although by 1950, when the will was made, Shaw was already 94 years old, Harman J noted its 'youthful exuberance'. Having also commented that the author was an indefatigable reformer, Harman J went on to note the 'marriage of incompatibles' in the will between Shaw's own work and that of a skilled equity draftsman: 'The two styles, as ever, make an unfortunate mixture.' Only copyrights and royalties were settled in the will, but these were far greater than anticipated — hence the litigation.

The purposes included the following:

(1)   To institute and finance a series of inquiries to ascertain as far as possible the following statistics

(a)   the number of extant persons who speak the English language and write it by the established and official alphabet of 26 letters (hereinafter called Dr Johnson's alphabet);

(b)   how much time could be saved per individual scribe by the substitution for the said alphabet of an alphabet containing at least 40 letters (hereinafter called the proposed British alphabet) . . . ;

(c)   how many of these persons are engaged in writing or printing English at any and every moment in the world;

(d)   on these factors to estimate the time and labour wasted by our lack of at least 14 unequivocal single symbols;

(e)   to add where possible . . . estimates of the loss of income in British and American currency . . .

(2)   To employ a phonetic expert to transliterate my play entitled 'Androcles and the Lion' into the proposed British alphabet assuming the pronunciation to resemble that recorded of His Majesty our late King George V, and sometimes described as Northern English . . .

The purposes having been held non-charitable (on which see further 12.3.1), the settlement was struck down on the grounds that there were no identifiable beneficiaries who could enforce it.

In cases of this type, the courts may have been reluctant to uphold the trusts for other reasons also. For example, Roxburgh J in *Astor* thought that it was against public policy to allow large accumulations of private capital to be dispersed with no administrative State control. These reasons cannot be decisive, however, as they could be applied to all non-charitable trusts, whether or not purpose trusts. The courts in any case disallow trusts for useless or capricious purposes (see further chapter 6).

On the other hand, trusts to erect or maintain tombs and monuments have been upheld, as have trusts for the maintenance of specific animals (e.g., *Re Dean* (1889) 41 ChD 522), and in *Re Thompson* [1934] Ch 342 a trust for the promotion and furtherance of fox-hunting. It is difficult to reconcile these with the general principle; on the other hand too much reliance has been placed upon them for them now to be regarded as wrong, and they are usually regarded as exceptions: they were, for example, in *Re Astor ST,* and similarly in *Re Endacott* [1960] Ch 232, where a gift 'to North Tawton Devon Parish Council for the purpose of providing some useful memorial to myself' was held void by the Court of Appeal. *Dean* and *Thompson* were regarded as anomalous and not to be extended.

It may also be possible to make provision for a pure purpose indirectly, using a device. One such device is considered in 11.2.2. A gift is made to charity A so long as it maintains the testator's grave to the satisfaction of the testator's trustees, with a gift over to charity B. The gift over is exempt from perpetuity rules (see chapter 7), so long as B is a charity. If B is not a charity the gift over will fail for perpetuity unless the gift is appropriately limited in duration: *Re Wightwick* [1950] 1 Ch 260.

There is authority, however, that a trust to pay income to a corporation so long as the corporation maintains the testator's grave to the satisfaction of his trustees is not subject to perpetuity, at any rate at common law. In *Re Chardon* [1928] 1 Ch 464, the will provided:

> I give unto my trustees the sum of two hundred pounds free of duty upon trust to invest the same upon any of the investments hereinafter authorised and pay the income thereof to the South Metropolitan Cemetery Company West Norwood during such period as they shall continue to maintain and keep the graves of my great grandfather and the said Priscilla Navone in the said Cemetery in good order and condition with flowers and plants thereon as the same have hitherto been kept by me.

Romer J held the gift valid, and the decision was followed in *Re Chambers* [1950] 1 Ch 267. It depended on the gift of the income being absolute: *Re Wightwick* [1950] 1 Ch 260.

In *Re Chardon*, if the graves were not maintained the cemetery company would have ceased to be entitled to the income; a resulting trust would have arisen and the income fallen into residue. At common law, a resulting trust probably did not attract the perpetuity rules (*Re Chardon* was decided on the common law perpetuity rule). Today, the disposition would be caught under the Perpetuities and Accumulations Act 1964, s. 12, so this device no longer works: see further 5.3.4.

5.1.2 Purpose trusts for benefit of identifiable objects

Sometimes, on the other hand, identifiable people are intended directly to benefit, but the gift is nevertheless limited for a particular purpose. Here the problem is different. There are people (who must be ascertainable within the certainty of object tests discussed in chapter 4) with an interest in enforcing the trust. It may be possible to regard these people as entitled to a full beneficial interest, subject to a condition (e.g., direction to the trustees to apply the fund only for a particular purpose), in which case these are simply ordinary private trusts.

For example, *Re Abbott* [1900] 2 Ch 326, which concerned a trust for the maintenance of two old ladies, was upheld (see further 2.4.2.1). There was no question of the trust being invalid, even though the fund is clearly intended to be used for a purpose, rather than simply given to the two ladies. Yet the case is probably best analysed as an ordinary trust for the two ladies, with a direction to the trustees to apply the fund only for their maintenance. In other words, this is not, in reality, treated as a purpose trust at all. Other examples, where the courts have construed trusts for purposes as ordinary trusts for beneficiaries, can be found in 2.3.3.

Suppose, however, that although objects can be found with an interest in enforcing the trust, none is entitled to a full beneficial interest. Although the contrary view is arguable, it is probable that only where a full beneficial interest is granted to the identifiable objects will the disposition be valid. In *Leahy* v *Attorney-General for New South Wales* [1959] AC 457, property was to be held on trust for 'such order of nuns of the Catholic Church or the Christian brothers as my executors and trustees shall select'. The trust was not charitable, and Viscount Simonds in the Privy Council thought that it failed as a private trust on the ground that, even though the individual members had an interest in enforcing the trust, they were not granted a full beneficial interest:

> If the words 'for the general purposes of the association' were held to import a trust, the question would have to be asked, what is the trust and who are the beneficiaries? A gift can be made to persons (including a corporation) but it cannot be made to a purpose or to an object; so also, a trust may be created for the benefit of persons as *cestuis que trust*, but not for a purpose or object unless the purpose or object be charitable. For a purpose or object cannot sue, but, if it be charitable, the Attorney-General can sue to enforce it. . . . It is therefore by disregarding the words 'for the general purposes of the association' (which are assumed not to be charitable purposes) and treating the gift as an absolute gift to individuals that it can be sustained.

A gift can therefore be made to a person, but not to an object.

Viscount Simonds's views in *Leahy* are technically *obiter dicta*, because the case is also explicable on other grounds. The gift ought also to have failed for perpetuity (although in the event it was validated by the New South Wales Conveyancing Act). Obviously, however, the reasoned views of the Judicial Committee of the Privy Council must be regarded as very strong authority, in the absence of authority to the contrary.

Somewhat inconclusive contrary authority can be found in *Re Denley's Trust Deed* [1969] 1 Ch 373, where Goff J thought that the *Astor/Endacott* principles invalidated only 'abstract or impersonal' purpose trusts:

> I think there may be a purpose or object trust, the carrying out of which would benefit an individual or individuals, where that benefit is so indirect or intangible or which is otherwise so framed as not to give those persons any *locus standi* to apply to the court to enforce the trust, in which case the beneficiary principle would, as it seems to me, apply to invalidate the trust, quite apart from any question of uncertainty or perpetuity. Such cases can

be considered if and when they arise. The present is not, in my judgment, of that character, and it will be seen that . . . the trust deed expressly states that, subject to any rules and regulations made by the trustees, the employees of the company shall be entitled to the use and enjoyment of the land. Apart from this possible exception, in my judgment the beneficiary principle of *Re Astor's ST* [1952] Ch 534, which was approved in *Re Endacott* [1960] Ch 232, CA — see particularly by Harman LJ — is confined to purpose or object trusts which are abstract or impersonal. The objection is not that the trust is for a purpose or object *per se*, but that there is no beneficiary or *cestui que trust*.

He went on to say that:

Where, then, the trust, though expressed as a purpose, is directly or indirectly for the benefit of an individual or individuals, it seems to me that it is in general outside the mischief of the beneficiary principle.

These quotations are unfortunately not entirely clear. One view is that the test is not whether a full beneficial interest is granted, but whether individuals who are ascertainable have *locus standi* to sue. They will have so long as the benefit is not too indirect or intangible. The trust (which was upheld by Goff J) was 'for the purpose of a recreation or sports ground primarily for the benefit of the employees of the company', with a gift over at the end of the perpetuity period to the General Hospital, Cheltenham. This view of *Denley* was adopted by Megarry J in *Re Northern Developments (Holdings) Ltd*, unreported, 6 October 1978 (see 2.3.3.5).

Another view of *Denley*, however, is that Goff J construed it as a trust for individuals, and not as a purpose trust at all. If this view is correct then the case breaks no new ground, and all private purpose trusts remain void, apart from the anomalous exceptions discussed above. This view was taken, for example, by Vinelott J in *Re Grant's WT* [1980] 1 WLR 360 (at p. 370):

That case [*Denley*] on a proper analysis, in my judgment, falls altogether outside the categories of gifts to unincorporated association and purpose trusts. I can see no distinction in principle between a trust to permit a class defined by reference to employment to use and enjoy land in accordance with rules to be made at the discretion of trustees on the one hand, and, on the other hand, a trust to distribute income at the discretion of trustees amongst a class, defined by reference to, for example, relationship to the settlor. In both cases the benefit to be taken by any member of the class is at the discretion of the trustees, but any member of the class can apply to the court to compel the trustees to administer the trust in accordance with its terms.

This case is further considered in 5.2, although not on this particular issue. A similar view can be found in (1985) 101 LQR 269, at pp. 280–82 (P.J. Millett QC).

Given that the trust was enforceable in *Denley*, and that similar trusts will continue to be enforceable, does it matter how the case is analysed? It could. Consider, for example, the question of enforcement. If the trustees decided to use the fund to install a kidney machine for the benefit of the patients, then that can be relatively easily prevented by injunction. Suppose, however, the trustees do nothing, and no trustees can be found to build and/or maintain the sports ground. Specific performance cannot be awarded, as constant supervision would be required, and an injunction is clearly of no use.

At the end of the day, it is difficult to see what solution can be adopted, apart from distribution of the income from the fund directly to the employees of the company (not the capital, because of the gift over). That puts them into exactly the same position as a beneficiary under an ordinary fixed or discretionary trust.

The issue could also arise if the objects of the trust wanted to terminate it on the basis of *Saunders* v *Vautier* (see chapter 18, and the discussion of discretionary trusts in chapter 4). Presumably, only beneficiaries in the conventional sense can invoke this doctrine, and if the objects of a *Denley*-style purpose have a lesser interest, they will be unable to do so.

Whatever *Denley* decides, pure purpose trusts, such as *Re Astor's ST* [1952] Ch 534 (above), are unaffected by it, and are still void. It is also clear that the individuals to whom direct or indirect benefit is given must be ascertainable within the certainty of object requirements: in *R* v *District Auditor, ex parte West Yorkshire Metropolitan County Council* [1986] RVR 24 (see 4.4.5.5), an alternative argument that the disposition created a valid private purpose trust failed, since whatever *Denley* decided, and indeed even if there were objects with full beneficial interests, they were not ascertainable under the certainty of objects rules.

5.2 GIFTS TO (NON-CHARITABLE) UNINCORPORATED ASSOCIATIONS

Another related problem occurs where property is conveyed to an unincorporated association (e.g., a society, social club or religious group), which will, of course, exist to use the property for a particular purpose. Unincorporated associations cannot themselves own property, not having legal personality (unlike companies). If the purposes of the association are charitable, its officers may hold property as charitable trustees, so no difficulties arise over gifts to charitable associations.

On the conventional view, it might be thought that a *Denley*-style purpose trust might be a good method of allowing property to be conveyed to a non-charitable unincorporated association. On this view the property would be held in trust for the members of the association, for the purposes of the association, and it would be necessary only that the identity of those members was sufficiently certain. Unfortunately, however, a gift to members for the time being (i.e., present and future, assuming a fluctuating membership) will usually infringe the perpetuity rules (another difficulty in *Leahy* v *Attorney General for New South Wales* [1959] AC 457 see 5.1.2), so the purpose trust solution is not generally appropriate. The problem with a fluctuating membership is the need to vary beneficial interests as the membership varies, and if this could occur outside the perpetuity period (on which, see chapter 7), the disposition will be void. It should be noted that in *Re Denley's Trust Deed* [1969] 1 Ch 373 itself the grant was only effective until 21 years from the death of the last survivor of a number of specified persons (with a gift over to a hospital), so no perpetuity difficulty arose. There are also, of course, no perpetuity difficulties where the association is charitable.

Undoubtedly it is possible for any association, by clever drafting of its rules, also to avoid the perpetuity problem (see, e.g., Warburton [1985] Conv 318, 321), but most existing associations have not in fact drafted their rules so as to allow a purpose trust solution which avoids these difficulties.

The purpose trust solution also depends upon it being generally possible to make gifts for non-charitable purposes, so long only as there exist persons with *locus standi* to enforce the trust, even where they do not have a full beneficial interest. As has already been noted in the previous section, this is by no means certain.

Perpetuity difficulties can be avoided by construing the gift to present members only. The problem is that, if it is construed simply as a gift to them as joint tenants, then a retiring member (or indeed any member) is perfectly at liberty to sever and sell his or her share. New members could only obtain any benefit from association property by acquiring shares (or part shares) from existing members. No doubt it would be theoretically possible to run an unincorporated association on that basis, but it would be very inconvenient.

For this reason gifts to non-charitable unincorporated associations are usually construed as being to the existing members only, but subject to their contractual duties as members of the society or club. These will be determined by the rules of the association, but usually a member will be prevented from severing his share, and it will accrue to other members on death or resignation. Thus, although present and future members of a fluctuating body will benefit *de facto*, because the gift is construed as one to existing members alone, there is no perpetuity problem.

This was Cross J's analysis in *Neville Estates* v *Madden* [1962] Ch 832, where (at pp. 849–50) he analysed in detail the methods by which property can be conveyed to a non-charitable unincorporated association:

> The question of the construction and effect of gifts to or in trust for unincorporated associations was recently considered by the Privy Council in *Leahy* v *Attorney-General for New South Wales* [1959] AC 457. The position, as I understand it, is as follows. Such a gift may take effect in one or other of three quite different ways. In the first place, it may, on its true construction, be a gift to the members of the association at the relevant date as joint tenants, so that any member can sever his share and claim it whether or not he continues to be a member of the association. Secondly, it may be a gift to the existing members not as joint tenants, but subject to their respective contractual rights and liabilities towards one another as members of the association. In such a case a member cannot sever his

share. It will accrue to the other members on his death or resignation, even though such members include persons who became members after the gift took effect. If this is the effect of the gift, it will not be open to objection on the score of perpetuity or uncertainty unless there is something in its terms or circumstances or in the rules of the association which precludes the members at any given time from dividing the subject of the gift between them on the footing that they are solely entitled to it in equity.

Thirdly, the terms or circumstances of the gift or the rules of the association may show that the property in question is not to be at the disposal of the members for the time being, but is to be held in trust for or applied for the purposes of the association as a quasi-corporate entity. In this case the gift will fail unless the association is a charitable body.

This passage is interesting in a number of respects. Cross J (whose views are technically *obiter*, because the property was in the event held on charitable trusts: see 12.4) first sets out the difficulties of construing a gift to an unincorporated association as a gift to the members of the association at the relevant date as joint tenants. Secondly, he sets out the usual solution to the problem, that of a gift to the existing members not as joint tenants, but subject to their respective contractual rights and liabilities towards one another as members of the association. In that case, he points out that a member cannot sever his share. Thirdly, he reiterates the orthodox position that a trust for purposes is valid only if charitable.

A similar approach was taken by Brightman J in *Re Recher's WT* [1972] Ch 526, where the limits of the contractual analysis can be seen. The testatrix left some of her residuary estate to a non-charitable unincorporated association which, on the construction of her will, was identified as the London and Provincial Anti-Vivisection Society. By the date of the will, however, that society had ceased to exist, but had amalgamated with the National Anti-Vivisection Society. The question was whether the gift could take effect in favour of the National Anti-Vivisection Society.

Brightman J held that the gift could not be construed as a trust for the purposes of the London and Provincial Anti-Vivisection Society. It would have been possible to construe the gift, on the basis of Cross J's views in *Neville Estates*, as a gift to the members of the London and Provincial Anti-Vivisection Society, subject to the contract towards each other to which they had bound themselves as members, had the Society been in existence at the date of the testatrix's will. By then it had been dissolved, however, and the contract between the members terminated. The gift could not be construed as a gift to the members of a different association (i.e., the National Anti-Vivisection Society), and accordingly failed.

A similar difficulty arose in *Re Grant's WT* [1980] 1 WLR 360, where a grant to the Chertsey Constituency Labour Party could not be construed as a grant to the Chertsey and Walton Constituency Labour Party, the old Chertsey CLP having been dissolved in 1971, upon the redistribution of Parliamentary constituency boundaries. Another difficulty in *Re Grant* was that the members of the Chertsey and Walton Constituency Labour Party did not have control over their own property, because they were also bound by the rules of the Labour Party nationally. Thus, a gift to the CLP could not be construed as a gift to the members of the CLP beneficially, since they could not direct that the bequest be divided among themselves as beneficial owners. The gift could take effect, if at all, only as a private purpose trust, in which case it infringed the rule against perpetuities.

The second of Vinelott J's reasons in *Re Grant's WT* merits further examination, since the relationship between national and local Labour Parties was unusual, in that the local association appeared to have virtually no control over its own funds. Indeed, the national Party could itself take direct control of the local Party's funds, and it is not at all surprising, therefore, that Vinelott J held that the funds were owned by the national, rather than the local Party. It does not follow that gifts can never be made to local branches of federated societies, however. In *News Group Newspapers Ltd* v *SOGAT 1982* [1986] ICR 716, the local branch of SOGAT could unilaterally secede from the national union (Society of Graphical and Allied Trades) and was therefore held still to control its own property. Presumably, therefore, it would have been possible to make a donation to the local branch. Many federated societies adopt an intermediate position, where although the local branches cannot unilaterally secede, the national society has no direct control over the local funds, the local society instead paying an annual membership subscription and agreeing to be bound, to a greater or lesser extent, by national rules. It is not clear whether the reasoning in *Re Grant's WT* applies in this situation.

5.3   WINDING UP UNINCORPORATED ASSOCIATIONS

The correct analysis of a gift to an unincorporated association, such as a club or society, also controls the distribution of its assets when it is wound up, since that question depends upon who are the owners of the fund.

5.3.1   When is a fund wound up?
It is necessary first to consider when a fund may be wound up. According to Brightman J in *Re William Denby & Sons Ltd Sick & Benevolent Fund* [1971] 1 WLR 973, winding up of a fund is not at the discretion of the treasurer or trustees of the fund, but may occur only when:

(a)   the rules allow for dissolution, or
(b)   all interested parties agree, or
(c)   a court orders dissolution, or
(d)   the substratum upon which the fund is founded is gone. An example is *Re St Andrew's Allotment Association* [1969] 1 WLR 229, where an allotment association was wound up when the land for allotments was sold to developers for £70,000.

Many of the cases arise when the club or association has simply been inactive for a number of years, but no positive moves have been made to wind it up. The courts are reluctant in these circumstances to infer that the substratum has gone. In *William Denby* itself the substratum had not disappeared, although after an industrial dispute many of the company's employees left, and for some time (about four and a half years) nobody had contributed to the fund. But before the dispute the fund was viable, and indeed increasing, and mere inactivity by the members did not necessarily lead to the conclusion that they had acquiesced in the dissolution of the fund, since a less drastic interpretation was possible, namely that they had acquiesced in the temporary suspension of contributions and grants.

A similar dispute arose in *Re GKN Bolts and Nuts Ltd Sports and Social Club* [1982] 2 All ER 855, noted [1983] Conv 315, where Megarry V-C allowed what he called 'spontaneous dissolution', that is to say, the winding up of a club without any resolution or court order to that effect. He observed, however, that mere inactivity is not enough, unless it is so prolonged that dissolution is the only reasonable inference. A cataleptic trance, he said, may look like death without being death, and suspended animation may be continued life, not death. Here, however, spontaneous dissolution had occurred, but it required a positive act, in this case a resolution to sell the club's only remaining asset, the sports ground.

5.3.2 Basis upon which funds are held

The types of fund with which this section is concerned are members' clubs or friendly societies, which are unincorporated associations. As we saw in 5.2, the property of unincorporated associations is not normally held in trust for the members. Instead, the relationship between the members is contractual. Members' contributions or subscriptions are regarded as out-and-out gifts, each member retaining contractual rights (based upon the rules) to use the property of the club or society. On resignation from the club or society, although the gift of the subscriptions remains (otherwise a retiring member could claim back a share of these), the retiring member gives up any contractual claim on the property of the association.

It ought to follow, therefore, that when such an association is wound up, only existing members have a right to claim any part of the fund. The basis of their claim is a contractual right to share in the property, and the method by which the division is calculated is considered in the next subsection.

It is nevertheless possible in theory for funds to be held by trustees on trust for the members, even though this is rare in practice. The main difficulty is the rule against perpetuities (see chapter 7), at any rate if membership is likely to fluctuate, since dispositions in favour of future members might fall outside the perpetuity period. This difficulty will not necessarily apply where the fund is intended only for the benefit of existing members or is of short-term duration (e.g., limited to 21 years from the death of the last survivor of a number of specified persons, like the trust in *Re Denley's Trust Deed* [1969] 1 Ch 373, considered in 5.1). Otherwise, the normal requirements for constitution of an express trust will apply.

If such a fund is dissolved, the *surplus of the contributions themselves* will be held on resulting trust. All contributors, including those who have ceased to contribute, will be entitled to a share, and division will be in proportion to the *total amount* they have contributed. Thus, assuming everyone pays subscriptions at the same rate, a person who has contributed for 10 years is entitled to twice as much of the share of the proceeds as someone who has contributed for only five.

This was the basis of division in *Re Hobourn Aero Components Air Raid Distress Fund* [1946] Ch 86, affirmed [1946] Ch 194. From 1940 to 1944 employees of a company situated in Coventry made weekly contributions to a fund to assist employees who had suffered damage as a result of air raids. Only contributors to the fund could benefit. The fund was closed in 1944, and the question arose what to do with surplus moneys. The Crown did not claim the fund as *bona vacantia*. The contributors wanted the surplus back. The Charity Commissioners wanted to adopt a cy près scheme, which they could do only if the fund was charitable (see chapter 13).

At first instance, Cohen J held that the purposes of the organisation were not charitable, since there was an insufficient element of public benefit. It followed that a cy près scheme could not be directed. That being so, the contributors were entitled to distribute the fund among themselves, in proportion to the total amount each had contributed, on resulting trust principles:

> [The] basis on which the contributions are returned is that each donor retained an interest in the amount of his contributions except so far as they are applied for the purposes for which they were subscribed.

In other words, a proportion of the *total* contribution of each individual contributor is held on resulting trust, the assumption being that he retains an interest in his contribution. On a contractual analysis, however, anyone ceasing to contribute to the scheme loses any benefits he or she had under the scheme, and also loses any property interest in the fund. All those who are still contributors at the date of closure of the fund are usually entitled to an *equal* share in the surplus, not a share which is based upon their past contributions (see further below).

The Crown in *Hobourn Aero* appealed on the issue of the charitable status of the fund alone, and the Court of Appeal upheld Cohen J's decision. On this aspect of the case, see further 12.8.2. Nothing was said in the Court of Appeal about the distribution of the funds, however.

One of the problems with Cohen J's analysis is that the rule against perpetuities appears to be infringed, unless either the fund is expressly limited in duration, or there are no fluctuations in membership. Arguably the fund in *Hobourn Aero* did not infringe the rule, although there were fluctuations in the identity of the individual contributors, because of its essentially temporary nature. Presumably, however, nobody knew how long the fund would continue at its inception, and no express limit appears to have been put on its duration.

In *Re West Sussex Constabulary's Widows, Children & Benevolent (1930) Fund Trusts* [1971] Ch 1, Goff J thought that it was not part of the *ratio* of the case, but I would suggest that it was. He also pointed out that there were no contractual benefits in *Hobourn*, so that the usual contractual analysis may well not be applicable, but that does not in any way answer the perpetuity difficulties inherent in Cohen J's analysis.

I would respectfully suggest that Cohen J's analysis set out above is wrong. At any rate, the case cannot be regarded as laying down any principle applicable to the majority of fund cases, since their duration is not limited, and fluctuating membership is assumed.

Walton J's analysis in *Re Bucks Constabulary Widows' & Orphans' Fund Friendly Society (No. 2)* [1979] 1 WLR 936 will usually be more appropriate. The case involved a fund which was made up of voluntary contributions from its members, for the relief of widows and orphans of deceased members of the Bucks Constabulary. In April 1968 the Bucks Constabulary was amalgamated with other constabularies to form the Thames Valley Constabulary, and in October 1968 the society was wound up. The trustee applied to court to determine how the funds were to be distributed. Walton J thought that the members' rights to share in the fund were governed by their contractual rights and duties *inter se* and that, in the absence of evidence to the contrary, members who resigned lost all claim on the fund. Therefore, division should be made among only those who were still members at the time of the dissolution of the fund and, in the absence of evidence to the contrary, they were entitled to an equal share in the fund. Accordingly, he held that the surplus should be held by the trustees for the members at the time of dissolution in equal shares.

It cannot be assumed, however, that the courts have finally resolved in favour of a contractual basis for the holding of funds. We saw in 2.4.2.2 that in *Re West Sussex Constabulary's Widows, Children and Benevolent (1930) Fund Trusts* [1971] 1 Ch 1, Goff J held that the proportion of the surplus attributable to identifiable donations and legacies was held on resulting trust. He thought these indistinguishable from *Re the Trusts of the Abbott Fund*. Presumably, then, before the dissolution of the constabulary, they had been given to the association on trust. The problem is that this is not at all like *Re the Trusts of the Abbott Fund*, which concerned a trust for two identifiable ladies, living at the time the trust was set up. There could not possibly be any perpetuity problems with such a trust. Nor could there, I would suggest, in *Re Gillingham Bus Disaster Fund* [1958] Ch 300 (see 2.4.2.2), where the purposes (or at any rate, valid purposes), were taken to be defraying the funeral expenses of the identifiable boys who had just died, and caring for identifiable living boys who were disabled. But if there was a trust of donations in *Re West Sussex Constabulary's Widows, Children and Benevolent (1930) Fund Trusts*, the beneficiaries would have been the fluctuating body of present and future members, and exactly the same perpetuity problems arise as in the *Hobourn Aero* case (above).

Similar reasoning was adopted by Scott J in *Davis v Richards and Wallington Industries Ltd* [1991] 2 All ER 563, where a pension fund was wound up. The *ratio* of the case was that distribution of the assets was by a definitive deed which was executed by the trustees, but Scott J went on to consider the position if he were wrong. There were three main sources of contributions to the fund, employers, employees and money transferred from other funds. Scott J thought that the employers' contributions should be held on resulting trust for them, since they were similar to the legacies in *West Sussex*. There was no reason to rebut the conclusion that there was a resulting trust. But the problem is exactly the same as above. What was the trust upon which the funds were held prior to the winding up of the fund? It must have been a trust for a fluctuating body of individuals. Surely, similar perpetuity problems arise as before, although perhaps in this case the trust could have been saved by the Perpetuities and Accumulations Act 1964, on which see chapter 7, and in particular for this issue 7.9.5.

Re Bucks Constabulary Widows' and Orphans' Fund Friendly Society (No. 2) was not mentioned by Scott J, although according to the report the case was cited, and there was some consideration given to a contractual analysis (at pp. 589–90). No obvious reason was given for its rejection, however. I would suggest, however, that the trust analysis in these cases simply cannot work, and it is greatly to be hoped that the courts adopt the analysis of Walton J in *Re Bucks Constabulary Widows' and Orphans' Fund Friendly Society (No. 2)*.

5.3.3 Calculation of shares

In spite of the cases considered at the end of the last section, I would suggest that a contractual basis of division is usually the only tenable basis, as in the *Bucks Constabulary* case (see 5.3.2), in which case, if the rules provide for the contingency of dissolution of the fund, division will be according to the rules, as they will form the basis of the contract.

Often the rules do not so provide, however, and in this event the courts are left to imply terms. In accordance with normal contractual doctrine, this will be on the basis of inferred intention and, since this is largely a question of fact, no rigid rules of law can be stated. Nevertheless, certain presumptions appear to apply:

(a) Only existing members can claim, because it is assumed that past members gave up all claims on the fund on resignation (*Re Bucks Constabulary Widows' & Orphans' Fund Friendly Society (No. 2)* [1979] 1 WLR 936). Sometimes the rules expressly so provide, as in *Re West Sussex Constabulary's Widows, Children & Benevolent (1930) Fund Trusts* [1971] Ch 1.

(b) Generally speaking, in the case of members' clubs, division is equally among existing members. In mutual benefit or friendly society cases, the prima facie rule also appears to be equal division (*Bucks Constabulary*), although there have also been cases where division has been proportional to total constributions — this seems appropriate where the benefit contracted for while the fund subsists is also proportional to total contributions. In *Re Sick & Funeral Society of St John's Sunday School, Golcar* [1973] Ch 51, there were two distinct clases of membership, one class of which (adults) paid and received twice the benefit of the other (children). Division was such that adults received twice as much as children. It must be emphasised, however, that inferred intention is a question largely of fact, and that it would be a mistake to deduce rigid principles of law from these cases.

(c) If the assumption can be made that a contributor has made an out-and-out gift of his contributions, retaining no rights in the fund at all, then the property will go to the Crown as *bona vacantia*, because nobody has a claim on it. This conclusion has sometimes been drawn where only third parties could benefit from the fund (for example, in *Cunnack* v *Edwards* [1896] 2 Ch 679, where only the widows of contributors were entitled to benefit). The same result was reached in the *West Sussex* case: Goff J thought that the contributors had parted with their property out and out, and had retained no interest in the fund since it was held for the benefit of third parties (the widows and dependants of the deceased members), but on this point the case was criticised in the *Bucks Constabulary* case. In the later case, Walton J observed that merely because the members have contracted between themselves to provide benefits for third parties does not mean (in the absence of a valid trust in favour of the third parties) that they have relinquished their property in the fund. They can still, after all, collectively agree to distribute the fund among themselves, or to vary the benefits under the scheme. The position is essentially analogous to *Beswick* v *Beswick* [1968] AC 58, where although two parties had contracted to provide a benefit for a third party, they could at any time agree to vary the benefit to be provided for the third party, and the third party had no enforceable claim against either of them. If they had set up enforceable trusts in favour of the third parties, of course, the position would be different, but in that case the third parties would have the beneficial interest in the surplus: see 2.3.2. In neither case should the property go to the Crown as *bona vacantia*.

5.3.4 Perpetuities since 1964

In 5.3.2, I suggested that there are perpetuity difficulties with the trusts cases, such as *Hobourn Aero* and *West Sussex*, because with a fluctuating membership it is necessary to provide for transfers of beneficial interests into the indefinite future, unless a maximum duration is placed on the fund. Where a donation is made to a non-charitable unincorporated association, therefore, and it is not expressed to be by way of trust, in principle the courts ought to adopt the contract analysis in order to validate the gift.

Unfortunately, the contract analysis in *Neville Estates* (see 5.2) depends on the members of the society at any time having the entire beneficial interest in the funds, so that they can, if they so wish, dissolve the society and use the assets as they wish. Furthermore, because since 1964 reverters after a condition subsequent are subjected to the rule against perpetuities, by s. 12 of the Perpetuities and Accumulations Act 1964 (see 5.1.1), donors cannot impose any conditions on their donation to prevent dissolution, for example by making a gift for the purposes of the association unless those purposes are charitable. In *Re Hopkins* [1965] Ch 669, a gift was made to the Bacon-Shakespeare Society, not out-and-out but for the purposes of finding the Bacon-Shakespeare manuscripts. In order to validate the gift, Wilberforce J had to hold finding the Bacon-Shakespeare manuscripts to be charitable for the advancement of education (see 12.3.1.3). Otherwise, either the donation will not take effect at all, or the courts will (if they can) validate the gift by striking out the condition; in *Re Lipinski's WT* [1976] 1 Ch 235, Oliver J was able to give effect to a gift to the Hull Judeans (Maccabi) Association to be used solely for the construction and improvements of the association's buildings, but only by striking out the condition relating to buildings, and holding that the present members of the association were absolutely entitled and could use the property in any way they liked.

It is sometimes argued (e.g., *Gardner* [1991] Conv 41) that if donors wish to make gifts on trust, or conditional gifts to unincorporated associations they should be free to do so, but, at any rate prior to 1964, the law did not allow this (note that both *Hobourn Aero* and *West Sussex*, criticised at 5.3.2, involved pre-1964 dispositions which, if made on trust, ought to have been void). The Perpetuities and Accumulations Act 1964 has relaxed the position in two respects (see 7.9.5), namely by providing for the possibility of stipulating an 80-year perpetuity period and by providing for the 'wait and see' principle. The application of 'wait and see' could lead to considerable difficulties at the end of the period, however, if it became clear that the rule against perpetuities would indeed be infringed; and although it may be useful to validate temporarily gifts expressed to be made on trust, it is not a satisfactory solution where the gift is silent as to how it is to take effect. Since the contractual analysis clearly works, it should be used in preference to a trust analysis, except where the donor has made it quite clear that a trust is intended.

SIX

Formalities and Other Requirements for Validity

This chapter looks further at requirements for validity not considered in chapter 4. Only express trusts (whether charitable or not) are subject to all the requirements considered in this chapter, implied, resulting and constructive trusts (see chapters 8 and 9) being expressly exempted from the statutory formality requirements of the Law of Property Act 1925, s. 53.

6.1 INTRODUCTION TO THE FORMALITIES REQUIREMENTS

There are no formality requirements for trusts, except those laid down by statute; these are now contained in the Law of Property Act 1925 s. 53. The important distinctions to bear in mind are between land and other property, and between declarations and dispositions.

Implied, resulting and constructive trusts are expressly exempted from the statutory requirements, and so, it appears, are variations of trust carried out under the Variation of Trusts Act 1958 (on which see chapter 18). As appears below, however, the distinction between implied, resulting and constructive trusts on the one hand, and express trusts on the other, may be less important than appears at first sight; it is probable that express trusts can also, in some circumstances, fall outside the operation of s. 53, even though they are not expressly exempted.

6.1.1 Reasons for the rules
Land is subject to special rules because of its value, and also because real property (i.e., land) transactions are sufficiently complex for it to be undesirable for them to be taken lightly. So far as other property is concerned, the purpose of legislation on formalities is twofold. Bear in mind that equitable interests are intangible, and that it may not be possible to trace their movement unless that movement is evidenced by written documents. The primary purpose of a writing requirement is to prevent fraud — indeed the original statute was entitled the Statute of Frauds 1677. The secondary purpose is to enable the trustees to ascertain where the equitable interests lie, to enable them to carry out the trusts.

6.1.2 The tax angle

The litigation has borne little relation to these primary and secondary purposes, however. It will become apparent that whereas declarations of trusts do not (generally) require writing, dispositions of equitable interests do. The question of what amounts to a disposition has received attention from the courts in recent years, due in part to attempts by settlors to avoid payment of *ad valorem* stamp duty (now abolished on *inter vivos* gifts). Stamp duty is imposed, not upon a transaction itself, but upon the written instrument by which property is transferred. All documents under seal, whatever their value, require a nominal 50p stamp, but more important was the additional *ad valorem* duty, whose amount was calculated as a proportion of the value of the interest being transferred. If the value of such interest was nothing, as (for example) where a bare legal estate carrying no right to beneficial enjoyment was transferred, no *ad valorem* duty was payable. It is the beneficial interest which is valuable, and if that was transferred in writing, then substantial *ad valorem* duty was payable on the written instrument. Taxpayers therefore obviously preferred to avoid transferring the valuable beneficial interest in writing if they could, arguing instead that only the legal interest had been transferred by the written instrument, the beneficial interest having been transferred orally.

With the abolition of *ad valorem* stamp duty on *inter vivos* gifts in 1985, the practical implications of much of the discussion in the first part of this chapter have disappeared. The theoretical basis remains, however, and the *Vandervell* litigation (see 6.4.3 to 6.4.5) still raises (albeit incidentally) live taxation issues.

6.2 LAND

All the formalities which are required in the case of personalty are also needed in the case of land, but there are additional requirements also. Section 53(1)(b) of the Law of Property Act 1925 provides:

> A declaration of trust respecting any land or any interest therein must be manifested and proved by some writing signed by some person who is able to declare such trust or by his will.

This provision applies to freehold and leasehold land, and also to a share in the proceeds of sale of land. The trust need not actually be declared in writing, since what is necessary is that the declaration should be evidenced in writing, and no special form of document is needed — indeed, the necessary writing may be supplied by an exchange of correspondence or the like. The writing must, however, bear the signature of the settlor and not merely his agent. Failure to comply with s. 53(1)(b) will probably not render the trust void, but only unenforceable in the absence of evidence in writing.

For further discussion of s. 53(1)(b), see 8.1.

6.3 DECLARATIONS OF TRUST: PERSONALTY

As far as personalty is concerned, a settlor (assuming he is *legal* owner) may create a trust merely by manifesting the intention to create it, and no special formalities are required. So, for example, the simple declaration by the owner of, e.g., a stamp collection that he holds it in trust for his nephew will be effective to create a trust of the collection. Even personalty of great value may, in theory, be settled with no greater formality than this. This is true only for *inter vivos* gifts, however. If it is desired to create a trust by will, then the will itself must comply with the provisions of s. 9 of the Wills Act 1837, as amended by the Administration of Justice Act 1982, s. 17, which will be dealt with in the chapter on secret and half-secret trusts (chapter 9).

In fact, as a matter of practice, even with *inter vivos* gifts, the intention to create a trust will usually be declared in a written document setting out in detail the terms of the trust: a major motive for the creation of settlements is tax planning, and documentary evidence for this purpose is often highly desirable.

6.4 DISPOSITIONS OF EQUITABLE INTERESTS

Dispositions of equitable interests are void, whether in land or personalty, unless in writing. Section 53(1)(c) of the Law of Property Act 1925 provides:

> [A] disposition of an equitable interest or trust subsisting at the time of the disposition must be in writing signed by the person disposing of the same, or by his agent thereunto lawfully authorised by writing or by will.

This provision covers both land and personalty, and even in the case of land it is much more stringent than s. 53(1)(b). The disposition must *itself* be in writing, not merely manifested and proved by writing, and failure to comply probably renders the disposition void, not merely unenforceable.

If the law were to accord with the policy discussed above, dispositions would be defined so as to include dealings with the beneficial interest which can be kept secret from the trustees, but to exclude other dealings. After all, the whole reason for treating dispositions of equitable interests differently from other dispositions is precisely because of the difficulties which would ensue were the trustees to be kept unaware of them. The precursor to this section, s. 9 of the Statute of Frauds 1677, caught 'grants and assignments', clearly reflecting this policy, but the term 'disposition' is at least theoretically wider.

Nevertheless, generally speaking the definition of 'dispositions' accords in general with the policy described. The creation of a trust, by declaration, is outside the scope of the section. So, in general, is its extinguishment (by merger with the legal interest). If the purpose of formality rules is to prevent hidden transactions which prevent trustees from ascertaining who the beneficiaries are, there is no reason ever to require them where the legal and equitable interests merge. The same ought also to apply to the extinguishment of equitable interests.

Transfers or assignments of existing equitable interests, on the other hand, normally require writing. They are within the mischief covered by the legislation if the trustees are not party to the arrangement, but not, one would have thought, if the trustees themselves are directed to transfer the interests. Nevertheless, *Grey* v *IRC* [1960] AC 1 suggests that writing is required even in this situation, and I would suggest that the decision is not in accord with the policy described above.

The position is not clear for a surrender of an equitable interest. A surrender cannot, of course, be kept secret from the trustees, and on the principles discussed above surrender should probably not be a disposition. The Court of Appeal held in *Re Paradise Motor Co. Ltd* [1968] 1 WLR 1125 that a disclaimer of an equitable interest is not a disposition. Danckwerts LJ commented that 'a disclaimer operates by way of avoidance and not by way of disposition'. A surrender, however, differs from a disclaimer in that surrender requires a transfer of equitable interest, whereas with a disclaimer there is never any movement of the beneficial interest at all. I would suggest that a surrender may well be a disposition, even though this does not accord with the policy described above.

6.4.1   *Grey* v *IRC*

The usual interpretation of the House of Lords case of *Grey* v *IRC* [1960] AC 1 is that a transfer of an equitable interest on its own constitutes a disposition, even if the trustees are directed to make it, and therefore must be in writing. Until recently, therefore, it would have attracted liability for *ad valorem* stamp duty.

Mr Hunter was beneficial owner of 18,000 shares of £1 each, the legal title being held by nominees. In order to transfer his beneficial interest, Mr Hunter orally directed the nominees (one of whom was Grey) to hold the shares on trust for beneficiaries under six settlements (the nominees were also the trustees under these settlements). Later the trustees/nominees executed six deeds of declaration to this effect, which were of course in writing.

In effect the whole scheme was a tax-avoidance device. If the oral direction had transferred the shares, no *ad valorem* stamp duty was payable; if the transfer had been effected by the written declaration, however, it was.

In deciding in favour of the Inland Revenue, the House of Lords held that a direction, by a beneficiary to the trustees, to transfer his interest to someone else constituted a disposition and must therefore be in writing. Lord Radcliffe did not think that s. 53(1) merely consolidated the earlier Statute of Frauds, and thought that this was a disposition, whether or not it was also within the mischief of the old s. 9. While on a literal interpretation this conclusion may well be inevitable, the transfer in *Grey* does not fall within the mischief of the legislation, as a request to trustees can hardly constitute a secret transaction.

6.4.2   Variations on *Grey*

Suppose a beneficiary declares that he himself will hold his interest on trust for another (rather than directing the trustees to do so), so creating, in effect, a subtrust. A commonly held view is that the issue depends on whether the equitable owner effectively gives away the totality of his interest, so that he, like the trustees who hold the legal title, becomes in turn a merely nominal owner. If so, this is in reality a case of substitution of a new beneficiary, for which on policy grounds formality ought to be required.

If, on the other hand, the equitable owner purports to assume the active role of a trustee of his equitable interest, for example, by declaring discretionary trusts, the case resembles a straightforward subtrust, and should arguably be regarded as a declaration of trust, and not a disposition of an equitable interest at all.

Suppose that Mr Hunter had surrendered his interest, and asked the trustees immediately to declare new trusts, these not of course requiring writing. Suppose also that the trustees were happy to comply with Hunter's request. If surrenders of equitable interests do not require writing (on which, see above), this would have allowed for an easy way to achieve a *Grey* disposition without attracting stamp duty. If surrenders do require writing, however, the surrender is caught by the writing requirement, even if the declaration of new trusts is not.

6.4.3 The *Vandervell* litigation

I suggested above that, in principle, the merger of legal and equitable interests, extinguishing rather than disposing of the equitable interest, should not require writing, on the grounds that it is not a hidden transaction of the type which the law would wish to prevent. On the same principle, it should also be possible for an equitable owner orally to direct the trustees to transfer *both* their legal and his equitable interest to a single third party. In this event also, his equitable interest is extinguished, and the transaction cannot be secret from the trustees. The House of Lords came to this conclusion in *Vandervell* v *IRC* [1967] 2 AC 291.

There are two *Vandervell* cases, both arising out of a scheme which was originally intended to transfer money to endow a chair without attracting taxation, in this case surtax.

6.4.4 *Vandervell* v *IRC*

Mr Vandervell wished to make a gift of £150,000 to the Royal College of Surgeons in order to endow a chair of pharmacology. He was equitable owner of a substantial number of shares in Vandervell Products Ltd, a private limited liability company which he controlled, and which produced, among other products, the Vanwall racing car which competed in Formula 1 races from 1954–1958, and won the Manufacturers' Championship in 1958. The legal interest in Vandervell's shares was held by a bank as nominee.

In order to endow the chair, he arranged with the bank orally (presumably to avoid stamp duty) to transfer both legal and equitable interests in these shares to the Royal College of Surgeons (RCS). It was not Vandervell's intention that the college should receive the shares absolutely, with all the implications that would have had for control of Vandervell Products Ltd. The intention, rather, was that it should receive dividends on the shares large enough to provide £150,000, upon which, as a charity, it was not liable to pay tax.

Vandervell retained an option to repurchase the shares themselves for a nominal amount (£5,000), however. He did not retain it in his own name, for that would have left him liable to pay surtax on the dividends. Instead, he set up a trustee company, Vandervell Trustees Ltd, to whom the option was granted.

The RCS actually received some £266,000 by means of this device.

At this stage, therefore, the legal interest in the shares had been transferred to the RCS. Vandervell Trustees Ltd had the legal interest in the option. If the equitable interest in either remained in Vandervell himself, however, he would be liable to surtax, on the basis of s. 415 of the Income Tax Act 1952. Clearly Vandervell had to show that he had divested himself of the entire benefit of the shares, therefore.

Although the particular income tax provision at issue in *Vandervell* has been long since replaced, the principles of using trusts, and in particular charities, as a means of avoiding taxation, still survive. The principle is essentially that liability to income tax can be minimised by ensuring that the income is received by those whose taxation liability is least. The so-called 'granny trust', where the income is paid to infant grandchildren, is a good example of this principle. Further examples of the use of the trust to avoid taxation are considered in chapter 18.

Figure 6.1

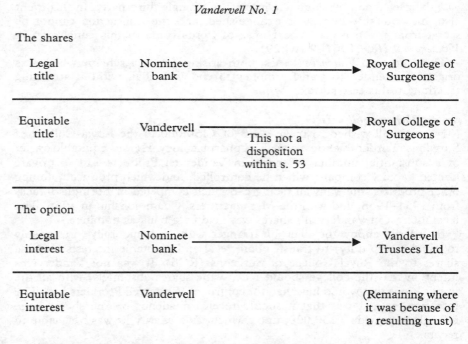

Vandervell No. 1

The shares

| Legal title | Nominee bank ————————————————▶ | Royal College of Surgeons |

| Equitable title | Vandervell ————————————————▶ | Royal College of Surgeons |

This not a disposition within s. 53

The option

| Legal interest | Nominee bank ————————————————▶ | Vandervell Trustees Ltd |

| Equitable interest | Vandervell | (Remaining where it was because of a resulting trust) |

In *Vandervell* itself, as a high earner Mr Vandervell's personal liability to income tax was very high (note that surtax was being claimed, at well over the marginal rates that would have been applicable for standard-rate payers).

The RCS as a charity, however, paid no income tax at all. It was important to show, therefore, that it was the charity and not Vandervell himself who was entitled to the income from the shares. The same principle applies today, where trusts are being used as a device to save income tax: the settlor must ensure that he divests himself effectively of all interest in the trust property, since even the most tenuous connection with the trust may result in the income being deemed to be that of the settlor.

That was essentially the issue in *Vandervell* itself. The shares and the option should be considered separately.

6.4.4.1 The shares

The Revenue initially claimed surtax from Mr Vandervell on the ground that he remained the equitable owner of the shares (although the legal title had clearly been vested in the RCS), in the absence of a separate disposition, in writing, of his equitable interest. This argument was rejected by the House of Lords, which held that s. 53(1)(c) had no application to the case where a beneficial owner, solely entitled, directs his bare trustees with regard to the legal and equitable estate. This is the most important part of the *Vandervell* litigation for formality purposes, and is in line with the policy discussed. As far as the shares themselves were concerned, therefore, both legal and equitable interests had been validly transferred despite lack of writing.

An interesting aside is that *Re Rose* [1952] Ch 449 was approved (see 3.1.3): the transfer was effective as soon as Vandervell had performed his last act.

6.4.4.2 The option

Vandervell was liable to surtax nevertheless, because the House of Lords also held (Lords Reid and Donovan dissenting) that he had not succeeded in divesting himself of the equitable interest in the option (the legal title to which was now in the trustee company), as this was held on resulting trust for him, along with liability to pay surtax on the dividends. Vandervell was not entitled to the benefit of s. 415(1)(d) because the strict requirements of that section had not been satisfied.

This did not raise a formalities point, however, but was the result simply of Vandervell's failure to state where the equitable interest was to go. Lord Wilberforce noted that the trusts upon which the option was supposed to be held were undefined and in the air, possibly to be defined later. The trustee company itself was clearly not a beneficiary, and an equitable interest cannot remain in the air, and so the only possibility was a resulting trust in favour of the settlor. See further, chapter 2.

6.4.5 *Re Vandervell's Trusts (No. 2)*

In order to avoid further surtax liability, Vandervell in 1961 instructed the trustee company to exercise the option and repurchase the shares, and this gave rise eventually to further litigation (*Re Vandervell's Trusts (No. 2)* [1974] Ch 269) about whether Vandervell had divested himself of the option and the whereabouts of the equitable interest in the shares thereby purchased.

Clearly the legal interest in the shares was now vested in the trustee company, Vandervell Trustees Ltd, because it had purchased them. They were also trustees under a separate trust for Vandervell's children: the £5,000 purchase money came from the children's settlement and the trustee company regarded themselves as holding the shares on trust for the children under this settlement. In other words, they regarded the equitable interest in the shares as being in the children.

Liability to surtax now depended on the whereabouts of the equitable interest in the shares during that period (although in the event the Inland Revenue was excluded as a party to the action, and the taxation point was not in fact the main issue). It was argued that, as before, it remained with Vandervell. Again, let us consider separately the option and the shares.

6.4.5.1 The option The Court of Appeal held that the option was destroyed when it was exercised by the trustee company in 1961, so Vandervell's equitable interest in it (resulting from the earlier litigation) was extinguished. This was not a disposition within s. 53.

6.4.5.2 The shares The Court of Appeal held that the children had the equitable interest. The shares had been placed by the trustee company on the trusts of the children's settlements, and the Court of Appeal held that Vandervell had now succeeded in divesting himself of the entire interest in these shares, there being no longer a resulting trust in his favour. This was because the later trusts were precisely defined, in favour of the children's settlements, so that it was no longer necessary for the equitable interest to remain in the settlor.

Lord Denning analysed the position as a termination of the resulting trust of the option in favour of Vandervell, and a fresh trust of the shares declared (presumably by the trustee company) in favour of the children. He thought that as to the first part, writing is not required to terminate a resulting trust, and that since the new trust was not of land no formalities were required for its creation.

So far as the formality aspects of the *Vandervell* decisions are concerned, at no stage did s. 53 operate to defeat a transaction in either case. Since none of the transactions could have been kept secret from the trustees this is in accord with the policy of the section.

In 1965 Vandervell, presumably by now justifiably fed up with his scheme, clearly relinquished by deed any interest, legal or equitable, he may still have had in the shares.

6.4.6 *Oughtred* v *IRC*

The point which arose in this third important House of Lords case is logically quite separate from that which arose in the above cases. It is virtually a pure taxation case, and it is difficult to argue either for or against the result from any general policy standpoint on formalities.

Contracts for the sale of personalty do not require writing, but in cases where the equitable remedy of specific performance is available, equity recognises that the buyer has an interest as soon as the contract is made. A possible route round s. 53 (and therefore stamp duty) might therefore be to have an oral contract for the sale of (say) shares, followed later by a formal transfer. The argument is that the oral contract, not the written transfer, conveys the equitable title; the formal transfer merely conveys the bare legal title, which is worth hardly anything for the purposes of *ad valorem* stamp duty.

This was the essence of the scheme in *Oughtred* v *IRC* [1960] AC 206. Mrs Oughtred owned 72,700 shares in William Jackson and Son Ltd absolutely.

Figure 6.2

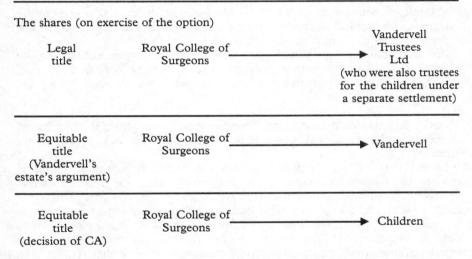

Vandervell No. 2 (1961–5)

The option was extinguished when exercised

200,000 shares in the same company were held on trust for Mrs Oughtred for life, thence for her son, Peter absolutely. The parties orally agreed to exchange their interests, so that Mrs Oughtred would obtain Peter's reversionary interest (she would then have 200,000 shares outright), and in exchange Peter would obtain Mrs Oughtred's 72,700 shares. The contract was later performed.

The Revenue claimed stamp duty on the transfer of the reversionary interest in the 200,000 shares, the actual transfer of which involved writing. Oughtred's argument was that the equitable interest was transferred on the oral contract for sale, and that the later writing transferred only the bare legal title.

The argument was rejected by the House of Lords, Viscount Radcliffe and Lord Cohen dissenting. The essence of the majority view was that, although equity in appropriate circumstances can grant specific performance of a contract for the sale of shares (at any rate in a private company, where the shares are unique, but not in a public company, where equivalent shares are freely available on the stock market), and although in that case a constructive trust arises immediately in favour of the purchaser, the buyer does not have a full beneficial interest until the formal transfer. The situation was regarded as analogous to a sale of land, where the deed of conveyance is the effective instrument of transfer (and so liable to stamp duty). The minority view, on the other hand, was that the purchaser obtained a full beneficial interest immediately.

In the case of shares in a limited company, Lord Jenkins observed that:

> . . . the title secured by a purchaser by means of an actual transfer is different in kind from, and may well be far superior to, the special form of proprietary interest which equity confers on a purchaser in anticipation of such transfer . . . Under the contract, the purchaser is, no doubt, entitled in equity as between himself and the vendor to the beneficial interest in the shares, and (subject to due payment of the purchase consideration) to call for a transfer of them from the vendor as trustee for him. But it is only on the execution of the actual transfer that he becomes entitled to be registered as a member, to attend and vote at meetings, to effect transfers on the register, or to receive dividends otherwise than through the vendor as his trustee.

Transfer of legal title definitely confers additional privileges on the purchaser, therefore, and can reasonably be said to confer a superior form of proprietary interest.

In the case of land, between contract and conveyance the vendor is constructive trustee for the purchaser, but there remains a conflict of interest between the two parties. This therefore differs from a normal trust (see further 14.3), and it can reasonably be argued that at this stage the purchaser has received less than a full beneficial interest. In *Lloyds Bank plc* v *Carrick*, CA, 28 February 1996, however (see 1.6.2), the purchaser had paid the entire purchase price and gone into occupation, so that all that remained to do was to transfer the bare legal title. Morritt LJ expressed the view (*obiter*) that in these circumstances the vendor held on bare trust for the purchaser, so that presumably the purchaser had a full beneficial interest even prior to the conveyance.

6.5   EQUITABLE DOCTRINE OF PART PERFORMANCE

6.5.1   Part performance and the Law of Property (Miscellaneous Provisions) Act 1989

The equitable doctrine of part performance allows for limited avoidance of formality provisions. It developed originally from the principle that equity would not allow a statute to be used as a cloak for fraud (see further 10.2). In recent years, however, it appeared to be developing away from a purely fraud-based doctrine into an evidential doctrine, with its own detailed rules. These rules were arguably both unsatisfactory and uncertain, and the Law

Commission (Law Com No. 164: 'Formalities for Contracts for Sale, etc. of Land') accordingly recommended the abolition of the doctrine, at any rate in relation to contracts for the sale or other disposition of land, or interests in land. Their proposals were brought into effect by the Law of Property (Miscellaneous Provisions) Act 1989, which also tightened up on formality provisions affecting land.

It seems generally to be accepted that insofar as part performance had become a rigid evidential doctrine, that has not survived the 1989 Act. But the question still arises: what if formality provisions are being relied upon to promote a fraud? It seems unlikely that the 1989 Act was ever intended to affect the fundamental principle that equity will not permit a statute to be used as a cloak for fraud. Or suppose the provisions of the 1989 Act itself are used to promote fraud? It must be presumed that the original fraud basis of the doctrine survives the 1989 Act.

It should also be noted that the 1989 Act applies only to formality provisions concerning contracts for the sale of estates and interests in land. Insofar that the part performance doctrine applies to other dispositions, and declarations of trust, it has not been affected by the 1989 Act. There are also contracts, apart from those involving land, that require writing. For example, s. 90 of the Copyright, Designs and Patents Act 1988 provides that '[a]n assignment of copyright is not effective unless it is in writing signed by or on behalf of the assignor', and under the Consumer Credit Act 1974 many consumer credit agreements must be in a prescribed written form and signed. No doubt, it would be possible to apply a doctrine based on part performance if these provisions were not complied with. So, although the cases considered in this section concern land, and may therefore not survive the 1989 Act, the principles discussed still apply to other contracts. Thus, for example, an unwritten assignment of copyright may be effective, in spite of the statutory provision to the contrary, if supported by acts of part performance pointing unequivocally to the existence of such an assignment. Also, the payment of money could presumably have the same effect as described here.

Though the doctrine can be used to avoid s. 53 of the Law of Property Act, 1925, by virtue of s. 55(d), the main cases arose from attempts to enforce a contract for a leasehold or freehold estate in land, despite non-compliance with the formalities required by the (now repealed) Law of Property Act 1925, s. 40:

(1)   No action may be brought upon any contract for the sale or other disposition of land or any interest in land, unless the agreement upon which such action is brought, or some memorandum or note thereof, is in writing, and signed by the party to be charged or by some other person thereunto by him lawfully authorised.

(2)   This section applies to contracts made before or after the commencement of this Act and does not affect the law relating to part performance, or sales by the court.

Like s. 53, s. 40 replaced earlier provisions deriving from the Statute of Frauds 1677, so cases before 1925 were equally authoritative on s. 40.

There are two important points to note about s. 40. First, in the absence of the required formalities it merely prevented an action being brought upon a contract for the sale or other disposition of land or any interest in land, but did not render the contract void. Secondly, s. 40(2) expressly preserved the old equitable doctrine of part performance.

Developments in the law of part performance and in particular the House of Lords decision in *Steadman* v *Steadman* [1976] AC 576 clearly worried the Law Commission, not least because it had left the law in an extremely uncertain state. They also took the view (at page 3) that whereas the part performance doctrine was a blunt instrument for doing justice despite non-compliance with statutory formalities, equity had developed more flexible ways (see 6.5.2) of dealing with the position if formalities were not observed. Accordingly, they recommended the abolition of the part performance doctrine.

The recommendations of the Commission led to the enactment of the Law of Property (Miscellaneous Provisions) Act 1989, s. 2 of which provided:

> (1)   A contract for the sale or other disposition of an interest in land can only be made in writing and only by incorporating all the terms which the parties have expressly agreed in one document or, where contracts are exchanged, in each . . .
>
> (8)   Section 40 of the Law of Property Act 1925 (which is superseded by this section) shall cease to have effect.

Apart from the tightening up of the formalities provisions in this section, it differs from its precursor in not making any provision for the part performance doctrine. However, although s. 40 was repealed and s. 40(2) not replaced, the part performance doctrine was not abolished expressly. It should also be remembered that the doctrine did not derive from s. 40(2), but from an earlier, fundamental equitable principle. Since it does not derive from statute, and since it has not been expressly abolished, is it therefore possible to argue that it still survives?

No doubt in interpreting the new statute the courts will take account of the Law Commission's recommendations, which clearly favoured the abolition of the doctrine. It is also worth noting that the section does not merely render unenforceable any contract which does not comply with its provisions, but that contracts failing to comply are void. The Commission took the view (at p. 23) that the doctrine of part performance would cease to have effect in contracts concerning land, presumably because there would be nothing for it to operate on. This was also the view taken by Professor P.H. Pettit ([1989] Conv, at p. 441):

> It is an inevitable consequence of section 2 that the doctrine of part-performance no longer has a role to play in contracts concerning land. The simple fact is that under the new law if section 2 is not complied with there is no contract for either party to perform.

I would suggest that, insofar (if at all) as the doctrine had evolved from its fraud-based beginnings, the effect of the 1989 Act is to curtail those developments. Where, however, reliance on the statutory formality provisions could perpetrate a clear fraud, it is surely unlikely that equity will allow that to happen because of a new statute, which does not expressly abolish the doctrine. Nor is it a bar to the operation of the fraud doctrine that the contract is rendered void rather than merely unenforceable, since it is only rendered void by the operation of a formality statute whose provisions are being used as a cloak for fraud. The doctrine that equity will not allow a statute to be used as a cloak for fraud was applied by the Court of Appeal in *Rochefoucauld* v *Boustead* [1897] 1 Ch 196 to avoid s. 7 of the Statute of Frauds 1677 (the precursor to s. 53(1)(b) of the Law of Property Act 1925), which like s. 53(1)(b) and s. 2 of the 1989 Act, rendered non-complying dispositions void. I would suggest, therefore, that at any rate to the extent that part performance is based on the equitable fraud doctrine (see 10.3), it is unaffected by the 1989 Act.

It is arguable, however, that equity has evolved other devices for dealing with the genuinely fraudulent case, and no longer needs to rely on the part performance doctrine. To that argument we turn in the next section.

6.5.2   Alternatives to part performance

6.5.2.1   Proprietary estoppel   In its report, the Law Commission took the view (at page 18) that if the part performance doctrine were abolished, many of the cases where injustice might be caused by an inability to plead the doctrine could be resolved by the application either of the equitable doctrine of estoppel, or various common law actions. For example, recovery of money paid by a prospective purchaser would normally be recoverable on the grounds of total failure of consideration. If work had been carried out, a *quantum meruit* claim might be made.

So far as estoppel is concerned, the effect of the doctrine (in essence) is that where one party makes a representation upon which another party relies to his detriment, the party making the representation may be estoped from later denying it. Proprietary estoppel, and its limitations, are discussed more fully at 8.5.3. There is no doubt that it is less effective for the injured party than enforcement of the unwritten contract would have been, but the Commission was of the view (at page 19) that the remedies for proprietary estoppel were sufficient to prevent injustice in most situations where previously the part performance doctrine may have operated. While this may be so, in as much as the Law Commission was worried about uncertainty in its criticism of the part performance doctrine, it can hardly be said that the equitable estoppel doctrine is a particularly certain alternative.

There may also be difficulties with estoppel reasoning where third parties are involved. In the part performance cases there was no third party (e.g., purchaser) and the only question was whether the other party to the contract was bound. But estate contracts can also bind third parties (subject to the registration requirements of the Land Charges or Land Registration Acts, the former having been recently considered by the Court of Appeal in *Lloyds Bank plc* v *Carrick*, CA, 28 February 1996, (1996) NLJ 405), whereas estoppels cannot be guaranteed to do so (see further 8.5.3).

6.5.2.2 Constructive trust Another possibility, closely related to the discussion in the previous section, is that a constructive trust might protect against any injustice that might arise from the abolition of the part perform- ance doctrine. It seems that constructive trusts *may* arise in similar circum- stances to proprietary estoppels, and there is no doubt that a full range of equitable remedies is available to protect a beneficiary under a constructive trust. Constructive trusts also give rise, unlike (probably) proprietary estop- pels, to full beneficial interests, and so are capable of binding third parties also.

Constructive trusts arising from inequitable conduct are considered in detail in chapter 10, and the constructive trust may well be an alternative to part performance — like equitable estoppel, however, it is no more certain in its operation!

Alternatives to the part performance doctrine are analysed in detail by Lionel Bently and Paul Coughlan in (1990) 10 Legal Studies, at p. 325.

6.6   CAPACITY

As a general rule, anyone who has the capacity in law to hold a legal or equitable interest in property has also the capacity to declare a trust of it. The old rules which placed married women in a special position have long been abolished, and the repeal of the Mortmain Acts (by s. 38 of the Charities Act 1960) has removed former restrictions on trusts for corporate bodies. Two special classes of person require consideration, however: minors and persons suffering from mental abnormality.

6.6.1 Minors

A minor may hold the legal title to property other than land and can therefore create a trust of such property *inter vivos*. Any such settlement is, however, voidable and the minor may repudiate it during his minority or within a reasonable time of attaining his majority.

Because a minor cannot make a valid will, he cannot therefore create a trust by will. Statutory exceptions are made in the case of soldiers on military service and sailors while at sea.

Since 1925 (Law of Property Act 1925, s. 1(6)) a minor cannot hold a legal estate in land. He therefore cannot settle such an estate, but he may hold an equitable interest in land and can settle this, subject to the possibility of repudiation of the settlement.

Before the passing of the Family Law Reform Act 1969, s. 9 of which reduced the age of majority from 21 to 18 years, the High Court had the power to approve settlements of real and personal property made upon or in contemplation of marriage by males not under 20 and females not under 17 and such approval made the settlement binding. These provisions were repealed by the Family Law Reform Act 1969, s. 11, without, however, affecting anything done before that Act came into force.

6.6.2 Persons suffering from mental abnormality

A mentally abnormal person may be unable to effect a valid disposition of his property where his condition can be shown to affect his understanding of the transaction. Some transactions call for a higher degree of understanding than others. In order to make a valid will, the testator must understand not only the nature of the document itself, but be able also to evaluate the claims of all the potential donees in relation to the sum of property to be disposed of. *Inter vivos* transactions may demand a lower degree of understanding, which depends upon the size of the contemplated transfer relative to the total assets of the donor. A low degree of understanding will be sufficient if the amount of the gift is relatively trivial, but if it comprises the donor's only assets of value, so as to pre-empt the devolution of his property after his death, then the same degree of understanding is required as in the case of a will.

The Mental Health Act 1983, replacing the 1959 Act of the same title, gives the Court of Protection wide powers to manage the affairs of a person whom the judge is satisfied is incapable of managing his property and affairs by reason of mental disorder. A judge may make orders or give directions for the settlement of any property of a patient of full age. These powers may provide for the maintenance or benefit of the patient or members of his family, or for persons or purposes for which the patient might be expected to provide but for his disorder, or otherwise for the management of his affairs. Such a settlement can be varied at any time up to the death of the patient if it appears that any material fact was not disclosed when the settlement was made or that there has been some substantial change of circumstances.

In exercising these powers, the court will be guided by consideration of what the patient would be likely to do if he were not under disability. In *Re TB* [1967] Ch 247 the court approved a revocable settlement of the whole of the patient's property in favour of the patient's illegitimate son and his family, the effect of which was to prevent the property passing to collateral relatives under the rules of intestacy in the anticipated event of the patient's failure to recover testamentary capacity in his lifetime.

Since the Administration of Justice Act 1969 the court has had the power to make a will for a patient of full age whom the judge has reason to believe lacks testamentary capacity.

Applications for approval of schemes to deal with patients' property commonly have the aim of reducing tax liability, although the scheme must be for the benefit of the patient. It is not essential to provide for revocation if the patient should recover: it is sufficient that it is the sort of settlement which he would be likely to make in favour of his family if he were not subject to the abnormality.

6.7 PUBLIC POLICY; CAPRICIOUS TRUSTS

6.7.1 Public policy; void conditions

Various trusts which would otherwise be valid are held to be void for reasons of public policy, in which case the property will be held on resulting trust for the settlor. Trusts for future-born illegitimate children fell into this category before 1970, because it was supposed that they tended to encourage immorality, and the old law still applies to pre-1970 dispositions. Since that date trusts for future-born illegitimate children have been validated, the present provisions being contained in the Family Law Reform Act 1987.

Conditions affecting dispositions may also be struck down on public policy grounds, in which case the result depends on whether the condition is construed as a condition precedent or a condition subsequent. If the former, the entire gift generally fails (although this statement must be qualified in relation to personal property) and the property results to the settlor. If the latter, the gift, but not the condition, is valid.

Examples of invalid conditions are trusts tending to prevent the carrying out of parental duties, trusts in restraint of marriage and trusts which are fraudulent. Testators sometimes leave property to children subject to a condition subsequent relating to their religious upbringing. In *Blathwayt* v *Lord Cawley* [1976] AC 397, for example, a large estate (valued in 1975 at 2 million) was left in 1936 on various entailed trusts, but such that any person who became entitled was to forfeit his interest if he became a Roman Catholic (or ceased to use the name and arms of Blathwayt). It was argued that with respect to the present children, the religious condition tended to restrain the carrying out of parental duties, and was therefore void on public policy grounds, but the House of Lords held otherwise. The effect of the clause may have been to force the parents to choose between material and spiritual welfare for their offspring, but this was not necessarily contrary to public policy. In the event, however, the House of Lords held by a 3-2 majority (Lords Wilberforce and Fraser of Tullybelton dissenting) that the clause did not apply on its construction.

Conditions subsequent can still be struck down on the grounds of uncertainty, as in *Clayton* v *Ramsden* [1943] AC 320, which concerned a forfeiture on marriage to a person 'not of Jewish parentage and of the Jewish faith'. This was held to be conceptually uncertain. But it seems that so long as a clause is not uncertain the courts will be slow to strike it down on grounds of public policy, and a somewhat similar clause to the above was upheld by the Court of Appeal in *Re Tuck's ST* [1978] Ch 49, where 'an approved wife' of Jewish blood was precisely defined, cases of dispute being dealt with by the Chief Rabbi in London. Names and arms clauses (such as the other clause in *Blathwayt*) have also been upheld (for example, *Re Neeld* [1962] Ch 643). It may be, though, that such leniency by the courts is misplaced, because social conditions change and clauses of this nature arguably allow the dead too much freedom to interfere in the lives of the living.

6.7.2 Capricious or useless trusts

There is no doubt that the courts can also strike down capricious or useless trusts. An early example is *Brown* v *Burdett* (1882) 21 ChD 667, which was an attempt to create a trust to block up windows — surprisingly, this was not an attempt to avoid window tax.

It is to be hoped that the courts tread warily where the validity of a trust is at issue, however. Public policy tests are inherently vague, and in this area in particular there is an acute shortage of judicial definition. Certainty as to the law is important in property transactions, especially for testamentary dispositions, where there is no opportunity for the settlor to correct any mistakes or failures. Public policy is always supposed to be an unruly horse and I would suggest that extensive use of such a jurisdiction would be most inappropriate in this area.

6.7.3 Insolvency Act 1986

The Insolvency Act 1986, replacing earlier complex provisions, empowers the court to set aside certain transactions (called 'transactions at an undervalue') whereby a debtor's property has been placed beyond reach of his creditors. Such transactions include voluntary settlements made by the debtor as well as gifts or sales made for inadequate consideration. Marriage is not regarded as adequate consideration for this purpose.

Section 339 of the Act applies only where a debtor has been adjudged bankrupt. On application by the trustee in bankruptcy, the court may set aside a 'transaction at an undervalue' made by the debtor in the two years preceding the bankruptcy, without need to show that the debtor was already insolvent (i.e., unable to meet his liabilities) at the time of the transaction. Further, a transaction made more than two but less than five years prior to the bankruptcy may be set aside on proof that the debtor was insolvent at the time.

Section 423 applies irrespective of whether the debtor has been adjudged bankrupt. Its effect is to allow any person prejudiced by a transaction at an undervalue (referred to as 'the victim' — usually a creditor) to apply to have the transaction set aside, provided he can establish that the debtor's intention was to place his assets beyond the reach of the victim or otherwise to prejudice the victim's claims against the debtor's property.

In either case, the court has a wide discretion to restore the situation to what it would have been but for the transaction in question.

SEVEN

Perpetuities

In addition to the requirements for validity set out in chapters 4 and 6, any private trust will be invalid if it infringes the Rule against perpetuities. The Rule applies only to a lesser extent to charitable trusts (see 11.2.2).

In this chapter, 'Rule' with a capital 'R' indicates the Rule against perpetuities, in order to distinguish it from any other rule.

7.1 RATIONALE FOR THE RULE

We saw in 1.3 how the Statute of Uses 1535 executed many uses and vested the legal estate in the *cestui que use*. At that time, equity allowed the creation of future interests, whereas the common law did not. Because the uses were executed, however, the *common law* was faced with the problem of dealing with future interests in land, which previously had been recognised only in equity. In summary, then, an incidental effect of the Statute of Uses was to enable successive future interests to be created at common law.

One consequence of this was that land could more easily be rendered unsaleable, and in particular testators could ensure that large estates remained in the family for many generations, since, by creating a succession of limited estates, it was possible to ensure that nobody was in a position to convey an entire unencumbered fee simple. The reasons for wishing to do this, and the difficulties caused by it, are considered in greater detail in chapter 10. The creation of potentially infinite successive future interests was eventually curbed by the development of the common law Rule against perpetuities.

The Rule represents a compromise between the policy of assisting the prudent management of family wealth across generations on the one hand, and the prevention of schemes for tying up property for unacceptably long periods on the other.

Since its original inception, however, the policy of the Rule has undergone modification. The Rule affects all kinds of property, both real and personal, but was originally developed in the context of settlements of land. Since nowadays settlements of land are very rare, mainly for reasons which are unconnected with perpetuities and which are considered in chapter 10, it could be argued that early fears about tying up land for generations should no longer govern modern policy.

The chief scope of the Rule today is in fact within settlements of personalty, which are mostly set up with a view to tax saving. But because fiscal law alters fairly rapidly, there is in any case an inbuilt disincentive to create long-term, immovable arrangements. There is thus less need for a rigid prohibition against such settlements and, by the same token therefore, less justification for a stringent Rule against perpetuities.

7.2   HOW THE 1964 ACT TIES IN

As developed by the common law, the Rule tended to invalidate many perfectly reasonable family arrangements, which could never have produced the lengthy ties feared in the 17th century. The Perpetuities and Accumulations Act of 1964 thus introduced (among other provisions) a new policy of 'wait and see', which allows certain arrangements which would have been void from the outset at common law to take effect unless and until it is obvious that they must infringe the Rule.

It is still necessary, however, to understand the common law position as well. In the case of pre-1964 settlements, the common law Rule is the only rule applicable, along with the minor modifications introduced by the Law of Property Act 1925. Settlements made before 1964 may well give rise to litigation for some considerable time yet: for example, *Re Drummond* [1988] 1 WLR 234 (see 7.4.7) concerned a *1924* settlement, so we might reasonably expect pre-1964 dispositions to continue to be litigated well into the 21st century.

Even in the case of post-1964 dispositions, the Act only applies to those which are void under the common law Rule. The result is therefore a two-stage process, in which the common law Rule must first be applied. If the disposition is valid at common law, that is the end of the matter. Only if it would have been void at common law are the provisions of the Act applied, in which case a 'wait and see' period must be allowed to run, to see whether the gift does in fact vest within the permitted period. This period, for reasons to be explained, differs from that permitted at common law in certain crucial respects which need to be appreciated.

The following discussion will consider the two stages in turn, beginning with the common law Rule.

7.3   COMMON LAW POSITION

The Rule against perpetuities affects only contingent, and not vested interests. The distinction has already been touched upon in 2.1.1, and is further elaborated in 7.3.1 and 7.3.2.

At common law, a contingent interest (i.e., an interest which will arise only upon the happening of some future event, which may or may not occur) must be certain to vest, if at all, within 21 years from the death of some person who is living at the date when the disposition creating that future interest comes into effect. If there is any possibility that the event in question can happen outside that time, the interest is void right from the outset. See further 7.3.3.

The law allows for a period of gestation to be added on to the 21 years, if gestation actually occurs.

Whether the event in fact occurs within the permitted period is a matter of total indifference. Unless it is possible to say, at the moment when the instrument containing the disposition acquires legal force, that such an event *must* occur within that period, then the future interest is absolutely void. Nothing that happens in the real-life world can affect this result.

Because the crucial date from which the period is measured is that of the instrument which contains the disposition creating the future interest, the form of the instrument itself may be important. If the disposition is contained in a deed, executed *inter vivos*, the crucial date is the date of its execution. If it is contained in a will, however, the crucial date is that of the testator's death, since his will can have no legal effect until then. This has repercussions when we come to consider who are the persons living at the date of the disposition, for clearly a person who executes an *inter vivos* deed must be alive, and is therefore a living person for the purposes of the Rule. By definition, however, a testator is never a living person for the purpose of measuring the time allowed to the dispositions contained in his will.

7.3.1 Contingent and vested interests

It should be emphasised at this point that not every kind of future interest is subject to the Rule. The Rule applies only to *contingent* interests, that is, interests which will only arise if an event which is *not absolutely certain to occur* does in fact occur.

This is most easily explained by example. Some kinds of future interests are certain to take effect sooner or later. A simple settlement of land, creating a succession of life interests followed by a remainder in fee simple, does not create any contingent interests at all, because sooner or later, each of the people who take a life interest must die, and then the next interest in the chain will inevitably arise. Death is not a contingency, because it is bound to occur.

Consider a simple settlement: 'to X for life, remainder to Y'. Clearly in one sense Y's interest in the land can be described as a future interest, because he will have to wait until X dies before he can personally enjoy any benefit from the land. Y's interest will not therefore vest *in possession* until X and his life interest have expired.

However, because X's death must occur eventually, from the very moment when the settlement was made, Y has been granted the certainty that, sooner or later, he (or his heirs, should he not live to enjoy it) will come into possession of a fee simple. This certainty is, in itself, a valuable bit of property which has an economic value. So in this sense, Y owns something here and now (a fee simple in remainder). Although not yet vested *in possession*, this remainder is vested *in interest*, and he can deal with it just as he can deal with anything else he owns. Even if he never physically enjoys the land, his interest exists from the moment the settlement was made. Y's interest, then, is not a contingent interest. Nothing has to happen before he can become entitled to the remainder. He already has it.

The Rule never applies to any interest which is vested, even if it is only vested 'in interest', and not yet vested 'in possession'. A possible reason for this is that the Rule, whose purpose was to prevent property being tied up for unacceptably long periods, needed only to prevent *unsaleable* interests being created. A vested interest is saleable, even if the right of enjoyment is deferred until the future.

In order for an interest to vest, three factors must be present. First, the person who is to have the interest must be in existence, and identifiable as the person entitled. Secondly, the size of the interest must be known for certain. Thirdly, nothing further must need to happen before the person in question becomes entitled to the interest. In the case of Y in our example, all three factors are clearly present — he is alive and identified by name in the settlement; the size of his interest is certain (a fee simple in remainder) and there are no conditions which have to be fulfilled. It would be different if, for example, he only obtained the interest if he married (since unlike death, marriage need not occur).

7.3.2   Examples of contingencies

Contrast, however, a gift to Y's first son (as yet unborn). Such a gift cannot vest until the son is born (because the identity of the beneficiary is unknown): it is necessarily contingent. A gift to a class of persons, e.g., 'my grandchildren' must also be contingent until it is no longer possible for any more members of the class to come into being. This is because until all the members of the class are finally known (in effect, until I and all my children are dead), it is not possible to calculate with certainty the *size* of each grandchild's interest: his or her share of the property, as a proportion of the whole, obviously cannot be calculated before the entire class is known. Finally, even if the identity of a beneficiary is known, and the size of his interest is certain, the gift will still be contingent if there is some outstanding condition yet to be fulfilled, such as his reaching the age of majority, getting married, or whatever.

Gifts to unincorporated associations are particularly prone to perpetuity difficulties (see chapter 5), unless the gift is limited in its terms to present members. If future members may become entitled to a share, it cannot be said for certain that all such future members will have been identified, and their shares ascertained, before the period of a life plus 21 years runs out. In other words, it is not certain that the gift will vest in all of those who are entitled to it according to its terms within the permitted period, and so at common law it will be void. So a gift to an unincorporated association must either be drafted in terms which make it clear beyond doubt who is entitled, in what shares, and when, or (more commonly) construed as a gift to present members alone, subject only to their *contractual* rights and obligations (see chapter 5).

Clearly any gift which is not vested must necessarily be contingent. A contingency is anything which (unlike death) is not absolutely bound to occur. The law is concerned only with theoretical possibilities, not with real-life probabilities, and it is irrelevant that the event is very likely to occur.

For example, though most people nowadays survive to reach their majority, reaching it remains a contingency right up to one's 18th birthday. Similarly, at least at common law, many things which were unlikely to happen, but in theory might happen, were sufficient to prevent a gift being vested. Though it is very unlikely that the class of 'X's children' will be increased if X is 86 years old and kept alive on a life-support machine, nevertheless until the moment of his death it is possible that it may. A gift to 'X's children' is therefore contingent right up until his death.

To illustrate the extent to which this principle is taken, suppose a gift to X's grandchildren at 21 (both X and his wife are alive and 80, and have grandchildren). The common law would not assume that X and his wife would not have more children, despite their age, and as will appear below the gift fails at common law for this reason.

7.3.3   The life plus 21 years rule
The basic principle of the common law is as follows. If a contingent interest is to be valid at common law, it must be possible to say, at the date when the disposition creating the interest takes effect, that the contingency in question is one which *must* occur (if it ever does) within the period of a life plus 21 years. Note the phrase '*if it ever does*'. Whether or not the contingency actually occurs is irrelevant. What the Rule demands, in essence, is that the contingency should be something which *could not possibly occur* at a date later than the end of the life-plus-21-years period.

Thus, a gift to A when he marries is perfectly valid. A may never marry, but it is certain that if he does, he must do so in his own lifetime. There is no chance that the contingency might be fulfilled at a date beyond the expiry of the permitted period. If A never marries, the gift will of course fail, but this will be because A did not satisfy the condition attached to the gift, and not because the gift itself infringes the Rule against perpetuities.

Similarly a gift to the first child of A to marry a person now living (A is alive), or to the first of A's great-grandchildren to shake hands with Michael Schumacher, is valid. The contingencies may never occur, and may even be most unlikely to occur. Yet neither of these gifts falls foul of the common law Rule. The first must occur, if at all, during the lifetime of the person now living to whom A marries, and the second must occur, if at all, during the life of Michael Schumacher.

7.4   HOW DO YOU KNOW WHO IS A LIFE IN BEING?

The courts have never laid down a single authoritative test of who *is* a 'life' for the purposes of the Rule, and it is not at all easy to formulate the principle on which the selection should be made. While not all writers would agree with the following approach, it is at any rate rational, and consistent with the authorities.

Since every living person must sooner or later die, it is obvious that the permitted period will expire *at the latest* 21 years after the death of the last survivor among all those people who were alive when the disposition took effect. If the contingency specified in the disposition is one which, by its nature, *could* happen later than that, it will necessarily infringe the Rule.

Though anyone in the world who was alive at the date the disposition was created could, in theory, be a 'life' for the purpose of measuring the permitted period, in practice the law will not embark upon the impossible exercise of discovering who, from the entire population of the world, was the survivor of all those living at the date of the disposition. In practice, therefore, the class of 'lives' must be reasonably certain.

In any case, the common law courts were never prepared to wait to find out if the gift did or did not vest within 21 years of anybody's death. For the gift to be valid, it has to be obvious right at the moment the gift is made that it cannot, under any circumstances, infringe the Rule. So we need some method of deciding which, out of all possible lives, have some relevance to the gift under consideration.

A person (or persons, for there might be several) can be relevant to a particular gift in one of two senses. Either the donor can expressly designate him as a 'measuring life', or it may be possible to assert with total certainty that the date of his death will affect the date at which the contingency mentioned in that gift will occur.

7.4.1 Expressly selected lives

A donor may expressly select some person or persons to be used for measuring the permitted period. A fairly common way of doing this is to employ a 'royal lives' clause, the effect of which is to terminate the period applicable to the vesting of the gift 21 years after the death of the survivor of all those members of the royal family who are alive at the date of the disposition. Such a clause always validates the gift, since it cannot vest more than 21 years after the death of somebody living at the date of the disposition.

In the 19th century it was usual to select the lineal descendants of Queen Victoria who were alive at the date of the disposition, but in *Re Villar* [1928] Ch 471, problems arose in identifying those descendants, who were scattered around the world following the First World War. The trust was valid, however, and such clauses have subsequently been upheld in *Re Leverhulme (No. 2)* [1943] 2 All ER 247 and in *Re Warren's WT* (1961) 105 SJ 511. Nowadays, however, it is thought wiser to refer to the descendants of George V.

No doubt royal lives clauses are commonly used because royalty tend to be long-lived. In principle, anybody can be selected as a 'life', though obviously it is better to select at least one person who is healthy and young.

If the donor takes the trouble to select his own lives, they need have no other connection with the gift. Anyone will do, so long as the 'lives' can be identified with reasonable certainty. Nor is there any limit upon the number of lives which may be specified, so long as they are not so numerous or so difficult to ascertain that the task of determining the date of death of the survivor becomes impracticable. In *Re Moore* [1901] 1 Ch 936, a testatrix specified a period '21 years from the death of the last survivor of all persons who shall be living at my death'. This was held void, not because it infringed the Rule — all those people alive at the lady's death were indeed 'lives in being' — but on the ground of uncertainty.

The only other restriction on the donor's choice is that his 'lives' must be human lives, and not the lives of plants or animals.

7.4.2 No lives expressly selected

Although when the donor selects his own lives, they need have no connection with the gift, when no lives are expressly selected, it becomes necessary to ascertain who, out of all possible 'lives', should be taken as a measuring life for the purposes of the particular gift. The objective is to ascertain at what future time the gift in question must, in the nature of things, vest. In effect, we are looking for the latest possible date at which vesting could occur. If that date is within the permitted period of a life plus 21 years, then the gift is incapable of infringing the Rule, and must consequently be valid. If it is *remotely conceivable* that the gift might vest outside that time, it is void. So, the only lives which are relevant are those which in some way *affect* the date when the gift will vest.

Although the Rule is always stated in terms of a 'life' or lives which can affect the time of vesting, in actual fact we are looking for someone whose *death* affects the time of vesting. What is required is someone whose death will *guarantee* that the gift cannot vest outside the permitted period. It is therefore necessary that the death has some connection with the date of vesting.

7.4.3 Examples of 'lives'

The connection between the death of some person and the date of vesting has to be sought from the standpoint of logic alone. The degree to which it is merely likely that a gift *might* vest at any given time is neither here nor there. For example, consider a disposition 'to A upon his call to the Bar'.

Assuming that A is a living person at the date of the disposition, he must be the 'life' for the purposes of this gift. This is because A's call to the Bar must take place, if it ever does, in A's own lifetime. Obviously, once he is dead there is no chance of the gift vesting if it has not already done so. Therefore, this gift cannot infringe the Rule and must be valid. It does not matter whether A ever qualifies for the Bar. The only element in the example which has the slightest relevance to perpetuity is the immutable logic of the proposition that once A is dead, the contingency which causes the gift to vest can no longer occur.

It follows that a gift to a *named* person will always be valid (provided, of course, that the nature and amount of the gift itself are certain). Anyone having a name must be in existence at the date of the disposition, and if he is ever to take the gift, he must do so during his own lifetime. So, gifts to named persons on their marriage, on reaching a specified age, walking on the moon, or whatever, will be valid provided only that the gift itself is certain.

Similarly, a gift which can only vest during the lifetime of a *named* person, or anybody living at the date of the disposition, will also be valid. See, for example, the gifts referred to at the end of 7.3.

Consider now a gift 'to the first child of A to attain the age of 21'. Assuming that A is alive at the date of the disposition, he is a relevant life because, again, the time of his death affects the latest date at which the gift could vest. Another way of putting this is to say that A's life 'validates' the gift. For the gift to be valid, we have to be certain that it cannot vest outside the period of a life plus 21 years. A's life provides this certainty — or, rather, the inevitability of his death does. As a matter of logic, he cannot have children after his death, so if any child of A's reaches 21 years of age, this event must occur at the latest 21 years after A's death. In other words, it must occur at the latest 21 years after the death of a 'life in being'.

It is therefore clear for the gift 'to the first child of A to attain the age of 21' that A at any rate is a relevant life. This is all it is necessary to know, for if there is anyone at all of whom it can be said with certainty that his death will affect the date of vesting, the gift must be valid. However, it might seem at first sight that there is more than one potential 'life' in being. For the sake of completeness, therefore, note that any existing children of A who are already living at the date of the disposition cannot be counted as lives also. They are not relevant to the date of vesting (unless, of course, the donor specifically chooses them to be his measuring lives). This is simply because the date of their deaths cannot have any effect upon the time when the *first* child of A to reach 21 in fact does so. The first child of A to reach 21 may not yet have been born, and all the existing children may die before reaching that age. Obviously, in that event the vesting date is entirely independent of the deaths of any of the existing children.

The position is of course different if A is dead. Now, obviously, no further children of A can be born, and the existing children become measuring lives. As a matter of logic, one of them must reach 21 (if at all) before they have all been dead for 21 years!

On the other hand, the date of A's death, or the length of his life, whichever way you care to look at it, can have no effect (assuming that A is still alive) on the time at which his children marry, seek call to the Bar, walk on the moon or whatever. It is not certain, as a matter of logic, that they must do these things, if at all, within 21 years of A's death. They might do them much later than this, so A could not be a life for the purpose of a gift 'to the first child of A to marry'.

Nor can A's existing children be 'lives' (assuming A has children who were in existence at the date of the disposition and none of them are married as yet). The crucial question, remember, is: can the date of death affect the time of vesting? and the answer must again be no. The date at which any of A's children happens to die can have no effect on the date at which the first child to marry does this. All we can say for sure is that none of the children could marry after his or her own death, but this tells us nothing about the time when the *first* child to marry will do so. Indeed, the first child of A to marry might not be an existing child at all. He might be born after the date of the disposition, in which case he could not, by definition, be a 'life'.

For a gift 'to the first child of A to marry', then, where A is alive, there is nobody whose length of life could affect the time when the gift vests. If the child who marries first was still unborn at the date of the disposition, the gift might not vest until a time when A, and all those of his children who were alive at the date of the disposition, have been dead for more than 21 years. In consequence, we cannot say for certain that the gift *must* vest within 21 years of the death of someone who was alive at the date of the disposition, and that gift will be void at common law.

A gift 'to the first child of A to attain the age of 25', where A is alive, appears to be similar, but is subject to a statutory amendment (see below).

However, if A himself were dead by the date of the disposition taking effect, as in a gift 'to the first child of A to attain the age of 25', where A is dead, things would be different. A has now had all the children he is ever going to have, so if anyone is ever going to qualify for this gift, it will be one of those children. They are now the 'lives', because the date at which *they* die must determine the date by which the gift will have vested, if it ever does. The example is now exactly like the first one we examined: 'to A upon his call to the Bar', and the gift is valid.

7.4.4 Gifts to grandchildren
If a rough 'family tree' is drawn, it will be immediately obvious to you why a gift made by a living settlor, in favour of his grandchildren, is bound to fail unless it is limited to only those grandchildren who are already in existence at the date of the disposition. This would be tantamount to making separate gifts to each one individually, and thus would be valid. So long as the settlor is still alive, he can in theory have more children who, not having been born by the date of the disposition, could not be 'lives'. They in turn might grow up to have children of their own, more than 21 years after the death of their father. This would mean that the class of 'grandchildren' could not be finally determined until more than 21 years after the death of anyone living at the date of the disposition. (Remember that the settlor's existing children are no use as 'lives'; the dates of their deaths cannot affect the date at which their future-born brothers or sisters produce their own children.)

Figure 7.1

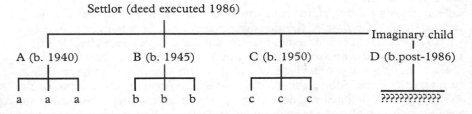

As can be seen from figure 7.1, it is impossible to say for certain when the children of the imaginary child D might be born. The fact that it might be unlikely that our settlor will have any more children is quite beside the point (to judge from the ages of his children, he can hardly be under 60 when he executes the deed). So long as he is alive, he is at common law deemed capable of reproduction.

However, if the gift had been contained in a will, it would have been valid. If the settlor in figure 7.1, and the imaginary child D who will never be born now that the settlor is dead, are covered up, it is immediately clear that A, B and C are 'lives'. By the time the last of this trio dies, it will be possible to say with certainty that no more grandchildren of the original settlor can be born. A testamentary gift to the donor's grandchildren must therefore vest at the end of a life in being, and it will be valid.

This example also emphasises the importance of the *form* of the disposition — deed or will! Incidentally, *inter vivos* trusts in favour of the settlor's grandchildren are surprisingly common, given the trouble involved in drafting the settlement so as to avoid infringing the Rule, because they carry considerable tax advantages. These matters are by no means purely academic, therefore.

7.4.5 The 'unborn spouse' problem
The 'unborn spouse' problem arose in *Re Frost* (1889) 43 ChD 246. This involved a gift to a lady (Emma) for her life, and after her death to any husband whom she might marry if he survived her, and then to those of their children who should be alive at the death of the survivor of Emma and her husband. Again, a diagram (see figure 7.2) illustrates how it is possible for the gift to the children to vest beyond the period of a life plus 21 years, thereby rendering the gift void. For ease of explanation, imaginary dates are used in this diagram.

Figure 7.2

Re Frost (1889) 32 ChD 246 (NB: Dates are imaginary)

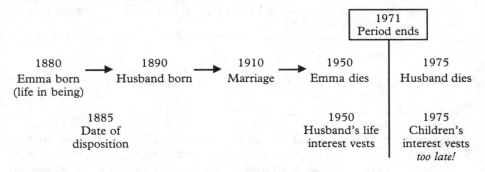

The gift to Emma is valid, because that vests immediately. So is the gift to her imaginary husband, because this must vest, if it ever does, when Emma dies. But the gift to the children is void. The contingency upon which this gift is to vest is the death of the survivor as between Emma and her husband. If the survivor happened to be Emma herself, then the gift to the children would necessarily vest within a 'life' (Emma's).

At the date of the disposition, however, it cannot be known with certainty that this is what will happen. It might equally be the husband who outlives Emma, and whose death thus determines the date when the children's gift vests. And Emma could conceivably marry someone who had not yet been born at the date of the disposition, i.e., not a 'life' at all. Moreover, he might not die until more than 21 years after Emma's death. Since Emma is the only possible 'life', once she is dead there is only 21 years to go until the period runs out. Thus the gift to the children must be void, as it could *conceivably* vest more than 21 years after the death of anyone who was alive at the date of the disposition. Until then, it may be impossible to say *how many* children will be still be alive on the death of the survivor, and hence the size of each share.

Suppose that instead of Emma being unmarried at the date of the disposition, we imagine her married to a man who is many years older than herself. Even then, the children's gift would not be valid. In theory at least, Emma's elderly husband may die, and Emma may remarry, to a man who was *not* alive at the date of the disposition. It is exactly the same as in the case itself, therefore.

Suppose that Emma is 90 at the date of the disposition. It still makes no difference. In theory she might still marry a young man and bear him children (or so the common law assumed). And, as before, the young husband might then survive her for more than 21 years.

However, if the gift to the children were limited to vest upon the death of an ascertained individual, such as Emma herself, it would be valid. This was what saved the gift in *Re Garnham* [1910] 2 Ch 415. The children's interests were limited to vest upon the death of the principal beneficiary (Thomas) and so would necessarily vest in time. The fact that their interests would not vest *in possession* until the death of Thomas's widow if she survived him was immaterial. A similar example might be a gift 'to X [a bachelor] for life, then to any wife he may marry for her life, then to X's children at 21'. The gift vests *in interest* when X's children become 21, even though it does not vest *in possession* until the death of his widow.

The unborn spouse problem was finally solved, in a roundabout fashion, by the 1964 Act (see 7.9).

7.4.6 Nephews and nieces

Gifts to grandchildren are not the only potential victims of the Rule. A gift to nephews or nieces may fail, even if contained in a will. A good illustration is provided by the facts of *Ward* v *Van der Loeff* [1924] AC 653. Here, a testator tried to leave a gift for his nephews and nieces at the age of 21. Stripped of its complexities, the problem in the case was this: the testator had two brothers and two sisters, all over 30 at his death and all with children of their own. He clearly meant to benefit his existing nephews and nieces, for he could hardly have expected his parents, who were 66, to have further children who might, in turn, produce more nephews or nieces. Indeed, by the date of the trial, the testator's father had also died.

The gift failed for essentially the same reason as that in *Re Frost* (see 7.4.5). The testator's elderly parents (or surviving parent) remain (at common law) in theory capable of reproduction until the end of their lives. Even a sole surviving parent might remarry and then produce offspring. So, another child, a new brother or sister for the testator, could come into existence after the testator's death. This new brother or sister could not, of course, be a 'life', not having been born at the time the testator's will took effect. If he or she in due course has children of his or her own, these children are nephews or nieces of their (deceased) uncle, and potentially entitled to share in the gift upon reaching 21. But they need not reach that age within 21 years of the death of anyone who was alive when the will came into effect. By the time they reach 21, the testator's parents, his other brothers and sisters, and all their offspring, may have died. So it is impossible to say *with certainty* that the gift to these imaginary nephews and nieces will vest within 21 years of the death of any person who was alive at the date of the disposition. Figure 7.3 is a diagrammatic representation.

Figure 7.3

Ward v *Van der Loeff* [1924] AC 653

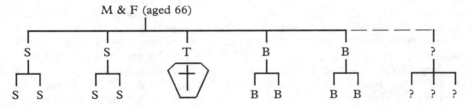

As can easily be seen by drawing a family tree like figure 7.3, if there is even a single ancestor still alive at the time the will takes effect, his or her assumed capacity for subsequent reproduction may invalidate any class gift which the testator had sought to make in favour of his brothers or sisters, or their children.

7.4.7 'Issue' cases
There has been a certain amount of recent litigation involving issue cases, for example, a gift 'to A for his life and then to his issue at 21'.

'Issue' means linear issue through all degrees (i.e., children, grandchildren, great grandchildren, and so on). At first sight, therefore, it would seem that this disposition ought to fail for precisely the same reason as a gift to the grandchildren of a living person.

However, in *Re Cockle's WT* [1967] Ch 690, Stamp J took the view that to construe 'issue' literally, in a pre-1964 disposition, would be absurd. It could not have been what the settlor intended. His lordship therefore construed the gift as excluding any issue born after the death of the tenant for life (A in the example). A therefore became a measuring life and so, *on the construction of this particular gift*, the disposition was not void for perpetuity. *Re Cockle's WT* was followed by Goff J in *Re Deeley's Settlement* [1974] Ch 454, a case which was in all its essentials identical.

However, this construction of 'issue' will not always be appropriate, and depends on it being possible to construe the settlor's intention as excluding any issue born after the death of a measuring life, for example, the tenant for life. The Court of Appeal adopted such a construction in *Re Drummond* [1988] 1 WLR 234. The settlement, made in 1924, was (in its essentials) as follows: to the settlor for his life, then (subject to conditions) to any of his daughters who were living at his death, and the issue of any daughter who predeceased him (again, on attaining the age of 21 or marrying under that age). The settlement also provided that if a daughter died without a child, her share was to be divided equally 'amongst such of the daughters as shall then be living and the issue of any of them who may then be dead such issue taking their parent's share only on attaining the age of 21 or marrying under such age'.

The problem here was the additional clause. Suppose that a daughter (let us say B) had died, leaving an only child (C), who was not yet born at the date of the disposition (hence not a life in being), nor was she yet, at the time of B's death, 21 or married. Suppose C then died before reaching 21 or getting married — then the additional clause would come into operation. The issue (who could have been born after B's death) themselves had to reach 21, or marry below that age, for their interest to vest (although they would become *identifiable* on C's death, which must occur within 21 years of B's death). At first sight, therefore, the interests of any issue born after B's death would vest more than 21 years after her death. The majority in the Court of Appeal (Nourse and Fox LJJ) held, however, that the issue who could benefit were limited to those who were alive on B's death. But Nourse LJ emphasised that the case depended on the particular wording of the settlement, and it should not be assumed that it will always be possible to construe the settlor's intention as excluding any issue born after the death of a life in being.

7.4.8 The precocious toddler

Just as no-one is too old to reproduce at common law, so probably nobody is too young. In *Re Gaite's WT* [1949] 1 All ER 459, Roxburgh J was able to avoid tackling the question of whether the Rule contemplates that a lady aged 65 might have a baby who in turn might, before its fifth birthday, have a child of its own, because the Age of Marriage Act 1929 made it impossible for a person under 16 to contract a valid marriage in this country. Because of this provision, the hypothetical child could not have produced a *legitimate* child who could qualify for inclusion within the class of beneficiaries, so the gift was safe.

However, marriages contracted in other jurisdictions by parties under 16 years of age may be valid, and since 1969 there is a presumption that illegitimate children are intended to be included within the class of children (the present provisions are contained in the Family Law Reform Act 1987). It would be difficult to avoid the issue today, therefore, although the policy of 'wait and see' introduced by the 1964 Act (see 7.9.5) has reduced the importance of such questions.

7.5 CLASS GIFTS

As we have seen, class gifts are especially problematic, for if the interest of even one potential member might vest outside the permitted period, the whole gift fails and even those who qualify well within that period get nothing. It is vital to be able to recognise a class gift. Its distinguishing feature is that the number of persons in the class determines the share that each receives (e.g., three members, one third each — four members, one quarter each).

If, however, the beneficiaries are to receive distinct shares which are not liable to be diminished or increased according to the number of other members, the gift is not a class gift, but rather a series of individual gifts to persons who just happen to be designated by some common label. Thus, a gift of '£10 to each of my sons' is not a class gift, but a number of gifts to individuals. As each son is born, he becomes entitled to his £10 quite irrespective of how many brothers he has.

7.5.1 The rule in *Andrews v Partington*

At common law, a class gift which would otherwise be invalid because it is not possible to say, at the date of the disposition, that all the members will be ascertained within the period, can sometimes be saved, quite fortuitously, by the rule of construction known as the rule in *Andrews* v *Partington* (1791) 3 Bro CC 401. A gift 'to those children of X who graduate from Oxford' is validated by this rule, if, for example, X, who is alive, has one child who is an Oxford graduate.

The rule was devised to make the administration of estates easier, but it applies also to gifts by deed. It amounts to a presumption that, if there was some member of the class who had already qualified for his share by the time the disposition came into effect, the donor must have intended that only those potential members of the class who were already born by that date should have the opportunity to qualify for the gift. Any who are born later are presumed to be excluded. So, if a testator leaves property 'to the sons of X', only those sons of X who had been born at the testator's death could be included in the class and any later-born sons would be excluded.

When this rule applies, it can have the incidental effect of saving a class gift from being void for perpetuity. A gift 'to those sons of A who are called to the Bar' would clearly be void if A is still alive, for the only sons of A to become barristers might be sons born after the date of the disposition, and their calls might take place more than 21 years after everyone who was alive at the date of the disposition had died. But if, at the date of the disposition, A already had a son who was a barrister, the rule in *Andrews* v *Partington* will presume that the donor only meant to benefit such of A's sons as had already been born by that time. The son who is already a barrister may take his share immediately, and his existing brothers (including any who happen to be en ventre sa mère) will receive their shares if and when they meet the condition of being called. But any later-born son of X would be excluded, and since this exclusion eliminates the very possibility that would have rendered the gift void, the gift is saved.

The rule is merely a rule of construction, resting on an assumption about what the donor intended, so if there is evidence that he actually meant to include later-born sons, the gift will not, after all, be saved. In recent years the courts have been more willing to discern an intention to exclude the operation of the rule, and indeed it may be excluded expressly nowadays. This is because, under the 1964 Act, recourse to the rule will only rarely be necessary to save a gift. Now that it is possible to wait and see whether the shares of all members will in fact vest in time, there is no point in closing the class at the outset.

7.6 NO RELEVANT LIVES

It is possible that there may be no lives at all which could affect the date of vesting. This could be because the donor has deliberately chosen some contingency which is quite independent of human longevity, such as a natural event (the next eruption of Vesuvius), a social event unconnected with the gift (the date of the next royal wedding) or simply a date, as a gift 'to be given equally to the issue of X, living on 1 January 2030'.

The common law Rule allows the period of 21 years 'in gross' (i.e., without reference to anyone's life) as the measuring period. So, if it can be said with total certainty that the contingency *must* happen within 21 years, the gift can stand; otherwise, it will fail.

The choice of a fixed date for vesting is considered in greater detail below in the context of the Perpetuities and Accumulations Act 1964. At common law, however, the conventional view is that so long as the date of vesting is within 21 years of the disposition, the gift will not fail on grounds of perpetuity. This is clearly not the case in the 1 January 2030 example above, so the gift there would fail, but as will appear below it would be saved by the operation of the Act, in the case of a 1980 disposition.

Another situation in which it may be impossible to find measuring lives is if the transaction is not a straightforward gift to human beneficiaries. An example might be the anomalous 'purpose trusts' for the upkeep of tombs or pet animals which provide exceptions to the general principle that a trust for non-charitable purposes will be void (see chapter 5). Again at common law, if there are no available lives by which to measure the period, then 21 years only is allowed and this is also the case under the Perpetuities and Accumulations Act 1964, unless the donor has taken advantage of the 80-year period which may be chosen under the Act. In the case of a trust for a specific animal, the courts have occasionally taken judicial notice that a particular kind of animal (e.g., a dog or a cat) does not live beyond 21 years (despite the fact that sometimes they do) and hence saved the gift from the operation of the Rule, but presumably this would not be possible in the case of very long-lived species. A trust 'for the maintenance of my Galapagos tortoises for their lives', for example, can be valid if limited to 21 years only (at common law), so it would be difficult to use a private trust to protect such animals for the 500 years or so they are believed to live. However, since charitable trusts may continue for ever, and most zoos are charitable, donation to a zoo is a better solution to this particular problem.

Another possibility is that directions given to trustees in the trust instrument fall foul of the Rule. It cannot be said that such directions are necessarily limited to the lifetime of the trustee, for trusteeship is an office, and its powers may be exercised by successors. *Re Wood* [1894] 2 Ch 310 is the classic example. A testator had left directions that his trustees should continue working his gravel pits until the pits were exhausted, and then sell them and divide the proceeds between beneficiaries then living. He had assumed, correctly as it turned out, that his pits would be exhausted in a very few years after his death, but the direction was void because it was impossible to say *with total certainty* that this would be so.

On the other hand, if the specified event is one which is required by law to occur within the period, the direction will be valid. It is not rendered void merely because we can imagine that someone may breach his legal obligations. In *Re Atkins's WT* [1974] 1 WLR 761, the contingency in issue was that of a bank complying with its duty to sell land within a specified time, and this was valid.

7.7 POWERS AND DUTIES

Generally, any power which creates an interest in property will be subject to the Rule and this applies also to duties. Thus, a trust for sale (see chapter 10) which could be exercised beyond the period would be void but it is not necessary to affix a special time-limit upon such powers as they are anyway limited by the interests to which they relate.

Powers conferred by statute are subject to the Rule inasmuch as they may result in the creation of beneficial interests; for example, the statutory power of advancement is treated as analogous to the exercise of a power of appointment. Mere administrative powers which create no beneficial interests, however, are mostly outside the Rule.

Although the rules appear complex, they are actually based on the very nature of general and special powers. A general power, which permits the donee of the power to appoint in favour of anyone he likes, including himself, is tantamount to an outright gift of the property to the donee of the power, and only attracts the Rule in a limited fashion. Special powers, on the other hand, operate rather as if the original donor of the power had left a blank in his trust instrument which he intended to be filled in later by the exercise of the power. Exercising the power is therefore tantamount to inserting an extra disposition within the original document, so the period must be measured from the date of that original instrument.

Where the Perpetuities and Accumulations Act 1964 applies, s. 7 treats a power as being special *unless* it is exercisable by one person acting alone and empowers him to transfer the whole property to himself without the consent of anyone else and without having to meet any further conditions. The full text of s. 7 is as follows:

For the purposes of the rule against perpetuities, a power of appointment shall be treated as a special power unless—

(a) in the instrument creating the power it is expressed to be exercisable by one person only, and

(b) it could, at all times during its currency when that person is of full age and capacity, be exercised by him so as immediately to transfer to himself the whole of the interest governed by the power without the consent of any other person or compliance with any other condition, not being a formal condition relating only to the mode of exercise of the power:

Provided that for the purpose of determining whether a disposition made under a power of appointment exercisable by will only is void for remoteness, the power shall be treated as a general power where it would have fallen to be so treated if exercisable by deed.

A power may infringe the Rule in one of two ways. It may not come into existence until too remote a date, and even if it arises in time, its exercise may create interests which are themselves too remote. This means that we have to consider these matters separately for both types of power.

7.7.1 General powers

It must be possible to exercise a power within the period of a life plus 21 years after its creation. In the case of a general power, this means that the person who is to exercise it must be ascertainable within that period and any condition which needs to be satisfied before he can exercise the power must be fulfilled.

So long as the power becomes exercisable within the period, it does not matter that the donee may not in fact exercise it within the period, for he is regarded as having an absolute interest in the property on the basis that he could dispose of it at any time he pleased.

The only exception to this principle occurs where the power, though 'general' in the sense that the donee could appoint to anyone he likes, is limited by the requirement that he can exercise it only in his will. This is clearly not tantamount to absolute ownership, for the donee cannot dispose of the property during his life. The Rule therefore says that the power will be void if its exercise could take place outside the period. This means that a power exercisable only in the will of some person as yet unborn will be void, even though the person in question must be born within the period. A power given to the (unborn) son of X, exercisable only by will, must be void, even though it is certain that all X's children will be born within X's own lifetime, and so within the period. The son cannot exercise the power until his own death, which of course may be more than 21 years after the death of his father X.

If the power can be exercised by will or by deed, as the donee likes, this problem does not arise.

Assuming that the power arises within the period, the donee may exercise it how and when he pleases, but just as any other settlement which he might create would be subject to the Rule, so any settlement which he creates of the property subject to the power must also comply with the Rule. In relation to any such settlement, the period will be reckoned from the date when he exercises the power. In effect, the exercise of the power is tantamount to being a settlement of his own property, so the same rules apply to this settlement as to any other.

Even where the power is one which can only be exercised by will, both the common law and the Act reckon the period from the date of the will in which it is exercised. Logically, however, one might have thought that this power is only notionally 'general' and so should fall under the rules for special powers, see 7.7.2.

7.7.2 Special powers

Since these have an in-built tendency to restrain the free alienation of property, it is not surprising that the rules are more stringent.

Just as with a general power, a special power must become exercisable within the period, which means that the donee must be ascertainable, and any necessary conditions fulfilled, within that time. But since special powers, by definition, are exercisable only in favour of a limited class of persons, it has to be possible to ascertain all of these potential beneficiaries, or 'objects' of the power, within that same period. Unless and until the objects of a special power are known for certain, the power cannot be exercised at all.

Assuming that the power becomes exercisable, the appointments made under it must, as you would expect, also conform to the Rule. Whereas the law regards an appointment made under a general power as a disposition of the donee's own property, the donee who exercises a special power is, in effect, making the appointment on behalf of the original donor. The crucial date, therefore, is the date of the instrument which created the power in the first place. The appointments made by the donee are, as is said, 'read back' into the original instrument, just as though the original donor had made them himself.

However, an element of latitude is allowed to the court when considering the validity of an appointment made under a special power, inasmuch as it can take account of the facts as they existed *at the time of the exercise,* and not as they were at the date of the original instrument.

Thus, in *Re Paul* [1921] 2 Ch 1, a lady exercised a testamentary power in favour of her son upon his reaching 25. The son had not yet been born when the original instrument creating the power came into effect, and if the gift had been contained in that instrument, it would have been void (because the son might reach 25 more than 21 years after the death of anyone then alive). As the facts stood, however, the boy was already 18 years old when his mother died, so he would inevitably reach 25 within 21 years of her death, she being the 'life' for the purpose of this gift. In reading back the appointment into the original instrument, the court took account of the reality of the situation and held the appointment to the son valid.

Except for a few minor details, the wait-and-see policy of the Perpetuities and Accumulations Act 1964 applies to powers just as to other dispositions, but note that the Act only applies to special powers where the *original instrument itself* takes effect after 15 July 1964.

7.8 DISCRETIONARY AND PROTECTIVE TRUSTS

Discretionary trusts are subject to the Rule and, in the case of post-1964 instruments, to the Perpetuities and Accumulations Act 1964. The interests which the trustees create in the exercise of their discretion must vest within the period, otherwise they will be void. Since it is very common nowadays to give trustees the power virtually to create subsettlements out of the original trust property, the issue has considerable practical importance.

Protective trusts are, in essence, composed of a life interest which is determinable upon the alienation of the interest by the life tenant, or upon his bankruptcy, with a discretionary trust tagged on to provide a limitation over in the event of the life interest coming to an end (see further 2.6). The life interest must of course vest within the period. So, a protective trust created in favour of a person not yet born must be carefully scrutinised, to see whether it will vest in time. This is also an area in which the difference between the common law rules and the Act produces a dramatically different result.

If the position falls to be governed by the common law rules alone, it is possible that a protective trust in favour of someone as yet unborn might be partly valid and partly void. Provided the life interest must vest in time, the protective trust will be valid as regards this interest. So long as the life interest vests within the period, it does not matter that it might come to an end outside the period. The Rule is not concerned with the determination of interests, only with their beginning. But, of course, the whole point of a protective trust is to bring the discretionary trust into effect at the moment the life interest comes to a premature end, so the Rule will affect this. The discretionary trusts will be void if it is conceivable that the determining event could occur beyond the period. The life interest will duly determine but the discretionary trusts cannot take effect.

Where the Act applies, the position is affected by the policy, incorporated into the Act, of making determinable interests absolute if they do not in fact determine within the period. So, if the life interest has not yet determined by the time the period expires, that life interest will become absolute, and no longer subject to be determined by alienation or bankruptcy. The discretionary trusts will be void. If, however, the determining event *does* occur within the period, the life interest will duly determine and the discretionary trusts will be valid until the expiry of the period. After that date, they will be void.

7.9 REFORMS MADE BY THE 1964 ACT

The Perpetuities and Accumulations Act 1964 came into force on 16 July 1964 and applies to any disposition contained in an instrument taking effect on or after that date. It made important changes in the operation of the Rule.

The Act provides specific solutions to some of the more obvious absurdities raised by the strict application of the common law Rule. These can be easily summarised.

7.9.1 Fertility presumptions

Section 2 of the Perpetuities and Accumulations Act 1964 creates a presumption that male persons are capable of begetting children at 14 or older and that female persons may bear children at no younger than 12 and no older than 55. Evidence of the capacity or otherwise of a living person to have children may be introduced and the court has a discretion to make such order as may be necessary if it should happen that injustice results from the application of these presumptions. The presumptions also apply to acquiring children by adoption, legitimation, or 'other means', which may offer an escape from any difficulties arising in the context of artificially aided reproduction.

The full text of s. 2 if as follows:

(1) Where in any proceedings there arises on the rule against perpetuities a question which turns on the ability of a person to have a child at some future time, then—

(a) subject to paragraph (b) below, it shall be presumed that a male can have a child at the age of 14 years or over, but not under that age, and that a female can have a child at the age of 12 years or over, but not under that age or over the age of 55 years; but

(b) in the case of a living person evidence may be given to show that he or she will not be able to have a child at the time in question.

(2) Where any such question is decided by treating a person as unable to have a child at a particular time, and he or she does so, the High Court may make such order as it thinks fit for placing the persons interested in the property comprised in the disposition, so far as may be just, in the position they would have held if the question had not been so decided.

(3) Subject to subsection (2) above, where any such question is decided in relation to a disposition by treating a person as able or unable to have a child at a particular time, then he or she shall be so treated for the purpose of any question which may arise on the rule against perpetuities in relation to the same disposition in any subsequent proceedings.

(4) In the foregoing provisions of this section references to having a child are references to begetting or giving birth to a child, but those provisions (except subsection (1)(b)) shall apply in relation to the possibility that a person will at any time have a child by adoption, legitimation or other means as they apply to his or her ability at that time to beget or give birth to a child.

7.9.2 Age reduction provisions

At common law, the postponement of vesting to an age greater than 21 was a common cause of failure of a gift. Section 163 of the Law of Property Act 1925 (which was repealed by the Perpetuities and Accumulations Act 1964 for instruments taking effect after 15 July 1964) introduced a partial reform which applies to any disposition taking effect between 1925 and 1964. The section substitutes the age of 21 for that specified by the donor, if this would save the gift.

The 1964 Act will often obviate the need for any reduction of a specified age simply by virtue of allowing us to wait and see whether the gift vests in time. If wait and see alone will not save the gift, in the case of post-1964 dispositions the age may be reduced, *not* automatically to 21, but to whatever age nearest to the specified age would have the effect of saving the gift. The age cannot, however, be reduced below 21.

The relevant provision is s. 4(1):

(1)   Where a disposition is limited by reference to the attainment by any person or persons of a specified age exceeding 21 years, and it is apparent at the time the disposition is made or becomes apparent at a subsequent time—

(a)   that the disposition would, apart from this section, be void for remoteness, but

(b)   that it would not be so void if the specified age had been 21 years, the disposition shall be treated for all purposes as if, instead of being limited by reference to the age in fact specified, it had been limited by reference to the age nearest to that age which would, if specified instead, have prevented the disposition from being so void.

If an age is reduced in order to save a gift to one member of a class, s. 4(2) provides that the same reduction must be applied to those other members whose gifts would in any case have vested in time, unless the class has already closed (see 7.9.3).

7.9.3   Class exclusion provisions

Section 4 also abolishes the rule that a gift to a class must fail if there is any possibility that the interests of some members may vest outside the period. The all-or-nothing approach of the common law is replaced by a rule that if, even after applying wait and see, fertility presumptions and age reduction provisions, it still cannot be said that *every* possible member of the class will have attained a vested interest in time, the gift is to be treated as valid in relation to those members who have in fact qualified, while those who have not are excluded.

The basic principle is simple, but in practice it may be complicated by the existence of the class-closing rule in *Andrews* v *Partington* (see 7.5.1). If that rule applies, the class will close as soon as one member obtains a vested interest, which may be sooner than would be the case under wait and see. Remember that the Act does not apply at all if the rule in *Andrews* v *Partington* validates the gift at common law. Hence the readiness of the courts, as we saw, to discover an intention to exclude this rule.

The relationship between the rules and the Act is best shown by illustration. Take a gift 'to the grandchildren of A at 25'. A is alive and has three grandchildren, aged 22, 15 and 2. When the eldest reaches 25, the rule in

Andrews v *Partington* would close the class to exclude any further grand-children born after that date, even though they may in fact attain 25 within 21 years of the death of all available lives. Those who were already born are allowed to take when they themselves reach 25. Suppose a new grandchild is born, after the date of the disposition but before the class closed. If it is obvious that he cannot reach 25 before the period expires, age reduction may be applied to save his gift. But age reduction will not be applied to those grandchildren who were already alive at the date of the disposition. This is because under s. 3 of the Act (see 7.9.5), they are themselves measuring lives, and so must necessarily reach 25 before the expiry of a period measured by their own lifetimes.

7.9.4   The 'unborn spouse' problem

Section 5 of the Perpetuities and Accumulations Act 1964 provides that in a situation of the kind we discussed in connection with *Re Frost* (1889) 43 ChD 246 (see 7.4.5), if the gifts to the children have not already vested by the time the period expires (i.e., if the surviving spouse continues to survive more than 21 years after the death of the lives in being), the disposition is to be treated as if the gift had been limited to vest upon the expiry of the perpetuity period:

> Where a disposition is limited by reference to the time of death of the survivor of a person in being at the commencement of the perpetuity period and any spouse of that person, and that time has not arrived at the end of the perpetuity period, the disposition shall be treated for all purposes, where to do so would save it from being void for remoteness, as if it had instead been limited by reference to the time immediately before the end of that period.

This does not mean that the children will physically obtain the property; this remains to be enjoyed by the surviving spouse until his or her death. But they get a vested interest and their gifts are safe. The solution is something of a departure from the policy of wait and see, but it offers a practical escape from a notorious trap.

Note that the problem could not have been solved by treating the 'unborn spouse' as a measuring life on the ground that he or she is a parent of a benificiary since, by definition, a real-life unborn spouse would not have been born by the date of the disposition.

7.9.5   Wait and see

By far the most radical reform introduced by the Perpetuities and Accumulations Act 1964 is the principle of wait and see, which applies in the case of post-1964 dispositions which would have been void *ab initio* under the common law rules.

It does not affect any disposition which would have been valid anyway at common law. Hence the cumbersome necessity for examining every post-1964 disposition to see whether or not it is valid at common law, even though we know for a virtual certainty that the Act will save it if it is not. The exercise is not necessarily academic, as we have already seen with the class-closing provisions.

The position is further complicated because the draftsman of the Act felt that the lives which were appropriate at common law were not necessarily appropriate to wait and see (see, on this point, R.L. Deech (1981) 97 LQR 593). The lives which can be used under the Act are set out in s. 3(5). Arguably, in order to operate wait and see, you need defined measuring lives (otherwise you may not know what you are waiting for).

There are basically four categories of measuring lives set out in s. 3(5):

(a)   The donor himself, assuming he is living.

(b)   The donees. This includes anyone who is a 'potential' donee, i.e., someone who satisfies some of the conditions attached to the gift, and who may in time satisfy the rest (e.g., 'to X when he qualifies for the Bar'). It applies to class gifts as well as to individual gifts, so in a gift to 'grandchildren', those grandchildren already living at the date of the disposition will be 'lives'. Note also that this applies to powers of appointment and that anyone on whom a power, option or other right is conferred may be a 'life'. This would include the trustee of a special power of appointment.

(c)   The parents and/or grandparents of donees, except for those who are 'donees' only in the sense of having a 'power, option or other right'. Persons whose children or grandchildren would, if subsequently born, be 'donees' are included under this head.

(d)   Anyone who has a prior interest on the failure or determination of which the disposition is limited to take effect, e.g., a life tenant.

It will be evident that a person may count as a life under the Act by virtue of falling under more than one head and it is not possible to discuss here all the possible permutations. The important thing is to know the heads themselves, so that you can be confident of recognising a 'life', even if you are unsure how many heads he or she fits.

The Act can yield a large number of lives in any given example and it is crucial to appreciate how wait and see works. Unlike the position at common law, each successive disposition must be approached separately. Each disposition has to be considered on its own merits and allowed a separate opportunity of vesting within the period.

At common law, this is not so. If a disposition is void at common law, any subsequent disposition which follows it might or might not be void, depending upon its relationship to the earlier, void disposition.

If the subsequent gift has already vested, it will be valid. It will be valid also if it is independent of the prior, void disposition and will vest in terms regardless of the validity of any prior disposition. But if the subsequent disposition will only vest upon the happening of some contingency which itself is void for perpetuity, it would be void also, even though it is made in favour of some living person who meets all the conditions of the gift. The Act allows a far simpler process, but do not forget that if the gift is valid at common law the Act never applies.

Also, the available lives may be different from those available at common law. Space prevents detailed examination here, but it will be clear that the range of lives under the Act is in most respects wider than at common law since it includes people who could not have been relevant in the sense examined earlier in this chapter. However, the Act does not provide for such alternatives as the 'royal lives' clause. Such clauses can still be used and if properly drafted will render the gifts valid at common law without recourse to the Act.

Under the Act, the donor may expressly stipulate for a period not exceeding 80 years. It used to be thought this had to be done expressly and it would not be enough simply to fix a date, so that, for example, a gift 'to be given equally to the issue of X, living on 1 January 2030' would be void even in the case of a 1980 disposition. However, in *Re Green's WT* [1985] 3 All ER 455, Nourse J upheld a similar disposition, made in 1976, for the establishment of a charitable foundation on 1 January 2020 unless an event stated in the gift had occurred before then. A mother believed that her son, who as one of the crew of a bomber had been killed in the Second World War, was still alive, and the gift to the charity took effect only if he had not claimed the property by the date stipulated. The court held that the gift to charity was not void for perpetuity.

Where the Act applies, the period during which the trustees may wait and see is calculated as follows, assuming that the 80-year period or other express choice has not been made. A list of all those who count as 'lives' by virtue of s. 3(5) is made and, upon the death of the last survivor of them all, a further 21 years is added. This gives the maximum time for which wait and see is permitted. If at any time before the expiry of that period it becomes evident that a disposition cannot vest in time, then and only then is it treated as being void. Otherwise, the period is allowed to run its course to see if it will vest in time.

7.9.6 Determinable interests

A typical determinable interest might arise from a grant 'to X charity for so long as it shall continue to [whatever]' followed by a gift over to some other person or body in the event of X charity ceasing to do the prescribed act.

At common law, it was of no consequence that the interest given to X might cease at some date beyond the period, provided only that it vested within that time. So, the determination of the interest might take place at any time. But the property has to go somewhere when it is taken back from X, either by way of gift over or simply on a resulting trust to the estate of the original donor. One would have expected that the Rule would apply to prevent this further vesting and, in a sense, it did. Any gift over was void, and the property passed back to the original donor on a resulting trust, whether or not he had specified that this should happen. Some writers thus assert that resulting trusts are exempt from the Rule and, in any case, the property has to go somewhere.

So, in the case of a pre-1964 disposition, a limitation like the one above would be valid to the extent that X's gift would duly determine, but the gift over was void and the property resulted back to the donor. This was regarded as anmalous and the Act made a radical change. In the case of post-1964 dispositions, it is necessary to wait and see whether the determining event in fact happens within the period (which, in the absence of lives, must be 21 years only). If it does, then the gift over can take effect: if it does not, the determinable interest becomes absolute and X owns the property for ever.

7.9.7 Accumulations

The accumulation of property adds to the orignal amount any profits which that property produces instead of paying it out to beneficiaries. Accumulations are a very common feature of modern trusts, the idea being to provide a healthy capital sum for the beneficiaries on their coming of age, marriage or whatever, but it is most important to limit the time during which the accumulation is directed to take place to one of the periods permitted by statute.

If an accumulation is directed for longer than the common law perpetuity period of a life plus 21 years, the direction is void *ab initio* and no accumulation can be undertaken at all. If, however, the direction does not infringe the rule, it will be allowed to take place for a period not exceeding one of the periods specified by statute. Should it overrun, it will be void with regard to the excess, and in this event the surplus accumulated income will pass to the persons who would have been entitled to receive that income if the accumulation had not been directed.

The statutory periods are contained in the Law of Property Act 1925, ss. 164 to 166, and in the Perpetuities and Accumulations Act 1964, s. 13. Section 164 of the 1925 Act sets out four periods and only these can apply to pre-1964 dispositions. In the case of post-1964 dispositions the additional two periods contained in s. 13 are available. Only one period can be used and it is usual in a modern, professionally drafted trust, to specify which it should be. In any other case, the court will determine which period is most appropriate on the proper construction of the instrument.

The four periods in s. 164 are:

(a)   the life of the grantor or settlor;
(b)   21 years from the death of the grantor or settlor;
(c)   the minority or respective minorities only of any person or persons living or en ventre sa mère at the death of the grantor, settlor or testator;
(d)   the minority or respective minorities only of any person or persons who, under the limitations of the instrument directing the accumulation, would for the time being, if of full age, be entitled to the income directed to be accumulated.

The two periods added by the 1964 Act are, in effect, a rationalisation. A peculiarity of s. 164 is that it allows periods (b) and (c) to run only from the death of the settlor and not from the date of the instrument. This is unnecessarily restrictive so s. 13 of the 1964 Acts adds:

(e)   21 years from the making of the disposition;
(f)   the minority or respective minorities of any person or persons in being at that date.

EIGHT

Beneficial Interests of Cohabitees

Chapters 4 to 7 cover the requirements for validity of express non-charitable trusts. The trusts in chapters 9 and 10 are probably best described as constructive; at any rate, the trust is imposed against the will of the trustee. Chapters 11 to 13 cover charitable trusts.

Most of the trusts considered in this chapter can, like those in chapters 9 and 10, be categorised as constructive; but equally, however, some of the cases are clearly based on resulting trust principles. Furthermore, even where there is a constructive trust, it does not, in my view, have an independent existence, but is used solely to avoid the formality provisions of s. 53(1)(b) of the Law of Property Act 1925. All the features of an express trust are present as well, apart from the necessary writing.

This chapter is therefore conceptually rather diverse, but the developments described here are self-contained, in the sense that the cases on cohabitation tend to refer to other cases on cohabitation, but make little reference to the law of trusts as described in the remainder of this book. That justifies the separate chapter, in my view, but it is also a pity; one of the main reasons for difficulties in this area is that judges and academics alike seem to forget that the applicable principles are those of the ordinary law of trusts. Perhaps this chapter can help redress the balance.

For the purposes of the discussion in this chapter, I am going to consider the following problem in all hypothetical examples. Mr A and Miss B, an unmarried couple, purchase a home in which they intend to live. Legal title is conveyed to Mr A alone. The issues are in what circumstances can Miss B claim an equitable interest in the home and, if she can, how large is her interest? The parties are unmarried to avoid the necessity to deal with the legislation covered in 8.1.10. I have assumed A to be male and B to be female simply for convenience, and because that appears to be the commonest situation in the cases. It would make no difference if the sexes were reversed.

Of course, it is possible, and the courts have frequently expressed the view that it is desirable, for the transfer of the property to contain an express declaration of trust concerning the beneficial interests. For the purposes of this chapter, we must assume that that has not been done. It is also worth observing that the law in this area is widely regarded as unsatisfactory, and in 1995, the Law Commission announced that it was to examine the property rights of home-sharers (Item 8, Sixth Programme of Law Reform: Law Com. No. 234). The report commented, at p. 34, that 'The present legal rules are uncertain and difficult to apply and can lead to serious injustice'.

Until 1990, the law in this area was indeed very difficult to state with any degree of certainty. The House of Lords then stepped in, with a remarkably clear statement by Lord Bridge in *Lloyds Bank plc* v *Rosset* [1991] 1 AC 107. The starting point for discussion will be this important House of Lords decision, but before we examine it there are some preliminary points to make. About a year ago, the Court of Appeal muddied the waters again, at any rate for quantification of the interest, with *Midland Bank plc* v *Cooke* [1995] 4 All ER 562, noted Glover and Todd, [1995] 4 Web JCLI (see 8.6.2 and 8.7.1), but this decision is difficult to reconcile with other Court of Appeal decisions, including in particular, *Springette* v *Defoe* (1992) 24 HLR 552, [1992] 2 FCR 561, noted [1992] Conv 347 (see 8.1.6.1 and 8.6.2) and *Huntingford* v *Hobbs* [1993] 1 FCR 45 (see 8.4.1). *Midland Bank* v *Cooke* allows the courts a great deal of flexibility over quantification and benefits the person claiming the beneficial interest (Miss B in our hypothetical example). It is difficult at the time of writing (May 1996) to predict how the law will develop, but I shall argue here that *Midland Bank* v *Cooke* is wrong. The main basis for this argument is as follows:

First, it has been clear since at least the decision of the House of Lords in *Gissing* v *Gissing* [1971] AC 886 (see 8.4.3), and in particular Lord Diplock's speech at p. 904H, that the applicable principles are those of the general law of trusts. This is not, then, an area of law which is governed by its own special principles. *Midland Bank* v *Cooke* is difficult, if not impossible, to reconcile with this proposition.

Secondly, it might be argued that the law has moved on since *Gissing*, that we should now regard as definitive Lord Bridge's speech in *Lloyds Bank plc* v *Rosset*, and that *Rosset* is silent as to quantification, the decision being that no interest was acquired by Mrs Rosset (see 8.4.3). However, the whole tenor of Lord Bridge's speech is conservative. His intent was to clarify, rather than to alter the law. Certainly, the case can hardly be seen as a charter for people claiming beneficial interests. Furthermore, although it is true that none of the House of Lords cases deals with quantification as part of the *ratio*, there is quite a lot of discussion of quantification in *Gissing*, especially at p. 908.

This chapter analyses the law on the assumption that it is governed by the ordinary law of trusts (detailed analyses of how the ordinary law of trusts actually applies have rarely been attempted).

8.1   THE TWO DIFFERENT TYPES OF CASE

The only sensible starting point today for a discussion of this area of law is the following passage, which distinguishes between two completely different types of case, taken from Lord Bridge's speech in *Lloyds Bank plc* v *Rosset*:

> The first and fundamental question which must always be resolved is whether, independently of any inference to be drawn from the conduct of the parties in the course of sharing the house as their home and managing

their joint affairs, there has at any time prior to acquisition, or exceptionally at some later date, been any agreement, arrangement or understanding reached between them that the property is to be shared beneficially. The finding of an agreement or arrangement to share in this sense can only, I think, be based on evidence of express discussions between the partners, however imperfectly remembered and however imprecise their terms may have been. Once a finding to this effect is made it will only be necessary for the partner asserting a claim to a beneficial interest against the partner entitled to the legal estate to show that he or she has acted to his or her detriment or significantly altered his or her position in reliance on the agreement in order to give rise to a constructive trust or proprietary estoppel.

In sharp contrast with this situation is the very different one where there is no evidence to support a finding of an agreement or arrangement to share, however reasonable it might have been for the parties to reach such an arrangement if they had applied their minds to the question, and where the court must rely entirely on the conduct of the parties both as the basis from which to infer a common intention to share the property beneficially and as the conduct relied on to give rise to a constructive trust. In this situation direct contributions to the purchase price by the partner who is not the legal owner, whether initially or by payment of mortgage instalments, will readily justify the inference necessary to the creation of a constructive trust. But, as I read the authorities, it is at least extremely doubtful whether anything less will do.

In this passage Lord Bridge clearly distinguished between two types of case. The first type is where there is evidence of an agreement to share the property beneficially. The agreement need not be formal and its terms need not be particularly precise, but it appears that it must be based on evidence of express discussions between the partners (but see further 8.6.2). More importantly, the evidence of the agreement must be independent of the conduct of the parties in the course of sharing the house as their home (conduct for this category is any detrimental reliance and is wider than that for the second category, considered at 8.4.3 and 8.6.1). If there is such evidence, then in principle it is not necessary to look at the conduct of the parties in order to establish either the existence of a beneficial interest, or its size. The agreement tells you both of those.

The second type of case is where there is no evidence, independently of the conduct of the parties (e.g., contributions to the home), of any such agreement. *Rosset* itself was such a case. Here, if any inference is to be drawn of an intention to share the beneficial interests, it can be drawn only on the basis of the contributions themselves. Thus, the contributions are used to establish the existence of Miss B's beneficial interest, and also (I shall argue) its size, there being no other evidence for either. Lord Bridge is of the opinion that in this situation, it is likely that only direct contributions to the purchase price by the partner who is not the legal owner, whether initially or by payment of mortgage instalments, will do (see further 8.4.3 and 8.6.1).

The conduct of the parties is also relevant in the first type of case, but it is of far less importance than in the second type. Also, the conduct need not necessarily be in the form of direct contributions to the purchase price. Since the agreement to share is shown independently of the parties' conduct, the only function of the conduct is to get around the formalities requirements of s. 53(1)(b) of the Law of Property Act 1925 (see 6.2). It should be borne in mind that there is unlikely to have been any written agreement in this type of case, and the inference to be drawn is that Mr A has declared himself trustee for himself and Miss B (see 8.5.2). Section 53(1)(b) of the Law of Property Act 1925 requires such a declaration to be in writing, unless there is an implied, resulting or constructive trust, in which case by virtue of s. 53(2), the provisions of s. 53(1)(b) do not apply. There will be a constructive trust if the female cohabitee has acted to her detriment or significantly altered her position in reliance on the agreement (the principles are probably similar to those in 10.3). All that is required, therefore, is to show detrimental reliance, in order to get around the formality provisions.

This is made clear elsewhere in Lord Bridge's speech in *Rosset*:

> Even if there had been the clearest oral agreement between Mr and Mrs Rosset that Mr Rosset was to hold the property in trust for them both as tenants in common, this would, of course, have been ineffective since a valid declaration of trust by way of gift of a beneficial interest in land is required by s. 53(1) of the Law of Property Act 1925 to be in writing. But if Mrs Rosset had, as pleaded, altered her position in reliance on the agreement this could have given rise to an enforceable interest in her favour by way either of a constructive trust or of a proprietary estoppel.

It also follows from this analysis that no detrimental reliance is required if the agreement is in writing, for example where the parties communicate by signed letters, or where the property is not land (e.g., a caravan or houseboat, but see also 8.9).

It is a matter of some importance to establish into which of the two categories a particular case falls, since generally speaking Miss B will do better under the first category than under the second. We are now going to expand on the fundamental distinction drawn by Lord Bridge, but in the reverse order. It is easier to consider first cases where there has been no independent agreement, and then to look at the independent agreement cases by way of contrast.

First, however, we need to consider some general principles. Much (but not all) of the second category can be explained in terms of resulting trusts, and it is there that we need to turn next. We will begin with an explanation in general terms, and then apply that explanation to the second category in *Lloyds Bank* v *Rosset*.

8.2 PRESUMPTION OF RESULTING TRUST

As we saw in 2.4, resulting trusts arise either where some or all of the beneficial interest is undisposed of, or because of the actual or presumed intention of the parties. In this section we are concerned only with the presumed resulting trust.

In general, where there is a voluntary transfer of the legal title to property (i.e., not a transfer for value) then unless there is a presumption of advancement (see below), the presumption is that the equitable title does not follow the legal title but remains in the settlor, i.e. there is a resulting trust. The presumption is very old, going back at least as far as *Dyer* v *Dyer* (1788) 2 Cox Eq Cas 92 where Eyre CB said (at 93):

> . . . [T]he trust of a legal estate, whether freehold, copyhold, or leasehold; whether taken in the names of the purchasers and others jointly, or in the name of others without that of the purchaser; whether in the name of one or several; whether jointly or successive, results to the man who advances the purchase money. This is a general proposition supported by all the cases, and there is nothing to contradict it; and it goes on a strict analogy to the rule of the common law, that where a feoffment is made without consideration, the use results to the feoffor.

In *Hodgson* v *Marks* [1971] 1 Ch 892, an old lady (Mrs Hodgson) was cajoled by her lodger (Evans) to convey the legal title of her house to him. He told her that the conveyance was just a device to protect him against her nephew, who disapproved of him. This was a voluntary transfer of the legal title, and in the Court of Appeal, Russell LJ took the view that only the bare legal title was conveyed to Evans. Equitable title remained with Mrs Hodgson, who thereby had an interest by way of a resulting trust, which as an overriding interest also bound Marks, the purchaser (on which see 1.6.2).

The presumption is said to be fairly weak and therefore easily rebutted, and indeed it must be rebutted whenever a gift is to take effect.

8.3 PRESUMPTION OF ADVANCEMENT

The opposite presumption (i.e., that the equitable title *does* follow the legal title) prevails where there is a presumption of advancement. As with the presumption of resulting trust, the origin of the presumption of advancement is almost certainly very old.

Presumptions of advancement occur where the relationship between the parties is such as to impose a moral obligation upon one to provide for the other. Examples are the obligation of a husband to support his wife, and the obligation of a father to support his children.

The effect of the presumption is that where there is a voluntary conveyance of the legal title (i.e., without consideration, in effect a gift), the equitable title passes also. In other words, the presumption is that an out-and-out gift is intended, to fulfil the moral obligation to give, whereas in other voluntary conveyances there is a presumption of resulting trust.

The presumption applies only between husband and wife and between father and son or daughter (or any other person to whom he stands *in loco parentis*, e.g., an adopted child). It does not apply from wife to husband, or at all between unmarried couples.

The position as between mother and son, or mother and daughter, is less clear. In *Bennet* v *Bennet* (1879) 10 ChD 474, Jessel MR, having observed (at 476) that the presumption of gift arises from the moral obligation to give, went on to say:

> [T]he father [of a child] is under that obligation from the mere fact of his being the father, and therefore no evidence is necessary to shew the obligation to provide for his child. In the case of a father, you have only to prove that he is the father, and when you have done that the obligation at once arises . . .

He continued (at 480):

> In the case of a mother . . . it is easier to prove a gift than in the case of a stranger: in the case of a mother very little evidence beyond the relationship is wanted, there being very little additional motive required to induce the mother to make a gift to her child.

In other words, a weaker form of the presumption applies, it being easier to prove an intention to make a gift than in the case of a stranger.

The presumption is based upon intention, and can therefore be rebutted. In *Marshal* v *Crutwell* (1875) LR 20 Eq 328, a wife was allowed to draw cheques on a joint banking account for the convenience of the husband, because the husband was ill. Clearly in such a case there is no intention to make a gift to the wife, unlike, for example, in *Re Figgis* [1969] 1 Ch 123, where an otherwise similar arrangement on a joint account was not merely for convenience. It also appears that bank guarantees, for example where a husband guarantees his wife's overdraft, do not attract the operation of the presumption, but that ordinary rules of contract apply: *Anson* v *Anson* [1953] 1 QB 636.

It may be wondered why there is any need for the presumption of advancement at all. There is, of course, no need for presumptions at all where the actual intention can be easily ascertained, but evidential problems can arise, especially when the donor has died. Suppose Mr X marries Mrs X1 and gives her valuable jewellery. The marriage breaks down and X marries again, Mrs X2. X dies intestate. Mrs X2 claims the jewellery on the grounds that the equitable title remained in X. It may be difficult to prove that the presumption of resulting trust has been rebutted, and this is a possible explanation for the development of the presumption of advancement.

8.4 *ROSSET* SECOND CATEGORY

8.4.1 Application of presumption of resulting trust
A definition of a resulting trust is where 'the beneficial interest "results" to the settlor or his estate' (see, e.g., A.J. Oakley, *Parker & Mellows, The Modern Law of Trusts*, 6th ed., Sweet & Maxwell (1994), at p. 189). It follows that for Miss B to obtain an interest by way of resulting trust, she must settle property; or in other words, she must start with legal and equitable title to

some property, legal title to which she transfers to Mr A. One possibility would be where she starts off with legal and equitable title to the home itself, and transfers the bare legal title to Mr A, as in *Hodgson* v *Marks* [1971] 1 Ch 892. This is clearly not the normal *Rosset* situation, but it is easy to see how a resulting trust can arise from Miss B's contributions to the purchase money. If Miss B pays the purchase money (in which she has legal and equitable title) over to Mr A, then in the absence of a presumption of advancement or consideration moving from him, she is presumed to retain equitable owner-ship in the money: *Dyer* v *Dyer* (1788) 2 Cox Eq Cas 92, *per* Eyre CB at p. 93. If the money is referable to the acquisition of property, then on its acquisition by Mr A, Miss B's interest in the money becomes converted into an interest in the property (on the principles stated by Sir George Jessel MR in *Re Hallet's Estate* (1880) 13 ChD 696, an equitable tracing case considered at 19.2, at p. 708). Alternatively, if both Mr A and Miss B separately pay the vendor, V, then V becomes trustee of the money for him and her in the proportions in which he and she has paid it, until such time as the property is conveyed, when again the equitable interests are converted into interests in the property.

For these purposes the origin of the money advanced by Miss B is irrelevant. If it is obtained by a loan, with her undertaking liability to repay the loan, the position is exactly the same; and similarly if she obtains the money through a mortgage on the property itself, accepting liability to repay the mortgage debt. This explains, for example, *Huntingford* v *Hobbs* [1993] 1 FCR 45, where the entirety of Mr Huntingford's undertaking to repay the mortgage debt was taken into account in calculating his share, although he had not actually paid off any of the capital.

8.4.2 Application of presumption of advancement
If the presumption of advancement is applicable to this area of law, it can be relevant whether or not the parties are married. Suppose, for example, a matrimonial home is purchased in the name of the husband alone, but his wife has contributed to the purchase price (either the deposit or mortgage repayments). There being no presumption of advancement from wife to husband, on the principles discussed above, the equitable interests remain in proportion to the contributions, and the husband will therefore hold the legal estate on trust for both himself and his wife in proportion to their contribu-tions. They will thus hold the land as joint tenants or tenants in common in equity, and a statutory trust for sale will arise under the provisions of the Law of Property Act 1925, ss. 34–36 (see further 8.9). The same result obtains, of course, if the parties are living together but not married.

Suppose instead, however, that the man contributes to the purchase money, the property being conveyed into the woman's name alone. It now matters whether the parties are married. If so, and if the presumption of advancement applies, the wife will obtain both legal and equitable title. If the parties are unmarried, the opposite result obtains, the presumption being that the man retains an equitable title under a resulting trust.

All this presupposes that the presumption of advancement has any appli-cation in this area of law (there is no doubt that the presumption of resulting trust applies — see *Tinsley* v *Milligan*, below). Obviously, the justification for the presumption at the end of 8.3 applies to a set of circumstances very different from that being considered here. Indeed, the presumption may well be regarded as very old fashioned. In *Pettitt* v *Pettitt* [1970] AC 777, a cottage was purchased in the name of the wife, Mrs Pettitt providing the entirety of the purchase money. The husband significantly improved the property, using his own labour and money. He claimed an equitable interest, but the House held that he had no interest in the cottage (see further 8.6.1). The House refused to decide the case simply on the basis of the presumption of advancement, however, which would have led them to the same conclusion. Lord Diplock did not think the presumption applied at all in shared home cases, observing that:

> It would, in my view, be an abuse of the legal technique for ascertaining or imputing intention to apply to transactions between the post-war gener- ation of married couples 'presumptions' which are based on inferences of fact which an earlier generation of judges drew as to the most likely intentions of earlier generations of spouses belonging to the propertied classes of a different social era.

The other judges appeared to favour a weak presumption, so that as Lord Diplock observed in *Gissing* v *Gissing* [1971] AC 886 see 8.4.3):

> . . . as I understand the speeches in *Pettitt* v *Pettitt* four of the members of your Lordships's House who were parties to that decision took the view that even if the 'presumption of advancement' as between husband and wife still survived today, it could seldom have any decisive part to play in disputes between living spouses in which some evidence would be available in addition to the mere fact that the husband had provided part of the purchase price of property conveyed into the name of the wife.

In *McGrath* v *Wallis* [1995] 2 FLR 114, Nourse LJ began his judgment as follows:

> Ever since the decision of the House of Lords in *Pettitt* v *Pettitt* [1970] AC 777, it has been my understanding that, in its application to houses acquired for joint occupation, the equitable presumption of advancement has been reclassified as a judicial instrument of last resort, its subordinate status comparable to that of the *contra preferentem* rule in the construction of deeds and contracts; see *per* Lords Reid, Hodson and Diplock at pages 793, 811 and 824 respectively; see also *Gissing* v *Gissing* [1971] AC 886, *per* Lord Diplock at page 907 . . . For myself, I have been unable to recollect any subsequent case of this kind in which the presumption has proved to be decisive, even where one of the parties has since died.

He continued:

> In *Pettitt* v *Pettitt* Lord Upjohn, more loyal to the presumption of advance- ment than the others of their Lordships, while maintaining that that

presumption and the presumption of a resulting trust, when properly understood and properly applied to the circumstances of today, remained as useful as ever in solving questions of title (see page 813H), nevertheless accepted that they were readily rebutted by comparatively slight evidence (see page 814H).

In that case the presumption between father and son was easily rebutted, there being no evidence that the father intended to make a gift of the house to his son.

It is clear, therefore, that the presumption of advancement will rarely, if ever, be decisive in matrimonial property cases, but whether there is no presumption at all, or a very weak presumption, a matter on which the courts have reached no definite conclusion, can make a difference. In *Tinsley* v *Milligan* [1994] 1 AC 340 (see 1.4.6.4), Stella Tinsley and Kathleen Milligan jointly purchased a home which was registered in Tinsley's name alone. On the principles set out at 8.4.1. above, the beneficial interest would have been shared between Tinsley and Milligan in equal shares, but to both Tinsley and Milligan's knowledge, the home was registered in Tinsley's name alone to enable Milligan to make false claims to the Department of Social Security for benefits. After a quarrel Tinsley moved out and claimed possession from Milligan. Milligan counterclaimed, seeking a declaration that the house was held by Tinsley on trust for both of them in equal shares. Tinsley argued that Milligan's claim was barred by the common law doctrine *ex turpi causa non oritur actio* and by the principle that he who comes to equity must come with clean hands.

The House of Lords held (Lord Keith and Lord Goff dissenting) that because the presumption of resulting trust applied, Milligan could establish her equitable interest without relying on the illegal transaction, and was therefore entitled to succeed. However, it is also clear that if she had had to rebut a presumption of advancement, however weak, she would have failed, because she would have had to plead the fraud in order to do so. In *Tribe* v *Tribe* [1995] 4 All ER 236, the Court of Appeal allowed evidence to rebut a presumption of advancement where the fraud had not actually been carried out, but this decision will not apply where the fraud has been carried out. Where a husband has conveyed a house to his wife (for example) to perpetrate a capital gains tax fraud, and the fraud has been successfully perpetrated, it matters whether there is a weak presumption or none at all.

8.4.3 Contributions definitely outside second category
The exact scope of the second category in *Lloyds Bank* v *Rosset* is considered below (8.6.1), when its juristic basis has been made clearer, but the important point about this category is that apart from the contributions of the parties, there is no independent evidence of their intention. It is therefore not surprising that only contributions which are referable to the property, and indeed to its acquisition, count. These will usually (perhaps necessarily) be financial contributions, as in the previous sections.

By comparison, other contributions are arguably undervalued. Generally speaking, this operates to the disadvantage of the woman living in the home, since it is still far more likely that the man will earn more money than the woman, and it is accordingly likely that his financial contributions will be the greater. On the other hand, the woman may contribute in other ways. She may, for example, give up her job to bring up the children, pay the household expenses, or provide furniture or domestic services. Because it undervalues these other contributions, the law appears to work unjustly against the woman (which is presumably why legislation was thought necessary for married couples — see further 8.10).

Yet (subject to possible new developments discussed at 8.7) the courts appear to attach little weight to non-financial contributions. In the 1970s it was argued that the courts should exercise a discretion based on some abstract notion of justice. It was also argued that equity is a flexible instrument. 'Equity,' said Lord Denning MR in *Eves v Eves* [1975] 1 WLR 1338, at 1340, 'is not past the age of child bearing'. The facts of *Eves v Eves* are set out at 8.5.2.

It is now reasonably clear that the courts will not exercise the sort of discretion envisaged by Lord Denning MR in *Eves v Eves* (although the actual decision in the case was implicitly approved in *Lloyds Bank v Rosset*). Indeed, a rigidly property-based approach was taken by the House of Lords in *Pettitt v Pettitt* [1970] AC 777 (see 8.1.4.2) and *Gissing v Gissing* [1971] AC 886. Mrs Gissing had been married to Mr Gissing for 16 years and had paid a substantial sum towards furniture and the laying of a lawn, but the house had been conveyed into the name of Mr Gissing alone, and Mrs Gissing had made no direct contributions towards its purchase. On their divorce, the House of Lords held that she had no interest (the position would possibly have been different after the enactment of the Matrimonial Causes Act 1973 — see 8.10). The main importance of the case is that the House refused to exercise a discretion simply in order to do 'justice'. The interests of the parties were determined on the basis of their intentions at the time of acquisition of the property, and not by their subsequent conduct. It was also clear that normal principles of property law would be applicable.

In *Eves v Eves*, Lord Denning MR relied on the following passage from Lord Diplock's speech in *Gissing v Gissing* [1971] AC 886, as authority that the courts had a great degree of flexibility. The nature of the interest depended on all the equities of the case, and the law might consider not merely financial contributions at the time of acquisition of the property, but all types of contribution, whether at that time or subsequently:

A resulting, implied or constructive trust — and it is unnecessary for present purposes to distinguish between these three classes of trust — is created by a transaction between the trustee and the *cestui que trust* in connection with the acquisition by the trustee of a legal estate in land, whenever the trustee has so conducted himself that it would be inequitable to allow him to deny to the *cestui que trust* a beneficial interest in the land acquired. And he will be held so to have conducted himself if by his words or conduct he has induced the *cestui que trust* to act to his own detriment in the reasonable belief that by so acting he was acquiring a beneficial interest in the land.

The quotation was taken out of context, since from the previous paragraph in Lord Diplock's speech it is clear that he was referring to the constructive trust here merely as a device to get round s. 53(1)(b) of the Law of Property Act 1925, where all the other requirements of a trust are already present. In other words, this passage merely referred to what has now become detrimental reliance for the purposes of the first category in *Rosset* (see 8.5.2), and Lord Diplock did not intend this reasoning to be used to create a trust in the first place.

The Court of Appeal restated the conventional view in *Burns* v *Burns* [1984] Ch 317, the facts and result of which were similar to *Gissing*, except that though the parties had lived together as husband and wife for many years, they were unmarried. The plaintiff, Valerie Burns, had been living with the defendant for 19 years, 17 in the house which was the subject of the dispute. She and the defendant, Patrick Burns, had never married. The house had been purchased in the name of the defendant, and he paid the purchase price. The plaintiff made no contribution to the purchase price or the mortgage repayments, but had brought up their two children, performed domestic duties and recently contributed from her own earnings towards household expenses. She also bought various fittings and a washing machine, and redecorated the interior of the house. The plaintiff left the defendant and claimed a beneficial interest in the house.

Since the couple had never married the provisions of the Matrimonial Causes Act 1973, ss. 24–25 (see 8.10) did not apply, and the Court of Appeal held that the plaintiff's case rested on orthodox property principles. In the absence of a financial contribution which could be related to the acquisition of the property, for example to the mortgage repayments, or a contribution enabling Patrick Burns to pay the mortgage instalments, Valerie Burns was not entitled to a beneficial interest in the house. *Burns* v *Burns* was upheld by the House of Lords in *Winkworth* v *Edward Baron Development Co. Ltd* [1988] 1 WLR 1512. The House refused to infer that Mrs Wing had an equitable interest in the matrimonial home, which was owned by a company of which she and her husband were sole directors, where she had used the proceeds from her share of her former matrimonial home to pay off the company overdraft, because the payment was not referable to the acquisition of the house in Hayes Lane.

Lastly, there is *Lloyds Bank plc* v *Rosset* [1991] 1 AC 107 itself. Mr and Mrs Rosset decided to purchase a semi-derelict farmhouse for £57,000. Mrs Rosset understood that the entire purchase money was to come out of a family trust fund, the trustees of which insisted that the house be purchased in the husband's sole name (this appears to have been the only reason for the legal title being vested in Mr Rosset alone). The house required renovation, and it was intended that this should be a joint venture. The vendors allowed Mr and Mrs Rosset to enter the property a number of weeks before completion in order to begin repairs and render the house habitable.

During this period Mrs Rosset spent a lot of time at the house, urging on the builders and attempting to co-ordinate their work (until her husband insisted that he alone should give instructions), going to builders' merchants to obtain material required by the builders, delivering the materials to the site, assisting her husband in planning the renovation and decoration of the house (she was a skilled painter and decorator), wallpapering two bedrooms, arranging the insurance of the house, arranging a crime prevention survey, and assisting in arranging the installation of burglar alarms.

Unbeknown to Mrs Rosset, Mr Rosset was unable to fund the purchase and repairs entirely from the trust fund, and obtained an overdraft of £18,000 from Lloyds Bank, executing a legal charge on the property in their favour on the same day as completion. He later defaulted on the repayments and the bank sought possession. Mrs Rosset claimed a beneficial interest in the property, binding the bank by virtue of her actual occupation as an overriding interest under the Land Registration Act 1925, s. 70(1)(g) (on which see further, 10.3).

In the Court of Appeal in *Rosset*, most of the discussion revolved around whether Mrs Rosset was in actual occupation when the charge was created, in order to be able to rely upon s. 70(1)(g). The House of Lords were able to avoid all discussion of s. 70(1)(g), simply holding that Mrs Rosset had no beneficial interest. There was no evidence of any agreement between the parties to share the beneficial interest, and the wife's contributions were regarded as *de minimis*. The principles discussed in this section were applied.

The cases suggest, then, that for a beneficial interest to be acquired in this type of case, the contributions must be referable to the *initial* acquisition of the property. There is no such requirement under the first category in *Rosset*, where there is independent evidence of the intentions of the parties.

The resulting trust reasoning explained above (8.4.1) also suggests that for the second category, the extent of Miss B's interest depends solely on her contributions (but see further below, 8.7.1).

8.5   *ROSSET* FIRST CATEGORY

8.5.1   Trust or estoppel
By contrast with the second category in *Lloyds Bank* v *Rosset*, where the intention of the parties is inferred from the contributions themselves, under the first category there *is* independent evidence of intention.

Lord Bridge does not make clear, however, whether the analysis should be in terms of constructive trust or proprietary estoppel, or even whether the concepts are intended to be the same or distinct. Professor Hayton, for example, argues that Lord Bridge is equating these concepts ([1990] Conv 370, at p. 376), a view apparently shared by Morritt LJ in *Lloyds Bank plc* v *Carrick*, CA, 28 February 1996 (see 1.6.2), and Lord Oliver of Aylmerton in *Austin* v *Keele* (1987) 61 AJLR 605, at p. 609. However, this is by no means clear from the judgment itself (see P. Ferguson, (1993) 109 LQR 114, at p. 118), and even Morritt LJ in *Lloyds Bank plc* v *Carrick* seemed prepared to accept that estoppel might raise different issues, and actually dealt with estoppel separately, when considering (and rejecting) the *Rosset* argument advanced by Mrs Carrick, on the ground that her estate contract (see 1.6.2) precluded the co-existence of a *Rosset* interest.

Unfortunately, an investigation of the cases cited by Lord Bridge throws little more light on the issue, and both estoppel and constructive reasoning can be found, for example, in *Grant* v *Edwards* [1986] Ch 638 (see 8.5.2). The courts have tended to prefer trusts to estoppel reasoning, as in *Ungurian* v *Lesnoff* [1990] 1 Ch 206 (see 8.5.2 and 8.8), decided a few months prior to *Lloyds Bank plc* v *Rosset*, and *Stokes* v *Anderson* [1991] 1 FLR 391 see 8.7.2). However, Professor Hayton argues for a pure estoppel approach to the first category, and estoppel reasoning was adopted in *Baker* v *Baker* [1993] 25 HLR 408. The reality, I would suggest, is that some cases within the first category are properly categorised as trust cases, while for others estoppel is a more appropriate classification. Facts which give rise to an estoppel will not necessarily suffice for a trust, and the consequences of trusts and estoppel reasoning are different (see also 8.8).

8.5.2 Constructive trust requirements

The trust requirements were analysed by Lord Diplock in *Gissing* v *Gissing* [1971] AC 886, at pp. 904H–905D, in terms of a declaration of trust by Mr A for Miss B. The declaration would (if oral) be void for want of writing, which is required by s. 53(1)(b) of the Law of Property Act 1925, unless it were acted upon by her so as to render it inequitable to allow him to deny the trust. It would then take effect as a constructive trust, to which, by virtue of s. 53(2), s. 53(1)(b) has no application. The explanation in *Lloyds Bank plc* v *Rosset*, at p. 129C, is similar: see also *Re Densham* [1975] 1 WLR 1519. As was observed in 8.1, it follows that there is no need for detrimental reliance by Miss B if either s. 53(1)(b) is satisfied, or the property is not land (on which see further 8.9).

The important point about this analysis is that the constructive trust does not have any independent existence, in that it assumes that all the incidents of an express trust are also present. If the trust is in writing then you do not even need detrimental reliance, and if not then the only function of detrimental reliance is to invoke s. 53(2), and hence avoid the formality requirements. It is similar to the analysis at 10.3, and also in chapter 9, where again all the elements of an express trust (apart from writing) are present, and the constructive trust is imposed as a device to avoid a formality requirement. Lord Denning MR's view in *Eves* v *Eves* [1975] 1 WLR 1338 (see 8.4.3 and 8.5.2), that the constructive trust might exist on its own, is inconsistent with *Gissing* v *Gissing*, and has received no support from later authorities.

A consequence of all the incidents of an express trust being present is that Miss B's interest ought to be capable of binding a third party, such as a purchaser or mortgagee (see, e.g., 1.4.6 and 1.6.2). A second consequence is that the quantification of Miss B's interest ought to depend on the discussions alone, and not on the extent of her detrimental reliance, since the function of the detrimental reliance is simply to avoid the formality provisions of the Law of Property Act 1925. Quantification is discussed separately below, however (8.7.2), since there is recent authority suggesting that a broad brush can be taken to quantification (though not to acquisition, which remains governed by the rigid principles discussed here).

The leading cases cited by Lord Bridge as examples of this category were the Court of Appeal decisions in *Grant* v *Edwards* [1986] Ch 638 and *Eves* v *Eves* [1975] 1 WLR 1338. In *Grant* v *Edwards*, a house was purchased in 1969 for the plaintiff, Mrs Linda Grant, and the defendant, George Edwards, to live in as if married (although Linda Grant was actually married to someone else). The house was purchased in the name of Edwards and his brother. Edwards told Grant that her name would not go on the title for the time being because it would cause prejudice in the matrimonial proceedings pending between Mrs Grant and her husband. In reality, Edwards had no intention of conveying any legal title to the plaintiff.

The defendant paid the deposit on the house and most, but not all, of the repayments on the two mortgages. He paid the deposit and all the mortgage instalments on the first mortgage, but Mrs Grant paid some instalments under a second mortgage. The plaintiff also made substantial contributions towards general household expenses, provided housekeeping and brought up the children. In 1980 the couple separated, and the plaintiff claimed a beneficial interest in the property.

The Court of Appeal held that Edwards's statement that Mrs Grant's name would have appeared on the title except that it could cause prejudice in the matrimonial proceedings was evidence of a common intention that Mrs Grant should have a beneficial interest (a half share) in the property. Mrs Grant had relied to her detriment on the common intention, so that she was entitled to a half share on a resulting or constructive trust.

It must be observed that Linda Grant's contributions were not particularly significant, and would certainly not have justified a half share, or probably any share, on the principles discussed in the previous section. The crucial element in the case was the statement by the defendant as to why the plaintiff's name would not go on the title. The Court of Appeal took the view that this statement could be explained only on the basis of a common intention that she was to have a half share. At first sight this seems rather a surprising conclusion, since Edwards clearly intended no such thing, but the representation was interpreted (in effect) as meaning: 'Your name would go on the title but for the fact that it would prejudice your matrimonial proceedings'. Had Edwards intended to say 'The house is to be mine alone', there would have been no need for an excuse. By this somewhat tortuous reasoning, therefore, the Court was able to infer, independently of her contributions, a common intention that Mrs Grant was to have a half share, and the case depended on this.

Because there was evidence of a common intention (independent of the contributions themselves), Linda Grant's contributions (unlike those of Valerie Burns), were relevant only in order to get round the formality provisions of s. 53 of the Law of Property Act 1925. It was only necessary for Grant to show that she had relied on the agreement to her detriment, by acting in a manner which was explicable only on the basis that she was to have an interest in the house, for a constructive trust to arise in her favour.

This is a far less stringent requirement than that adopted in *Burns* or *Rosset*, where there was no outside evidence of any agreement so that evidence of intention could be inferred only from the contributions themselves. Furthermore, the value of the beneficial interest was determined by the common intention (as evidenced by the defendant's statement) and not by the value of Linda Grant's contributions.

Mention has already been made (in the previous section) of *Eves* v *Eves* [1975] 1 WLR 1338. In that case, Lord Denning MR reasoned that equity was still capable of developing, and that the courts had a discretion to depart from strictly property-based criteria in order to achieve what they saw as 'justice'. It is now clear that the case cannot be explained on that basis, but while in *Grant* v *Edwards* Lord Denning MR's reasoning in *Eves* v *Eves* was expressly rejected, the decision itself was upheld, and in *Lloyds Bank* v *Rosset* the case was explained as one of this type.

Janet Eves, who was under 21 and separated from her husband, went to live with a man whose marriage had also broken down. They had a child together and shortly afterwards found a house with the intention that they would live there together. The man told her that if she had been 21 he would have arranged for the house to be conveyed into their joint names, but in reality this was simply an excuse for having the house conveyed into his name alone. The house was in a dilapidated state and Janet did a great deal of heavy building work improving it, including wielding a 14-lb sledge-hammer to break up the concrete in the front garden so that it could be levelled and turfed. When the relationship broke down, Janet Eves was held to be entitled to a quarter-share. As in *Grant* v *Edwards*, the case depended upon the representation made by the man: there would have been no need for him to make an excuse had he intended to say: 'The house is to be mine alone'. As Brightman J explained (at p. 1345):

> The defendant clearly led the plaintiff to believe that she was to have some undefined interest in the property, and that her name was only omitted from the conveyance because of her age.

Grant v *Edwards* and *Eves* v *Eves* were explained by Lord Bridge in *Rosset*, who also made clear what inference was to be drawn from the representations and what was the importance of the subsequent conduct of the female partner:

> Outstanding examples on the other hand of cases giving rise to situations in the first category are *Eves* v *Eves* [1975] 1 WLR 1338 and *Grant* v *Edwards* [1986] Ch 638. In both these cases, where the parties who had cohabited were unmarried, the female partner had been clearly led by the male partner to believe, when they set up home together, that the property would belong to them jointly. In *Eves* v *Eves* the male partner had told the female partner that the only reason why the property was to be acquired in his name alone was because she was under 21 and that, but for her age, he would have had the house put into their joint names. He admitted in evidence that this was simply an 'excuse'. Similarly, in *Grant* v *Edwards* the female partner was told by the male partner that the only reason for not

acquiring the property in joint names was because she was involved in
divorce proceedings and that, if the property were acquired jointly, this
might operate to her prejudice in those proceedings. As Nourse LJ put it
(at p. 649):

> Just as in *Eves* v *Eves*, these facts appear to me to raise a clear inference
> that there was an understanding between the plaintiff and the defend-
> ant, or a common intention, that the plaintiff was to have some sort of
> proprietary interest in the house otherwise no excuse for not putting
> her name onto the title would have been needed.

The subsequent conduct of the female partner in each of these cases,
which the court rightly held sufficient to give rise to a constructive trust
or proprietary estoppel supporting her claim to an interest in the
property, fell far short of such conduct as would by itself have supported
the claim in the absence of an express representation by the male
partner that she was to have such an interest. It is significant to note that
the share to which the female partners in *Eves* v *Eves* and *Grant* v
Edwards were held entitled were one-quarter and one-half respectively.
In no sense could these shares have been regarded as proportionate to
what the judge in the instant case described as a 'qualifying contribution' in terms of the indirect contributions to the acquisition or
enhancement of the value of the houses made by the female partners.

In *Grant* v *Edwards*, Nourse LJ (at p. 647) drew the following distinction,
which essentially summarises the above discussion, between the relevance of
the woman's conduct in *Grant* v *Edwards* itself, and its relevance in a case like
Burns v *Burns*:

> In most of these cases the fundamental, and invariably the most difficult,
> question is to decide whether there was the necessary common intention,
> being something which can only be inferred from the conduct of the
> parties, almost always from the expenditure incurred by them respectively.
> In this regard the court has to look for expenditure which is referable to the
> acquisition of the house (see . . . *Burns* v *Burns* [1984] Ch 317). If it is
> found to have been incurred, such expenditure will perform the two-fold
> function of establishing the common intention and showing that the
> claimant has acted upon it.
>
> There is another and rarer class of case, of which the present may be one,
> where, although there has been no writing, the parties have orally declared
> themselves in such a way as to make their common intention plain. Here
> the court does not have to look for conduct from which the intention can
> be inferred, but only for conduct which amounts to an acting upon it by
> the claimant. And although that conduct can undoubtedly be the incurring
> of expenditure which is referable to the acquisition of the house, it need
> not necessarily be so.

Elaborating on the question of what conduct would suffice, he referred to
Eves v *Eves* and said (at p. 648):

So what sort of conduct is required? In my judgment it must be conduct on which the woman could not reasonably have been expected to embark unless she was to have an interest in the house. If she was not to have such an interest, she could reasonably be expected to go and live with her lover, but not, for example, to wield a 14 lb sledge-hammer in the front garden. In adopting the latter kind of conduct she is seen to act to her detriment on the faith of the common intention.

The requirement for this type of case is detrimental reliance, therefore. In *Burns* v *Burns*, by contrast, the court had to look for expenditure which was referable to the acquisition of the house. It is obvious that it is far easier to satisfy the requirement in *Grant* v *Edwards* than it is to satisfy the requirement in *Burns* v *Burns*.

These cases have been criticised on the grounds that the agreement is entirely fictitious, because in each case the man clearly did not intend the woman to have any interest in the property. Thus, Simon Gardner writes ((1993) 109 LQR 263, at p. 265):

But the fact that the men's statements were excuses (i.e., neither objectively valid nor even sincerely uttered) does not mean that the men were thereby acknowledging an agreement whereby the woman should have a share. If I give an excuse for rejecting an invitation to what I expect to be a dull party, it does not mean that I thereby agree to come: on the contrary, it means that I do not agree to come, but for one reason or another find it hard to say so outright. The fallacious quality of the reasoning in *Eves* v *Eves* and *Grant* v *Edwards* is thus clear. It is hard to think that the judges concerned really believed in it. . . .

He contrasts these cases with *Hammond* v *Mitchell* [1991] 1 WLR 1127 (below), where it appears that Hammond really did intend Vicky Mitchell to have a share (Vicky Mitchell obtained a half share on the basis of statements that had been made to her by Hammond, which are set out below).

Gardner's objection is clearly valid if a subjective view is taken of intention, but the cases, considered in chapter 3, on declaration of trusteeship, suggest that intention is judged objectively. The courts appear to adopt the position of a reasonable observer. In *Richards* v *Delbridge* (1874) LR Eq 11, Sir George Jessel MR concentrates on the words used, as opposed to the actual intention, observing that 'however anxious the Court may be to carry out a man's intention, it is not at liberty to construe words otherwise than according to their proper meaning'. This suggests that the actual intention is irrelevant. In *Re Kayford* [1975] 1 WLR 279, Megarry J, at p. 282A, also talks in terms of an intention being manifested, rather than merely held.

For these reasons, Nicola Glover and I (Glover and Todd, [1995] 5 Web JCLI) felt that Gardner's objection was misplaced. To take *Grant* v *Edwards* as the example, what George Edwards was saying, in effect, was that although legal title must be vested in himself alone, this was for purely formal reasons (so as not to cause prejudice in the matrimonial proceedings pending between Linda Grant and her husband), and the reality was that the property (i.e., equitable title) was to belong to both of them. Once it is accepted that the test is objective, and does not depend on what George Edwards actually thought, it is difficult to imagine a clearer declaration of trusteeship than that.

There are, however, other constraints on the constructive trust analysis. A trust operates as an immediate and irrevocable commitment, so that statements as to future intention will not suffice. The cases in chapter 3 show that before a trust can be inferred, Mr A must evince an intention to deal with the property in such a way as to deprive himself of his beneficial ownership, and to declare that he will hold it from that time forward on trust for Miss B. Another limitation of some importance is that the property must be identified as existing property: *Re Ellenborough* [1903] 1 Ch 697. A trust analysis should not work, therefore, where the property has not been identified (i.e., where the statement concerns a house to be purchased at some future time). On this basis, there are difficulties with *Ungurian* v *Lessnoff* [1990] 1 Ch 206, which is surely wrongly categorised as a constructive trust case.

Mrs Lesnoff, who was a Polish academic, gave up a flat in Poland of which she could have remained in occupation for life, her Polish nationality and her career, in order to live with Mr Ungurian. Ungurian bought a house in London, registered in his sole name, in which he and Mrs Lesnoff lived as man and wife for four years. During that time Mrs Lesnoff installed or supervised the installation of central heating, and the re-wiring and re-plumbing of the house, in addition to other works of improvement and redecoration (had this been a second category case, she would probably have failed to get an interest). Mrs Lesnoff remained in occupation; and when Ungurian brought an action for possession and the case finally came to court many years later, Vinelott J held that Mrs Lesnoff had an interest, but clearly did not want to give her the fee simple. Perhaps for this reason, he did not think that Mr Ungurian's words when handing over a cheque for the balance of the purchase price ('This is your house; you had better sign it') constituted a declaration of trusteeship (at pp. 214F and 220F). If they had done, and it is not at all clear why they did not, Vinelott J would have had no option but to grant Mrs Lesnoff the fee simple. Instead, he relied on obscure recollections of conversations which had occurred over 20 years before the case was heard, in Beirut. I would suggest, however, that unlike the statement made when the cheque was handed over, the conversations relied on ('We will have to look for and buy a house for us in London so that you will feel secure and happy, having lost your house in Poland', and 'You'll have to decide and find the house which you like. I want you to feel that you have something to rely on if anything happens to me') cannot, in principle, amount to a declaration of trust, both because there was no trust property at the time they were made, and because they were statements of future intention, not therefore amounting to a present irrevocable commitment.

Ungurian v *Lesnoff* is also notable in showing how substantial property interests can depend on obscure recollections. Coming as she did within the first category, Mrs Lesnoff obtained a life interest (see further 8.8), whereas without the Beirut conversations she would have come within the second category and obtained little or nothing.

By contrast with *Ungurian* v *Lesnoff*, both types of statement were present in *Hammond* v *Mitchell* [1991] 1 WLR 1127, noted [1992] Conv 218. On its own, Hammond's promise (at p. 1131E):

> Don't worry about the future because when we are married it will be half yours anyway and I'll always look after you and [the boy]

is a statement of future intent which ought not to lead to the inference of a trust. However, Hammond also said (at p. 1131D):

> I'll have to put the house in my name because I have tax problems due to the fact that my wife burnt all my account books and my caravan was burnt down with all the records of my car sales in it. The tax man would be interested, and if I could prove my money had gone back into a property I'd be safeguarded.

This is similar to the statements in *Eves* v *Eves* [1975] 1 WLR 1338 and *Grant* v *Edwards* [1986] Ch 638, considered above, where a trust analysis is entirely appropriate. In both cases the property was identified, and in *Eves* v *Eves* the statement appears to have been made at the time of purchase, so that the declaration of trust is of existing property. The statement may have been made earlier in *Grant* v *Edwards*, but there is no problem in construing the defendant's intention as continuing until title was conveyed to him, at which point it became irrevocable. This would also therefore be a declaration of trusteeship of existing property.

8.5.3 Estoppel requirements

For the above discussion it will be seen that a trusts analysis will not always be appropriate, but this will not necessarily preclude the alternative of an estoppel. Estoppels differ from constructive trusts in a number of significant respects. Whereas a trust is based on an irrevocable commitment, estoppel is based on the notion of A misleading B, and A is prevented from going back on his or her assurances only to the extent necessary to do justice to B. The commonly-accepted formula for proprietary estoppel, adopted by Oliver J in *Taylors Fashions Ltd* v *Liverpool Victoria Trustees Co. Ltd* [1982] QB 133, at pp. 151H–152A, requires only that 'it would be unconscionable for a party to be permitted to deny that which, knowingly or unknowingly, he has allowed or encouraged another to assume to his detriment', and in *Moorgate Mercantile Co. Ltd* v *Twitchings* [1975] QB 225 Lord Denning MR took the view (at p. 241) that encouragement can be by words or conduct (see also 8.6.2). This is less stringent than the requirements for a declaration of trusteeship. A statement as to future intent will suffice, even where the property is not as yet identified (*Re Basham* [1986] 1 WLR 1498, at pp. 1508-1509).

The quantification of B's interest is considered in greater detail below (8.7.2), but it will not always be the same for estoppels as for constructive trusts. The main difference between the two, however, is in the extent to which they can affect third parties. This is especially a problem where a mortgagee is involved, since as Ferguson states (at p. 122), 'the consensus of opinion favours' the view that estoppels do not bind third parties, at any rate until the extent of the interest has been crystallised by a court. The consensus is by no means unchallenged, and Morritt LJ took a different view in *Lloyds Bank plc* v *Carrick*, CA, 28 February 1996 (see 1.6.2 and 8.5.1), but Nicola Glover and I have argued it in greater detail elsewhere: Glover and Todd, [1995] 5 Web JCLI.

8.6 FURTHER CONSIDERATION OF *LLOYDS BANK* v *ROSSET*

8.6.1 Exact scope of second category

We have already seen (8.4.3) that certain types of contribution are incapable of giving rise to the inference necessary to create a trust. It is also clear that direct contributions to the purchase price will give rise to the necessary inference. There are, however, grey areas, such as indirect financial contributions and improvements to the property.

In the passage from *Lloyds Bank* v *Rosset* already quoted, Lord Bridge observes that:

> . . . direct contributions to the purchase price by the partner who is not the legal owner, whether initially or by payment of mortgage instalments, will readily justify the inference necessary to the creation of a constructive trust. But, as I read the authorities, it is at least extremely doubtful whether anything less will do.

This passage, which is not part of the *ratio* of the case, may appear at first sight clearly to state what is, and what is not, within the second category; but not only does Lord Bridge not analyse the authorities to which he refers, but he is not absolutely ruling out a lesser contribution. Other authorities (and in particular statements by Fox and May LJJ in *Burns* v *Burns* [1984] Ch 317 suggest that indirect financial contributions, referable to the acquisition of the property will also suffice. The following passage is taken from Fox LJ's judgment in *Burns* v *Burns*, at p. 327:

> What is needed, I think, is evidence of a payment or payments by the plaintiff which it can be inferred was referable to the acquisition of the house. . . . If there is a substantial contribution by the woman to the family expenses, and the house was purchased on a mortgage, her contribution is, indirectly, referable to the acquisition of the house since, in one way or another, it enables the family to pay the mortgage instalments. Thus, a payment could be said to be referable to the acquisition of the house if, for example, the payer either (a) pays part of the purchase price or (b) contributes regularly to the mortgage instalments or (c) pays off part of the mortgage or (d) makes a substantial financial contribution to the family expenses so as to enable the mortgage instalments to be paid.

This is obviously wider than Lord Bridge's view, in that Lord Bridge would not recognise category (d) as justifying the inference necessary for the creation of a trust. Lord Bridge does not however make clear whether his intention is to alter the law or merely to re-state it, a point made by Patricia Ferguson (1993) 109 LQR 114, at p. 116:

> [Lord Bridge's] requirement of 'direct contributions' where there is no express agreement runs contrary to previous authorities which held that indirect financial contributions which were 'referable to the acquisition of the house' — such as F's payment of all household expenses to free M's income for mortgage instalments — were sufficient. It is difficult to know . . . whether he intends to depart from this view of the law or not.

Another area on which *Lloyds Bank* v *Rosset* is inconclusive (indeed silent) is that of improvements by Miss B to Mr A's property.

Where authorities conflict (as in the case of Fox LJ's category (d)), or are silent (as in the case of improvements), it is necessary to examine the juristic basis of the category and deduce from that what should be included and what should not.

It is clear from 8.4.1 that where Miss B provides cash contributions to the purchase price, the interest that she obtains can be explained in resulting trust terms. It does not matter where the money comes from, so that if, for example, she obtains the money by accepting liability to repay a mortgage debt, the entire capital liability can be explained in resulting trust terms. It is not possible, however, to explain the whole of the second category in this way. It is also noteworthy that Lord Bridge's analysis in the above passage is in constructive, rather than resulting, trust terms.

Thus, even on Lord Bridge's view, payment of mortgage instalments (and not merely undertaking liability to repay the mortgage) counts, but there are serious difficulties in the way of analysing these in resulting trust terms. Where Miss B pays the instalment to Mr A, for example, Miss B might be presumed to retain beneficial title to the money, which will be converted into an interest in the property as each mortgage instalment is made by A. This would result in the undesirable situation where the extent of B's interest alters every month, but in any event, the explanation works only where B pays the instalment to A, who then pays it to the mortgagee. If both parties pay the instalments directly to the mortgagee, then it is impossible to devise a resulting trust mechanism.

There is also Court of Appeal authority, which nobody has seriously doubted, that Miss B can obtain an interest even if her contribution is in the form of a discount from the purchase price, rather than an actual cash payment. In *Springette* v *Defoe* [1992] 2 FCR 561, the Court of Appeal took into account in assessing the size of her share Springette's 41 per cent discount, attributable to her council tenancy under a 'right to buy' scheme. Although the Court purported to adopt a resulting trust analysis, it is difficult to see how Springette settled anything (a requirement for the analysis in 8.4.1). In *Springette* v *Defoe*, her discount arose from a legal chose in action enforceable against the council, and it might be possible to argue that she had transferred the bare legal title to the chose in action; but even this could not explain *Marsh* v *Von Sternberg* [1986] 1 FLR 526, where the discount depended on increased bargaining power as a statutory tenant under the Rent Act 1974, and did not arise from a cause of action at all. It follows that resulting trust reasoning cannot explain the discount cases.

An alternative analysis is that of Staughton LJ in *Evans* v *Hayward* [1995] 2 FCR 313, at p. 319D:

> . . . I do consider that the facts as to the existence of a discount and the source from which it is derived must be taken into account, and are capable of leading to the inference that the parties have made an agreement as to how the purchase price is provided.

In other words, the discount leads to the inference that the parties have made an agreement that they are to be treated as having provided the purchase price in proportions which take into account the discount. Conceptually, this is far closer to the analysis we have already seen, in the first category, than it is to the resulting trust.

Once it is accepted that the true explanation of the discount cases is in terms of an inferred agreement, and does not depend on a resulting trust, then we can see that similar reasoning can also apply to the non-financial contributions mentioned in *Burns*. In principle, therefore, it may seem that there is no particular reason to prefer Lord Bridge's views to those of Fox LJ. However, the requirements of the second category are that B's interest can be inferred from the contributions alone, in the absence of other evidence of an agreement to share. Whereas in the discount and mortgage repayment cases this inference can be made automatically, nothing in *Burns* v *Burns* suggests that any automatic inference should be drawn from indirect contributions. They could lead to many different types of inference, depending on the other evidence available. In terms of the categorisation in *Lloyds Bank* v *Rosset*, therefore, indirect financial contributions are not correctly placed in the second category, since the court cannot rely entirely on the conduct of the parties to infer A's intention. Nor do these contributions fit happily into the first category, since there may be no evidence of express discussions between the parties.

If Lord Bridge's categories are exhaustive, therefore, indirect financial contributions cannot create an interest outside the first category. In principle, however, surely such contributions should nevertheless be capable of being taken into account in inferring A's intention; to refuse to do so is to place artificial constraints on the evidence that will be accepted.

The same arguments can be used in the case of capital improvements. It is difficult to see why they should be ruled out, but it is clear that no automatic inference can be drawn, since all sorts of inferences can be reached in the absence of further evidence. Clearly, if Miss B improves Mr A's property without his permission, B should not obtain an interest in that property (*Ramsden* v *Dyson* (1866) LR 1 HL 129). Even if A gives permission, or acquiesces, a possible inference is that B makes a gift of the work. This was the view taken by the House of Lords in *Pettitt* v *Pettitt* [1970] AC 777 (see 8.4.1), where the husband as improver failed to obtain an interest in his wife's property. A stronger case is *Thomas* v *Fuller-Brown* [1988] 1 FLR 237, where the Court of Appeal held that a man had no interest in the house in which he lived with a woman (who had legal title), although in the view of Slade LJ (at p. 240):

> [The work he did] was obviously quite substantial . . . *inter alia*, he designed and constructed a two-storey extension, created a through lounge, carried out minor electrical and plumbing works, replastered and re-decorated the property throughout, landscaped and reorganised the gar-den, laid a driveway, carried out repairs to the chimney and the roof and repointed the gable end of the property, constructed an internal entry hall at the property, rebuilt the kitchen and installed a new stairway.

Again, however, the inference must have been that he intended to make a gift of his work.

It does not necessarily follow that this will always be the inference, however. Another possibility is an implied contract for reimbursement of the value of the work done, a solution which was apparently adopted by the Court of Appeal in *Huntingford* v *Hobbs* [1993] 1 FCR 45 (see 8.4.1) in respect of the money spent on the conservatory. Another possibility would be to give Miss B an estoppel interest, as was envisaged by Lord Oliver of Aylmerton in *Austin* v *Keele* (1987) 61 AJLR 605, at p. 609. He also drew another distinction, between capital improvements and the other types of contribution, which clearly fall within the second category, observing that there is no reason why the interest should be acquired at the time of acquisition of the property.

There is indeed no reason in principle why a full beneficial interest might not be inferred, either from the time of acquisition or from a later date, an approach contemplated by Lord Reid in *Pettitt* v *Pettitt* [1970] AC 777, at pp. 794–795. Although as we have seen (at 8.4.2), he rejected Pettitt's claim to a beneficial interest, this was solely on the ground that his improvements were of an ephemeral character and that it would be unreasonable for him to obtain a permanent interest in the house in return for making improvements of this nature: at p. 796E. Other views expressed in *Pettitt* are more equivocal, particularly that of Lord Upjohn (whose views were expressly adopted by the Court of Appeal in *Thomas* v *Fuller-Brown*). However, an inference that improvements to the property could give rise to a beneficial interest was actually adopted by Karminski LJ in *Cooke* v *Head* [1972] 1 WLR 518, where Miss Cooke, who had contributed only about one-twelfth of the purchase price, was nevertheless granted a third share, one of the factors in assessing Miss Cooke's share (from acquisition) being the value of her labour, and by the majority of the Court of Appeal in *Hussey* v *Palmer* [1972] 1 WLR 1286 where the inference here must have been a declaration of trust by Mr A post-acquisition. It cannot be said, therefore, that improvements to property can never give rise to the inference of a trust.

However, it follows from so many different approaches being possible that although the work may provide relevant evidence of intention, it cannot be conclusive, and that which approach is adopted is going to depend on all the facts of the case. As with indirect contributions, to rule out entirely this type of contribution would seem to be an unnecessary and artificial limitation.

8.6.2   Communication requirements — first category

For the first category, Lord Bridge stated that 'The finding of an agreement or arrangement to share in this sense can only, I think, be based on evidence of express discussions between the partners, however imperfectly remembered and however imprecise their terms may have been'. A similar view was adopted by the Court of Appeal in *Springette* v *Defoe* (1992) 24 HLR 552, [1992] 2 FCR 561 (see further above, 8.6.1), Miss Springette and Mr Defoe purchased a house, Miss Springette being able to obtain a 41 per cent discount under a 'right to buy' scheme under Part V of the Housing Act 1985, the discount being based on her 11 years as a tenant. The property was conveyed into joint names, there being no declaration of trust in the transfer, and both were liable to repay the mortgage instalments, and in fact both contributed equally to the repayments. Both Springette and Defoe also provided other moneys, the result being that, taking into account her 41 per cent discount (see 8.6.1), Miss Springette's financial contributions were about 75 per cent, and Mr Defoe's 25 per cent.

The relationship broke down and proceedings were commenced to determine the respective beneficial interests of the parties. Miss Springette claimed a 75 per cent share on the basis of her financial contributions, whereas Mr Defoe claimed 50 per cent on the basis that the couple understood that they were to share the property equally. Mr Defoe claimed that the case should be decided on the basis of the first category in *Lloyds Bank plc* v *Rosset*.

The Court of Appeal held in Miss Springette's favour, applying Lord Bridge's remarks in *Rosset* that the finding of such an agreement, arrangement or understanding could only be based on evidence of express discussions between the partners. Steyn LJ observed ((1992) 24 HLR 552, at p. 558), that '[o]ur trust law does not allow property rights to be affected by telepathy. Prima facie, therefore, the alleged actual common intention was not established'.

Springette v *Defoe* was distinguished in *Savill* v *Goodall* [1993] 1 FLR 755. Mrs Goodall was entitled to a 42 per cent discount under a 'right to buy' scheme, the entirety of the remainder of the purchase money being raised on a mortgage for which Mr Savill accepted liability to repay. As in *Springette* v *Defoe*, the property was transferred into the joint names of the parties. The Court of Appeal held, on the basis of express discussions between the parties, that the beneficial interests should be divided equally, but also accepted that Mr Savill's *quid pro quo* for being granted a beneficial interest was his agreement to repay the mortgage capital and costs of redemption. The net proceeds, after repayment of the mortgage by him, were therefore divided equally.

The only substantive difference between *Springette* v *Defoe* and *Savill* v *Goodall* was the absence of any discussion in the former and its presence in the latter case.

In *Midland Bank plc* v *Cooke* [1995] 4 All ER 562, however, Waite LJ did not regard *Springette* v *Defoe* as laying down any general principle, for the following reasons: that Dillon LJ, who had given the leading judgment in *Springette* v *Defoe*, had taken a very different approach in *McHardy & Sons* v *Warren* [1994] 2 FLR 338; that no such requirement for express discussion could be gleaned from *Gissing* v *Gissing* [1971] AC 886 or *Grant* v *Edwards* [1986] 1 Ch 638 and that the couple in *Springette* v *Defoe* were 'a middle aged couple already established in life whose house-purchasing arrangements were clearly regarded by the Court as having the same formality as if they had been the subject of a joint venture or commercial partnership'.

If Waite LJ is correct, we can no longer assume that the presence or absence of discussions will be decisive. In principle, however, it is not easy to see how a declaration of trusteeship can occur without at least some form of communication (there was none at all in *Midland Bank* v *Cooke*). In any case, in order to render it fraudulent for Mr A to deny the existence of the trust, Miss B must rely on the declaration, or significantly alter her position. Again, this necessitates communication between the parties, and is again a justification for the requirement for discussion. There are also certainty arguments for requiring communication. Waite J's decision in *Hammond* v *Mitchell* [1991] 1 WLR 1127 (see 8.5.2) shows how much can turn on A's declaration of trusteeship: Vicky Mitchell obtained a half share under the first category in *Lloyds Bank plc* v *Rosset*, having contributed nothing at all to the house itself, solely because of statements that had been made to her by Hammond. Any beneficial interest thereby created will also bind third parties. It should also be borne in mind that a declaration of trusteeship constitutes an irrevocable and onerous commitment. Prior to an act of commitment, it ought to be possible for A to change his or her mind, however much, at that time, he or she is determined to become a trustee. It is not unreasonable to require the act of commitment to be in some sense public, or at any rate to be communicated to the other party.

There is nothing in the *Springette* v *Defoe* line of cases to indicate what needs to be communicated. It follows from the above that Mr A needs to communicate something which leads Miss B to suppose that A is making an immediate and irrevocable commitment, whether or not this is A's actual intention (see the discussion of Gardner, above, 8.5.2). But in *Re Kayford* [1975] 1 WLR 279 (see 8.5.2), Megarry J required only that the intention to declare oneself trustee be manifested. While detrimental reliance requires some form of communication, it may not necessarily require words. If the evidence showed that the parties really were capable of communicating by telepathy, there is no obvious reason why the law should not allow this method of communication to be used to create beneficial interests within this category.

In *Savill* v *Goodall*, the Court of Appeal distinguished *Springette* v *Defoe* on the basis that there were discussions in the later case. The Court did not pay particular regard to the nature of the discussions, however, and it is surprising, I would suggest, that they led to the inference of a beneficial interest. The content of the discussions was tenuous, and certainly there was no substantial discussion of beneficial interests in the property. I would suggest, therefore, that there were no obvious grounds for distinguishing *Springette* v *Defoe*, and that the case was incorrectly decided.

The requirement in *Lloyds Bank* v *Rosset* (at p. 132F) was for evidence of express discussions, not express evidence of discussions. This suggests that inferred evidence of discussions ought to be sufficient, and indeed, in *Gissing* v *Gissing* Lord Diplock suggested (at p. 906A) that the parties' intentions could be inferred from their conduct, even in the absence of express words. No doubt is thereby cast on the correctness of *Springette* v *Defoe*, where there was no evidence at all of discussions.

All the above discussion is in terms of a trust analysis. The commonly-accepted formula for proprietary estoppel, adopted by Oliver J in *Taylors Fashions Ltd* v *Liverpool Victoria Trustees Co. Ltd* [1982] QB 133, at pp. 151H-152A, requires only that 'it would be unconscionable for a party to be permitted to deny that which, knowingly or unknowingly, he has allowed or encouraged another to assume to his detriment'. There is no express communication requirement in this formula, and there is authority for the proposition that encouragement can be by words or conduct: e.g., *Moorgate Mercantile Co. Ltd* v *Twitchings* [1975] QB 225, per Lord Denning MR at p. 241.

Indeed, it is universally accepted that Oliver J's formulation is intended to broaden the definition of estoppel, and there is no doubt that it still suffices to satisfy Fry J's five *probanda* from *Willmott* v *Barber* (1880) 15 ChD 96, at pp. 105–106, recently applied by Roch LJ in *Matharu* v *Matharu* (1994) 26 HLR 648, at pp. 656–657 (see 8.8). Fry J's fifth element, encouragement of B in the expenditure of money, or in other acts, can be satisfied by A merely abstaining from asserting a legal right. A can therefore be estopped, in theory, having taken no positive acts to communicate at all. So although in many cases communication will be necessary to establish an estoppel, we cannot assert that it will be necessary in every case. It will, however, remain necessary to establish reliance by Miss B to her detriment.

To conclude, then, for a trust to arise there must be communication between the parties, but the requirement for express discussion may be too stringent. Any form of communication which is fully understood by both parties ought to suffice. It should not be necessary to use express words. To allow a complete lack of communication, however, as in *Midland Bank* v *Cooke*, seems impossible to justify, especially as it was common ground that there had been no discussions between the parties. For an estoppel, it is possible, albeit exceptionally, to envisage circumstances where the communication requirement is unnecessary, but there still has to be reliance by the representee to her detriment.

8.7 QUANTIFICATION

In *Lloyds Bank plc* v *Rosset*, Lord Bridge set out the two methods where the person without legal title could acquire a beneficial interest. The remarks do not expressly address the issue of quantification. If, as I have argued, the applicable principles are those of the ordinary law of trusts, then they should be relatively easy to deduce. Nevertheless, there is recent Court of Appeal authority for the application of a broad brush approach to quantification. The broad brush approach is inconsistent with other authorities, however, and I would suggest that it is wrong.

8.7.1   *Rosset* second category
As we saw in 8.4.1, where Miss B contributes directly to the purchase price, the presumption will be that she retains the equitable interest in her contribution, and hence a share in the house which will be in proportion to her contribution. The courts calculate these contributions with a fair degree of accuracy. For example, in *Huntingford* v *Hobbs* [1993] 1 FCR 45 (see 8.4.1), the shares were calculated at 39 per cent and 61 per cent, hardly an authority for a broad brush approach. Sir Christopher Slade observed:

> In the absence of any declaration of trust, the parties' respective beneficial interests in the property fall to be determined not by reference to any broad concepts of justice, but by reference to the principles governing the creation or operation of resulting, implied or constructive trusts which by section 53(2) of the Law of Property Act 1925 are exempted from the general requirements of writing imposed by section 53(1).

Even where resulting trust reasoning is inappropriate, as in the discount cases and where Miss B contributes by repaying mortgage instalments, the contributions are the only evidence for her share, and the courts again calculate shares in proportion to the contributions, as in *Springette* v *Defoe* (1992) 24 HLR 552, [1992] 2 FCR 561 (see 8.6.2).

However, in *Midland Bank plc* v *Cooke* [1995] 4 All ER 562, Mrs Cooke was granted a half share in the property, although she had contributed only 6.47 per cent of the purchase price, and there were no discussions about beneficial interests. The case appears to be authority for a broad brush approach to quantification, once the existence of the beneficial interest has been established. As we saw in 8.6.2, *Springette* v *Defoe* was distinguished in *Midland Bank* v *Cooke*, but it is impossible to reconcile *Midland Bank* v *Cooke* with *Huntingford* v *Hobbs*. If this area is governed by the general law of trusts, then *Midland Bank* v *Cooke* is impossible to justify. Mrs Cooke's interest under a resulting trust was only 6.47 per cent, and there was no evidence of any transfer to her, or declaration of trust in her favour, regarding the other 43.53 per cent.

An inevitable consequence of *Midland Bank* v *Cooke* is that beneficial interests will be difficult to determine with any reasonable degree of certainty, a most unsatisfactory consequence bearing in mind that Mrs Cooke's interest took priority to that of a third party. Since it is not possible to reconcile all the cases, I would suggest that *Midland Bank* v *Cooke* is wrong, and that if the issue goes to the House of Lords, it will be overruled.

8.7.2   *Rosset* first category
By contrast with the second category, where a trusts analysis is appropriate in a first category case, then quantification should be determined from the

declaration of trust, or in other words from the discussions or representation. Miss B's contributions are relevant only to s. 53(1)(b), and not to quantification of her share. This can clearly be seen in cases such as *Hammond* v *Mitchell* [1991] 1 WLR 1127; Vicky Mitchell had not really done a great deal, and had contributed nothing at all to the house, but as a result of the discussions was entitled (following *Grant* v *Edwards* [1986] Ch 638), to a half share in the home. The half share could be inferred from the declaration (Hammond stated expressly that the house would be half hers). In *Ungurian* v *Lessnoff* [1990] 1 Ch 206 (see 8.5.2), the life interest may have been justified by the statement 'We will have to look for and buy a house for us in London so that you will feel secure and happy, having lost your house in Poland', since Mrs Lesnoff had had a life interest in the house in Poland.

Thus, the quantification of Miss B's interest should depend on the declaration and not on the reliance, since the latter acts only to overcome the fraud hurdle. In *Gissing* v *Gissing*, Lord Diplock, adopting the reasoning based on s. 53(2), suggested that effect is given to the original declaration, from which it can be inferred that quantification depends on the declaration rather than the reliance.

All this assumes that B's share can be inferred from A's declaration. There are cases where, although a trust is declared, B's share is not agreed at the outset, but is to be settled at some time in the future. It may even be agreed that Miss B's share will depend on her contribution. *Stokes* v *Anderson* [1991] 1 FLR 391 seems to be a case of this type, as is (probably) *Passee* v *Passee* [1988] 1 FLR 263. In such cases B's contribution will be relevant to her share, but only because the parties have so agreed from the outset. For there to be certainty of subject matter, presumably there has to be some formula, irrevocably agreed from the outset, for calculating B's share. In *Cowcher* v *Cowcher* [1972] 1 WLR 425, Bagnall J observed, at p. 430D, that '[t]here can be no trust unless the nature and *quantum* of the several beneficial interests are certain at the inception, and during the whole life, of the trust'.

Yet another possibility is that no share can be inferred from A's declaration. In *Grant* v *Edwards* the Court of Appeal presumed a half share, but the presumption can be rebutted in appropriate circumstances. A quarter share was awarded in *Eves* v *Eves*, but it is difficult to discern why the presumption was rebutted in that case.

Thus, where a trusts analysis is appropriate, the size of Miss B's interest is not at the discretion of the courts but depends on A's declaration. In the event that A's declaration is silent as to the share, the courts presume a half share. The size of B's interest does not generally depend on the size of her contributions, which are relevant only to trigger s. 53(2), except in cases such as *Stokes* v *Anderson* and *Passee* v *Passee*.

In *Drake* v *Whipp*, *The Times*, 19 December 1995, Mrs Drake was awarded a third share, Peter Gibson LJ observing that 'in constructive trust cases, the court can adopt a broad brush approach to determining the parties' respective shares'. This appears similar to the reasoning in *Midland Bank* v *Cooke*, discussed above, and is subject to the same criticism. In *Drake* v *Whipp*, however, Whipp's intention was not clear from his declaration, and Mrs

Drake's share appears to have been determined from all the evidence, including the respective contributions of the parties. Since she had never claimed more than a 40 per cent share, it would clearly have been reasonable to rebut the half share presumption in the light of contrary evidence. The parties' entire course of conduct together was considered relevant, and maybe this can be justified on an analysis similar to that in *Stokes* v *Anderson*, above. In that case, *Drake* v *Whipp* breaks no new ground.

The trust basis of quantification may not work without modification for estoppels; the quantification of B's interest may not depend on A's representation alone, but also on the extent of B's reliance. In *Crabb* v *Arun District Council* [1976] Ch 179, Scarman LJ (at p. 198G–H) took the view that quantification should be on the basis of 'the minimum equity to do justice to the plaintiff'. A's representation is undoubtedly relevant in that B cannot get more than was contemplated by the parties: *Baker* v *Baker* (1993) 25 HLR 408. However, while B's entitlement cannot be more than would be accorded on the basis of A's representation, it can certainly be less, as in *Dodsworth* v *Dodsworth* (1973) 228 EG 1115 (see further 8.8), and in principle there seems no reason why in satisfying the equity it would be inappropriate to consider the extent of B's reliance.

8.8   PARTICULAR PROBLEMS WITH LIFE INTERESTS

In *Ungurian* v *Lesnoff* [1990] 1 Ch 206 (see 8.5.2), Vinelott J held that Mrs Lesnoff was entitled to a life tenancy. Therefore, because Ungurian's interest was subject to Mrs Lesnoff's prior life interest, there were thereby necessarily successive interests in the property, and the house therefore became settled land within the Settled Land Act 1925 (see 1.6.4). The result of this was that Mrs Lesnoff as tenant for life was entitled to call for the execution of a vesting deed and the appointment of trustees, and, once the house was vested in her, to sell it and to re-invest the proceeds in the purchase of another house or to enjoy the income therefrom. This is a consequence infinitely more far-reaching than anything envisaged in the obscurely-recollected conversation that took place in Beirut in December 1968.

It seems most unlikely that the draftsmen of the 1925 legislation intended this. It is rather an accidental consequence of legislation, which originated with the Settled Land Act 1882, whose purpose had nothing to do with the problem in *Ungurian* v *Lesnoff*; it was enacted to curtail the strict settlement, which had developed as a means of keeping landed estates within the same family, but was giving rise to difficulties in the latter part of the nineteenth century.

The detailed mechanism of the strict settlement is beyond the scope of this book (but see generally Harvey, *Settlements of Land*, Sweet & Maxwell Modern Legal Studies Series (1973)). Essentially, its purpose was, by resettling the land every generation, to ensure that the person in possession of the land was always a life tenant. A tenant in tail in possession could bar the entail, creating a saleable fee simple interest. Obviously, this would have defeated the purpose of the settlement, so it was essential to ensure that the tenant in tail never got possession.

The problem was that, in the absence of express provision in the settle-ment, the powers of the life tenant in possession were extremely limited. Not only was he (as intended) unable to sell any part of the land, but (because the length of his interest was uncertain) he was also unable to lease it, or (because of the doctrine of waste) to develop the land, for example by quarrying and tree-felling. By the latter part of the nineteenth century this was creating difficulties, stultifying land use at a time when agricultural land values were declining and when it would often have been more profitable to turn some or all of the land over to industrial use.

The cure for the problem was legislation. The Settled Land Act 1882, amended in small particulars in 1884, 1887, 1889 and 1890, gave extensive powers, including sale of the fee simple, to the tenant for life in possession, whatever the provisions of the settlement. If the land was sold, all interests in it were overreached by the purchasers (see 1.6.3 and 8.9), as long as the purchase money was paid to trustees of the settlement.

The 1925 legislation continued the policy of the earlier Acts, but also required the legal estate in fee simple to be vested in the life tenant in possession. This was necessary because of the restriction placed on possible legal estates by the Law of Property Act 1925, s. 1 (see 1.6.1). A settlement typically required a life interest followed by an entail, with ultimate remain-ders over, so that in the absence of some legislative provision nobody would have had a fee simple absolute in possession and hence a legal estate in the land.

The effect of the Settled Land Act 1925, therefore, is that a life tenant is given extensive powers, including the power to sell the land, and is entitled to call for the fee simple to be vested in him or her. Given the mischief with which the legislation was intended to deal, to give such powers to the tenant for life, and indeed the fee simple, is a rational approach. However, to return to our hypothetical problem at the start of the chapter, suppose that under the first category Miss B is granted a life interest. For Miss B to be treated as a life tenant within the Settled Land Act is to give her far more than the parties ever intended. So the question is whether the Settled Land Act can be avoided: see further Glover and Todd [1995] 5 Web JCLI.

It seems that avoidance is not possible where a trusts analysis is appropri-ate. The definition of a settlement for present purposes is contained in s. 1(1)(i) of the Settled Land Act 1925, which triggers the provisions of the Act whenever the land stands 'limited in trust for any persons by way of succession'. It can be argued that the phrase 'limited in trust' implies an active limitation by the settlor (Harvey, at p. 54), in which case a life tenancy arising under a constructive trust ought to be excluded, although there will inevitably be a succession whenever there is a life tenancy. Unfortunately, this argument appears not to be supported by the authorities.

In *Bannister* v *Bannister* [1948] 2 All ER 133 (see 10.4), the Court of Appeal held that the plaintiff held the cottage as constructive trustee of the defendant for her life. Scott LJ observed (at p. 137C) that a 'trust in this form has the effect of making the beneficiary a tenant for life within the meaning of the Settled Land Act', a conclusion which was technically *obiter* as the defendant was concerned only to resist an action for possession by the plaintiff.

A similar conclusion was reached by two members of the Court of Appeal in *Binions* v *Evans* [1972] 1 Ch 359 (see 10.4), where the defendant (Mrs Evans) was again concerned to resist a possession action by the plaintiffs (Mr and Mrs Binions). The vendors had, by an agreement in writing, granted the defendant a right to occupy a cottage rent-free for the rest of her life, and the plaintiffs had purchased the cottage expressly subject to her rights. The decision was that the plaintiffs held the house on trust for the defendant for her life, and although, as in *Bannister* v *Bannister*, the discussion was technically *obiter*, the effect of the Settled Land Act was again considered. Only Lord Denning MR (at p. 366E) took 'limited in trust' to mean 'expressly limited', which would have excluded the constructive trust from the operation of the Settled Land Act. Megaw and Stephenson LJJ, respectively at pp. 370D-G and pp. 372E-G, simply adopted Scott LJ's views from *Bannister* v *Bannister*, but it is not clear that they also rejected Lord Denning MR's views, since their own view as to how the trust arose was different (see 10.4). Whereas Lord Denning clearly reasoned by way of a constructive trust, which arose only on the sale of the land to the plaintiffs, Megaw and Stephenson LJJ thought that the settlement arose from the earlier (written) agreement between the vendors and the defendant (this point is also made by Goff LJ in *Griffiths* v *Williams* (1978) 248 EG 947, at p. 949 (col. 2)). It is arguable that the agreement indeed operated as an express limitation in trust, in which case there is no necessary inconsistency between Lord Denning MR's views on the operation of s. 1 of the Settled Land Act 1925 and those of his brethren. In *Ungurian* v *Lesnoff* [1990] 1 Ch 206, however, Vinelott J (at pp. 224D—226D) thought that there was a conflict, and preferred the views of Megaw and Stephenson LJJ to those of Lord Denning MR. It seems probable, therefore, that a life tenancy under a constructive trust is caught by the Act.

However, from the definition of settled land already considered, it follows that if there is no trust then there is no settlement within the Act. A purely personal right to occupy ought not to be caught by the Act, therefore: *Re Anderson* [1920] 1 Ch 175 (criticised by Harvey, at p. 84). It further follows that a contractual or estoppel licence allowing B the right to reside for his or her life does not invoke the Settled Land Act provisions. In *Dent* v *Dent* [1996] 1 All ER 659, David Young QC (sitting as a Deputy Judge of the High Court) held that the Act did not apply to a personal licence. In *Matharu* v *Matharu* (1994) 26 HLR 648, the Court of Appeal held that the defendant, who had successfully argued on the basis of a proprietary estoppel, had no beneficial interest, but merely a licence for life. It was not even argued that the Settled Land Act ought to apply: see also *Inwards* v *Baker* [1965] 2 QB 29.

It might therefore be thought that the solution for the courts to adopt is to use, as far as possible, estoppel rather than constructive trust reasoning; but this assumes that estoppel and trusts reasoning are interchangeable, an argument that I rejected at 8.5. In any case, where a trust is appropriate, estoppel reasoning gives Miss B too little protection, because if the argument at 8.5.3 is correct, it does not bind third parties until crystallised by the court; and whether or not the argument at 8.5.3 is correct, it would have to be crystallised as a personal right only to avoid the Act. This was done by the Court of Appeal in *Dodsworth* v *Dodsworth* (1973) 228 EG 1115, expressly to avoid an interest arising that was much greater than intended, but a purely personal right cannot give sufficient protection where the facts justify a proprietary interest.

8.9   EFFECT OF STATUTORY TRUSTS FOR SALE

Discussion so far rests on the assumption that legal title vests in A alone. In many of the cases it vests jointly in A and B. This affects the analysis, but makes no significant difference in principle.

The starting point where A and B have joint title, and where the conveyance does not state the whereabouts of the equitable title, is that A and B share equally. Also, the effect of rebutting the resulting trust presumptions will be that the parties share equally, the equitable title then following the legal. One effect of this is that for Miss B to obtain a 50 per cent share where A has paid more requires only rebuttal of the normal resulting trust presumptions. There is no need for A to declare himself trustee of any part of his share. Consequently, no reliance is required on B's part (excepting where her claim is based on estoppel) where she claims a 50 per cent share.

If Miss B is claiming a share greater than 50 per cent, then assuming that she has not paid more than 50 per cent of the purchase price, and again, apart from estoppel, A must, on the basis of the analysis at 8.5.2, declare himself trustee of part of his share. The same problem can arise in a case like *Midland Bank plc* v *Cooke* [1995] 4 All ER 562 (see 8.7.1), if the analysis is accepted that Miss B definitely has a share (having contributed something to the purchase price) but claims a greater share. The issue is whether the writing requirement of s. 53(1)(b) still applies, even assuming no reliance by B.

The argument at 8.5.2 leads to the conclusion that in each case A would have to declare himself trustee of part of his share, but now, since we know that there are concurrent interests in the land, his interest arises under a statutory trust for sale (see 1.6.3). It might be argued that the equitable doctrine of conversion (see 2.8) converts his interest into an interest in personalty, to which, of course, s. 53(1)(b) does not apply. The effect of this would again be to remove the need for detrimental reliance by Miss B.

The courts have been reluctant to take the conversion doctrine to its logical conclusion, and it seems more likely that A's interest would still be regarded as an interest in land within s. 53(1)(b). In *Williams & Glyn's Bank* v *Boland* [1979] 1 Ch 312 (in the Court of Appeal), Ormrod LJ (at pp. 333H and 336G) observed that the statutory trust for sale is a legal fiction, which should not be pressed to its logical conclusion beyond the point which is necessary to achieve its primary objective. It is one thing for equity to regard as done that which ought to be done where the parties have expressly provided for a trust for sale, but quite another where the only reason for the existence of such a trust is because Parliament has deemed that it would simplify conveyancing. Mrs Boland's interest was held capable of binding the bank, a third party, as an overriding interest under the Land Registration Act 1925 (see 1.6.2), the decision later being upheld in the House of Lords ([1981] AC 487). This looks very much like an interest in land, therefore, although s. 70(1)(g) of the Land Registration Act 1925 requires only that it be a right 'subsisting in reference to the land', wording which, as Browne LJ observed in *Boland*, is wider than the 'interest in land' under s. 53(1)(b). However, in *National Provincial Bank Ltd* v *Ainsworth* [1965] AC 1175, another s. 70(1)(g) case, the House of Lords held that only interests in land are capable of binding third parties at all, and in *Kingsnorth Trust Ltd* v *Tizard* [1986] 1 WLR 783, an interest under a statutory trust for sale bound a third party purchaser of unregistered land, and hence must have been an interest in land. The conclusion must be, therefore, that A is declaring himself trustee of an interest in land, for which either writing or detrimental reliance is required.

Apart from these possible formality consequences, the fact that the land is conveyed to A and B jointly, or that B who definitely has some interest, is claiming a greater one, makes no difference to the analysis in this chapter.

8.10 LEGISLATION AFFECTING SPOUSES

The legislature reacted to the House of Lords decisions in *Pettitt* v *Pettitt* [1970] AC 777 (see 8.4.2) and *Gissing* v *Gissing* [1971] AC 886 (see 8.4.3), by enacting legislation which allows the courts to take into account additional considerations when the parties are married.

Section 37 of the Matrimonial Proceedings and Property Act 1970, entitled 'Contributions by spouse in money or money's worth to the improvement of property', was a reaction to *Pettitt* v *Pettitt*. It allows for the beneficial interests of husbands and wives (and by virtue of s. 2(1) of the Law Reform (Miscellaneous Provisions) Act 1970, fiancées, but not those of other unmarried couples) to be varied by substantial contributions 'in money or money's worth to the improvement of real or personal property in which . . . both of them has or have a beneficial interest'.

Sections 24 and 25 of the Matrimonial Causes Act 1973 were a reaction to *Gissing* v *Gissing*. The sections allow the courts significantly to alter the property interests of married (but not unmarried) couples in the event of divorce, a decree of nullity of marriage or a decree of judicial separation. In that event, the importance of the prior property interests of the spouses is reduced, since they will no longer be conclusive. The Matrimonial Causes Act 1973 applies only on the breakdown of marriages, however, and if the question of the existence or otherwise of a beneficial interest arises during the course of the marriage (as is usually the case, for example, where a third party is involved, as in *Lloyds Bank plc* v *Rosset* itself, see 8.1.5), the issue will be determined on the basis of the ordinary principles of equity discussed in this chapter.

NINE

Secret and Half-secret Trusts

9.1 WHAT ARE SECRET AND HALF-SECRET TRUSTS?

9.1.1 Formality requirements of the Wills Act 1837, section 9 (as amended)

As with *inter vivos* transactions (see chapter 6), there are formality requirements where property is left by will. To be valid, under s. 9 of the Wills Act
1837 (as amended by s. 17 of the Administration of Justice Act 1982) wills
have to be made in writing, and properly signed and witnessed. The full text
of s. 9, as amended, is as follows:

No will shall be valid unless—

(a) it is in writing, and signed by the testator, or by some other person
in his presence and by his direction; and
(b) it appears that the testator intended by his signature to give effect
to the will; and
(c) the signature is made or acknowledged by the testator in the
presence of two or more witnesses present at the same time; and
(d) each witness either—
(i) attests and signs the will; or
(ii) acknowledges his signature, in the presence of the testator (but
not necessarily in the presence of any other witness),
but no form of attestation shall be necessary.

If the provisions of s. 9 are not complied with, the will is completely void and
any trusts which it purports to create will be invalid also. As will be seen,
however, a secret or half-secret trust may take effect on the death of the
testator without any need to specify the terms of the trust in the will, or even
to reveal its existence.

The purpose of s. 9 (as amended) is to prevent fraud. To make a will is to
enter into a major transaction. This must not be done in a light-hearted
manner but must be the result of a deliberate act. Formality requirements are
supposed to ensure this. It is also more important than with *inter vivos* gifts
to remove the possibility of false claims as the testator himself obviously

cannot refute them. As in other areas, however, formalities can sometimes encourage fraud. But 'equity will not permit a statute to be used as a cloak for fraud' (see the equitable maxims in 1.4.1) and the doctrines of secret and half-secret trusts have evolved in this area to prevent this.

9.1.2 Reasons for testators wishing to avoid formality requirements

There are at least two reasons why a testator may wish to avoid formality provisions (see, e.g., Sheridan (1951) 67 LQR 314).

First, he may wish the identity of the beneficiary to remain secret. This was especially common in the 19th century, if a gift of land to a charity was intended, when the Statutes of Mortmain (which prevented testamentary gifts of land to charities between 1736 and 1891) were in force. Another common situation was (and still is) where the beneficiary is to be a lover or mistress, or illegitimate child. Possibly the need for secrecy in this situation has diminished since 1969, because until then there was a presumption that a gift to 'children' in a will excluded illegitimate children. Thus it was necessary to identify them to include them. That presumption was reversed in 1969, so that a gift to 'children' on its own will now include illegitimate children (the relevant provisions can now be found in the Family Law Reform Act 1987). Even so, secrecy may still be desired if the testator wishes to keep their very existence secret.

Secondly, the testator may simply not have made up his mind at the time of making the will about the details of all the dispositions. It has been argued (e.g., Watkin [1981] Conv 335) that whereas the law should indulge secrecy, it should discourage indecision, and to at least a partial extent, it has taken this line.

9.1.3 Methods of avoiding formality provisions of Wills Act

There are two methods by which the Wills Act can effectively be avoided. A can leave property by will to B, in a manner which complies with the provisions of the Act, but having come to an (unwritten) understanding with B that he is merely trustee of it in favour of C. The understanding does not, of course, comply with the formality requirements of the Act. This is called a fully secret trust.

Alternatively, A can leave property by a valid will 'to B on trust', but where the beneficial interest under the trust (for example, in favour of C) is undeclared. This is called a half-secret trust because, while the details of the trust are secret, it is made clear that B holds as trustee and not beneficially.

For clarity, A, B and C will be used in the same fashion throughout the chapter.

In general, the principles for the enforcement of fully secret and half-secret trusts are probably the same (although some argue otherwise). Thus, most of what follows in the next section (on fully secret trusts) applies equally to half-secret trusts. However, because it is necessary to refute arguments that their basis of enforcement is different, and because there are respects in which half-secret trusts are treated differently, there is also a separate section (9.4) on half-secret trusts.

9.2   ENFORCEMENT OF FULLY SECRET TRUSTS

Subject to the constraints on the doctrine outlined in the remainder of this section, fully secret trusts will be enforced by the courts — C can enforce the trust against B. The question therefore arises: on what basis does equity allow the clear provisions of the Wills Act to be avoided?

9.2.1   Fraud theory

The leading authority on fully secret trusts is the House of Lords decision of *McCormick* v *Grogan* (1869) LR 4 HL 82 which clearly states that the basis of their enforcement is fraud. The precise nature of the fraud is discussed in 9.2.2.3 but at the very least, if it would be fraudulent for B to take beneficially, he will be required to enforce the trust in favour of C. This would be the case, for example, if the only reason why the property was left to B in the will was because of the unwritten understanding that he would hold it on trust for C.

The facts in *McCormick* v *Grogan* were that in 1851, the testator had left all his property by a three-line will to his friend Mr Grogan. In 1854 he was struck down by cholera. With only a few hours to live he sent for Mr Grogan. He told Mr Grogan in effect that his will and a letter would be found in his desk. The letter named various intended beneficiaries and the intended gifts to them. The letter concluded with the words:

> I do not wish you to act strictly on the foregoing instructions, but leave it entirely to your own good judgment to do as you think I would, if living, and as the parties are deserving.

An intended beneficiary (an illegitimate child) whom Mr Grogan thought it right to exclude sued.

The House of Lords held that although in principle the courts will enforce secret trusts, the terms of the letter in this particular case were not such that equity would impose on the conscience of Mr Grogan, and the secret trust alleged would not be enforced.

Although in *McCormick* v *Grogan* itself it was held that no secret trust was created in favour of C (an illegitimate child), but merely a moral obligation imposed on B, the court made it clear that had the facts been different a fully secret trust would, in principle, have been enforceable by C, in spite of the provisions of the Wills Act. In fact, the principles of enforcement of secret trusts go back at least as far as *Thynn* v *Thynn* (1684) 1 Vern 296 (see 9.2.2.1).

It is by no means self-evident that equity should uphold a trust despite a clear statutory provision to the contrary. In *McCormick* v *Grogan,* Lord Hatherley LC and Lord Westbury emphasised that the justification for the doctrine is personal fraud. In several places in his speech, Lord Westbury in particular emphasised the need for a '*malus animus*' to be 'proved by the clearest and most indisputable evidence' (at p. 97):

> . . . the jurisdiction which is invoked here . . . is founded altogether on personal fraud. It is a jurisdiction by which a court of equity, proceeding

on the ground of fraud, converts the party who has committed it into a trustee for the party who is injured by that fraud. Now, being a jurisdiction founded on personal fraud, it is incumbent on the court to see that a fraud, a *malus animus,* is proved by the clearest and most indisputable evidence.

On one view, this means that a deliberate intention to deceive must be shown on B's part (for example, where B had deliberately induced the testator to leave the property to him in the will, on the clear representation that he would hold it in trust for C), and it could also be argued that the standard of proof is as in common law fraud; in other words, a very high standard indeed is required. It may well be that this was what Lord Westbury meant. However, the statement has recently been explained in different terms. As will be explained below, *malus animus* may mean no more than the state of mind required for equity to impose a constructive trust on B's conscience, a very different proposition from common law fraud. Further, clearest and most indisputable evidence may mean no more than the standard of proof which the court will require before rectifying a written instrument. This is, at any rate, how the passage was interpreted by Brightman J in *Ottaway* v *Norman* [1972] Ch 698 (see 9.2.3.1).

The fraud basis of enforcement could operate in one of two ways. Either equity imposes upon the conscience of the secret trustee, B, and forces him to hold the property received under the will on constructive trust for the secret beneficiary, C, or alternatively secret trusts are express trusts to which the Wills Act 1837 does not apply, because equity will not allow a statute intended to prevent fraud to be used as a cloak for fraud (see the equitable maxims in 1.4.1). The question whether secret or half-secret trusts are express or constructive is considered in 9.8.

9.2.2 Why no resulting trust?
The principles enunciated in *McCormick* v *Grogan* (1869) LR 4 HL 82 beg an important question. If the only basis of the doctrine is to prevent B from fraudulently keeping the property for himself, why is it necessary to enforce the trust in C's favour? If the defeat of the intended trustee's (B's) fraudulent profit is all that was desired, surely it should be sufficient merely to compel him to hold the property on a resulting trust for the testator's estate? This solution would deprive B of his personal gain and the policy of the Wills Act 1837 would appear to be effected. Why should equity further disregard the requirements of the Wills Act 1837 to the extent of giving effect to the testator's oral instruction that the property should go to someone not named in the will?

Clearly, however, the House of Lords in *McCormick* v *Grogan* would have been prepared to enforce a secret trust on its terms (although on the facts no trust was held to have been created). Indeed, even long before *McCormick* v *Grogan* it was clear that the courts did not favour the resulting trust solution and that equity would enforce the trust in favour of C. There are in fact three answers to the resulting trust argument.

9.2.2.1 The residuary legatee argument A historical reason why a resulting trust would not have provided a satisfactory solution is that, prior

to the Executors Act of 1830, an executor was entitled to take as residuary legatee all property not specifically disposed of in the will. If, as might well happen, the intended trustee (B) was also the executor, a resulting trust would merely have the effect of granting him indirectly what the court refused to allow him to take directly.

An early example is *Thynn* v *Thynn* (1684) 1 Vern 296. The testator (A) had made his wife sole executrix. The son (B) persuaded the wife to make him sole executor instead, upon a completely fraudulent pretext. The Lord Keeper held that the property must be held in trust for the wife (C). If the court had not enforced the trust but allowed the property to result to the estate, the fraudulent son B (as executor) would himself have benefited from that as residuary legatee and indeed would have taken beneficially. Clearly, therefore, this solution would have been inappropriate and the only way to prevent personal fraud was to enforce the secret trust.

By the time *McCormick* v *Grogan* was decided, the Executors Act 1830 had altered the rule. Nowadays, the effect of a resulting trust in favour of the testator's estate will be to pass the property to the person named as residuary legatee, or if there is none, to those persons (usually close relatives of the testator) who are entitled to take in the event of his total or partial intestacy.

Hence, were the same facts to have arisen as in *Thynn* v *Thynn* today, B may not have personally benefited in the same way from a resulting trust. Yet *McCormick* v *Grogan* applied the same principles to a case under the Wills Act 1837. This appears to go further than necessary and to defeat the intention behind the Act. There can still be similar problems today, as in *Re Rees* [1950] Ch 204 (see 9.7.3), where the intended trustee, B (the solicitor who had drafted the will), was also the *named* residuary legatee. Where B is named as residuary legatee the arguments advanced in *Thynn* v *Thynn* retain their full force. Any argument favouring a resulting trust must at any rate make an exception to cover this situation, therefore.

9.2.2.2 The policy argument It is also possible to justify enforcing the secret trust on policy grounds. A common reason for setting up a secret trust is the desire to benefit someone whose existence the testator would prefer to keep hidden from his family, such as a mistress or, as in *McCormick* v *Grogan* an illegitimate child. A resulting trust in favour of the estate would divert the property to the very last people whom the testator wished to benefit (his legitimate family).

But for the court to give weight to this sort of consideration involves accepting that the testator's wishes are of sufficient importance to justify ignoring the clear terms of a statute in order to enforce the trust. The policy argument alone cannot justify enforcement, as opposed to a resulting trust, although if there are other justifications as well, it is a significant additional factor.

9.2.2.3 The nature of the fraud More importantly, however, we must examine the nature of the fraud upon which the doctrine is based. Just because Lord Westbury insisted on an element of intention to deceive, it does not follow that the nature of that deceit rests only in the personal gain of B.

Hodge [1980] Conv 341 has a different explanation. It should be remembered that the gift to B depended in the first place on B's promise to carry out the wishes of the testator. Hodge argues that the nature of B's fraud lies not simply in keeping the property personally, but in the fact that it was the promise to carry out the testator's wishes *in their exact terms* which induced him to leave his property to the intended trustee. It is the intended trustee's (B's) failure to do this which makes the fraud, not the element of greed.

B's fraud then, in equity, lies in the defeat of the testator's wishes, not necessarily in his own personal gain. He would be just as fraudulent with regard to the testator's confidence if he gave the property to a charity as he would be if he kept it for himself. And the testator would be no less defrauded if the intended trustee were (say) to hand over the gift intended for the testator's mistress to his innocent and long-suffering wife. A deception practised out of high moral principle is still deceit. Therefore, nothing less than the enforcement of the testator's wishes will suffice to avert a fraud in this situation.

On this argument, had the facts in *McCormick* v *Grogan* suggested fraud, it could only have been resolved by the enforcement of the trust in C's favour: a resulting trust would not have sufficed.

This line of reasoning is not universally accepted, but is clearly the basis on which at any rate *Blackwell* v *Blackwell* [1929] AC 318 was decided in the House of Lords (see further 9.4). A similar statement can be found in Lord Sterndale's judgment in *Re Gardner* [1920] 2 Ch 523 (at p. 529): 'The breach of trust or the fraud would arise when [the secret trustee] attempted to deal with the money contrary to the terms on which he took it.' It is not necessary for him to attempt to keep it beneficially, and indeed, in *Re Gardner* itself, he had no intention of so doing.

9.2.3 Developments since *McCormick* v *Grogan*

Lord Westbury's requirement in *McCormick* v *Grogan* was for a *malus animus* to be proved by clearest and most indisputable evidence. This seems to suggest that a deliberate intention to deceive must be shown on the legatee's part (for example, where he had deliberately induced the testator to leave the property to him in the will, on the clear representation that he would hold it in trust for the secret beneficiary). It also appears that the standard of proof is as in common law fraud; in other words, a very high standard indeed is required.

There is limited authority that since *McCormick* v *Grogan* (1869) LR 4 HL 82, their Lordships' stringent requirements concerning *malus animus* have been relaxed. Before considering the law itself, however, which is not yet clear, it is useful to consider why Lord Westbury was so concerned to limit the doctrine as he did, and what has altered since 1869.

As we have seen, *McCormick* v *Grogan* concerned an attempt to make a secret gift in favour of an illegitimate child. Secret trusts were also frequently used, however, in providing for charity. Testamentary gifts of land in favour of charities were, at that time, void. The practice therefore grew up whereby A left property to B, who was a trusted friend, on the understanding that he would later give the property to the charity (C).

It must be appreciated that it was not the intended beneficiary (C) in these cases who brought the action. Rather, it was A's family who attempted to show that the secret trust was enforceable. This can be seen from *Wallgrave* v *Tebbs* (1855) 2 K & J 313, where the secret trust failed, for reasons discussed in the next section.

The reason for this extraordinary state of affairs was this. If the secret trust was unenforceable, B took the property beneficially, and he could be relied upon, as a friend of the testator, to carry out A's wishes. If, however, it was enforceable, then by virtue of the Statutes of Mortmain, it was void. Thus, there would be a resulting trust to the estate (i.e., A's family)! This accounts for the surprising circumstance that it was the very last people who might at first sight be expected to benefit from the secret trust being enforceable, who argued that it was. On the other hand, it was in the interests of the charity for it not to be enforceable, because the charity could rely on B carrying out A's wishes.

It is likely that the House of Lords in *McCormick* v *Grogan* did not wish to allow gifts to charities to be defeated in this way. On the other hand, if B had procured a bequest dishonestly, they did not wish to see a mistress or illegitimate child deprived of his or her rightful interest because of the provisions of the Wills Act 1837. In the first case B was far from being fraudulent — indeed, he only wished to carry out the trust. In the second case, he was. Hence the stringent limits placed on the doctrine in that case.

The position changed in 1891, and the last vestiges of the mortmain legislation disappeared in 1960. Only the second type of secret trust remains today, therefore. Arguably, their lordships' limits to the doctrine are no longer appropriate. Their status is, of course, *obiter dicta*, albeit from the House of Lords, because in the event C lost on other grounds, and there is some authority that the limitations will no longer be stringently applied.

For example, although it seems that the basis of enforcement is still based on fraud, insofar that equity will not allow a statute intended to prevent fraud to be used to perpetrate fraud, it is possible that fraud in equity is nowadays a wider concept than it was in 1869. Today, there is some authority that it bears little relation to the common law or criminal law concept of the same name. It imposes on B's conscience, but may not necessarily demand the same degree of *mens rea* as fraud in the common law or criminal sense. Because of this, it may also demand a lower standard of proof.

Lord Westbury's remarks were not essential to the decision in *McCormick* v *Grogan*, and indeed, seem not to have been adopted in later cases. For example, in the later House of Lords authority, *Blackwell* v *Blackwell* [1929] AC 318, Lord Buckmaster thought that all that was required to show a fraud was:

(a)   the intention of the testator to subject the intended trustee to an obligation in favour of the intended beneficiary;

(b)   communication of that intention to the intended trustee; and

(c)   the acceptance of that obligation by the intended trustee, either expressly or by acquiescence.

Blackwell v *Blackwell* concerned a half-secret trust, but it is clear that the reasoning was intended to apply equally to fully secret trusts.

9.2.3.1 *Ottaway* v *Norman*

In *Ottaway* v *Norman* [1972] Ch 698, Brightman J enforced an oral secret trust of land without any suggestion that the intended trustee (B) had procured her prior life interest by deceit. Miss Hodges's (B's) employer, Mr Ottaway (A), left her his bungalow in his will, on terms that she would leave it by her own will to Mr Ottaway's son (C). Brightman J was prepared to enforce that agreement by imposing what he described as a constructive trust upon the bungalow in the hands of Miss Hodges's executor (she having later changed her mind and left her property to a cousin).

At the time of the arrangement between Miss Hodges (B) and the testator Ottaway (A), she clearly intended to carry out her promise to leave the land to Ottaway's son (C) in her own will. Although she later changed her mind, there was no evidence that she had procured the bequest by deceit: certainly, the evidence was insufficient to surmount the stringent standard of proof required for common law fraud. Her failure in the event to carry out her promise is clearly a fraud in the sense that it defeats the intention of the testator, but no question of *malus animus* arose. Far from requiring fraud in the sense required by Lord Westbury, Brightman J held that enforcement of a secret trust in C's favour depended only on those criteria derived from *Blackwell* v *Blackwell* [1929] AC 318 (see 9.2.3). Brightman J also thought that it was immaterial whether these elements precede or succeed the will. This seems correct in principle: if acceptance of an obligation by B persuades A not to revoke an existing will in B's favour, for B to break this obligation is quite as clearly a fraud on A, as it would have been had A been persuaded by B's acceptance of the obligation to make a will in his favour.

Nor did Brightman J see any reason to depart from the ordinary civil standard of proof, i.e., balance of probabilities.

Brightman J called the trust which he imposed upon the legatee of the (by then deceased) trustee a 'constructive' trust. This is a description of the mechanism by which secret trusts are enforced, not the basis of their enforcement. The constructive trust is simply a device of equity to protect beneficiaries where trust property has found its way into the hands of someone who, even if personally innocent, cannot assert a better right to that property.

The fact that the trust (of land) was oral was not a bar to its enforcement, despite the Law of Property Act 1925, s. 53(1)(b), because the executor was held to be a constructive trustee of the bungalow. Whether or not this analysis was correct, in principle a fully secret trust of land should be enforceable despite the absence of writing, either on the assumption that such trusts are to be regarded as constructive since they are imposed on the ground of conscience or because equity will not allow a statute intended to prevent fraud to be used as a cloak for fraud. See further 9.8.

So much for the trust of land in *Ottaway* v *Norman*. According to the evidence given by the son and his wife, Miss Hodges also undertook to leave them the furniture and other contents, including her money. Brightman J accepted that the secret trust comprised such furnishings and fixtures as Miss Hodges had received under Mr Ottaway's will, but not that it included all Miss Hodges's other property and cash from whatever source.

In respect of the last, it seems that he was not convinced that so far-reaching an obligation had in fact been envisaged in the agreement, but if the intended trustee (B) has clearly accepted such an obligation, it would appear, on analogy with mutual wills (on which, see 10.5), that this obligation also could be enforced against her estate.

This raises the issue of the status of the trust during Miss Hodges's lifetime. In *Ottaway* v *Norman,* Brightman J employed the concept of a 'floating trust', derived from the Australian case of *Birmingham* v *Renfrew* (1937) 57 CLR 666, which would remain in suspense during the life of the trustee and crystallise on her death, attaching to whatever property was comprised within her estate. This, as the learned judge noted, would seem to preclude Miss Hodges from making even a small pecuniary legacy in favour of her relatives or friends. This reasoning is similar to that of Nourse J in *Re Cleaver* [1981] 1 WLR 939 in the context of mutual wills (see 10.5).

9.2.3.2 *Re Snowden* Sir Robert Megarry V-C partially dissented from Brightman J's view in *Re Snowden* [1979] Ch 528. He thought that a higher standard of proof was required where fraud (which he seemed to view in the narrower Lord Westbury sense) had to be proved, as was necessary for some, but not all secret trusts. In other words, in his view, there are two classes of secret trusts, some of which require a more stringent burden of proof than others. Unfortunately, he did not go on to elaborate on the distinction, which appears to have been a desperate attempt to reconcile Brightman J's views with the apparently irreconcilable views of Lord Westbury, but perhaps he had in mind that if the only way that a would-be beneficiary can assert the existence of a trust in his favour is to allege facts which necessarily impute fraud to the alleged trustee, then the higher standard of proof applies. If the three elements listed earlier can be shown without proof of fraud, however, presumably he may succeed on the ordinary civil standard of balance of probabilities.

In the event, it was not necessary for Sir Robert Megarry V-C to elaborate, because there was really no evidence at all on which a secret trust could be established. His views are therefore *obiter*. In any case, if the criteria in *Blackwell* v *Blackwell* and *Ottaway* v *Norman* are sufficient, it is difficult to see why it is ever necessary to allege fraud in the Westbury sense, in which case the higher standard ought never to be required. If, on the other hand, Lord Westbury is correct, it is difficult to see why the higher standard is not always required.

9.3 LIMITATIONS ON ENFORCEMENT OF SECRET TRUSTS

The limitations on the enforcement of half-secret trusts are mainly concerned with the time of communication of the terms of the trust. It appears to be necessary for the existence of the secret trust to be communicated to the trustee before the death of the testator, and there is some authority that the terms also have to be communicated before the testator's *death*. Whether or not these communications precede or succeed the date of the *will* is irrelevant to the enforcement of a fully secret trust (although it is probably different in the case of half-secret trusts: 9.5).

The authorities are *Wallgrave* v *Tebbs* (1855) 2 K & J 313, and *Re Boyes* (1884) 26 ChD 531.

9.3.1 *Wallgrave v Tebbs*

Whether the stringent limitations of *McCormick* v *Grogan* (1869) LR 4 HL 82 still apply, or whether the law was correctly stated by Brightman J in *Ottaway* v *Norman* [1972] Ch 698, it is clear that once B has received a gift absolutely, any subsequently imposed obligations cannot deprive him of that gift. Apart from the principle that gifts are irrevocable, there is no reason, in such a case, to impose on B's conscience.

Thus, in *Wallgrave* v *Tebbs* (1855) 2 K & J 313, the existence of the secret trust, in favour of a charity, was not communicated to B until after A's death. B was entitled to the property absolutely. The testator had left property to close friends (B) without informing them in his lifetime that he wished the land to be used for a religious charitable purpose (i.e., in favour of C). The court held that the friends (B) were entitled to the property beneficially — a decision which, surprisingly enough, was most likely to give effect to the wishes of the testator, since if a secret trust had been found to exist it would have been void under the (now repealed) Statutes of Mortmain.

As it was, the friends were free to carry out the testator's wishes. If, as the testator's relatives had argued, a secret trust had been created, they would have had to hold the property on resulting trust *for those relatives*, the purpose of the trust being unlawful. Hence the surprising situation that the very last people who might be expected to argue for a secret trust (the relatives) did so in that case, and in other cases to which the Statutes of Mortmain applied.

The case is authority for the proposition that for a fully secret trust to be enforced, the intended trustee must be told of the existence of the trust before the testator's death. There is no particular difficulty in justifying the decision in *Wallgrave* v *Tebbs*, since if the intended trustee knew nothing about the trust until after the testator's death, there could have been no fraud in the procuring of the bequest, and thus no reason for the court to compel the intended trustee to do anything in particular with what is now his own property.

Another justification is that any other decision would have permitted the testator (A) to derogate from his grant. A bequest ought not to be 'snatched back' after it has been made, any more than a birthday present could be later reclaimed.

9.3.2 *Re Boyes*

A more difficult case is *Re Boyes* (1884) 26 ChD 531. Here, the intended trustee (B) was told of the existence of the trust before the testator's death, but was not told its terms until after the death of the testator.

A legacy was given to the testator's solicitor, who was told, before the testator's death, that he was to hold the residuary estate upon trust. However, he was not told its terms until a letter was found, after the death of the testator, which directed him to hold the residuary estate on behalf of a lady who was not the testator's wife. The solicitor wished to carry out the testator's wishes, but the validity of the trust was challenged by the testator's family. Kay J held that the solicitor held the property as trustee, but on resulting trust for the testator's estate.

If *Re Boyes* is correct, then not only the existence, but also the terms of a fully secret trust must be communicated to the trustee before the death of the testator. Kay J said (at p. 536):

> If the trust was not declared when the will was made [i.e., fully secret trust], it is essential in order to making it binding, that it should be communicated to the devisee or legatee in the testator's lifetime and that he should accept that particular trust.

This is a difficult case to fit into the general scheme of things, and the result was arguably a fraud on the testator, because A obviously did not intend the property to go to his estate, but it is clear from Kay J's judgment that his understanding of the basis of enforcement was substantially that outlined in the previous sections:

> The essence of [the early cases on secret trusts] is that the devisee or legatee accepts a particular trust which thereupon becomes binding upon him, and which it would be a fraud in him not to carry into effect.

There is nothing in the fraud basis of enforcement, however, which would require that an intended trustee must know the terms of the trust *by the time the will is executed*. There is no real difference between making a bequest on the strength of the intended trustee's promise, and leaving that bequest unrevoked on the strength of his later assurance. So, there is no reason to refuse to enforce the trust where the intended trustee becomes aware of its terms only after the execution of the will. All that is necessary is that he should be aware of them, or where they are to be found, before the bequest takes effect, i.e., *upon the testator's death*.

Further, in *Re Boyes* the intended trustee (B) was willing to carry out those terms. It seems that the case must be explained as one in which the scope of any possible fraud was limited to denying the existence of the trust. The intended trustee could hardly be said to have procured the bequest by a promise to adhere to its terms since he did not know them. All he knew was that the testator wished him to take the property in the capacity of trustee and not beneficially, so by compelling him to hold as trustee the court had done all it needed to in order to make him comply with the terms on which the bequest had been granted.

There may also be sound policy considerations for not enforcing a trust on its terms in a *Re Boyes* situation, sufficient to outweigh that of enforcement of the trust in C's favour. In particular, to enforce the trust would sanction indecision by A, which is arguably bad policy, since to allow a testator to establish a trust whose terms he may change from moment to moment is to permit the very luxury of indecision which the Wills Act 1837 sought to circumscribe (see 9.1.2 and 9.5.2.2). Furthermore, the court has to set a limit on the time for which trustees are required to hold property without knowing who the objects are, and it is a reasonable solution to insist that they know from the outset (although this may be not until the estate has been administered, i.e., later than death, so arguably this rather than death should be the deadline).

Another possibility is that the case is simply wrong: after all, it is a High Court case only, which has not been followed. I suggest that *Re Boyes* is correct, however, and is explicable on one or both of the bases outlined above.

It is enough, incidentally, for the intended trustee (B) to be aware of where the terms of the trust could be found (for example, if the terms of the trust are to be placed in a sealed letter to be opened only after the testator's death). Then it could be said that he accepted those terms and was bound by them. In this situation, he would hold the property on the terms of the secret trust (*Re Keen* [1937] Ch 236, 242; see 9.5.1). Further, although B is not informed of them until after A's death (as in *Re Boyes*), the policy reasons discussed above against enforcing the secret trust in C's favour do not apply. A is not being indecisive and B is not being asked to hold property for any length of time as trustee without knowing the identity of the objects of the trust.

9.4 HALF-SECRET TRUSTS

Half-secret trusts are also valid in principle, and like secret trusts, can be enforced by the intended beneficiary. The leading House of Lords authority is *Blackwell* v *Blackwell* [1929] AC 318. The justification for enforcement of half-secret trusts is exactly the same as that for fully secret trusts, that equity imposes upon the conscience of the secret trustee for the prevention of fraud. This is clear from the speech of Viscount Sumner in *Blackwell* v *Blackwell* (at pp. 335–6):

> For the prevention of fraud equity fastens on the conscience of the legatee a trust, a trust, that is, which otherwise would be inoperative; in other words it makes him do what the will in itself has nothing to do with; it lets him take what the will gives him and then makes him apply it, as the court of conscience directs, and it does so in order to give effect to wishes of the testator, which would not otherwise be effectual.

From the quote three propositions can be gleaned. First, the reason equity fastens on the conscience of the legatee is for the prevention of fraud. Secondly, the effect of the trust is to make the legatee 'do what the will in itself has nothing to do with'; in other words, the trust operates independently of the will. Thirdly, in order to prevent fraud, equity directs the legatee to give effect to wishes of the testator. This point is of some importance. The fraud whose commission is being prevented is not the taking of the property beneficially by the legatee, but having taken it, not giving effect to the wishes of the testator.

The facts of *Blackwell* v *Blackwell* were that, by a codicil to his will a testator transferred £12,000 to five trustees, to apply the income 'for the purposes indicated by me to them', with power to pay over the capital sum of £8,000 'to such person or persons indicated by me to them'. He had given detailed oral instructions on the codicil to one of the trustees, and all five knew the general object of the codicil before its execution. The trustees accordingly proposed to pay the income to a lady who was not the testator's wife. The testator's legitimate family challenged the validity of the half-secret trust. The House of Lords held that the half-secret trust was valid.

9.4.1 Fraud theory

It is sometimes argued that the fraud theory ought to draw a distinction between fully and half-secret trusts, on the ground that there is no possibility of an intended trustee of a half-secret trust claiming the property for himself since the fact of the trust is plain from the will. All that is needed to avert fraud, therefore, is to compel him to hold on resulting trust for the testator's estate.

Some writers have argued that fraud cannot be the justification because B cannot in any event take beneficially himself, whereas he could if fully secret trusts were not enforced. This is because half-secret trusts differ from the fully secret variety in that the will makes it clear that B takes as trustee only. So, if half-secret trusts are not enforced, B holds the property, not beneficially, but on resulting trust for the residuary legatee. Therefore, there is no possibility of personal gain by B (unless, of course, B is also residuary legatee).

It is no answer to say that a resulting trust would be a fraud on C, the intended beneficiary. As an argument in favour of enforcement, the reasoning is circular, because if a half-secret trust is not enforceable there is no beneficiary to make the argument work. C is only a beneficiary if the conclusion has already been reached that half-secret trusts are to be enforced.

The answer to the resulting trust argument, however, is exactly the same as that for fully secret trusts. The resulting trust is a fraud on the testator (A), and the property has only been given to B because of an express or implied promise, made by B to A. This is clear from the facts of *Blackwell* v *Blackwell* itself. A intended to benefit his mistress and illegitimate son. A resulting trust would have given the property to his wife and legitimate child — indeed, it was they who argued for a resulting trust. Clearly, A did not intend that they should benefit. He would not have settled the property on B had he thought that the result would be a gift in favour of his wife and legitimate child. B's acceptance of the property would have been a fraud on A unless the trust was enforced in favour of C. The justification for the enforcement of half-secret trusts, therefore, is exactly the same as that for fully secret trusts.

It is in any case clear from Viscount Sumner's speech that the basis of the enforcement of half-secret trusts is fraud, and that the fraud lies not in the personal gain of the intended trustee (B) but in not giving effect to the promise made to the deceased testator.

The case also contains statements to the effect that the law does not distinguish between enforcement of fully and half-secret trusts.

9.5 LIMITATIONS ON ENFORCEMENT OF HALF-SECRET TRUSTS

9.5.1 *Re Keen*

It appears, however, that half-secret trusts differ from their fully secret cousins in one respect. It is necessary for their enforcement for B to have accepted the obligation before the will is made. This distinction is difficult to justify in principle because a will is a revocable instrument having no legal status until death. And if it is argued that the contrary result allows the testator to alter the identity of the beneficiaries every day, at any time up his death, then why not have the same rule for fully secret trusts?

Nevertheless, there are *dicta* which appear to support the distinction in *Blackwell* v *Blackwell* itself, where Viscount Sumner observed (at p. 339):

A testator cannot reserve to himself a power of making future unattested dispositions by merely naming a trustee and leaving the purposes of the trust to be supplied afterwards, nor can a legatee given testamentary validity to an unexecuted codicil by accepting an indefinite trust, never communicated to him in the testator's lifetime . . .

It is possible that Viscount Sumner meant no more here than to restate the general principle that there must be acceptance by the secret or half-secret trustee and that such acceptance must take place within the lifetime of the testator, but this passage clearly can be taken to support the distinction made in the previous paragraph. *Blackwell* v *Blackwell* was used as authority for that distinction in *Re Keen* [1937] Ch 236. It is arguable that the time of communication was not the true basis of the decision in *Re Keen*, since the alleged communication did not anyway match the description given in the will, but the rule derived from *Re Keen* has since been applied in *Re Bateman's WT* [1970] 1 WLR 1463.

In *Re Keen*, a clause in the testator's will gave £10,000 on trust to two persons, who were directed to dispose of it 'as may be notified by me to them or either of them during my lifetime'. In fact, some months prior to the will, the testator had given one of the two trustees a sealed envelope containing a sheet of paper on which he had written the name and address of the proposed secret beneficiary (a lady to whom the testator was not married).

The Court of Appeal held that no valid half-secret trust had been created, and the £10,000 fell into residue. One reason was that, simply as a matter of construction, the clause in the testator's will referred to a *future* direction, whereas the direction had by then *already* been communicated to one of the two trustees. Therefore, the express terms of the will were inconsistent with the terms of the trust being contained in the sealed envelope. Had that been the only ground for the decision, the case would have created no difficulties, and the position for half-secret trusts would have been identical to that for fully secret trusts.

Lord Wright MR also said, however, that the testator having declared the existence of the trust in the will, should not be able to reserve to himself the power of making future dispositions without a duly attested codicil simply by notifying them during his lifetime. If that is correct, it follows that the terms of a half-secret trust must be finalised by the date of the will. In *Re Bateman's WT*, the trustees were directed by a clause in the will to pay the income from the testator's estate 'to such persons and in such proportions as shall be stated by me in a sealed letter in my own handwriting and addressed to my trustees'. As in *Keen*, this refers to a *future* direction, but unlike *Keen*, the trustees in *Bateman* received their instructions by means of a sealed letter after the will, but before the death of the testator. Therefore, the express terms of the will were not inconsistent with the timing of the communication.

Nevertheless, the Court of Appeal held that the direction to the trustees was invalid. The only possible explanation for the case, and indeed the one actually adopted by Pennycuick V–C, was that as a general principle, a half-secret trust is enforceable only where its terms are known at the date of the will.

The distinction drawn in *Keen* and *Bateman* has not been adopted in the Republic of Ireland: *Re Prendiville (dec'd)* , Irish High Court, 5 December 1990, noted [1992] Conv 202, where the alternative view of the *Blackwell dictum*, above, was adopted.

9.5.2 Justifications for *Re Keen*

9.5.2.1 Analogy with incorporation by reference
A possible explanation is that there is a second principle at work in addition to the fraud principle already discussed. This is that where reference is made in a will to a document, that document must already be in existence, otherwise the possibility exists of testators creating unattested codicils. It may be that of the two principles, the latter prevails where there is conflict.

With fully secret trusts, the question does not arise because the will is silent. It only applies to half-secret trusts because the existence of a half-secret (but not fully secret) trust is openly declared in a formal testamentary bequest. The argument proceeds that the testator having availed himself of this luxury, later additions or changes to the statement that the property is to be held on trust must also be made in a properly attested will or codicil. Therefore, if the testator chooses to declare the terms of his trust later than the date of executing his will, he is committed to using the correct formalities. Thus the distinction between half and fully secret trusts is justified.

This argument has a superficial attraction, taking account as it does of the fact that the problem of adequate proof is one which bedevils the whole area of secret trusts. If a testator has blandly asserted that property is to be held on trust, it is obviously vital to ensure that any other statements he may have made regarding the precise terms of that trust are indeed referable to that particular trust and no other. B. Perrins [1985] Conv 248 explains the timidity of the courts in accepting evidence which post-dates the will.

In this, they appear to have been influenced by the probate doctrine of incorporation by reference. This, in brief, permits the incorporation into the will of any document which was in existence at the time the will was executed, and was referred to as such in the will itself. It is a useful doctrine in that it saves the bother of copying out lengthy trust documents in the will itself merely for the purpose of adding a fresh sum to those trusts by way of bequest. The testator can instead simply refer to those documents and rely on a short declaration that the bequest is to be held on the terms set out in those documents. He cannot, however, incorporate a document which is not yet in existence at the time of making the will: to allow this would be to tempt fraudulent claims that this or that document was the one to which the testator meant to refer.

It is therefore easy to see why the courts, conscious of the wisdom of these limits to the doctrine of incorporation by reference, may have thought it prudent to import those limits into the enforcement of half-secret trusts. But as a principled justification for the communication rules, the explanation has defects.

For example, it is not necessary to the enforcement of a half-secret trust that any document at all should exist to declare the terms of the trust. So long as he communicates the terms before signing his will, the testator is free to rely on a purely oral communication, which must be even more susceptible to later misrepresentation than a document. If the courts are prepared to accept the existence of fully secret trusts on quite slender evidence, e.g., *Ottaway* v *Norman* (see 9.2.3.1), it would be odd if they refused to accept oral evidence to show the terms of a half-secret trust, where the chance of fraud is if anything less.

In any case, to argue that the testator, having once committed himself to formality, remains bound by the need for further formality if he wishes to expound the terms of his trust later than the date of making his will, is merely to penalise him for partial compliance with the Wills Act 1837, while allowing the testator who ignores that Act entirely (by creating a fully secret trust) to have his wishes enforced. This seems to fall short of being a rational justification, therefore.

9.5.2.2 Policy against indecision

Another, related argument which was stated in *Blackwell* v *Blackwell,* and repeated in *Re Keen,* is that to permit a testator simply to state the existence of a trust and communicate its terms at his leisure would be to permit a will to be freely altered by unattested dispositions, thus defeating the policy of the Wills Act 1837.

Thus, for example, Watkin [1981] Conv 335 argues for the *Bateman* position on policy grounds, namely that whereas the law should and does not object to secrecy, it should not encourage indecision. A testator should have made up his mind by the time the will is made.

The argument reflects a respect for the policy of the Wills Act 1837, and the logic of this reasoning (if correct) applies to fully secret trusts also.

Indeed, Watkin argues that they should be brought into line by statute. This, it is argued, would allow the testator who has made up his mind where he wants his property to go, but wishes its destination to be secret, to fulfil his desires by making his communication prior to the will, while defeating the testator who is merely indecisive and wants the luxury of changing his will without the trouble and expense of making fresh testamentary provisions. As Watkin acknowledges, however, the practice of permitting indecisive behaviour via a fully secret trust is so firmly entrenched that a statute would be required to effect the change.

9.5.3 Codicils

As we have seen in 9.5.1, half-secret trusts must be communicated prior to, or contemporaneously with, the execution of the will. Suppose that the trusts are communicated after the date of the will but before a later codicil. This raises the question of the effect of the codicil. Another issue is whether additional property can be added to an existing secret or half-secret trust by codicil.

In *Blackwell* v *Blackwell* [1929] AC 318 itself, the gift which was subject to the half-secret trust was contained in a codicil, but in that case the gift was created for the first time by the codicil and the trustees had been duly informed in advance. Suppose, however, that the half-secret trust is originally created earlier, in the will, and the intended trustee (B) has not been informed in advance. There is no direct authority whether the later reference to that trust in the codicil will suffice first to create the trust contained in the will and secondly to add extra property to this trust.

In favour of allowing the trust, it can be argued that the policy of the *Re Keen* rule ([1937] Ch 236) is merely to ensure that the trust is communicated prior to some properly executed testamentary disposition which indicates its terms, and that therefore the mention of the trust in the codicil should be good enough. A codicil has the effect of republishing a will, in other words it is as though the will itself had been made at the date of the later codicil.

The position is different where additional property is added by the codicil, since the trustees may not have accepted any obligations regarding the additional property. In *Re Colin Cooper* [1939] Ch 811, a testator had left £5,000 to trustees on half-secret trust in his will, having duly informed them in advance and obtained their agreement, and later added a further £10,000 to this trust in a codicil. The Court of Appeal held that only the first amount mentioned in the will could be subject to the half-secret trust, and that the amount added by the codicil fell into residue. In *Re Colin Cooper*, the trustees had agreed to hold £5,000, and that was the limit of their obligation, since they never knew of the further obligation imposed in the codicil. As Sir Wilfred Greene MR said (at p. 818):

> it was not with regard to any sum other than the £5,000 that the consciences of the trustees (to use a technical phrase) were burdened.

He seemed to envisage, however, that if the agreement had been that the trustees would hold £5,000 or whatever sum the testator finally chose to bequeath, it would have been enforceable on those terms. This also accords with the view taken by the courts that a sealed envelope may be sufficient communication, despite the fact that the terms are, *ex hypothesi*, unknown to the trustee, who assents to carry them out whatever they might turn out to be.

9.6   SECRET AND HALF-SECRET TRUSTS TAKE EFFECT INDEPENDENTLY OF THE WILL

It is also clear from *Blackwell* v *Blackwell* [1929] AC 518 that secret and half-secret trusts operate independently of the will. It is possible that they operate as express trusts created *inter vivos* by the agreement reached between the testator and the intended trustee, the function or relevance of the will being to vest the property in the intended trustee at the agreed time for the assumption of his office. From the passage in Viscount Sumner's speech, however, to which allusion has already been made (at 9.4), it seems more likely that after the will has transferred legal title to the legatee, the court fastens on the conscience of the legatee by imposing on him a trust. This is probably best analysed as a constructive trust, imposed in order to prevent fraud.

A similar analysis was adopted by Lord Westbury in *McCormick* v *Grogan* (at p. 97):

> The court of equity has, from a very early period, decided that even an Act of Parliament shall not be used as an instrument of fraud; and if in the machinery of perpetrating a fraud an Act of Parliament intervenes, the court of equity, it is true, does not set aside the Act of Parliament but it fastens on the individual who gets a title under that Act, and imposes upon him a personal obligation, because he applies the Act as an instrument for accomplishing a fraud.

Whichever analysis is correct, whether secret and half-secret trusts are express *inter vivos* trusts or constructive trusts imposed once the legatee has received the property (on which, see further 9.8), the will does no more than constitute the trust, transferring the legal property to the secret trustee. It seems likely that the trust could also be constituted by intestacy, in the absence of any will, if the settlor refrains from making a will in the knowledge that the property will pass to the intended trustee by virtue of the Administration of Estates Act 1925, rather than using a more usual form of transfer for an *inter vivos* trust.

It is sometimes argued that if secret and half-secret trusts are ordinary *inter vivos* trusts, the Wills Act has no application to them. If this is so, then fraud ought not to be strictly necessary for their enforcement. The mere fact of an existing trust should be enough for equity to intervene to enforce it, irrespective of any '*malus animus*' on the part of the trustee.

Yet while it is undoubtedly correct to say that the *mechanism* by which secret and half-secret trusts are enforced has nothing to do with the will, merely to describe the mechanism is not the same thing as providing a reason for their enforcement. The reason that equity imposes on the conscience of the legatee is fraud, and the mere fact that the mechanism operates independently of the will in no way affects that requirement.

The operation of secret and half-secret trusts independently of this will does have other consequences, however. In *Re Young* [1951] Ch 344 a half-secret trust was enforced despite the fact that the beneficiary had witnessed the will, which under s. 15 of the Wills Act 1837 would normally have the effect of invalidating the gift to the witnessing beneficiary. Since he took outside the will, however, this rule did not apply. Danckwerts J commented:

> The whole theory of the formation of a secret trust is that the Wills Act has nothing to do with the matter . . . , since the persons do not take by virtue of the gift in the will, but by virtue of the secret trusts imposed upon the beneficiary, who does in fact take under the will.

In *Re Gardner* (*No. 2*) [1923] 2 Ch 230, a secret trust in favour of a beneficiary who had predeceased the testator was upheld. It is not possible to leave property to a dead person by will, and it is difficult to justify this decision even on the basis that the will has nothing to do with the matter. The usual analysis is that, at the very least, the will constitutes the trust by transferring legal title to the secret trustee, but Romer J saw no reason why a declaration of trust by the secret trustee should not have occurred at the moment of communication of the trust to him (at p. 233):

> The rights of the parties appear to me to be exactly the same as though the husband [secret trustee], after the memorandum had been communicated to him by the testatrix . . . , had executed a declaration of trust binding himself to hold any property that should come to him upon his wife's [settlor's] partial intestacy upon trust as specified in the memorandum.

If Romer J's view is correct, then the consequences are not limited to an ability to make a secret or half-secret trust in favour of a beneficiary who predeceases the testator. If the trust comes into force from the moment of communication, then it must also follow that it is irrevocable from that moment, and that neither the testator nor the secret trustee would be able later to change his mind. This would be an unfortunate consequence if the communication was made many years before the testator's death and circumstances had changed radically in the meantime. Suppose, for example, the secret beneficiary ran off with the secret trustee's wife. Could not the secret trustee inform the testator that he was no longer prepared to accept the property on the original terms? Or, if he were no longer able to get in touch with the testator, could he not refuse to take the property under the will? One would have thought that, in principle, he should be able to change his mind, but if Romer J is right, and the trust is created from the moment of communication, then it may well be that he cannot.

Romer J's view is in any case inconsistent with views expressed in the Court of Appeal in *Re Maddock* [1902] 2 Ch 220, to the effect that the trust only becomes binding once the legatee accepts the legacy. For example, Collins MR said (at p. 226):

> But the right of the [beneficiary] is wholly dependent on whether the legatee accepts the legacy with knowledge of the mandate, and no right for them arises at all unless and until the legatee has, with notice, accepted the legacy.

Cozens-Hardy LJ took a similar view (at p. 231):

> Now, the so-called trust does not affect the property except by reason of a personal obligation binding the individual devisee or legatee. If he renounces and disclaims, or dies in the lifetime of the testator, the persons claiming under the memorandum can take nothing against the heir-at-law or next of kin or residuary devisee or legatee.

These statements clearly imply that the trust is not constituted until the testator has died, and the legatee has accepted the trust property.

There is another difficulty with Romer J's analysis. The secret trustee must be declaring himself trustee of after-acquired property, since only on the testator's death is legal title vested in him. The conventional view is that trusts of future property are void (see further chapter 3).

The orthodox view is that *Gardner* (*No. 2*) is wrong.

9.7 MISCELLANEOUS ISSUES

9.7.1 *Re Stead*

In *Re Stead* [1900] 1 Ch 237, Farwell J (at p. 241) made various distinctions where property was given to two or more persons (let us call them B1 and B2) as joint tenants or tenants in common, but where only one (B1) had promised to hold the property on a secret trust. The question at issue is whether B2 is bound by the trust.

Where a gift is made to trustees as joint tenants, the orthodox view, as stated in *Re Stead*, is that if communication is made before the execution of the will, all will be bound, whereas if communication is made after the execution of the will but before the death of the testator, only those who have accepted the trust are bound by it, on the basis that the gift to an intended trustee who does not consent is not tainted with any fraud in procuring the execution of the will. Where the gift is to the intended trustees as tenants in common, only those who are aware of the trust are bound, whether they obtain this knowledge before or after the will is executed.

The distinctions were said to be based on older cases but are difficult to support as a matter of policy. However, B. Perrins (1972) 85 LQR 225 argues, at p. 228, that Farwell J's distinctions are wrong and that the true rule rests on the principle of *Huguenin* v *Baseley* (1807) 14 Ves Jr 273, that no man may profit from the fraud of another. On this argument, B2 would be bound if the testator was induced to leave the property to him on the strength of

B1's promise, but not otherwise, and the question of when communication occurred would be a matter of evidence only. The argument has much to commend it, and if Perrins is correct then these cases fit into the general scheme of things, so long as the criteria for enforcement advanced in *Ottaway* v *Norman* [1972] Ch 698 (see 9.2.3.1) are correct.

9.7.2 Absence of intended trustee, or renunciation by him of the legacy

Suppose B has died before A. This makes it necessary to consider whether a secret trust can be enforced in the absence of the intended trustee (B). It is undoubted law that a legacy cannot take effect where the legatee predeceases the testator, and the statements already considered from *Re Maddock* [1902] 2 Ch 220 (see 9.6), and in particular that of Cozens-Hardy LJ, suggest that the trust will not be enforced in this case, nor where the secret trustee renounces the legacy.

On the other hand, the fraud on the testator is no less in these cases than in the conventional situation, and there is a general principle that 'equity will not allow a trust to fail for want of a trustee'. It might be thought, therefore, that where the intended trustee has predeceased the testator, a trust should be imposed upon the property in the hands of A's executor.

There are also *dicta* of Lord Buckmaster in *Blackwell* v *Blackwell* [1929] AC 318, at p. 328, that the intended trustee will not be allowed to defeat the testator's purpose by renouncing the legacy.

The *dicta* in *Re Maddock* cannot be reconciled with those of Lord Buckmaster in *Blackwell* v *Blackwell*. It is true that *Re Maddock* concerned a fully secret trust, whereas the trust in *Blackwell* v *Blackwell* was half-secret. One could argue for a distinction on that basis, since the trust is plain on the face of the will in the latter, but not the former case. It is clear, however, that both sets of *dicta* are intended to apply to both types of trust, and we can only conclude that neither issue has been finally decided.

If the secret trustee cannot renounce the legacy, then on the assumption that the trust is not fully constituted before the death of the testator (but see 9.6), there must be a general principle that a trustee cannot renounce his obligations once he has accepted trusteeship, even before the trust is fully constituted. There appears to be no authority for or against the existence of such a general principle, but I have already suggested (see 9.6) that significant problems could arise if there was a long period of time between acceptance of the trust and the death of the testator, and circumstances had changed radically in the meantime.

9.7.3 Residuary legatees

Suppose B is directed to dispose of only some of the property acquired under the will and to keep the rest for himself. In effect, the will makes him residuary legatee.

The issue seems to turn on the construction of the will. If it can be said that the will creates a conditional gift then the trustees may take, subject to fulfilling the condition. If, however, on its true construction it imposes a trust, the courts have shown themselves reluctant to allow the trustees to introduce evidence to contradict its terms. In other words, the trustees will be unable to adduce evidence that they were intended to take as residuary legatees.

In *Re Rees* [1950] Ch 204, the testator had left his whole estate on half-secret trust and privately informed his trustees (B) that they were to make certain payments and retain the surplus for themselves. Since one of the trustees was the solicitor who had drafted the will, the court was, perhaps, especially disposed towards caution in this case, holding that on the proper construction of the will, the half-secret trust was imposed upon the entire estate. The trustees would not therefore be allowed to introduce extrinsic evidence to contradict this by showing that they were intended to take beneficially subject only to making the payments.

The reasoning in *Re Rees* applies only to half-secret trusts, since with a fully secret trust the will itself will be silent. There can therefore be no question of additional evidence *contradicting* the will. *Re Rees* was doubted in *Re Tyler* [1967] 1 WLR 1269, but *Re Tyler* was distinguishable because the trustees were claiming only a specified sum (£500), and were not claiming to take as residuary legatees: the £500 was apparently treated as a conditional gift. In any case, this was a fully secret trust, so that in principle *Re Rees* should not have been applicable.

9.8 EXPRESS OR CONSTRUCTIVE TRUSTS: DOES IT MATTER?

We have seen that the basis of enforcement of both fully and half-secret trusts is B's fraud, defined in a wide equitable sense. Additionally, both varieties implement the express intentions of the testator, even though those intentions may not be expressed correctly, in writing, signed and attested etc. Each takes effect outside the will. It is said that it matters whether they are classified as express or constructive trusts because the formality requirements of the Law of Property Act 1925, s. 53(1) (see chapter 6), apply to express, but not (by virtue of s. 53(2)) constructive trusts.

Section 53(1)(b) requires express trusts of land to be declared in writing, yet a fully secret trust of land was enforced in *Ottaway* v *Norman* [1972] Ch 698 despite being oral (see 9.2.3.1). Further, that case ostensibly rested on constructive trust principles. This is therefore apparently authority that fully secret trusts at least are constructive. Yet some writers distinguish between the two varieties, and argue that *Ottaway* v *Norman* applies only to fully secret trusts. Indeed, *Re Baillie* (1886) 2 TLR 660 suggests that writing is required for half-secret trusts of land, although perhaps not too much emphasis should be placed on cases prior to *Blackwell* v *Blackwell* [1929] AC 318, and there can be no justification for the distinction if the basis of enforcement of half and fully secret trusts is the same.

I would suggest that writing is never required for any secret trust of either variety. The mechanism appears to be that B obtains property under the will and that equity, operating outside the will, imposes on his conscience and requires him to hold as constructive trustee for C. On this basis, both fully and half-secret trusts are constructive (see also 10.3 and 10.4).

I would also suggest that the issue is wholly academic and of no practical importance whatever. The classification is relevant only to the formality requirements of s. 53. Yet the validity of half and fully secret trusts depends on a principle of equity, which is not defeated by s. 9 of the Wills Act 1837. Surely it will also not be defeated by s. 53 of the Law of Property Act 1925 or any other statutory formality provision intended to prevent fraud. If equity will not permit a statute intended to prevent fraud to be used as an instrument for fraud, there is no reason why it should distinguish between statutes for these purposes. The principle applies as much to the Law of Property Act 1925, s. 53, as to the Wills Act 1837, s. 9. This will be so however secret trusts are classified because it is not therefore necessary that they fall within the s. 53(2) exception to avoid the requirements of s. 53(1). See further on this point, Perrins [1985] Conv 248, 256–7.

Further support for the view that s. 53(1)(b) is treated in a similar fashion to the Wills Act itself can be found in *Sen* v *Headley* [1991] Ch 425 (see 3.5.1.1).

The conclusion is, then, that whether secret and semi-secret trusts are express or constructive, they are not affected by any statute requiring formality.

TEN

Equitable Fraud Doctrine

This chapter is concerned primarily with constructive trusts: whereas express and implied trusts give effect to the express or implied wishes of the settlor, and resulting trusts are also a consequence, albeit more remote, of the settlor's intention, constructive trusts are imposed by the courts as a matter of law. They depend on principles of equity and conscience, and are independent of the settlor's intention.

The circumstances in which constructive trusts can arise are many and varied, and rather than attempt to cover all situations in any single chapter, many have been dealt with elsewhere in the book. Some trusts which are arguably constructive (for example, secret trusts in chapter 9) are dealt with not in this chapter, but in their appropriate place in the book. Trusts imposed on third parties, in connection with the equitable doctrines of tracing, knowing receipt and knowing assistance, are dealt with in chapter 19.

If there are common general principles explaining all constructive trusts, then this form of organisation would be counter-productive. But my impression is that the areas covered in this book, where constructive trusts arise, have developed largely independently of each other. They all arise (except perhaps in cases such as *Re Rose* in chapter 3) because the conscience of the defendant is affected, however, and the cases in this chapter are the most extreme examples of this: the trusts here are imposed by the courts specifically because of the conduct of the legal owner of property.

10.1 CRIMINAL ACTS

Equity will not allow a person to retain the benefit of criminal activities, and holds property so received on constructive trust for those entitled to it. Thus in *Re Crippen* [1911] P 108, Crippen murdered his wife and attempted to escape abroad with his mistress, Miss Ethel le Nève. He was apprehended while at sea (the first murderer to be brought to justice as a result of a wireless communication) and was subsequently hanged, leaving his property to Miss le Nève. The question arose regarding that part of Crippen's property to which he was apparently entitled on the death (intestate) of his murdered wife. Evans P held that Crippen could not take the property and that it could not therefore pass to Miss le Nève. Instead it passed to his wife's next of kin. It must be assumed that if Crippen had actually received the property he would have held it on constructive trust for his victim. (There was no evidence, incidentally, that the murder was in any way motivated by a desire to inherit Mrs Crippen's property.)

The principle applies not only to property inherited directly by the killer, but also where killer and victim are joint tenants, so that the victim's share passes to the killer by virtue of the right of survivorship (see 1.2.6). In *Re K (decd)* [1985] 2 WLR 262, a wife (whose name was not disclosed) killed her husband with a shotgun after suffering many years of violent attacks by him. She was convicted of manslaughter and sentenced to two years' probation. Vinelott J held that both the money inherited under the husband's will and his share as joint tenant of the matrimonial home were subject to the forfeiture rule.

It is also clear from *Re K* that manslaughter is capable of attracting the *Crippen* principle. Obviously crimes requiring an element of intention, such as murder, ought to attract the principle, because of the connotation of unconscionable conduct. Manslaughter does not necessarily require any subjective element of intention, however, and it is equally clear that the *Crippen* principle will not always apply in a manslaughter case. However, in *Re K* the killer had deliberately threatened the victim with a loaded gun with the safety catch removed, and this was sufficient to attract the equitable forfeiture rule.

The position has been altered, however, by the Forfeiture Act 1982 which allows the court a discretion to grant relief from forfeiture except in a case of murder. Vinelott J was prepared to grant relief under the Act, forming a view based on the degree of moral culpability in view of the violence the killer had suffered at the hands of her victim. The case went to the Court of Appeal on the application of the 1982 Act only, and Vinelott J's decision was affirmed ([1986] Ch 180).

10.2 FRAUD

There are certainly two principles by which fraud is relevant to the creation of a trust. The first is that equity will not allow a statute to be used as a cloak for fraud, and the second is that where somebody obtains legal title to property by agreeing to take it expressly subject to the rights of another party, equity will require him to hold the property subject to those rights. The second works by the imposition of a constructive trust. It is less clear whether this is also the explanation of the first principle, which may simply be one of statutory interpretation, but if it does indeed work by the imposition of a constructive trust, that would prevent any conflict arising between the equitable jurisdiction and the statute.

There is some authority for a more general fraud doctrine, and also for extensions of the second principle in the preceding paragraph. These are examined at the end of the chapter.

10.2.1 Equity will not allow a statute to be used as a cloak for fraud
This principle was developed by the courts of equity to prevent people from taking unfair advantage of statutory formality provisions, which are of course

intended to prevent, rather than encourage, fraud. We have already seen two examples: the part performance doctrine (see 6.5), which has usually been used to prevent reliance on the now-repealed s. 40 of the Law of Property Act 1925; and secret trusts (see chapter 9), which prevent reliance on s. 9 of the Wills Act 1837, as subsequently amended. This is probably also the principle that operates to avoid s. 53(1)(b) of the Law of Property Act in first category *Rosset* cases (see 8.5.2).

The principle is of more general application, applying whenever there is an attempt to use a statute intended to prevent fraud as a means of perpetrating fraud. However, there are limits to the principle. It probably applies only to formality provisions. Certainly, it would be difficult to argue that it applies to the Land Charges Act 1925 (which was intended to simplify conveyancing, not prevent fraud) following the House of Lords decision in *Midland Bank Trust Co. Ltd* v *Green* [1981] AC 513 (see 1.6.2). In this case, a sham sale between husband and wife, intended specifically to defeat a third party's valuable option to purchase a farm, succeeded in its purpose solely because the option had not been properly registered under the Act. Lord Wilberforce said (at p. 531) that in general it is not 'fraud' to rely on legal rights conferred by Act of Parliament.

Furthermore, the principle operates only where all the requirements for a trust (or contract) are already present, apart from writing. The part performance doctrine operates only where the contract is in all respects otherwise valid, and would be enforceable if in writing. We also saw in 8.5.2 that all the elements of a trust (apart from writing) must be present in a first category *Rosset* case.

In the discussion at 9.8, I suggested that the mechanism upon which the doctrine operated, at least for secret and half-secret trusts, was the imposition of a constructive trust, and a similar explanation was adopted in 8.5.2, in the later case in order to trigger s. 53(2). However, the fact that constructive trusts are not exempted from the Wills Act suggests that it would have made no difference in 8.5.2 had s. 53(2) never been enacted. The mechanism by which the part performance operates may also be the constructive trust; certainly a constructive trust arises, on the principles of 1.4.4 and 6.4.6. It is interesting that s. 2 of the Law of Property (Miscellaneous Provisions) Act 1989, which is often said to have abolished the part performance doctrine as far as it related to land, does not apply (by virtue of s. 2(5)) to the creation or operation of resulting, implied or constructive trusts. This strengthens the argument I advanced at 6.5, that is, to the extent that part performance is a fraud-based doctrine, it survives the enactment of the 1989 Act.

However, it is not clear beyond doubt that the mechanism is always the imposition of a constructive trust; it could, as previously observed, simply be an interpretation of a statute which was intended to prevent fraud — it cannot be used to promote fraud. For similar reasoning to that advanced at 9.8, it probably does not matter whether the mechanism is one of constructive trust or not, unless it were intended to use these cases to advance a more general principle connecting fraud with constructive trusts.

10.2.2   Obtaining legal title expressly subject to rights of another

There is now a clear line of authority that where somebody obtains legal title
to property by agreeing to take it expressly subject to the rights of another
party, equity will require him to hold the property as constructive trustee, to
give effect to the rights of the other party.

This development is not particularly startling, and can again be seen as a
generalisation of the secret trusts doctrine in chapter 9. It is also not that
dissimilar to ordinary express trusteeship, since trustees ordinarily accept
legal title subject to the terms of the trust, except of course that in these cases,
formality provisions are avoided. In so far as these cases cause problems, it is
because the trusts which thereby arise are full property interests capable of
binding third parties. The problems of life tenancies are considered at 8.8.
Conveyancing problems might also arise where a bare trust is created, since
this would not require registration under the Land Charges Act 1972 and,
since the beneficiary would often be in occupation, could be an overriding
interest under s. 70(1)(g) of the Land Registration Act 1925. That would
seem to be an argument for amending the conveyancing provisions, however,
rather than curtailing the development of the equitable doctrine.

In *Bannister* v *Bannister* [1948] 2 All ER 133, the plaintiff, who was the
defendant's brother-in-law, was able to obtain two cottages from the defendant, at well below their market value, on the understanding that after the sale
the defendant would be able to continue to live in one of the cottages rent
free for as long as she wished. She relied on his oral statement — 'I do not
want to take any rent, but will let you stay [in one of the cottages] as long as
you like rent free' and consequently the plaintiff obtained the cottages for only
£250, as compared with their true market value of around £400. No written
agreement to this effect was included in the conveyance. The plaintiff
thereafter occupied the whole cottage save for one room which was occupied
by the defendant. Troubles arose between the parties a few years later and
the plaintiff sought possession of the cottage, claiming that the defendant was
a mere tenant at will. The Court of Appeal took the view that the plaintiff
had obtained the property cheaply by fraud, and therefore decided that he
held it as constructive trustee of the defendant for her life (see 8.8 on the
effect of the life interest).

In *Binions* v *Evans* [1972] Ch 359 Mrs Evans's husband was employed by
the Tredegar Estate (near Newport in South Wales) and lived rent free in a
cottage owned by the estate. The husband died when the defendant (Mrs
Evans) was 73. The trustees of the estate then entered into a written
agreement with the defendant that she could continue to live in the cottage
during her lifetime as tenant at will rent free; she undertook to keep the
cottage in good condition and repair. The trustees later sold the cottage to
the plaintiffs, Mr and Mrs Binions, expressly subject to Mrs Evans's 'tenancy
agreement'. The plaintiffs, having thereby obtained the cottage more cheaply,
six months later sought possession from Mrs Evans, claiming that she was a
tenant at will. The Court of Appeal held in favour of Mrs Evans, but although
the decision was unanimous, the reasoning of the Master of the Rolls was
quite different from that of Megaw and Stephenson LJJ.

Lord Denning MR started with the assertion that Mrs Evans had a contractual licence, which bound the purchasers with notice. This is inconsistent with the later Court of Appeal decision in *Ashburn Anstalt* v *Arnold* [1989] 1 Ch 1 (see further below) and is almost certainly incorrect. Indeed, Stephenson LJ doubted whether this line of reasoning was correct in *Binions* v *Evans* itself.

Lord Denning MR's alternative grounds were that because Mr and Mrs Binions had purchased expressly subject to the agreement, equity would impose upon their conscience and require them to hold the property on constructive trust for Mrs Evans. This approach, based on *Bannister* v *Bannister*, differs from the views of the other two judges, in that the trust arose not under the original agreement, but only on the sale of the property to the plaintiffs.

Lord Denning MR's constructive trust approach, narrowly interpreted, is probably the *ratio* of *Binions* v *Evans*, and has been followed in subsequent cases. However, parts of Lord Denning's judgment are more radical. He thought that to take property *impliedly* subject to an enforceable agreement would also be enough, and that a constructive trust could be imposed whenever the trustee had conducted himself in an inequitable manner. As with the contractual licence reasoning, this part of the judgment probably cannot survive the criticism in *Ashburn Anstalt* v *Arnold*.

The reasoning of Megaw and Stephenson LJJ was entirely different. In their view, the original agreement between the trustees and the defendant created a life tenancy. Thus, even at this stage the trustees held the property on trust for Mrs Evans for her life, thereafter for the Tredegar Estate in fee simple. Because this was a succession of equitable interests, Mrs Evans had an interest in land coming within the provisions of the Settled Land Act 1925 (see 8.9). The purchasers were therefore bound by an existing trust, on the ordinary principles of the equitable notice doctrine (see 1.4.6).

The majority view has never been followed and there is a problem with it, i.e., that it is difficult to see why the sale to the plaintiffs was not caught by the 'paralysing section' which should have prevented the sale to Mr and Mrs Binions from taking effect: Settled Land Act 1925, s. 13. On the Settled Land Act question, however, we saw at 8.8 that in *Ungurian* v *Lesnoff* [1990] Ch 206, Vinelott J preferred the view of the majority to that of Lord Denning MR (who thought that the Act did not apply to interests created under a constructive trust). It is reasonably clear, therefore, that the imposition of a trust creates a property interest so as to trigger the Settled Land Act 1925.

Cases subsequent to *Binions* v *Evans* suggest that the very broad views of Lord Denning MR, that a constructive trust could be imposed whenever the trustee had conducted himself in an inequitable manner, have not gained favour. However, there is now a reasonable body of authority supporting his view that a constructive trust may be imposed on a purchaser (probably of land or chattels: see, for example, Browne-Wilkinson J's judgment *Swiss Bank Corporation* v *Lloyds Bank Ltd* [1979] 1 Ch 548) who purchases expressly subject to a prior agreement.

Lord Denning MR's view was adopted by Dillon J in *Lyus* v *Prowsa Developments Ltd* [1982] 1 WLR 1044 (see also 1.6.2), but Dillon J limited

Binions v *Evans* to the situation where the purchaser took *subject to* a right. It is not enough that he merely knew of it.

The decision of the Court of Appeal in *Ashburn Anstalt* v *Arnold* [1989] 1 Ch 1, comprehensively noted by M.P. Thompson ([1988] Conv 201), is probably more important to students of land law than to those of trusts, but nevertheless it contains important *dicta* which bear on the present discussion. Fox LJ thought that contractual licences are not interests in land and do not bind third party purchasers. The relevance of this point to the present discussion is that if Lord Denning MR's judgment in *Binions* v *Evans* can be justified, it can only be on the basis of the constructive trust reasoning, and not on the basis of the contractual licence reasoning alternatively advanced.

A constructive trust was argued in *Ashburn Anstalt* v *Arnold* on the basis of Lord Denning MR's reasoning in *Binions* v *Evans*. The court, however, took the view that it would be imposed only where it was satisfied that the conscience of the purchaser was affected. This required more than mere notice, even express notice of the contractual licence. Even a purchaser who took 'subject to' a contractual licence would not necessarily be bound. There must be a clear undertaking on the part of the purchaser, and the obligation must be imposed expressly in the conveyance. While Fox LJ supported the decision in *Binions* v *Evans*, he would virtually have limited it to its facts. On his view, a constructive trust will be imposed only where the conveyance to the purchaser is made *expressly* subject to the contractual licence, and he also thought that the fact that the purchaser had paid a reduced price in *Binions* v *Evans* significant. None of these factors was present in *Ashburn Anstalt*, so no constructive trust arose.

The actual decision in *Ashburn Anstalt* has been overruled by the House of Lords in *Prudential Assurance Co.* v *London Residuary Body* [1992] 2 AC 386, but no doubt has been cast on the statements in the previous paragraph, which were *dicta* and not necessary for the decision; the Court of Appeal's decision in *Ashburn Anstalt* was that there was a valid lease, and that aspect of the case can no longer be supported.

10.3 MUTUAL WILLS

The principles of mutual wills are similar to those that operated in the previous section, but an extension is the floating trust, which crystallises on the death of the survivor.

Mutual wills are agreements, usually (but not necessarily) between husband and wife. Wills are made (or the parties agree to make them) by each party in (usually) the same terms, and there is a mutual agreement that neither party will revoke, but the essence of the transaction is an agreement that each party will settle his or her property in a particular (usually the same) way.

Mutual wills create enforceable contracts, but we are not concerned here with them as contracts. Let us suppose that the agreement is between A and B, and that B is the survivor. B accordingly receives property under A's will; and, of course, he receives it only because he has agreed to settle it in a certain way. If the condition attaches merely to the property received under A's will, then the principles of the previous section, or indeed those discussed in chapter 9, suffice. B has taken property expressly subject to conditions, and equity will, by the device of the constructive trust, require him to carry out those conditions.

Suppose, for example, that as with the land in *Ottaway* v *Norman* [1972] Ch 698 (see 9.2.3.1), B has agreed that he will leave the property received to C. B simply obtains a life interest in the property. This is also a possible explanation of *Re Oldham* [1925] Ch 75, a mutual wills case. A more problematic situation is where A and B agree that each will leave all his property to the survivor on the understanding that the survivor will leave all his property to C. *Re Hagger* [1930] 2 Ch 190 suggests (contrary to *Re Oldham*) that a trust attaches to all the survivor's property, as long as the survivor accepts the legacy under the other's will. This is an extension of the reasoning we have seen so far, in that the obligation extends beyond the property actually received by B. It also suggests that unlike express trusts (see 3.2.1), constructive trusts can cover future as well as existing property.

As we saw at 9.2.3.1, a similar concept was envisaged in *Ottaway* v *Norman*, in respect of the furniture and other contents, including Miss Hodges's money. In fact, Brightman J thought that the obligation extended only to such furnishings and fixtures as Miss Hodges had received under Mr Ottaway's will, but also thought that if the agreement had included all Miss Hodges's other property and cash from whatever source, this obligation also could be enforced against her estate. He employed the concept of a 'floating trust', derived from the Australian case of *Birmingham* v *Renfrew* (1937) 57 CLR 666, which would remain in suspense during the life of the trustee and crystallise on her death, attaching to whatever property was comprised within her estate. This, as the learned judge noted, would seem to preclude Miss Hodges from making even a small pecuniary legacy in favour of her relatives or friends.

Similar reasoning was adopted, by Nourse J in a mutual wills context, in *Re Cleaver* [1981] 1 WLR 939. However, it is not clear from the report whether the trust imposed actually bound any property not received under Arthur Cleaver's will. If it did not then the *ratio* goes no further than *Re Oldham* [1925] Ch 75 (the widow, who survived her husband, would simply have enjoyed a life interest in the property received under Arthur Cleaver's will). But in *Re Dale* [1994] Ch 31, Morritt J applied the mutual wills doctrine in a situation where the second testator had received no benefit at all under the first testator's will, the mutual agreement having been that their children should share equally. There the trust clearly applied to the whole of the widow's estate, since the widow had received no property to which it could apply.

In *Re Goodchild* [1996] 1 All ER 670, Carnwath J accepted the notion of the floating trust, holding also that the floating trust so created was not destroyed by the remarriage of the second testator after the death of the first. On the facts, however, he found insufficient evidence of a specific agreement that the wills were to be mutually binding. Nonetheless, this case provides further authority for the floating trust concept.

10.4   A WIDER FRAUD-BASED DOCTRINE?

I would suggest that the equitable fraud doctrine is probably limited to the cases we have considered. However, in *Re Sharpe (a bankrupt)* [1980] 1 WLR 219, an 82-year-old lady, who was in poor health, loaned a large sum of money (£12,000) to her nephew to enable him to purchase a house in which they could both live. The nephew later went bankrupt, and the question arose as to whether the old lady's money was secured, or whether it formed part of the nephew's assets, to be divided among his general creditors. Browne-Wilkinson J found for the old lady, on the basis that she was a beneficiary under a constructive trust, which bound the trustee in bankruptcy. He thought that a constructive trust can be imposed simply because a licensee expends money or otherwise acts to his detriment. If the reasoning in this case is correct, almost any reliance on a promise relating to the occupation of property could give rise to a constructive trust, and the constructive trust could exist in a pure form in the situations discussed at 8.5.2.

This seems to be confusing the constructive trust with a proprietary estoppel (see Jill Martin, [1980] Conv 207), and indeed, I argued at 8.5 and 8.8 that trust and estoppel concepts are entirely different. *Re Sharpe* looks wrong as an estoppel case, if the reasoning at 8.5.2 is correct, since it ought not be capable of binding a trustee in bankruptcy. Indeed, Sir Nicholas Browne-Wilkinson himself took this view in his Holdsworth Club Address 1991, observing that 'only if the third party's conduct is such as to raise an estoppel against the third party individually will the third party be affected'. If this is correct, the trustee in bankruptcy as the third party could hardly have been affected by an estoppel in *Re Sharpe*.

The constructive trust reasoning in *Re Sharpe* was treated dismissively by Fox LJ in *Ashburn Anstalt v Arnold* [1989] 1 Ch 1, but he did not elaborate, since the case before him was sufficiently different as not to be affected directly by *Re Sharpe*. Nonetheless, the confusion between trust and estoppel concepts appears wrong in principle; and *Re Sharpe*, unsupported by other authority, is probably wrong.

ELEVEN

An Introduction to Charity

11.1 CHARITIES AND THE TRUST

It is usual to deal with charities as an integral part of the law of trusts. It is not necessarily the most appropriate classification, however, because though many charities exist in the form of a trust, this is not universal. Also, historically the law has recognised charities for even longer than the trust itself.

In its earliest institutional form, charity was the province of the medieval Church, and its supervision the responsibility of the ecclesiastical courts. It was the secularisation of charitable donation during the Tudor period and the contemporaneous growth of the jurisdiction of the Court of Chancery by way of the use (see 1.2) which brought the administration of charity under the control of the Chancellor. He began to enforce uses for 'pious purposes' at around the same time as he began to enforce uses relating to land. The attractive simplicity of the use, and later the trust, for philanthropic donors, coupled with the effectiveness of equitable remedies (see 1.4.5), meant that the trust rapidly became the commonest method of dedicating property to worthy causes.

Charitable trusts are, of course, a variety of purpose trust and, as we saw in 5.1, there are difficulties in the enforcement of purpose trusts, especially as with charities there will probably not be easily identifiable human benefici-aries. However, since the early 17th century the Attorney-General has undertaken the enforcement of charitable trusts, as representative plaintiff, and since 1960 the Charity Commissioners have been given supervisory powers over charities. Because the Attorney-General has powers of enforce-ment, there is no need for charitable trusts to be subject to the same certainty of objects requirements as private purpose trusts and they are not. Indeed, because of the public character of charitable trusts, they are also exempt from other requirements to which private trusts are subject and in addition enjoy certain privileges.

Although not all charities exist in the form of a trust, the trust is still the most common medium of charity today, both numerically and in terms of the value of their funds. The trust seems to be most favoured on the one hand by private individuals and on the other by the largest and wealthiest of charitable enterprises, the foundations which often originate within international commercial corporations.

From the viewpoint of the private donor, the trust form is simple to create and sufficiently flexible to allow for a degree of individuality to be expressed in its provisions. For a large and well-funded organisation, the trust form offers the opportunity to maintain large capital funds producing high levels of income, which can be distributed on a discretionary basis. For these reasons the trust will probably remain the most usual form of charitable enterprise and charity law will continue to take its direction from the doctrines developed in equity. Indeed, the courts have always shown a preference for treating all charities as partaking in the nature of a trust, even where their institutional arrangements are of a quite different sort.

The most common alternative forms for charity are the charitable corporation and the unincorporated association.

11.1.1 Charitable corporations
An increasing number of charitable ventures nowadays operate within a corporate structure and this form is particularly well suited to collective, active enterprises. A corporate charity will usually be a company limited by guarantee and will usually have a constitution forbidding the distribution of profit among its members. Otherwise, the establishment of a company limited by guarantee is broadly similar in terms of formality to the setting up of an ordinary commercial company. As with a commercial company, the liability of the charity is limited to its assets, thus protecting its members from unlimited personal liability in the event of the charity becoming insolvent.

The advantage of corporate status is that the charity can operate as a legal person. So it has the capacity to make contracts, incur liabilities and hold property in its own right without the need to involve trustees. Also, it does not need to effect alterations in the documents of title to its property at every change in personnel. Corporate status is therefore well suited to charities which undertake extensive long-term operations. These often have considerable assets, sufficient to make the expense of incorporation worthwhile.

11.1.2 Unincorporated associations
These are the other most common form, which may convert to corporate status if and when it becomes convenient. The less rigid framework offered by this form makes it attractive to groups of people wishing to undertake active charitable work in accordance with broadly democratic and flexible policies which may change and develop over time. Control of the organisation and its funds, if any, will typically be vested in a committee of managers who will probably be elected in conformity with the wishes of the current membership.

As we saw in 5.2, the basis of this form of organisation is usually a contract between the members, formulated as the rules which are contained in the constitution of the association. This carries the advantage of extreme flexibility, allowing the terms of the contract to be modified to meet new situations. The main disadvantage is that the managers and members are exposed to unlimited personal liability incurred in the course of the organisation's activities. Nevertheless, the unincorporated association accounts for a moderate proportion of old established charities, as well as some of the newer and most active charitable undertakings.

11.1.3 Other, unusual forms

Mutual benefit organisations maintaining funds collected by subscription from members, and being intended to provide benefits during sickness, old age etc., may be registered under the Friendly Societies Act 1974, and those which qualify as charitable according to the legal definition of that term (see chapter 12) may have the status of 'benevolent societies'. Their significance appears to be declining in view of the growth in State welfare provision.

Another form available to charities, and apparently favoured by the growing number of housing associations, is the industrial and provident society, a kind of hybrid with some of the features of both the friendly society and the guarantee company, and registrable under the Industrial and Provident Societies Acts 1965 to 1978.

Finally, there is the charitable corporation, which is not related to the guarantee companies discussed above. These include universities, hospitals and the British Museum, and they are established either by charter from the Crown or else by legislation (for example, the Charitable Trustees Incorporation Act 1872, and the British Museum Act 1963). Such institutions are diverse in nature, and there is no standard form — each is endowed with a constitution specific to its own requirements. These charities are generally considered to enjoy high prestige by virtue of their unique character, and represent something of an elite category within the range of charitable organisations.

11.2 LEGAL REGULATION OF CHARITIES: CONSEQUENCES OF CHARITABLE STATUS

Before considering the legal definition of charity (see chapter 12), we should consider the consequences that flow from charitable status. The cases considered in chapter 12 arose for a diversity of reasons, and this may have led to a confusion on the part of the courts as to the policy they should adopt.

For the consequences outlined here to apply it is necessary to show that the property is to be held beneficially for charitable purposes. It is insufficient for the recipient merely to covenant to use the property for purposes which happen to be charitable purposes. In *Liverpool City Council* v *Attorney-General, The Times,* 1 May 1992, Allerton Hall had been conveyed (in 1926) to Liverpool City Council subject to covenants that it would be used only as a public park. It was accepted that the provision of a public park or recreation ground was a charitable purpose (presumably on the principles in 12.6, below). The Attorney-General nevertheless failed in his contention that the land was held on charitable trusts, so that the City Council were able to treat it as part of its corporate property. No doubt, the covenants remained valid, but presumably since the original covenantees had long-since died, there was nobody in a position to enforce them.

11.2.1 Tax advantages

Charities enjoy exemption from income tax on all income, rents, dividends and profits, provided these are applied for charitable purposes, and may reclaim from the Revenue any income tax already paid prior to receipt of the income. Nor is income tax chargeable on the profits of any trade carried out by the charity, so long as these are applied for charitable purposes only and the trade is either exercised in carrying out the primary purposes of the charity or the work is carried out mainly by its beneficiaries (e.g., workshops for the handicapped). Charitable corporations are exempt from corporation tax.

Gifts to charity are largely exempt from inheritance tax, and capital gains tax is not payable where gains are applied to charitable purposes. All charities are exempt from half of the rates on premises occupied in connection with the charity, including charity shops, and premises used for religious purposes are entirely exempt from rates. Generally, charities must pay VAT on goods and services, but certain goods, such as some equipment for the handicapped, are zero rated.

Some conception of the importance of the taxation consequences of charitable status may be gleaned from the number of cases considered in chapter 12 involving the Inland Revenue. In addition, charitable status is often claimed for rates advantages, for example, in *Re South Place Ethical Society* [1980] 1 WLR 1565 (see 12.4.1) and *United Grand Lodge of Ancient Free & Accepted Masons of England and Wales* v *Holborn Borough Council* [1957] 1 WLR 1080 (see 12.4.2).

The annual cost to the Revenue of these tax concessions is of the order of half a billion pounds or, to put it into perspective, about £50 for every average-sized family in the UK.

11.2.2 Validity

Another common reason for litigation on charitable status is to ascertain whether the gift is valid at all. Probably the commonest situation is where the next of kin challenge the validity of a testamentary bequest (e.g., *Re Shaw* [1957] 1 WLR 729 and *Re Pinion* [1965] Ch 85, on which see 12.3.1, and *Re Koeppler's WT* [1986] Ch 423, see 12.8.1). Charitable status has three main consequences for validity.

First, charitable trusts are trusts for purposes, which would often be void if non-charitable (see 5.1). Yet as we saw in 11.1, charities are public trusts enforceable at the suit of the Attorney-General, so their lack of human beneficiaries is not fatal, as it is to private trusts. Indeed, only the Attorney-General can enforce charitable trusts; individuals who may benefit have no *locus standi*, by virtue of the Charities Act 1960, s. 28. The Attorney-General can be substituted as plaintiff for individuals, however (*Hauxwell* v *Barton-upon-Humber Urban District Council* [1974] Ch 432, where he was substituted as plaintiff for two individuals).

Secondly, it is not necessary for the purposes of a charitable trust to be defined with certainty. A gift on trust 'for charitable purposes' will be valid, and the court and Charity Commissioners have jurisdiction to create a scheme for the application of the property donated. A gift to charity which is not expressed as a trust will be similarly disposed of by the Crown.

Thirdly, charitable trusts, unlike private trusts, may exist indefinitely. This being so, a gift over from one charity to another may take effect at any time in the future: *Christ's Hospital* v *Grainger* (1849) 1 Mac & G 460. Once property is dedicated to charity, there is no infringement of the perpetuity rules merely because it passes from one charitable body to another. However, the rule against perpetuities applies as usual to prevent a too remote vesting of a gift to a charity in the first instance, and also to a gift over from a charity to a non-charity.

Private conveyancers were quick to make use of the exemption from the rule against remoteness of vesting. Suppose, for example, a gift is made by X to the trustees of charity A on trust for A's purposes for so long as they continue to maintain X's tomb, and thereafter to the trustees of charity B for B's purposes. The gift over to charity B is valid even if it may vest outside the perpetuity period, but of course the trustees of charity A have an incentive to continue to maintain X's tomb. Thus X can secure the maintenance of his tomb far beyond the period he could achieve under a private purpose trust.

11.2.3 Registration of charities

Though the definition of charitable status is at the end of the day a matter for the courts, the process of obtaining recognition as a charity today is primarily administrative, and largely outside the direct control of the courts. The Charities Act 1960 provided for the comprehensive registration of charities, and an organisation seeking charitable status must normally apply for registration to the Charity Commissioners, who have power under the Act to grant or withhold registration according to their decision as to whether the proposed purposes are, in law, charitable.

The modern Charity Commission, charged with supervising supervision of charitable endowments, came into being in 1853, although originally it was given only limited powers.

The duty to maintain the register is placed on the Commissioners themselves by virtue of s. 4(1) of the Act but a duty to apply for registration is also placed on the charity trustees by virtue of s. 4(6). Registration is conclusive evidence of charitable status.

Therefore, though the importance of judicial decisions has not been diminished since 1960, some knowledge is also required of the work of the Commissioners, who exercise a quasi-judicial function in this area. In reaching their decisions, they may consult with other bodies, such as the Inland Revenue, which may also be called upon to judge the validity of claims to be treated as a charity. The overall effect of the procedure has been to reduce the number of reported court decisions on the boundaries of charity to a handful of test cases which raise significant issues of law.

Refusal by the Commissioners to register an organisation gives rise to a right of appeal, under s. 5, which is in the first instance an informal appeal to the board of Charity Commissioners. Such appeals are rare, usually single figures each year. Further appeal lies through the courts (as in, e.g.,

Incorporated Council of Law Reporting for England and Wales v *Attorney-General* [1972] Ch 73, on which see 12.3.1.1, and *McGovern* v *Attorney-General* [1982] Ch 321, on which see 12.8.1), initially the High Court, and thence to the Court of Appeal and House of Lords. The smooth functioning of the system is aided by the openness of the Commission's practices, which are made public through annual reports, and by the advice and assistance which are offered to applicants seeking to frame their trusts so as to meet the necessary criteria.

Viewed from the perspective of the saving thus effected in money and time, the registration process must be regarded as an improvement upon *ad hoc* litigation as a method of establishing charitable credentials. From the standpoint of the well meaning donor or charity activist, however, the process of registration may appear as a system of gate keeping, limiting the range of altruistic enterprises to settled and uncontentious fields already blessed by judicial decisions and the precedents of the Commission.

Further, although achieving charitable status carries numerous advantages, it also has the effect of bringing the organisation under the supervision of the Commissioners, who are given wide-reaching powers by the Act. Much of the routine work of the Commissioners consists of making schemes and orders to assist the efficiency of charity trustees, and in practice little use has been made of the powers to demand accounts, institute inquiries and if necessary to remove trustees. It is not, however, unknown for the Commissioners to warn organisations who engage in activities falling outside the legal definition of charitable purposes that they risk deregistration by so doing. This may be a serious curb, as we shall see in 12.8.1, upon the actions of those charities which involve them in campaigns falling foul of the requirement that charities must not be political. Certain organisations therefore prefer to forgo the privileges of charitable status in favour of greater freedom of action, or seek registration only in the name of sub-branches which clearly limit themselves to charitable works such as education or the alleviation of poverty and distress.

The supervisory powers of the Commissioners, and their powers of inquiry, have been strengthened by the Charities Act 1992, a provision whose main aim (as with a great deal of charities legislation over the centuries) seems to have been to curb abuses by and maladministration of charitable bodies.

It is relatively rare for the supervision of the Charity Commissioners to be the reason for litigation, but in *Neville Estates* v *Madden* [1962] Ch 832 (see 12.4.1), the trustees of the Catford Synagogue were able to resist an action for specific performance for the sale of land owned by the synagogue: as a consequence of the synagogue being held to be charitable, the consent of the Charity Commissioners was required before the sale could go ahead.

In *Mills* v *Winchester Diocesan Board of Finance* [1989] 2 All ER 317, Knox J held that the Charity Commissioners owed no duty of care of the potential objects of charity.

11.2.4   Cy près

If a charitable organisation is wound up, any surplus property may be applied cy près. If, on the other hand, the organisation is not charitable, any surplus property will go to the Crown as *bona vacantia,* or to the donors on resulting trust, on the principles discussed in 2.4, or in the case of an unincorporated association, to the members of the association, on the principles discussed in 5.3. In *Re Hobourn Aero Components Ltd's Air Raid Disaster Fund* [1946] Ch 194 (see 12.8.2), the sole consequence of the fund being held non-charitable was that a cy près scheme was not directed, and that the surplus was distributed among the contributors.

11.2.5 The political dimension to charities
The political dimension to charities has possibly influenced their development and cannot be altogether avoided.

The role adopted by charities 100 or so years ago has to some extent been superseded by State provision for the least fortunate in society. Some might even go so far as to argue that charities have no value alongside a State-funded system. Most, however, would probably hold that the freedom of individuals to decide whether to distribute any of their property to philanthropic purposes, and if so which purposes, is an important freedom, which is in no way in opposition to the welfare State provision (in which, of course, individuals have very little direct say).

At the very least, however, it is more difficult nowadays to justify tax concessions to charities, when at the same time many of the least fortunate are provided for by the welfare State. Also, if the State has decided not to fund a particular purpose through the welfare scheme, it is odd that it should be required to fund it through the back door, by virtue of the tax concessions given to charitable enterprise. Probably such an argument has to some extent been taken on board by the courts and the legislature, the former by laying down more stringent conditions for charitable status, and excluding 'undesirable' forms of altruistic activity, the latter by requiring registration and to some extent supervision by a public body, viz. the Charity Commissioners (see 11.2.3).

There is also no doubt that the terms of a gift to charity are controlled by the donor, and some might argue that, at any rate where very large sums are concerned, the power that goes with such control is better administered by public bodies than private individuals.

11.3 THE LAW OF CHARITY: CONFLICTING POLICIES ADOPTED BY THE COURTS

11.3.1 Today
Courts today are generally unwilling to frustrate the wishes of a settlor and prefer to hold gifts valid if they can. This leads to a tendency to expand the legal definition of charity. On the other hand, jealousy of the tax concessions tends towards the opposite result. In other words, there is a tension between two conflicting tendencies, which to some extent explains the haphazard development of the law.

The jealousy over the tax position may also explain why the public benefit requirement for charitable status figures so largely. Lord Cross of Chelsea in

Dingle v *Turner* [1972] AC 601 (see 12.7.3), a case where only the validity of the trust was at issue, would have preferred different tests for validity on the one hand and tax concessions on the other. The law adopts the same test, however.

It is not only today that tensions between conflicting policies are felt, and it should be remembered that the legal definition of charity is the result of the development of several centuries, at any rate from the Statute of Charitable Uses 1601 onwards. At certain periods, charity was viewed with extreme suspicion, particularly where, as in the case of the medieval Church, the power of charitable donation could be seen in rivalry to the claims of the then nascent secular State, or where, as in the 17th and 18th centuries, charity was blamed for taking away the rightful expectations of heirs.

11.3.2 Elizabethan times to 18th century

With the decline during this period of the influence of the Roman Catholic Church, and other economic factors, poor relief during Elizabethan times became something of a problem to the State. Statutory provision for the poor, to be administered by the parish and paid for out of local rates, was introduced in 1572, and comprehensive poor codes were enacted in 1597 and 1601. However, it was in the interests of the State to encourage charitable donation in order to reduce the burden of poor rates. The development of charity law at this time, therefore, was geared primarily towards relief of the poor, rather than other forms of philanthropic enterprise.

This can be clearly seen by examination of the preamble to the Statute of Charitable Uses 1601 (set out in full in 12.1). The primary purpose of this Act was to provide for commissioners to be appointed to investigate administration of charities, and in particular misappropriation of trust property. This procedure continued in operation for about 200 years.

Of greater importance for present purposes, however, was that a number of charitable uses (or, in other words, charitable purposes) are listed in the preamble to the Act, and the preamble was later used by the courts to provide the basis for the legal definition of charity. Indeed, under the fourth head of charity (see 12.5), this is still the case today.

The preamble in fact contains quite a divergent list of charitable purposes, sufficiently diverse to provide for the expanding definitions of charity in the 18th and 19th centuries. However, the list as a whole is clearly intended to be confined to provision for the poor, to reduce the burden of the poor rates, and early development of charity was heavily influenced by this bias.

The notion of public benefit also appears clearly in the preamble.

11.3.3 The 18th and 19th centuries

This period of development is important because it was then that the legal definition of charity was consolidated. The modern law of charity is based on developments during this period. The two main influences are the decline in importance of genuine poverty charities and the influence of the mortmain legislation.

The decline in the importance of poverty relief in charitable giving was partly connected with notions of the 'undeserving' poor. At the same time, there was a move towards other types of charitable donation. For example, the NSPCC, Dr Barnado's Homes and the National Trust are all creatures of this period.

A major influence on the law of charity at this time was judicial hostility to bequests for charitable purposes which threatened to deprive testators' families from their 'rightful due'. It might be thought that this judicial hostility would lead to a narrowing of the legal definition of charity, but in fact the reverse was often the case. It should not be forgotten that the mortmain legislation (Mortmain and Charitable Uses Act 1736) made many testamentary gifts of land to charity void during this period (from 1736 to 1891), and this may paradoxically have resulted in a *wider* definition of charity being adopted in order not to frustrate the claims of disappointed relations (if the gift was held void, there was a resulting trust of the property for the estate).

Examples of cases where the adoption of a wide definition of charity led to a gift being struck down under the mortmain legislation were *Townlee* v *Bedwell* (1801) 6 Ves Jr 104, on the establishment of botanical gardens, *Thornton* v *Howe* (1862) 31 Beav 14, on the advancement of religion (see 12.4), and *Tatham* v *Drummond* (1864) 3 De G J & Sm 484, on animal charities (see 12.5).

Also during this period, the original notion of public benefit underwent a change. Originally a benefit to the poor was required, but now almost any public purpose would do. For example, it became clear that a school to educate the sons of gentlemen may be charitable, whereas it had previously been thought that the preamble covered only free schools. Also apparent, even at the height of philanthropic activity in the 19th century, was that middle-class social values of the time were strongly in evidence in an attempt to limit the distribution of charity to the 'deserving'. Hence the modern definition of relief of poverty for charitable purposes is by no means limited to the relief of the destitute.

11.3.4 Late 19th and 20th centuries

Two further developments are important during this period: first, the growing tie between tax concessions and charitable status, and secondly further changes in the nature of charitable donation, especially with the development of increased welfare provision.

In *Commissioners for Special Purposes of the Income Tax* v *Pemsel* [1891] AC 531 (see 12.1), the case which really forms the basis of the present-day definition of heads of charity, it became clear for the first time that relief from taxation might be tied in to the definition of charity. The judges themselves do not appear to have appreciated the importance of the connection, however.

There was an exemption in the Income Tax Act 1842 for rents and profits of lands vested in trustees for 'charitable purposes', and the House of Lords held (by a 4-2 majority) that this exemption applied to a trust for the maintaining, supporting and advancing of missionary establishments (known as Unitas Fratrum, or United Brethren, whose purpose was to convert people among the 'heathen nations' to Christianity).

This case laid down the heads of charity as relief of poverty, advancement of education, advancement of religion, and other purposes beneficial to the community. These heads are described in detail in chapter 12.

There has also been a further change in the nature of charitable donation. In the 20th century, relief of poverty has become more clearly a State function, and accordingly charities for the relief of poverty have declined to a greater extent even than in the 19th century. On the other hand, gifts to social welfare, disaster appeals, and especially pressure groups, have increased. Also, a far greater proportion of charitable income comes from fees and government grants, as opposed to voluntary donations.

It is questionable whether the law has altered significantly to take account of these developments, although Lord Cross clearly faced the taxation issue in *Dingle* v *Turner* (see 12.7.2). On the changing emphasis of charity, the Recreational Charities Act 1958 added a new head of charity, in line with the greater emphasis on social welfare (see 12.6). Also, the fourth head of charity (12.5) may still be developing, in line with modern social conditions. For example, Lord Wilberforce said in *Scottish Burial Reform & Cremation Society Ltd* v *Glasgow Corporation* [1968] AC 138, 154 (a case on the fourth head):

> But three things may be said about [the *Pemsel* classification], which its author [Lord Macnaughten] would surely not have denied: first that, since it is a classification of convenience, there may well be purposes which do not fit neatly into one or other of the headings; secondly, that the words used must not be given the force of a statute to be construed; and thirdly, that the law of charity is a moving subject which may well have evolved even since 1891.

Similar statements can be found, also in the House of Lords, in *IRC* v *McMullen* [1981] AC 1, a case concerning the playing of football at schools and universities (see 12.3.1.2). This is a case on the second head of charity, and again it is clear that the legal conception of charity is not static but changes with ideas about social values.

11.3.5   Validity of non-charitable purposes

Lord Cross's desire to see different tests for validity on the one hand, and tax concessions on the other (see 11.3.1) to some extent pre-supposes that it is difficult to achieve valid dispositions for purposes which are not charitable. It is by no means impossible, however, and the methods by which this can be achieved are described in chapter 5. It is, for example, common nowadays for disaster appeals to be expressly made non-charitable, to free them from the fetters of Charity Commissioners' supervision, and in particular the requirement that the funds must be distributed so as to relieve poverty (see 12.2).

That being so, the main consequence of charitable status today may well be taxation privileges. Perhaps the law should not be too free in the granting of those privileges. This probably explains the personal nexus rule in *Oppenheim* v *Tobacco Securities Trust Co. Ltd* [1951] AC 297 (see 12.7.1).

The position is more difficult for pure purpose trusts, like *Re Astor's ST* [1952] Ch 534 (see 5.1), where trustees were instructed to hold a fund upon various trusts including 'the maintenance of good relations between nations [and] . . . the preservation of the independence of newspapers', or *Re Shaw* [1957] 1 WLR 729, a trust to research the development of a 40-letter alphabet. Both were void, and such trusts can still only be validated by being charitable.

In conclusion, it should come as no surprise that the legal definition of charity has fluctuated over the centuries, depending on the prevailing social philosophies of the time, and that this, coupled with the conflicting policies of the present law, has resulted in a less than logical legal position obtaining today.

TWELVE

Legal Definition of Charity

12.1 INTRODUCTION

12.1.1 Sources of law

There is no formal statutory definition of charity, despite occasional proposals. Nor does it appear likely that a statutory definition will appear in the near future. The courts in the past, however, used the preamble to the Statute of Charitable Uses 1601, sometimes referred to as the Statute of Elizabeth (which was part of a scheme intended to curb abuses), as a guideline to simplify their task of determining which purposes were charitable. The preamble listed purposes which were regarded as charitable at the time. Purposes which fell within the 'spirit and intendment' of the preamble were accepted by the courts as being charitable. Those which did not were not, however much they may have been regarded as beneficial to the public.

By operation of the doctrine of precedent, what had originally been simply a convenient practice by the courts crystallised into rigid legal doctrine, and thus the preamble came, in effect, to have direct legal force. This was most unusual, because preambles to statutes usually have no legal force. Of course, the authority for the present law cannot be the preamble itself, but the cases which subsequently adopted it.

The purposes laid down in the preamble are many and diverse, but fortunately in the House of Lords in *Commissioners for Special Purposes of the Income Tax* v *Pemsel* [1891] AC 531, Lord Macnaughten categorised them under four main heads:

1. Relief of poverty (see 12.2).
2. Advancement of education (see 12.3).
3. Advancement of religion (see 12.4).
4. Other purposes which are beneficial to the community (see 12.5).

Any given charitable purpose may, of course, fall within more than one of these heads.

Generally, therefore, there is no need to go back before 1891 for a judicial definition of charity. As we shall see, however, for head 4 the test still depends

on the spirit and intendment of the preamble: *Scottish Burial Reform &*
Cremation Society Ltd v *Glasgow Corporation* [1968] AC 138. In that case,
Lord Wilberforce also sounded a general note of caution about over-rigorous
application of the *Pemsel* heads (see 11.3.4), noting in particular that the law
of charity is a moving subject which may well have evolved even since 1891.

The Statute of Charitable Uses was repealed by subsequent legislation, so
that for a time only the preamble remained. The preamble itself was repealed
by the Charities Act 1960 and was not replaced. This repeal had no legal
effect, however, because the cases which used the preamble as a guideline can
still be taken to be authoritative. Indeed, Lord Wilberforce in the *Scottish
Burial Reform* case, mentioned above, used the spirit and intendment of the
preamble as a test of charitable status as late as 1968.

Because reference still therefore occasionally needs to be made to the
preamble, it is here set out in full:

> Whereas Lands, Tenements, Rents, Annuities, Profits, Hereditaments,
> Goods, Chattels, Money and Stocks of Money, have been heretofore given,
> limited, appointed and assigned, as well as by the Queen's most excellent
> Majesty, and her most noble Progenitors, as by sundry other well disposed
> persons; some for Relief of aged, impotent and poor People, some for the
> Maintenance of sick and maimed Soldiers and Mariners, Schools of
> Learning, Free Schools, and Scholars in Universities, some for the Repair
> of Bridges, Ports, Havens, Causeways, Churches, Sea-Banks and High-
> ways, some for the Education and Preferment of Orphans, some for or
> towards Relief, Stock or Maintenance for Houses of Correction, some for
> the Marriages of Poor Maids, some for Supportation, Aid and Help of
> young Tradesmen, Handicraftsmen and Persons decayed, and others for
> the Relief or Redemption of Prisoners or Captives, and for Aid or Ease of
> any poor Inhabitants concerning Payments of Fifteens [a tax on moveable
> property], setting out of Soldiers and other Taxes; which Lands, Ten-
> ements, Rents, Annuities, Profits, Hereditaments, Goods, Chattels, Money
> and Stocks of Money, nevertheless have not been employed according to
> charitable Intent of the givers and Founders thereof, by reason of Frauds,
> Breaches of Trust, and Negligence in those that should pay, deliver and
> employ the same: For Redress and Remedy whereof, Be it enacted . . .

Nevertheless, in spite of the caution sounded in *Scottish Burial Reform*, the
main source of the modern law can be taken to be Lord Macnaughten's
classification in *Pemsel*. In addition to judge-made law, a body of precedent
has now been built up by the Charity Commissioners in exercising their
jurisdiction under s. 4 of the Charities Act 1960 (see 11.2.3). This body of
precedent is not technically authority but may be assumed to govern the
process of registration in practice, unless and until it is successfully challenged
in a court.

Recreational charities are a special case, by virtue of the Recreational
Charities Act 1958 (see 12.6), which provides a limited extension to the
general law.

12.1.2 The requirement of public benefit

We have seen that charitable trusts are of a public nature, in that they are publicly enforced and controlled, and have certain tax concessions. There is also a requirement that to be charitable a purpose must, in addition to falling within the *Pemsel* heads outlined above, involve a public benefit. There are therefore two requirements for a purpose to be charitable. It must confer a benefit upon those who are directly the objects of the charity, and it must also confer an additional benefit upon the public at large.

For example, if a charitable purpose such as education is to be advanced, it must not only confer a benefit on those in direct receipt of the education, but must also be advanced in some way that benefits the public, or at least a substantial section thereof, rather than providing benefits for some artificially limited class of people. However, as we shall see in 12.7, this requirement is not applied with the same rigour to each of the four heads of charity, and in the case of the relief of poverty, its role is minimal. For this reason, the public benefit requirement will be dealt with separately under each head.

12.1.3 Overseas benefits

There is no rule of law which prevents the benefits of a charity being directed overseas, as opposed to being confined within the UK or primarily directed within the UK. For example, in *Re Niyazi's WT* [1978] 1 WLR 910, a trust to construct a hostel for working men in Cyprus was held charitable as being for the relief of poverty. Missionary societies operating abroad always seem to have been regarded as religious charities, and these will often involve advancement of education also. There are, however, two qualifications concerning overseas benefits.

First, although the Charity Commissioners (Annual Report for 1963, paras 69–76) take the view that trusts to relieve poverty or to advance religion will be charitable wherever found, a trust which falls within the fourth head must involve a benefit, even if indirect, to persons within the UK.

Secondly, charity must not be tainted with political activity (see 12.8.1), and the large-scale charities which aim at assisting developing nations must avoid this pitfall. It seems that whereas it can be charitable to provide direct relief of observable poverty among a population, it is not charitable to seek to raise the total economy of an overseas country, or to alter its laws in order to alleviate poverty.

12.1.4 Purposes must be exclusively charitable

A further point to be noted is that a trust must not merely be capable of application to charitable purposes; it must be exclusively so. If it is possible to benefit an object which is not charitable, then the trust will not be exclusively charitable, and will fail unless the courts feel able to sever the offending objects from the main corpus of the otherwise charitable purpose, or to declare that the non-charitable purposes are merely subsidiary.

A great deal therefore depends on whether drafting of the trust is construed conjunctively or disjunctively. For example, if a purpose is described as 'Charitable *and* benevolent', it is probable that these will be construed conjunctively: 'benevolent' merely qualifies 'charitable', so only charitable purposes are included. But in *Chichester Diocesan Fund & Board of Finance* v *Simpson* [1944] AC 341, the words 'charitable *or* benevolent' would have permitted the trustees to devote all the funds to benevolent ends which were not also charitable. The trust therefore failed, leading to further litigation because funds had already been distributed by the trustees (*Ministry of Health* v *Simpson* [1951] AC 251). A gift to 'benevolent, charitable and religious' purposes was treated in *Williams* v *Kershaw* (1835) 5 Cl & F 111 n as allowing the trustees to select purposes which were benevolent, but not necessarily charitable and religious. In other words, the comma was treated as allowing the trustees to select alternatives (i.e., as '*or*').

Although each case calls for independent construction, as a general guide it may be said that a comma, or the word 'or', is likely to lead to the listed purposes being interpreted disjunctively (i.e., as alternatives), while the word 'and' is usually read conjunctively. 'Charitable and . . .' succeeds; 'charitable or . . .' fails.

This is not invariably the case. In *Attorney General of the Bahamas* v *Royal Trust Co.* [1986] 3 All ER 423, the Privy Council held not charitable a bequest for 'any purposes for and/or connected with the education and welfare of Bahamian children and young people', on the grounds that education and welfare should be interpreted disjunctively, and that a trust for welfare was not charitable. Therefore, although it may be possible to draw up guidelines to construction, categoric statements should be treated with caution.

In *Chichester Diocesan Board of Finance* v *Simpson*, it was impossible to construe the gift as being confined to charitable purposes, rather than benevolent purposes. Sometimes it is possible to construe the gift as a whole as being to charitable purposes, however, and as a matter of construction to exclude all purposes which are not charitable: see, for example, *Re Hetherington* [1990] Ch 1, at 12.7.4. If so, the trustees will be restrained from using trust property for purposes which are not charitable, even where by so doing they are not contravening the *express* terms of the donation. In *Webb* v *O'Doherty*, *The Times*, 11 February 1991 (see 12.8.1), the officers of a students' union were restrained from making any payments to the National Student Committee to Stop War in the Gulf, or to the Cambridge Committee to Stop War in the Gulf, whose purposes were not charitable. The union was an educational charity, and the officers were therefore entitled to use its property only for charitable purposes, even though there was nothing in the constitution of the union itself prohibiting such payments.

12.1.5 Profit-seeking
Generally speaking, it is incompatible with charitable status actively to seek profit as a primary objective, although fees may be charged, and incidental acquisition of profit should not disqualify. In *Scottish Burial Reform & Cremation Society Ltd* v *Glasgow Corporation* [1968] AC 138, the House of Lords held a society charitable for rating purposes (under the fourth *Pemsel* head — see 12.5), whose main object was the promotion of sanitary methods of disposal of the dead. The society charged fees but was not profit-making.

12.2 RELIEF OF POVERTY

12.2.1 What is poverty?

The courts have not attempted to define poverty in precise terms (e.g., a particular level of income), but as we saw in chapter 11, have been influenced by notions of 'the deserving poor' (see 11.3.3). Hence, poverty is not as extreme a concept as destitution (i.e., people can be poor who are not destitute) and it varies depending upon one's status in life. People who are sufficiently well off to be able to live without State aid can be regarded as being poor for these purposes. Paradoxically, it is nowadays actually very difficult to relieve poverty among the poorest sections of society, because a claimant of State benefit can suffer a reduction in that benefit if he receives more than a small donation from charity.

12.2.1.1 Relative nature of poverty   In *Re Coulthurst* [1951] Ch 661, Evershed MR said of poverty (at pp. 665–6):

> It is quite clearly established that poverty does not mean destitution: it is a word of wide and somewhat indefinite import; it may not be unfairly paraphrased for present purposes as meaning persons who have to 'go short' in the ordinary acception of that term, due regard being had to their status in life, and so forth.

Poverty, therefore, is a relative matter, depending on one's status in life, and the courts have been willing to allow trusts to assist such categories as 'distressed gentlefolk'. In *Re De Cartaret* [1933] Ch 103, a trust for annual allowances of £40 each to widows and spinsters 'whose income otherwise shall not be less than 80 or more than 120 pounds per annum' was held charitable, even though there was a minimum income qualification, and £80 a year was at any rate a moderate income then.

12.2.1.2 Exclusively for the poor   Subject to the width of the definition of poverty, it is essential that poverty should be imposed as a qualification for benefit and that only the poor can benefit. Whereas a trust under any of the other four heads can be charitable even where affluent people can enjoy its benefits, a trust which may benefit rich persons as well as poor will fail under this head. This is the reason why disaster fund appeals are often not charitable (see 12.8.3), but the organisers of recent appeals have sometimes preferred to forgo charitable status, and the consequent tax exemptions, rather than limit compensation expressly to the poor.

The rich must usually be expressly excluded, the courts being very reluctant to infer their exclusion even where the nature of the benefit is unlikely to make it attractive except to the destitute. Thus in *Re Gwyon* [1930] 1 Ch 255, a clergyman had provided in his will for the distribution of trousers to the boys in the Farnham area. Though the trousers were described in such a way as to be unlikely to appeal to any but the very needy, because the rich were not expressly excluded, the provision was not charitable (see 12.1.4), and therefore failed. Another case is *Re Drummond* [1914] 2 Ch 90, where a bequest of shares on trust to provide holidays for employees failed, even though the actual wages received by those employees was very low. In *Re Sanders's WT* [1954] Ch 265, Harman J thought that the provision of dwellings for 'the working classes' in the Pembroke Dock area was not sufficient to limit the benefit to poor persons. Nor will a gift for 'deserving' persons, or 'those in need of financial assistance' suffice, but 'indigent' and 'needy' can be regarded as synonyms for poverty. Poverty can also often be implied in the case of gifts to elderly or disabled recipients.

As with any question of construction, however, no hard and fast rules can be laid down. Whereas the courts are reluctant to infer exclusion of the rich in the absence of an express limitation to the poor, it would be wrong to assume that they never do so. For example, in *Powell* v *Attorney-General* (1817) 3 Mer 48, it was assumed that the widows and children of Liverpool seamen would necessarily be poor, even though the word 'poor' itself was not used. More recently, in *Re Niyazi's WT* [1978] 1 WLR 910 (see 12.1.3), Megarry V-C held charitable a bequest of £15,000 'for the construction of or as a contribution towards the cost of a working men's hostel' in Famagusta, Cyprus, although there was no express limitation to the poor. He accepted that persons requiring such accommodation would necessarily be poor. *Re Niyazi's WT* is probably not of general application, however. The amount of money left for the purpose was relatively small, and the word 'hostel', rather than 'dwelling' suggested very inferior accommodation. 'Working men' is more limited than 'working classes', excluding, for example, battered wives and students, and Megarry V-C had regard to the deplorable housing shortage in Famagusta. It follows that it would be inadvisable for settlors to rely too heavily on this decision, and an express limitation to the poor is safer.

12.2.1.3 Methods of relieving poverty The measures must actually relieve poverty, so merely to provide amusement for the poor will not suffice under this head, although it might under the second head, if educational (see 12.3).

It used to be thought that relief of poverty had to be on-going, rather than by way of an immediate distribution of property. It was thought that an immediate distribution was indistinguishable from an ordinary private bequest. It is now clear from the Court of Appeal decision in *Re Scarisbrick* [1951] Ch 622 that this is no longer the case and that it is possible to relieve poverty by way of one-off payment or distribution. The question of whether or not a trust is perpetual in nature could, in the view of Jenkins LJ in that case, be relevant to the question of public benefit (see 12.7) because an immediate gift would be less likely to be in favour of a class of persons, as opposed to individuals. But on the assumption that the public benefit test is satisfied, it is not fatal that the disposition is once and for all rather than perpetual.

Indeed, the growth in State welfare provision has reduced the attractiveness of hand-outs, for reasons explained at the beginning of the section. Yet many old trusts to relieve poverty still bind trustees to distribute money or goods. This problem and the solution to it are considered in 13.6.

Relief need not even necessarily be in the form of direct hand-outs of money, goods or services, but could, for example, allow access to necessary amenities at reduced cost. So it was accepted in *Joseph Rowntree Memorial Trust Housing Association Ltd* v *Attorney-General* [1983] Ch 159 that the sale of homes to elderly persons at 70 per cent of cost was charitable.

12.3   ADVANCEMENT OF EDUCATION

12.3.1   What constitutes education?

12.3.1.1   Wide range of activities covered   The scope of charitable educational activities is surprisingly wide. In other areas (see, e.g., 12.4 and 12.5.2) a wide definition of charitable activity has been motivated by the mortmain legislation (see 11.3) but this legislation rarely affected educational charities, many of which were incorporated by royal charter.

The preamble to the Act of 1601 (set out in 12.1.1) speaks only of 'schools of learning, free schools, scholars in universities' and the 'education and preferment of orphans', but in modern times this category has grown to cover a very wide range of educational and cultural activities extending far beyond the administration of formal instruction.

Schools and universities are clearly charitable, and so now are nursery schools, adult education centres and societies dedicated to promoting training and standards within a trade or profession. Education is not limited to teaching, however, and learned societies which bring together experts in a field to share and exchange knowledge may be charitable. Museums, zoos and public libraries may be educational to the public at large, quite apart from their research activities. Even cultural activities such as drama, music, literature and fine arts can come within this head, on the ground that they have a role in the cultivation of knowledge and taste.

As with other heads of charity, it is essential that the organisation should not be profit-seeking and the purposes must be exclusively charitable. Thus a trust for 'artistic' purposes may be too wide (see *Associated Artists Ltd* v *IRC* [1956] 1 WLR 752).

It is also necessary that education be advanced, so that although research can be charitable, probably it will not be if, for example, it is carried on in secret. Scholarship for its own sake is also not charitable, and this is one of the reasons why researching the advantages of a new 40-letter alphabet was held non-charitable by Harman J in *Re Shaw* [1957] 1 WLR 729. The validity of a bequest under George Bernard Shaw's will, which also provided for the transcription of *Androcles and the Lion* into the proposed 40-letter alphabet, was successfully challenged.

Learned societies are charitable, and professional and vocational bodies which advance education, such as the Royal College of Surgeons, are also charitable, even though one of the ancillary purposes is the protection and assistance of its members. Other examples include the Royal College of

Nursing, the Institution of Civil Engineers, and the Incorporated Council of Law Reporting (in *Incorporated Council of Law Reporting for England & Wales v Attorney-General* [1972] Ch 73, the Attorney-General tried unsuccessfully to argue that the citation of law reports in court could not be educational because judges are deemed to have complete knowledge of the law). Bodies whose chief purpose is to further the interests of the members and to promote the status of the profession will not, however, be charitable, for example the General Nursing Council (see *General Nursing Council for England & Wales v St Marylebone Borough Council* [1959] AC 540).

12.3.1.2 Physical education As we shall see in 12.5.3 and 12.6, physical activity which is of a purely recreational nature will not be charitable unless it falls within the provisions of the Recreational Charities Act 1958. Games and other leisure-time pursuits can be charitable under this head, however, if educational. Thus in *Re Marriette* [1915] 2 Ch 284, a gift to provide squash courts at a public school was held charitable, Eve J remarking (at p. 288) that the playing of games at boarding schools was as important as learning from books, and that the proper education of young people can include a physical element:

> No one of sense could be found to suggest that between those ages [10 to 19] any boy can be properly educated unless at least as much attention is given to the development of his body as is given to the development of his mind.

On the same principle, the provision of toys for small children can be charitable (the National Association of Toy Libraries is a registered charity) as are youth movements, such as the Boy Scout Movement, or trusts to provide school outings. In *Re Dupree's Deed Trusts* [1945] Ch 16, Vaisey J held charitable a chess contest for young men in the Portsmouth area, though leaving the issue open for less intellectually demanding pursuits:

> I think that the case before me may be a little near the line, and I decide it without attempting to lay down any general propositions. One feels, perhaps, that one is on a slippery slope. If chess, why not draughts; if draughts, why not bezique, and so on, through to bridge and whist, and, by another route, to stamp collecting and the acquisition of birds' eggs? Those pursuits will have to be dealt with if and when they come up for consideration in connection with the problem whether or no there is in existence an educational charitable trust.

These cases have been approved and followed by the House of Lords in *IRC v McMullen* [1981] AC 1, a case involving the playing of football at schools and universities. The House, holding that the Football Asociation Youth Trust was charitable, also made it clear that the legal conception of charity was not static but changed with ideas about social values (see 11.3.4).

All the above cases concerned the education of children or young persons. There is no reason, in principle, why adult education should not also be charitable, but a different approach seems to be taken to adult *physical* education: a police athletic association was held to be a trust for recreational purposes, and therefore not charitable (see 12.5.3). Nor has it been suggested that driving schools or flying schools should be charitable, although their purposes are undoubtedly, in a sense, educational.

12.3.1.3 Value judgments   Inevitably with a wide definition of educational purposes, the courts and Commissioners may be involved in subjective value judgments as to whether a particular purpose falls within or without the definition. There appear to be two separate issues. First, does the activity have any educational value at all? Secondly, in the case of research, on the assumption that any discoveries made will be of value, to what extent should the courts take account of the likelihood of finding nothing?

It is clear that the courts are prepared to embark upon value judgments on the first question. The views of the donor will of course not be conclusive, and expert evidence will be admitted in order to assist in evaluating the merit of artistic and cultural work.

In *Re Pinion* [1965] Ch 85, for example, the testator left his 'studio' for the purposes of a museum to display his collection of what were claimed to be 'fine arts'. However, expert witnesses thought that the paintings were 'atrociously bad', and one 'expresse[d] his surprise that so voracious a collector should not by hazard have picked up even one meritorious object'. The question arose as to the validity of the trust, and this depended on whether it was charitable. Harman LJ described the collection as 'a mass of junk' and, reversing Wilberforce J, the Court of Appeal held the trust void. In *Re Hummeltenberg* [1923] 1 Ch 237 the court held void a trust to train spiritualistic mediums (though perhaps disciplined research into the paranormal, undertaken on scientific principles, could be charitable). On the other hand, in *Re Delius* [1957] Ch 299 a trust for the appreciation of the works of the composer was held charitable, but Roxburgh J made it clear that the undoubted merit of Delius's music was crucial, and the same view would not be taken of a 'manifestly inadequate' composer.

Where research is concerned, the courts will also presumably assess the value of the ultimate aim of the project, but on the assumption that any findings would be of value, it does not seem to be a bar to charitable status that nothing might be found at all. Of course, it is often difficult to know in advance whether or not the results of research will be useful (after all, if you did know the conclusions, the research would be pointless).

Perhaps this point was in Wilberforce J's mind in *Re Hopkins* [1965] Ch 669, where he upheld as charitable a bequest to the Francis Bacon society for the purposes of finding the Bacon-Shakespeare manuscripts. Though he observed that if found the discovery would be 'of the highest value to history and to literature', the search could equally have been futile, as not only were the manuscripts not known to exist, but Wilberforce J thought their discovery unlikely. Value judgments are very difficult to operate when the outcome of the quest is uncertain, as will usually be the case where genuine research is concerned.

12.3.1.4 Political purposes A trust for the advancement of political purposes will not be charitable. Education, however, can undoubtedly cover political theory and philosophy. The borderline appears to fall at the point where partisan propaganda is seen to be masquerading in the guise of instruction. In *Re Hopkinson* [1949] 1 All ER 346, a trust for adult education in socialist principles fell foul of the line. The political angle was another reason why the trust in *Re Shaw* [1957] 1 WLR 729 failed. The Charity Commissioners commented on the problem in their Annual Report for 1967, para. 8, but seem to take a fairly generous view, regarding, for example, the promotion of racial harmony as charitable. For greater detail on the problem of political purposes generally see 12.8.1.

12.4 ADVANCEMENT OF RELIGION

12.4.1 What religion?

The law adopts a tolerant stance towards religion, and seems reluctant to enter into value judgments in this area. As Cross J remarked in *Neville Estates* v *Madden* [1962] Ch 832, a case already considered in another context in 5.2, in which a trust for the members of the Catford Synagogue was held charitable: 'As between different religions the law stands neutral, but it assumes that any religion is at least likely to be better than none'. Another example is *Church of the New Faith* v *Commissioner of Payroll Tax* (Victoria) (1983) 83 AJC 4652, a case concerning Australian Scientology, where the High Court of Australia held that:

> There can be no acceptable discrimination between institutions which take their character from religions which the majority of the community recognises as religions and institutions which take their character from religions which lack that general recognition.

Generally speaking, it seems, the courts are unprepared to engage in value judgments as to the relative worth of different religions.

In *Bowman* v *Secular Society Ltd* [1917] AC 406, Lord Parker of Waddington thought that a trust for the purpose of any kind of monotheistic theism would be a good charitable trust.

The preamble to the Statute of Charitable Uses 1601 gave little support for the tolerant approach the law has taken, the only reference to religion within it concerning the repair of churches (see 12.1.1). It may be that the explanation lies in the mortmain legislation in force from 1736 to 1891 which as we have seen (11.3.3) rendered many gifts to charity void. Religious tolerance in this area, therefore, may have been used simply as a device to strike down testamentary gifts, though the authorities from that period still have validity today.

In *Thornton* v *Howe* (1862) 31 Beav 14, for example, charitable status was extended to a devise of land to promote the writings of Joanna Southcote, the founder of a small but fervent sect in the West of England, who had proclaimed that she was with child by the Holy Ghost and would give birth to a second Messiah. The practical effect of the decision was to bring the trust within the invalidating provisions of the mortmain legislation, but the case is still seen as a landmark in establishing that any theistic belief, however obscure or remote, will fall within the meaning of religion for the purposes of charity law. A recent example to the same effect is *Re Watson* [1973] 1 WLR 1472, where Plowman J held charitable a trust to publish the religious writings of a retired builder who was virtually the sole remaining adherent of a small, fundamentalist group of believers. Expert testimony regarded the theological merits of the works as very small but confirmed the genuineness of the writer's beliefs.

It is not necessary that the religious beliefs in question should be Christian. Certainly the Jewish, Sikh, Hindu and Muslim faiths have been accepted. Faith healing was held to be a charitable purpose in *Re Le Cren Clarke* [1996] 1 WLR 288. In *Re South Place Ethical Society* [1980] 1 WLR 1565, however, Dillon J remarked that religion is concerned with man's relations with God, so it seems therefore that one qualification is the need for a belief in some kind of God (or gods). The South Place Ethical Society was held not to be a religious charity, because although its objects included 'the study and dissemination of ethical principles', and 'the cultivation of a rational religious sentiment', its beliefs were non-theistic. Dillon J observed:

> Religion, as I see it, is concerned with man's relations with God, and ethics are concerned with man's relations with man. The two are not the same, and are not made the same by sincere inquiry into the question, what is God? If reason leads people not to accept Christianity or any known religion, but they do believe in the excellence of qualities such as truth, beauty and love, or believe in the Platonic concept of the ideal, their beliefs may be to them the equivalent of a religion, but viewed objectively they are not religion.

In an old case in the Privy Council, *Yeap Cheah Neo* v *Ong Cheng Neo* (1875) LR 6 PC 381, a provision for the performance of ancestor worship was held non-charitable. High ethical principles or moral philosophy, being concerned with man's relations with man, cannot amount to a religion, though they may of course be educational and so charitable under that head. Plowman J also thought in *Re Watson*, considered above, that doctrines which were averse to the foundations of all religion, and subversive of all morality, would not be charitable under this head.

It seems that the gift must be exclusively for religious purposes, so that a gift for 'missionary work' or 'parish work' will be too wide, since such work may involve elements not wholly religious. On the other hand, in *Re Simson* [1946] Ch 299, a gift to a named clergyman 'for his work in the parish' was held to be impliedly confined to his religious duties.

Buddhism poses a problem in this context, since although it is generally accepted as being a religion, it is not clear (at any rate to the judiciary) whether or not Buddhists believe in a supernatural or supreme being. It is possible that it should be treated as an exception, since a trust to advance

Buddhism is clearly charitable. Difficulties could also presumably arise where a human being sets himself up as a deity, and is worshipped as such — such religions exist, and it is unclear whether or not their advancement is charitable.

12.4.2   Advancement of religion

It is not enough merely to practice religion. Religion must also be advanced. As with education, the means by which religion may be advanced may be many and various. Apart from the provision and maintenance of churches, and provision of or for the benefit of clergymen, such matters as church choirs, Sunday school prizes, and even exorcism, have all been held to advance religion.

The advancement of religion seems also to require some positive action. For example, in *United Grand Lodge of Ancient Free & Accepted Masons of England* v *Holborn Borough Council* [1957] 1 WLR 1080, Donovan J, in denying charitable status to freemasons (who attempted to claim rates advantages), commented that:

> There is no religious instruction, no programme for the persuasion of unbelievers, no religious supervision to see that its members remain active and constant in the various religions they may profess, no holding of religious services, no pastoral or missionary work of any kind.

Religion may have been a necessary qualification for membership of the lodge, as it might be for a church squash club, for example, but the lodge did not advance religion any more than a church squash club would.

12.4.3   Reform of the law?

The Government, in its White Paper *Charities: A Framework for the Future*, HMSO (May 1989), the recommendations of which led to the enactment of the Charities Act 1992, later consolidated in 1993, considered whether the law in this area should be altered. The White Paper noted that:

> Anxieties have been expressed, in particular, about a number of organisations whose influence over their followers, especially the young, is seen as destructive of family life and, in some cases, as tantamount to brainwashing.

Nevertheless, although considerable sympathy was expressed for these anxieties, reform of the law was not recommended, mainly because it was considered too difficult to formulate adequate proposals. Removal of charitable status from all trusts established for the advancement of religion was rejected because of the difficulties in which it would leave many existing trusts. Denial of charitable status only to new organisations, established after the legislation came into force, was rejected on the grounds that it would be difficult to justify denying charitable status to new trusts for religious purposes of an existing denomination. Replacing the presumption of public benefit (see 12.7.4) with a positive test of worth, which those seeking charitable status would need to satisfy, was rejected on the grounds that it would be difficult to define any criteria upon which a test of worth could be based. Problems would also occur where there was a single objectionable feature in a complex body of doctrine. The Paper also notes that the public anxieties which have been expressed have generally been addressed to the *conduct* of a movement rather than its *objects*, and that these matters can be dealt with administratively by the Charity Commissioners.

The result is, therefore, that the substantive law in this area has been unaffected by the Charities Act 1993.

12.5   OTHER PURPOSES BENEFICIAL TO THE COMMUNITY

This provides a residual category of charitable purposes which it is almost impossible to define precisely. Not every purpose which might, by common consensus, be considered beneficial to the community can come within this head. What the law admits as charitable under this head is still governed (see 12.1.1), by the general statement of charitable purposes which was set out in the preamble to the Statute of Charitable Uses 1601, for although this has itself been repealed, the cases which have relied upon its guidance over centuries are still themselves authority. If some wholly novel purpose appears, the question is not whether it is beneficial in some general sense, but whether it falls within the 'spirit and intendment' of the preamble, or can be held to do so by analogy with the principles developed through the cases.

It should therefore be obvious that it is not always possible to state whether a particular purpose is charitable under this head or not. Some cases are expressly mentioned in the preamble, however, and there are also classes of trust which have been specifically considered by the courts. About these, at least, it is possible to state conclusions.

12.5.1   Specifically included in the preamble
The preamble (which is set out at 12.1.1) makes specific mention of the relief of aged, impotent (meaning disabled or handicapped) and poor people, and it has never been necessary to show that the recipients possess all three characteristics simultaneously. Trusts to assist the elderly are common, as are trusts for the handicapped, and no further requirement of poverty in the recipients is imposed. In other words, this head is wider than the relief of poverty head.

It must be the case, however, that the proposed purpose will offer some relief to the recipients. Since many of the disadvantages which accompany age or general disability can in fact be eased by material provision in the form of money or special equipment, this general requirement usually poses no problems. Probably, however, a gift of money which was wholly confined to such elderly or disabled people as are already wealthy could not be charitable, because it would fail to relieve the disadvantage of their condition. It is also likely that the class of recipients would not amount to a section of the public so as to satisfy the additional public benefit requirements.

Trusts to benefit the sick are prima facie charitable and before the introduction of the National Health Service in 1946, charitable gifts were the main source of provision for those needing hospital care but unable either to afford it or to insure against illness or injury. Today, gifts to private hospitals will still be charitable, since they help to ease the pressure upon the public services, as was noted in *Re Resch's WT* [1969] 1 AC 514. It is no objection that such hospitals tend to be of direct benefit to those who are relatively rich, though as under other heads a purely profit-making institution will not be charitable. There is no need to confine the benefits of the trust directly to the patients, and gifts which improve the efficiency of the service by providing homes for nurses, or accommodation for visiting relatives, are included under this head. Even organisations offering help with family planning, and those which seek to promote health by encouraging temperance, have been accepted for registration, but the Commissioners have found difficulty (see their Annual Report for 1975, para. 70) with fringe methods of healing, not generally recognised by the medical profession. Methods which are widely recognised, such as acupuncture, osteopathy and faith healing, are acceptable, but in other cases some evidence of the method's effectiveness will be demanded.

Another category of benefits mentioned in the preamble was the 'setting out of soldiers', which has been extended to include the well-being and morale of the forces, or specific units thereof, charities for ex-servicemen, and the promotion of the efficiency of the police and the maintenance of law and order. Gifts to the Inland Revenue and for 'my country England' have been held charitable (*Re Smith* [1932] Ch 153), but gifts expressed to be for 'public' or 'patriotic' purposes have failed as being too wide and not exclusively charitable.

Gifts for the 'repair of bridges, ports, havens, causeways, sea-banks and highways' were included in the preamble, and now that the State assumes responsibility for such matters, this category has grown to include such miscellaneous amenities as the National Trust, museums, art galleries, parks and community centres. In *Scottish Burial Reform & Cremation Society Ltd* v *Glasgow Corporation* [1968] AC 138 (see 12.1.5), a crematorium was held charitable. And while it is not charitable to erect a monument to oneself, the commemoration of significant people or events (e.g., war memorials) will qualify. The Earl Mountbatten of Burma Statue Appeal Trust has been registered as being 'likely to foster patriotism and good citizenship' (Charity Commissioners' Annual Report 1981, paras 68–70).

The 'preferment of orphans' mentioned in the preamble has its modern counterpart in the provision of orphanages and local authority homes, but in *Re Cole* [1958] Ch 888 a majority of the Court of Appeal held non-charitable a trust for the general welfare and benefit of children in such a home out of fear that this might permit the provision of amenities not of an educational nature, such as radios or television sets, and this decision was followed in *Re Sahal* [1958] 1 WLR 1243. In this respect, therefore, purposes are unlikely to succeed under this head unless they will also succeed under the educational head.

Trusts to aid the rehabilitation and reform of prisoners have been accepted as charitable since the 19th century, but it is not easy to envisage circumstance in which the reference in the preamble to the ransom of captives has any application today, unless perhaps hostages taken by terrorists are encompassed within the term 'captives'.

A gift for the benefit of a locality such as a town, county or parish, or for its inhabitants, will be charitable although one might have expected it to fail either because of failure to specify exclusively charitable purposes or on the ground that there is an insufficient public benefit. The explanation may lie in an analogy with gifts to local authorities. These have long acted in the capacity of trustees of various charities and so such gifts may be *impliedly* confined to charitable purposes. In any event, gifts to localities were probably within the spirit of the reforms of 1601 historically as these reforms were largely directed towards easing the burden of local poor rates. The trust must, it seems, be cast in terms of benefit for an area or its residents for the time being (not, for example, a trust for expatriate Welshmen, unless the purposes were charitable for some other reason).

12.5.2 Animal charities
Animal charities are among the most popular with the public. Their inclusion within this head of charity owes nothing to the preamble to the Statute of Charitable Uses 1601 but rests upon a process of reasoning by analogy. As with religious toleration, the motive may well have lain in the mortmain legislation, but precedents of that period are of course still followed today.

In *London University* v *Yarrow* (1857) 1 De G & J 72, a trust to study the diseases of animals useful to mankind was held charitable, but this would probably have been a valid educational charity anyway. A more general authority is *Tatham* v *Drummond* (1864) 4 De G J & S 484, in which a bequest for the relief and protection of animals taken to be slaughtered was held charitable so that the gift failed under the mortmain legislation. Romer J held a gift to a named lady to aid her work in caring for cats and kittens to be charitable in *Re Moss* [1949] 1 All ER 495.

It is not, however, the benefit to the animals themselves which has been fastened upon, to provide principled justification for the inclusion of animal charities under this head (although in Ireland, the good of animals requires no further justification). Rather, the assumed benefit is to humans, by encouraging them in 'feelings of humanity and morality generally' (see the judgment of Swinfen Eady LJ in *Re Wedgwood* [1915] 1 Ch 113, 122).

Homes for lost dogs, needy horses, donkeys etc., have been accepted as charitable, along with well-known organisations such as the RSPCA and the PDSA. On the other hand, the need to benefit humans leads to the conclusion that the protection of creatures harmful to man could not be charitable under this head, nor, according the Court of Appeal in *Re Grove-Grady* [1929] 1 Ch 557, would be the creation of a sanctuary where animals would be protected from all human intrusion. No doubt, however, both these could, in the case of trusts appropriately drafted, be valid as educational charities, for example, by the inclusion of a provision that the wildlife be studied.

Whereas it is usually assumed that a purpose falling under the first three heads of charity is a benefit, no such assumption is made for purposes falling under the fourth head, and indeed, sometimes the courts will be faced with value judgments as to the relative merits of competing benefits. On the issue of whether the abolition of vivisection might be a public benefit, for example, the House of Lords in *National Anti-Vivisection Society* v *IRC* [1948] AC 31 was not prepared to depart from the view of the Special Commissioners for Income Tax, that any assumed public benefit in the suppression of vivisection, in the advancement of morals was outweighed by a detriment to medical science and research, which was itself of undoubted public benefit. The purposes of the National Anti-Vivisection Society not therefore being charitable, it was not entitled to exemption from income tax. This case is further considered in 12.8.1.

Private trusts for pet animals are not charitable because there is no public benefit, but they may nevertheless be valid as private purpose trusts as an anomalous category (see 5.1).

12.5.3 Trusts for recreational purposes

Until the 1950s it was assumed that while some recreational purposes, such as boys' clubs, women's institutes and parish halls, were potentially charitable, sporting facilities were not, unless they were either educational or promoted efficiency in the armed forces. A series of cases in the 1950s, however, suggested that no recreational purpose will be charitable at common law. As we shall see in 12.6, however, a fifth (limited) head of recreational charities has now been added by statute.

In *IRC* v *Glasgow Police Athletic Association* [1953] AC 380, the encouragement and promotion of athletic sport and general pastimes for officers and ex-officers of the City of Glasgow police force was held non-charitable, although it might have been allowed had the purpose been merely incidental to improving police efficiency. It had been found as a fact that the athletic association played an important part in the maintenance of health, morale and *esprit de corps* within the police force, and in attracting recruits to the force. The leisure element bulked too large, however, to be merely incidental to maintaining the efficiency of the police force. Lord Reid said:

I do not doubt that the purpose of increasing or maintaining the efficiency of a police force is a charitable purpose within the technical meaning of those words in English law. It appears to me to be well established that the purpose of increasing the efficiency of the army or a part of it is a charitable purpose. It may be that in some cases the facts hardly justified the conclusion that this was the purpose of the gift in question, but that does not affect the principle. I can see no valid distinction between the importance or character of the public interest of maintaining the efficiency of the army and that of maintaining the efficiency of the police.

But it is not enough that one of the purposes of a body of persons is charitable: the Act requires that it must be established for charitable purposes only. This does not mean that the sole effect of the activities of the body must be to promote charitable purposes, but it does mean that that must be its predominant object and that any benefits to its individual members of a non-charitable character which result from its activities must be of a subsidiary or incidental character.

. . . I have come to the conclusion that conferring such benefits [leisure and enjoyment] on its members bulks so large in the purposes and activities of this association that it cannot properly be said to be established for charitable purposes only. . . .

In *Williams's Trustees* v *IRC* [1947] AC 447, the London Welsh Association, whose objects were to promote social and recreational purposes among Welsh people living in London had also been held non-charitable, partly on the basis that purely social activities could not be charitable within the spirit of the preamble to the Statute of Charitable Uses 1601. Finally, in *IRC* v *Baddeley* [1955] AC 572, a reduction in stamp duty on a conveyance of land was refused because the purposes of the conveyance were not charitable. The conveyance was to a Methodist mission and the purposes were essentially those of promoting the 'religious, social and physical well-being' of residents of an area by providing facilities for 'religious services and instruction; and for the social and physical training and recreation' of such people. The inclusion of purely social purposes prevented these purposes from being exclusively charitable.

12.6 RECREATIONAL CHARITIES ACT 1958

We have seen in 12.5.3 how doubt was cast by a number of decisions in the 1950s on the charitable status of a number of social trusts which had always been assumed to be charitable. The Recreational Charities Act 1958 was enacted to restore what was assumed to be the *status quo ante* in respect of those trusts. The London Welsh Association (see 12.5.3), for example, was validated by the Charity Commissioners in 1977.

Section 1 states that it shall be and be deemed always to have been charitable to provide, or assist in the provision of, facilities for recreation or other leisure–time occupation, if the facilities are provided in the interests of social welfare. A proviso adds that nothing in the section shall be taken to derogate from the principle that to be charitable a trust or institution must be for the public benefit. Under s. 1(2), the requirement that the facilities are provided in the interests of social welfare is not to be satisfied unless the facilities are provided with the object of improving the conditions of life for the persons for whom the facilities are primarily intended, and either:

(a)   those persons have need of such facilities as aforesaid by reason of their youth, age, infirmity or disablement, poverty or social and economic circumstances, or

(b)   the facilities are to be available to the members or female members of the public at large.

Subject to the requirement of social welfare, there is specific reference to the provision of facilities at village halls, community centres and women's institutes, and to the provision and maintenance of grounds and buildings to be used for the purposes of recreation or leisure-time occupation, extending to the provision of facilities for these purposes by the organising of any activity.

There is also express provision (in s. 2) for miners' welfare trusts.

Where the Act applies, the spirit of the preamble to the Statute of Charitable Uses 1601 seems no longer to be relevant, and it must therefore be taken that the statute has added a fresh head of charity.

Section 1(2)(b) above allows for the provision of facilities for recreation or other leisure-time occupation where the facilities are made available to the public at large, but under s. 1(1) they have also to be provided in the interests of social welfare. In *IRC* v *McMullen* (considered in a different context in 12.3.1.2), Walton J at first instance ([1978] 1 WLR 664, [1978] 1 All ER 230) held that the requirement of social welfare in s. 1(1) implied that for a charity to succeed under the Act, the recipients must be limited to those who are in some way be 'deprived persons'. The Court of Appeal ([1979] 1 WLR 130, [1979] 1 All ER 588) split on the issue, the majority (Stamp and Orr LJJ) holding that the class to be benefited must be disadvantaged in such a way as to have a special need for the facilities. There was no such limitation in *McMullen* itself, where the gift was to the Football Association Youth Trust. Bridge LJ dissented, preferring a wider view that social welfare may be promoted by benefits which extend to the better off as well as the socially deprived, observing that he could

> see no reason to conclude that only the deprived can have their conditions of life improved. Hyde Park improves the conditions of life for residents in Mayfair and Belgravia as much as for those in Pimlico or the Portobello Road, and the village hall may improve the conditions of life for the squire and his family as well as for cottagers.

The House of Lords ([1981] AC 1) left the issue open, allowing the appeal on the grounds that the trust was charitable under head 2 (see 12.3.1.2). Indeed, their lordships expressly refused to decide which of the approaches adopted in the Court of Appeal was correct, but the issue has now been resolved in *Guild* v *IRC* [1992] 2 AC 310, where the House of Lords came down in favour of Bridge LJ's view. It is therefore not fatal that benefits are not limited to deprived persons.

Presumably, social welfare indicates some element of provision for others, so that a group acting purely to benefit themselves would fail to qualify. In any event, such an enterprise would lack the necessary element of public benefit preserved by the Act.

12.7 PUBLIC BENEFIT

An additional requirement for all charities is that they be for the public benefit.

The logic of the order in which I propose to consider public benefit may not be immediately apparent — heads 2, 4, 1 and 3, in that order. The reason for proceeding in this manner is that the test of public benefit for educational charities has been clearly stated, and one of the main issues is the extent to which that test also applies to the other heads of charity. Most of the cases are on head 4, which is why this head is dealt with immediately after head 2.

12.7.1 Educational charities

In the case of relief of poverty, even benefiting a small number of people may be regarded as conferring a public benefit (see 12.7.2). Yet whereas education is clearly a benefit to those in immediate receipt of it, it is not self-evident that educating a few people constitutes a benefit to the general public. Indeed, given that many of the cases under this head are in reality disputes over tax relief, it would be quite wrong if the education of a privileged few were to be regarded as charitable. Under this head it is therefore necessary that there is some additional benefit to the general public or some appreciable sector thereof.

That is not to say that a particular form of education has to be capable of being enjoyed by everyone, so long as access to it is reasonably open. Thus public schools may be charitable as long as they are not operated as profit-making ventures, although their fees may place them beyond the means of the majority. Even scholarships or endowed chairs, which can be enjoyed only by one person at a time, present no difficulty. The problems arise where it is sought to limit the potential beneficiaries within a class which is insufficiently wide to constitute a section of the public.

It is clear that it may be charitable to provide, e.g., scholarships, open to:

(a)   persons following a common profession or calling, or their children and dependants, or

(b)   people of common nationality, religion or sex, or

(c)   the inhabitants of a given area, provided this is reasonably large, such as a town or county.

Special provisions for people suffering disability are also permissible, since they are a section of the public in a meaningful sense.

12.7.1.1 The *Oppenheim* personal nexus test
However, under this head, and probably under all the *Pemsel* heads except relief of poverty, it will be fatal if the class of potential beneficiaries (however large) is defined in terms of relation to particular individuals or a company. This approach originated in *Re Compton* [1945] Ch 123, where charitable status was denied to a trust to educate the children of three named families. It is understandable that the courts are reluctant to allow an essentially private arrangement to enjoy charitable privileges, especially tax advantages, but it seems that the principle extends to cases where the class of potential beneficiaries is defined in terms of a relationship with an employer, even where the employer is a substantial concern.

The most authoritative statements, however, are those of Lord Simonds in *Oppenheim* v *Tobacco Securities Trust Co. Ltd* [1951] AC 297, where *Re Compton* was approved in the House of Lords. Lord Simonds said that first, the number of possible beneficiaries must not be negligible, and secondly, that the class must not be defined so as to depend on any relationship to a particular individual or employer:

> Then the question is whether that class of persons can be regarded as such as a 'section of the community' as to satisfy the test of public benefit. The words 'section of the community' have no special sanctity, but they conveniently indicate first, that the possible (I emphasise the word 'possible') beneficiaries must not be numerically negligible, and secondly, that the quality which distinguishes them from other members of the community, so that they form by themselves a section of it, must be a quality which does not depend on their relationship to a particular individual. . . . A group of persons may be numerous, but, if the nexus between them is their personal relationship to a single *propositus* or to several *propositi*, they are neither the community nor a section of the community for charitable purposes.

In the trust with which the House of Lords was concerned, the number of potential beneficiaries (at least in theory) was certainly not negligible. The income of the trust fund was directed to be applied 'in providing for . . . the education of children of employees or former employees of the British-American Tobacco Co. Ltd . . . or any of its subsidiary or allied companies in such manner . . . as the acting trustees shall in their absolute discretion . . . think fit'. The number of present employees alone exceeded 110,000, so it was only the personal nexus rule which was fatal (because they were all connected with the same company).

As Lord MacDermott pointed out in his dissenting speech, however, the rule is by no means easy to apply, and produces odd results when the *'propositus'* is an employer. For example, a trust to educate the sons of railwaymen, not expressed as limited to a single company, would have been valid before the nationalisation of the railways, and void when British Rail became the sole employer. In any case the test is arguably inappropriate in large companies. Though perhaps the special tax concessions of charitable status should not be given to any arrangement for a private class, the personal link between employees is not as obvious as that between members of a family, among whom considerations of mutual interest might be considered to negate the altruistic status of the trust.

Perhaps the real, if unstated, justification for the result in *Oppenheim* was the extent of the trustees' discretion in that case. The benefit to 110,000 or more people may in fact have been entirely theoretical — for example, if the trustees had used the funds to pay 15 per cent of fees to those employees who sent their sons to boarding school, only the relatively small number who could afford the other 85 per cent would actually have benefited. The problem is that the test in *Oppenheim* may not achieve the desired result in all cases; the House of Lords should have concentrated, I would suggest, on the extent of the trustees' discretion to limit the number of people who could in practice have benefited, rather than the nexus with the company.

Nevertheless, the personal nexus rule is law, certainly for trusts under this head. There may however be loopholes, as for example in *Re Koettgen's*

WT [1954] Ch 252, in which an educational trust succeeded despite a direction that the trustees should give preference to the families of employees, up to a maximum of 75 per cent of income. On the other hand, doubts have been expressed and, for example, a preference for the grantor's family rendered a gift non-charitable in *Caffoor* v *Income Tax Commissioner* [1961] AC 584. In *IRC* v *Educational Grants Association Ltd* [1967] Ch 123, affirmed [1967] Ch 993, between 76 per cent and 85 per cent of the income of a fund (varying from year to year) was paid out for the education of persons connected with the Metal Box Co. Ltd. In a dispute with the Inland Revenue, it was held that the money had not been paid exclusively for charitable purposes. Pennycuick J found 'considerable difficulty in the *Koettgen* decision' and thought that a preference for a private class might always be fatal (although he did not actually need to decide that). The problem with laying down a clear rule of this nature would be that extreme cases could be envisaged (e.g., a preference up to 5 per cent of income) where its application would further no obvious policy (unless again, of course, an objection is taken in principle to charitable status for an arrangement with any purely private content).

This problem is similar to that in *Oppenheim* itself, i.e., that the rule is arguably too rigid. The real problem in *Oppenheim*, as has been seen, was the extent of the trustees' discretion to limit the number of people who could in practice have benefited rather than the nexus with the company (unless again, objection is taken to *any* private arrangement). It would have been difficult to formulate a clear rule on trustees' discretion, however, where the problem is essentially one of where to draw the line, just as it is difficult to draw the line in the *Koettgen* situation. In both cases, therefore, a rigid rule may well be the only answer.

12.7.1.2 Class must be a section of the community *Oppenheim* v *Tobacco Securities Trust Co. Ltd* [1951] AC 297 also required that it must be possible to describe the class genuinely as a section of the community, rather than simply a body of private individuals. There are in effect two separate requirements. First, the class must be capable of being genuinely described as a section of the community, rather than simply a fluctuating body of private individuals. Persons following a common profession or calling, people of common nationality, religion or sex, or the inhabitants of a town or county can be described as a section of the community. Special provisions for people suffering disability are also permissible, since they are a section of the public in a meaningful sense. But in *Davies* v *Perpetual Trustee Co. Ltd* [1959] AC 459, the Privy Council held non-charitable a trust which was confined to Presbyterian youths who were descended from settlors in New South Wales who had originated from the North of Ireland. Although quite large in number, this category of potential beneficiaries was held not to be a section of the public. It was merely a fluctuating body of private individuals.

12.7.2 Public benefit under the fourth head
Lord Simonds thought in *Oppenheim* v *Tobacco Securities Trust Co. Ltd* [1951] AC 297 that the test of public benefit may vary between the four heads of

charity (in particular he excluded the 'poor relations' cases entirely from consideration: see 12.7.3). It is clear that the personal nexus test applies to the fourth head, but arguably the requirement that the trust benefits a section of the public is more stringent under the fourth head than under the second.

For example, in *Williams's Trustees* v *IRC* [1947] AC 447 (see also 12.5.3), doubt was expressed by Lord Simonds about whether Welsh people living in London could be a section of the public under the fourth head. In *IRC* v *Baddeley* [1955] AC 572 (see also 12.5.3), the House of Lords held that the persons to be benefited must either be the whole community or the inhabitants of a particular area. If some further restriction is imposed, thus creating in effect a class within a class, the test of public benefit will not be satisfied.

Viscount Simonds in *IRC* v *Baddeley* thought 'that a different degree of public benefit is requisite according to the class in which the charity is said to fall', and that public benefit considerations 'have even greater weight [than in the case of educational trusts] in the case of trusts which by their nominal classification depend for their validity upon general public utility':

it is possible, particularly in view of the so-called 'poor relations' cases, the scope of which may one day have to be considered, that a different degree of public benefit is requisite according to the class in which the charity is said to fall. But it is said that if a charity falls within the fourth class, it must be for the benefit of the whole community or at least of all the inhabitants of a sufficient area.

The *Baddeley* test seems therefore to be a different, and additional, test to that adopted in *Davies* v *Perpetual Trustee Co. Ltd* [1959] AC 459 for the second head. Indeed, the very definition of charity under the fourth head (purposes beneficial to the community) would seem to demand a more stringent test of public benefit than under any other head. However, Lord Reid thought otherwise in his dissenting speech in *IRC* v *Baddeley* .

It is also likely that what constitutes a section of the public depends on the purposes of the particular trust, and the courts are more likely to strike down arbitrary restrictions which are irrelevant to those purposes, but which simply serve to exclude other sections of the public. For example, in *IRC* v *Baddeley*, the limitation was to Methodists living in West Ham and Leyton, and the trust included the provision of playing-fields. Lord Simonds clearly thought that the restriction to Methodists living in West Ham and Leyton was completely irrelevant to the provision of playing-fields. Referring (at p. 592) to a rhetorical question put in argument: 'Who has ever heard of a bridge to be crossed only by impecunious Methodists?' he went on to say that what is true of a bridge for Methodists is equally true of any other public purpose falling within the fourth head, and of the adherents of any other creed. The limitation merely operated to prevent the purpose from being a public purpose; it could have had no other effect. A purpose which is not a public purpose cannot be charitable within the fourth head.

There is some authority that the test of public benefit can vary even within the fourth head itself. In *Re Dunlop* [1984] NI 408 (noted by Norma Dawson

[1987] Conv 114), Carswell J upheld as charitable a bequest 'to hold the remainder of my residuary estate for the Presbyterian Residential Trust . . . to found or to help to found a home for old Presbyterian persons', and a cy près scheme (see chapter 13) was ordered. There was earlier Northern Irish authority that the Presbyterians of Londonderry were not a sufficient section of the public under the fourth head, and it was accepted that there was no difference between Irish and English definitions of charity. Carswell J took the view, however, that public benefit depended upon the nature of 'the advantage which the donor intends to provide for the benefit of all of the public'. A 'bridge to be used only by Methodists should clearly fail to qualify, whereas a gift for the education of the children of members of that church might be a valid charity'. But he was also prepared to distinguish between purposes within the fourth head itself.

It should perhaps finally be observed that neither *IRC* v *Baddeley* nor *Williams's Trustees* v *IRC* actually turned on the issue of public benefit. In the former case the purposes were not exclusively religious, but included social purposes and the provision of playing-fields, and in the latter case purposes were exclusively social and recreational. They would therefore have failed because of the inclusion of a social content, whatever view had been taken on the public benefit issue.

12.7.3   Relief of poverty

It is unquestioned law that to relieve poverty is to confer a benefit upon the public at large, if only by mitigating the burden of support for the poor which would otherwise fall upon the community. The House of Lords in *Oppenheim* v *Tobacco Securities Trust Co. Ltd* [1951] AC 297 (see 12.7.1) exempted 'poor relations' cases as anomalous and left open the question whether the personal nexus test applies to them.

The 'poor relations' anomaly stems from the practice of Chancery in the 19th century when faced with trusts expressed to be for poor relations; rather than allow these to fail for uncertainty (at a time when the class ascertainability test applied: see 4.4.5) or perpetuity, the courts rescued such trusts by holding them charitable. Since then the 'poor relations' cases have been consistently followed, which is probably why the House of Lords left them alone in *Oppenheim*. Since then the House of Lords has considered them directly in *Dingle* v *Turner* [1972] AC 601, and expressly upheld them. In that case a trust for 'poor employees of E. Dingle & Co.' was held charitable, although it would have failed under the personal nexus test. The same reasoning must apply to 'poor relations'. It is clear, therefore, that the personal nexus test does not apply to this head of charity.

In order for a trust to be charitable under this head, it is, however, necessary that the trust should be intended to benefit a class of persons, and not simply to make a gift to an individual, or group of individuals, who happen to be poor. In *Re Scarisbrick* [1951] Ch 622, Jenkins LJ stated the rule thus:

I think the true question in each case has really been whether the gift was for the relief of poverty amongst a class of persons, or . . . a particular description of poor, or was merely a gift to individuals, albeit with relief of poverty amongst those individuals as the motive of the gift, or with a selective preference for the poor or poorest amongst those individuals.

This statement received the approval of Lord Cross of Chelsea in the leading case of *Dingle* v *Turner,* considered below. In *Re Scarisbrick* itself the class of potential recipients was sufficiently wide to be incapable of exhaustive ascertainment ('such relations of my said son and daughters as shall be in needy circumstances . . .') so the trust was charitable.

Assuming that Jenkins LJ's test is satisfied, however, the public benefit requirements are less stringent under this head than under the others and the class to be benefited can be quite small.

12.7.4 Advancement of religion

There are *dicta* in *Oppenheim* that the public benefit tests advanced in that case apply to all heads of charity except the relief of poverty. Certainly, for religious charities, there must also be an element of public contact. Private salvation, however commendable, is not charitable. This is another explanation of *Yeap Cheah Neo* v *Ong Cheng Neo* (1875) LR 6 PC 381 (see 12.4.1) because a provision for the performance of ancestor worship could benefit only the family group. The leading case is *Gilmour* v *Coats* [1949] AC 426, where the House of Lords had to consider a gift of £500 towards a Carmelite priory. The priory housed about 20 cloistered nuns who devoted themselves to intercessory prayer and had no contact at all with the outside world. This was held non-charitable on the grounds that there was no contact with the outside world. Arguments based on Catholic doctrine, to the effect that everyone benefited from the intercessory prayers, were rejected as being not susceptible to legal proof. Nor could any benefit be found merely in the example of the piety of the women, as it was too vague and intangible. The House of Lords also rejected the argument that, entry being open to all women, the priory should be treated on analogy with an educational institution offering scholarship entry, holding that an educational establishment which required its members to withdraw from the world and leave no record of their studies would not be charitable either.

On the other hand, in *Re Caus* [1934] Ch 162, Catholic masses for the dead were held charitable. This case was doubted in *Gilmour* v *Coats,* but in principle the case seems correct, and *Caus* was applied by Brown-Wilkinson V-C in *Re Hetherington* [1990] Ch 1. The point is that Catholic masses are open to the public at large even where a private function, such as a funiary rite, is incorporated into the celebration, so in principle *Caus* is distinguishable from *Gilmour* v *Coats.*

In *Re Hetherington,* Browne-Wilkinson V-C was called upon to consider a gift for the saying of masses, which did not exclude the possibility that the masses would be said in private. In practice, however, all or most of the masses would be open to public. Reviewing the cases, he said (at pp. 134–5):

1.   A trust for the . . . advancement of religion is *prima facie* charitable, and assumed to be for the public benefit . . . This assumption of public

benefit can be rebutted by showing that in fact the particular trust in question cannot operate so as to confer a legally recognised benefit on the public, as in *Gilmour* v *Coats*.

2. The celebration of a religious rite in public does confer such a benefit because of the edifying and improving effect of such celebration on the members of the public who attend. As Lord Reid said in *Gilmour* v *Coats* [1949] AC 426 at 459:

> 'A religion can be regarded as beneficial without it being necessary to assume that all its beliefs are true, and a religious service can be regarded as beneficial to all those who attend it without it being necessary to determine the spiritual efficacy of that of that service or to accept any particular belief about it.'

3. The celebration of a religious rite in private does not contain the necessary element of public benefit since any benefit by prayer or example is incapable of proof in the legal sense, and any element of education is limited to a private, not public, class of those present at the celebration: see *Gilmour* v *Coats* itself . . .

4. Where there is a gift for a religious purpose which could be carried out in a way which is beneficial to the public (i.e., by public masses) but could also be carried out in a way which would not have sufficient public benefit (i.e., by private masses) the gift is to be construed as a gift to be carried out only by the methods that are charitable, all non-charitable purposes being excluded . . .

Applying these principles to the case before him, he concluded that:

> a gift for the saying of masses is *prima facie* charitable, being for a religious purpose. In practice, those masses will be celebrated in public, which provides a sufficient element of public benefit . . . The gift is to be construed as a gift for the saying of public masses only . . ., private masses not being permissible since it would not be a charitable application of the fund for a religious purpose.

In other words, he construed the gift in such a way as to exclude purposes which were non-charitable.

It follows that the mere attendance by the public at a prayer service is sufficient to distinguish *Gilmour* v *Coats*. Suppose, on the other hand, the religious organisation conducts all its affairs in private, but unlike *Gilmour* v *Coats* its members have not cut themselves off entirely from the outside world, but mix with it. This also seems sufficient to distinguish *Gilmour* v *Coats*. In *Neville Estates* v *Madden* [1962] Ch 832 (considered in a different context at 5.2), Cross J held charitable a trust for the members of Catford Synagogue. He thought that the rejection of example as a benefit in *Gilmour* v *Coats* would not apply to a restricted religious group if its members lived in the world and mixed with their fellow citizens, because they could thereby extend their example of religious living to the public at large:

The trust with which I am concerned resembles that in *Gilmour* v *Coats* in this, that the persons immediately benefited by it are not a section of the public but members of a private body. All persons of the Jewish faith living in or about Catford might well constitute a section of the public, but the members for the time being of the Catford Synagogue are no more a section of the public than the members for the time being of a Carmelite Priory. The two cases, however, differ from one another in that the members of the Catford Synagogue spend their lives in the world, whereas the members of a Carmelite Priory live secluded from the world. If once one refuses to pay any regard — as the courts refused to pay any regard — to the influence which these nuns living in seclusion might have on the outside world, then it must follow that no public benefit is involved in a trust to support a Carmelite Priory. As Lord Greene said in the Court of Appeal ([1948] Ch 340, at p. 354): 'Having regard to the way in which the lives of the members are spent, the benefit is a purely private one'. But the court is, I think, entitled to assume that some benefit accrued to the public from the attendance at places of worship of persons who live in this world and mix with their fellow citizens.

On this view, religion can be advanced by example, so long as one mixes in the world in a *physical* sense. *Neville Estates* is authority that no more is required.

On the other hand, Harman J in *Re Warre* [1953] 1 WLR 725 had refused to accord charitable status to an Anglican house of retreat open to all members of the public wishing to retire from the world for a short period of meditation and spiritual renewal. On Cross J's reasoning one might have expected this to be charitable, because the meditators would return to the world after their spiritual renewal. It is not possible to state a clear conclusion, therefore, on the question of short-term private meditation since there are conflicting High Court views. Nevertheless, Cross J's view seems more in accord with recent High Court decisions and the recent practice of the Charity Commissioners.

12.8 PURPOSES WHICH CREATE PROBLEMS UNDER ANY HEAD

12.8.1 Political purposes

A trust cannot be charitable under any head if its purposes are, directly or indirectly, political. A trust to promote the aims of a particular political party is clearly not capable of being charitable, and attempts to disguise such objectives as educational trusts have generally failed.

The definition of 'political' in this context is somewhat wider than the layman might expect, however. Where the objectives involve attempting to bring about a change in the law, they will be considered political and therefore non-charitable, unless change in the law is merely ancillary to the main purpose of the trust. This was one of the reasons for the failure of the National Anti-Vivisection Society to achieve charitable status in *National*

Anti-Vivisection Society v *IRC* [1948] AC 31 (see also 12.5.2). Lord Simonds gave as the ostensible rationale that it is for Parliament, not the courts, to decide whether any change would be for the public benefit. He also rejected the contention that alteration in the law was merely ancillary to the purposes of the trust, since in order to abolish vivisection it would have been necessary to repeal the Cruelty to Animals Act 1876 (since replaced by the Animals (Scientific Procedures) Act 1986) and pass an Act prohibiting vivisection altogether. He said at p. 61–63:

> Here, the finding of the Commissioners is itself conclusive. 'We are satisfied', they say, 'that the main object of the society is the total abolition of vivisection . . . and (for that purpose) the repeal of the Cruelty to Animals Act 1876 [now replaced by the Animals (Scientific Procedures) Act 1986], and the substitution of a new enactment prohibiting vivisection altogether.' This is a finding that the main purpose of the society is the compulsory abolition of vivisection by Act of Parliament. What else can it mean? And how else can it be supposed that vivisection is to be abolished? Abolition and suppression are words that connote some form of compulsion. It can only be by Act of Parliament that that element can be supplied.
> . . .
>
> I would remind your lordships that it is the King as *parens patriae* who is the guardian of charity and that it is the right and duty of his Attorney-General to intervene and inform the court, if the trustees of a charitable trust fall short of their duty. So too it is his duty to assist the court, if need be, in the formulation of a scheme for the execution of a charitable trust. But, my Lords, is it for a moment to be supposed that it is the function of the Attorney-General on behalf of the Crown to intervene and demand that a trust shall be established and administered by the court, the object of which is to alter the law in a manner highly prejudicial, as he and His Majesty's government may think, to the welfare of the State? . . . I conclude upon this part of the case that a main object of the society is political and for that reason the society is not established for charitable purposes only.

It follows, therefore, that any trust whose main object includes a change in the law of the United Kingdom cannot be charitable. In *Re Bushnell* [1975] 1 WLR 1596, money was left to advance awareness of the benefits of socialised medicine and to show that its realisation was fully possible only in a socialist State. The testator had died in 1941, before the introduction of the National Health Service. One of the grounds upon which the trust was held void was its political bias in favour of socialism. Another ground for the failure of the trust in *Re Bushnell* was that in 1941 legislation would have been needed (and was of course later enacted) to introduce socialised medicine.

This was also an additional reason for the failure of Shaw's 40-letter alphabet (see 12.3.1.4), and accounts for the inability of, e.g., the Campaign against Racial Discrimination and the National Council for Civil Liberties to be registered. Charities may, however, campaign *against* changes in the law, which may enable some political purposes of a generally conservative nature to obtain registration.

Lord Simonds's reasoning in *National Anti-Vivisection Society* v *IRC*, above, applies only to changes to the law in the United Kingdom, but in *McGovern* v *Attorney-General* [1982] Ch 321, Slade J frustrated Amnesty International's attempt to procure charitable status for some of its activities by creating a trust of those parts which were thought most likely to be accepted as charitable, on the grounds that a main object of the trust was to secure the alteration of the laws of foreign countries. The objects of the trust were as follows:

(a)   The relief of needy persons within any of the following categories:

(i)   prisoners of conscience
(ii)   persons who have recently been prisoners of conscience
(iii)   persons who would in the opinion of the trustees be likely to become prisoners of conscience if they returned to their country of ordinary residence
(iv)   relatives or dependants of the foregoing persons;
by the provision of appropriate charitable (and in particular financial educational or rehabilitational) assistance.

(b)   Attempting to secure the release of prisoners of conscience.

(c)   Procuring the abolition of torture or inhuman or degrading treatment or punishment.

(d)   The undertaking promotion and commission of research into the maintenance and observance of human rights.

(e)   The dissemination of the results of such research by (a) the preparation and publication of the results of such research (b) the institution and maintenance of a library accessible to the public for the study of matters connected with the objects of this trust and of the results of research already conducted into such matters (c) the production and distribution of documentary films showing the results of such research.

(f)   The doing of all such other things as shall further the charitable purposes set out above *provided always* that the foregoing objects shall be restricted to those which are charitable according to the law of the United Kingdom but subject thereto they may be carried out in all parts of the world.

The trustees applied to the Charity Commissioners for registration as a charity under s. 4 of the Charities Act 1960, and the Commissioners refused. Amnesty International unsuccessfully appealed to the High Court under s. 5(3). The problem was the inclusion of objects (b) and (c), seeking release of prisoners of conscience and the abolition of torture, which necessarily involved securing changes in the laws of foreign countries.

The decision represents an extension of the principles laid down in the House of Lords in *National Anti-Vivisection Society* v *IRC* [1948] AC 31. The reasoning adopted by Lord Simonds could not be applied directly here, but

Slade J thought that to grant charitable status to such purposes might prejudice the relations of the British Government with foreign countries, and this consideration of policy could not be overlooked by the court:

> The point with which I am at present concerned is whether a trust of which a direct and main object is to secure a change in the laws of a foreign country can ever be regarded as charitable under English law. Though I do not think that any authority cited to me precisely covers the point, I have come to the clear conclusion that it cannot.
>
> I accept that the dangers of the court encroaching on the functions of the legislature or of subjecting its political impartiality to question would not be nearly so great as when similar trusts are to be executed in this country. I also accept that on occasions the court will examine and express an opinion on the quality of a foreign law. . . .
>
> Furthermore, before ascribing charitable status to an English trust of which a main object was to secure the alteration of a foreign law, the court would also, I conceive be bound to consider the consequences for this country as a matter of public policy. In a number of such cases there would arise a substantial *prima facie* risk that such a trust, if enforced, could prejudice the relations of this country with the foreign country concerned. . . .

A political taint will in any case be fatal to charitable status, whether or not a trust's direct and main object is to secure a change in the law of the United Kingdom, or of a foreign country. This can apply even to trusts seeking to promote aims which most civilised nations hold to be high aspirations. In *Re Strakosch* [1949] Ch 529, the promotion of racial harmony between English and Afrikaans communities in South Africa was held non-charitable, and registration of community councils is refused where their principal aims are the promotion of interracial accord. The same will apply where the aims are harmony and peace, if such movements overtly or covertly call upon governments to promote specific policies, such as disarmament. One reason sometimes given for denying charitable status to attempts to promote moral objectives is that they necessarily involve a propagandist element biased in favour of only one side of the argument.

12.8.1.1 Discussion of political issues, and campaigning On the other hand, it is legitimate for an educational charity to discuss political issues, and a political object which is merely incidental will not be fatal. In *Re Koeppler's WT* [1986] Ch 423, a testamentary gift to Wilton Park, whose main function was to organise educational conferences, was upheld by the Court of Appeal as a gift for charitable purposes, although the Wilton Park's objects included the promotion of informed international public opinion and the promotion of greater co-operation between East and West. The objects of the trust were:

> (1) An enquiry into the 'quality of life'; ecology and the environment; participation in government and industry; tensions in free societies; (2)

Europe and the emergent pattern of superpower relationships; (3) the unification of Europe; a balance sheet; (4) the requirements of Western defence and the possibilities of arms control; (5) the European Community and its external relations; (6) the media, public opinion and the decision-making process in government; (7) security issues as a factor in domestic and international politics; (8) labour and capital and the future of industrial society.

In upholding the trust, Slade LJ distinguished *McGovern v Attorney-General* on the grounds that a political purpose which is merely incidental to the objects of a trust will not necessarily be fatal where the purposes are otherwise educational. In *McGovern v Attorney-General*, by contrast, alteration in the law was not incidental to the objects of the trust, but was essential to Amnesty International's aims:

the activities of Wilton Park are not of a party political nature. Nor, so far as the evidence shows, are they designed to procure changes in the laws or governmental policy of this or any other country: even when they touch on political matters, they constitute, so far as I can see, no more than genuine attempts in an objective manner to ascertain and disseminate the truth. In these circumstances I think that no objections to the trust arise on a political score, similar to those which arose in the *McGovern* case.

Another authority that discussion of political issues is not necessarily fatal to charitable status is *Attorney-General v Ross* [1986] 1 WLR 252, where Scott J commented at p. 263 that 'there is nothing the matter with an educational charity in the furtherance of its educational purposes encouraging students to develop their political awareness or to acquire knowledge of and to debate and to form views on political issues'. He also observed that there is no reason why a charitable student organisation should not affiliate to a non-charitable organisation if that enables it to further its own charitable activities for the benefit of students. That is the basis upon which student unions are entitled to affiliate to the National Union of Students, a non-charitable organisation. It is, however, essential that the purpose of the affiliation should be to benefit the student body in their capacity as students.

It may also be that it is legitimate to go beyond discussion and take tentative steps into the arena of persuasion. The following passage is taken from the White Paper, *Charities: A Framework for the Future*, HMSO (May 1989):

Charities can, for example, quite properly respond to invitations from Government to comment on proposed changes in the law. Where a Bill is being debated, they can legitimately supply members of either House with such relevant information and arguments as they believe will assist the attainment of their objects. Where this kind of action is in furtherance of their purposes, charities are free to present to government departments reasoned memoranda advocating changes in the law.

The White Paper continues a few paragraphs further on:

> Ministers welcome the advice and the guidance which charities offer to
> Members of Parliament, to central and local government, and to other
> public authorities on a wide range of social problems. Charities should feel
> free to take the initiative in offering advice and opinions and in proposing
> changes to the law and should not need to wait to be invited to do so.

There is the qualification, however, that such activities must remain ancillary
to the charity's primary purposes.

There are limits to the extent to which a charity can go in this direction,
however. Political discussion may not be fatal to charitable status, but
campaigning, in the sense of seeking to influence public opinion on political
matters, undoubtedly is. In *Webb* v *O'Doherty, The Times,* 11 February 1991,
Hoffman J, distinguishing *Attorney-General* v *Ross*, granted an injunction
restraining the officers of a students' union, which was an educational charity,
from making any payments to the National Student Committee to Stop War
in the Gulf, or to the Cambridge Committee to Stop War in the Gulf. The
union had passed a resolution in January 1991 which mandated the executive
in the following terms:

> 1. To affiliate to the National Student Committee to Stop the War in the
> Gulf and the Cambridge Committee to Stop the War in the Gulf. 2. To
> campaign on the above issues. 3. To support and publicise national and
> local demonstrations, speaker meetings and non-violent direct actions
> organised by CND and Committee to Stop War in the Gulf. 4. To support
> the teach-in on the Gulf Crisis organised by the Student Committee to
> Stop War this Thursday. 5. To allocate £100 from the Campaign budget
> to the anti-Gulf War campaign. 6. To write to the Prime Minister and
> Ministry of Defence outlining this policy.

In restraining the officers from making the payments, Hoffman J observed:

> There is . . . a clear distinction between the discussion of political matters,
> or the acquisition of information which may have a political content, and
> a campaign on a political issue. There is no doubt that campaigning, in the
> sense of seeking to influence public opinion on political matters, is not a
> charitable activity. It is, of course, something which students are, like the
> rest of the population, perfectly at liberty to do in their private capacities,
> but it is not a proper object of the expenditure of charitable money.

The Charity Commissioners exercise supervisory control over charities (see
11.2.3), and one area is the permissible limits to political involvement by
charities. Their Annual Reports of 1969 and 1981 point out that charity
trustees who engage in political activities risk personal liability to repay trust
funds expended in breach, and that charities whose purposes are found to be
wide enough to permit political action may be de-registered. Charities may

aid governments on particular issues by giving information and by rational persuasion, but must avoid seeking to remedy the causes of poverty which lie in social, economic and political structures, or to eliminate other social injustice.

The advice of the Commissioners has also been published in the form of a booklet, *Political Activities by Charities*, which is intended for the guidance of trustees. In the White Paper *Charities: A Framework for the Future*, the Government summarises the position as follows:

The Charity Commission's guidance is, broadly, to the effect that:

governing instruments should not include a power to exert political pressure except in a way which is ancillary to a charitable purpose;

the powers and purposes of a charity should not include the power to bring pressure to bear on the Government to adopt, to alter, or to maintain a particular line of action, although charities may present reasoned argument and information to Government;

where the objects of a charity include the advancement of education or the power to conduct research, care must be taken that both objectivity and balance is maintained and that propaganda is avoided.

12.8.1.2 Reform of the law? Since reform of the law has recently been considered and rejected, it is perhaps pertinent to make reference to criticisms that have been made of the law in this area. In his excellent contextual work, *Charities, Trusts and Social Welfare* (1979), Chesterman observes (at pp. 357–8) that it has ultimately conservative implications, particularly where a welfare organisation takes the view that its role is that of a catalyst, its long-term aim being to encourage state funding:

The irony here, however, is that if they are too vociferous in urging the state to take over from them, they risk being deemed non-charitable because they are 'political' in one of the senses which charity law does not recognise. In the eyes of the law, a statement by a charity such as Shelter that 'it exists to put itself out of business' has non-charitable implications.

He also observes that overseas welfare charities, such as Oxfam and War on Want, are restricted by the law to distribution of food and other basic amenities, which is unlikely to have any long-term impact on the problems being addressed. They cannot, under the present law, become involved in projects of a more strategic nature, such as stimulation of local food production, or attempts to persuade a foreign government to distribute the country's resources more equitably or the British government to grant more foreign aid. In short, they cannot do that which would be most effective.

The Government took a different view in 1989, commenting in *Charities: A Framework for the Future* that:

the safeguards which the law provides are indispensable to prevent what are essentially political factions or pressure groups from assuming the guise of charity. It is vital, in the long term interests of the public and charities alike, that political and charitable purposes should remain distinct. It would be wrong if taxpayers, through the Government, were to find themselves unwittingly distorting the democratic process by subsidising bodies whose true purpose was to campaign not so much for their beneficiaries as for some political end. Nor do the Government believe that the public would for long continue to display their generosity if charities were to ally themselves to causes with which individual donors might well differ strongly on political grounds.

No *substantive* change to this area of law was therefore made by the Charities Acts 1992 or 1993, although the strengthening in that provision of the Commissioners' powers of investigation (see 11.2.3) could well affect in practice the political activities of charities.

There are three final observations which are worth making. First, Chesterman also observes (at p. 359) that long-established political charities, such as the Howard League for Penal Reform, the Anti-Slavery Society and the Lord's Day Observance Society, have not been denied charitable status. He comments that the present ban on political activity is of comparatively recent origin, and that the Charity Commissioners are not disposed to refuse registration to organisations long believed to be charitable: indeed, an undertaking to this effect was in fact given when the Charities Act 1960 was going through Parliament. Secondly, there is no restriction on officers of charities making their personal views known, even allowing it to be known that they happen to be officers of the particular charity. Thirdly, it is perfectly legitimate for groups to split up their activities among various distinct organisations with their own separate legal structures. Some, but not all, of these organisations might engage in political activity, in which case charitable status can still be claimed for those which do not. This was what Amnesty International tried to do in *McGovern* v *Attorney-General*, by claiming charitable status only for their Prisoners of Conscience Fund, but they failed because even the purposes of that sub-group were held to be non-charitable.

12.8.2 Self-help
Although self-help organisations may possibly have been regarded as charitable in the 19th century when, for example, friendly societies contributed considerably to the then limited provisions for welfare, Hall V-C held in *Re Clark* (1875) 1 ChD 497 that a friendly society was not charitable because of the absence of any stipulation that benefits should be restricted to those members who were poor as well as old, disabled or sick.

If they are not poverty charities, self-help organisations clearly fail on the *Oppenheim* personal nexus test (see 12.7.1.1). Hall V-C envisaged that they may succeed as poverty charities, where as we have seen public benefit tests are less stringent, but there may be a second principle that the benefits of charity must be provided by bounty and not bargain. Where, as is the case with many friendly societies, the beneficiaries have, in effect, bought their entitlement in a contractual arrangement, the element of altruism essential to charity is lacking.

In *Re Hobourn Aero Components Ltd's Air Raid Distress Fund* [1946] Ch 194 (see 5.3.2), a fund established by employees to relieve members suffering in consequence of air raids on Coventry was held by the Court of Appeal to be non-charitable on the ground that the employees among whom benefit was confined could not be a section of the public. It was not argued as a poverty charity, and the issue was left open whether it could have been charitable had it been so limited. Nevertheless, there are passages in Lord Greene MR's judgment which suggest that it could not have been charitable even as a poverty charity because the members' entitlement to benefit turned upon the fact of their having subscribed to the fund. This was, in his view, a private trust. If this is correct, then no self-help organisation will be charitable.

It should perhaps be observed that the contributors did not want the fund in *Re Hobourn Aero Components Ltd's Air Raid Distress Fund* to be charitable, since if it had been the Charity Commissioners would have applied their contributions cy près (see chapter 13) when the fund was wound up.

12.8.3   Disaster appeals
These will be valid if for the relief of poverty, otherwise, like self-help organisations, they will fail on the grounds of public benefit. This leaves the organisers of such funds with two alternatives. One possibility is that they can apply a means test criterion to the receipt of benefit, which they may regard as invidious. For example, in the Aberfan coal-tip disaster of 1966, the majority of victims were children, and far from it being easy to show that their deaths produced material deprivation among the relatives, one could actually argue that the cost of rearing the children was saved. In fact, the Commissioners eventually held that the fund was charitable, when money was paid to enable people to move away from the area altogether. Chesterman, *Charities, Trusts and Social Welfare,* gives an extremely comprehensive coverage of this appeal (pp. 339ff) and see also (1982) NLJ 223.

The other possibility, often favoured by fund organisers (e.g., Penlee lifeboat disaster fund in 1982), is to avoid the means test and draft the appeal in such a way as to avoid charitable status altogether. In that event, of course, the tax concessions will also be forgone. Perhaps more importantly, the cy près doctrine described in chapter 13 will not apply and there may be difficulties over distribution of any surplus left over after the purposes have been achieved (see 2.4.2). It may even be that the Crown will take some or all of the surplus as *bona vacantia,* not perhaps the most fitting consequence of the altruism of the donors.

One of the problems with disaster appeals is that they are usually set up very quickly after the disaster has occurred, often before the full legal consequences have been considered. They may well be described as charitable, and donors may believe that their contributions are going to a charitable fund, only for the organisers later to change their minds and draft the purposes so as to avoid charitable status. An interesting question might then arise as to what happens to the money already contributed, in the (probably unlikely) event of a dispute (for example, if somebody who had contributed on the assumption that the fund was charitable objected when he discovered that it was not).

THIRTEEN

Cy Près

13.1 GENERAL PRINCIPLES

The Anglo-Norman phrase cy près (which is sometimes hyphenated) meant
something like 'as near as possible', and the doctrine of cy près in charity law
lays down that where property given on trust for charitable purposes cannot
be used in the precise manner intended by the donor, the court (and since
about 130 years ago the Charity Commissioners) may make a scheme for the
application of the property to purposes resembling as closely as possible the
donor's original intention. The idea, in other words, is not to frustrate the
intention of the donor (who cannot be consulted if the gift is testamentary)
any more than necessary. The doctrine dates back at least as far as the 17th
century. It only applies to charities — if private purposes fail, the results are
as discussed in 2.4 and chapter 5.

The question whether cy près can be applied can arise either because it is
clear from the outset that the donor's intention cannot be fulfilled, as where
the organisation which he has singled out for benefit has already ceased to
exist, or because at some later time, during the continuance of the trust, it
turns out that the purposes cannot be achieved. Cy près is more easily
invoked in the latter case, for once property has been dedicated to charity,
there is no possibility of a resulting trust to the donor.

Where, however, a gift fails from the start, the courts have since the early
19th century insisted that before the property can be applied cy près, a
general or 'paramount' charitable intention must be shown.

The application of the doctrine has been significantly widened by the
Charities Act 1960. This may reflect a difference of emphasis. The equitable
doctrine was probably based on the presumed intention of the donor, and
could in some circumstances militate against the efficient operation of
charitable enterprises (see, e.g., 13.4.1). The 1960 Act, on the other hand, is
concerned more with the efficient running of charities, even at the expense of
the donor's intentions.

13.2 INITIAL FAILURE

The question turns on whether the intention of the donor was specific or
general. If it was to further some specific purpose which cannot be carried

out, or benefit some specific institution no longer in existence, then the gift fails and the property will return to the settlor, or his estate, on a resulting trust, as discussed in 2.4.

If, however, the intention is a more general one, which might be satisfied by applying the property to a purpose or institution similar to that specified, a cy près scheme may be ordered. The test, then, is whether a general or 'paramount' charitable intention can be found.

13.2.1 Gift to a charity which has never existed at all

13.2.1.1 Operation of cy près doctrine: general charitable intention
In *Re Rymer* [1895] 1 Ch 19, a gift for a specific seminary which had ceased to exist failed. This is the general position where no paramount (or general) charitable intention can be found. Whether a general charitable intention can be shown is a question of fact. The cases in this section are illustrations of the factors that can be taken into account but do not lay down general rules.

If the charity specified by the donor has never existed at all, it is usually easier to discover a general charitable intention than where the charity once existed but has since ceased (as in *Re Rymer*), since only a general intention can be attributed to the donor who fails correctly to specify the beneficiary. For example, in *Re Harwood* [1936] Ch 285, a gift was made to the Peace Society in Belfast, which could not be shown ever to have existed. Farwell J found that there was an intention to benefit societies aimed at promoting peace, and the gift was therefore applied cy près. A second gift in the will, in favour of the Wisbech Peace Society, which had once existed but had ceased to do so prior to the testatrix's death, was held, however, to have lapsed. Although the case is a good illustration of the operation of the cy près doctrine, doubt may perhaps be cast on the assumption that the promotion of peace is in fact capable of being charitable (see 12.8.1).

In *Re Satterthwaite's WT* [1966] 1 WLR 277, a will listed a number of organisations concerned with animal welfare. The list had been thoughtlessly compiled from the London telephone directory, the testatrix's chief concern being to divert her estate to animal charities, because she hated the whole human race. One of the named institutions, the London Animal Hospital, had never existed as a charity. The Court of Appeal held that the gift to the London Animal Hospital should be applied cy près: a general charitable intention could be inferred from the testatrix's known attitude towards the human race, and from the fact that all but one of the other dispositions were made in favour of genuine animal charities. In the opinion of Russell LJ, therefore, a general intention to benefit animal charities could easily be inferred.

Harman LJ expressed 'the gravest doubts', however, and a better explanation of this case may be that, as with the Peace Society in Belfast in *Re Harwood* [1936] Ch 285, the London Animal Hospital had never existed as a charity. Sir Robert Megarry V-C refused to apply what he described as the doctrine of 'charity by association' in *Re Spence's WT* [1979] Ch 483, on the grounds that *Re Satterthwaite* only applied where the body had never existed.

It is also necessary for the other donations to be to charitable organisations of the same type; merely for a non-charitable body to be included among a general list of charities is not evidence of a general charitable intent. In *Re Jenkins's WT* [1966] Ch 249 Buckley J declined to hold that a gift to the British Union for the Abolition of Vivisection (which did exist but was not charitable) could be taken as charitable simply by being included in a list of gifts to unquestionably charitable organisations.

It must be emphasised, however, that the question is ultimately one of fact, and the above cases should not be treated as authorities.

13.2.1.2 Non-existent body, but no initial failure Even where the charity specified does not exist, it may be possible to save the gift if the institution can be said to continue to exist in some other form. In recent years many small charities have amalgamated, and it is sometimes possible to regard the new body thus formed as being the same as the old. In *Re Faraker* [1912] 2 Ch 488, for example, a gift to 'Mrs Bailey's charity, Rotherhithe' (which was taken to mean 'Hannah Bayly's Charity') passed to the new charity formed by an amalgamation of Hannah Bayly's Charity with several others.

Another approach is to find that the gift was made for the *purpose* of the named charity, rather than for the body itself. If the body is unincorporated then by definition the gift cannot be to it but must be to its purposes, and if those purposes can still be fulfilled the gift will not fail. Since there is no failure there is no need to show a general charitable intention. Indeed, this is not an application of cy près as such, but rather an instance of finding a substitute trustee to carry out the purposes of the trust. Where the body is a corporation, however, a gift to it will prima facie lapse if the corporation has ceased to exist, just as a gift to a human individual would lapse if the person concerned had died before the gift was made. The gift may be rescued only on the cy près principles already outlined, i.e., if the court is able to find a general charitable intention going beyond the specific aim of benefiting the named corporate charity.

In *Re Finger's WT* [1972] Ch 286, for example, testamentary gifts were made to the National Radium Commission, an unincorporated association, and to the National Council for Maternity and Child Welfare, which was a corporate charity. Both had ceased to exist by the time the testatrix died. Goff J held that the gift to the National Radium Commission was interpreted as a gift to its purposes, and since these still continued, the gift did not fail. The gift to the National Council for Maternity and Child Welfare would have failed, as a gift to a corporate charity, in the absence of a general charitable intention, which in the event it was, however, possible to discern.

Similar principles were applied in *Re Koeppler's WT* [1986] Ch 423 (see 12.8.1), where Slade LJ construed a gift to a non-existent body as a valid trust for educational purposes. The case concerned the validity of a testamentary gift to the warden of the institution known as Wilton Park. At the time of the testator's death there was no entity called Wilton Park, nor was there a warden of Wilton Park, but there was a Wilton Park project, which organised a series of conferences. The gift was construed as a gift for the purposes of the Wilton Park project, the non-existent body in *Re Koeppler's WT* being treated as analogous to the National Radium Commission in *Re Finger's WT*.

13.2.2 Gifts with conditions attached

Even where the institution to which the donation is made exists there may be an initial failure if there is a condition in the gift which the donee body finds unacceptable. In *Re Lysaght* [1966] Ch 191, the testatrix left £5,000 to the Royal College of Surgeons in order to establish and maintain one or more studentships. There was a condition, however, which would have disqualified Jews and Roman Catholics, and the College declined to accept the gift on these terms. The gift was saved because the court found a general charitable intention on the part of the testatrix, to establish medical studentships. The cy près doctrine therefore operated; the condition could be deleted as not being essential to the fulfilment of the general intention. A scheme was ordered on the terms of the will as it stood without the condition.

Recently, in *Re Woodhams* [1981] 1 WLR 493, a general charitable intention to foster musical education was found, allowing the court to remove the restriction which would have limited scholarships to boys from two named children's homes and would have also prevented the donees from accepting the gift.

It may be wondered why the gift fails unless the conditions are deleted. After all, a trust should not fail merely because the trustee refuses to accept the trust property. 'Equity will not allow a trust to fail for want of a trustee', and in principle it might be thought that the court should find a trustee who is prepared to carry out the terms of the trust on the settlor's terms. In other words, it should not be necessary to delete the repugnant condition.

In a case like *Re Lysaght,* however, the identity of the donee is essential to the purposes of the trust, and were the Royal College to decline the gift another trustee simply could not be found to carry out the testatrix's intention. As Buckley J pointed out in the case:

> Obviously a trustee will not normally be permitted to modify the terms of his trust on the ground that his own opinions or convictions conflict with them. If his conscience will not allow him to carry out the trust faithfully in accordance with its terms, he must make way for a trustee who can and will do so. But how, if the identity of the trustee selected by the settlor is essential to his intention? It is of the essence of a trust that the trustees selected by the settlor and no one else shall act as the trustees of it and if those trustees cannot or will not undertake the office, the trust must fail.

13.3 SUBSEQUENT FAILURE

Cy près has a much wider application in the event of a subsequent failure, and none of the difficulties which arise in the event of an initial failure arise here.

Once property has been dedicated to charitable purposes, it remains so, and if those purposes cease to be capable of achievement, there can be no resulting trust to the settlor or his estate unless the terms on which the gift was originally made provide for this to happen. It is not necessary to search for a general charitable intention on the part of the settlor. The only relevant consideration is whether there was an outright disposition in favour of charity. Where this is so, funds which cannot be applied to the original purpose, whether because that purpose is impossible, or because there is a surplus left over after the purposes have been achieved, may be applied cy près.

In *Re Slevin* [1891] 2 Ch 236, a legacy had been left to the Orphanage of St Dominics, Newcastle-upon-Tyne. The orphanage ceased to exist after the date of the donor's death, but before the legacy could be paid over. Since the orphanage had survived its benefactor, by however short a time, the gift was effective in favour of charity and could be applied cy près. In *Re King* [1923] 1 Ch 243, a surplus was left after the purpose (the setting of a stained-glass window in a church) was carried out. Finding that the whole fund, and not just the sum sufficient for the window, had been dedicated to charity, Romer J applied the surplus cy près (to the setting of a second window).

Nor will it matter that the gift to charity was intended to be postponed until some future date under the terms of the will or gift. In other words, the relevant date is that of the original donation, even though the charity may only at that time obtain a future interest in the property. If A dies leaving property to B for his life, thereafter to C (a charity), and C ceases to exist after A's death but before B's, this is regarded as a subsequent, not an initial, failure.

Thus, in *Re Moon* [1948] 1 All ER 300, the testator directed that a legacy should be paid to the trustees of a Methodist church for the purposes of missionary work after the death of his widow. The purposes were no longer practicable by the time of the widow's death and Roxburgh J held that the question of whether the gift had lapsed must be resolved in relation to the time when the gift was made, that is, at the death of the testator. Since the purposes would have been practical then, there was an effective gift to charity at that time, and the failure was subsequent and not initial. A similar result was reached in *Re Wright* [1954] Ch 347, where a testamentary gift for the founding of a convalescent home was to take effect after a life interest, at the end of which time the property was insufficient for this purpose. The date of the testatrix's death was taken to be crucial in determining the question of whether the gift was practicable.

In *Re Welsh Hospital (Netley) Fund* [1921] 1 Ch 655, a surplus of £9,000 remained after the winding up of a (charitable) hospital erected at Netley, and the question arose what to do with the surplus. P.O. Laurence J held that it should be applied cy près, but only after concluding that the donors must be taken to have parted with their donations out and out to charity (much of the money had been derived from anonymous sources, and the issues were essentially those discussed at 2.4.2.2). There was no suggestion, in other words, that a cy près scheme ought to have been automatic, on the basis of subsequent failure. However, in *Re Ulverston and District New Hospital Building Trusts* [1956] Ch 622, Jenkins LJ explained *Re Welsh Hospital (Netley) Fund* as a straightforward case of subsequent failure. The earlier case was distinguished because, in *Re Ulverston*, the hospital had never been built and none of the funds ever expended, so the failure was regarded as an initial failure. There being no evidence of general charitable intention, the fund was not applied cy près.

13.4 ALTERING CHARITABLE OBJECTS

13.4.1 At common law

Whereas no difficulties have ever arisen in the case of a clear failure, such as a charitable body ceasing to exist, when the cy près doctrine could operate on the subsequent failure, there could be problems before 1960 where a charitable purpose simply became outdated and obsolete although the original charitable body continued in existence. There was no effective system whereby moribund charities could be modernised and of course the cy près doctrine could not apply if there was no failure.

Until the reforms introduced by the Charities Act 1960 the courts' only jurisdiction was their inherent jurisdiction to apply funds cy près, but the inherent jurisdiction is confined to rather narrow limits, being available only where it is 'impossible' or 'impracticable' to carry out the terms of the trust. Some very peculiar trusts were kept on foot by the limits of the cy près doctrine before 1960, obliging trustees to distribute bread, linen, stockings, boots etc., among the poor. One old trust specified the distribution of green waistcoats in memory of the testator's surname. The courts' main concern was not to depart too far from the original wishes of settlors, rather than to promote the efficient administration of charities.

For example, in *Re Weir Hospital* [1910] 2 Ch 124, a testator left two houses to be used as a hospital. The premises were not suitable, and the Charity Commissioners approved a scheme to use them as a nurses' home instead, perpetuating the testator's name by renaming a hospital in his honour. The Court of Appeal held that the scheme was *ultra vires*, since the original purpose was not impossible to fulfil, merely difficult. Sir Herbert Cozens-Hardy MR's view (at p. 131) was that the court's primary duty was to give effect to the charitable intentions of the donor, rather than to seek the most beneficial application of the property:

> The first duty of the Court is to construe the will, and to give effect to the charitable directions of the founder, assuming them not to be open to objection on the ground of public policy. The Court does not consider whether those directions are wise or whether a more generally beneficial application of the testator's property might not be founded.

Similar sentiments were echoed by Kennedy LJ at pp. 140–41:

> But neither the Court of Chancery, nor the Board of Charity Commissioners, which has been entrusted by statute, in regard to the application of charitable fund, with similar jurisdiction, is entitled to substitute a different scheme for the scheme which the donor has prescribed in the

instrument which creates the charity, merely because a coldly wise intelli-
gence, impervious to the special predilections which inspired his liberality,
and untrammelled by his directions, would have dictated a different use of
his money . . . If the charity can be administered according to the directions
of founder or testator, the law requires that it should be so administered.

It is permissible under the courts' inherent jurisdiction, however, to
eradicate a condition of the trust which, with the passage of time, has become
inimical to its main purpose. In *Re Robinson* [1923] 2 Ch 332, a condition in
a gift of an endowment for an evangelical church requiring a preacher to wear
a black gown in the pulpit was cut out, since it was thought likely to offend
the congregation and reduce attendance: with the passage of time, the
condition had become inimical to the main purpose of the gift. Another
example is *Re Dominion Students' Hall Trust* [1947] Ch 183, where a colour
bar was removed from a trust for the maintenance of a hostel for male
students of the overseas dominions of the British Empire, since the main
purpose of the trust was to promote community of citizenship among
members of the Commonwealth.

Re Robinson was applied by Buckley J in *Re Lysaght* (13.2.2), the same test
being used there in an initial failure case to strike out a condition. Unlike
Robinson, of course, which is a subsequent failure case, in *Lysaght*, it was
necessary to find a general charitable intention, in order to invoke the cy près
doctrine in the first place.

In *Re J. W. Laing Trust* [1984] Ch 143, Peter Gibson J was prepared to
strike out a term requiring trustees to distribute, within 10 years of the
settlor's death, a fund which by then had risen significantly in value (from
some £15,000 in 1922 when the trust was set up, to over £24 million in
1982). The increase in value had been quite unforseen when the trust was set
up, partly because the settlor had lived much longer than expected (to the age
of 98). The recipients of the income from the charity (Christian evangelical
bodies) had come to depend upon it, whereas it would have been impossible
to distribute such a large amount of capital in such a way as to ensure
continuance of the causes which the settlor wished to support. The term was
struck out on the basis that it was 'inexpedient in the very altered circumstances of the charity since that requirement was laid down 60 years ago'. It
is not entirely clear whether this expediency test is the same as that being
applied in the earlier cases, or whether a wider principle is being adopted.

There may also be situations where no scheme is required. In *Oldham
Borough Council* v *Attorney-General* [1993] Ch 210, the Clayton Playing Fields
in Oldham had been conveyed to the council (or more accurately, to the
bodies which preceded it prior to the local government reorganisation in
1974) in 1962, for recreational purposes. The Borough Council proposed to
sell the land for development, but also to provide a new site which (it was
assumed) would be used for exactly the same charitable purposes. The
council expressly disclaimed reliance on the Charities Act 1960, since clearly
none of the heads (enumerated below) could apply in this case. Dillon LJ,
who gave the only substantive judgment in the Court of Appeal, took the view

that the sale of the land would have been approved prior to the Charities Act, since there was no requirement to use *that particular land*. Since the charitable purposes would still be carried out, there was no need for a scheme, and the court was prepared to approve the sale.

13.4.2   Charities Act 1993, section 13

Following a recommendation of the Nathan Committee on the Law and Practice Relating to Charitable Trusts (1952, Cmd 8710), para. 365, s. 13 (which replaces a similar provision in the 1960 Act) extends, presumably in the interests of more efficient administration of charities, the circumstances in which property may be applied cy près.

The purpose of this section is to modernise outmoded trusts; as we have seen this was difficult using only the inherent jurisdiction of the courts. Section 13(5) places a duty upon trustees to seek the application of property cy près if and when appropriate circumstances arise. Much of the work of the Commissioners consists in settling and approving schemes of this kind.

The precise circumstances are set out in s. 13(1). No longer is it necessary to show that it is 'impossible' or 'impracticable' to carry out the terms of the trust. It is enough that the original purpose has been fulfilled as far as possible, or cannot be carried out according to the directions given and the spirit of the gift, or if there is a surplus left over, or if the purposes have been adequately provided for by other means, or become useless or harmful to the community. Cy près may also apply where the original purposes relate to an area, or class of persons, which has ceased to have any relevance, having regard to the spirit of the gift. There are also provisions for the amalgamation of small charities if that is more efficient.

Section 13(1) is in the following terms:

(1)   Subject to subsection (2) below, the circumstances in which the original purposes of a charitable gift can be altered to allow the property given or part of it to be applied cy près shall be as follows:—

(a)   where the original purposes, in whole or in part,—

(i)   have been as far as may be fulfilled; or

(ii)   cannot be carried out, or not according to the directions given and to the spirit of the gift; or

(b)   where the original purposes provide a use for part only of the property available by virtue of the gift; or

(c)   where the property available by virtue of the gift and other property applicable for similar purposes can be more effectively used in conjunction, and to that end can suitably, regard being had to the spirit of the gift, be made applicable to common purposes; or

(d)   where the original purposes were laid down by reference to an area which then was but has since ceased to be a unit for some other purpose, or by reference to a class of persons or to an area which has for any reason since ceased to be suitable, regard being had to the spirit of the gift, or to be practical in administering the gift; or

(e)   where the original purposes, in whole or in part, have, since they were laid down,—

(i)   been adequately provided for by other means; or

(ii)   ceased, as being useless or harmful to the community or for other reasons, to be in law charitable; or

(iii)   ceased in any other way to provide a suitable and effective method of using the property available by virtue of the gift, regard being had to the spirit of the gift.

Subheads (a) to (e) of s. 13(1) will generally be wider than the pre-1960 definition of failure, and apparently supersede it; in *Oldham Borough Council v Attorney-General* [1993] Ch 210, Dillon LJ took the view that the s. 13 heads were exhaustive, at any rate where alteration of the 'original purposes' is sought (on which, see further below):

Broadly the effect of that section is that an alteration of the 'original purposes' of a charitable gift can only be authorised by a scheme for the *cy près* application of the trust property and such a scheme can only be made in the circumstances set out in subheads (a) to (e) of subsection (1) of section 13.

Section 13 defines failure and arguably applies to define initial as well as subsequent failure. However, the section begins by talking of 'the original purposes of a charitable gift', which supposes that a charitable gift has taken place. It will not have in many cases of initial failure. In that case the question of whether there has been a failure will be determined on the basis of the pre-1960 law.

In any case s. 13 (by virtue of s. 13(2)) only affects the definition of when failure occurs for cy près purposes, and all the other requirements of the doctrine remain. Thus, for example, it is still necessary to show a paramount charitable intention in the case of an initial failure.

In interpreting the section, the Commissioners attempt, so far as possible, to effect the intentions of the donor, these being understood in the context of modern conditions (see their Annual Report 1970, para. 41).

In *Re Lepton's Charity* [1972] Ch 276, Pennycuick V-C invoked ss. 13(1)(a)(ii) and 13(1)(e)(iii) (above) to increase payment to a church minister from £3 per year to £100 per year. Under the original will of 1715 the testator left land, whose profits amounted to £5 a year, with a direction to trustees to pay £3 a year to the minister, and the residue to the poor of Pudsey. In 1967 the income from the investments representing the land was £791 14s 6d. Pennycuick V-C approved an application under s. 13 to increase the income of the minister to £100 a year, the residue going, as before, to the poor of Pudsey. The court felt that after the change the relative distribution between the minister and the poor of Pudsey remained as in the spirit of the gift. The main argument in the case was whether s. 13 applied to the trusts in the will as a whole, or to each of the two trusts separately (a trust to pay the £3 a year to the minister, and a separate trust to pay the residue to the poor of Pudsey). Only if (as Pennycuick V-C held) the spirit of the gift related to the will as a whole could the court alter the relative proportions of each part.

Section 13 allows only the original purposes of a charitable gift to be altered, and for this reason it could not be used in *Re J. W. Laing Trust* [1984] Ch 143 (13.4.1) to delete a provision relating to distribution, which was essentially administrative in nature. Peter Gibson J observed (at p. 153) that 'it cannot be right that any provision, even if only administrative, made applicable by a donor to his gifts should be treated as a condition and hence part of its purpose'. The same view was taken in *Oldham Borough Council* v *Attorney-General* [1993] Ch 210, above, where Dillon LJ considered that the requirement that the actual land given should be used as playing fields was not part of the 'original purposes' within s. 13. In *J. W. Laing* the condition was struck out under the inherent jurisdiction, whereas in *Oldham* there was no need for a scheme at all, so these are both cases where the common law applied but the statute did not.

13.4.3 Limit to Commissioners' scheme-making powers

One of the problems perceived with the Charities Act 1960 was the inability of the Commissioners to make a scheme of their own volition where no trustees could be found who were able or willing to apply for one. It is true that under s. 18(6), the Commissioners can apply to the Secretary of State to refer to them cases where the trustees have unreasonably refused or neglected to make a scheme, but apparently this provision has never been invoked. The Commissioners have also since 1960 had wide-ranging powers under s. 20 in the event of misconduct or mismanagement in the administration of the charity, for example to suspend trustees and to appoint additional trustees as necessary for the proper administration of the charity, but under the original legislation they had no power to make a cy près scheme themselves. This has now been catered for by the Charities Act 1993, s. 18.

13.5 CHARITIES ACT 1993, SECTION 14

Section 14 provides reform to cope with the problems which may arise if property is given for charitable purposes which fail and where it is difficult to find the donors. This is a form of initial failure and often there will be no paramount charitable intention. This most frequently arises in disaster appeal funds.

13.5.1 Position in the case of non-charitable trusts

In the case of private (non-charitable) trusts, the operation of the resulting trust doctrine usually results in a proportion of the funds passing to the Crown as *bona vacantia*. This is because where a donation to such a fund is anonymous (e.g., small change in a street collecting box) and no means of tracing the donor has been left, it is reasonable to construe the contribution as an out-and-out gift. It is difficult to infer that the donor intended any surplus left over to be held on resulting trust for him since he has left the organisers no means of finding him. That part of the surplus attributable to his donation will therefore have no owner and so goes to the Crown as *bona vacantia*.

It is true that in *Re Gillingham Bus Disaster Fund* [1958] Ch 300 (see 2.4.2.2), such donations were directed to be held on resulting trust, so that such a result was avoided, but apart from being administratively inconvenient this result is probably wrong. Undoubtedly the usual inference would be that if people give money in an anonymous collection, they intend an out-and-out gift, not to see it back again.

This result (i.e., the out-and-out gift construction) was in fact reached by Goff J in *Re West Sussex Constabulary's Widows, Children & Benevolent (1930) Fund Trusts* [1971] Ch 1 (see 2.4). The fund was not a disaster fund but was for widows and dependants, and there were outside contributions in addition to those of the members themselves. It came to an end upon amalgamation with other police forces in 1968, and the court was asked to decide how to distribute the surplus.

So far as identifiable donations and legacies were concerned, the proportion of the surplus attributable to that source was held on resulting trust. But there were also the proceeds of street collecting boxes and in relation to those Goff J declined to follow Harman J's earlier judgment on the ground that the intention to be inferred was also that of an out-and-out gift (see further 2.4). Thus, nobody could lay claim to the proportion of the surplus attributable to the last two categories, so it went to the Crown as *bona vacantia*.

13.5.2 Position where purposes charitable

The *West Sussex* result (see 13.5.1) will be the norm not only in the case of non-charitable donations where a surplus is left over after the fund is wound up or its purposes achieved but also where money is given for charitable purposes which initially fail (unless a paramount charitable intention can be found). It does not apply where a charitable fund *subsequently* achieves its purposes because this will be a subsequent failure and there will be no difficulty applying the cy près doctrine. So had the Gillingham Bus Disaster Fund (see. 13.5.1) been charitable, cy près would have applied in the normal way on a subsequent failure.

13.5.3 Operation of section 14

Section 14 of the Charities Act 1993, replacing a similar provision from the 1960 Act, is intended to prevent the *West Sussex* result (see 13.5.1) where money is given for charitable purposes which fail. The section has application only in the case of initial failure, as in the case of subsequent failure (as we have seen) no question of returning the gifts to the donors would arise.

Section 14(1) allows the application of such property cy près, regardless of charitable intention, when the property has been given:

(a) by a donor who, after such advertisements and inquiries as are reasonable, cannot be identified or cannot be found (donors may claim within one year of the scheme), or;

(b) by a donor who has executed a written disclaimer of his right to have the property returned.

There is a conclusive presumption (in s. 14(3)) that property raised by cash collections by way of collecting boxes or other methods which make it hard to tell one gift from another, or as the proceeds of lotteries, competitions, sales, entertainments or similar fund-raising activities, belongs to unidentifiable donors without the need for instituting any inquiries:

(3) For the purposes of this section property shall be conclusively presumed (without any advertisement or inquiry) to belong to donors who cannot be identified, insofar as it consists—
(a) of the proceeds of cash collections made by means of collecting boxes or by any other means not adapted for distinguishing one gift from another; or
(b) of the proceeds of any lottery, competition, entertainment, sale or similar money-raising activity, after allowing for property given to provide prizes or articles for sale or otherwise to enable the activity to be undertaken.

Allowance must, however, be made for property given to provide prizes or articles for sale, or otherwise to allow the activity to be undertaken, and the donors of such items are entitled to the return of the property or its proceeds, should they so wish.

In any other case, the court may direct the property to be considered as belonging to unidentifiable donors if it would not be reasonable to return it in view of the amounts involved or the lapse of time since the gift was made.

It would seem then that the law is thus improved to the degree that it is no longer necessary to impute a fictitious general charitable intention to the donors or else attempt the return of the property — a result which, as has been seen, often results in the fund passing to the Crown as *bona vacantia*.

However, David Wilson has argued ([1983] Conv 40) that s. 14 is 'a dead letter of English law', and it is indeed arguable that it made no difference to the pre-1960 law. The argument essentially is that s. 14(1) applies only where the property belongs to a donor. But if Goff J was correct in *Re West Sussex Constabulary's Widows, Children and Benevolent (1930) Fund* [1971] Ch 1, doubting Harman J in *Re Gillingham Bus Disaster Fund* [1958] Ch 300, anonymous contributors do not intend to retain any interest in the property, and hence s. 14 is never triggered. It might be thought that the presumption in s. 14(3) cures the problem, but arguably the presumption goes only to the question of identification, rather than to whether the property also 'belongs to donors'. Indeed, it is natural to read s. 14(3) as applying to identification only. In that case, the property will, as in *West Sussex*, still go to the Crown as *bona vacantia*, and s. 14 will make no difference.

If, on the other hand, any of the fund has actually been applied towards a charitable purpose, then on Jenkins LJ's views (see 13.3) in *Re Ulverston and District New Hospital Building Trusts* [1956] Ch 622, the failure would be a subsequent failure, and a cy près scheme would be ordered. In that case, there would be no need for s. 14 anyway. If this argument is correct, in the only situation where s. 14 is needed, it is worded in such a way that it cannot operate.

13.6 SMALL POVERTY CHARITIES

There are particular problems with old charities for the relief of poverty. Many of these required trustees to distribute money or goods, but the growth of State welfare has reduced the attractiveness of these, and even rendered them counter-productive in some cases, because hand-outs can lead to a reduction in State benefit. As long ago as 1967 the Annual Report of the Charity Commissioners (paras 17–20 and App. B) recognised the problem involved in cash hand-outs by commenting on the undesirability of using charity funds to relieve the burdens of the DHSS and local authorities, and instead suggested other schemes, for example outings or home decoration.

Yet many old trusts to relieve poverty bound trustees to distribute money or goods. One example required the trustees to spend the income in buying bread and linen for the poor of East Barning — in 1983, the fund available was £5.12p! Obviously, by the 1980s a trust of this type had come to serve little useful purpose.

A possible solution to this problem obviously existed under the provisions of the Charities Act 1960, but the mechanisms for the full scheme-making powers contained therein were arguably too complicated for very small charities. Following a report of a House of Lords Select Committee in 1984, the Charities Act 1985 addressed this problem. Section 2 allowed trustees of charities more than 50 years old, by a simplified procedure, to change the objects to more suitable ones, so long as they were within the spirit of the original donor's intentions. Under s. 3, where the annual income of a charity was less than £200, the trustees could transfer its property to another charity having similar aims, or if its income was less than £5 a year, the trustees under s. 4 could wind it up, by spending the capital as if it were income.

The Government, in its White Paper *Charities: A Framework for the Future*, HMSO (May 1989), proposed to extend the policy of the 1985 Act, by standardising the application of ss. 2 and 3, and applying both these sections to all charities with an income of less than £1,000 a year, without distinction of age, locality or purpose, the sole exception being those holding land for the purposes of the charity. It was proposed that trustees wishing to modify their objects or amalgamate with another charity need to be satisfied:

that the original purposes had, since they were laid down, ceased to provide a suitable and effective method of using the property; and

that the new objects specified, or the objects of the charity to which property was being transferred, were as similar as practicable to the charity's original objects having regard to the spirit of the gift.

The Charities Act 1993 has for the most part put these recommendations into effect, but the ss. 2 and 3 financial limits have been raised to £5,000 per year (rather than £1,000 as recommended), and the s. 4 limit has been raised to £1,000. Section 74 of the 1993 Act replaces the old ss. 2 and 3, and s. 75 replaces the old s. 4.

Trustees are required to act by unanimous resolution and with the Commissioners' concurrence, and to give reasonable public notice of their intentions. Transfers of property under what used to be s. 3 obviously require the consent of the trustees of receiving charities.

FOURTEEN

The Office of Trustee

Up to now we have been concerned largely with different types of trust and requirements for their validity. Chapters 14 to 17 are about trusteeship and the actual administration of trusts. This chapter is about the general nature of the office of trustee. The next covers how trustees are appointed and removed (or retire). Chapter 16 takes a much more detailed look at their main powers and duties. Chapter 17 is about what happens when something goes wrong — what can the beneficiaries do about it?

There are a number of general points to appreciate before embarking on the administration of trusts.

First, it will soon become clear how onerous the office of trusteeship is. Legal title, without its equitable counterpart, is by no means a privilege. It is no wonder that the courts require very clear evidence, for example, that a settlor has constituted himself trustee (see 3.1.4). Nor will it come as a surprise that trusteeship is often undertaken on a professional basis and that the charges can be very high.

Secondly, whereas some of what follows in chapters 14 to 16 is inherent in the nature of any trust, many of the powers and duties described in chapter 16 represent simply a fall-back position where nothing to the contrary is provided in the trust instrument. In reality, the precise scope of such powers and duties will, in the case of most express trusts, be governed by the terms of the trust instrument and not by the fall-back legal position. Provision is also frequently made in the trust instrument for the remuneration of trustees, on which see 14.3.2, and it is usual to include clauses designed to limit the trustees' liability for breach of trust. The trust instrument may therefore contemplate considerable deviation from the rules to be considered in chapters 14 to 16.

That is not to deny the importance of the general law. As long as people set up trusts without taking proper legal advice the fallback position remains a material consideration. Also, of course, trust instruments can be considerably shortened to the extent that powers and duties are provided anyway, in the absence of provision to the contrary.

Thirdly, it is less certain how far these rules apply to constructive trustees, whose powers and obligations may depend upon the circumstances in which the trust arises. See further 16.1.3.

Quite a lot of the material on the administration of trusts is statutory, but usually the provisions only restate the previous law, or re-enact, either exactly or with slight differences, earlier provisions. Occasionally, therefore, cases are cited as authority on the interpretation of a section where the cases actually pre-dated the section now in force.

14.1 STANDARD REQUIRED OF TRUSTEES

14.1.1 Creation of the trust

Upon creation of the trust, the trustees become the legal owners of the trust property. Where the trust is created *inter vivos,* they will normally be parties to the deed which creates it, and which has the effect of vesting the trust property in them. In the case of a testamentary trust, it is usual to appoint the same persons to be both executors and trustees, so the acquisition of the legal title to the testator's property is automatic inasmuch as it vests in his personal representatives from the moment of death. Upon completion of the administration of the estate, it may be necessary, depending on the nature of the property, to execute additional formalities signifying that they now hold in the capacity of trustees, or if other persons are to act as trustees, to vest the property in them (see 15.2).

In any event, it is the duty of those who take property as trustees to familiarise themselves with the nature of the property and the terms of the trusts upon which it is held. They must also ensure that all formalities necessary to vest the property have been complied with, such as procuring registration as shareholders etc. At this stage, it may also be necessary to consider the conversion and disposal of any unproductive assets, and the settling of any liabilities outstanding against the trust estate. Trustees appointed to an existing trust, for example, in replacement of a retiring trustee, must satisfy themselves that the affairs of the trust are in order and that no breach of trust has occurred: if it has, steps must be taken as soon as possible to put matters right and recoup any loss.

14.1.2 Day-to-day running of the trust

The duty of the trustees in the day-to-day running of the trust is to manage the property so as to preserve the value of the capital and produce an income for the beneficiaries. In effecting administrative functions, they may employ the services of agents such as solicitors, accountants and stockbrokers. There are, however, some discretions which must be exercised personally, such as distributions to be made under a discretionary trust. Details on powers of delegation are given in 14.2.

In managing the affairs of the trust, the trustees must act honestly and must take (according to Lord Blackburn in *Speight* v *Gaunt* (1883) 9 App Cas 1, 19) 'all those precautions which an ordinary prudent man of business would take in managing similar affairs of his own'. The selection of investments involves additional considerations, for although ordinary business prudence may sometimes involve accepting a degree of risk or speculation, trustees must confine themselves to securities which are authorised by the trust instrument or by statute, and avoid hazardous investments. This was further elaborated upon in *Re Whiteley* (1886) 33 ChD 347, at p. 355:

> The duty of a trustee is not to take such care only as a prudent man would take if he had only himself to consider; the duty rather is to take such care as an ordinary prudent man would take if he were minded to make an investment for the benefit of people for whom he felt morally bound to provide.

This suggests that a more conservative approach is in order than might be considered appropriate for investments on the trustee's own behalf.

A modern application of these principles can be found in *Bartlett v Barclays Bank Trust Co. Ltd (No. 1)* [1980] Ch 515, where the trustee was a bank (i.e., a professional, paid trustee). Essentially, the bank, as trustee under a settlement of shares in a private company, failed adequately to supervise a hazardous investment policy embarked upon by that company, although as trustee of the shares it had a controlling interest in the company. Brightman J thought that a higher standard of care is required of paid trustees than of unpaid, non-professional trustees, in that the former will be held to the standards of skill and expertise which they claim to possess. At p. 534, he said:

> A trust corporation holds itself out in its advertising literature as being above ordinary mortals. . . . so I think that a professional corporate trustee is liable for breach of trust if loss is caused to the trust fund because it neglects to exercise the special care and skill which it professes to have.

One of the investments proved disastrous, and the company sustained a large loss. The beneficiaries under the settlement successfully sued the bank.

In *Bartlett*, however, the bank would have been liable on the standard applied in *Speight v Gaunt*, and it was unnecessary to rely on the higher standard owed by professional trustees. Of the ordinary standard, Brightman J said:

> The prudent man of business will act in such manner as is necessary to safeguard his investment. He will do this in two ways. If facts come to his knowledge which tell him that the company's affairs are not being conducted as they should be, or which put him on enquiry, he will take appropriate action. Appropriate action will no doubt consist in the first instance of enquiry of and consultation with the directors, and in the last but most unlikely resort, the convening of a general meeting to replace one or more directors. What the prudent man of business will not do is to content himself with the receipt of such information on the affairs of the company as a shareholder ordinarily receives at annual general meetings. Since he has the power to do so, he will go further and see that he has sufficient information to enable him to make a responsible decision from time to time either to let matters proceed as they are proceeding, or to intervene if he is dissatisfied.

The bank having failed to do any of these things, would have been liable even on the standard applicable to non-professional trustees.

Another authority on the high standard required (again in an investment context) is *Cowan* v *Scargill* [1985] Ch 270 (see 16.6.2.4). Sir Robert Megarry V-C held that trustees must not refrain from acting in the best interests of the beneficiaries on grounds of personal conscience, and even thought that:

> Trustees may even have to act dishonourably (though not illegally) if the interests of their beneficiaries require it. Thus where trustees for sale had struck a bargain for the sale of trust property but had not bound themselves by a legally enforceable contract, they were held to be under a duty to consider and explore a better offer that they received, and not to carry through the bargain to which they felt in honour bound. . . . In other words, the duty of trustees to their beneficiaries may include a duty to 'gazump', however honourable the trustees.

14.1.3   Position where more than one trustee
All trustees (if more than one) are required to be active in the management of the trust, and equity makes no concession to any notion of a 'sleeping trustee'. A trustee who concurs in the decisions of the rest is treated as having acted in the same degree as the rest, and is equally liable if a breach is committed since he might have prevented it by exercising his independent judgment. However, a trustee who, after giving proper consideration to the matter, reasonably defers to the knowledge of his fellow trustees may be excused from liability (see 17.1).

Trustees of private trusts must act unanimously and not by majority vote, unless the trust instrument authorises them to act upon a majority decision. This rule in effect gives each trustee a veto in the exercise of powers and discretions arising under the trust. The veto does not apply to duties because there is, of course, no question of deciding whether or not to comply with a duty since to do otherwise will be a breach. As we have already seen, for example, in chapter 10, in the case of trusts for sale, where there is normally a power to postpone sale, the power to postpone has to be exercised unanimously, otherwise the trust to sell will prevail.

14.1.4   Termination of the trust: distribution among beneficiaries
Sooner or later a private trust will come to an end and the trustees will be required to distribute the property among the beneficiaries. Needless to say, they must distribute it to those who are properly entitled, and failure in this regard will be a breach for which they may be liable.

The onus is heavy, and trustees have been held liable where they made payment on the strength of a forged marriage certificate (*Eaves* v *Hickson* (1861) 30 Beav 136) or in the erroneous belief that a valid charitable trust was created (*Ministry of Health* v *Simpson* [1951] AC 251). They may even be liable where they acted upon legal advice (*National Trustee Co. of Australia Ltd* v *General Finance Co. of Australasia Ltd* [1905] AC 373), although this may be a factor which would induce the court to exercise its discretion under s. 61 of the Trustee Act 1925 to excuse the trustees from liability (see 17.2.5).

The problems of wrongful payment are dealt with more fully in chapter 17, but it may be noted here that trustees may apply to court for directions in doubtful cases or, in the last resort, protect themselves by paying money into court.

Section 27 of the Trustee Act 1925 gives trustees power to advertise for claimants, in accordance with certain formalities, and to distribute the whole of the fund to those who come forward. By this procedure they obtain the same protection as if they had administered the trust under a court order. The rights of those properly entitled to follow the property (see chapter 17) are not thereby prejudiced. Other potential liabilities can be met by setting aside a fund, distributing under a court order, or obtaining an indemnity from the beneficiaries before distributing.

A special problem may arise by virtue of the statutory reforms made by the Family Law Reform Act 1987, which give new rights to illegitimate children in some circumstances. The trustees or personal representatives could be unaware of the existence of such children and the legislation therefore provides protection for the trustees without diminishing the rights of the person entitled to recover their property.

14.2 PERSONAL NATURE OF TRUSTEESHIP

We have seen how the duty of trustees regarding the exercise of their discretions is essentially of a personal nature. Yet since trustees need not be experts in finance etc., it is obviously very important for trustees to be able to employ others to carry out the more specialised aspects of trust management.

Equity has therefore always allowed the employment of agents in effecting specialised administrative functions, for example, solicitors, accountants and stockbrokers. Prior to the intervention of the Trustee Act 1925 two principles had been established by the House of Lords in *Speight* v *Gaunt* (1883) 9 App Cas 1. First, it was permissible to employ an agent where this was reasonably necessary, or in accord with normal business practices. Secondly, where such an agent was employed, trustees would not be liable for losses attributable to the agent so long as they took proper care in his selection, employed him within his proper sphere and exercised reasonable general supervision over his work.

14.2.1 Sections 23 and 30 of the Trustee Act 1925

14.2.1.1 Section 23 The Trustee Act 1925 considerably widened the scope of the power of delegation. First, on the question of when it is permissible, by virtue of s. 23 of the Act, it is no longer necessary to justify the employment of an agent by reference to the needs of the trust or normal business practice. Instead, s. 23(1) provides:

Trustees or personal representatives may, instead of acting personally, employ and pay an agent, whether a solicitor, banker, stockbroker, or other person, to transact any business or do any act required to be transacted or done in the execution of the trust, or the administration of the testator's or intestate's estate, including the receipt and payment of money, and shall be entitled to be allowed and paid all charges and expenses so incurred, and shall not be responsible for the default of any such agent if employed in good faith.

Clearly, the effect of s. 23(1) is considerably to reduce the burdens of trusteeship by permitting trustees to reduce their own work-load at the expense of the trust.

The section applies only to executive or administrative functions, and does not alter the fundamental principle, at least where the property is within the UK, that trustees may not delegate the powers and discretions which belong to them alone by virtue of their office. These discretions are not of a purely executive nature but involve real choices, for example, deciding how to distribute under a discretionary trust. They may, and sometimes must, take expert advice before exercising these discretions, but the decision must be theirs alone.

In respect of property outside the UK, however, s. 23(2) allows trustees to delegate not only their powers of sale, management etc., but also their discretions. Such delegation had been accepted as justified since the middle of the 19th century where property had to be administered abroad.

Section 23(3) permits the delegation to a limited class of professional agents certain functions which are most conveniently performed by such agents, but which would not otherwise be permissible. They sanction practices that have now become normal. Section 23(3)(a) meets the case where a receipt for money is contained in the body of a deed, a common practice in conveyances of land. The solicitor acting for the vendor will typically hold the deed until completion, when he will hand it over to the purchaser in exchange for the purchase price. Were it not for this section, it would probably be improper for trustees to employ an agent to hold a receipt, in case he absconds with the purchase money. Because of the Act trustees who engage in this normal (and usually harmless) practice will not be liable merely because they appointed the solicitor. Similar protection is conferred by s. 23(3)(c) where solicitors or bankers employed to receive money under insurance policies are granted custody of the policy and the trustees' signed receipt.

14.2.1.2 Section 30 A second question then arises as to whether trustees can be held liable in the event of the agent defaulting and causing loss to the trust. It is clear that trustees will be liable for the default of an agent whose appointment is not proper. It also seems clear that if the trustees purport to delegate their own discretions, any purported exercise of those discretions by the agent will be void and the trustees will be liable for any resulting loss.

What is less clear is the extent to which trustees who properly appoint an agent may be vicariously liable for the default of that agent. Is it sufficient that the appointment itself should be a valid exercise of the power to employ an agent, or must the trustees also use special care in selecting the agent, and perhaps exercise supervision over his actions?

A failure to take reasonable care in selecting the agent, or delegation of that choice to someone else, will render the trustees liable for loss arising from his default. This follows from the fact that the choice of agent is within the trustees' own, non-delegable discretion, so that to select without proper care or to shuffle off that choice is a default on the part of the trustees.

Since 1925, however, s. 30(1) of the Trustee Act 1925 provides that:

> A trustee . . . shall be answerable and accountable only for his own acts, receipts, neglects, or defaults, and not for those of any other trustee, nor for any banker, broker, or other person with whom any trust money or securities may be deposited . . . nor for any other loss, unless the same happens through his own wilful default.

14.2.2 Was the law altered by the 1925 amendments?

Section 30 of the Trustee Act 1925 (see 14.2.1.2) replaced with amendments the Trustee Act 1893, s. 24, which itself re-enacted the Law of Property (Amendment) Act 1859, s. 31, and under those provisions, 'wilful default' was treated as a failure to do what was reasonable, so that failure to supervise an agent might render a trustee liable. However, s. 23(1) of the 1925 Act (which replaced with amendments the Trustee Act 1893, s. 17), states that trustees 'shall not be responsible for the default of any such agent if employed in good faith', which suggests that so long as the appointment was made in good faith, liability will not arise where loss is due to inadequate supervision.

In *Re Vickery* [1931] 1 Ch 572, Maugham J attempted to resolve the issue where the executor of a will had employed a solicitor to wind up the estate, giving the solicitor signed authority to collect money on deposit with the Post Office. About six months later, a beneficiary under the will informed the executor that the solicitor had previously been suspended from practice and objected to his being employed in connection with the estate. The executor pressed the solicitor for settlement, finally placing the matter with another solicitor, but by this time the original solicitor, and the money, had disappeared. Maugham J held the executor not liable, finding that the appointment had been made validly and in good faith. In interpreting the meaning of 'wilful default' within s. 30(1), he relied upon the construction reached by Romer J in *Re City Equitable Fire Insurance Co. Ltd* [1925] Ch 407. In that case it was said that a person guilty of wilful default 'knows that he is committing and intends to commit a breach of his duty, or is recklessly careless in the sense of not caring whether his act or omission is a breach of duty'. In other words, it is virtually necessary to show that the trustee is fraudulent, unless the original appointment was wrongful.

Not everybody to whom money is entrusted comes within s. 30, however. Cross J did not apply the section in *Re Lucking's WT* [1968] 1 WLR 866, where large sums of money were entrusted to a managing director who was an old friend of the trustee and who went bankrupt having spent the money. A manager of a business is not a 'person with whom any trust money or securities may be deposited' within s. 30, so the section could not operate to protect the trustee from the consequences of the manager's default. Where the section does not apply, as in *Re Lucking's WT*, the relevant standards are those applied in *Speight* v *Gaunt* (see 14.1.2).

The decision in *Re Vickery* has been much criticised on the grounds, among others, that it imported the common law meaning of 'wilful default' into equity and that it so widens the protection of trustees under s. 23(1) as to make the rest of that section redundant. It is only a decision at first instance, of course, and so could be wrong. Nonetheless it may be suggested that, since the whole tenor of s. 23 is to allow trustees to repose confidence in their properly appointed agents, it would be a strange interpretation which required them to supervise activities which they have properly chosen to delegate as being beyond their own competence to perform.

For the sake of completeness, reference ought also to be made to s. 25 of the Trustee Act. Originally, this section applied only when the trustee was absent from the United Kingdom, but (as substituted by the Powers of Attorney Act 1971, s. 9) it allows trustees, by power of attorney, generally to delegate all or any of their powers and discretions for a period not exceeding 12 months. Section 25(5), however, provides that:

A donor of a power of attorney given under this section shall be liable for the acts or defaults of the donee in the same manner as if they were the acts or defaults of the donor.

There is no equivalent, therefore, to s. 30 protection where a trustee delegates under s. 25, as opposed to appointing an agent under s. 23: trustees are vicariously liable for the defaults of those to whom the power has been delegated under s. 25.

The Law Reform Committee, in its 23rd Report, on the powers and duties of trustees (Cmnd 8733, 1982), approved the construction given to 'wilful default' but recommended that the reference to good faith in s. 23 should be replaced with a provision that trustees should not be liable if it was reasonable to employ an agent, and if reasonable steps were taken to ensure that the agent was competent, and that the work was competently done. On the whole, the committee recognised the extent to which trusteeship is undertaken professionally today and considered that the problem lay more with the power to delegate in the first place being presently too easily available. It therefore recommended that trustees should only be able to charge the trust with the expenses of employing agents where those charges are reasonably incurred, taking into account the trustees' knowledge, qualifications, experience and level of remuneration.

In an article entitled 'Developing the Law of Trusts for the Twenty-First Century' (1990) 106 LQR 87, Professor David Hayton argues also for wider powers of delegation, in particular to investment managers, but without the trustees becoming vicariously liable for the defaults of the manager. Although he calls this approach 'modernist' (as opposed to 'traditionalist'), presumably the fundamental issues are the same as they have always been: while there may well be benefits in more extensive powers of delegation to professional investment managers, there can also be greater risks, especially given the exhortation to trustees in *Re Whiteley* (1886) 33 ChD 347 (14.1.2) to be more cautious than they would be, were they acting merely for themselves. The question is therefore to what extent, in the absence of express powers of delegation in the trust instrument, beneficiaries should be exposed to those risks. Professor Hayton suggests (at p. 91) that the risk might be reduced if powers of delegation were restricted to managers authorised under the Financial Services Act 1986.

14.3 FIDUCIARY NATURE OF TRUSTEESHIP

14.3.1 What relationships are fiduciary and what is their nature?

The nature of a trustee's duty towards a beneficiary is fiduciary. We are concerned in this book primarily with the duties of trustees, but it should be noted that the law also recognises other fiduciary relationships. Many of the cases considered in this section relate to other fiduciary relationships, but these cases are authoritative on trustees also.

Examples of other fiduciary relationships are those of agent and principal, company director and company, and partner and copartner. Additionally, the duties owed by solicitors, accountants, guardians and receivers are sometimes regarded as fiduciary. As will appear, the term may also encompass wider relationships, and its precise extent is not entirely clear.

A distinguishing feature of a fiduciary relationship is that the fiduciary is expected to act impartially in the interests of his principal. Ordinary commercial relationships, where the parties act independently in their own interests, are not fiduciary relationships. In *Re Goldcorp Exchange Ltd* [1995] 1 AC 74, the Privy Council refused to recognise the existence of any fiduciary relationship between a company which had sold gold bullion for future delivery, and its customers. Lord Mustill observed that 'the essence of a fiduciary relationship is that it creates obligations of a different character from those deriving from the contract itself', and that that was not the case here. One effect of the lack of a fiduciary relationship between the parties was that the customers were unable to trace in equity (see further chapter 19).

It is of the essence of any fiduciary relationship that the fiduciary has no personal interest in the way the duty is performed. In other words, where a fiduciary has a discretion, he must not have a personal interest in exercising the discretion in a particular way. A trustee, for example, must be motivated to benefit the trust, not himself. That is not to say that fiduciaries are not entitled to receive any benefit for their services; banks, accountants and solicitors are after all unaccustomed to working for nothing, and it will be apparent by now that trusteeship is an onerous business. The amount of their reward must not depend, however, on the manner in which their discretion is exercised.

14.3.2 Payment of trustees

In many parts of the United States, statutory rates of payment are established, but in this country only the Public Trustee and a number of other trustees acting in an official capacity have any statutory entitlement to charge fees.

There are a number of ways in which trustees and other fiduciaries may be entitled to payment, but these should be regarded as exhaustive. If a trustee does not come within one of the following heads, he is not entitled to any money for the performance of his duties:

(a) The right to remuneration may be fixed by contract between settlor and trustee at the outset; banks' charging clauses are an example of this. Similarly, a director of a company who owes a fiduciary duty to the company may enter into a contract with the company for remuneration. The contract must be one that the company is empowered to make. In *Guinness plc* v *Saunders* [1990] 2 AC 663, two Guinness directors, Thomas Ward and Ernest Saunders, claimed that they were contractually entitled to fees of £5.2 million for advice and services rendered to Guinness in connection with a take-over bid for Distillers Co. plc. The purported contract was made by a committee of three of Guinness's directors (two of whom were Ward and Saunders), but under Guinness's articles of association the committee had no power to authorise reimbursement, and the House of Lords held that the directors were not entitled to keep the £5.2 million that they had received.

(b) Section 30(2) of the Trustee Act 1925 entitles a trustee to reimbursement for expenses from trust funds.

(c) The courts have a jurisdiction to authorise payment. In one of the cases involving a breach of fiduciary duty considered below, *Boardman* v *Phipps* [1967] 2 AC 46, although a solicitor as fiduciary to a family trust was not entitled to keep profits received as a result of his position, he was held to be entitled to liberal remuneration on a *quantum meruit* basis, which is to say, on a reasonable basis for work done for the benefit of the trust, including work that had been performed gratuitously. The Court of Appeal took a similar view in *O'Sullivan* v *Management Agency & Music Ltd* [1985] QB 428, another case involving a breach of fiduciary duty. The remuneration included even a reasonable profit element, but was not related to the *actual* profits obtained in breach of fiduciary duty, which had to be accounted for.

In *Re Duke of Norfolk's ST* [1982] Ch 61, the Court of Appeal was prepared to exercise this jurisdiction to increase the remuneration of a trustee over the amount agreed in the original settlement. The quantity of work had increased because new property had been added to the settlement, and the tax position had been substantially altered by the introduction of capital transfer tax in 1975 (see further on the effects of this tax 18.3.3.2). The trustee was held entitled to extra remuneration for the increase in work.

A possible justification for the *quantum meruit* claim is that it is founded on an implied contract, in which case it is simply a variation on the express contractual provision already considered. In that case, it ought not to be possible for a fiduciary to claim on a *quantum meruit* basis where the express contract would be void. The directors in *Guinness plc* v *Saunders* (above) claimed an alternative *quantum meruit* entitlement, and failed, in Lord Templeman's view for precisely the same reasons that their claim in contract failed (that the company has no power to authorise payment): Guinness were no more empowered to enter into an implied contract to pay for the services of the two directors, then they were to enter into an express contract for the same.

However, in *Westdeutsche Landesbank Girozentrale* v *Islington London Borough Council* [1996] 2 All ER 961, Lord Browne-Wilkinson, disapproving the reasoning in the earlier House of Lords decision in *Sinclair* v *Brougham* [1914] AC 398, on which see further chapter 19, doubted whether a money had and received claim, for total failure of consideration, was based on implied contract. Instead, he said, it is based on unjust enrichment, and is therefore entirely independent of the underlying contract. It is difficult to see why similar reasoning should not apply to the *quantum meruit* claim in *Guinness plc* v *Saunders*. An alternative ground for rejecting the *quantum meruit* claim in *Guinness plc* v *Saunders*, particularly in Lord Goff's view, was that it contradicted the long-established principle that a director (or other fiduciary) may not make an unauthorised profit out of his position (see further below). The problem with this is that it is then necessary to explain why a *quantum meruit* claim was available in *Boardman* v *Phipps* and *O'Sullivan* v *Management Agency and Music Ltd*. One (not very satisfactory) possibility is that it is a matter of degree: the conflict of interest was much more extreme than in the other two cases (indeed, it is questionable whether there was really any conflict at all in *Boardman* v *Phipps*). See further generally Burrows, *The Law of Restitution*, Butterworths (1993), p. 308.

In none of the above cases, however, is the amount of remuneration dependent on the manner in which the discretion (if any) of the trustee is exercised. Thus there can be no conflict between the interests of the trust and the personal interests of the trustee. Otherwise, trustees must not benefit in any way from their position as trustees. The courts refuse to allow *any possibility* that a conflict of interest may occur. Whether any conflict occurs in fact is not relevant. In other words, it is immaterial that the trust does not suffer, or even that it gains, from the activities of the trustee. The trustee has to show that there is no possible causal connection between his position and any profit made by him (outside the categories outlined above).

It will be seen, therefore, that the law is extremely strict. Some argue that it is too strict, and can stifle entrepreneurial spirit; in some of the cases below such stifling appears indeed to have occurred. This is inevitable if the law insists that a trustee is to exercise truly independent judgment, but it is arguable that the law accords too high a value to the principle of independence and too little to the encouragement of initiative by trustees. It should be remembered that many equitable principles developed in the days when family settlements were the main variety of trust and initiative was not therefore an especially valued asset in a trustee. Some would argue that to apply similar principles today is inapposite.

On the other hand, the law has the advantage of certainty. It is fairly clear what trustees may and may not do, and it is possible for prospective trustees to negotiate terms freely before accepting appointment.

There are three main situations where a conflict of interest may arise between the trust and the personal interest of the trustee, which the law therefore prevents from arising. First, a trustee may not purchase trust property (or sell property to a trust). Secondly, he must not set himself up in competition with the trust. Thirdly, he must not make any profit by virtue of his position.

So far as remedies are concerned, any property or money acquired which can be regarded as being trust property (as in 14.3.3 and 14.3.5.1) will be held on constructive trust by the trustee for the beneficiaries. Where a trustee has obtained incidental profits from his office, to which he is not entitled on the basis of the principles discussed below, he can be required to 'account' for (i.e., pay over to the trust) those profits. In many of the cases either remedy would be available, but in the case of the remedy of account it is unnecessary to show that the profits obtained by the trustee have ever been the property of the trust. Thus it is often a more appropriate remedy in the cases described in 14.3.4, 14.3.5.2 and 14.3.5.3.

14.3.3 Profiting from the trust

Apart from the methods described above whereby a trustee (or other fiduciary) becomes entitled to payment, a trustee will rarely, if ever, be allowed to profit from the office of trusteeship. The words 'rarely, if ever' are used deliberately, because it is not clear whether the law ever allows a trustee to profit from his trusteeship. It is just about arguable that the law only prevents profits being obtained by wrongdoing, or where there is a clear conflict of duty and interest; but it is also arguable that the law never allows profits to be made by trustees.

Breach of a fiduciary duty is a breach of trust, so where profits are wrongfully obtained all the remedies in chapter 15 also apply here. Often, however, the trust will have suffered little or no loss; but where a trustee has obtained incidental profits from his office, to which he is not entitled on the basis of the principles discussed below, he can be required to 'account' (i.e., pay over to the trust) those profits. In most of the cases discussed in this chapter the remedy sought is account of profits. This is, however, a personal remedy, which is of no use if the trustee is bankrupt. Further, if the trustee invests the profits which have been wrongfully obtained, the account of profits remedy on its own does not allow the trust to claim the investment, which may have increased in value. However, any profits so acquired can be regarded as being trust property, which should have been paid over to the trust. Since equity treats as done that which ought to be done, the profits will therefore also be held on constructive trust by the trustee. The effect of this is that the trust can claim any investment into which the profits can, on the principles discussed in chapter 19, be traced in equity, thereby protecting the trust in the event of the trustee's bankruptcy, and also giving the trust any increase in the value of the investment, as in *Attorney-General for Hong Kong v Reid* [1994] 1 AC 324.

14.3.3.1 Wrongdoing cases

There is at any rate no doubt that where the trustee, or other fiduciary, has acted in bad faith, he will not be allowed to benefit from his wrongdoing. In *Reading v Attorney-General* [1951] AC 507,

Reading had been a sergeant in the British army and had made at least £19,000 illegally by helping smugglers to transport smuggled goods, by riding in the lorries in his uniform. Unfortunately for Reading, the £19,000 was confiscated and he was forced into the role of plaintiff, petitioning for its return. He failed because as a fiduciary he was liable to account for his profits to the Crown. An army sergeant would probably not normally be regarded as a fiduciary, but the use in the case of the uniform to deceive the authorities may have been the decisive factor.

Reading v *Attorney-General* was considered and followed in *Attorney-General* v *Guardian (No. 2)* [1990] 1 AC 109 (the *Spycatcher* case, where the *Sunday Times* was required to account the profits that it had received from Peter Wright's deliberate breach of confidence). It was also followed in *Attorney-General for Hong Kong* v *Reid* [1994] 1 AC 324, where a fiduciary who accepted bribes was required to hold them on constructive trust for the Crown (his employer). Because he held them on constructive trust, the Crown's claim was not limited to the value of the bribes, but extended to any property purchased with the secret commissions. Thus the Crown was able to obtain the value of three houses, which had substantially increased. There was old Court of Appeal authority, including in particular *Lister & Co.* v *Stubbs* (1890) 45 ChD 1, to the contrary, which was disapproved by the Privy Council in *Reid*.

The principles in *Reid* apply only where there is a fiduciary relationship between the parties. In *Halifax Building Society* v *Thomas* [1996] 2 WLR 63, the defendant mortgagor had obtained a 100 per cent mortgage advance from the plaintiff building society to finance the purchase of a flat, having made fraudulent misrepresentations as to his identity and creditworthiness. He fell into arrears and the building society exercised its power of sale, but because of a rising property market, there was a surplus after discharging the mortgage. The building society claimed this, arguing on the basis of *A-G* v *Reid* that the defendant was constructive trustee for the mortgagee of all the profits made as a result of his fraud. The Court of Appeal held that the remedy of account of profits, and the imposition of a constructive trust were not applicable where there was no fiduciary relationship between the parties. Accordingly, the defendant was not required to account to the plaintiff for the profit he had made from the rising market.

Where there is bad faith there need not be any harm to the plaintiff. Indeed, in none of the above cases had the Crown suffered any obvious loss. In *Industrial Development Consultants* v *Cooley* [1972] 1 WLR 443, the defendant, a managing director for the plaintiff company, had been negotiating on its behalf a contract with the Eastern Gas Board. The negotiations failed and it was clear that the Eastern Gas Board objected to the plaintiff company particularly. In other words, it appeared that whatever the defendant had done, the negotiations would have failed, and so the plaintiff company suffered no loss as a result of the defendant's subsequent action.

The Eastern Gas Board then began negotiations with the defendant personally, and the end result was that he terminated his contract with the plaintiff company, obtaining a release on the false representation that he was ill, and contracted with the Eastern Gas Board himself, on terms similar to those originally proposed on behalf of the plaintiff company. Roskill J held that the defendant was constructive trustee of the benefit of the contract for the benefit of the plaintiff company.

It is noteworthy that the plaintiff company had lost nothing, and as a result of the case gained only as a result of the defendant's breach of duty.

14.3.3.2 Conflict of interest cases The wrongdoing cases may be an application of a wider principle that a fiduciary should not put himself into a position where his duty and interest conflict. After all, it is obviously not in the interests of someone accepting bribes or secret commissions to act in an impartial, or fiduciary, manner. A conflict of interest was also assumed to exist in *Industrial Development Consultants* v *Cooley*, since the defendant had negotiated for his own benefit in the plaintiff's time.

But conflicts of interests can arise even in the absence of *mala fides*. There are two other clear situations where a conflict of interest may arise between the trust and the personal interest of the trustee, which the law therefore prevents from arising. First, a trustee may not purchase trust property (or sell property to a trust). Secondly, he must not set himself up in competition with the trust.

14.3.3.2.1   A trustee may not purchase trust property It is possible, particularly in the light of Harman LJ's views at least in *Holder* v *Holder* [1968] Ch 353 (below), to distinguish self-dealing (trustee purchasing trust property for himself) from fair dealing (trustee purchasing from beneficiary). Self-dealing renders the transaction voidable at the option of the beneficiaries. Fair dealing renders the transaction voidable only if the trustee has behaved unfairly.

The distinction is not universally accepted, and both are arguably part of a wider principle that a trustee should not profit from his office as trustee (on which again, see further below).

The rationale for the self-dealing rule is that if a trustee purchases trust property, he can abuse his position and buy at less than the best price obtainable. Similarly if he sells to the trust, he may be able to demand too high a price.

The self-dealing rule is very strict where trustees are concerned, so that there must be no possibility of the trustee taking advantage of his position, whether he does so in fact or not. The lengths to which the law goes are shown by *Wright* v *Morgan* [1926] AC 788, where a trustee who had resigned his trusteeship purchased trust property at a price that had been fixed by independent valuers. One might have thought that not even a possibility of conflict arose here. The arrangements had been made while he was still trustee, however, and the Privy Council held that this sale must be set aside.

It is possible for purchases by trustees to be valid, but only in very exceptional circumstances. It is essential not only that the trustee paid a fair price, as he had in *Wright* v *Morgan*, but also that he took no advantage of his position and made full disclosure of his interest. For example, in *Holder* v

Holder [1968] Ch 353, an executor (Victor) purchased two farms that were part of the estate at a fair price at an auction. The Court of Appeal refused to set aside the sale, although as executor Victor was acting in a fiduciary capacity. It was clear, however, that Victor had not been active in his role as executor, had indeed purported to renounce it and had acquired no information as a result of it. He took no part in instructing the valuer who fixed the reserves or in the preparations for the auction. Additionally, the plaintiff beneficiary had accepted his share of the purchase money in full knowledge of the facts, and so was disentitled from taking the action on the grounds of acquiescence.

Both Sachs and Danckwerts LJJ expressed doubt whether today the self-dealing rule should apply where trust property is sold at public auctions, at least in a case where the sale is arranged by trustees other than the purchasing trustee. However, *Holder* v *Holder* was limited almost to its own unusual facts by Vinelott J in *Re Thompson's Settlement* [1986] Ch 99, a case which concerned the purchase of leases of farms owned by a trust, by a company whose director was one of the trustees. Vinelott J explained *Holder* v *Holder* on the narrow ground that the defendant had never acted as executor in a way which could be taken to amount to acceptance of a duty to act in the interests of the beneficiaries under his father's will. He said that the self-dealing rule is an application of the wider principle that a man must not put himself in a position where duty and interest conflict, or where his duty to one conflicts with his duty to another. If Vinelott J is right, *Holder* v *Holder* should not be regarded as laying down more than the narrowest of exceptions to the rule.

The same principles apply to sales of property to trusts by trustees.

14.3.3.2.2   A trustee must not set himself up in competition with the trust   Similar principles apply here, because the trustee may gain for himself the benefit of any goodwill acquired by the trust, and possibly also useful information. It is not necessary to show that he has in fact done so, however.

In *Re Thomson* [1930] 1 Ch 203, an executor was restrained from carrying out a yacht broking business in competition with the estate. The substantive issue did not come before Clauson J, because the executor had, as a consequence of an earlier interlocutory injunction granted by the Court of Appeal, transferred the business to the sole beneficiary. The question of costs was still outstanding, however, and depended on whether the original action was justified. The point of interest about the case is that Clauson J, in finding against the executor, did not think it would have made any difference if he had resigned his executorship, so long as he had contemplated starting a competing business while still an executor. There is a logic in this approach, because such contemplation may have affected the manner in which his duties as executor were performed. It has been argued that Clauson J's view depends on the specialist nature of the business, but it is difficult to see why this should make any difference.

14.3.3.3   Other cases (if any)   It is not clear whether the above cases are all part of a wider principle, that a trustee (or other fiduciary) may not make any profit from his position. If so, then all that should be necessary is to establish a causal connection between the profit and the position. It should not be necessary to go further and show either *mala fides* or a conflict of interest.

In *Re Macadam* [1946] Ch 73, trustees who used their position to appoint themselves to directorships of a company were held liable to account to the trust for all the fees they received as directors. This type of situation can commonly arise in private companies, because eligibility for appointment to directorships can depend on the legal ownership of a minimum number of shares, and indeed trustees may be under a duty to procure their representation on the board if it is necessary in order to safeguard the value of the trust shares.

Arguably, all that is necessary is to establish the causal connection between position and profit. No such connection was established in *Re Dover Coalfield Extension* [1908] 1 Ch 65, a case similar to *Re Macadam*, but where a trustee had already become a director before becoming trustee. *Re Gee* [1948] Ch 284 is similar, where a trustee became a director after refraining from using his vote, which he had by virtue of holding trust shares. He would have been elected anyway, due to the votes of the other shareholders, however he had voted himself; he would even have been elected if he had voted against himself. Harman J held that the remuneration received as director was not accountable to the trust. In neither of these cases could it be said that the trustees had made any profit by virtue of their position.

A closer examination of these cases suggests that they are, in reality, conflict of interest cases, since clearly a trustee who stands to gain from the choice of himself as director cannot advise the trust impartially as to the choice of who to appoint.

A stronger case is *Keech* v *Sandford* (1726) Sel Cas Ch 61, where the trustee took over the benefit of a lease which had been devised to the trust, when that lease expired. Since the lease had expired, this is not a case of dealing in trust property. The causal connection between position and profit was presumably established, in that he would not have been in a position to take the lease had he not been trustee. The lessor had refused to renew the lease for the trust, on the ground that the beneficiary was an infant against whom it would be difficult to recover rent. The trustee thereupon took the lease for his personal benefit, and profited from it.

There cannot have been any actual conflict of interest, because the trust itself could not have benefited, given the views of the lessor. Nor would Lord King LC say that there was any fraud in the case. Yet he held that the trustee had to assign the benefit of the lease to the infant, and account for profits received. The trustee was the one person in the world who could not take the lease for his own benefit, because by so doing he would be profiting from his position. The same principle may apply where a trustee of a lease purchases for himself the freehold reversion: *Protheroe* v *Protheroe* [1968] 1 WLR 519 (CA) (but there are contrary authorities).

There was no *mala fides* in *Regal (Hastings) Ltd* v *Gulliver*, originally reported in [1942] 2 All ER 378 and only in the official reports in [1967] 2

AC 134n. Regal were considering applying for shares in a subsidiary company, but were unable to afford them, whereupon the directors subscribed themselves and made a profit. The directors would not have been in a position to profit had they not been directors, but arguably there was no conflict of interest, given that Regal were not in a position to subscribe for themselves. Yet the directors were held liable to account. Lord Russell of Killowen said:

> The rule of equity which insists on those, who by use of a fiduciary position make a profit, being liable to account for that profit, in no way depends on fraud, or absence of *bona fides*; or upon such questions or considerations as whether the profit would or should otherwise have gone to the plaintiff, or whether the profiteer was under a duty to obtain the source of the profit for the plaintiff, or whether he took a risk or acted as he did for the benefit of the plaintiff, or whether the plaintiff has in fact been damaged or benefited by his action. The liability arises from the mere fact of a profit having, in the stated circumstances, been made.

This is a fairly clear statement that all that needs to be established is the causal connection between position and profit. Arguably, however, there was in fact a conflict of interest, as the directors themselves must have determined that the company could not afford to subscribe for the shares. It would have been difficult for them to advise impartially where they intended to subscribe for themselves, and hence obtain a profit.

The leading case is *Boardman* v *Phipps* [1967] 2 AC 46, but it is not clear on what principle it was decided. Boardman was solicitor to a trust, which owned 8,000 of 30,000 shares in a private textile company with whose performance Boardman was dissatisfied. The trust had no wish to buy the remaining shares, and in any case was unable to buy them, although it could have applied to court for power to do so. Boardman decided to purchase them himself, undoubtedly benefiting from information he had received in his fiduciary capacity (in knowing what price to offer), and did not obtain the consent of all beneficiaries (on which see further 17.2.1). The shares later increased in value (partly perhaps because of Boardman's management in selling off some of the assets of the newly acquired company), so Boardman made a large profit for himself. Additionally, however, because the trust still had a large share in the same company, his activities resulted in a large profit for the trust. There was no claim of bad faith, or any obvious conflict of interest, since the trust did not have the power to purchase the shares itself; and in any case, the trust had positively benefited from Boardman's intervention.

By a 3-2 majority, the House of Lords nevertheless held that Boardman held the shares as constructive trustee for the trust, and was therefore liable to account profits. It is not easy to discern the *ratio*, although it seems that whereas the majority thought it enough simply to profit from the trust, Viscount Dilhorne and Lord Upjohn (dissenting) thought that this was insufficient in the absence of a clear conflict of interest. They took the view that there was no conflict or possibility of a conflict between the personal interests of the appellants and those of the trust. Unfortunately, the position is muddied because the majority also took the view that there was a (somewhat theoretical) conflict of interest also: the trust might have changed its mind and sought to buy the shares itself, in which case Boardman as solicitor to the trust would have had to advise on the application to court. It may be, therefore, that the case does not extend existing principles, except in showing how willing the courts are to find even the most theoretical possibility of a conflict of interest.

14.3.3.4 Information as trust property A further difficulty about *Boardman* v *Phipps* is that in the Court of Appeal ([1965] Ch 992), Russell LJ had decided the case on an entirely different ground, that all the information acquired by Boardman in his fiduciary capacity became trust property. Lords Hodson and Guest also seemed to be of this view. Lord Cohen appeared less sure about the trust property point, but was happy to decide the case on causation alone.

The property reasoning raises serious difficulties (see, e.g., Gareth Jones (1968) 84 LQR 472), especially where information is obtained by somebody who is trustee to several trusts, or where the information is passed on to other, innocent recipients who also profit from it. Partly for these reasons, Viscount Dilhorne, adopting the views of Lindley LJ in *Aas* v *Benham* [1891] 2 Ch 244, said that information was not the property of the trust, and Lord Upjohn's views were similar. Certainly, the information as trust property reasoning is not part of the *ratio* in the House of Lords.

14.3.3.5 Conclusions Although the *ratio* of *Boardman* v *Phipps* is not very clear, the weight of authority probably supports the proposition that all that is required is to find a causal connection between the fiduciary's position and the profit obtained. If Boardman would have purchased the shares anyway, even without the information acquired by virtue of his fiduciary position, there would have been no causal connection between the position and the profit, and the case would have been like *Re Gee*. If not, the case is similar to *Re Macadam*, and Boardman was properly held to account.

It may be objected that the law deters entrepreneurial activity which may well benefit the trust. However, Boardman was liberally rewarded on a *quantum meruit* basis for benefiting the trust, on the principles discussed in 14.3.2. What he could not do was to keep any additional profits he made. The law allows private speculators to do so, but takes the view that those who are acting as fiduciaries accept, by taking on fiduciary positions, that their remuneration is limited to the categories described in 14.3.2, however much they benefit the other party. Though this view may appear harsh, it at least has the merit of ensuring that their discretion will be exercised in an independent manner.

FIFTEEN

Commencement and Termination of Trusteeship

15.1 APPOINTMENT OF TRUSTEES

Usually, trustees will be appointed by the document which brings the trust into existence, and this document ought also to make provision for any additional appointments which may be necessary during the continuance of the trust. In addition, however, the Trustee Act 1925 makes provision for any additional appointments which may be necessary, unless the operation of the Act is expressly excluded. The Trustee Act provisions are necessary if the trust instrument does not make the necessary provision or if there is no trust instrument at all.

The settlor will usually name those whom he wishes to act as trustees, and where the settlement is *inter vivos,* the trustees themselves will normally be parties to the deed of settlement, since the purpose is both to declare the trusts and to vest the property in the trustees. In the uncommon case where the settlor simply declares his intention henceforth to hold some of his property on trust, he will himself be the sole trustee. Alternatively, he may decide to appoint other trustees as well and take steps to vest the property in himself and his co-trustees jointly.

Where trusts are created by will, it is usual to appoint the same persons to be both executors and trustees. The fiduciary duties of executors are very similar to those of trustees, but they are not identical and it may be important to know at what point an executor has ceased to act as such and become a trustee. Generally, this will occur when the executors assent to the vesting of property in themselves as trustees, although in the case of personalty, this assent may be implied since no formalities are necessary. In the case of land, an assent in writing is required, since this is an essential document of title.

15.1.1 No trustee available

It may happen that for some reason a trust comes into existence without there being anyone able or willing to act as trustee, for example, if the trustees appointed by the will have predeceased the testator or if the trust arises by operation of law. An instance of the latter is where an outright bequest of property is made to a minor, who cannot give a good receipt for the property until he comes of age. The absence of trustees will not invalidate the trust. If the trust is *inter vivos,* the settlor himself will be the trustee. If it arises by will, the personal representatives of the testator will hold the property on trust. Where an instrument creating the trust names someone as having power to appoint trustees, he may use that power to fill the gap. If all else fails, the court will appoint trustees.

15.1.2 Acceptance once and for all

No one can be compelled to accept office as a trustee under an express trust, although a person may find himself a trustee against his will by operation of law, e.g., a constructive trustee. Once the office is accepted, it cannot later be renounced, although retirement is possible under certain conditions. In theory, the office of trustee is lifelong, and if a trustee dies in office, any liabilities which he has incurred will persist against his estate. Should the trustee wish to disclaim, he should do so as soon as possible, and preferably by deed, for failure to disclaim may lead to a presumption that he has accepted. Acceptance will also be presumed once the trustee has started to act in relation to the property.

15.1.3 Who may be trustee?

Anyone who has the legal capacity to hold the legal title to property may be appointed a trustee of that property. A corporation may thus be a trustee provided its constitution authorises it so to act. An infant may become a resulting or constructive trustee of personalty (*Re Vinogradoff* [1935] WN 68) although not of land, but s. 20 of the Law of Property Act 1925 declares the express appointment of an infant trustee void, and s. 36(1) of the Trustee Act 1925 permits his replacement by a person of full age. These restrictions apart, the settlor may appoint as he pleases. Traditionally, certain appointments, such as that of a beneficiary or one of his relatives, or the solicitor to the trust, have been regarded as undesirable by the courts, but they are not invalid and are commonly made in practice.

Certain special categories of trustee exist, the most important in practice being the trust corporation, usually but not always the executor and trustee company of a bank. The main advantages of appointing a trust corporation are its longevity, financial stability and expertise, and the fact that it may act alone in circumstances where two individual trustees would be necessary. The chief disadvantage is that its fees are likely to be high. The qualifications necessary for a company to be a trust corporation are contained in the Public Trustee Rules 1912 (SR&O 1912 No. 348), r. 30 as amended.

Other special trustees include custodian trustees, the public trustee and judicial trustees. They perform specialist functions which in practice are rare.

15.1.4 Appointment of new trustees during the continuance of the trust

If an occasion for the appointment of new trustees arises during the continuance of the trust, rather different considerations apply than those governing the initial appointments.

15.1.4.1   Role of the settlor   It should be recalled that once a settlor has completed the steps necessary to create a trust, he has no further interest in the trust property. It follows that he retains no rights in regard to the appointment of trustees in the future. If he wishes to control future appointments, he must nominate himself in the trust instrument as being the person having power to appoint new trustees, and any appointments that he makes will be in this capacity and not by virtue of his being settlor.

Alternatively, he may prefer to nominate some other person to exercise the power of appointing trustees, particularly where the trust is intended to extend beyond his lifetime. A well drafted trust instrument will be required for this, because the terms of any power to appoint will be strictly construed. It is usual nowadays, when nominating a person in the trust instrument to exercise the power of appointing new trustees, to draft the power in very simple terms, since in the event of an inconsistency between the terms of the trust instrument and the statutory power considered below, the latter will prevail.

15.1.4.2   Trustee Act 1925, section 36   It is obviously desirable that there should always be some person having power to appoint new trustees, and usually such powers will be contained in the trust instrument itself. Even where there are no powers in the instrument itself, however, s. 36(1) of the Trustee Act 1925 makes provision for new appointments. As with other sections of the Act, however, its operation can be expressly excluded: Trustee Act 1925, s. 69(2):

> The powers conferred by this Act on trustees are in addition to the powers conferred by the instrument, if any, creating the trust, but those powers, unless otherwise stated, apply if and so far only as a contrary intention is not expressed in the instrument, if any, creating the trust, and have effect subject to the terms of that instrument.

Where s. 36 applies, its effect is to create a hierarchy of categories of persons having power to appoint. There is an order. Persons falling into the first category have the first right to make the appointment, and only if there is no one in that category, or no one able and willing to act, will the power become exercisable by the persons within the next category. By virtue of the section, the following persons, in this order, may appoint:

(a)   The person(s), if any, nominated in the trust instrument.
(b)   The existing trustees, if any.
(c)   The personal representatives of the last, or only surviving trustee.

If there is no one in any of these categories who is able and willing to act then the power given by s. 36(1) cannot be exercised at all (although the court may have jurisdiction to appoint under s. 41 of the Act, considered in 15.1.4.3).

The circumstances which give rise to a power under s. 36(1), on the part of the appropriate person to appoint fresh trustees in replacement for the original trustees, are also specified in the section, and are as follows:

(a)   Where a trustee has died. This covers not only the situation of a trustee dying while in office, but also that of a trustee dying before assuming office, as where a trustee named in a will predeceases the testator. The Act makes no provision for the perhaps unlikely case of all trustees dying before the will comes into effect, as noted above.

(b)   Where a trustee remains out of the United Kingdom for more than 12 months. The absence must be for a continuous period, so that a trustee who occasionally returns for short visits cannot be removed under this head (*Re Walker* [1910] 1 Ch 259). So long as the absence is continuous, its cause is immaterial, so that a trustee who remains abroad involuntarily by reason of illness or imprisonment may be replaced. Where it is intended that the trust should operate in another jurisdiction, care should be taken expressly to exclude the operation of this part of s. 36(1), to protect the tenure of foreign residents who have been specifically selected as trustees.

(c)   Where a trustee desires to be discharged from all or any of the trusts or powers reposed in or conferred on him. Although it is not permitted to disclaim in relation to part only of the trust before assuming office, a trustee who accepts office and later seeks to be discharged may be relieved of his duties with regard to a part only of the trust, while retaining a say in the management of those parts in which he has an interest.

(d)   Where a trustee refuses. This seems apt to permit an appointment to be made in replacement of a trustee who disclaims, although strictly, of course, such a person never becomes a trustee. Old authorities on the predecessor of s. 36 favour this interpretation.

(e)   Where a trustee is unfit to act. This appears to refer to defects of character, and although no precise description can be given of the circumstances in which a trustee can be described as unfit for the purposes of s. 36(1), the courts will remove a trustee as unfit where he has been convicted of a crime of dishonesty, or has become bankrupt and his continuation in office is opposed by the beneficiaries, or he has been imprudent in the management of his own affairs. A bankrupt trustee who is free from moral blame may, however, be permitted to remain in office.

(f)   Where a trustee is incapable of acting. This covers the case where a trustee is unfit due to mental or physical incapacity, and also where some legal incapacity is imposed, as where wartime regulations forbid certain foreign nationals to hold property in this country. Special provisions apply where a trustee has also a beneficial interest under the trust and is a patient under the Mental Health Act 1983. In this case, the leave of the authority having jurisdiction over him under Part VII of the Act will be required before a new trustee can be appointed in his place.

(g)   Where the trustee is an infant. The express appointment of an infant trustee is void, but a trust could be deprived of an active trustee because of the infancy of a person named as a trustee, and the section appears to cover this contingency.

(h)   By virtue of s. 36(3), where a corporate body acting as trustee has been dissolved. It is deemed to be incapable of acting from the date of dissolution.

In addition to the power of appointing new trustees by way of replacement, there is also power to appoint additional trustees, the existing trustees remaining in office. Where there are currently three trustees or less, none of whom is a trust corporation, and it is thought desirable to have more, appointment may be made by the person nominated in the trust instrument for the purposes of appointing new trustees, or by the existing trustee or trustees, in that order. The total number of trustees must not be raised beyond four, although more than one at a time may be appointed. The power is contained in s. 36(6), and is independent of the power to appoint replacement trustees under s. 36(1).

An appointment under s. 36 must be in writing, and in practice it will be made by deed to take advantage of the vesting provisions of s. 40 (see 15.2.2).

15.1.4.3 Appointment by the court under section 41

The court has an inherent power to appoint trustees as part of its supervisory jurisdiction over trusts, which is supplemented by s. 41 of the Trustee Act 1925. Under this section, the court may appoint whenever it is expedient that an appointment should be made and it is inexpedient, difficult or impracticable to bring this about without the assistance of the court.

Application to the court may be made by a beneficiary or by a trustee, but if it is possible to appoint under a power in the trust instrument or under s. 36, this should be done in preference. If there is some person having power to appoint and seeking to exercise that power in good faith, the court will not interfere even if the proposed appointment is not one which it would itself have made.

Where allegations of misconduct against a trustee are being made, the court may act under its inherent jurisdiction, but the proper course is to begin the action by writ so that the trustee knows what accusations he has to meet.

The court's assistance may properly be sought when no one has power to appoint, or no one is willing and able to exercise it, or where there is some doubt about whether the power has become exercisable. Recourse to the court may be the only way of replacing elderly or sick trustees who have become incapable of acting for the trust, as in *Re Phelp's ST* (1885) 31 ChD 351, where the sole trustee was 85 years old, deaf, and failing in intellect, or of meeting the case where the only person having power to appoint is too old or ill, or too young, to be able to exercise it. In practice, application is sometimes made by trustees who wish to avoid later argument over the propriety of a particular appointment.

Certain principles govern the court's selection in appointing trustees. At one time, a beneficiary, or even one of his relations, would have been unsuitable because of the possibility of a conflict between duty and self-interest. Nor would the family solicitor be chosen, ostensibly to avoid the indelicate task of assessing the probity of a member of the legal profession. Both kinds of appointment are commonly made out of court, however, and the attitude of the courts appears to be changing.

The court will not, however, make an appointment which favours the interests of certain beneficiaries above others, nor will it willingly appoint against the known wishes of the settlor. For example, in *Re Tempest* (1866) LR 1 Ch App 485 a trustee had predeceased the testator, and there was strong disagreement between the surviving trustee and a faction among the beneficiaries over who should replace him. It was clear that the surviving trustee would be unwilling to act with the person appointed by the court at first instance. Turner LJ considered that it would be going too far to say that a court would refuse to appoint a person with whom the existing trustees refuse to act since that would amount to giving them a veto. The court should inquire whether the objection is well founded and act accordingly. Regard will be had to whether a proposed appointment will promote or impede the execution of the trust.

Persons permanently resident abroad will not normally be suitable, but where the beneficiaries have emigrated and the trust property is situated abroad, the court may make such an appointment (*Re Windeatt's WT* [1969] 1 WLR 692).

15.1.4.4 Role of the beneficiaries Where a sole beneficiary is absolutely entitled to the entirety of the trust property, or where all the beneficiaries are *sui iuris* (i.e., not children or people who are mentally incapacitated) and together so entitled, the rule in *Saunders* v *Vautier* (1841) 10 LJ Ch 354, considered in greater detail in 18.1.2, permits the beneficiaries to terminate the trust. They may then, if they so wish, set up a new trust to which they, now as settlors, have the right to appoint the trustees. This course of action, however, will require transfers of title attracting *ad valorem* stamp duty, and may well give rise to liability for capital transfer or other tax upon the dissolution and fresh settlement.

However, although the beneficiaries may make new appointments in this roundabout fashion they may not do so directly. In *Re Brockbank* [1948] Ch 206, a trustee wished to retire and the beneficiaries sought to have a trust corporation appointed in place of the remaining trustees, who opposed the change on the ground of the cost to the trust of the trust corporation's fees. The beneficiaries argued that since they were all *sui iuris* and collectively entitled, the trustees were obliged to appoint in accordance with their wishes. Vaisey J rejected this argument. The beneficiaries might terminate the trust if they so wished but they were not entitled to control the trustees' exercise of their statutory power to appoint while the trust subsisted. For further discussion of this case see 18.1.2.

Further, it seems that those who have the right to appoint under s. 36 may do so regardless of the wishes of the beneficiaries. In *Re Higginbottom* [1892] 3 Ch 132, an illiterate lady of no means, and having no interest in the trust, became executrix of the last survivor among the trustees, and therefore was entitled by virtue of the statute to appoint new trustees. The majority of the beneficiaries opposed this and requested the court to appoint trustees of their choosing, but Kekewich J refused to interfere with the lady's right to make the appointment herself.

15.2 FORMALITIES FOR VESTING OF TRUST PROPERTY IN NEW TRUSTEES

As we saw in chapter 2, where a settlement is created *inter vivos,* the trust property will be vested in the trustees as part of the transaction. If the settlor declares himself sole trustee, there is of course nothing more to be done. In a testamentary trust, where the same persons are appointed as executors and trustees, the change of role involves the executors in vesting the property in themselves as trustees, which is notional in the case of most kinds of personalty but requires a formal assent in the case of land. If other persons are to take over as trustees, the property must be vested in them with whatever degree of formality is appropriate to that property. Similarly, when new trustees are appointed to an existing trust, the property must be vested in them so that they hold it jointly with the existing trustees.

15.2.1 The formalities themselves
In brief, formalities are required as follows (all those relating to land are dealt with in greater detail in land law textbooks):

(a) Unregistered freehold land — a conveyance must be executed.

(b) Unregistered leasehold land — the lease must be assigned.

(c) Registered land, either freehold or leasehold — the appropriate transfer and its registration at the land registry must be completed (Land Registration Act 1925, s. 47).

(d) Stocks and shares — these must be formally transferred, and the transfer registered in the books of the company or other body issuing the shares.

(e) Where the property is a debt, it must be formally assigned and notice given to the debtor, to secure priority over future assignees.

(f) Negotiable instruments (e.g., cheques) — these must be delivered and (unless payable to bearer) indorsed.

(g) Personal chattels (i.e., ordinary goods) — these may be physically handed over unless there are specific documents of title to be transferred, e.g., a car or an aeroplane.

15.2.2 Consequences of improper vesting
Proper vesting is vital, since the trustees may be held personally liable for any loss arising from failure in this regard. A newly appointed trustee must satisfy himself that all is in order and cannot say that it should have been attended to by the other trustees. However, in the case of a newly appointed trustee, some of the formalities of vesting are obviated by s. 40 of the Trustee Act 1925. The effect of this section is that where he is appointed by deed containing a declaration in appropriate terms, the trust property vests automatically in the new trustee and his co-trustees as joint tenants.

Unfortunately, certain types of property are excluded from the operation of s. 40. This is inconvenient, since they include the most common types of property held in trust, but there are good reasons for the exclusion. These are:

(a) Land held by way of mortgage. The reason for requiring formality is probably simply to ensure that the mortgagor knows who to pay.

(b) Land held under a lease which contains a covenant against assignment (i.e., transfer of the lease to any but the original lessor), unless permission to assign was obtained prior to executing the deed of appointment. This is because if vesting was automatic upon appointment of new trustees, there would necessarily be a breach of the covenant against assignment, and this might render the lease liable to forfeiture (i.e., termination by the landlord).

(c)   Stocks and shares must be formally transferred and registered in the company's books. This is because under the Companies Acts, legal title to stocks and shares depends upon registration, and companies can recognise as shareholders only those who appear in their books.

15.3   TERMINATION OF TRUSTEESHIP

15.3.1   Retirement

We saw in 15.1.2 that in principle the office of trustee is lifelong. Nevertheless, a trustee may voluntarily retire in one of several ways. First, he may take advantage of any power to retire contained in the trust instrument, although such a power is nowadays uncommon. Secondly, if someone can be found to replace him, he may retire under the provisions of s. 36(1) of the Trustee Act 1925 (see 15.1.4.2).

Thirdly, he may retire under the provisions of s. 39 of the Act even without replacement, under the following conditions:

(a)   his retirement must leave the trust with not less than two individual trustees or a trust corporation to act for it, and

(b)   the remaining trustees must consent to his retirement, and

(c)   anyone empowered to appoint trustees must consent.

Retirement, and any necessary consents, must be in the form of a deed. Unlike s. 36(1), s. 39 does not permit retirement from part only of a trust.

Fourthly, the beneficiaries may consent to his retirement, so as to debar themselves from holding the trustee accountable for any event arising after the date of such consent. This is only an aspect of the rule that a beneficiary who consents to a breach of trust has no right of action in respect of that breach (see 17.2.1). Unless all are *sui iuris* (i.e., suffering from no incapacities, such as infancy or mental handicap) and collectively entitled to the entire trust property, the trustee will not obtain his discharge from the trust. It will also be prudent to obtain the consents of the other trustees, to avert any claim by them to an indemnity.

Fifthly, the court may discharge a trustee without replacing him under its inherent jurisdiction, but will not do so if this would leave the trust without a trustee. In such a case it may make an order for administration of the trust by the court, so that the trustee remains in office but is relieved of responsibility. Alternatively, if the trustee pays the entire trust fund into court, he thereby loses the right to exercise any of his discretionary powers in the trust, which amounts to virtual retirement. He remains in office for the purpose of receiving notices of dealings with the trust property, however, and may be made a party to any action brought by the fund.

Although the once-and-for-all nature of trusteeship looks harsh in theory, in practice the statutory provisions for retirement are almost always sufficient.

15.3.2 Death of a trustee

Trustees hold their office, and the trust property, jointly. There is a right of survivorship so that upon the death of a trustee, his office and the trust estate devolve on the survivors. As we saw in 1.2.6, one of the attractions of the early use was its ability to allow estates to pass from generation to generation with few conveyances of legal titles. This was achieved in part by vesting the legal title in a number of feoffees to use jointly, and relying on the right of survivorship on the death of any one of them. Trusts today operate in the same way and for essentially similar reasons.

The equitable rule was codified in s.18(1) of the Trustee Act 1925, which provides:

> Where a power or trust is given to or imposed on two or more trustees jointly, the same may be exercised or performed by the survivors or survivor of them for the time being.

If one trustee dies, then, the rest may carry on the trust without interruption, subject to the possible need to appoint a replacement if the numbers have been reduced below what is required for effective management.

Although the trust property vests automatically in the survivors, due steps should be taken to ensure that any register or document of title is brought up to date.

When a sole surviving trustee dies, the trust property devolves on his personal representatives and is held by them on the terms of the trust. Section 18(2) enables the personal representatives to exercise all the powers of the former trustee, although they are not obliged to do so. The personal representatives can only act until new trustees are appointed. Often, they will themselves be the persons having the power to appoint (see 15.1.4.2).

15.3.3 Removal of a trustee

A trustee may be removed against his will in any of the following ways:

(a) Under an express power in the trust instrument. Such power is almost never inserted in a domestic trust, and if it exists it will be strictly construed. More commonly it is found in certain commercial transactions. A common example is an equitable mortgage effected by depositing the title deeds with the lender, where the mortgagor may declare himself a trustee of the legal estate for the lender. In turn, the lender is likely to reserve a power to remove and replace the mortgagor as trustee, simply a means of protecting himself.

(b) He may be removed under s. 36(1) (see 15.1.4.2) if he remains out of the United Kingdom for more than 12 months, refuses, or is unfit to act or incapable of acting, by the appointment of some other person to act in his place.

(c) He may be removed by the court either in the exercise of its jurisdiction under s. 41 (see 15.1.4.3), where the appointment of a new trustee may involve removing an existing trustee, or under its inherent jurisdiction where an action for the administration of the trust is brought.

Removal is not a step to be taken lightly, but it is not necessary to show misconduct. Friction between trustees may be a ground for removing one (*Re Henderson* [1940] Ch 764). A mere dispute between the trustee and the beneficiaries over the manner in which the trustee exercises his discretions will not generally suffice, but it may be proper to take this into account. The main consideration will always be the welfare of the beneficiaries (*Letterstedt* v *Boers* (1884) 9 App Cas 371, PC).

15.3.4 Proposals for change

When the Trusts of Land and Appointment of Trustees Act 1966 comes into force, additional powers will be given to the beneficiaries, where they are all of full age and capacity, and are together absolutely entitled to the trust property. Section 19 empowers the beneficiaries, by written direction to the trustees, to appoint a person or persons as trustee(s), and to direct the retirement of a trustee. Section 20 allows them to substitute for a trustee who is incapable by virtue of mental disorder of exercising his functions as trustee.

SIXTEEN

Powers, Discretions and Duties of Trustees

16.1 GENERAL DESCRIPTION AND OVERVIEW

16.1.1 Powers and duties

Equity equips trustees with a number of powers, and imposes also a range of duties, most of which may be modified or excluded by the express terms of the particular trust. Modern trusts created by deed of settlement or will, prepared under expert legal advice, generally seek to give the trustees the widest possible powers, being almost invariably drafted with tax saving in mind. It is important to bear in mind that the powers described in this chapter are generally subject to the terms of the trust instrument, and apply only to the extent that wider powers are not expressly given: see Trustee Act 1925, s. 69(2), at 15.1.4.2.

The distinction between trusts and powers has been considered in 2.5. A similar distinction exists between the duties of the trustee's office on the one hand, and his powers or discretions on the other. Trustees have a discretion as to whether or not they will exercise a power, and if after proper consideration they decide in good faith not to exercise it, the beneficiaries have no ground for complaint. Generally speaking, however, there will be a duty to undertake such consideration where it would be appropriate. There is of course no discretion as to whether to fulfil a duty, but there may be an element of discretion as to how precisely a duty is fulfilled, as in the selection of investments.

16.1.2 What are the powers and duties?

In view of the different types of situation in which trusts come into being, it is only to be expected that powers and duties will vary according to the character of the trust, for example, whether the trustees are required to accumulate or distribute income and so on.

However, it will be seen that some kinds of power are in principle widely available to trustees. Most of these are now statutory and they are chiefly concerned with facilitating the management of the trust.

Generally, therefore, trustees will be under an obligation to invest the funds in authorised securities according to the powers given to them by the trust instrument or under the Trustee Investments Act 1961, discussed in 16.6. In so doing, they must take expert advice where necessary, and make any adjustments required by the equitable rules of apportionment, which, as we shall see in 16.7.2, are designed to preserve a fair balance between capital and income. They must also ensure the proper payment of tax. At some stage, they have to consider matters such as the sale of trust property, provision for infant beneficiaries, and the exercise of any powers of appointment. Accounts must be kept and copies supplied to the beneficiaries. It is usual and desirable for trustees to meet at appropriate intervals to transact the trust business and minutes of these meetings, and a trust diary or minute book, will be kept.

The trust instrument itself will usually give additional powers appropriate to the particular trust, which in the case of the modern tax-saving trust may be very wide indeed. Older trusts are somewhat less likely to grant extensive additional powers, and here the statutory powers are more important. They are still of some relevance in the modern style of trust, for they will be incorporated into the trust to the extent that they are not expressly excluded by the trust instrument, and may be useful if for any reason it proves impossible to rely upon a specially given power.

The duties of trustees will similarly vary, depending on the nature of the trust. Here, though, there are certain fundamental duties arising from the fiduciary nature of the trustee, and these affect all trustees. The duty of loyalty, i.e., the duty not to make a personal profit from the trust, considered in 14.3, is an example.

Other duties relate to the safe keeping of the trust property, and include the duty to maintain proper custody of documents of title, the duty to invest etc. The extent to which these apply depends upon the character of the trust property. Trustees also have duties towards the beneficiaries (see 16.7), such as the duty to inform them of their rights and to provide them with information regarding the affairs of the trust, and the duty to distribute the property in accordance with their entitlements. They must also consider the need to maintain fairness between the beneficiaries, and select investments which preserve a balance between the interests of the income beneficiaries and those interested in the capital of the fund.

Some duties may be, and frequently are, modified by the trust instrument: the insertion of a charging clause, also considered in 14.3 is an example. Others, such as the duty to make proper distribution, are inherent in the nature of any trust, although even here the trust instrument may limit the personal liability of the trustees in the event of a breach.

It will be apparent that the administration of all but the simplest trusts calls for a considerable degree of business competence, and nowadays most trusts of any size will have a professional trustee such as a bank or trust corporation to act for them. The professional may act either as sole trustee or in conjunction with one or more individuals. This sort of mixture can be useful in family settlements, combining the expertise of the professional with the more intimate knowledge of family circumstances supplied by the private trustee.

A recent illustration of the difficulties which can arise where private trustees lack professional guidance arose in *Turner* v *Turner* [1984] Ch 100, where private trustees exercised powers of appointment at the behest of the settlor, not appreciating the duty to consider the exercise of the power which attached to their office (the nature of which is discussed in chapter 2). They thus acted in breach of trust and most of the appointments so made were held void.

16.1.3 Constructive trusts

The powers and duties described in this chapter apply to express trusts. Constructive trustees are in a peculiar position for they hold under a trust imposed by operation of law, and although the circumstances may be such that it is perfectly obvious to the constructive trustee that he is holding the legal estate in the property on trust for someone else (as might occur, for example, on facts similar to those in *Hodgson* v *Marks* [1971] Ch 892, see 8.4.1.2), it is equally possible that the constructive trustee may be entirely ignorant of the fact that he holds on trust until such time as the issue is determined by a court. Such may be the case, for example, where he takes property as a purchaser with constructive notice of a trust, or takes as a volunteer (i.e., not giving value) with no notice at all.

It is improbable that a constructive trustee is under comparable duties to those of an express trustee in the matter of investing trust property, and it would certainly be harsh to hold him liable for, e.g., non-investment or non-apportionment when he may be entirely unaware of the beneficiaries' claims.

The duties of constructive trustees are uncertain, and it may be that the only duty is that of holding the property or its proceeds (and perhaps any profits) on behalf of the beneficiaries. But much may turn upon the conduct of the trustee, and a constructive trustee who fraudulently misapplies property subject to a trust may be placed under a more onerous liability than one who has acted innocently.

16.2 SALE OF TRUST PROPERTY

A power to sell some or all of the trust property is usually given by the trust instrument, either expressly or by implication, and even in the absence of such power, trustees will often be permitted to sell by statute or, as a last resort, by order of the court. Some specific cases require consideration.

16.2.1 Settled land

The powers and duties which derive from the Settled Land Act 1925 are unique, and quite different from those which operate under any other trust.

As was explained in chapter 10, settled land today is very rare (although land is sometimes accidentally settled, especially by people who make wills without taking legal advice). We saw in that chapter how the Settled Land Act 1925 creates in effect a statutory trust of the land. It is an unusual type of trust, however, because virtually the sole function of the trustees of the settlement is to take the proceeds if the land is sold, so as to protect the (overreached) interests of the beneficiaries under the trusts of the settlement.

The legal estate (fee simple absolute in possession) and the powers of sale are vested not in them but in the tenant for life. Further, very little limit is placed on the power of the tenant for life to sell the land — he has far more extensive powers than a normal trustee in this regard.

16.2.2 Trusts for sale of land
The nature of the trustees' powers to sell in this case have been covered in chapter 10.

16.2.3 Other trusts of land
It is possible to have a trust of land which involves neither a strict settlement nor a trust for sale, e.g., a sole trustee holding the land on a simple bare trust. An example is *Hodgson* v *Marks* [1971] Ch 892 (see 8.4.1.2), which is a very unusual case. Indeed, from a land law perspective, one of the difficulties of that case was precisely that it was so unconventional and did not therefore fall within the overreaching or registration provisions of the 1925 legislation.

Even with this type of trust, the trustee will have a power to sell under s. 1(1) of the Trustee Investments Act 1961 (considered below) unless the trust instrument, assuming there is one (there was not in *Hodgson* v *Marks*), specifically prohibits sale.

Trustees (except of settled land) are given further powers to sell or mortgage property, where they are required to pay out or apply capital, by the Trustee Act 1925, s. 16.

16.2.4 Personal property
Section 16 of the Trustee Act 1925, or s. 1(1) of the Trustee Investments Act 1961, will generally be wide enough to enable trustees to raise money from the sale of chattels where necessary, even if no such power is expressly or impliedly given by the trust instrument itself.

Chattels which are heirlooms, i.e., intended to devolve with land subject to a settlement through successive generations, are governed by the Settled Land Act 1925 and may be sold only by the tenant for life upon obtaining a court order.

Section 57 of the Trustee Act 1925 (considered in chapter 18) empowers the court to authorise the sale, lease, mortgage, surrender, release or other disposition of property subject to a trust whenever it considers such a transaction expedient but where the trustees lack the necessary power. Again, the section does not apply to a strict settlement.

16.2.5 Standard of care
In exercising their powers of sale, trustees have an overriding duty to obtain the best price they can on behalf of the beneficiaries, and while there may be circumstances in which it will be proper to reject the highest offer, if this is suspect, the trustees will be in breach of their duty if they permit ethical considerations to entice them into accepting a lower price. This may require trustees to resile from an agreement on later receiving a better offer.

Trustees may thus be faced with a difficult choice between a quick and sure sale on the one hand and holding on for a better price on the other. For example, in *Fry* v *Fry* (1859) 28 LJ Ch 591 the testator, owner of an inn, directed that it should be sold 'as soon as convenient'. His executors refused an offer of £900 and held on in the hope of a better one. In the meantime, however, the coming of the railway took away the inn's trade, and the inn was finally sold at a much lower price, leaving the executors liable to make up, out of their own pockets, the difference between the actual selling price and the offer of £900.

16.2.6 Power to give receipts

The power to sell or otherwise deal with trust property is of little value unless the purchaser can obtain a valid receipt for his money and so s. 14(1) of the Trustee Act 1925 gives a power, notwithstanding anything to the contrary in the trust instrument, to give an effective receipt. The receipt in writing of a trustee is thus effective to exonerate a purchaser from any obligation to see that the trustees apply the money in accordance with the trust — a necessary provision, since a purchaser who was aware that the property was held on trust might otherwise be taken to hold it as constructive trustee under the equitable notice doctrine (see 1.4.6).

It is likely that nothing in the section affects the principle that if there is more than one trustee, a receipt to be valid must be given by all jointly. Also, in the case of settled land or trusts for sale of land, the purchase money must be paid to two trustees in order effectively to overreach the beneficial interests.

16.3 POWER TO INSURE

In the absence of any express provision in the trust instrument, trustees are under no duty to insure the trust property, and will not be liable for failure to insure if subsequent loss or damage occurs. Nor, in general, does a trustee have any power to insure unless given expressly by the trust instrument.

An exception is s. 19 of the Trustee Act 1925, which gives trustees a limited power to insure against loss or damage by fire (but not against other insurable risks) any building or other insurable property, up to three quarters of its value, and pay the premiums out of the trust income. The section does not apply where property is held on a bare trust.

The rationale, it seems, for the absence of any implied duty or power to insure, is to guard against the possibility that the premiums will make significant inroads into the trust income. It should be remembered that the principles developed before the introduction of modern forms of insurance, and many prudent commercial men today would regard insurance as a most elementary precaution. The Law Reform Committee, in its 23rd Report, on the powers and duties of trustees (Cmnd 8733, 1982), recommends that trustees should be under a positive duty to insure whenever a prudent man of business would do so, up to the full value of the property if necessary.

All the above applies only to first-party insurance of the trust property. There is nothing to stop the trustees insuring *themselves* for third-party liability towards the trust in the event of their own breach, although they cannot reimburse themselves from the trust property for the premiums they pay on insuring themselves.

16.4 POWER TO COMPOUND LIABILITIES

As legal owner, a trustee has the right to maintain an action with regard to the trust property. Where the claim is itself a legal claim, only the trustee as legal owner will be able to sue. This is of importance where debts are owed to the trust. It may be the duty of the trustee, for example, to pursue the claims of the trust by proving in the bankruptcy of a debtor.

The pursuit of legal claims, and the possibility of compromise, are not easily amenable to absolute duties but require a discretionary element. Litigation is, after all, a risky business. Even in an apparently cut-and-dried situation like the bankruptcy of a debtor, the costs of proving in bankruptcy may outweigh any likely benefits to the trust, in which case a trustee should not pursue the matter.

Section 15 of the Trustee Act 1925 therefore provides trustees with an element of discretion in dealing with persons who are involved in contention with the trust, who in practice will usually be persons who owe it money. As they think fit, trustees may enter into a range of transactions of the sort which business people would often enter into, for example, accepting compositions of debts, allowing time for payment of debts and so on. Provided the trustees act in good faith, they will not be responsible for any loss arising from the exercise of these powers.

In exercising their discretion, the trustees should consider the wishes of the beneficiaries but are not bound to act in accordance with them. The section also applies to personal representatives.

16.5 MAINTENANCE AND ADVANCEMENT

The powers of maintenance and advancement are appropriate to family-type settlements, which are described in 2.1. They have the object of providing for infant beneficiaries (under 18) who are not as yet entitled to any of the income or capital, but who require financial support during their minority.

Payments by way of maintenance are payments out of income, in theory to provide for routine necessities such as education or board and lodging, while payments by way of advancement are sums advanced from capital, in theory to cover major costs such as setting up the infant in his profession.

Originally such payments were made for their theoretical purposes, but in recent decades, significant use has also been made of these powers in reducing the tax liability of trusts. For example, early advancements of capital could until 1975 be effective to avoid liability to estate duty entirely (see, e.g., *Pilkington* v *IRC* [1964] AC 612 below, 16.5.2), and even now can be used to reduce inheritance tax liability (see 16.5.2) while the purpose of mainten- ance payments is often to reduce liability for income tax. The real (but often hidden) issues arising in relation to maintenance and advancement are the extent to which schemes intended purely to save tax can be valid.

16.5.1 Maintenance

A power to maintain is not implied into the trust instrument. Therefore it must be expressly given, or advantage may be taken of the power contained in s. 31 of the Trustee Act 1925 (see below). The statutory power operates provided no contrary intention is expressed. But where the statutory power is expressly excluded it cannot be used, even if an express power turns out to be useless. In *Re Erskine's ST* [1971] 1 WLR 162, a settlement contained a provision for accumulation which was void for perpetuity. But since the statutory power to maintain was excluded by the provisions of the trust instrument, the income which the trustees had accumulated could not be applied for the beneficiary, and resulted to the settlor's estate.

16.5.1.1 The statutory power

The power to maintain under s. 31(1) can only arise where the beneficiary is entitled to receive intermediate income under the trust. This will be the case either where his interest is vested (unless a contrary intention is shown, as by a specific grant of that income to someone other than the beneficiary) or where it is a contingent interest which carries the intermediate income. If there are prior interests, or if the beneficiary's interest is as a member of a class of discretionary beneficiaries, the power will not be available at all.

The question of whether contingent gifts carry the intermediate income is dealt with by complex rules, which seem to reflect no coherent policy and are beyond the scope of this book. These rules derive from a combination of case law, s. 175 of the Law of Property Act 1925 and s. 31(3) of the Trustee Act 1925.

Assuming income to be available, the trustees have a discretion as to whether to maintain the beneficiary. Section 31 directs them to have regard to the age and requirements of the infant, whether any other income is available for his maintenance, and generally to the circumstances of the case. The money may be paid to the parent or guardian of the infant or directly for his benefit, e.g., school fees. If the infant is married, they may pay it directly to him.

Subject to contrary intention in the trust instrument, the power to maintain ceases when the beneficiary reaches the age of majority. Even if his interest is still contingent, the trustees must pay the whole of the income to him until he obtains a vested interest or dies.

16.5.1.2 Court's inherent jurisdiction

The court has inherent jurisdiction to approve the use of income or even capital for the maintenance of infant beneficiaries, but in practice this is rarely necessary.

16.5.2 Advancement

The power of advancement permits trustees to pay capital sums to or on behalf of a beneficiary some time before he is entitled to claim the fund. The power may be given by the trust instrument or, subject to contrary intention, the power contained in s. 32 of the Trustee Act 1925 may be used.

Section 32 allows trustees at any time to pay or apply capital money for the 'advancement or benefit' of any person entitled to that capital or a share thereof. Subject to that limitation, the powers are wide, applying, for example, whether the interest is vested or contingent, or whether in possession, remainder or reversion. Up to one half of the beneficiary's share may be advanced.

The trustees' discretion whether to exercise their power of advancement is absolute, so long as it is for the 'advancement or benefit' of the beneficiary. The ambit of the power is very wide and it is possible to use it for schemes which are intended only to save taxation. In order to explain how this works, it is necessary to explain briefly how taxes on capital transfers operate.

16.5.2.1 Taxes on capital transfers
Estate duty, which was originally introduced in 1894, was the only tax on transfers of private capital from 1949 to 1975.

It was originally payable only upon property passing upon a death. As an inevitable consequence, therefore, it could be avoided by giving away one's property before death. In an attempt to prevent circumvention, the legislature countered by extending the ambit of the tax to gifts made within a certain period prior to death, which by 1968 was seven years. It was therefore desirable from the point of view of tax-avoidance to transfer as much capital from a life tenant to his or her children as early as possible (see, e.g., *Pilkington* v *IRC* [1964] AC 612 (below, 16.5.2.2).

Because the tax was frequently avoided, by this and other means, estate duty was replaced by Capital Transfer Tax (CTT) in the Finance Act 1975, with retroactive effect from 26 March 1974. It operated upon capital transfers whether on death or *inter vivos* (so as to catch estate duty avoiders), and it was designed to tax family capital at least once a generation. It was no longer possible, simply by early transfer of capital, to avoid liability to taxation altogether, but the tax was levied on two scales, the first applicable to transfers on death and within three years of death, and a second (lower rate) to all others. Also, from 1981 onwards, the rates which applied to any particular gift were calculated, on a steeply progressive scale, by reference to the total value of gifts made over a 10-year period. In addition, there were threshold limits on amounts transferred, below which no CTT was payable on either scale.

The result of all this was that it was still generally advantageous, from a tax point of view, to transfer capital early from a life-tenant to his or her children. Not only did this increase the chance of attracting taxation on the lower scale, but if a settlor settled some of his estate *inter vivos*, and survived (after 1981) for 10 years, both the *inter vivos* transfer and that on death could be more easily kept below the minimum threshold, whereas, had the entire settlement been delayed until death, the amount may have been sufficient to attract CTT liability. Nevertheless, any settlement made between 1975 and 1986 required careful planning. See, for example, the discussion of *Re Robinson's ST* [1976] 1 WLR 806 (see 18.3.3.2).

The Finance Act 1986, which purported merely to amend the law on capital transfer tax, and rename it inheritance tax, in fact negated many of the principles of capital transfer tax. To a large extent, the position has reverted to that which obtained before 1974. The changes came into effect on 18 March 1986.

The most important change was the abolition of CTT on out-and-out lifetime gifts to individuals. Another change was the further reduction in the cumulation period from 10 years to seven. In effect, therefore, as before 1974, out-and-out gifts (with no benefit reserved to the donor) are exempt from tax if made seven years or more before death. There was originally a sliding scale on gifts from three to seven years before death (in four equal 20 per cent steps), but these were replaced in 1988 by a single rate of 40 per cent on all chargeable transfers, subject to a threshold below which no inheritance tax is payable.

It is obvious that in general terms, therefore, the tax-avoidance devices which were used before 1974 still operate today.

16.5.2.2 *Pilkington* v *IRC* In *Pilkington* v *IRC* [1964] AC 612, the trustees proposed to advance, under the powers contained in s. 32, one half of the share of a two-year-old girl (Penelope) and resettle it. The child was in no need of the moneys advanced, and too young for the traditional purposes of advancement to be relevant. The only benefit to her would be the effect of saving estate duty, and one of the issues was whether this was a sufficient 'benefit'. The House of Lords held it was, and that the advance made was not for this reason objectionable. There was no need to show that the advance was to meet some personal need of the beneficiary: the saving of estate duty was itself a sufficient benefit. Nor was it relevant that other persons might also benefit from the resettlement if the provision as a whole would benefit Penelope.

In fact, however, the resettlement in *Pilkington* (which was actually disadvantageous to Penelope) infringed the rule against perpetuities as it then stood. Thus, although the advance was valid, the resettlement was not.

A diagrammatic representation of *Pilkington* v *IRC* can be found in figure 16.1.

Figure 16.1

Advancement and re-settlement of capital in Pilkington v *IRC* [1964] AC 612

Capital

	Life tenant	Penelope
Before proposed advancement	Life interest on 100%	None now. Remainder on all, but subject to substantial estate duty on death of life tenant
After proposed advancement	Life interest on 50%	50% now, saving on estate duty, but resettled on disadvantagous terms

16.5.2.3 Advance must be for benefit of advancee However widely expressed is the power of advancement, the Court of Appeal held in *Re Pauling's ST* [1964] Ch 303 that the trustees must be satisfied that the advance will be for the benefit of the advancee. Further, if the trustees decide to make him an advance for a particular purpose, they must ask themselves whether he will carry it out: they should not make a payment for a purpose and then leave him free to do with it as he pleases. The question was left open as to whether trustees can recover money which the beneficiary requests but then applies for some quite different purpose.

In that case, the life tenant and her husband habitually spent well in excess of their income, and consequently their account at the defendant bank was considerably overdrawn. The defendant bank was also trustee under the settlement, under which the plaintiffs were remaindermen. As the plaintiffs reached their majority, the life tenant and her husband persuaded them to consent to various advances, which were ostensibly made for a specific purpose, for example, the purchase of a house or furniture, or house improvements, but which were in fact given to the life tenant and her husband, and used to reduce their overdraft. The bank was held to have acted in breach of trust in making the advances.

16.6 DUTY TO PROTECT THE TRUST ASSETS: INVESTMENT

This is a continuing duty which begins with the collection of the assets upon assuming office and ends only with the final distribution of the property among those entitled to it.

16.6.1 Initial duties

From the outset, trustees must acquaint themselves with the terms of the trust and the state of the property they are to hold, ensure that funds are appropriately invested and see that all securities and chattels are in proper custody. If there is property outstanding, all proper steps must be taken to gather it in.

In *Re Brogden* (1888) 38 ChD 546, trustees were held liable where they refrained from suing to enforce a covenant to pay £10,000 into the settlement, although their motive was their reluctance to endanger the family business, of which the covenantor's estate formed the major part. In *Ward v Ward* (1843) 2 HL Cas 777 n, trustees were not liable for failure to sue a beneficiary who might have been ruined by the action, along with his family who were also beneficiaries, but this is probably an extreme case. In *Re Brogden,* the Court of Appeal held that the only excuse for failure to enforce payments due to the trust was the well founded belief that action would be fruitless.

As we saw in 16.4, however, trustees have power by s. 15 of the Trustee Act 1925 to compromise actions, compound liabilities and allow time for payment of debts, and will not be liable for the exercise of these powers in good faith.

16.6.2   Protection of assets by investment

16.6.2.1   General principles   Once the assets are in, they must be protected, and an important aspect of this is the selection of proper investments. Two main principles operate. First, trustees have a general duty to act fairly as between the beneficiaries, and secondly there are limitations on the making of risky investments.

The first principle dictates, for example, that investments must be selected which produce income for the income beneficiaries while at the same time preserving the capital for those ultimately entitled to it. This rules out certain forms of investment such as antiques or a wine cellar, since these produce only capital appreciation and no income.

There is also a general duty to diversify, that is, to spread the risks of investment by spreading the funds between different investments.

So far as the second principle is concerned, the general law is cautious compared with present-day investment practice. Nowadays it is therefore usual expressly to give trustees wide powers of investment, and further authority to amend if necessary. The general law is therefore of limited practical application, save where the express power fails to cover all the property in the trust. Usually, the Trustee Investments Act 1961 is expressly excluded. If the trustees consider that their investment powers are still too narrow, the court may be persuaded to extend them beyond the provisions of the 1961 Act, under the Variation of Trusts Act 1958. This was the outcome in *Trustees of the British Museum* v *Attorney-General* [1984] 1 WLR 418 (see 18.3.1), but that case depended on investment practices considered safe in 1983 and the position may be different today, in the light of the 1987 stock market crash.

16.6.2.2   Trustee Investments Act 1961   The following discussion is concerned with the unusual position where no express provisions are made in the trust instrument.

Until 1961, there was no general power to invest in equities (ordinary shares) at all. The Trustee Investments Act 1961, which repealed and replaced s. 1 of the Trustee Act 1925, was designed to give trustees the power to invest a portion of the trust fund in equities (i.e., the purchase of ordinary shares in companies), which otherwise would have required express power in the trust instrument.

Trustees who wish to take advantage of the Act are required (by s. 2) to divide the fund into two parts, in the ratio 75:25 at the time of division and called the narrower-range part and the wider-range part. Only the wider-range part can be invested in ordinary shares, so the provision limits the proportion of the fund that can be invested in that way. For the purpose of this division, they should obtain a valuation, which, if made in writing by a person believed by the trustees to be qualified, will be conclusive. After the initial division, there is no need to ensure that both parts remain equally valuable but any additions to the fund must be equally split between the two parts.

A list of authorised investments is provided in Sch. 1 to the Act, Parts I and II of which both deal with narrower-range investments. Those in Part I are fixed-interest investments whose capital value does not fluctuate, and trustees may select these without taking any expert advice. They include such things as National Savings certificates and National Savings indexed-income bonds. The income from the investments listed in Part II may fluctuate, and expert advice must be obtained before selecting these investments, which include government securities, deposits with building societies and mortgages of freeholds or long leaseholds.

Part III deals with wider-range investments, in which the trustees may invest the wider-range part of their fund. There is no obligation to do so, and even after making a division they may decide to keep all investments within the narrower range. If they decide to invest the wider-range part in ordinary shares, they must select shares which are quoted on a recognised investment exchange (such as the International Stock Exchange), are fully paid up (or required to be so within nine months of issue) and are issued by a company whose issued capital is at least £1 million and which has paid a dividend on all its shares which rank for dividend within each of the immediately preceding five years.

If property accrues to either part of the fund, such as a bonus issue of shares accruing to the wider-range part, the accrual remains with that part. Any other addition to the trust fund, however, such as where the trustees choose to purchase under a rights issue, must be apportioned between the two parts so that each is increased in value by the same amount. This can be done directly or by making a compensating transfer from one part to the other.

If the trustees decide to withdraw property from the trust fund in the exercise of any of their powers or duties, they have a discretion as to which part they will use, and no compensating transfer is necessary. They may wish to do this, for example, to set up a separate fund by way of provision for an infant beneficiary. If they set up a separate fund out of a fund which is already divided into narrower-range and wider-range parts, the new fund must also be divided, either into equal halves, or into the same proportions as the two parts of the original fund bore to each other when the separate fund was removed, or in some proportion intermediate between these two, if the trustees wish to use the powers of the Act in relation to the new separate fund.

In May 1996, HM Treasury issued a Consultation Document, *Investment Powers of Trustees*, which was a proposal to replace the Trustee Investments Act 1961 with an Order made under s. 1 of the Deregulation and Contracting Out Act 1994. The main proposals, taken from para. 16, are as follows:

(i)   the TIA will be repealed;

(ii)   trustees will be given the same power to make an investment of any kind as they would have if they owned the trust in their own right. There will be no list or lists of authorised investments;

(iii)   trustees will continue to be under an obligation to have regard to the need for diversification of investments, so far as appropriate to the circumstances of a trust, and to the suitability of any proposed investment;

328 Powers, Discretions and Duties of Trustees

(iv) in exercising the power of investment, trustees will remain subject to the existing duties and standards of care established by trust law, including the duty to take advice where necessary and to review portfolios . . . The new wider power will be without prejudice to these duties and standards, and also to the more general rules and duties applicable to trustees under trust law, for example to avoid any conflict between their position as trustees and their personal interests;

. . .

16.6.2.3 Investment outside the 1961 Act Express powers to invest outside the Act are known as special powers, usually given to allow trustees to invest in private companies which would not otherwise be authorised investments or in the purchase of land. If the whole property of the trust is encompassed by these special powers, then the Act will be irrelevant, but if not, the trustees must, if they wish to use the investment powers of the Act, divide the trust property into three parts. The special-range part will consist of such property as is encompassed by the express powers, and the rest will be split into equal narrower-range and wider-range parts, to which the rules mentioned above will then apply. Accruals to special-range property join the special range, but if any special-range property is to be converted out of the special range, it must be apportioned equally between the narrower-range and wider-range parts of the fund, or a compensating transfer must be made.

16.6.2.4 Criteria for choice of investment Trustees must not of course make unauthorised investments, but even in selecting those which are authorised they must exercise the usual standard of care, bearing in mind that the trustees are not acting for themselves, but for others. This standard of care applies to investments under express powers, as well as those granted under the 1961 Act.

In this context, the usual standard of care is that which 'an ordinary prudent man would take if he were minded to make an investment for the benefit of other people for whom he felt morally bound to provide': see the judgment of Lindley MR in *Re Whiteley* (1886) 33 ChD 347, 355, adopted by Brightman J in *Bartlett* v *Barclays Bank Trust Co. Ltd (No. 1)* [1980] Ch 515: see 14.1.2.

This may require the trustees to set aside their personal views as to the desirability of particular investments. They must not refuse to invest in, e.g., armaments, if such investment is in the best financial interests of the beneficiaries, although if all the beneficiaries were adult they might take into account their views on the impropriety of a proposed investment.

In *Cowan* v *Scargill* [1985] Ch 270, Mr Scargill, President of the National Union of Mineworkers, was one of the trustees of a pension fund with wide powers of investment. He and five other trustees (the defendants) appointed by the union refused to approve an annual investment plan unless it was amended to prohibit any increase in overseas investments, to provide for withdrawal from existing overseas investments and to prohibit investments in industries which were in direct competition with coal. Their action was in line with the policy of the National Union of Mineworkers. The plaintiffs (five trustees appointed by the National Coal Board) applied to the court for directions that the defendants were in breach of their fiduciary duties as trustees. Sir Robert Megarry V-C held that the defendants were in breach of their fiduciary duties in refusing to approve the investment plan.

By s. 6(1) of the Trustee Investments Act 1961, trustees are required to have regard both to the need for diversification and the suitability of the proposed investment to the trust. Presumably, then, trustees might reasonably refrain from investments which are at odds with the purposes of a charitable trust. However, Browne-Wilkinson V-C observed in *Bishop of Oxford* v *The Church Commissioners* [1991] PLR 185, noted [1992] Conv 115, that the starting point for investment even by charitable trustees must be the pursuit of maximum financial returns, and minimum financial risk, and that even where they felt that such investment was contrary to the purposes of the charity they could only relax the pursuit of financial aims to the extent that this did not create a risk of significant financial detriment.

Any investment in a manner specified in Part II or Part III of Sch. 1 must be made on the basis of advice, even if the power to invest in that manner derives from an express special power. The advice must be in writing, and must come from someone whom the trustee reasonably believes is qualified to advise, unless the advice is being given by a trustee to his fellow trustees, or where, as in the case of a trust corporation, the decisions on investment are in the hands of employees competent to advise.

Obtaining advice does not permit the trustee to place blind faith in his adviser because the final decision cannot be delegated. He must consider the advice, and reach his own decision as a prudent man of business (essentially, the principles considered in chapter 14 apply). Where advice was initially required, trustees must also consider at what intervals further advice should be sought upon the retention of the investment and may incur liability if failure to exercise due consideration results in a loss.

Special considerations apply where an investment by way of mortgage is proposed.

Trusts which comprise a controlling interest in a company also require brief mention since shares in a private company are a fairly common form of trust property. Since the trustees as legal owners of the shares may be in a position to control the activities of the directors, the question arises as to whether their duty to safeguard trust assets extends to attempting to direct the policy of a commercial enterprise. In *Bartlett* v *Barclays Bank Trust Co. Ltd (No. 1)* [1980] Ch 515 (14.1.2), a series of speculations by a private company in which the bank, as trustee, had a controlling interest, led to a large overall loss to the trust, and Brightman J was of the view that the bank should, if necessary, have been prepared to remove the board. Certainly, it should have insisted on representation on the board and availed itself of the fullest possible information on the state of the investments. The principle seems clear: trustees in this situation must, if necessary, curb possible beneficial speculations to avoid the risk of their going wrong. They cannot shelter behind the acts of the directors where they themselves are in a position to control those acts.

Trustees are obliged to invest within a reasonable time, and in the meantime the fund should be placed on deposit with a bank so as to produce at least some interest. If the trustees unreasonably fail to find an investment for the trust funds, they will be liable themselves to pay interest to the fund.

16.6.2.5 Retaining an investment Liability may arise not only through the making of unauthorised investments but also from the improper retention of an investment.

The retention of even an authorised investment may in certain circumstances be improper. Where the 1961 Act applies, and the trustees have made investments for which advice is required (i.e., those within Parts II and III of sch. 1 to the Act) they must also determine at what intervals advice should be sought on the question of retaining the investment (s. 6(3)).

By s. 4 of the Trustee Act 1925, trustees are protected from liability for breach arising only from continuing to hold an investment which has ceased to be authorised. There will still be a duty to consider the propriety of retaining the investment, however, for the section does not confer protection when a duty to realise the investment has arisen on some other ground than the investment having become unauthorised.

These provisions apart, the standard of care is the same as in the previous section, so the trustees will not be liable, according to Lindley LJ in *Re Chapman* [1896] 2 Ch 763, 776, if they have acted 'honestly and prudently, in the belief that [retention] was the best course to take in the interests of all the parties'. A mere error of business judgment will not therefore amount to a breach of trust in these circumstances.

In order to meet the standards of the prudent man of business, of course, it may be necessary to take advice and periodically to review the trust investments, quite apart from the requirements of s. 6(3) of the 1961 Act.

In the unusual case of the trustees being restricted by the trust instrument to a single investment (as in the case, perhaps, of a private company or a pension fund limited to investment in a single industry), the lack of power to switch investments could in theory pose serious problems for the trustees. It seems unlikely that they must passively watch the funds deteriorate; business prudence would appear to require that they should apply to the court under s. 57 of the Trustee Act 1925, or s. 1 of the Variation of Trusts Act 1958, for any necessary additional powers to preserve the funds.

16.7 DUTIES OF TRUSTEES TOWARDS BENEFICIARIES

16.7.1 General principles of control by beneficiaries

Although the ultimate benefit under a trust goes to the beneficiaries, the trustees are concerned not only with their wishes but also those expressed by the settlor on creation of the trust. There is therefore no general principle which permits the beneficiaries to control the way in which trustees exercise their discretions. Were it otherwise, the trustees would be hopelessly handicapped in fulfilling their overriding duty towards the trust as a whole, and the court will never compel the trustees to act under orders from the beneficiaries where a power or discretion has been entrusted to the trustees alone. This will hold as long as the trust continues, although if the beneficiaries collectively wish, they can bring the trust to an end and resettle the property on any terms they wish, under the *Saunders* v *Vautier* doctrine (see further chapter 18).

Tempest v *Lord Camoys* (1882) 21 ChD 571 shows the position while the trust continues. The beneficiaries desired the trust to purchase an estate but one of the trustees objected. Jessel MR refused to interfere with that trustee's bona fide decision. Strictly, the trustees are under no obligation even to consult with the beneficiaries as to how a power or discretion should be exercised, although of course they will often do so in practice.

An exception arises by virtue of s. 26(3) of the Law of Property Act 1925, which requires trustees of land under a statutory trust for sale to consult beneficiaries in possession and to give effect to their wishes so far as is consistent with the general intentions of the trust. The reason is, as we saw in chapter 10, that these are really fictitious trusts for sale whose main purpose is to simplify the conveyancing of shared land, but even in this limited case there is no overriding obligation to follow the beneficiaries' directions.

16.7.1.1 Disclosure of reasons for decisions The need to protect trustees from importuning beneficiaries is evident. However, the courts have gone further and established that trustees will not be compelled to disclose the reasons behind the exercise of a discretion. In *Re Beloved Wilkes's Charity* (1851) 3 Mac & G 440, charity trustees were required to select a boy to be educated for the ministry, preference to be given to boys from four named parishes if a fit candidate could be found. The trustees, without giving reasons, selected a boy who did not come from one of the named parishes but whose brother had put forward his merits to the trustees. It was held that in the absence of evidence that the trustees had exercised their discretion unfairly or dishonestly, the court would not interfere.

This poses an obvious problem for any beneficiary wishing to challenge a decision made by trustees. If trustees are not required to give reasons for their decisions, it will generally be impossible to know whether they have exercised their discretions in a proper manner.

If on the other hand the trustees choose to disclose their reasons, then the court may consider their adequacy. In *Klug* v *Klug* [1918] 2 Ch 67, a trustee whose daughter was a beneficiary refused to consider the exercise of a power of appointment in her favour, and from the correspondence it appeared that her reason was annoyance that the daughter had married without her consent. Neville J held that the trustee had not exercised her discretion at all, and that it was the duty of the court to interfere. Where the trustees take steps to keep the basis of their decisions private, however, there appears to be little that a beneficiary can do if the decision is not obviously unreasonable or fraudulent.

This leads to the question of whether the beneficiaries are entitled to have access to any written records of how the trustees have conducted the trust business. It is usual practice for trustees to keep a trust diary or minute book in which decisions affecting the trust are kept, but there is no requirement that the reasons for trustees' decisions should be recorded. The beneficiaries are, however, entitled to access to documents connected with the trust, known as 'trust documents', and indeed have a proprietary interest in such documents. If those documents disclose the reasons for a decision, this would seem to offer the beneficiaries a way round the difficulty that trustees will not be compelled to disclose reasons.

The Court of Appeal, however, in *Re Londonderry's Settlement* [1965] Ch 918, effectively closed this door. In that case a beneficiary, dissatisfied with the sums appointed to her by trustees, pressed them to disclose various documents connected with the settlement. The trustees sought directions from the court. The Court of Appeal found that the category of 'trust documents' had not previously been defined with any degree of clarity, but concluded that all documents held by trustees *qua* trustees are prima facie trust documents, but that documents containing confidential matters which a beneficiary is not entitled to know about should not be disclosed, either (in the view of Harman J) because they are protected by analogy with the rule that trustees need not disclose reasons, or (according to Salmon LJ) because a document which a beneficiary is not entitled to see cannot be a trust document.

It would appear, then, that the only way in which a beneficiary can gain sight of documents disclosing the trustees' reasons is to bring a hostile action against the trustees, as a preliminary to which an order for discovery of documents can be sought from the court. Unless the beneficiary already has substantial evidence of misconduct, this course will be fraught with difficulties.

16.7.1.2 Trust accounts   There is no argument here: beneficiaries are entitled to be informed of the condition of the trust property and trustees must be ready at all times to produce trust accounts. Normally, the beneficiaries will be supplied with copies, perhaps in a simplified form, although strictly they are entitled to see the original accounts and to have copies made at their own expense. Income beneficiaries (e.g., life tenants under a family settlement) are entitled to see the accounts relating to the entire property of the trust, but remaindermen are entitled only to those accounts which relate to capital transactions and may therefore affect their interests.

It is not obligatory or even usual to have trust accounts subjected to an audit, but this may be done, at the absolute discretion of the trustees, who may employ an independent accountant and charge the costs to the trust fund. By s. 22(4) of the Trustee Act 1925, an audit is not to be carried out more frequently than once every three years, unless the nature of the property or other special difficulties so require. Any trustee or beneficiary may apply for an investigation and audit of the trust accounts by virtue of s. 13 of the Public Trustee Act 1906. A copy of the auditor's report is supplied to the applicant and to each trustee.

16.7.2 Apportionment
The general duty of trustees to act even-handedly as between the beneficiaries entails the necessity, where there are successive interests under a trust, to take

certain steps to ensure that a fair balance is maintained between the capital and income of the trust, so that the former is preserved for those entitled in the future while at the same time allowing a reasonable income to those currently entitled. The rules relating to apportionment are an instance of this principle, and although it is nowadays usual practice to exclude their operation where possible, they are by no means without relevance, particularly in their application to accretions to the trust fund. It has been said that in special circumstances the court itself may direct an apportionment (*Re Kleinwort's Settlement* [1951] Ch 860), but this does not appear to have been done in practice.

16.7.2.1 *Howe* v *Earl of Dartmouth* Some types of property are inherently unsuited to being held for successive interests. A wasting asset, which will soon be used up, provides no benefit to the remaindermen, while a reversionary interest which may not accrue for many years will provide no present income for the life tenant. The obvious way to achieve fairness as between the beneficiaries is therefore to sell the property and invest the proceeds so as to produce an income for the life tenant and an addition to capital for the benefit of the remainderman.

Obviously no problem arises if the trust instrument so directs, e.g., in the case of a trust for sale, but *Howe* v *Earl of Dartmouth* (1802) 7 Ves Jr 137 compels trustees to sell in other circumstances, even if there is no express direction, in some testamentary trusts of personal property (not land). The principle in the case only applies to settlements of the types of property considered in the previous paragraph, and where there is no contrary intention expressed in the will.

Where a duty to convert (i.e., sell) arises under this principle, the normal date at which the property should be converted is one year from the death of the testator, that is, at the end of the 'executors' year' allowed for the administration of the estate to be carried out. If there is power to postpone the sale and conversion, however, this cannot apply, and the valuation for the purposes of apportionment is taken to be the date of the death.

It will usually not be possible to convert and reinvest on either of these specific dates, so some principle is needed for apportioning the income from the asset until actual conversion. This is unnecessary if there is a clear intention that the tenant for life should have the actual income, or if the property is realty (and so not subject to the rule in *Howe* v *Earl of Dartmouth*) and no contrary intention appears, in which event the life tenant will receive the actual income.

Otherwise complex actuarial calculations are required, which turn on the precise nature of the property. For property which produces no present income, such as a reversionary interest, the principles deriving from the decision in *Re Earl of Chesterfield's Trusts* (1883) 24 ChD 643 apply, and apportionment between capital and income is calculated by a formula. In effect, an assumption is made of 4 per cent interest, compounded annually. Thus, suppose the property produces £1,000 at sale. The capital element will be the amount which if invested at 4 per cent compound interest would have produced £1,000. This will be less than £1,000, and the income will be the rest.

Where the asset produces income, the life tenant is entitled to 4 per cent of its value as interest, and if extra income is actually produced, it accrues to capital.

There is also a formula, based on an assumption of 4 per cent compound interest, for apportioning the payments of liabilities out of the fund (e.g., funeral expenses, debts of the testator) to capital and income. This formula derives from *Allhusen* v *Whittell* (1887) LR 4 Eq 295.

It seems likely that none of these formulae could easily be applied without employing the services of an accountant, to the obvious detriment of the fund. Perhaps for this reason, they are in fact frequently ignored. Another difficulty is that 4 per cent is a very low rate of return today, and it is possible that if the issue were to come again before a court, a higher rate would be considered appropriate, on the principles discussed in chapter 17. This in turn gives rise to a third problem, which is that until that occurs, trustees do not know which interest rate to apply.

It is no surprise, therefore, that the Law Reform Committee, reviewing these principles in its 23rd Report (1982), advocated their replacement with a statutory duty of a more general nature, to hold a fair balance between beneficiaries, with express power to trustees to convert capital to income and vice versa, and a duty to have overall regard to the investments of the trust. The effect of this if enacted would simplify the actuarial calculations required in these situations.

16.7.3 Duty to distribute
This has already been mentioned in 14.1.3. The remedies available to those who suffer as a result of wrongful distribution are considered in chapter 17.

SEVENTEEN

Breach of Trust

17.1 LIABILITY

17.1.1 What is breach of trust?

Generally speaking, any failure to comply with the duties laid upon the trustee by the trust instrument, if there is one, and of the obligations laid upon him by equity, as described in chapters 15 and 16, will be a breach of trust. Such failure may take the form of some positive action, such as investing in unauthorised securities, or an omission, such as neglecting to have the trust property placed in the name of the trustee. Even a merely technical act of maladministration may result in liability if in fact it causes a loss to the trust estate.

Nor, at least in the case of an express trust, does it matter how the trust was created (although the duties imposed on constructive trustees, as we saw in 16.1, may be less). Volunteer beneficiaries are entitled to have their interests protected to the same extent as those who have given consideration, and it is of no relevance either that the trust was created voluntarily by the same person who, in his capacity as trustee, is now charged with breach of trust. In other words, a settlor-trustee is liable to the same extent as any other trustee.

17.1.2 Basis of liability

The basis of a trustee's liability is compensation to the beneficiaries for whatever loss may have resulted from the breach, or, if an unauthorised profit has been made, the restoration to the beneficiaries of property rightfully belonging to the trust. The objective is not to punish the trustee and so his personal fault is immaterial once a breach is established. Of course, fault in an objective sense may be relevant to the question whether there has in fact been a breach, there being, as we have seen, a general standard of care based on normal business practice.

In many of the cases considered at 14.3, the trust had generally not suffered a large loss, and the remedy sought against the defendant was account of profits. In most of the cases considered in this chapter, the remedy sought is compensation for breach. In *Target Holdings Ltd* v *Redferns* [1995] 3 WLR 352, the House of Lords held that this is governed by principles similar to damages at common law. The plaintiffs, Target Holdings Ltd, were persuaded to advance approximately £1.5m on a mortgage, on the assumption that the selling price of the property was to be £2m. In fact the property was sold for £775,000. The defendant solicitors acted for both vendor and purchaser. They had taken the money advanced and paid it over to the purchaser and associated companies before the purchase and mortgage were executed, and in this respect (because they had paid the money away before being authorised to release it) were clearly in breach of trust with the plaintiffs.

The purchasers later became insolvent, and the plaintiffs sold the property, but for only £500,000 (so that they had lost around £1m), and sued the defendants for breach of trust. The defendants argued that the plaintiffs had suffered no loss, because the defendants had obtained for the plaintiffs exactly the mortgages to which they were entitled. The plaintiffs would have suffered exactly the same loss, whether or not the defendants had paid out the money in breach of trust. The House of Lords held in principle in favour of the defendants, that a trustee who committed a breach of trust was not liable to compensate the beneficiary for losses which the beneficiary would, in any event, have suffered if there had been no such breach. The defendants would therefore not be liable on the assumed facts, that the transaction would have gone through anyway, even in the absence of Target's advance. If the assumed facts were wrong, and Target's advance was necessary for the transaction to go through at all, then Target would be entitled to be compensated for the entire loss that they had suffered, since in that event, but for the breach of trust, nothing would have been paid over.

There are no degrees of breach, however. Liability can attach to a trustee who has acted honestly in the beneficiaries' interests, just as it can to a trustee who has acted fraudulently for his own ends. Further, since the standard of care is objective (i.e., measured against the level of competence of a notional reasonable man, rather than that of the particular trustee), liability can attach to a trustee who lacks the knowledge or skills to avoid the breach and is doing his incompetent best, if that best is not up to the objective standard required. Protection of the beneficiaries, and not the nature of the wrongdoing, is the crucial element.

The court may, however, take into account degrees of culpability in exercising its discretion to grant relief from liability (see 17.2), or in fixing the amount of interest which the trustee may be liable to pay on the sum lost to the trust estate (see 17.3.3).

17.1.3 Personal nature of trustee's liability

A trustee is liable personally for his own breach of trust, and not vicariously for breaches committed by his fellow trustees. In *Re Lucking's WT* [1968] 1 WLR 866, Lucking had committed a breach of trust in entrusting large sums of money to a manager, without adequately supervising him (14.2.2). His fellow trustee, Block, was not liable for Lucking's breach of trust, but was entitled to rely on what Lucking had told him about the company's affairs, unless he had a positive reason to disbelieve him.

However, a trustee who passively permits a breach to occur may thereby put himself in breach of his own duties because, though trustees are not required to police each other's conduct, they are expected, as we have seen, to be active in the administration of the trust. Thus, a trustee who leaves funds under the control of a fellow trustee without enquiry, or fails to take steps to obtain redress if he discovers a breach, will be in dereliction of his own duty to the beneficiaries.

We saw in 14.2.1.2, how s. 30 of the Trustee Act 1925 provides that:

A trustee . . . shall be answerable and accountable only for his own acts, receipts, neglects, or defaults, and not those of any other trustee, . . . nor for any other loss, unless the same happens through his own wilful default.

In *Re Vickery* [1931] 1 Ch 572, discussed in 14.2.1.3, Maugham J assumed that s. 30 had altered the law, at least in relation to liability for agents, for he interpreted the phrase 'wilful default' as meaning 'a consciousness of negligence or breach of duty, or recklessness in the performance of duty'. If this meaning is applied in relation to co-trustees, the section clearly confers extra protection. But *Re Vickery* concerned the liability of an executor for the default of an agent, not a fellow trustee. As we saw in 14.2 the decision has been criticised, so it is unlikely that it will be extended so as to affect what is after all the personal liability of a trustee.

Apart from *Re Vickery*, it is generally accepted that s. 30 did not alter the previous law: the section does not alter the principle that a trustee remains liable for his own acts, upon which the liability in the extract set out above is based. Under the previous law liability was incurred where a trustee handed over money without securing its proper application, or permitted a fellow trustee to recover money without enquiring what he did with it, or refrained from taking steps to obtain redress for a breach of which he was aware. It has yet to be decided whether, in these circumstances also, it will be necessary to prove that a passive trustee was guilty of 'wilful default' as defined in *Re Vickery*, but I would suggest that this is unlikely.

A trustee will not, upon accepting office, become liable for breaches committed prior to his appointment. His first steps upon taking office, however, should be to examine the documents and accounts of the trust, and if he discovers that a breach has occurred, he should take action against the former trustee to recover the loss. Failure to do so may itself amount to a breach for which he will be liable, save perhaps in the rare case where he can show that action would have been futile (because there would then be no causal relationship between the breach and the loss).

A trustee cannot escape liability for his own breach of trust by retiring from office, for even after his retirement he remains liable for breaches committed while he was in office, and his estate remains liable after his death. He will not be liable for breaches committed after the date of his retirement, unless it can be shown that he retired in order to facilitate a breach of trust (*Head v Gould* [1898] 2 Ch 250).

17.1.4 Liability as between trustees

The liability of trustees is said to be joint and several, which means that if two or more trustees are liable, a beneficiary may choose to sue some or all of them, or perhaps only one, and recoup the entire loss from those against whom he chooses to proceed. Similarly, he may levy execution against any one of them for the whole amount.

As between themselves, however, the trustees were until 1978 regarded by equity as being equally liable, so that a trustee who was compelled to pay more than his fair share of the loss could in turn enforce a contribution from the others. In enforcing equal contribution, equity disregarded any differing degrees of involvement in the breach. Thus in *Bahin* v *Hughes* (1886) 31 ChD 390 a passive trustee was liable to the same extent as an active one.

There were exceptions to the principle of equal contribution, which are unaffected by the 1978 legislation (considered below):

(a)   Where there has been fraud. A fraudulent trustee is solely liable, and can claim no contribution from the honest trustees.

(b)   Where a trustee has got money into his hands and made use of it, he will be liable to indemnify a co-trustee who is obliged to replace the funds.

(c)   Where one trustee was a solicitor and the rest relied on his judgment (*Re Partington* (1887) 57 LT 654). The mere fact that a trustee happens also to be a solicitor will not make him liable to indemnify the other trustees, for it is necessary also that the others rely on his judgment. Thus, he will not be liable if it is shown that the other trustees were active participators in the breach, and did not participate merely in consequence of the advice and control of the solicitor (*Head* v *Gould* [1898] 2 Ch 250).

(d)   Where a trustee is also a beneficiary he will be required to indemnify his co-trustees to the extent of his beneficial interest, and not merely to the extent that he has personally received some benefit from the breach (*Chillingworth* v *Chambers* [1896] 1 Ch 685). Only after that interest is exhausted will further liability be shared equally. The principle seems to be that a beneficiary may not claim any share of the trust estate until he has discharged his liabilities towards it.

The equitable position has been affected by the Civil Liability (Contribution) Act 1978. Under this Act, any person liable in respect of damage suffered by another person, including damage arising from breach of trust, may recover a contribution from any other person in respect of the same damage. By s. 2(1) the amount of the contribution is:

> such as may be found by the court to be just and equitable having regard to the extent of that person's responsibility for the damage in question

and may by virtue of s. 2(2) amount to a total indemnity. The Act therefore gives the court a discretion (but not a mandatory duty) to depart from the rule of equal distribution and have regard to degrees of fault.

The Act does not apply to the limited number of exceptions to the general equitable principle described above, and may indeed not affect the equitable position at all, since it is left to the court to determine what is 'just and equitable'. One other situation is clearly unaffected by the 1978 Act. If all the trustees were involved in a fraud, equity would not allow those who paid the damages to claim any contribution from the rest, on the ground that a plaintiff could not base a claim upon his own wrongdoing. The 1978 Act makes no special provision for such a case, but though the court is theoretically free to exercise its discretion in allocating liability to contribute, it is inconceivable that a fraudulent trustee would be allowed to sue.

Where some but not all of the trustees are excused from liability under s. 61 of the Trustee Act 1925 (see 17.2.5), it would seem to follow that those who are not excused can claim no contribution from them. Under the 1978 Act, the excused trustees would seem not to be persons who are liable in respect of any damage, so presumably the court cannot direct them to make contribution.

17.1.5 Criminal liability of trustees

In the course of a breach of trust criminal offences may be committed, but breach of trust is not of itself a criminal offence. There used to be a difficulty about theft, because the trustee as legal owner of the trust property could not be guilty of stealing it, and a special offence of conversion by a trustee had to be created in order to make him punishable. Under the Theft Act 1968, he may now be guilty of ordinary theft, however, by virtue of s. 5(2).

17.1.6 Bankruptcy of a defaulting trustee

If a trustee who is liable for a breach becomes bankrupt, the claim in respect of the breach is provable in his bankruptcy. His duties towards the trust are not affected by his bankruptcy, so the odd situation arises whereby he has a duty (as trustee) to prove in his own bankruptcy (as debtor to the trust). If he fails to do this, he commits a further breach of trust which is not affected by any subsequent discharge from bankruptcy and he will be liable to the trust for the resulting loss (i.e., dividend that he would have received in the bankruptcy).

17.2 QUALIFICATIONS TO LIABILITY AND DEFENCES

17.2.1 Consent or participation by beneficiaries

A beneficiary who consents to or participates in a breach of trust will not usually be able to succeed in a claim against the trustees, even if he has obtained no personal benefit from the breach. The consent or participation of one beneficiary will not, of course, prevent those who did not consent from claiming, and if it is uncertain which beneficiaries have consented, the court may order an inquiry. No particular form of consent is required.

To be effective, consent must be that of an adult who is *sui iuris* and not acting under an undue influence which prevents him from making an independent judgment. In *Re Pauling's ST* [1964] Ch 303, trustees of a marriage settlement had made a series of advances in breach of trust because the trustees did not ensure that the moneys advanced were used for their proper purpose (see further 16.5.2.3). A wide range of defences was argued, both before Wilberforce J and in the Court of Appeal, but on this issue several of the payments which went to benefit the parents were presumed to have been the result of undue influence over the children. Whether undue influence has been exercised is a question of fact, depending on circumstances. The trustees will not be liable if it cannot be shown that they knew, or ought to have known, that the beneficiary was acting under such influence.

In *Re Pauling's ST* itself, the Court of Appeal held that where a presumption of undue influence existed, as between a parent and child who was still subject to parental influence (albeit a child who had reached his or her majority), an advance to the child which was given to his or her parents, could not be retained by the parent unless it was clear that:

(a)   the gift was the spontaneous act of the child; and
(b)   the child knew what his or her rights were. It was also desirable that the child had obtained independent and, if possible, professional advice.

In this regard, the courts treat with suspicion gifts from children to their parents, whereas the reverse was true of gifts the other way round (see e.g., the presumption of advancement, 8.3).

Consent involves more than mere awareness of what the trustees are proposing to do. Otherwise, trustees could protect themselves by simply telling the beneficiaries beforehand. In *Re Pauling's ST* [1962] 1 WLR 86, Wilberforce J (at p. 108) explained that:

[T]he court has to consider all the circumstances in which the concurrence of the cestui que trust was given with a view to seeing whether it is fair and equitable that, having given his concurrence, he should afterwards turn round and sue the trustees.

He went on to say that it is not necessary that the beneficiary should know that what he is concurring in is a breach of trust, provided that he fully understands what he is concurring in. Nor is it necessary that he should personally benefit from the breach. This statement of the law was neither approved nor disapproved by the Court of Appeal in *Re Pauling's ST* itself [1964] Ch 303, but was approved by the Court of Appeal in *Holder* v *Holder* [1968] Ch 353, in which a beneficiary was held unable to set aside a sale after affirming it and accepting part of the purchase money.

17.2.2   Release or acquiescence by beneficiaries

A beneficiary will also be unable to succeed in his claim if, on becoming aware of the breach, he acquiesced in the breach or released the trustee from liability arising therefrom. A partial defence succeeded on the basis of the acquiescence doctrine in *Re Pauling's ST* [1964] Ch 303 (see 17.2.1).

Release suggests some active waiver by the beneficiary of his rights. A waiver requires a positive act which is intended to be irrevocable. It is like making a gift and, as with gifts, no consideration need move from the donee (in this case the trustee). As with consent, there need not be any particular formalities and release may even be inferred from conduct.

If a release cannot be shown, it may still be possible to show that the beneficiary acquiesced in the breach. It is usually accepted that the acquiescence doctrine is based on an implied contract, whereby the beneficiary is taken to have agreed not to rely on his rights. The evidence required for this intention to be inferred is less than in the case of release, and the doctrine is often applied where a beneficiary has done nothing to pursue his claim.

Delay in making the claim is not in itself evidence of acquiescence, but where the length of time between the breach and the claim is very great, slight additional evidence will suffice. As in the case of consent, the release or acquiescence must be that of an adult who is *sui iuris*.

Undue influence or lack of full knowledge will prevent the trustee from relying upon these defences, the test being as in the consent doctrine, above.

17.2.3 Impounding the beneficiary's interest

The court has an inherent power to impound the interest of a beneficiary, thus providing the trustee with an indemnity to the extent that the beneficiary's interest will suffice to replace the loss to the trust.

The power can arise where a beneficiary has merely consented to the breach, but only if some benefit to him can be proved, and then only to the extent of that benefit. If the beneficiary has gone further, and actually requested or instigated a breach, the power can be exercised whether or not he has received a personal benefit from the breach.

Needless to say, the trustee has to show that the beneficiary acted in full knowledge of the facts, but it is not necessary to show that he knew that the acts he was instigating or consenting to amounted to a breach.

There is also a statutory discretion to impound. Section 62(1) of the Trustee Act 1925 (replacing an earlier enactment) provides:

> Where a trustee commits a breach of trust at the instigation or request or with the consent in writing of a beneficiary, the court may, if it thinks fit, make such order as to the court seems just, for impounding all or any part of the interest of the beneficiary in the trust estate by way of indemnity to the trustee or persons claiming through him.

The courts seem to have treated this largely as a consolidating section, rather than extending their powers, except that Wilberforce J in *Re Pauling's ST (No. 2)* [1963] Ch 576 thought that it gave an additional right, among other things, to deal with a married woman beneficiary. This additional right is no longer necessary, because of changes in legislation on family property, and that part of the section was repealed in 1949.

The effect of the court making an order impounding a beneficiary's interest is that the beneficiary is not only debarred from pursuing his own claim against the trustee, but also liable to replace the losses suffered by the other beneficiaries, to the extent ordered by the court, and perhaps up to the full value of his own interest. To this extent, the trustee is protected at the beneficiary's expense.

The discretion is a judicial discretion, and though the section appears to extend the inherent power of the court by giving a discretion to impound a beneficiary's interest regardless of whether he obtained a benefit, it has received a restrictive interpretation. It seems that the court will make an impounding order in any case where it would have done so before the Act; generally speaking, in any case where the beneficiary has actively induced the breach (for which it has never been necessary to show benefit).

It must, of course, be shown that the beneficiary was fully aware of what was being done. In *Re Somerset* [1894] 1 Ch 231, a beneficiary had urged the trustees to invest in a mortgage of a particular property, but had left them to decide how much money they were prepared to invest. Lindley MR said (at p. 265):

> In order to bring a case within this section the cestui que trust must instigate, or request, or consent in writing to some act or omission which is itself a breach of trust, and not to some act or omission which only becomes a breach of trust by reason of want of care on the part of the trustees.

The words 'in writing' have been held to apply only to consent, and not to instigation or request (*Griffith* v *Hughes* [1892] 3 Ch 105). So a request or instigation need only be oral.

The power to impound will not be lost upon an assignment of the beneficial interest. Nor is it lost when the court replaces the trustees in consequence of the breach. In *Re Pauling's ST* [1962] 1 WLR 86, the trustees resisted removal because they were claiming an indemnity out of the interests of the parents. Wilberforce J held that they were entitled to such indemnity and that this would be unaffected by their replacement. They were therefore unable to use this as a ground for continuing in office: see *Re Pauling's ST (No. 2)* [1963] Ch 576.

Apart from statute, it is the practice, where trustees have under an honest mistake overpaid a beneficiary, for the court to make allowance for the mistake in order to allow the trustee to recoup as far as possible (*Re Musgrave* [1916] 2 Ch 417). An overpaid beneficiary is not compelled to return the excess but further payment may be withheld until the accounts are adjusted.

If a payment is made by mistake to someone who is not entitled, the trustee may recover on an action for money had and received if the mistake was one of fact, but not if it was a mistake of law (*Re Diplock* [1947] Ch 716). It is also certain that the error must be corrected where trustee-beneficiaries overpay themselves.

17.2.4 Lapse of time

Lapse of time may protect a trustee in one of two ways. By the Limitation Act 1980, limits are set upon the time within which certain actions for recovery may be brought, while in cases not covered by statutory limitation, a defendant may rely upon the doctrine of laches.

17.2.4.1 Limitation Act 1980 By s. 21(3) of the Limitation Act 1980, any action by a beneficiary to recover trust property or in respect of any

breach of trust (other that situations covered by the self-dealing and fair-dealing rules) must be brought within six years from the date on which the right of action accrued.

A right of action in respect of future interests is not treated as having accrued until the interest falls into possession: this was also part of the *ratio* in *Re Pauling's ST* [1964] Ch 303 (see 17.2.1).

Under s. 21(1), no period of limitation applies where the action is in respect of any fraud to which the trustee was a party, or privy, or where (in summary) it is sought to recover from the trustee trust property still in his possession, or the proceeds of sale of such property. Protection is also lost where the trustee converts trust property to his own use. Conversion to the trustee's own use, however, implies application in his own favour, so that if the funds have been used to maintain an infant beneficiary, or dissipated by a fellow trustee, the protection of limitation remains available.

Where fraud is the issue, this must be fraud by the trustee himself. In *Thorne* v *Heard* [1894] 1 Ch 599 a trustee was protected by a section in similar terms of an earlier Act, where he had left trust funds with a solicitor who had embezzled them, the trustee himself being no more than negligent. Where the trustee is in possession of trust property or its proceeds, however, no dishonesty need be shown. Fraud for these purposes is wider than common law fraud or deceit, but nevertheless requires unconscionable conduct on the part of the trustee, something in the nature of a deliberate cover up: in *Bartlett* v *Barclays Bank Trust Co. Ltd (No. 1)* [1980] Ch 515 (14.1.2), the bank was held able to rely on what is now s. 21(1) of the 1980 Act, in respect of income lost outside the limitation period, since, being unaware that it was acting in breach of trust, it could not be guilty of fraud for these purposes.

Section 22 prescribes a limitation period of 12 years for actions in respect of any claim to the personal estate of a deceased person. It is often hard to determine at what point executors have completed the administration of an estate and become trustees, but it is thought that the 12-year period will apply although for all other purposes the executors would be regarded as trustees.

Plaintiffs under disability are permitted an extended period in which to bring an action by s. 28, and by s. 32, where fraud, concealment or mistake is alleged, time runs only from the point when the plaintiff discovers the fraud or mistake, or could with reasonable diligence have discovered it.

It should be noted that a person other than a bona fide purchaser for value without notice who receives property from a trustee also falls within these rules.

17.2.4.2 Laches Where no statutory limitation period applies, the defendant may rely on the equitable doctrine of laches, that is, he may show that it would be unjust to allow the plaintiff to pursue his claim in view of the time that has elapsed since it accrued. The court has a discretion to allow or refuse the defence, and mere delay may suffice, but, where possible, the courts have preferred to regard delay as furnishing evidence of acquiescence by the plaintiff.

17.2.5 Section 61 of the Trustee Act 1925

This section gives the court a wide discretion to excuse honest and reasonable trustees from liability for breach of trust. It applies also to executors. The section provides:

> If it appears to the court that a trustee . . . is or may be personally liable for any breach of trust, whether the transaction alleged to be a breach of trust occurred before or after the commencement of this Act, but has acted honestly and reasonably, and ought fairly to be excused for the breach of trust and for omitting to obtain the directions of the court in the matter in which he committed such breach, then the court may relieve him either wholly or partly from personal liability for the same.

Dishonesty will obviously disqualify a trustee from obtaining relief, but a trustee is also required to act 'reasonably'. The standard applied appears to be the same as that for breach of trust itself, that of the prudent man of business in relation to his own affairs, and the bank failed on this test in *Bartlett* v *Barclays Bank Trust Co. Ltd (No. 1)* [1980] Ch 515 (see 14.1.2). Failure to obtain directions might be thought to fall below this standard, but the section implies that relief may nonetheless be granted.

Unauthorised investments appear to be the most common circumstances in which applications are made, and it may not be easy to show that this sort of risk-taking meets with the standard of the prudent business person. Reasonable conduct may be more easily shown where the breach consists in some error made in the course of a complex administration. Professional trustees may claim the protection of the section, but the courts have been less ready to excuse failure where a high standard of expertise is professed by the trustee. See again *Bartlett* v *Barclays Bank Trust Co. Ltd (No. 1)* [1980] Ch 515.

It may be that, even if the trustee is shown to have acted honestly and reasonably, the question of whether he ought fairly to be excused will be separately considered.

17.3 PERSONAL REMEDIES AGAINST TRUSTEES

All the usual equitable remedies (described in chapter 19) are available to guard against breach of trust, so it is possible, for example, to prevent such a breach by injunction. This section deals with the problems where a financial remedy, for example, an account of profits, is sought once a breach has been committed.

17.3.1 Measure of liability

This is the actual loss to the trust estate which arises, directly or indirectly, from the breach, usually with interest. Where an unauthorised profit has been made, the trustees must account for this profit, but this will be the limit of their liability. It should also be noted that the trustees are liable only for losses which arise causally from a breach of trust. They are not required to act as insurers for the beneficiaries, and any losses which arise despite the exercise of due diligence on the part of the trustees must be borne by the trust estate.

Subject to the above limitations, assuming the plaintiff can establish a causal connection between the breach and the loss, there are no rules governing remoteness of damage such as apply in tort or contract. Inquiries as to what a reasonable trustee ought to have foreseen or contemplated are not relevant in this context. This may not matter as much as in, for example, a tort action, because the spectre of virtually unlimited liability, such as could occur in a negligence action, for example, if a cigarette end negligently thrown away causes a large ship to explode, is unlikely to arise. The value of the trust property, and profits from its use, provide a natural limit to liability without the need for additional remoteness rules, but trustees could find themselves in difficulties where, for example, the property unexpectedly increases in value. Nor, incidentally, can a trustee set off against the amount which he is obliged to restore to the trust funds the tax which would have been payable on that amount, had he not lost it through his breach (*Re Bell's Indenture* [1980] 1 WLR 1217).

Further, a trustee cannot set off a profit made in one transaction against a loss made in another. The reason is that any profits made out of the trust property belong to the beneficiaries, so the trustees have no claim against those profits to lessen their own liability for loss caused by a breach. A frequently quoted authority is the old case of *Dimes* v *Scott* (1828) 4 Russ 195.

If the profit and loss can be seen to be part of the same transaction, however, the principle of *Dimes* v *Scott* will not apply. In *Bartlett* v *Barclays Bank Trust Co. Ltd (No. 1)* [1980] Ch 515 (see 14.1.2), loss had resulted from a disastrous development, but another development had produced a profit. Although acknowledging the general rule, Brightman J allowed that gain to be set off against the loss, remarking that it would be unjust to deprive the bank of an element of salvage in the disaster. The explanation was that the loss and gain arose from the same policy of speculation in the *Bartlett* case, and that, where gains and losses arise in a single dealing or course of dealing, the trustees will be liable only to the extent that a net loss results.

17.3.2 Investments

Many of the cases concern losses arising from improper use by the trustees of their powers of investment, and some specific points should be noted:

(a) If trustees make an unauthorised investment, they will be liable for any loss which is incurred when that investment is realised. There are, however, qualifications to this principle.

First, if the beneficiaries are all *sui iuris* and collectively entitled to the entire trust property, they may adopt the unauthorised investment as part of the trust property. It is not clear whether, if they do this, they may nonetheless call upon the trustees to make good any loss which arises from that investment: *Re Lake* [1903] 1 KB 439 seems to suggest that they may, but this result appears contrary to principle. If the beneficiaries do not unanimously agree to adopt the investment, the trustee's duty is to sell it and to make good any loss.

Secondly, the trustee is alternatively entitled to take over the investment for himself, subject to refunding the trust estate, the beneficiaries having a lien on the investment until the refund is made.

If an unauthorised investment brings in a greater income than an authorised one would have done, and this income has already been paid over to a beneficiary, the trustees cannot, it seems, require him to repay the excess above what he should have received, or set off this excess against future income.

Lastly, in *Nestle* v *National Westminster Bank plc* [1993] 1 WLR 1260, Staughton LJ observed that trustees will not be liable if, although they applied the wrong criteria in their choice of investments, their decision is nonetheless justifiable on objective grounds, since then there will be no loss to the trust.

(b) Where unauthorised investments are improperly retained, the measure of liability is the difference between the present value of the investment and the price it would have raised if sold at the proper time. For example, in *Fry* v *Fry* (1859) 28 LJ Ch 591 (see 16.2.5), the trustees were liable for the difference between the offer of £900 and the sum eventually obtained.

(c) If the trustees are directed by the trust instrument to make a specific investment, and either they make no investment at all, or else they invest the fund in something else, their liability is to supply the same amount of the specific investment as they could have acquired with the trust funds had they purchased it at the proper time. Account will, however, be taken of any payments which the trustees would have had to make regarding the investment if they had acquired it at the correct time.

Where the trustees are given a choice of investments but make no investment at all, they will only be liable to replace any deficit in the trust fund, with interest. This is simply because it cannot be assumed that any particular investment would have been chosen by the trustees if they had acted properly, and it is therefore impossible to base their liability upon the value of any particular investment.

(d) A trustee who uses trust money in his own business will be liable to hold any profit which he makes as a constructive trustee for the beneficiaries, or to account for the money with interest, whichever happens to be the greater. If he mixes trust money with his own, the beneficiaries may demand the return of the trust money with interest, or else claim a share in the profits proportionate to the amount of the trust money employed in the venture. Any loss must, of course, be borne by the trustee, and where he has become insolvent, the beneficiaries may have a proprietary claim for the return of the trust fund, in preference to his creditors (see chapter 19).

17.3.3 Interest

Normally, a trustee will be required to replace a loss with interest. Traditionally, the rate of interest was 4 per cent, which was in line with the rate produced on old-style trustee securities, but this is now recognised as unrealistic, and the proper rate at present appears to be that allowed from time to time on the court's short-term investment account established under s. 6(1) of the Administration of Justice Act 1965 (*Bartlett* v *Barclays Bank Trust Co. Ltd (No. 1)* [1980] Ch 515).

A trustee may be liable for a higher rate, at the discretion of the court. If he has actually received more than the standard rate, he will be liable for what he has actually received. Similarly, if it can be shown that he ought to have received more than he did, he will be liable for what he should have received, for example, where proper investment producing a higher rate has been wrongfully terminated. Traditionally, if the trustee was guilty of fraud or other active misconduct, the rate was raised from 4 per cent to 5 per cent, on the presumption that this represented what he had actually received. On the same presumption, compound interest may be charged nowadays, and it seems that this will be a matter of course if the trustee was under a duty to accumulate. Despite the frequent reiteration that higher rates are charged merely as reflecting the actual gain made by the defaulting trustee and not by way of penalty, the extent of the trustee's misconduct may be a relevant factor in the court's exercise of its discretion (see *Wallersteiner* v *Moir (No. 2)* [1975] QB 373).

EIGHTEEN

Variation of Trusts

18.1 INHERENT EQUITABLE JURISDICTION

As a general rule, as we have seen, trustees are bound to carry out the settlor's wishes, and any deviation from the terms of the trust will amount to a breach of trust. Nonetheless, circumstances may arise in which an extension of the trustees' powers, or even a substantial alteration in the beneficial interests of the trust, would be desirable in the interests of efficient administration, or for the sake of preserving the value of the beneficiaries' entitlements.

The main reason for wishing to vary trusts is to reduce liability to taxation, and that is what this chapter is really about. Yet although equity permits trustees discretion, as we have seen, in many aspects of performing the trust, it does not generally allow them to recast its terms. Until recent statutory reforms, therefore, powers to vary have been extremely limited, especially where tax planning is the motive.

There are nevertheless circumstances apart from those provided for by statute where variation is possible.

18.1.1 Express powers to vary
Obviously the trust instrument itself may have been drafted so as to confer upon the trustees powers far wider than those contemplated by the general law. Modern trust instruments generally contrive to allow the trustees considerable discretionary powers, and not uncommonly provide for variation of the beneficial interests themselves, by means of suitably drafted powers of appointment. The terms of such powers must, of course, be strictly observed, but it is often possible through careful drafting to obviate the need for recourse to more complex variation procedures. Reliance upon express powers contained in the trust instrument, needless to say, creates no exception to the duty not to deviate from the terms of the trust, for such powers are themselves among the terms of the trust.

18.1.2 *Saunders v Vautier*
In the absence of express powers, it may be possible to effect a variation in the trust by taking advantage of the rule in *Saunders* v *Vautier* (1841) 10 LJ Ch 354. Collectively, the beneficiaries, so long as they are all adult, *sui iuris*

and between them entitled to the entirety of the trust property, can bring the trust to an end and resettle the property on any terms they wish. Thus, in a simple settlement of property upon a life interest for X with remainder for Y, X and Y may agree to end the trust and divide the capital between them immediately. More complex settlements may require more sophisticated measures, involving perhaps the actuarial valuation of future entitlements, and possibly the need for insurance against any risk of loss, but the principles are basically the same.

The beneficiaries can also collectively consent to any act by the trustees which has the effect of varying the terms of the trust, without going through the process of dissolving and resettling the property which may involve a number of separate conveyances, all attracting stamp duty. It is very important, however, to appreciate the limits of the *Saunders* v *Vautier* doctrine.

First, it depends on the beneficiaries all being collectively entitled. Thus, donees under a power cannot use it, and though beneficiaries under a discretionary trust usually can, they will not be able to unless the entire class of objects is ascertainable. Secondly, it turns upon all the beneficiaries being able to consent to dissolve the trust, or to what would otherwise be a breach of trust by the trustees. If some of the beneficiaries are infants, or if the settlement creates any interests in favour of persons who are not yet born or ascertained, variation of the trust upon this basis will not be possible. This is a serious limitation when dealing with family settlements of the usual type, which almost invariably give interests to non *sui iuris* persons. As will appear below, this is the difficulty tackled by the Variation of Trusts Act 1958.

Thirdly, unless the trustees also agree, the beneficiaries cannot vary an existing trust, and keep it on foot, instead of dissolving it and resettling the property. *Re Brockbank* [1948] Ch 206 has already been discussed in 15.1.4.4. Although the *ratio* of the case is confined to the appointment of new trustees under s. 36 of the Trustee Act 1925, there are remarks by Vaisey J of a much wider scope:

> It seems to me that the beneficiaries must choose between two alternatives: either they must keep the trusts of the will on foot, in which case those trusts must continue to be executed by trustees . . . not . . . arbitrarily selected by themselves; or they must, by mutual agreement, extinguish and put an end to the trusts.

Walton J expressed similar views in *Stephenson* v *Barclays Bank Trust Co. Ltd* [1975] 1 WLR 88. One of the reasons he gave was that otherwise the beneficiaries could force upon the trustees duties quite different to those they had originally accepted.

18.1.3 Limited inherent jurisdiction of courts to vary trusts
The problem arises with persons unable to give consent, especially children and unborn persons. As will shortly be explained, the Variation of Trusts Act 1958 confers upon the court a discretion to give its approval to a proposed variation on behalf of such persons if the court is satisfied that such a

variation would be for their benefit. Before considering the effect of that Act and other statutory provisions, however, it is necessary to outline the extent to which the courts have traditionally been willing to permit a variation of trust under their inherent jurisdiction, where not all beneficiaries are adult and *sui iuris*.

It has long been recognised that the court may, in the case of necessity, permit the trustees to take measures not authorised by the trust instrument. In *Chapman* v *Chapman* [1954] AC 429, the House of Lords indicated that this inherent jurisdiction is narrow, encompassing for the most part only emergency and salvage. Originally, this seems to have been confined to cases where some act of salvage was urgently required, such as the mortgage of an infant's property in order to raise money for vital repairs. Gradually, it was widened to cover other contingencies not foreseen and provided for by the settlor, but the House of Lords reaffirmed in *Chapman* v *Chapman*, unanimously approving the formulation of Romer LJ in *Re New* [1901] 2 Ch 534, that some element of emergency still needs to be shown.

Chapman v *Chapman* applies only to variations in the *beneficial interests* as such. There is a wider inherent jurisdiction regarding the administration of the trust fund. For example, in *Re Duke of Norfolk's ST* [1982] Ch 61, the court authorised payment of remuneration to a trustee under its inherent jurisdiction. See further 14.3.2.

The courts may also approve compromises of disputes regarding the beneficial entitlements on behalf of infant or future beneficiaries. Arguably, this is not a matter of genuine variation of the trust, since by definition its terms are not clear: hence the dispute. The courts, however, showed a willingness to extend the term 'compromise' to cover situations where no real dispute had arisen, and approval was sometimes granted to what were, in reality, mere variations worked out between the beneficiaries. This broad conception of the inherent jurisdiction was firmly disapproved by the House of Lords in *Chapman* v *Chapman*, and held to be confined to instances where a genuine element of dispute exists.

Thus, in *Re Powell-Cotton's Resettlement* [1956] 1 All ER 60, the Court of Appeal decided that there were no disputed rights where an investment clause was ambiguous and it would have been advantageous to the beneficiaries to replace it with a new clause. In *Mason* v *Farbrother* [1983] 2 All ER 1078, genuine points of difference were found to have arisen where two contending interpretations of an investment clause had widely different implications for the permitted range of investments. The court, however, was reluctant to approve the substitution of a new clause under its inherent jurisdiction, preferring to rely upon s. 57 of the Trustee Act 1925 (see 18.2.3). In *Allen* v *Distillers Co. (Biochemicals) Ltd* [1974] QB 384, the court was asked to approve a settlement of the claims of the child victims of the drug thalidomide, and the question arose as to whether the court could postpone the vesting of capital in the children to an age greater than 18. Eveleigh J, on the basis of the rule in *Saunders* v *Vautier*, held there was no inherent jurisdiction to order such a postponement, but found it to be authorised by the terms of the settlement itself.

Clearly, therefore, the inherent equitable jurisdiction is of limited value to those whose main motive for variation is to reduce liability for taxation.

18.2 STATUTORY POWERS TO VARY TRUSTS APART FROM THE VARIATION OF TRUSTS ACT 1958

18.2.1 Matrimonial Causes Act 1973

The narrowness of the court's inherent jurisdiction to give approval to variations in the terms of trust is offset by several statutory provisions. A particularly useful and important addition to the jurisdiction was made by the Matrimonial Causes Act 1973, which, by ss. 24 and 25, gives a wide power to make orders affecting the property of parties to matrimonial proceedings, so as to avoid the unfairness which sometimes arose where the property of a married couple, in particular the matrimonial home, came under the rules governing resulting trusts (see 8.10). The court may order provision for either spouse to be made by payments in cash, by transfers of property or by the creation of a settlement for the benefit of a spouse and children.

More important in the context of variation, s. 24(1)(c) and (d) allow for variation of an ante or post-nuptial settlement, including settlements made by will or codicil, and also permit the making of an order extinguishing or reducing the interest of either of the spouses under such a settlement. The term 'settlement' has been widely interpreted to include any provision (other than outright gifts) made for the benefit of the parties to a marriage, whether by themselves or by a third party, and the acquisition of a matrimonial home has been held to be a settlement (*Ulrich* v *Ulrich* [1968] 1 WLR 180). Further, the court has the power to vary or discharge any order for a settlement or variation under s. 24(1) made on or after a decree of judicial separation if the separation order is rescinded or the marriage subsequently dissolved.

18.2.2 Mental Health Act 1983

The power given by s. 96(1)(d) of the Mental Health Act 1983 to the Court of Protection to make a settlement of a patient's property also allows the judge to vary the settlement as he thinks fit if it transpires that some material fact was not disclosed when the settlement was made, or if substantial changes in circumstances arise. See 6.6.2.

18.2.3 General powers in the 1925 legislation

The above provisions are designed to meet rather special situations. More general powers may be made available to trustees by virtue of provisions contained in the Trustee Act 1925 and the Settled Land Act 1925. Section 57(1) of the Trustee Act 1925 in effect widens the inherent jurisdiction with regard to 'emergency' by making the jurisdiction available in any case where it is 'expedient':

> (1) Where in the management or administration of any property vested in trustees, any sale, lease, mortgage, surrender, release or other disposition, or any purchase, investment, acquisition, expenditure, or other

transaction, is in the opinion of the court expedient, but the same cannot be effected by reason of the absence of any power for that purpose vested in the trustees by the trust instrument, if any, or by law, the court may by order confer upon the trustees, either generally or in any particular instance, the necessary power for the purpose, on such terms, and subject to such provisions and conditions, if any, as the court may think fit and may direct in what manner any money authorised to be expended, and the costs of any transaction, are to be paid or borne as between capital and income.

The section operates as though its provisions were to be read into every settlement, but it is clearly limited to matters falling within the management or administration of the trust property and does not permit the alteration of beneficial interests under the trust.

Applications under the section are usually heard in chambers and so are not generally reported, but the few reported cases show that it has been used to authorise a sale of settled chattels, to partition or sell land where necessary consents had been refused, to purchase a residence for the tenant for life, and to sell prematurely a reversionary interest.

Settlements of land do not fall within s. 57(1) of the Trustee Act 1925, but they may be varied by recourse to s. 64(1) of the Settled Land Act 1925, which allows the court to make an order authorising the tenant for life to effect any transaction affecting or concerning the settled land or any part of it, if the court is of the opinion that the transaction would be for the benefit of the settled land or any part of it, or of the persons interested under the settlement. The transaction must be one which could have been effected by an absolute owner. The section is not confined to cases of management or administration alone, although it includes such purposes and allows alteration of the beneficial interests with a view to reducing tax liability. In the days of estate duty, the especial vulnerability of the strict settlement to onerous charges might be mitigated by rearrangement of the beneficial interests under this section.

This section was invoked by Morritt J in *Hambro v Duke of Marlborough* [1994] Ch 158, to allow the eleventh Duke of Marlborough (as tenant for life) to execute a conveyance the effect of which was to disinherit the Marquis of Blandford, who (the trustees had concluded) displayed unbusinesslike habits and lack of responsibility.

The Settled Land and Trustee Acts (Court's General Powers) Act 1943, as amended by the Emergency Laws (Miscellaneous Provisions) Act 1953, permanently extends the court's jurisdiction to authorise the expense of any action taken in the management of settled land or land held on trust for sale in the context of ss. 57 and 64 to be treated as a capital outgoing where the action is beneficial and the income insufficient to bear the expense.

The inherent jurisdiction to make provision for infants is somewhat extended by s. 53 of the Trustee Act 1925, which allows the court to authorise dealings with the infant's property with a view to application of the capital or income for the infant's maintenance, education or benefit. 'Benefit' has been interpreted to cover dealings having the effect of reducing estate duty for the benefit of the infant (*Re Meux* [1958] Ch 154).

In that case, the proceeds of sale of property were to be resettled upon the infant, and so could be regarded as an 'application' for the infant's benefit. However, in *Re Hayworth's Contingent Reversionary Interest* [1956] Ch 364, a proposal to sell an infant's contingent reversionary interest to the life tenant for cash, thus ending the trusts, was thought not to be for the 'benefit' of the infant. Other types of dealing approved under the section have included the barring of entails to exclude remote beneficiaries (*Re Gower's Settlement* [1934] Ch 365) or to simplify a proposed application to the court for approval of a further variation under the Variation of Trusts Act 1958 (*Re Bristol's Settled Estates* [1965] 1 WLR 469).

18.3   VARIATION OF TRUSTS ACT 1958

The decision of the House of Lords in *Chapman* v *Chapman* [1954] AC 429 curtailed, as explained above, the broad approach previously developed by the courts in the exercise of the inherent jurisdiction to approve compromises or 'disputes', and the Law Reform Committee was asked to consider the question of the court's powers to sanction variations (see Law Reform Committee, *Court's Power to Sanction Variation of Trusts* (Cmnd 310, 1957)). The Variation of Trusts Act 1958 was based on these recommendations and provides a new statutory jurisdiction independent of the Trustee Act 1925 or the Settled Land Act 1925.

Under s. 1(1) of the 1958 Act, the court has discretion to approve, on behalf of the following categories of person, any arrangement varying or revoking all or any of the trusts, or enlarging the trustees' powers of management and administration over the property subject to the trusts. The categories are as follows:

(a)   infants or people who are mentally incapacitated, or
(b)   people who have a mere expectation of benefiting under the trusts, but those with interests, whether vested or contingent, should consent on their own behalf (see further below), or
(c)   any person unborn, or
(d)   any person with a discretionary interest of under a protective trust.

Proposals to vary the beneficial interests under a trust may be approved, provided (except in the case of para. (d) persons) that the court is satisfied that such variation will be for the benefit of the persons on behalf of whom approval is given. In deciding whether to approve a proposed settlement, the court will consider the arrangement as a whole since it is the arrangement which has to be approved and not just those aspects of it which happen to affect a person on whose behalf the court is being asked to consent.

18.3.1   Use of the 1958 Act
Where an extension of the trustee's powers of management is sought, the jurisdiction of the Act is invoked in preference to s. 57 of the Trustee Act

1925 wherever possible. The courts have shown themselves willing to approve the insertion of powers of advancement or a period of accumulation, or to terminate an accumulation, among other matters.

So far as investment is concerned, in *Trustees of the British Museum* v *Attorney-General* [1984] 1 WLR 418, Sir Robert Megarry V-C took the view that the powers conferred by the Trustee Investments Act 1961 (see 16.6.2) were becoming outdated, and that the effects of inflation and the character of the trust may amount to special circumstances in which it would be proper to give approval under the 1958 Act. The decision was based on the changes of investment pattern, including the movement from fixed interest investments to investments in equities and property, that had occurred between 1961 and 1983.

The reasoning is by no means of universal application, however, and indeed, Sir Robert Megarry V-C's judgment is in quite restricted terms. At the time of the case, investing in equities was relatively risk-free, and there had been a more or less continuous bull market for some eight years. That is not the case today. Sir Robert Megarry V-C also said:

> The size of the fund may be very material. A fund that is very large may well justify a latitude of investment that would be denied to a more modest fund; for the spread of investments possible for a larger fund may justify the greater risks that wider powers will permit to be taken.

It cannot by any means be said, therefore, that a variation beyond the terms of the 1961 Act will always be approved.

The main application of the Variation of Trusts Act 1958 has been to vary the beneficial interests for tax-saving purposes, and this has been assumed to be its natural sphere of operation. Some would argue that those who, like infants and the unborn, cannot give a valid consent to schemes which would be for their benefit, should not be deprived of the advantages which their adult counterparts could obtain on *Saunders* v *Vautier* principles; nor should their incapacity prevent the opportunity of gain to the trust as a whole.

18.3.2 Persons on whose behalf the court may give its approval

The way in which the statute works is to allow the court to give consent on behalf of non *sui iuris* beneficiaries, but the principles underlying the rule in *Saunders* v *Vautier* were preserved by the Act inasmuch as the court will not provide a consent which ought properly to be sought from an ascertainable adult, *sui iuris* beneficiary. Hence the limits placed on para. (b) of s. 1(1).

The difficulty with para. (b) arises with interests which are very remote, such as interests in default of appointment, or in the event of a failure of the trust. The subsection allows the court to consent on behalf of:

> any person (whether ascertained or not) who may become entitled, directly or indirectly, to an interest under the trusts as being at a future date or on the happening of a future event a person of any specified description or a member of any specified class of persons, so however that this paragraph

shall not include any person who would be of that description, or a member of that class, as the case may be, if the said date had fallen or the said event had happened at the date of the application to the court.

It is the words after 'so however' which cause the problem since those persons have to consent on their own behalf: the court cannot consent for them. There is no problem over, for example, potential future spouses, since they clearly have a mere expectation of succeeding. They clearly come within the first part of para. (b) and the court can consent on their behalf. But if somebody is named in the instrument as having a contingent interest, however unlikely that contingency is to arise, the court cannot consent on his or her behalf. They must consent themselves to any variation.

This can seriously limit the scope of the 1958 Act. For example, in *Re Suffert's Settlement* [1961] Ch 1, the court could not consent on behalf of a cousin who benefited only if Miss Suffert died without issue, and even then subject to a general testamentary power of appointment. Other examples are *Re Moncrieff's ST* [1962] 1 WLR 1344, and *Knocker* v *Youle* [1986] 1 WLR 934. In the latter case the court could not consent on behalf of sisters who would benefit only in the event of failure or determination of the trust, and Warner J felt constrained to adopt a fairly literal interpretation of the Act.

The application should be made by a beneficiary, preferably by the person currently receiving the income, but the settlor may also apply, and as a last resort the trustees may apply if no one else will apply and the variation is in the interests of the beneficiaries. Otherwise, it is undesirable for trustees to apply, as their position as applicants may conflict with their duty impartially to guard the interests of the beneficiaries. The settlor, if living, and all the beneficiaries, including minors, should be made parties, special attention being paid to ensure proper representation for minors and the unborn.

18.3.3   What is benefit?
The Variation of Trusts Act 1958 requires that, in general, the court must be satisfied that the arrangement will be for the benefit of the persons for whom it is consenting. Stamp J took the view in *Re Cohen's ST* [1965] 1 WLR 1229 that the benefit must be to those persons considered as individuals and not merely as members of a class. See further 18.3.3.3.

The benefit requirement does not extend expressly to a variation proposed on behalf of a beneficiary under a discretionary protective trust (s. 1(1)(d)) but the court has an unfettered discretion as to the exercise of its powers under the Act, and in *Re Steed's WT* [1960] Ch 407 the Court of Appeal refused its consent in such a case where it thought no benefit was shown.

18.3.3.1   Nature of benefit
It is not possible to state categorically what the court will regard as benefit, except that it will adopt the test of what a reasonable *sui iuris* adult beneficiary would have done in the circumstances.

Financial benefit is clearly included, and most tax-saving schemes will satisfy the requirement since such saving preserves the total quantum of property available for distribution among the beneficiaries.

In assessing financial benefit, the court may have to balance short-term against long-term factors, and take account of the character of the persons on whose behalf approval is sought. In *Re Towler's ST* [1964] Ch 158, Wilberforce J was prepared to postpone the vesting of capital to which a beneficiary was soon to become entitled, upon evidence that she was likely to deal with it imprudently. In *Re Steed's WT* [1960] Ch 407, the proposed scheme was for the elimination of the protective element in a trust relating to land. The principal beneficiary, who was a life tenant (but not *sui iuris* because of the protective element), wanted a variation such that the trustees held the property on trust for herself absolutely. Clearly this was in theory to her financial advantage, but evidence suggested that advantage would in fact be taken of the life tenant's good nature by the very persons against whose importuning the settlor had meant to protect her, and the Court of Appeal refused its consent.

It may be wondered why the court needed to be satisfied of a benefit in this case, since, as noted above, there is no express statutory requirement of benefit for para. (d) persons. However, even if it is clear that the court has jurisdiction to consent to a variation, it has an unfettered discretion to exercise its powers under the Act '*if it thinks fit*'. Thus, whereas the court obviously cannot approve a variation except where the Act so provides, it has an apparently unlimited discretion to refuse its approval where it is given jurisdiction under the Act.

Though it will be rare for the court to look beyond the financial advantages contained in the proposed arrangement, the unfettered discretion given by the Act to the courts can lead them to refuse a variation where there is a clear financial benefit. In *Re Weston's Settlements* [1969] 1 Ch 223, the Court of Appeal refused to approve a scheme which would have removed the trusts to a tax haven (Jersey), where the family had moved three months previously, on the ground that the moral and social benefits of an English upbringing were not outweighed by the tax savings to be enjoyed by the infant beneficiaries. Harman LJ said that 'this is an essay in tax avoidance naked and unashamed', and Lord Denning MR noted (at p. 245) that:

> There are many things in life more worth while than money. One of these things is to be brought up in this our England, which is still 'the envy of less happier lands'. I do not believe it is for the benefit of children to be uprooted from England and transported to another country simply to avoid tax . . . Many a child has been ruined by being given too much. The avoidance of tax may be lawful, but it is not yet a virtue.

Re Weston is perhaps atypical, and the court will not always refuse approval to the removal of a trust from the jurisdiction. It will depend on the circumstances. In *Re Windeatt's WT* [1969] 1 WLR 692, a similar scheme was approved by Pennycuick J, but there the family had already been in Jersey for 19 years and the children had been born there: there was no question of uprooting them. Similarly, in *Re Seale's Marriage Settlement* [1961] Ch 574, Buckley J approved a scheme removing the trusts to Canada, to which country again the family had moved many years previously, with no thought of tax avoidance, and had brought up the children as Canadians.

In reality, the use of the 1958 Act to export trusts is quite common, but *Re Weston* shows that all circumstances will be taken into account, and that the existence of a clear financial benefit will not necessarily be conclusive.

Another possibility, included for the sake of completeness, is that some beneficiaries will benefit at the expense of others. An example is *Re Remnant's ST* [1970] Ch 560, where Pennycuick J approved the deletion of a forfeiture clause in respect of children who became Roman Catholics. Some of the children were Protestant and others Roman Catholic, but the court approved the deletion of the clause on policy grounds (as being liable to cause serious dissension within the family) although this was clearly to the disadvantage of the Protestant children. The settlor's intentions were also not considered conclusive (indeed, they were overridden).

The courts may go further and approve schemes where there is a positive disadvantage in material terms. In *Re CL* [1969] 1 Ch 587, the Court of Protection held that there was a benefit to an elderly mental patient in giving up, in return for no consideration, her life interests for the benefit of adopted daughters. This was, in effect, giving approval to a straightforward gift by the beneficiary, from which in strictly material terms she could not possibly benefit. The lady's needs were otherwise amply provided for, however, and the court, in approving the arrangement, took the view that it was acting as she herself would have done, had she been able to appreciate her family responsibilities.

These cases should not be regarded as typical, however. Assuming that a proposed arrangement is otherwise unobjectionable, it will be rare for the court to look beyond the financial advantages contained therein.

18.3.3.2 Risks Sometimes, a proposed arrangement may involve some element of risk to the beneficiary for whom the court is asked to consent. An element of risk will not prevent the court from approving the arrangement if the risk is one which an adult beneficiary would be prepared to take. Such a test was applied by Danckwerts J in *Re Cohen's WT* [1959] 1 WLR 865.

In *Re Robinson's ST* [1976] 1 WLR 806, the fund was held on trust for the plaintiff for her life, with remainders over to her children, one of whom was under 21 (the age of majority at the time). The plaintiff was 55 and expected to live for many years. The variation proposed was to divide up the fund, giving the plaintiff an immediate capital share of 52 per cent (the actuarial capitalised value of her share), the children dividing the balance in equal shares. The children who got their share immediately, and those who were over 21 consented to the variation. The court was asked to approve variation on behalf of Nicola (who was 17).

Before the introduction of capital transfer tax in 1975 (see 16.5.2), division of the fund in this way, by giving the children their interests immediately rather than on the death of the life tenant, was almost certain to reduce liability to estate duty, because at that time there was no liability to estate duty on any advance made more than seven years before the death of the life tenant. The same is true today under inheritance tax (see 16.5.2). However, for a short period following the Finance Act 1975, which introduced capital transfer tax, all *inter vivos* gifts were also taxable, albeit that liability was lower so long as the transfer was made more than three years before the death of the life tenant.

At the time of *Re Robinson's ST,* therefore, the division would not necessarily have favoured Nicola. The transfer would have been taxed immediately so that the value of the fund would be reduced. On the other hand, Nicola would get her share immediately and not have to wait for the death of her mother. Whether this would be to her benefit or not would depend entirely on how long her mother was likely to live. If she died immediately, Nicola's share would be less than she would have received under the unvaried trust since tax would have been paid on it. It was calculated, however, that, given the mother's life expectancy, the deficiency would be made up in income on her share between the date of the variation and her mother's death.

Templeman J took the view that the court should require evidence that the infant would at least not be materially worse off as a result of the variation. He adopted as the test whether an adult beneficiary would have been prepared to take the risk: a 'broad' view might be taken, but not a 'galloping, gambling view'. The arrangement was approved subject to a policy of insurance to protect the infant's interests, but Templeman J did not require the entirety of the possible loss to be covered, the view being taken that the saving in premium on a lesser cover was worth the small risk.

A diagramatic representation of *Re Robinson's ST* can be found in figure 18.1.

Figure 18.1

Re Robinson's ST [1976] 1 WLR 806

		Mrs Robinson	Children
Before proposed variation	Capital	Life interest on 100%	Remainder on all, but subject to CTT
	Income	Income on all until death	Income on all, but only after Mrs R's death
After proposed variation	Capital	52% immediately	48% immediately, maybe lower CTT
	Income	Immediate income on 52%	Immediate income on 48%

A different type of case was *Re Holt's Settlement* [1969] 1 Ch 100. The trust provided for a life interest of personal property for Mrs Wilson, and then to her children at 21 in equal shares. The variation proposed was that Mrs

Wilson should surrender the income of one half of her life interest to the fund, but another effect of the proposed variation was to postpone the vesting of the children's interests until 30. The court was asked to approve the variation on behalf of Mrs Wilson's three children who were 10, 7 and 6.

The surrender of the income (whose real purpose was to reduce Mrs Wilson's liability to surtax) was also clearly to the advantage of the children, since the value of the trust property would be increased. However, the postponement to 30 (on the grounds that it would be undesirable for Mrs Wilson's children to receive a large income from 21) was clearly to their disadvantage. Megarry J approved the variation on the same test adopted in *Re Robinson*.

18.3.3.3 Benefit must be to individuals, not just class as a whole   In *Re Cohen's ST* [1965] 1 WLR 1229, Stamp J held that in considering questions of benefit under the 1958 Act, the court was being asked to consent on behalf of *non sui iuris* beneficiaries considered as individuals, and not merely as members of a class. It follows that if only one member of the class can be envisaged who cannot possibly benefit from the proposed variation, even if the class as a whole will benefit, the court will refuse its consent.

In *Re Cohen's ST*, the variation sought, with a view to saving estate duty, was to substitute for the death of the life tenant (who was an elderly lady), a specified date (30 June 1973) for the vesting of her grandchildren's interests. It was very unlikely that the life tenant would survive beyond 30 June 1973, although of course it was a theoretical possibility. Consent was sought on behalf of infant and unborn beneficiaries.

There was no problem regarding the infant beneficiaries, although even here, an element of risk was involved. They all stood to gain from the tax advantages of the proposed variation. If, however, the life tenant died before 30 June 1973, any infant grandchild who died between her death and the specified date would inevitably lose out (the grandchild would have taken under the unvaried, but not under the varied settlement). Also, the share of all the infant beneficiaries would be reduced if further grandchildren were born between her death and the specified date. On balance, however, these risks would be worth taking given the likely saving in estate duty (the principles applicable being those considered in the previous section).

The difficulty concerned unborn grandchildren. Although it was unlikely, it was theoretically possible for the life tenant to live beyond the specified date. Had she done so, it was also theoretically possible for an unborn grandchild to be born after 30 June 1973, but before the life tenant's death. Any such grandchild would take under the unvaried settlement, but not under the proposed variation, and therefore could not possibly benefit from the variation. Of course, the chances of *both* these events occurring were very low, and it may well be thought that the class of unborn grandchildren, as a whole, might be prepared to take the risk of the life tenant living beyond the specified date, and having further grandchildren before she died. Weighed against the tax advantages of the proposed variation, it might be thought that any reasonable unborn grandchild would be prepared to take this risk.

Stamp J held that it is not permissible only to consider the position of the class as a whole. If any individual grandchild was born after the specified date, but before the life tenant's death, then under the proposed variation, he or she would lose his or her entire interest. That individual would clearly not consent, since he or she would have no conceivable benefit. Since it was therefore possible to envisage unborn persons who could not possibly benefit, this was fatal to the proposed variation, and Stamp J refused his consent. It was not enough that the proposed variation would benefit the class as a whole, if it were possible to envisage *a single individual* who could not possibly benefit.

The argument that any unborn individual would have a greater chance of being born before 30 June 1973, because (since the life tenant was unlikely to live that long) more time would probably be available in which to be born, was also rejected on the ground that the court would not ascribe chances to a disembodied spirit. Stamp J observed:

Now it is of course perfectly true that as a result of this variation there would be a greater chance of there being some person or persons now unborn becoming beneficially interested in the trust fund [by being born], but to say that some particular unborn person will, immediately on the variation taking effect, have a better chance of being born within the qualifying period or a better chance of satisfying the necessary conditions seems to me to involve an excursion into metaphysics, on which I am unwilling to embark. Such a proposition seems to me to involve the logical conclusion that the court must regard one whose body may come into the existence in the future as having nevertheless such a present imaginary existence as to enable the court to ascribe to him a present chance of coming into existence at some specific time or during some specified period. My mind recoils at the idea of the unborn having prior to his birth such an identity as to enable the court to ascribe to him any such chance, or to enable one to say that he can more or less easily satisfy a condition of coming into existence during some particular period.

Only once birth (albeit in the future) had occurred could chances of benefit be ascribed to any individual.

Re Cohen's ST was distinguished in *Re Holt's Settlement* [1969] 1 Ch 100 (see 18.3.3.2). There, the settlement was in essence that Mrs Wilson gave up part of her income from the fund (so increasing the size of the fund), but vesting of the children's interest in possession would be postponed. If a child was born the year after the variation, and his mother died very soon afterwards, that child could not possibly benefit. The benefit from Mrs Wilson surrendering part of her income under the trust would be minimal if Mrs Wilson died soon after the birth, whereas the postponement would operate entirely to his or her disadvantage. *Re Cohen's ST* was distinguished, however, because here two chances had to occur: that of the unborn person being born next year, and secondly, that child having been born (and thus become a legal entity), his or her mother dying shortly afterwards. The first chance could be disregarded on *Cohen* principles, but not the second. Both were independently unlikely possibilities, so approval for the scheme was given. Even once the theoretical unborn child had been born, he or she would still have been well advised to agree to the variation, and accept the slight risk of his or her mother dying shortly afterwards.

It follows that the reasoning in *Cohen* applies only when the date of *vesting in interest* (or in other words the date on closing the class) is altered, and does not apply merely to alterations in *vesting in possession* (see further on this distinction, chapter 7).

It might be objected that two independent chances also had to occur in *Cohen* before an unborn beneficiary was certain to lose: first, the hypothetical beneficiary being born after 30 June 1973 and, secondly, the life tenant living beyond the date of his or her birth. However, no unborn beneficiary born after 30 June 1973 could possibly gain from the variation, and might lose, so there could be no advantage in the hypothetical beneficiary consenting to the variation. In this regard, the proposed variation in *Re Cohen's ST* differed from that in *Re Holt's Settlement*, where the hypothetical beneficiary had a good chance of benefiting from the variation.

18.3.4 Variation or resettlement?
According to Megarry J in *Re Ball's Settlement* [1968] 1 WLR 899, the courts will not approve a proposal for a total resettlement which alters completely the substratum of the trust. This is a question of substance not form.

18.3.5 Juristic basis of variation
The precise effect of the court giving its approval to an arrangement is not entirely clear. Does it merely provide consent or does the order of the court actually vary the trusts? The importance of the distinction has been greatly reduced in recent years. Until 1985, however, if all the court did was to provide consent, then any dispositions of equitable interests under the variation had to be in writing under s. 53(1)(c) of the Law of Property Act 1925, and hence attracted *ad valorem* stamp duty (see chapter 6). If the order of the court itself varied the trusts, then s. 53 was avoided, and no *ad valorem* duty was payable. With the abolition of *ad valorem* duty on *inter vivos* gifts, however, the practical significance of the juristic basis of variation effectively vanished.

In *Re Holmden's ST* [1968] AC 685, Lord Reid stated that the arrangement must be regarded as one made by the beneficiaries themselves, the court acting merely on behalf of those beneficiaries who are unable to give their own consent and approval. On this view of the matter, it seems that the adult beneficiaries at least ought to give their consents in writing so as to comply with s. 53(1)(c) of the Law of Property Act 1925.

There are two points to note about these remarks, however. First, the remarks do not form part of the *ratio* of the case, since this issue did not in fact arise. Secondly, we saw in 12.1.2 above, that even where all beneficiaries are *sui iuris* and consenting they may not be able to vary the trusts in all circumstances. This would not necessarily be a problem if the jurisdiction under the Act was regarded as being in the form of a *Saunders* v *Vautier* revocation, followed by a resettlement, rather than a variation.

In fact, however, variations are seldom in writing. In *Re Viscount Hambleden's WT* [1960] 1 WLR 82, it had been stated that the court's approval was effective for all purposes to vary the trusts, and this has been relied upon in countless subsequent instances. The problem was posed directly in *Re Holt's Settlement* [1969] 1 Ch 100, in which Megarry J, aware that possibly thousands of variations had been acted upon without writing conforming with s. 53(1)(c), accepted, though without enthusiasm, two grounds put forward by counsel in favour of the view that no writing was necessary.

First, it might be said that in conferring express power upon the court to make an order, Parliament had impliedly created an exception to s. 53. Secondly and alternatively, the arrangement might be regarded as one in which the beneficial interests passed to their respective purchasers upon the making of the agreement, that agreement itself being specifically enforceable. The original interests under the (unvaried) trusts would thus be held, from the moment of the agreement, upon constructive trusts identical to the new (varied) trusts and, as constructive trusts, would be exempt from writing under s. 53(2). Whether or not these reasons are regarded as adequate, the assumption that no writing is required has continued to prevail.

The point was also important in *Re Holt's Settlement* because the order of the court took effect after 15 July 1964, whereas the original trust had been set up in 1959, and Megarry J thought that the provisions of the Perpetuities and Accumulations Act 1964 (see chapter 7) could apply. If all the court had done had been to provide consent then the perpetuity period would have been that applicable to a 1959 instrument (i.e., the common law period).

NINETEEN

Remedies

The general principles applicable to equitable remedies have already been covered (see 1.4.5). In the first part of this chapter the personal remedies are examined in greater detail. There is no point, however, in 're-inventing the wheel', and it is reasonable to assume that students of equity and trusts are already familiar with the main equitable remedies. There is, for example, an excellent account in *The English Legal Process*, 6th edn (1996), by Terence Ingman, and there would be little point in repeating it here. In any case, space considerations do not permit more than outline discussion of the personal equitable remedies here.

The second part of the chapter deals with proprietary remedies, with which (unlike personal remedies) the student may not be familiar. Whereas a personal remedy is taken against a wrongdoer, for example, a trustee acting in breach of trust, a proprietary remedy amounts to an assertion to a right over (for example) trust property. The action will not necessarily be brought against the person responsible for the original wrong, but against a third party who has come into possession of the property. The remedy is proprietary in the sense that it goes with the property, and the liability of the third party depends upon his possession of that property.

The final part of the chapter considers the liability of third parties who may no longer be in possession of (for example) trust property, or where that property is no longer identifiable. The remedies here are again personal remedies, the third party being liable in his own right for breach of trust, as a constructive trustee.

In a review of the first edition of this book, C.E.F. Rickett objected to my linking in the same chapter remedies and constructive trusteeship: [1992] CLJ 172, 174. Undaunted, I am making the same link here. Tracing is a remedy; liability for knowing receipt is definitely based, and liability for knowing assistance possibly based, on constructive trusteeship. However, I am not intending to suggest, as Rickett thought I must thereby be suggesting, either that constructive trusteeship is in these cases really so close to tracing that it ought to be seen as remedial, or that this particular variety of constructive trust is remedial. Rather, the reason for lumping together in this chapter what may well be very disparate concepts is that the fact situations which can give rise to a tracing claim can also often give rise to a claim for knowing receipt or knowing assistance. An excellent (but by no means the only) example is *Agip (Africa) Ltd* v *Jackson* [1991] Ch 547, which is an important authority on common law and equitable tracing, and knowing receipt and knowing assistance. It might also be necessary to trace in equity, in order to establish receipt for a knowing receipt action, as in *El Ajou* v *Dollar Land Holdings plc (No. 2)* [1995] 2 All ER 213 (see further 19.2.2.5). For ease of explanation, therefore, I have decided to deal with the concepts in the same chapter, although I would accept that this might annoy conceptual purists.

19.1 PERSONAL REMEDIES

19.1.1 The range of equitable remedies
As was explained in chapter 1 (1.4.5), the primary remedy at common law is damages, which are available as of right, whereas equity developed its own range of remedies, which were discretionary. The most important equitable remedies are specific performance and the injunction, but we have also seen examples of other equitable remedies, for example, account of profits (see, e.g., 14.3.5) and rescission (see the misrepresentation section of any textbook on the law of contract).

19.1.2 Types of injunction
As was explained at the start of the chapter, the following discussion is intended to be an outline treatment only: detailed examination of the various types of injunction is beyond the scope of this book.

19.1.2.1 Prohibitory and mandatory injunctions A *prohibitory* injunction, the commonest type, simply orders the defendant to refrain or desist from doing something. A *mandatory* injunction orders the defendant to do some positive act, such as demolishing a building. A mandatory injunction is very like specific performance, but whereas specific performance usually arises out of contract, a mandatory injunction usually arises out of tort. However, it could be used to force the defendant to undo something which he has done in breach of contract.

Mandatory injunctions are uncommon, and will not be issued when damages would be an adequate remedy, or when the court would be required to exercise constant supervision. Mandatory injunctions will be issued only when it is possible to frame the order very precisely.

19.1.2.2 *Quia timet* injunctions '*Quia timet*' means 'because he fears', and this type of injunction may be granted if the plaintiff can show that there is a very real danger of substantial damage being done to his interests. The aim is to forestall the defendant from committing a wrong, and since by definition the defendant has not yet done anything unlawful, the plaintiff must make out a strong case, described in *Attorney-General* v *Nottingham Corpn* [1904] 1 Ch 673 as 'a strong probability almost amounting to moral certainty' of the threatened or apprehended infringement of the plaintiff's

rights. This type of injunction is rare, and its refusal will not debar the plaintiff from obtaining an injunction if the defendant actually goes ahead and commits the wrong.

19.1.2.3 Interlocutory injunctions

High Court cases can take many months to come to court, so courts can, through a swift procedure, grant interlocutory injunctions pending trial. These have the same effect as any other injunction, except that they last only until the full hearing.

Obviously, if an injunction is not eventually granted at the final trial the defendant may have been restrained from doing something he was perfectly entitled to do. Before 1975 it was thought that an applicant for an interlocutory injunction therefore had to prove not only that there was a serious question to be tried, but also that he had a strong prima facie case and that the balance of convenience was in favour of the grant of the remedy. The last point was likely to be satisfied if, for example, the plaintiff was likely to suffer irreparable damage, which could not be adequately compensated by an award of damages, were the defendant's actions allowed to continue until the full hearing. For example, any action which seriously affected a plaintiff's ability to trade would qualify on balance of convenience.

In *American Cyanamid Co.* v *Ethicon Ltd* [1975] AC 396, however, the matter was reviewed by the House of Lords and the requirements were relaxed. Lord Diplock noted (at pp. 407-408) that the whole point of the procedure was to allow a remedy to be granted *before* the full trial of the main issues:

> It is no part of the court's function at this stage of the litigation to try to resolve conflicts of evidence on affidavit as to facts on which the claims of either party may ultimately depend nor to decide difficult questions of law which call for detailed argument and mature considerations. These are matters to be dealt with at the trial. One of the reasons for the introduction of the practice of requiring an undertaking as to damages on the grant of an interlocutory injunction was that 'it aided the court in doing that which was its great object, *viz.* abstaining from expressing any opinion on the merits of the case until the hearing' (*Wakefield* v *Duke of Buccleuch* (1865) 12 LT 628, 629).

Yet the necessity to show a strong prima facie case meant that many of the main issues had to be decided at the interlocutory stage. He also noted that if an interlocutory injunction is wrongly granted the defendant may have a remedy at the full trial, because the plaintiff will normally be required to give an undertaking as to damages to cover that eventuality. Except in exceptional circumstances, therefore (which remain undefined), there is no longer any requirement that the plaintiff shows a a strong prima facie case. He only has to show that there is a serious question to be tried, although the balance of convenience test remains as before. In general, therefore, the merits of the case are not examined at the interlocutory stage.

Sometimes, however, the interlocutory stage is decisive, because the reality of the situation is that by the time of the full trial there will be nothing left to decide. Thus, for example, where an employer seeks to restrain strike action on the ground that it is tortious, it is unlikely that the industrial dispute will remain live until the full trial, so that success at the interlocutory stage is usually decisive. Yet it became clear as early as the decision of the Court of Appeal in *Hubbard* v *Pitt* [1976] 1 QB 142 that industrial disputes would not be treated as among the exceptional cases envisaged by Lord Diplock in *American Cyanamid*. However, in order to make the trade dispute immunities effective (which were in practice rather more extensive then than they are now), legislation (now contained in the Trade Union and Labour Relations (Consolidation) Act 1992, s. 221(2)), provided that where a defendant claimed a trade dispute immunity the court was obliged, in deciding whether or not to grant the interlocutory remedy, to consider the likelihood of a defence based upon that immunity succeeding at the full trial.

Since that legislation, which originated in the Employment Protection Act 1975, the House of Lords has held that, in cases where the interlocutory stage will in reality be decisive, the merits of the case may become a factor to be weighed up in assessing the balance of convenience. In *NWL Ltd* v *Woods* [1979] 1 WLR 1294, an interlocutory injunction was sought restraining industrial action. Lord Diplock noted (at p. 625) that *American Cyanamid*:

was not dealing with a case in which the grant or refusal of an injunction at that stage would, in effect, dispose of the action finally in favour of whichever party was successful in the application, because there would be nothing left on which it was in the unsuccessful party's interest to proceed to trial.

Cases of this kind are exceptional, but when they do occur they bring into the balance of convenience an important additional element . . . the degree of likelihood that the plaintiff would have succeeded in establishing his right to an injunction if the action had gone to trial, is a factor to be brought into the balance [of convenience] by the judge in weighing the risks that injustice may result from his deciding the application one way rather than the other.

The Court of Appeal applied these remarks in *Lansing Linde Ltd* v *Kerr* [1991] 1 WLR 251, upholding a judge's refusal to grant an interlocutory injunction to restrain a former employee from working for a competitor in alleged contravention of a restraint of trade clause in his contract of employment. The trial of the action was unlikely to occur until the period of restraint would have expired or almost expired, and the Court of Appeal held that the judge had been correct in these circumstances, in assessing the balance of convenience, to take account of the strength of the plaintiff's claim. The case should be contrasted with *Lawrence David Ltd* v *Ashton* [1991] 1 All ER 385, where the action was appropriate for a speedy trial, so that the (two-year) period of restraint would still have a significant time left to run, even after the full trial. In such cases, the Court of Appeal held that it is not open for the judge to consider the merits at the interlocutory stage, but that *American Cyanamid* should be directly applied. However, it should not be assumed that

Lansing Linde Ltd v Kerr is limited to the case where there will be nothing at all left to decide at trial, and a similar approach was adopted by Nolan LJ in *Hanover Insurance Brokers Ltd* v *Schapiro* [1994] IRLR 82, where about a third of the 12-month period of restraint would have run prior to the trial of the action. Although the earlier case was not explicitly mentioned by Dillon LJ, he was also prepared to consider the merits of the case at the interlocutory stage. Probably little more can be said than that it is a matter of degree, but clearly in restraint clause cases of this type, the length of time prior to trial is relevant to the balance of convenience issue.

19.1.2.4   *Mareva* injunctions   The *Mareva* injunction is also a form of interlocutory relief, but whose object is to prevent the defendant from removing his assets out of the jurisdiction, or otherwise dealing with them, until the action pending against him has been tried by a court. Although the original basis of the *Mareva* injunction was obscure, like the *Anton Piller* order considered below, the courts' jurisdiction now has a clear statutory footing, under the Supreme Court Act 1981, s. 37 (1) and (2) (powers of High Court with respect to injunctions and receivers), which read as follows:

> (1)   The High Court may by order (whether interlocutory or final) grant an injunction or appoint a receiver in all cases in which it appears to the court to be just and convenient to do so.
> (2)   Any such order may be made either unconditionally or on such terms and conditions as the Court thinks just.

The name *Mareva* comes from the case of *Mareva Compañia Naviera SA* v *International Bulk Carriers SA* [1975] 2 Lloyd's Rep 509 (although this is not in fact the first reported case in which the order appears). In *Mareva* itself, the plaintiffs were shipowners who time-chartered their ship, *The Mareva*, to the defendants. The hire was to be paid in instalments, but after the third instalment the defendants defaulted and claimed to repudiate the contract. The plaintiffs were afraid that the defendants would remove their assets from the jurisdiction before the plaintiffs' claim could be heard.

Since the *Mareva* injunction is a form of interlocutory relief, the courts are reluctant to allow themselves to be drawn into attempting to make a lengthy and detailed assessment of the strengths and weaknesses of the applicant's case at trial. In *Derby & Co. Ltd* v *Weldon (No. 1)* [1990] Ch 48, Parker LJ said (at p. 58):

> It is to be hoped that in future the observations of Lord Diplock and Lord Templeman [in *American Cyanamid*] will be borne in mind in applications for a *Mareva* injunction, that they will take hours not days and that appeals will be rare. I do not mean by the foregoing to indicate that argument as to the principles applying to the grant of a *Mareva* injunction should not be fully argued. With a developing jurisdiction it is inevitable and desirable that they should be. What, however, should not be allowed is (1) any attempt to persuade a court to resolve disputed questions of fact whether

relating to the merits of the underlying claim in respect of which a *Mareva*
is sought or relating to the elements of the *Mareva* jurisdiction such as that
of dissipation or (2) detailed arguments on difficult points of law on which
the claim of either party may ultimately depend.

Nonetheless, before a *Mareva* injunction can be granted, the plaintiff must
satisfy tests which are far more stringent than the *American Cyanamid* tests
considered above, the requirements being summarised by Rattee J (whose
views on the *grant* of the injunction were upheld in the Court of Appeal) in
Re BCCI (No. 9) [1994] 3 All ER 764 as follows:

> As has been said again recently by the Court of Appeal, there are three
> issues on which the court has to be satisfied before granting a *Mareva*
> injunction: (i) has the applicant a good arguable case; (ii) has the applicant
> satisfied the court that there are assets within and, where an extra-territorial
> order is sought, without the jurisdiction; and (iii) is there a real risk of
> dissipation or secretion of assets so as to render any judgment which the
> applicant may obtain nugatory?

Thus, the applicant must show a good arguable case, not merely (as in
American Cyanamid) that there is a serious issue to be tried. The second
requirement, that the applicant must show that there are assets within the
jurisdiction, are relaxed where a worldwide injunction is sought (see further
below).

Any kind of property belonging to the defendant may be the subject of a
Mareva order, and has included cars, jewels, and even aeroplanes. But the
court will not order delivery of the defendant's clothes, bedding, household
goods or tools of his trade, livestock, farm implements, or the like. The court
should take care not to put the defendant out of business or prevent him
earning his living. The remedy is also personal against the defendant, and is
not intended to give the plaintiff security so as to place him in a preferential
position in the event of the defendant's bankruptcy.

The last ten or so years have seen a number of frauds on a truly
international scale, but until recently it was thought that *Mareva* injunctions
were available only to prevent removal of assets from within the jurisdiction.
Since the jurisdiction is personal, however, as we saw in chapter 2, it should
not in principle matter where the assets are situated, and it is now clear (in
particular from *Babanaft International Co. SA v Basantine* [1990] Ch 13 and
Derby & Co. Ltd v Weldon (Nos 3 & 4) [1990] Ch 65) that *Mareva*
injunctions can be granted on a worldwide basis. However, since in reality
anybody with notice of the injunction can be affected by it, it is granted only
in exceptional circumstances, and the courts are careful to frame the order so
as to protect the position of third parties. In *Derby v Weldon (No. 1)* [1990]
Ch 48, Parker LJ said (at p. 57):

> In [exceptional] circumstances it appears to me that there is every justifi-
> cation for a worldwide *Mareva*, so long as, by undertaking or *proviso* or a

combination of both, (a) oppression of the defendants by way of exposure to a multiplicity of proceedings is avoided, (b) the defendants are protected against the misuse of information gained from the ordinary order for disclosure in aid of the *Mareva*, (c) the position of third parties is protected. Whether, ultimately, the order *in personam* will be converted into an order attaching some or all of the assets disclosed will of course depend on (i) the court here giving the plaintiffs leave to proceed in a jurisdiction in which assets have been found and (ii) the decision of the court in such jurisdiction whether to make an order.

19.1.2.5 *Anton Piller* orders These are a type of interlocutory mandatory injunction which (like the *Mareva* injunction) now derives its jurisdiction from the general power of the High Court, contained in the Supreme Court Act 1981, s. 37, to grant an injunction when it appears 'just and convenient' to do so. The order is named after the case of *Anton Piller KG* v *Manufacturing Processes Ltd* [1976] 2 WLR 162, which was the first case where the Court of Appeal approved the use of this kind of order. *Anton Piller* received House of Lords approval in *Rank Film Distributors Ltd* v *Video Information Centre* [1982] AC 380.

An *Anton Piller* order is obtained *ex parte* (i.e., in the defendant's absence), so as to catch him off his guard, and is used in cases where the court believes there is a danger that he will remove or destroy evidence in the form of documents or moveable property, such as money, papers or illegal copies of films. The evidence need not be the actual subject matter of the dispute. In addition to ordering the defendant not to move or destroy the evidence, the court may require him to allow the plaintiff to inspect the relevant evidence or property at the defendant's premises. It is not, however, a search warrant, and the defendant is merely required to allow the plaintiff to carry out an inspection of the property.

The order is very powerful and the courts are concerned to protect the interests of the defendant. As Lord Wilberforce observed in the *Rank Film* case:

Because they operate drastically and because they are made, necessarily, *ex parte* — i.e. before the persons affected have been heard, they are closely controlled by the court: see the judgment of Lord Denning MR in *Anton Piller* [1976] Ch 55, 61. They are only granted upon clear and compelling evidence, and a number of safeguards in the interest of preserving essential rights are introduced. They are an illustration of the adaptability of equitable remedies to new situations.

Among the safeguards are that the applicant shows a strong prima facie case, that the damage (potential or actual) must be very serious for the applicant, that there is a real possibility that the evidence will be destroyed, and that the injunction would do no real harm to the defendant or his case.

19.1.3 Specific performance and contracts
For breaches of most contracts the only available remedies are at common law, but sometimes (and subject to the discretionary nature of the remedy,

on which see 1.4.5) injunctions can be granted to restrain breaches of contract, and some contracts are enforceable by decree of specific performance.

Where the remedy of specific performance is granted, the court orders the party in breach to carry out his obligations under the contract. If he fails to do so, he will be guilty of contempt of court. Traditionally, the remedy has been granted only very sparingly in breach of contract cases, but that seems to be changing, and to some extent today the rigid requirements for specific performance have been abandoned in favour of the simpler requirement that specific performance be the most appropriate remedy. It seems sensible, then, to approach the question by considering some of the more rigid requirements, and seeing whether they have indeed been relaxed.

19.1.3.1 Damages not adequate remedy The traditional position is that if damages are an adequate remedy then an equitable remedy will not be available. Damages will generally be adequate in sale of goods contracts, because the buyer ought to be able to buy equivalent goods elsewhere, and indeed should do so in order to mitigate his loss (if specific performance were generally available then that would significantly weaken the contractual mitigation doctrine). However, it has long been recognised that contracts for estates and in land are enforceable in equity: e.g., *Walsh* v *Lonsdale* (1882) 20 ChD 9. Even contractual licences are specifically enforceable, as in *Verrall* v *Great Yarmouth Borough Council* [1981] QB 202. The Great Yarmouth council had agreed to hire out the Wellington Pier pavilion to the National Front, but there were elections before the date agreed for the hire. The Labour Party took control from the Conservatives and purported to repudiate the contract. The Court of Appeal held this contract to be specifically enforceable, and though it came as no surprise that contractual licences were specifically enforceable, this was the first case where that was actually part of the *ratio*.

Although specific performance is not usually available to enforce contracts for the sale of goods, it may be if the goods are unique, for example, a Van Gogh painting, or in other cases where the plaintiff could not reasonably be expected to find a substitute. Indeed, the courts are expressly empowered by the Sale of Goods Act 1979, s. 52 (re-enacting a similar provision in the Sale of Goods Act 1893), to grant specific performance of certain contracts for the sale of goods. The courts are, in general, reluctant to conclude that the goods in question are sufficiently unique. For example, in *Cohen* v *Roche* [1927] 1 KB 169, McCardie J refused to decree specific performance of a contract for the sale of a set of eight Hepplewhite chairs, on the ground that such chairs were merely ordinary items of commerce. Ordinary damages for breach of contract were awarded instead.

Arguably, there have been relaxations in recent years, where uniqueness of the goods has been held to be not the only criterion in establishing whether the plaintiff could reasonably be expected to find a substitute. For example, in *Sky Petroleum Ltd* v *VIP Petroleum Ltd* [1974] 1 WLR 576, Goulding J granted an injunction restraining the defendant from withholding supplies of petrol, in breach of his contract with the plaintiff. Although the actual remedy was an injunction, it was accepted that it amounted to a decree of specific performance. Although petrol is hardly unique, the case arose during a worldwide petrol shortage, when the plaintiff could not easily obtain supplies elsewhere. Were the remedy not granted, the plaintiff might have been forced out of business, so that it could not be said that damages were an adequate remedy. Goulding J observed:

> Now I come to the most serious hurdle in the way of the plaintiff company which is the well-known doctrine that the court refuses specific performance of a contract to sell and purchase chattels not specific or ascertained. That is a well-established and salutary rule and I am entirely unconvinced by counsel for the plaintiff company when he tells me that an injunction in the form sought by him would not be specific enforcement at all. The matter is one of substance and not of form and it is, in my judgment, quite plain that I am for the time being specifically enforcing the contract if I grant an injunction. However the *ratio* behind the rule is, as I believe, that under the ordinary contract for the sale of non-specific goods, damages are a sufficient remedy. That, to my mind, is lacking in the circumstances of the present case. The evidence suggests, and indeed it is common knowledge, that the petroleum market is in an unusual state in which a would-be buyer cannot go out into the market and contract with another seller, possibly at some sacrifice as to price. Here, the defendant company appears for practical purposes to be the plaintiff company's sole means of keeping its business going, and I am prepared so far to depart from the general rule as to try to preserve the position under the contract until a later date. I therefore propose to grant an injunction.

Beswick v *Beswick* [1968] AC 58 is another case where damages were considered inadequate, and specific performance granted to the estate, even though the obligation was only to pay money (an annuity). The problem was that the annuity was to be paid to a third party, and damages to the contracting party would therefore have been nominal only (because he personally had suffered no loss). There are, however, other justifications for the remedy in *Beswick* v *Beswick*. Lord Pearce thought that damages would not have been an adequate remedy even had it been an ordinary two-party contract, because a single award of lump sum damages is not appropriate where the contractual obligation had been to provide a continuing annuity. Further, the contract satisfied the mutuality requirement, since the obligation of the innocent party (whose personal representative was suing) was to transfer the goodwill of a business, and if he had failed to do so specific performance could have been awarded against him.

If, however, the courts regard the fact that a contract is intended to benefit a third party *per se* as a strong ground for the grant of the equitable remedy, then that provides support for the view that the requirements for specific performance have been relaxed.

19.1.3.2 Remedy discretionary It may be relevant to observe that specific performance will not be awarded where it is not the most appropriate remedy, and this may follow from the discretionary nature of the remedy. The

remedy of specific performance is, in principle, available to enforce a contract
for the sale of land, but it will not be granted, for example, where due to some
special circumstance to grant specific performance would be grossly unfair to
the defendant. *Wroth* v *Tyler* [1974] Ch 30 concerned a contract to sell a
bungalow, for which specific performance would normally be available. As far
as both parties to the contract knew, the only encumbrance on the title was
the vendor's mortgage, which would ordinarily not matter as the vendor
would use the purchase price to pay it off. Unfortunately, the vendor's wife
objected to moving, and subsequently tried to stop the sale by entering a
notice of her right of occupation under the Matrimonial Homes Act 1967.
This put the vendor into an impossible position, since in order to fulfil his
contract he would have had to sue his own wife in order to get the notice
removed, and he withdrew from the sale. Megarry J refused to grant specific
performance, and awarded the purchaser damages instead, which were based
on the difference between the market value of the bungalow at the date of the
contract and its value at the date of the judgment (since house prices had
risen considerably in in the meantime, the award was substantial).

19.1.3.3 Not granted where constant supervision required   A one-off
sale is one thing, but an order requiring the defendant to perform a series of
acts over a period of time is quite another. The courts have no machinery for
exercising continuous supervision to make sure that the defendant carries out
an order, and rather than risk the law being flouted, they will refuse to grant
an order in such circumstances.

In *Ryan* v *Mutual Tontine Westminster Chambers Association* [1893] 1 Ch
116, the lessor of a flat agreed in the lease that he would appoint a porter
who would be constantly in attendance to clean the passages, deliver mail,
etc. In fact, he appointed a porter who also worked as a chef in a nearby club,
and who was constantly absent. The plaintiff sought specific performance,
but the Court of Appeal held that his only remedy was damages for breach
of contract: the court would not attempt to supervise the daily goings-on in
a block of flats.

Contracts to build or repair will not normally be specifically enforced. This
is partly because the courts will not supervise, but also because the wronged
party can normally find another builder to do the work (in other words,
damages are an adequate remedy, on the principles discussed in the previous
section). Nevertheless, there are exceptional cases where specific performance
has been awarded. One such case was the Court of Appeal decision in
Wolverhampton Corporation v *Emmons* [1901] 1 KB 515, where the plaintiff
corporation had actually sold the land to the defendant, who had contracted
to erect a number of buildings on the land, in pursuance of a scheme of street
improvement. The defendant had defaulted on his obligations regarding the
buildings, but as purchaser had gone into possession of the land, so that the
corporation could not have sent in a different firm of builders without
committing a trespass. In this case, the court held that the corporation could
not be adequately compensated by damages, and ordered the defendant
actually to carry out the work. Another material factor was that the building

obligations had been defined in detail in the contract, so that the court could see what was the exact nature of the work required.

There are also a number of old cases involving railway companies. If the company had built a railway through a farmer's land, having undertaken to build a bridge to allow the farmer to go from one part of his farm to another, the courts used to regard damages as an inadequate remedy, and decree specific performance. The most important single factor in these cases is that the defendant is in possession of the land, so that it is impossible for the injured party to provide for the work to be done by other means.

19.1.3.4 Mutuality requirement In any case involving land the contract is specifically enforceable by *both* parties (vendor as well as purchaser), and generally speaking any contract which is specifically enforceable by one party is also specifically enforceable by the other. This is termed the mutuality requirement, and though there are exceptions, a common ground for specific performance of a contract being refused is that the contract could not be similarly enforced by the other party.

In *Flight* v *Bolland* (1828) 4 Russ 298, for example, a minor failed to obtain a decree of specific performance, since specific performance will not normally be ordered *against* a minor. A contract is specifically enforceable, however, as long as there is mutuality at the date of trial — it does not matter if mutuality did not exist at the time the contract was made. In *Price* v *Strange* [1978] Ch 337, the defendant had agreed to grant to the plaintiff a lease, which contained a provision that the plaintiff should carry out internal and external repairs. The courts will not normally enforce a contract to repair, so there was no mutuality at the time the contract was made. However, by the time of the trial, the plaintiff had carried out the internal repairs and although the external repairs had been carried out by the defendant, the plaintiff had expressed willingness to pay for them. By the time of the trial, therefore, repairs were no longer an issue, and the only question was whether the agreement to grant the lease should be enforced. The Court of Appeal held that mutuality was now satisfied, and that specific performance could be granted.

An exception to the mutuality requirement is that a victim of misrepresentation may enforce a contract, even though the contract could not be enforced against him because the misrepresentation would entitle him to avoid the contract.

19.1.4 Damages in lieu of injunctions and specific performance

19.1.4.1 Damages in lieu of specific performance Before the Chancery Amendment Act 1858, the Court of Chancery had no power to grant damages in lieu of specific performance, and a disappointed plaintiff was obliged to start his action all over again in the common law courts to recover damages. The 1858 Act gave the Chancery courts power to award damages in lieu, or even in addition to, specific performance. Additional damages are only awarded if there has been some special damage to the plaintiff.

The 1858 Act was repealed in 1883, but the power to award damages was preserved through a series of later enactments, and is now to be found in the Supreme Court Act 1981, s. 50.

Like specific performance itself, damages granted in lieu of specific performance are discretionary, and the plaintiff will only be able to obtain equitable damages where the court could have granted him specific performance at the date when the action was begun.

19.1.4.2 Damages in lieu of injunction As with specific performance, a court can award equitable damages in lieu of an injunction, by virtue of the same section of the Supreme Court Act 1981. Since in this event, the defendant is able to carry on as before, subject only to a payment of damages to the plaintiff, the court must take pains to ensure that the defendant cannot use damages in lieu simply as a licence to continue committing a wrong.

In *Shelfer* v *City of London Lighting Co.* [1895] 1 Ch 287, A.L. Smith LJ took the view that damages should be awarded in lieu only where the injury to the plaintiff was small, was capable of being estimated in money terms, and would be adequately compensated by a small payment, and where it would be oppressive to grant an injunction. The Court of Appeal there granted an injunction restraining excessive vibration, despite the fact that this might interfere with electricity supplies.

The *Shelfer* principles are obviously open to interpretation (for example, what is meant by small?), but the courts are generally very reluctant to grant damages in lieu, especially where a continuing trespass, or a continuing nuisance is complained of. For example, in *Kennaway* v *Thompson* [1980] 3 WLR 361, the Court of Appeal set aside the trial judge's refusal to grant an injunction against power-boat racing, where damages of £16,000 were awarded in lieu, and substituted an order restricting the racing to certain times and limited noise-levels.

19.2 TRACING

The remedies so far considered have been personal remedies, against the wrongdoer himself as an individual. The issues considered in this section differ in that the defendant is not the original wrongdoer. For example, money which has been stolen from the plaintiff may have found its way into the hands of the defendant, who may not have been in any way involved in the original theft. The defendant may nevertheless be liable if the plaintiff can trace the property into his hands.

In this section, we distinguish between common law and equitable tracing, and also between personal and proprietary claims. A proprietary tracing claim involves the plaintiff in identifying his property in the hands of the defendant. It is necessary for the defendant not only to have received but also to retain the plaintiff's property. Hence, if the defendant no longer has the property, a proprietary tracing claim will not be available. However, a proprietary claim is essential if the defendant is bankrupt, and is also useful if the property has increased in value, since the plaintiff by identifying the property can benefit from its increase in value.

At common law, there is also the action for money had and received. This is a personal claim, which requires the plaintiff to show only (subject to the complete and partial defences described below) that the defendant received the plaintiff's property, and not necessarily that he still retains it. Though it is conceptually entirely different from a proprietary tracing action, it is nevertheless usually described as a form of common law tracing, and is considered in this section. There is also a personal form of equitable tracing, which is more conveniently dealt with in 19.3, along with the other personal claims in equity.

A personal claim arises from the receipt by the defendant of the plaintiff's property, and the defendant remains liable even if he later divests himself of it, or indeed if the property is destroyed or is no longer identifiable. It is no use if the defendant is bankrupt, and unlike a proprietary claim, a personal claim will not allow the plaintiff to recover increases in the value of the property.

Knowing receipt (considered in 19.3) requires that the defendant has received property to which the plaintiff has equitable title. In order to establish this, it may be necessary to trace it into the defendant's hands using a proprietary equitable claim, as in *El Ajou* v *Dollar Land Holdings plc (No. 2)* [1995] 2 All ER 213 (see further 19.2.2.5).

19.2.1 Tracing at common law

19.2.1.1 Proprietary tracing at common law As we observed in 1.4.6, legal title is, in principle, enforceable against anybody in the world, and it might therefore be thought that if the plaintiff can establish that the defendant has his property, he should be able to recover it. However, whereas the common law developed an action for the recovery of a specific piece of land, it never extended this 'real' remedy to allow a plaintiff to recover a specific chattel. Although the common law acknowledged the plaintiff's ownership of the chattel, his action was a personal action in detinue, the remedy for which was damages. The defendant could therefore choose whether to return the plaintiff's chattel or pay him its full value as damages.

The Common Law Procedure Act 1854, s. 78, gave the court a discretion to order specific delivery of the chattel, and this power is retained by s. 3 of the Torts (Interference with Goods) Act 1977. But there is no absolute right to the return of the chattel. The importance of the proprietary claim lies rather in the fact that it entitles the plaintiff to the full value of the chattel, in preference to the claims of the defendant's other creditors.

The common law also concluded that the plaintiff's right should continue even if the defendant had exchanged the plaintiff's property for some other property, or sold it and purchased other property with the proceeds. So long as it was possible to 'trace' his original property — that is, to show that what the defendant now holds can be regarded as simply a substitute — his claim was unaffected. In *Re Diplock's Estate* [1948] Ch 465 (see 19.2.2.3), Lord

Greene MR explained the doctrine in terms of the plaintiff ratifying the wrongful sale of purchase, to enable the legal owner to claim the substitute.

In *Taylor* v *Plumer* (1815) 3 M & S 562, Sir Thomas Plumer had handed over money to a stockbroker with instructions to purchase exchequer bonds, but the stockbroker instead purchased American investments and bullion, and attempted to abscond with these. He was caught before he could leave England, and the investments and bullion were seized by Plumer. The assignees of the stockbroker then brought an action to recover them from Sir Thomas, but failed. The investments and bullion were held to be Sir Thomas's own property. In effect, Plumer's money was traced into the investments and bullion for, according to Lord Ellenborough at p. 575, 'the product of or substitute for the original thing still follows the nature of the thing itself, as long as it can be ascertained as such'.

Two other points need to be made about the substitution doctrine. First, if it depends on ratification, the plaintiff is equally entitled not to ratify the transaction and instead to claim the original property. Secondly, where (for example) money is paid into a bank account, at any rate where it is unmixed with other money, it is exchanged for a cause of action against the bank. In *Diplock*, Lord Greene MR thought that there was no reason why the common law would not allow the substitution of the money into the cause of action, and *vice versa*:

> If it is possible to identify a principal's money with an asset purchased exclusively by means of it, we see no reason for drawing a distinction between a chose in action such as a banker's debt to his customer and any other asset. If the principal can ratify the acquisition of the one, we see no reason for supposing that he cannot ratify the acquisition of the other.

This passage was approved by Millett J in *Agip (Africa) Ltd* v *Jackson* [1990] 1 Ch 265, but he thought that it was limited to following an asset into a changed form in the same hands, rather than following the same asset from one recipient to another. Millett J did not think that it necessarily followed that the common law allowed free tracing of causes of action from one person to another. See further below, 19.2.2.3.

19.2.1.2 Money had and received The proprietary tracing claim considered above depends upon the plaintiff being able to trace his actual property, or as in *Taylor* v *Plumer* its product or substitute, into the defendant's hands. In the case of currency, title will pass to the recipient, but the law imposes upon the recipient of (say) money stolen from the plaintiff an obligation to reimburse the plaintiff with an equivalent sum. From the recent House of Lords decision in *Lipkin Gorman* v *Karpnale Ltd* [1991] 2 AC 548, and in particular the speech of Lord Goff, the basis of the action appears to be that the defendant has been unjustly enriched at the expense of the plaintiff. The claim is established merely by showing that the defendant has received the plaintiff's property. The defendant's knowledge (or lack of it) is irrelevant. Nor is the action defeated by the recipient later disposing of the money, or mixing it with his own money, since the claim is a personal and not a proprietary one. It is defeated, however, if the recipient has not been unjustly enriched. Innocently to receive stolen money in return for full consideration is not to be unjustly enriched at all, so that for example, a shop which has innocently taken stolen money to pay for its goods is not liable to the victim of the theft.

Consideration recognised by the common law must be provided, however. In *Lipkin Gorman* v *Karpnale Ltd* [1991] 2 AC 548, Cass, a partner in the appellant firm of solicitors, by cashing cheques of which he was an authorised signatory, stole a large sum of money from the firm's clients' account. He took the cash to the Playboy Club, which was owned by the respondents, whereupon he gambled it away. The appellants successfully claimed the club's winnings from Cass, although property in the money had undoubtedly passed to the respondents and they no longer had the money. The owners of the club were unable to claim that they had provided consideration for the money, since contracts by way of gaming and wagering were rendered null and void by the Gaming Act 1845, s. 18. Gambling contracts were therefore not contracts for consideration.

Two further points arise from *Lipkin Gorman*. First, the plaintiffs (the firm of solicitors) never had legal title to the money in the clients' account, only a debt (i.e., a cause of action) against the bank. The House of Lords held that they were entitled to trace the cause of action, however, since that was a species of legal property (but see the criticism of this by Margaret Halliwell [1992] Conv 124). On the tracing of causes of action see further below, 19.2.1.3. There is, I would suggest, another possible explanation of the cause of action in *Lipkin Gorman*. There was nothing apparently wrong with the cheques that Cass presented to the bank, and the bank was entitled to pay him the money, as it did. But there is no reason to suppose that title to the money, which had, after all, been obtained by virtue of his position in the plaintiffs' firm, passed to Cass. The correct analysis must surely be that he drew out the plaintiffs' money, which he used to gamble at the Playboy Club.

Secondly, the case establishes a change of position defence to the restitutionary common law claim, where the defendant has altered his position in good faith, so that it would be inequitable to require him to make restitution or restitution in full. This defence was used in *Lipkin Gorman* to limit the plaintiffs' right to recover to the net winnings taken by the casino, rather than all the money gambled by the thief. Paying out money as winnings constituted a change of position by the club.

The change of position defence was applied by Tuckey J in *Bank Tejarat* v *Hong Kong and Shanghai Banking Corporation (Ci) Ltd and Hong Kong and Shanghai Bank Trustee (Jersey) Ltd* [1995] 1 Lloyd's Rep 239. Bank Tejarat had been induced, by a fraudulent transaction, to advance money (under a bankers' documentary credit) to the account of the fraudsters (CAK) at Hong Kong and Shanghai Banking Corporation (Ci) Ltd. Hong Kong later paid the money, in pursuance of an apparently legitimate instruction, to one Madame Parvin Farzaneh, a lady in Paris. When the fraud was discovered, Bank Tejarat sued Hong Kong for money had and received. They failed because they were unable to establish that Hong Kong had ever received any of their money (see 19.2.1.3), but also because Hong Kong had a change of position defence, having paid the money away, in good faith, before receiving any notice of Tejarat's claim.

It is not yet clear whether the change of position defence applies only to money had and received, or to any of the restitutionary claims considered in this and the following section.

It is also not clear what happens when money is paid to a second recipient, but Millett argues (convincingly, I would suggest) in (1991) 107 LQR 71, at p. 79, that since the action is personal and not proprietary, what happens to the money after it has been received by the first recipient is irrelevant. It becomes the property of the first recipient, and any subsequent recipient will be receiving the first recipient's money, rather than that of the plaintiff. It ought also to follow that the first recipient will be liable only to reimburse the value of what was received, and if he makes a favourable investment with it, he should be able to keep the benefit of that. There is, at the time of writing, very recent Court of Appeal opinion, apparently to the contrary, in *Trustee of the Property of F.C. Jones and Sons (a firm)* v *Jones, The Times*, 13 May 1996, but only the judgment of Nourse LJ — Millett and Beldam LJJ decided the case as a proprietary tracing case.

19.2.1.3 Identification of property at common law The main constraint on common law tracing is establishing that what the defendant has, or in the case of the money had and received claim, what he received, was in fact the plaintiff's property. While *Taylor* v *Plumer* (19.2.2.1) shows that tracing is available where a straightforward exchange of the property has occurred, the position is more complicated where the property or its proceeds have been placed into a bank account, and it is in this area where equitable rules appear to be more generous (see 19.2.2.1). However, as we saw in 19.2.1.1, in *Re Diplock's Estate*, Lord Greene MR saw no reason in principle why money should not be substituted for a chose in action, or *vice versa*, at any rate where the entirety of the money was substituted for a chose in action, for example where it was used to open a bank account in which there was no other money.

The leading authority is *Banke Belge pour L'Etranger* v *Hambrouck* [1921] 1 KB 321. Hambrouck, who was a cashier, stole cheques from his employer, altered them so as to make it appear that they were drawn by his employer on the plaintiff bank to Hambrouck's order, and used them to pay money into a new account (at Farrow's Bank) which he opened specifically for the purpose. Farrow's Bank collected the proceeds from the plaintiff bank and credited them to Hambrouck's account. Hambrouck then paid various sums, by cheque, from this account to Mlle Spanoghe, with whom he was living, either for no consideration, or in consideration for her future cohabitation, a consideration which would not be recognised at common law. She paid the cheques (and no other money) into a deposit account of her own at a different bank (London Joint City and Midland Bank). Mlle Spanoghe later spent most of the money in this account, but £315 remained, and the Court of Appeal held that the plaintiff bank was entitled to trace this money.

It is difficult precisely to ascertain the *ratio* of *Banque Belge* since the three judgments differ considerably. Scrutton LJ apparently took the view that the money could not be traced at common law, since it changed its identity when paid into the account at Farrow's Bank, but could be traced in equity (as is undoubtedly the case: see 19.2.2). Bankes LJ felt that tracing at common law was permissible, but only because the proceeds of Hambrouck's fraud had never been mixed with any other money, either at Farrow's or Mlle Spanoghe's bank. Atkin LJ appeared to take the view that the question of the property's identification was the same in common law and equity, in which case common law tracing would be possible even into mixed funds (on the same basis as in 19.2.2.2).

The orthodox view (but see Goode (1979) 95 LQR 360), is probably that of Bankes LJ, and it is impossible to support Atkin LJ's view in the light of the Court of Appeal decision in *Agip (Africa) Ltd* v *Jackson* [1991] Ch 547, considered further below. Bankes LJ appeared to treat the claim as a proprietary claim at common law. Clearly, the plaintiff bank started with legal title to the money, and since Bankes LJ rejected the proposition that the money passed between the banks as currency, the money would have remained the property of the plaintiffs when it was transferred to Hambrouck's account at Farrow. It is not clear that any cash was transferred from Farrow to London Joint City and Midland Bank (Mlle Spanoghe's bank), so presumably the plaintiffs could not continue to follow the money itself. However, since there was no other money in Hambrouck's account, they could presumably convert the money into the causes of action represented by the cheques, and convert back again into the money in Mlle Spanoghe's account (where again, there were no other funds). Bankes LJ did not accept that title ever passed to Mlle Spanoghe, so this must have been a proprietary common law tracing claim (since title passes with a money had and received claim — in any case, there would have been no reason to limit a personal claim to the £315 remaining in the account).

There are, however, serious restrictions on this analysis, which limit the value of common law tracing of money. We have observed the requirement in *Re Diplock* that the money must be exclusively converted into the cause of action, and *vice versa*. This implies (as Bankes LJ accepted) that if, at any stage, the plaintiff's money had become mixed with other funds belonging to Hambrouck or the defendant, it would have been impossible to trace it at common law. The common law will not trace into mixed bank accounts. Since mixing will often occur where funds are misappropriated, this severely curtails the usefulness of tracing at common law.

Another limitation was suggested by Millet J in *Agip (Africa) Ltd* v *Jackson* [1990] 1 Ch 265, that whereas the common law will substitute causes of action for tangible property, and *vice versa*, as long as the property remains in the same hands, it can only follow a physical asset, such as a cheque or its proceeds, from one person to another. Without the cheque, in other words, it would have been impossible to follow the chose in action it represented into Mlle Spanoghe's account. The inability to trace money into and out of mixed bank accounts, and to follow causes of action except where they are represented by a physical asset, such as a cheque, was fatal to the common law tracing claim (for money had and received) in *Agip (Africa)* itself.

In *Agip (Africa)*, the plaintiff company's chief accountant fraudulently altered payment orders which had been signed by an authorised signatory of the plaintiff, altering the name of the payee to that of a company (Baker Oil) of which the defendants were directors and shareholders. The forged payment order (for over US$ half a million) was taken to the Banque du Sud in Tunis, which debited the plaintiff's account and sent telexed instructions to a London bank (Lloyds) to credit the account which Baker Oil had there. The Banque du Sud also instructed its correspondent bank (Citibank) in New York to reimburse Lloyds with an equivalent sum. Lloyds duly credited Baker Oil with US$ 518,000, of which about US$ 45,000 remained in the account. The plaintiffs sued Baker Oil at common law for the full amount received by them. Had the claim succeeded it would have been irrelevant that Baker Oil had subsequently disposed of all but about US$ 45,000 of the money, but the plaintiffs failed to show that the money received by Baker Oil was the same money that had left the Banque du Sud. Both Millett J and Fox LJ in the Court of Appeal (which upheld Millett J's decision) held that the money could not be traced through the New York clearing bank system, since there it clearly became mixed with other money.

Since Lloyds must surely have had a contractual claim against the Banque du Sud at the latest when they had received and acted upon the telexed payment order, and Baker Oil a cause of action against Lloyds, the alternative would have been to trace the causes of action from Agip to Baker Oil, but at first instance Millett J distinguished between a payment order and a cheque, commenting that the payment order never moved from Tunisia, and that nothing passed between Tunisia and London but a stream of electrons. The common law can only follow a physical asset, such as a cheque.

Fox LJ did not adopt Millett J's distinction, relying instead upon the fact that Lloyds had credited the money to Baker Oil before it was reimbursed with the plaintiff's money. They thereby took a delivery risk, Fox LJ commenting that whereas the Banque du Sud could be regarded as having paid with the plaintiff's money, Lloyds must be regarded as having paid Baker Oil with its own (Lloyds') money, since at the time of payment it had no other money with which to pay. The money in Baker Oil's account could not therefore be identified as the plaintiff's money. This, however, would seem to be merely an additional reason why the *money* could not be traced through the New York banks. It does not explain why Agip could not follow the causes of action, and it is necessary to adopt Millett J's distinction to do that.

Millett J's reasoning was applied by Tuckey J in *Bank Tejarat* v *Hong Kong and Shanghai Banking Corporation (Ci) Ltd and Hong Kong and Shanghai Bank Trustee (Jersey) Ltd* [1995] 1 Lloyd's Rep 239, the facts of which have been set out at 19.2.1.2. As in *Agip (Africa)*, the money was paid by telegraphic transfer, through clearing banks, and for the same reason a common law tracing claim failed. Bank Tejarat also failed successfully to argue that since (as is common in documentary credit transactions) they had paid against presentation of a draft (i.e., a bill of exchange), that operated similarly to a cheque. The draft was not being used, as a cheque would be, as the method of making the payment. Its presentation to the plaintiff bank was merely the trigger for payment, so the analogy with the cheque failed. Tuckey J observed that:

> The simple answer to this submission is that the drafts were not the means by which Tejarat paid their money to CAK. The payment out of Tejarat's account . . . was probably made by telex instructions . . . (a stream of electrons). It was certainly not made by the drafts, so there is nothing from which Tejarat can trace.

Note incidentally that, since the common law does not recognise equitable interests in property, a beneficiary under a trust cannot follow trust property in the hands of a trustee, although he can in equity compel the trustee to trace the property at common law, where it has fallen into the hands of a third party.

19.2.2 Proprietary tracing in equity

Unlike the common law action for money had and received, tracing in equity is a proprietary claim. The plaintiff is claiming an equitable title to property in the hands of the defendant, so the remedy extends only to property in the hands of the defendant. If the defendant has parted with the property an equitable tracing action will fail (but see 19.3 on other possibilities for continuing liability).

Because the claim is proprietary, it will not be available if the property has ceased to be identifiable, for example where it has been dissipated, or where its identity has been lost by being mixed in a manufacturing process. An equitable tracing claim can also be defeated by transfers to third parties who give value and do not have the requisite knowledge to be bound (see further 19.2.2.5), whereas of course the common law recognises no such limitation. This is an application of the notice doctrine in 1.4.6.3; in *Agip (Africa) Ltd* v *Jackson* [1990] 1 Ch 265, Millett J held that the plaintiff's funds could be traced in equity into the hands of anyone still in possession of the funds, except for a *bona fide* purchaser for value without notice of the trust (this was not an issue when the case went to the Court of Appeal [1991] Ch 547). Note that it follows that an equitable claim will persist against a volunteer for as long as he retains the property, even if he has come by it innocently (i.e., without notice of the plaintiff's interest): see the discussion of *Re Diplock's Estate* at 19.2.2.3.

Both common law and equitable rights can in some circumstances exist simultaneously, of course, and plaintiffs often sue in the alternative (as in *Agip (Africa)* itself).

19.2.2.1 Identification of property in equity

When tracing in equity it is easier to establish that what the defendant has is the plaintiff's property. Thus, the equitable right is available not only in the common law situations where the plaintiff can identify his property *in specie*, or point to a fund representing its proceeds, but also where the defendant has created a mixed fund, and even when this fund has itself been converted into other property. The reason given in *Re Diplock* was that whereas common law ratification works only where it is possible to identify precisely which property is substituted for which other property, and therefore has no application where property is inextricably mixed, as in a mixed fund, equitable tracing works by the declaration of a charge on the property, which is not defeated by mixing.

In *Agip (Africa) Ltd* v *Jackson* (see 19.2.1.2) the plaintiffs were able to trace the money in equity (through the New York banking system, where it had certainly become mixed with other money), although the common law did not recognise that the money received by Baker Oil was the same money that had been stolen by the fraudster. The claim, being a proprietary claim, however, was only for the US$ 45,000 remaining in the account, not the entirety of the US$ 518,000 originally received, unlike the common law claim, which was personal, and was therefore for the entire amount.

Because tracing in equity works by the declaration of a charge on the property, in *Re Diplock* [1948] Ch 465 it was held that the remedy will not be granted where a charge upon the property would be inequitable, as where an innocent volunteer has spent the money on alterations or improvements on his land, or indeed in paying off mortgages or other loans on the property. In such cases, the imposition of a charge enforceable by sale would be unreasonable (not to mention the practical difficulties arising where the land is, e.g., a hospital). Of course, if the common law change of position defence also applied to equitable tracing claims, it would provide an alternative way of achieving the same result.

The reasoning in the last paragraph depends on the sale being unreasonable. It would not be if the innocent volunteer had mixed trust money with his own in order to make a purchase, since the sale would simply put him back into the position that he was in before receiving the trust money.

As we saw in 1.4.6.5, equity acts in personam. In *El Ajou* v *Dollar Land Holdings plc* [1993] 3 All ER 717, Millett J, whose decision on this point was upheld by the Court of Appeal ([1994] 2 All ER 685), held that it was possible to trace property through civil jurisdictions, such as Panama, which did not recognise equitable tracing, so long as the defendant was within the jurisdiction. It does not matter where the property actually is, therefore.

19.2.2.2 Requirements for fiduciary relationship

Unlike tracing at common law, tracing in equity requires that at some stage there must have existed a fiduciary relationship of some sort which was sufficient to give rise to an equitable proprietary right in the plaintiff. The clearest case is that of the relationship of trustee and beneficiary, so that in breach of trust cases there is no problem. As we saw in 14.3.1, agents and bailees (and others) may also occupy a fiduciary position.

The requirement of a fiduciary relationship for tracing in equity is not easy to justify in principle, because it means that a mere equitable owner may have a better action than someone who is both legal and equitable owner of property (since there will always be a fiduciary relationship in the former case, with the trustee). Thus a beneficiary can always trace in equity — someone who is both legal and equitable owner can do so only if he can find an additional fiduciary relationship.

The requirement appears to have arisen by historical accident. The original authority for tracing into mixed funds was *Re Hallett's Estate* (1880) 13 ChD 696, on which see further 19.2.2.4, which involved mixing by a trustee. The principle was extended in *Sinclair* v *Brougham* [1914] AC 398, from which (because the speeches of their Lordships differ substantially) it has always been difficult to extract a clear *ratio*, and indeed the case has recently been overruled in *Westdeutsche Landesbank Girozentrale* v *Islington London Borough Council* [1996] 2 All ER 961. However, as the case was interpreted in *Re Diplock's Estate*, the mixing was done by a fiduciary, and the case was interpreted as authority for the requirement of an initial fiduciary relationship. In *Re Diplock's Estate*, the plaintiffs also succeeded on a personal claim, on which see 19.3.5, so it might be thought arguable that remarks on the proprietary tracing claim were *obiter*, except that the proprietary remedy was necessary for the interest claim. *Re Diplock* was accepted by Millett J in *Agip (Africa)* as Court of Appeal authority for the requirement, and it has in any case been reiterated by the Privy Council in *Re Goldcorp Exchange* [1995] 1 AC 74, and most recently by the Court of Appeal in *Trustee of the Property of F.C. Jones and Sons (a Firm)* v *Jones, The Times*, 13 May 1996, so the requirement appears to be entrenched, whether or not justified on the basis of any coherent principle.

In *Chase Manhattan Bank NA* v *Israel-British Bank (London) Ltd* [1981] Ch 105, the plaintiff mistakenly paid a sum of money twice to the defendant, and on the defendant's liquidation was able to trace the money mistakenly paid into the hands of the liquidators. There was no fiduciary relationship initially between plaintiff and defendant, but Goulding J held it sufficient that a fiduciary relationship arose as a result of the mistaken payment. Nor need the fiduciary relationship exist between the parties to the action, so long as it originally existed. The usual authority is the important case of *Sinclair* v *Brougham* [1914] AC 398, but it also follows from *Re Diplock* [1948] Ch 465, considered above, where an action was successful against a volunteer.

In *Agip (Africa)*, Millett J observed that:

> In [*Chase Manhattan*] however, equity's assistance was not needed in order to trace the plaintiff's money into the hands of the defendant; it was needed in order to ascertain whether it had any of the plaintiff's money left. The case cannot, therefore, be used to circumvent the requirement that there should be an initial fiduciary relationship in order to start the tracing process in equity.

The general proposition, then, is that it is necessary for the fiduciary relationship to exist before the tracing process starts. In *Agip* itself, therefore, it was necessary to show a fiduciary relationship before the money got into the New York clearing system. However, as Tuckey J observed in *Bank Tejarat*, Millett J's analysis of *Chase Manhattan* is wrong, since the money became mixed (in another bank account) before it reached the defendant. Tuckey J therefore concluded that where a payment is made under a mistake of fact (in *Bank Tejarat* itself the bank had been deceived into thinking that the shipping documents tendered to it represented goods that had been shipped, whereas in fact they were simply forgeries), a fiduciary relationship arises as soon as the money has been paid out; it is not delayed until it has been actually received by the recipient. If *Chase Manhattan* is correct, then it must be authority for that proposition, but in *Re Goldcorp Exchange* [1995] 1 AC 74, the Privy Council refused to express an opinion on whether the case was correctly decided, so it cannot be assumed to be unassailable authority.

Millett has argued in (1991) 107 LQR 71, at pp. 75–76, that the fiduciary requirement is not particularly problematic in fraud cases, 'since the embezzlement of a company's funds almost inevitably involves a breach of fiduciary on the part of one of the company's employees or agents', as indeed in *Agip (Africa)* itself. Fraud by a stranger, such as that which occurred in *Bank Tejarat*, and such as would be typical in maritime frauds, presents greater difficulties in this regard, but if it can be established that the fraudster has induced the victim to convey property to him, then the fraudster may become a constructive trustee on the principles in *Bannister* v *Bannister* (see chapter 10). That would establish the fiduciary relationship for subsequent tracing purposes, but it would not help if, for example, it was necessary to trace through a mixed bank account to establish that the fraudster had received the victim's money in the first place. Victims of theft by a stranger will not normally be able to trace in equity, since the thief will not acquire legal title and therefore cannot become a trustee, whether constructive or otherwise. That is the main limitation of proprietary tracing in equity.

Establishing a fiduciary relationship may also be required for knowing receipt (see 19.3.3), where it is necessary to establish that the recipient received the plaintiff's equitable property: e.g., *El Ajou* v *Dollar Land Holdings plc* [1994] 2 All ER 685, and *El Ajou* v *Dollar Land Holdings plc (No. 2)* [1995] 2 All ER 213. A fiduciary relationship is also necessary for knowing assistance (see 19.3.4); this is why it was necessary to establish one in *Bank Tejarat* itself.

19.2.2.3 Quantifying shares in mixed funds: *pari passu* and *Clayton's case*   Once it is accepted that equity can trace into mixed funds, it is necessary to consider the basis upon which the fund is apportioned between rival claimants. Usually, the problem is that payments have been made out of the fund, leaving insufficient to satisfy all the claimants. But another possibility is that the payments out have been wisely invested, in which case claimants may prefer to claim a share of the payments out, rather than what remains in the fund.

The leading authority is probably again the Court of Appeal decision in *Re Diplock* [1948] Ch 465. The testator, Caleb Diplock, gave the residue of his property 'to such charitable institutions or other charitable or benevolent object or objects in England' as his executors should, in their absolute discretion, select. In the belief that this created a valid charitable trust, the executors distributed some £203,000 among 139 different charities. Then the next of kin successfully challenged its validity in *Chichester Diocesan Fund and Board of Finance* v *Simpson* [1994] AC 341. The next of kin, having exhausted their remedy against the executors, successfully recovered money from the various charities. The personal claim is considered at 19.3.5, but a proprietary claim also succeeded against some of the charities. The advantage of the proprietary claim was that it allowed the next of kin to claim interest.

On the proprietary claim, the Court of Appeal, extending the principles derived from *Re Hallett's Estate* and *Sinclair* v *Brougham*, held that the right to trace into a mixed fund is not limited to cases where the defendant is the person who has mixed the funds. Nor does there need to be a fiduciary relationship as between the parties to the action. The right to trace is available against an innocent volunteer. This is an application of the *bona fide* purchaser rule in 1.4.6; a volunteer is not a purchaser, and provides no value. Here, the volunteer charities had mixed Diplock money with their own, and hence the question of apportionment arose.

Where a trustee wrongly mixes trust money with his own, the principles in *Hallett's Estate*, in 19.2.2.4, apply, essentially to the disadvantage of the trustee, but the volunteers in *Diplock* were innocent and the Court of Appeal did not apply the same harsh principles to them. They were treated just like any other innocent claimant to a share in a mixed fund and, in particular, as being no less deserving than the next of kin. The volunteer's duty of conscience is regarded as akin to that of a person having an equitable interest in a mixed fund towards the other equitable owners, and so, for example, where Diplock money was used to purchase stocks, where the charity already had similar stocks, the charity ranked *pari passu* with the next of kin (i.e., in proportion to the amount each has contributed to the amalgam). This is clearly the fairest method of apportionment in such a case.

For current bank accounts, however, the Court of Appeal in Diplock applied the rule developed in *Clayton's case* (1816) 1 Mer 572, which enshrines the principle of 'first in, first out'. The first payment in is appropriated to satisfy the earliest debt. The basis of the rule is said to be the presumed intention of the person operating the account. A preferable solution, in the opinion of the authors of the Report of the Review Committee on Insolvency Law and Practice (Cook Report 1982, Cmnd 8558), paras 1076–1080, would be to divide the mixed fund rateably (i.e., in pari passu). However, in *Barlow Clowes International Ltd* v *Vaughan* [1992] 4 All ER 22, noted [1993] Conv 370, the Court of Appeal held that *Clayton's case* normally applied, the court being bound by the *ratio* of *Diplock*. Actually, in *Barlow Clowes* itself, the presumption in *Clayton's case* was rebutted (see 19.2.2.5), but it would normally be very difficult to operate *pari passu* distribution with a running bank account, because *pari passu* distribution assumes a starting date for the fund (otherwise how can you determine how much each has contributed to the amalgam).

19.2.2.4 Mixing by trustee or fiduciary The above principles assume that all claimants are equally innocent, or at any rate are treated as such, but as against a trustee who is in breach of trust, who has mixed trust money with his own, the beneficiary is entitled to a first charge over a mixed fund or property purchased with it. This will generally operate against the interests of the trustee.

In *Re Hallett's Estate* (1880) 13 ChD 696, Hallett, a solicitor, was a trustee of his own marriage settlement. He had paid some of the money from that trust into his own bank account, into which he also paid money which had been entrusted to him for investment by a client. He made various payments into and out of the account, which at his death contained sufficient funds to meet the claims of the trust and his client, but not those of his personal creditors as well. Hallett attempted to rely on *Clayton's case* to show that the payments out had been of the trust money, and that what was left was his own, but the Court of Appeal held (Thesiger LJ dissenting) that both the trust and the client were entitled to a charge in priority to Hallett's general creditors, and that the various payments out of the account must be treated as payments of Hallett's own money. The principle is that where an act can be done rightly, the trustee is not allowed to say that he did it wrongfully. Hallett had the right to spend his own money, but not that of the trust or the client, and was therefore unable to claim that he had done so. Therefore, he must have spent his own money, leaving that of the trust and the client in the account.

A different application of the same principle can be seen operating in *Re Oatway* [1903] 2 Ch 356. The trustee had withdrawn money from the mixed account and invested it in shares, leaving a balance which at that time was ample to meet the claims of the beneficiaries. Subsequently, however, he dissipated the balance further. The argument (based on *Hallett*) that he must be treated as withdrawing his own money first (so that his shares would be treated as his own property) was rejected. The beneficiaries' claim must be satisfied out of any identifiable part of the fund before the trustee could set up his own claim. They were entitled to the shares in priority to the general creditors. The principle is the same as before. The trustee was entitled to dissipate his own but not the trust money, so could not claim that what had been left in the account, and subsequently dissipated, was trust money, rather than his own.

However, there are limits to the rights of beneficiaries. Once it is clear that all money belonging to the trustee has been withdrawn, so that any further withdrawals must have been from trust money, they cannot claim that any subsequent payments in must be taken as intended to replace the trust money, unless the trustee shows an intention to make such repayment. In such a case, the right to trace will apply up to the lowest balance of the account in the period between the trust fund being paid into the account and the time when the remedy is sought. For example, if the trustee mixes £1,000 of his own money with £3,000 of trust money and later withdraws £2,000, the right to trace will not extend beyond the £2,000 which is thereby left in the account, even if the trustee later pays in further sums of his own.

In such a case, of course, the beneficiaries will have a personal claim against the trustee for any outstanding sum.

Another limit on the beneficiaries' right to trace is that there may not be any principle of proportionate entitlement. Suppose, for example, that the trustee has used the mixed fund to purchase property which has increased in value. Can the beneficiary claim any part of the increase? It appears not on the basis of *Re Hallett's Estate* and *Sinclair v Brougham*, where it was assumed that the beneficiary's remedy was limited to a charge upon the property for the amount of trust money expended in its purchase. This is a surprising result given the strict rule against profits by trustees, and some doubt has recently been cast on it (though only *obiter* in a first instance decision).

The discussion took place in *Re Tilley's WT* [1967] Ch 1179, where a sole trustee who was also the life tenant had mixed a small amount of trust money in her own bank account before embarking on a series of property speculations which were so successful that upon her death her estate was worth £94,000. The beneficiaries entitled in remainder claimed a share of this wealth in the proportion which the trust money in the account bore to the balance of the account at that time. Ungoed-Thomas J held them entitled only to the return of the trust money with interest.

His decision was based on a finding of fact, however, that Mrs Tilley had not invested the trust money in property but merely used it to reduce her overdraft. If a trustee has in fact laid out trust money towards a purchase, Ungoed-Thomas J thought that the beneficiaries would then be entitled to the property and any profit to the extent that it had been paid for with trust money.

The reasoning is that if the trustee draws on a mixed fund to purchase property but leaves enough in the account to cover the trust funds, the rule in *Re Hallett's Estate* requires that the purchase be treated as made entirely with his own money, in which case, should no further dissipations to the mixed fund occur, the property, and any profit, belong to him. But should he then go further and dissipate the remaining balance, the beneficiaries will have a charge on the property (*Re Oatway*), and this, according to Ungoed-Thomas J, may be for the proportionate part of the increased value and not merely for the original amount of the trust fund.

The solution is consistent with the rule applicable to unauthorised investment, where as we saw in 17.3.2, the beneficiaries may elect to adopt the investment. Its effect would be to allow the beneficiaries the choice of a charge for an amount of the trust money, which will be to their advantage where the funds are depleted, or a share in the property where its value has risen.

As we saw in 19.2.2.3, the Court of Appeal in *Re Diplock* did not apply the principles of this section to mixing by innocent volunteers, and there are other respects in which volunteers are treated differently. It seems that the volunteer is not liable to the full extent if any property purchased with the mixed fund has decreased in value, because otherwise he would be compelled to pay out of his own pocket for the mistake of the trustee who transferred the property to him in breach of trust. Nor is it obvious, if he purchases property with the mixed fund which increases in value, that justice requires him to share any increase, unless some allowance is made for his effort (see Hodkinson [1983] Conv 135).

19.2.2.5 *Clayton* presumption rebutted With current bank accounts *Clayton's case* is convenient to operate, and in any case, *pari passu* distribution is possible only where a start date can be given to the fund. Nevertheless, it is generally accepted that *pari passu* distribution is fairer. *Clayton's case* favours later contributions where the money that is paid out is dissipated, and earlier contributions where the money that is paid out is profitably invested but the distribution is fortuitous, in that it depends entirely on the relative timing of each contribution.

Clayton's case operates on presumed intention, which can therefore be rebutted. Indeed, it was rebutted in *Hallett's Estate*, considered in the last section. The courts have been reluctant to apply it outside the realm of current bank accounts. In *Re Hobourn Aero Components Air Raid Distress Fund* [1946] Ch 86, for example (see 5.3.2), where contributions had been made into, and moneys paid out of, a non-charitable unincorporated association, *Clayton's case* was argued by later contributors to suggest that all payments out were attributable to the earlier contributions. Cohen J rejected the argument, preferring what was, in effect, a *pari passu* distribution. There was, of course, a definite start date to the fund in *Hobourn Aero*, and in the earlier, similar case of *Re British Red Cross Balkan Fund* [1914] 2 Ch 419, so it was easy to make a *pari passu* calculation.

Barlow Clowes International Ltd v *Vaughan* [1992] 4 All ER 22, noted [1993] Conv 370, concerned the collapse of a deposit-taking company, where money had been invested in portfolios. Because the fund available for distribution was so much smaller than the totality of claims, *Clayton's case* would benefit only a few, late depositors. The Court of Appeal held that *Clayton's case* applied in principle to this type of case, Woolf LJ with some reluctance, and only because he felt constrained by authority. The rule in *Clayton's case* is just the starting point, however, and applies only where it provides a convenient method of determining competing claims. In the particular case, the presumed intention (from the application of the rule) was rebutted as being impractical and unjust, because a small number of investors would get most of the funds, and the fund was divided in *pari passu*.

There is no need to apportion where the defendant is solvent and the claim is based on knowing receipt of the plaintiff's money, since it is necessary only to trace the money into the hands of the defendant and not to apportion. In *El Ajou* v *Dollar Land Holdings plc (No. 2)* [1995] 2 All ER 213, the plaintiff was one of a number of victims of a fraud, and needed to trace money into the hands of the defendant in order to sue for knowing receipt. The defendant was solvent and had sufficient funds to satisfy the plaintiff's claim. The plaintiff could show that the amount of his claim (but not enough to satisfy all the possible claims from the fraud victims) could be traced into the defendant's hands, but the defendant claimed that the plaintiff could identify only a proportion of this money as his, as there were other victims of the fraud. Robert Walker J held that the need to apportion arose only where there were competing claimants to a fund that was too small to satisfy them all. There was no need to apportion where the sole reason for tracing was to establish receipt for the purposes of a personal equitable claim.

19.3 PERSONAL EQUITABLE REMEDIES

For an equitable tracing action to operate the trust property must still be identifiable in some form, albeit that at least in equity it need not be *physically* identifiable, so that if, for example, the trust property has been sold, it may still be possible to trace the *proceeds* of sale. There are also rules in equity for the tracing of trust money which has become mixed with other money (see 19.2.2).

Suppose, however, that the property no longer exists in any identifiable form. Trust money may have been spent, for example, with nothing identifiable to show for it. If the trust property no longer exists, then clearly it is not traceable. Alternatively, it may be that it has been mixed with other funds in such a way as no longer to be traceable on the principles elaborated in 19.2.2. We saw at 19.2.2 that the common law money had and received action depends only on receipt of the money by the defendant and that liability is unaffected by anything that later happens to the property, but that is not the case with proprietary equitable tracing.

This section is about the personal equitable actions, which do not depend on the defendant's continued retention of, or indeed in the case of knowing assistance even receipt of, the plaintiff's property. Knowing receipt and the personal action in *Re Diplock* are, if you like, the equitable equivalents of the common law money had and received claim.

19.3.1 Knowing receipt and knowing assistance compared

It is possible for a stranger to become liable as constructive trustee if he either assists a trustee (or other fiduciary) in breach of trust (or other fiduciary duty) regarding property under his control, or receives trust property with knowledge of breach of trust (or other fiduciary duty). The first type of case is categorised as 'knowing assistance', the second as 'knowing receipt'. A knowing receiver becomes constructive trustee of the property received. Since a knowing assister need never receive trust property, it is probably not correct to describe him as a constructive trustee, but he is liable as if he were.

The question at issue is usually the degree of knowledge required for imposition of a liability for knowing receipt or knowing assistance. The usual starting point is *Baden, Delvaux and Lecuit v Société Générale pour Favoriser le Devéloppement du Commerce et de l'Industrie en France SA* [1983] BCLC 325, where Peter Gibson J suggested five possible categories of knowledge sufficient to found constructive trusteeship:

(i)   actual knowledge;

(ii)   wilfully shutting one's eyes to the obvious;

(iii)   wilfully and recklessly failing to make such inquiries as an honest and reasonable man would make;

(iv)   knowledge of circumstances which would indicate the facts to an honest and reasonable man; and

(v)   knowledge of circumstances which would put an honest and reasonable man on inquiry.

It is clear that categories (ii) to (v) all represent varieties of constructive notice. Categories (i) to (iii) would normally suggest dishonesty, requiring either intention or something akin to criminal law recklessness. The test in categories (iv) and (v) is objective (i.e., akin to negligence), as opposed to the subjective test in (i) to (iii). Nevertheless, it is possible for someone to be dishonest even within (iv) and (v).

Yet although many of the cases take as their starting point these five categories, the courts have recently recoiled from using them as the only basis either for establishing liability, or for distinguishing between the two types of liability. It now seems that liability for both knowing receipt and knowing assistance can be founded on the basis of any of the five categories. In the case of knowing assistance, however, there, is an additional requirement for dishonesty (or lack of probity). In the case of knowing receipt there is no dishonesty requirement, but constructive knowledge is required, which may be narrower than notice satisfying categories (iv) and (v): see further 19.3.4.

It has long been clear that the test for knowing assistance is more stringent than that for knowing receipt. Indeed, in *Belmont Finance Corporation* v *Williams Furniture Ltd (No. 1)* [1979] Ch 250, and *(No. 2)* [1980] 1 All ER 393, a knowing assistance claim failed, whereas a claim for knowing receipt succeeded, on essentially the same facts. The first case ([1979] Ch 250) was heard on the pleadings only, the full hearing being on the second case ([1980] 1 All ER 393).

In the first hearing, the case was pleaded as a knowing assistance case; and on the pleadings, fraud or dishonesty on the part of the defendants could not be established. The Court of Appeal took the view that the defendants were not liable (on the pleadings) for knowingly assisting in a fraudulent design. In particular, the Court felt that constructive knowledge was not a sufficient basis for liability under that heading, Buckley LJ commenting (at p. 267):

> The knowledge of that design on the part of the parties sought to be made liable may be actual knowledge. If he wilfully shuts his eyes to dishonesty, or wilfully or recklessly fails to make such inquiries as an honest and reasonable man would make, he may be found to have involved himself in the fraudulent character of the design, or at any rate to be disentitled to rely on lack of actual knowledge of the design as a defence. But otherwise, as it seems to me, he should not be affected by constructive notice.

The views of Goff LJ were similar (at p. 275):

> Whilst wilfully shutting one's eyes to the obvious, or wilfully refraining from inquiry because it may be embarrassing is, I have no doubt, sufficient to make a person who participates in a fraudulent breach of trust without actually receiving the trust moneys, or moneys representing the same, liable as a constructive trustee, there remains the question whether constructive notice . . . will suffice.

He went on to say that in his opinion, it would not. The case clearly suggests, therefore, that at any rate in a knowing assistance case, constructive knowledge without dishonesty will not suffice.

The case then came back to the Court of Appeal on the second hearing, when the pleadings were amended, to include a knowing receipt claim which was successful. As in the first case, dishonesty could not be shown on the pleadings. Buckley LJ (quoting *Barnes* v *Addy* (1874) 9 Ch App 244) said (at p. 405b):

> If a stranger to a trust (a) receives and becomes chargeable with some part of the trust fund or (b) assists the trustees of a trust with knowledge of the facts in a dishonest design on the part of the trustees to misapply some part of a trust fund, he is liable as a constructive trustee.

Whereas dishonesty appears to be a requirement under part (b), there is nothing in this quote suggesting a need to show fraud or dishonesty under part (a).

Since the facts of the two cases, and the knowledge of the defendants, were (to all intents and purposes) identical, the case strongly suggests that the knowledge requirements for knowing assistance and knowing receipt are not the same. It appears, then, that whereas in the case of knowing assistance knowledge dishonesty is required, it is not for knowing receipt.

19.3.2 Knowing receipt
Belmont (No. 2) (above) clearly suggests that dishonesty is not required for a knowing receipt claim. It has often been assumed that something akin to constructive notice in land law (see 1.4.6) is sufficient, but doubt was cast on this by *dicta* in *Re Montagu's ST* [1987] Ch 264, where chattels were transferred to the defendant in breach of a trust created by a family settlement, and the defendant sold the chattels. The defendant certainly had constructive notice in the strict land law sense, since his solicitor was aware of the terms of the trust and therefore the defendant had imputed notice. However, Megarry V-C thought that while constructive notice might be appropriate for a tracing claim, where the actual money or property can still be identified, something more should be required before constructive trusteeship is imposed. He seemed inclined to the view that even for a knowing receipt claim, and against a volunteer at that, only the first three heads of *Baden* knowledge would suffice.

Megarry V-C's view was unnecessary to the actual decision in the case, since he did not think that the Duke had the requisite knowledge under any of the five *Baden* heads. At p. 286B he said that 'even if, contrary to my opinion, all of the five *Baden* types of knowledge are in point, instead of only the first three, I do not think that he had any such knowledge'. The distinction between constructive notice and the requisite knowledge for knowing receipt has also been criticised as being wrong in principle, for example by Harpum (1987) 50 MLR 217. It might also be argued that if, as Fox LJ thought in *Agip (Africa)* (19.3.3), all five *Baden* heads suffice for knowing assistance, it would be odd to require a *higher* standard of knowledge for knowing receipt. However, there is an additional dishonesty requirement for knowing assistance, which may deal with this criticism.

In (1991) 107 LQR 71, Millett at pp. 80ff, argued that *Montagu* is wrong in principle, because once property is traced into the defendant's hands, he becomes trustee of it for the plaintiff. Disposing of the property is therefore a breach of trust, and while it might deprive the plaintiff of his proprietary remedy, there ought to be a continuing liability for breach of trust. That argues that the knowledge requirement for each should be the same. Against that, it may be argued that tracing liability for volunteers is strict, whereas even for volunteers, some knowledge is required for knowing receipt, so there is no necessary tie in between the two.

Millett also argues for liability to be receipt-based, as at common law, rather than fault-based, subject to a change of position defence, but although the courts have shown some wariness of *Montagu*, they show no signs of following this route. Indeed, Millett J himself recognised that he was bound by authority in *El Ajou* v *Dollar Land Holdings plc* [1993] 3 All ER 717, and that the defendant did not have the requisite knowledge for knowing receipt (he was reversed on the facts in the Court of Appeal [1994] 2 All ER 685). Furthermore, the courts appear to be adopting a higher knowledge require-ment than the land law notice doctrine, but for different reasons. The notice doctrine developed in land transactions on the assumption that there would be a full and careful investigation of title, and the courts appear unwilling to impose constructive trusteeship in commercial transactions without some-thing more akin to constructive knowledge, as opposed to notice. In *Eagle Trust plc* v *SBC Securities Ltd* [1992] 4 All ER 488 and *Cowan de Groot Properties Ltd* v *Eagle Trust plc* [1992] 4 All ER 700 this was treated as being similar to the first three *Baden* heads, but it may be an oversimplification to assume that that will always be so.

Liability for knowing receipt probably requires more than mere possession of the trust property. In *Agip (Africa) Ltd* v *Jackson* [1990] 1 Ch 265, Millett J said of liability for knowing receipt that 'the recipient must have received the property for his own use and benefit'. It followed that a bank was not liable as a knowing receiver merely because money had been deposited in a customer's account.

Millett J's decision in *Agip (Africa)* was upheld by the Court of Appeal ([1991] Ch 547), but there was no appeal on the issue of knowing receipt and there is discussion only of knowing assistance (see 19.3.3). However, the same view was adopted in *Bank Tejarat* (see 19.2.1.2), where the fraudsters' bankers were held not liable as knowing receivers although Tejarat's money could be traced to them in equity and they had sufficient knowledge for knowing receipt, although not for knowing assistance.

19.3.3 Knowing assistance

It has been clear since at least *Belmont (No. 1)* that dishonesty, or lack of probity, is required for a knowing assistance claim. In *Lipkin Gorman* v *Karpnale Ltd* [1989] 1 WLR 1340 in the Court of Appeal (see 19.2.1.2 for the House of Lords decision), the bank was unsuccessfully sued for knowing assistance, May LJ taking the view, after approving statements from *Belmont (No. 1)*, that (at p. 1355D):

> In my opinion, therefore, there is at least strong persuasive authority for the proposition that nothing less than knowledge, as defined in one of the first three categories stated by Peter Gibson J in *Baden, Delvaux and Lecuit v Société Générale pour Favoriser le Développement du Commerce et de l'Industrie en France SA* [1983] BCLC 325, of an underlying dishonest design is sufficient to make a stranger a constructive trustee of the consequences of that design.

A different position was taken by Fox LJ in *Agip (Africa) Ltd v Jackson*, however. He appeared to accept that dishonesty was a requirement for knowing assistance, but that, subject to this requirement, any of the five *Baden* heads of knowledge would suffice. A similar view had been taken by Millett J at first instance, who suggested caution regarding the five *Baden* categories:

> I gratefully adopt the [*Baden*] classification but would warn against over refinement or a too ready assumption that categories (iv) or (v) are necessarily cases of constructive notice only. The true distinction is between honesty and dishonesty. It is essentially a jury question.

It seems fairly clear, therefore, that whereas any of the five *Baden* heads will probably suffice for liability, dishonesty or 'lack of probity' (a term used by May LJ in *Lipkin Gorman v Karpnale Ltd*, which requires more than mere negligence) is also required to found a constructive trusteeship claim based on knowing assistance. This has been reiterated by Vinelott J in *Eagle Trust plc v SBC Securities Ltd* [1992] 4 All ER 488 and by the Court of Appeal in *Polly Peck International v Nadir (No. 2)* [1992] 4 All ER 769. In *Eagle Trust* Vinelott J thought that knowledge of the fraudulent design had to be able to be imputed to the defendant, and that constructive notice of the fraudulent design would not be enough, although knowledge may be inferred in the absence of evidence if such knowledge would have been imputed to an honest and reasonable man.

Assuming that want of probity can be established, however, it does not appear to be necessary for the defendant to be aware of the precise details of the fraud. In *Agip Africa* the action succeeded against the money launderers' accountants, who may have believed only that they were participating in an illegal currency transaction, contrary to the exchange control laws of Tunisia. However, in *Bank Tejarat*, it was not enough simply for the defendants to be aware that CAK (who committed the fraud) was an offshore company of the type often used for fraudulent purposes, since anonymity is also a reason for operating through an offshore company.

In *Royal Brunei Airlines Sdn Bhd v Tan* [1995] 2 AC 378, the Privy Council held that the liability of the third party depended on the dishonesty of that party, and that the breach of trust (which was, of course, a prerequisite for accessory liability) need not itself be a dishonest and fraudulent breach of trust by the trustee. On the facts, however, both the trustee and the third party had acted dishonestly, the latter by causing or permitting the trustee to apply money in a way he knew was not authorised by the trust.

19.3.4 The personal action in *Diplock*

In *Re Diplock's Estate* [1948] Ch 465 (see 19.2.2.3), which was affirmed by the House of Lords on this issue in *Ministry of Health* v *Simpson* [1951] AC 251, the next of kin also succeeded in a personal action against the charities which, like the other personal actions considered in this section, was complete on receipt. Unlike knowing receipt, however, liability was strict, the defendants were innocent volunteers who took in good faith with no notice of the next of kin's title. The action appears to apply only to volunteers, but clearly cannot apply to all volunteers if *Re Montagu's ST* [1987] Ch 264 is correct (see 19.3.2), so we need to consider its limits.

In *Diplock*, the executors had made the payments to the charities under a mistake of law. The charities unsuccessfully argued that the personal action was limited to payments made under a mistake of fact (on analogy with the common law money had and received action) and where the administration of the estate had been made by the direction of the court. It is arguable that the action applies only to the administration of estates, but it seems more probable that it applies generally against volunteers. There is a requirement, however, that remedies against the wrongdoers (in this case the executors) should be exhausted first, which is presumably why no Diplock-based personal action was brought in *Montagu*. It is also possible (but not certain) that the change of position defence in *Lipkin Gorman* v *Karpnale Ltd* [1991] 2 AC 548 (see 19.2.1.2) applies to this equitable action also.

Index